fungus

ducklings

sloth

pollinate

knot

Oxford Primary Illustrated Dictionary

pagoda

immense

finches

basilisk

egg

OXFORD
UNIVERSITY PRESS

starfish

mistletoe

OXFORD
UNIVERSITY PRESS

Great Clarendon Street, Oxford, OX2 6DP, United Kingdom

Oxford University Press is a department of the University of Oxford.
It furthers the University's objective of excellence in research,
scholarship, and education by publishing worldwide. Oxford is a
registered trade mark of Oxford University Press in the UK and in
certain other countries

Copyright © Oxford University Press 2019

Database right Oxford University Press (maker)

All artwork by Jenny Wren except as detailed below.
Collaborate Agency: pages 218 (juggler), 234 (kittens), 304 (poppy), 352 (scorpion).
Dynamo Limited: pages 80 (concave), 86 (convex), 96 (cube), 356 (segment), 413 (cylinder).
Shutterstock: pages 14 (horses), 22 (asteroid), 76 (colour blind test), 87 (core), 110 (dice),
115 (dissolve), 119 (doughnut), 192 (hologram), 241 (wand), 296 (pictogram),
300 (planets), 309 (presents), 312 (prism), 401 (flies), 441 (virus), 446 (wavelength).
All photos courtesy of Shutterstock.

dragon

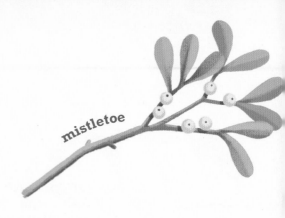

British Library Cataloguing in Publication Data

Data available

ISBN: 978 0 19 276845-2
10 9 8 7 6 5 4 3 2 1

Printed in China

Paper used in the production of this book is a natural,
recyclable product made from wood grown in sustainable forests.
The manufacturing process conforms to the environmental
regulations of the country of origin.

Chief lexicographer Rosalind Combley
The publishers would also like to thank Susan Rennie, Chief lexicographer
of the Oxford Primary Dictionary 2018 edition.

Oxford OWL

For school
Discover eBooks, inspirational
resources, advice and support

For home
Helping your child's learning
with free eBooks, essential
tips and fun activities

www.oxfordowl.co.uk

Oxford Corpus

You can trust this dictionary
to be up to date, relevant
and engaging because
it is powered by the
Oxford Corpus, a unique
living database of children's
and adults' language.

narwhal

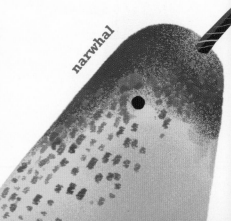

trophy

Contents

Find the answers for the questions at each alphabetical letter opener on page 481

invertebrate

acorn

mermaid

fan

Get to know your dictionary

WORD STORY
These notes tell you interesting facts about where a word came from.

alphabet
on every page to help you find your way around the dictionary easily

language fact
Every letter begins with an interesting fact and often a question—the answers are at the back of the book.

headword
in alphabetical order, in blue

word class
tells you what type of word it is, for example *NOUN*, *VERB*, *ADJECTIVE* or *ADVERB*

other forms
show you how to spell different forms of the word, such as plurals or past forms

definition
tells you what the word means; if there is more than one meaning, the definitions are numbered

A B C D E F G H I J K L M N O P Q R S T U V W X Y Z

Qq

Q is one of the rarest letters in the English language. Q is for **queueing**, which is the only word in English to have five vowels in a row.

quack *NOUN* **quacks**
the loud sound made by a duck
quack *VERB* **quacks, quacking, quacked**
When a duck quacks, it makes a loud sound.

quad *NOUN* **quads**
a rectangular courtyard with buildings round it

quadrant *NOUN* **quadrants**
a quarter of a circle

quadrilateral *NOUN* **quadrilaterals**
a flat shape with four straight sides

quail *NOUN* **quails**
a small bird that is hunted for sport and food

quail *VERB* **quails, quailing, quailed**
to feel or show fear

quaint *ADJECTIVE* **quainter, quaintest**
attractive in an unusual or old-fashioned way

quake *VERB* **quakes, quaking, quaked**
to tremble or shake

qualification *NOUN* **qualifications**
Your qualifications are the exams you have passed or certificates you have that show your skills and abilities.

qualify *VERB* **qualifies, qualifying, qualified**
❶ If someone **qualifies**, they pass a test or exam to show that they have the skills and abilities to do a job. • *She qualified as a doctor.* ❷ To **qualify** for a competition is to be good enough to be allowed to take part or compete.

quality *NOUN* **qualities**
❶ how good something is • *The work was of a high quality.* ❷ Someone's or something's qualities are what they are like.

quantity *NOUN* **quantities**
an amount that you can count or measure

quarantine *NOUN*
a period when a person or an animal is kept apart from others to prevent a disease from spreading

 WORD STORY
From the Italian word *quarantina* meaning 'forty days', because of a rule during the Black Death epidemic that people had to wait for 40 days before going ashore from a ship.

quarrel *NOUN* **quarrels**
an angry argument
quarrel *VERB* **quarrels, quarrelling, quarrelled**
to argue angrily with someone

quarrelsome *ADJECTIVE*
liking to quarrel or start arguments

quarry *NOUN* **quarries**
a place where stone or slate is dug out of the ground

quart (say kwort) *NOUN* **quarts**
a measurement of the volume of liquid, equal to 2 pints or about 1.136 litres

quarter *NOUN* **quarters**
❶ one of four equal parts into which something is divided. It can be written as $\frac{1}{4}$. ❷ Someone's quarters are where they live for a time.
► **quarter past** or **to** 15 minutes after or before the hour • *It's a quarter past three.*

quartet (say kwor-tet) *NOUN* **quartets**
❶ a group of four musicians ❷ a piece of music for four instruments or voices

quartz (say kworts) *NOUN*
a hard mineral, used in making accurate watches and clocks

quaver *VERB* **quavers, quavering, quavered**
to tremble

320

example
shows you how you might use a word; and helps you understand the meaning

phrase
shows you how the word is used in every day phrases and idioms

pronunciation
helps you to say the word (not how to spell it)

quaver NOUN quavers
a musical note equal to half a crotchet, written (♪)

> BUILD YOUR VOCABULARY
> Look at **crotchet**, **minim** and **semibreve**.

quay (say kee) NOUN quays
a place where ships can be loaded and unloaded

queasy ADJECTIVE queasier, queasiest
feeling slightly sick

queen NOUN queens
❶ a woman who has been crowned as the ruler of a country or the wife of a king ❷ a female bee or ant that produces eggs

queer ADJECTIVE queerer, queerest
strange or odd

quench VERB quenches, quenching, quenched
To quench your thirst is to drink until you are not thirsty any more.

query (say kweer-ee) NOUN queries
a question

quest NOUN quests
a long search, especially for something valuable
'Is this a proper quest we are on?' asked Tootles. 'A person could get killed!'–PETER PAN, J. M. Barrie

question NOUN questions
something you ask; a sentence asking for information • *If you don't understand, ask a question.*
➤ **out of the question** impossible
question VERB questions, questioning, questioned
❶ To question someone is to ask them questions. ❷ To question something is to doubt it.

question mark NOUN question marks
the punctuation mark (?) put at the end of a question

questionnaire (say kwess-chun-air) NOUN questionnaires
a set of questions for collecting information from a group of people

queue (say kew) NOUN queues
a line of people or vehicles waiting for something
queue (say kew) VERB queues, queueing, queued
to wait in a queue

> **WATCH OUT!**
> **Queue** has a tricky spelling—the letters **ue** appear twice!

quick ADJECTIVE quicker, quickest
taking only a short time • *We had a quick snack.*
➤ **quickly** ADVERB

quicken VERB quickens, quickening, quickened
If something quickens or you quicken it, it becomes quicker. • *She quickened her pace.*

quicksand NOUN quicksands
an area of loose wet sand that sucks in anything that falls into it

quid NOUN quid (informal)
a pound (£1)

quiet ADJECTIVE quieter, quietest
❶ without any noise • *It's very quiet here at night.*
❷ A quiet sound is not loud. • *He spoke in a quiet voice.*
➤ **quietly** ADVERB
quiet NOUN
silence • *Let's have a bit of quiet now.*

quieten VERB quietens, quietening, quietened
If something or someone quietens or you quieten them, they become quiet. • *The class quietened.*

quill NOUN quills
❶ A bird's quills are its large feathers. ❷ a pen made from a large feather ❸ A porcupine's quills are its long spines.

Using your dictionary

You can see all the features in the dictionary on the previous page.
You can use this dictionary:

- to find the meaning of a word you have read or heard
- to check the spelling of a word you want to use and
  if there are different ways of spelling the word too
- to find out the plural of a noun, the comparative of an adjective,
  or a past form of a verb
- to find out how to say a word
- to build your vocabulary
- to learn more about the history of words
- to discover related words through the illustrations and photographs.

At the back you will find a guide to **grammar, punctuation, spelling** and **word building**. You will also find lists such as **numbers, days of the week, months** and **Roman numerals**. There are also some activities that you can do with the help of the dictionary.

The *Oxford Primary Illustrated Thesaurus* is designed to be used with this dictionary and will help you with your creative writing.

If you love learning about new words and language, or if you want to find the meaning of a word that isn't in this dictionary, try a bigger dictionary, for example the *Oxford Primary Dictionary* or the *Oxford School Dictionary.*

A note for parents and teachers

This dictionary has been compiled with the help of the *Oxford Children's Corpus*, a large language database of many millions of words, which includes hundreds of fiction and non-fiction works written for children as well as children's own writing.

The reading corpus tell us words children which are are likely to want to look up. It also supplies real quotations which are used to provide lively contexts, models of good writing, and inspiration for children to read more.

The children's writing corpus helps us answer the questions: a) do children want to use this word in their writing and b) do they have problems spelling or using it correctly? This means we can make sure we include spelling notes or other helpful information at tricky words in the dictionary. We hope that all children will enjoy using this dictionary and having fun with language.

⚙ A is for **antonym**, which is a word that has the opposite meaning to another word. For example, *full* is an antonym of *empty*.

⚙ Do you know the antonym of *antonym*?

CLUE It begins with **s**.

a *DETERMINER*
❶ one or any • *I've bought you a present.* ❷ each or every • *I go swimming twice a week.*

⚙ **BUILD** YOUR VOCABULARY
The words **a** or **an** are called the **indefinite article**.

aardvark *(say ard-vark) NOUN* aardvarks
an African animal with a long snout that eats ants and termites

aback *ADVERB*
➤ **To be taken aback** is to be surprised and slightly shocked. • *We were taken aback by this silly idea.*

abacus *NOUN* abacuses
a frame with rows of sliding beads, used for counting and doing sums

abandon *VERB* abandons, abandoning, abandoned
To abandon something or someone is to go away and leave them, without intending to go back. • *The lioness had abandoned her cubs.*

abbey *NOUN* abbeys
a church with a group of buildings where monks or nuns live

abbreviate *VERB* abbreviates, abbreviating, abbreviated
To abbreviate a word or phrase is to write it with fewer letters so that it is shorter.

abbreviation *NOUN* abbreviations
a word or group of letters that is a shorter form of a word or phrase • *BBC is an abbreviation of 'British Broadcasting Corporation'.*

abdomen *NOUN* abdomens
❶ the part of your body below your chest, which contains your stomach and intestines ❷ the back part of the body of an insect or spider

⚙ **BUILD** YOUR VOCABULARY
Look at **thorax**.

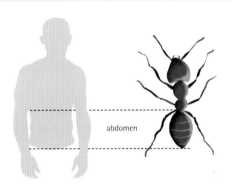

abdomen

ability *NOUN* abilities
❶ Ability is the fact that you can do something. • *the ability to see in the dark* ❷ An ability is a skill or talent. • *Different people have different abilities.*

ablaze *ADJECTIVE*
burning or shining brightly

able *ADJECTIVE* abler, ablest
❶ If you are able to do something, you can do it. • *No one was able to crack the code.* ❷ having a special talent or skill • *a very able swimmer*

aboard *ADVERB, PREPOSITION*
on or on to a train, ship or aircraft • *The ship's passengers were all aboard.* • *It's time to get aboard the train.*

abolish *VERB* abolishes, abolishing, abolished
To abolish a rule or custom is to get rid of it. • *The class voted to abolish homework.*

abominable *ADJECTIVE*
very shocking and bad • *an abominable crime*

Abominable Snowman *NOUN* Abominable Snowmen
another name for a **yeti**

a
b
c
d
e
f
g
h
i
j
k
l
m
n
o
p
q
r
s
t
u
v
w
x
y
z

Aborigine (say ab-er-rij-in-ee) NOUN
Aborigines
one of the people whose ancestors were living in
Australia before Europeans arrived
➤ **Aboriginal** ADJECTIVE

✴ WORD STORY

The words **boomerang** and **budgerigar** come
from Aboriginal words.

about PREPOSITION
❶ to do with or connected with • *The film is about a
family of superheroes.* ❷ approximately, roughly
• *The castle wall is about 10 metres high.*
about ADVERB
❶ in various directions or places • *People were
running about madly.* ❷ somewhere near by • *There
may be bears and wolves about.*
➤ **To be about to do something** is to be just going
to do it. • *They are about to announce the winner.*

above PREPOSITION
❶ in a position higher than • *on the shelf above the
fireplace* ❷ more than • *The temperature was just
above freezing.*
above ADVERB
at a higher point, overhead • *Fireworks lit up the
sky above.*

abracadabra EXCLAMATION
a word that people say when they are doing magic
tricks

abroad ADVERB
in a foreign country • *They live abroad now.*

abrupt ADJECTIVE
sudden and unexpected • *The bus came to an
abrupt halt.*
➤ **abruptly** ADVERB

abseil VERB abseils, abseiling, abseiled
to lower yourself down a steep cliff or rock by sliding
down a rope

✴ WORD STORY

Abseil is from the German words *ab* meaning 'down'
and *Seil* meaning 'rope'.

absent ADJECTIVE
not in a place where you are expected; away
➤ **absence** NOUN • *They noticed your absence.*

⚙ BUILD YOUR VOCABULARY

The opposite of **absent** is **present** and the opposite
of **absence** is **presence**.

absent-minded ADJECTIVE
forgetting things or not thinking about what you
are doing
➤ **absent-mindedly** ADVERB • *Lydia absent-
mindedly put too much sugar in her tea.*

absolute ADJECTIVE
total, complete • *I have absolute confidence
in you.*

absolutely ADVERB
completely

absorb VERB absorbs, absorbing, absorbed
To absorb something like liquid is to soak it up.

absorbed ADJECTIVE
very interested in something and giving it all your
attention • *I was so absorbed in my book I didn't
notice him.*

abstract ADJECTIVE
to do with ideas and not with physical things
• *abstract ideas like love and beauty*

absurd ADJECTIVE
silly or ridiculous • *What an absurd idea!*

abuse (say a-bewz) VERB abuses, abusing,
abused
❶ to treat someone or something badly or cruelly
❷ to say insulting or unpleasant things
to someone
abuse (say a-bewss) NOUN abuses
❶ bad or cruel treatment ❷ insulting or unpleasant
things said to someone • *The crowd were shouting
abuse.*

abysmal ADJECTIVE
very bad • *The weather was abysmal.*

abyss NOUN abysses
a deep dark hole that seems to go on forever

academic ADJECTIVE
to do with learning in a school or university
• *an academic subject*

academy NOUN academies
a college or school

accelerate VERB accelerates, accelerating,
accelerated
to go faster
➤ **acceleration** NOUN

accent NOUN accents
An accent is the way that people from a particular area pronounce words. • *He has a Yorkshire accent.*

accept VERB accepts, accepting, accepted
❶ to take or say yes to something that someone offers you • *She accepted my invitation.* ❷ To accept a fact or situation means to agree or realise that it exists. • *He had to accept his fate.*

acceptable ADJECTIVE
❶ good enough to accept • *We think it is an acceptable price.* ❷ all right; satisfactory • *Their behaviour was not acceptable.*

BUILD YOUR VOCABULARY
An opposite is **unacceptable**.

access NOUN accesses
a way to reach a place • *This road is the only access to the house.*

access VERB accesses, accessing, accessed
To access something is to be able to get it and use it. • *He can access all the information on his phone.*

accessible ADJECTIVE
easy to reach or get to

BUILD YOUR VOCABULARY
The opposite is **inaccessible**.

accident NOUN accidents
something unexpected that happens, especially when something is broken or someone is hurt
➤ **by accident** by chance, not intentionally

accidental ADJECTIVE
happening by chance and not because it was intended • *accidental damage*
➤ **accidentally** ADVERB • *I accidentally threw the paper away.*

accommodate VERB accommodates, accommodating, accommodated
to provide a place big enough for someone to sit, sleep, etc. • *The cottage easily accommodated five.*

WATCH OUT!
There is a double **c** and a double **m** in **accommodate**.

accommodation NOUN
a place to live or stay

WATCH OUT!
There is a double **c** and a double **m** in **accommodation**.

accompaniment NOUN accompaniments
the music played on a piano or another instrument while a singer sings

accompany VERB accompanies, accompanying, accompanied
❶ To accompany someone is to go somewhere with them. ❷ To accompany a singer is to play an instrument while they sing.

accomplish VERB accomplishes, accomplishing, accomplished
To accomplish something is to do it successfully.
➤ **accomplishment** NOUN • *I was proud of my accomplishments.*

according to PREPOSITION
❶ You say **according to** someone to show where a piece of information comes from. • *According to Katie, there is a party tomorrow.* ❷ following something such as a plan or rule • *Nothing went according to our plan.*

account NOUN accounts
❶ a description or story about something that happened • *a thrilling account of their adventures* ❷ If you have a bank account, you have money in a bank.
➤ **On account of something** means because of it.

account VERB accounts, accounting, accounted
➤ **To account for** something is to explain it. • *What could account for his odd behaviour?*

accountant NOUN accountants
a person whose job is to keep and organise records of the money a person or company makes and spends

accumulate VERB accumulates, accumulating, accumulated
❶ To accumulate things is to collect them or pile them up. ❷ Things accumulate when they collect or form a pile.

accurate ADJECTIVE
exactly correct or exactly in the right place • *an amazingly accurate guess*
➤ **accuracy** NOUN • *the accuracy of his shot*
➤ **accurately** ADVERB • *She described it accurately.*

BUILD YOUR VOCABULARY
The opposite is **inaccurate**.

a
b
c
d
e
f
g
h
i
j
k
l
m
n
o
p
q
r
s
t
u
v
w
x
y
z

A
B
C
D
E
F
G
H
I
J
K
L
M
N
O
P
Q
R
S
T
U
V
W
X
Y
Z

accuse *VERB* accuses, accusing, accused
To accuse someone is to say that they did something wrong.
➤ **accusation** *NOUN* • *They made false accusations against her.*

ace *NOUN* aces
❶ a playing card with an A in the corner and one large symbol on it ❷ In tennis, an ace is a serve that the other player cannot return.

ache *NOUN* aches
a dull steady pain
ache *VERB* aches, aching, ached
To ache is to feel a dull steady pain.

achieve *VERB* achieves, achieving, achieved
To achieve something is to succeed in doing it or getting it.
➤ **achievement** *NOUN* • *Winning the gold medal was a great* **achievement**.

acid *NOUN* acids
a substance that contains hydrogen and causes chemical change

🔧 **BUILD YOUR VOCABULARY**
Look at **alkali**.

acid *ADJECTIVE*
sour or bitter to taste

acid rain *NOUN*
rain that contains harmful acids because it has mixed with waste gases from the air

acknowledge *VERB* acknowledges, acknowledging, acknowledged
❶ To acknowledge something is to admit that it is true. ❷ To acknowledge a letter or message is to say that you have received it.
➤ **acknowledgement** *NOUN*

acne (*say* ak-nee) *NOUN*
a skin disease which causes red pimples and is common among teenagers

acorn *NOUN* acorns
the nut of an oak tree, which is oval and has a cup-shaped holder

acquaintance *NOUN* acquaintances
someone you know slightly
➤ **To make someone's acquaintance** is to get to know them.

⚠ **WATCH OUT!**
Don't forget the **c** before the **q** in **acquaintance**.

acre *NOUN* acres
an area of land measuring 4840 square yards (about 4047 square metres)

acrid *ADJECTIVE*
An acrid smell is sharp and bitter. • *a cloud of* **acrid** *smoke*

acrobat *NOUN* acrobats
an entertainer who gives displays of jumping and balancing
➤ **acrobatics** *NOUN* • *She performed amazing* **acrobatics**.

✳ **WORD STORY**
The word **acrobat** comes from Greek words meaning 'to walk on tiptoe'.

acronym *NOUN* acronyms
a word or name that is formed from the first letters of other words. For example *UFO* is an acronym of *unidentified flying object*.

across *ADVERB, PREPOSITION*
❶ from one side of something to the other
• *The table measures 1.5 metres* **across**. ❷ to the other side of something • *How can we get* **across** *the busy road?*

act *NOUN* acts
❶ something that someone does • *a very wicked* **act**
❷ a performance • *a magic* **act** ❸ one of the main sections of a play or opera ❹ a new law that a government makes
act *VERB* acts, acting, acted
❶ to do something useful or necessary • *We need to* **act** *now.* ❷ to behave in a particular way
• *Stop* **acting** *stupid.* ❸ To act in a play or film is to play a part in it.

action *NOUN* actions
❶ An action is something that someone does.
• *He regretted his* **actions**. ❷ Action is moving or doing things. • *The film is full of* **action**.

activate VERB activates, activating, activated
To activate a machine or device is to start it working.

active ADJECTIVE
❶ busy; moving or doing things

> ⚙ **BUILD YOUR VOCABULARY**
> The opposite of this meaning is **inactive**.

❷ An active volcano is erupting or likely to erupt.

> ⚙ **BUILD YOUR VOCABULARY**
> Look at **dormant** and **extinct**.

❸ (in grammar) An active verb is one where the subject does the action. For example in *I made a cake*, the subject is *I* and *made* is an active verb.

> ⚙ **BUILD YOUR VOCABULARY**
> Look at **passive**.

activity NOUN activities
❶ Activity is doing things. ❷ An activity is something someone likes to do. • *They enjoy outdoor activities.*

actor NOUN actors
someone who takes part in a play or film

actress NOUN actresses
a girl or woman who takes part in a play or film

actual ADJECTIVE
really there or really happening • *Is that an actual dinosaur bone?*

actually ADVERB
really, in fact • *Actually, I think you are wrong.*

acute ADJECTIVE
❶ sharp or intense • *an acute stomach pain*
❷ severe • *an acute shortage of food* ❸ An acute angle is less than 90°.

> ⚙ **BUILD YOUR VOCABULARY**
> Look at **obtuse**, **reflex** and **right angle**.

AD ABBREVIATION
short for Latin *Anno Domini*, used with dates that come after the birth of Jesus Christ • *The Romans left Britain in around AD 410.*

> ⚙ **BUILD YOUR VOCABULARY**
> Look at **BC**.

Adam's apple NOUN Adam's apples
the lump at the front of a man's neck

adapt VERB adapts, adapting, adapted
❶ to change something so you can use it for something different ❷ To adapt to something new is to get used to it. • *She adapted quickly to her new school.*

adaptable ADJECTIVE
able to change to suit different situations

add VERB adds, adding, added
❶ To add numbers or to add numbers up means to put them together to get a bigger number. • *If you add 7 and 3 you get 10.* ❷ To add one thing to another is to combine the things or put them together. • *Add the eggs.* • *Adding 'un-' to a word changes the meaning.*

adder NOUN adders
a small poisonous snake

addiction NOUN addictions
a habit that someone can't give up

addition NOUN additions
❶ Addition is the process of adding numbers together. ❷ An addition is something or someone that has been added. • *Matt was a late addition to the team.*

additional ADJECTIVE
extra, added on

additive NOUN additives
something that is added to food in small amounts

address NOUN addresses
❶ the details of the place where someone lives • *My address is 29 High Street, Newtown.* ❷ a set of letters and symbols that you type to find a website or to send an email • *What's your email address?*

address VERB addresses, addressing, addressed
❶ To address a letter or parcel is to write the address on it. ❷ To address a group of people is to make a speech to them. • *A man stepped forward and addressed the crowd.*

adhesive NOUN adhesives
something such as glue that you use to stick things together

Adi Granth (say ah-dee **grunt**) NOUN
the holy book of Sikhs

a
b
c
d
e
f
g
h
i
j
k
l
m
n
o
p
q
r
s
t
u
v
w
x
y
z

adjective NOUN adjectives

a word that describes a noun or adds to its meaning, for example *big*, *blue* or *friendly*

⚙ **BUILD** YOUR VOCABULARY

Adjective is a **word class**.

adjust VERB adjusts, adjusting, adjusted

❶ to change something slightly or change its position ❷ To adjust to something new is to get used to it. • *They found it hard to **adjust** to life in the city.*

➤ **adjustment** NOUN • *She made a few **adjustments** to the plan.*

administer VERB administers, administering, administered

To administer something is to give it to someone. • *The nurse **administers** medicine.*

administration NOUN

the work of managing and organising a business

admiral NOUN admirals

an officer of the highest rank in the navy

admiration NOUN

If you feel admiration for someone or something, you think they are very good or very impressive. • *I'm full of **admiration** for her courage.*

admire VERB admires, admiring, admired

to think someone or something is very good or very beautiful

➤ **admirer** NOUN

admission NOUN admissions

❶ Admission is being allowed to go into a place. • *Admission to the show is by ticket only.* ❷ An admission is something that someone admits or confesses. • *He is guilty by his own **admission**.*

admit VERB admits, admitting, admitted

❶ To admit something is to say that it has happened or that you have done it. ❷ To admit someone is to allow them into a place.

admittance NOUN

permission to go into a place • *The sign said 'No admittance'.*

ado NOUN

➤ **without more ado** or **without further ado** without wasting any more time

adolescent NOUN adolescents

a young person who is older than a child and not yet an adult, from about 15 to 18

➤ **adolescence** NOUN

adopt VERB adopts, adopting, adopted

To adopt a child is to take them into your family and make them legally your own child.

➤ **adopted** ADJECTIVE • *an **adopted** child*

➤ **adoption** NOUN

adorable ADJECTIVE

lovely and easy to love • *an **adorable** puppy*

adore VERB adores, adoring, adored

To adore someone or something is to love them or admire them very much.

➤ **adoration** NOUN

adrenaline (also **adrenalin**) NOUN

a hormone produced by your body in stressful situations, that makes your heart beat faster and gives you more energy

adrift ADJECTIVE

If something is adrift, it is loose and drifting about. • *The boat was **adrift** on the river.*

adult NOUN adults

a fully grown person or animal

advance NOUN advances

❶ An advance is progress. • *There have been amazing **advances** in technology.* ❷ An advance is a forward movement. • *The army's **advance** was stopped.*

➤ **in advance** beforehand

advance VERB advances, advancing, advanced

❶ to move forward ❷ to make progress

advanced ADJECTIVE

An advanced course or exam is one at a high level.

advantage NOUN advantages

something useful or helpful

➤ **To take advantage of someone** is to treat them unfairly when they are not likely to complain.

➤ **To take advantage of something** is to make good use of it.

Advent calendar NOUN Advent calendars

a decoration with numbered windows to open on each of the days of December before Christmas

adventure NOUN adventures
An adventure is something very exciting that someone does.
Not long ago there lived in Suffolk a hundred and one Dalmatians whose adventures had once thrilled all the dogs of England.—THE STARLIGHT BARKING, Dodie Smith

adventurous ADJECTIVE
An adventurous person likes to do exciting and new things.

> An opposite is **unadventurous**.

adverb NOUN adverbs
a word that tells you how, when, where or why something happens. In these sentences, the words in bold are adverbs: *He listened* **carefully**. • *I heard voices* **upstairs.**

BUILD YOUR VOCABULARY
> Adverb is a **word class**.

adverbial NOUN adverbials
An adverbial is a group of words that acts as an adverb. In these sentences, the phrases in bold are adverbials: *He moved* **as slowly as a snail**. • *You must leave* **before the clock strikes twelve.**

advert NOUN adverts *(informal)*
an advertisement

advertise VERB advertises, advertising, advertised
to tell people about something on television, in a magazine, on a website, etc. in order to make them want to buy it

advertisement NOUN advertisements
something such as a short film or a poster that tries to persuade people to buy something

advice NOUN
Advice is something you say to help someone decide what to do.

advisable ADJECTIVE
If something is advisable, it is sensible and you should do it.

BUILD YOUR VOCABULARY
> The opposite is **inadvisable**.

advise VERB advises, advising, advised
to tell someone what you think they should do
• *I* **advised** *her to ignore the email.*

aerial NOUN aerials
a wire or metal rod for receiving or sending radio or television signals

aerial ADJECTIVE
from or in the air • *an* **aerial** *view of the island*

aerobics NOUN
energetic exercises that strengthen your heart and lungs

aeroplane NOUN aeroplanes
a flying vehicle with wings and powerful engines

aerosol NOUN aerosols
a device that holds a liquid under pressure and lets it out in a fine spray

affair NOUN affairs
something that happens; an event • *The party was a very strange* **affair.**

affect VERB affects, affecting, affected
To affect someone or something is to cause them to change or to harm them. • *The dampness might* **affect** *his health.*

⚠ **WATCH OUT!**
> Do not confuse to **affect** (a verb) with an **effect** (a noun): *the effects of climate change.*

affection NOUN affections
love that you feel or show • *Her mum shows her a lot of* **affection.**
➤ **affectionate** ADJECTIVE • *She gave me an* **affectionate** *hug.*

affluent *(say af-loo-ent)* ADJECTIVE
wealthy • *This is an* **affluent** *part of the city.*
➤ **affluence** NOUN

afford VERB affords, affording, afforded
❶ If you can afford something, you have enough money to pay for it. ❷ If you can afford to do something, you have enough time to do it.
• *We can't* **afford** *to relax.*

afloat ADVERB
floating • *We managed to keep the raft* **afloat.**

afraid ADJECTIVE
frightened • *Don't be* **afraid.**
➤ **I'm afraid** I am sorry; I regret • *I'm afraid I can't help you.*

A
B
C
D
E
F
G
H
I
J
K
L
M
N
O
P
Q
R
S
T
U
V
W
X
Y
Z

after *PREPOSITION, ADVERB*
❶ later or later than; following • *I left after breakfast.* • *We saw her again the day after.*
❷ following or coming behind • *You got here after me.* ❸ To be named after someone is to be given their name. • *I was named after my grandmother.*

afternoon *NOUN* afternoons
the time from midday until evening

afterwards *ADVERB*
at a later time

again *ADVERB*
❶ once more; another time • *Can you say that again, slowly?* ❷ as before • *You'll soon be well again.*
➤ **again and again** lots of times

against *PREPOSITION*
❶ touching or hitting • *He was leaning against the wall.* ❷ If you are against something, you do not agree with or support it. • *Are you against eating meat?*

⚙ **BUILD YOUR VOCABULARY**
The opposite of the second meaning is **for**.

age *NOUN* ages
❶ Your age is how old you are. • *at the age of twelve* ❷ An age is a period of history. • *the Victorian age*
➤ **ages** (informal) a long time • *We've been waiting ages.*
age *VERB* ages, ageing, aged
To age is to become old.

aged *ADJECTIVE*
❶ *(say* ayjd*)* having the age of • *The girl was aged 9.* ❷ *(say* **ay**-jid*)* very old • *We saw an aged man.*

agency *NOUN* agencies
an office or business that organises something
• *an advertising agency*

agenda *(say* a-**jen**-da*) NOUN* agendas
a list of things to do or talk about at a meeting

agent *NOUN* agents
❶ a person or business that organises something
• *a travel agent* ❷ a spy • *a secret agent*

aggravate *VERB* aggravates, aggravating, aggravated
❶ To aggravate something is to make it worse.
❷ *(informal)* To aggravate someone is to annoy them.
➤ **aggravation** *NOUN* • *I've had enough aggravation for one day.*

aggressive *ADJECTIVE*
behaving in a very unfriendly or violent way • *That's a very aggressive dog.*
➤ **aggressively** *ADVERB*

aghast *ADJECTIVE*
horrified or shocked
'Travel in a balloon!' exclaimed the Duchess, aghast. 'William! Are you out of your mind?'–BLACK HEARTS IN BATTERSEA, Joan Aiken

agile *ADJECTIVE*
able to move quickly and easily • *Mountain goats are very agile.*
➤ **agility** *NOUN*

agitated *ADJECTIVE*
worried and nervous • *He seemed agitated.*
➤ **agitation** *NOUN*

agnostic *NOUN* agnostics
someone who believes that we cannot know if there is a God

ago *ADVERB*
in the past • *Dinosaurs lived on earth long ago.*

agony *NOUN* agonies
severe pain or suffering

agree *VERB* agrees, agreeing, agreed
❶ To agree with someone is to think the same as them. ❷ To agree to do something is to say that you are willing to do it. • *She agreed to show us the way.* ❸ Food does not agree with you when it upsets your stomach. • *Spicy food doesn't agree with me.*

agreeable *ADJECTIVE*
❶ willing to do something that someone suggests
• *He was agreeable to the idea.* ❷ pleasant

⚙ **BUILD YOUR VOCABULARY**
An opposite of the second meaning is
disagreeable.

agreement NOUN agreements
① Agreement is thinking the same. • *Are we in agreement?*

② An agreement is an arrangement that people have agreed on.

agriculture NOUN
Agriculture is farming or growing food on the land.
➤ **agricultural** ADJECTIVE

ahead ADVERB
forwards, in front • *He stared straight ahead.*

ahoy EXCLAMATION
a shout used by sailors to attract attention

aid NOUN aids
① Aid is help. • *He managed with the aid of his friends.* ② An aid is something that helps someone to do something. • *Uncle Ted wears a hearing aid.*
aid VERB aids, aiding, aided
To aid someone is to help them.

ailment NOUN ailments
a minor illness

aim VERB aims, aiming, aimed
① To aim something at someone or something is to point it at them or try to hit them with it. ② To aim to do something is to try to do it.
aim NOUN aims
Your aim is what you intend to do.

air NOUN airs
① Air is the mixture of gases which surrounds the earth and which everyone breathes. ② Travel by air is travel in an aircraft. ③ An air is a particular mood or atmosphere.
An air of gloom had settled upon the class.–THE DAY OF THE PSYCHIC SOCK, Steve Cole
air VERB airs, airing, aired
① To air washing is to put it in a warm place to finish drying. ② To air a room is to let fresh air into it. ③ To air your opinions is to tell them to people.

air-conditioning NOUN
a system for keeping the air in a building cool in hot weather

aircraft NOUN aircraft
an aeroplane or a helicopter • *The sound of enemy aircraft was getting closer.*

air force NOUN air forces
the part of a country's fighting force that uses aircraft

airline NOUN airlines
a company that takes people to places by aircraft

airport NOUN airports
a place where aircraft land and take off, with passenger terminals and other buildings

airtight ADJECTIVE
not letting air get in or out

airy ADJECTIVE airier, airiest
with plenty of fresh air

aisle (rhymes with **mile**) NOUN aisles
a passage between or beside rows of seats or shelves

ajar ADJECTIVE
slightly open • *Please leave the door ajar.*

alarm NOUN alarms
① a device that makes a warning sound ② a feeling of fear and worry • *He cried out in alarm.*
alarm VERB alarms, alarming, alarmed
To alarm someone is to make them frightened or worried.
➤ **alarmed** ADJECTIVE • *Don't be alarmed.*

alarm clock NOUN alarm clocks
a clock that can be set to make a sound to wake you up

a b c d e f g h i j k l m n o p q r s t u v w x y z

alas EXCLAMATION (old use)
a word people say when they are sad
'Aren't you also much loved in the world?' 'Alas, no,' Miss Spider answered, sighing long and loud.—JAMES AND THE GIANT PEACH, Roald Dahl

albatross NOUN **albatrosses**
a large seabird with long wings

album NOUN **albums**
❶ a book in which you keep things like photographs or stamps ❷ a collection of songs on a CD or record

alcohol NOUN
drinks such as beer, wine or whisky, that contain a substance that can make people drunk

alert ADJECTIVE
watching for something; ready to act
alert VERB **alerts, alerting, alerted**
to warn someone about a danger or problem

algae (say alg-ee or al-jee) NOUN
a group of plants that grow in water without roots or stems

algebra (say al-jib-ra) NOUN
mathematics in which letters and symbols are used to represent numbers

⭐ WORD STORY
The word **algebra** comes from an Arabic word meaning 'putting broken parts together'.

algorithm NOUN
a set of rules that a computer uses to solve a problem

alias (say ay-lee-ass) NOUN **aliases**
a false or different name that someone uses instead of their real name
alias (say ay-lee-ass) ADVERB
also named • *Clark Kent, alias Superman*

alibi (say al-ib-eye) NOUN **alibis**
If someone has an alibi, they can prove they were somewhere else when a crime was committed.

⭐ WORD STORY
Alibi is a Latin word meaning 'elsewhere'.

alien (say ay-lee-en) NOUN **aliens**
in stories, a creature from another world
alien (say ay-lee-en) ADJECTIVE
strange and unfamiliar • *an alien landscape*

alight VERB **alights, alighting, alighted**
❶ When a bird alights on a branch it lands on it.
❷ To alight from a vehicle is to get out of it.
alight ADJECTIVE
❶ on fire, burning ❷ lit up or shining
She sprang up, her face alight with laughter.—THE EAGLE OF THE NINTH, Rosemary Sutcliff

alike ADJECTIVE
similar, like each other
alike ADVERB
in the same way • *He treats everybody alike.*

alive ADJECTIVE
living; existing • *Is he alive?*

alkali (say al-kal-eye) NOUN **alkalis**
a substance that makes acids neutral or that combines with acids to form salts

⚙ **BUILD** YOUR VOCABULARY
Look at **acid**.

all DETERMINER, ADVERB, PRONOUN
everything or everyone • *That is all I know.*
• *She was dressed all in white.* • *All my friends are here.*

Allah NOUN
the Muslim name of God

allegation (say al-ig-ay-shun) NOUN **allegations**
If you make an allegation, you accuse someone of doing something wrong.

allege (say a-lej) VERB **alleges, alleging, alleged**
To allege that something is true is to claim that it is, without proving it.

allergic (say a-ler-jik) ADJECTIVE
If you are allergic to something, you become ill when you eat, drink or touch it. • *My sister is allergic to peanuts.*

allergy (say a-ler-jee) NOUN
a condition that makes someone ill if they eat, drink or touch particular things • *Victor has a peanut allergy.*

alley NOUN **alleys**
a narrow street or passage

alliance NOUN **alliances**
an agreement between countries or groups to support each other and work together

⚙ **BUILD** YOUR VOCABULARY
Look at **ally**.

alligator NOUN **alligators**
a large reptile like a crocodile but with a rounded snout, found in North America and China

✳ **WORD STORY**
The word **alligator** comes from the Spanish *el lagarto* meaning 'the lizard'.

alliteration NOUN
Alliteration is when several words are used together that begin with the same sound, as in *slugs slowly slithering* or *Vlad the Vampire*.

allocate VERB **allocates, allocating, allocated**
to give something to someone for a particular purpose • *We've been **allocated** this room.*

allotment NOUN **allotments**
a small rented piece of ground used for growing vegetables

allow VERB **allows, allowing, allowed**
To allow someone to do something is to let them do it. • *Will you **allow** me to take a photo?* • *Skateboarding is not **allowed**.*

⚠ **WATCH OUT!**
Do not confuse **allowed** with **aloud**.

alloy NOUN **alloys**
a metal formed from a mixture of other metals

all right ADJECTIVE
❶ satisfactory, quite good • *The film is **all right**, but the book is better.* ❷ acceptable, allowed • *Is it **all right** to sit here?* ❸ well • *Are you **all right**?*
all right EXCLAMATION
used for agreeing to something • *'Would you like to come?'—'**All right**.'*

ally (*say* al-eye) NOUN **allies**
a person or country that agrees to support and help another person or country

⚙ **BUILD** YOUR VOCABULARY
Look at **alliance**.

almond
(*say* ah-mond)
NOUN **almonds**
an oval nut that you can eat

almost ADVERB
nearly but not quite • *I am **almost** ready.*

aloft ADVERB
high up
When the wind blows and the rain comes down, it's jolly sitting up aloft in the snug tree-house.—THE MAGIC PUDDING, Norman Lindsay

alone ADJECTIVE, ADVERB
without any other people or other things • *She lives **alone**.* • *The drinks **alone** cost £10.*

along PREPOSITION, ADVERB
❶ on, forward • *They skipped happily **along**.* ❷ from one end of something to the other • *Crowds stood **along** the street.* ❸ with someone • *I brought my brother **along**.*

alongside PREPOSITION, ADVERB
next to something

aloud ADVERB
in a voice that can be heard

⚠ **WATCH OUT!**
Don't confuse **aloud** with **allowed** meaning 'given permission'.

alphabet NOUN **alphabets**
all the letters used in a language, that are written in a special order
➤ **alphabetical** ADJECTIVE • *Put the names in **alphabetical** order.*
➤ **alphabetically** ADVERB

✳ **WORD STORY**
The word **alphabet** comes from *alpha* and *beta*, the first two letters of the Greek alphabet.

already ADVERB
before now or by now • *I've **already** told you once.*

Alsatian (*say* al-say-shun) NOUN **Alsatians**
a large strong dog, also sometimes called a German shepherd

also ADVERB
as well, besides • *We **also** need some bread.*

altar *NOUN* **altars**
a table used in religious ceremonies

> ⚠ **WATCH OUT!**
> Do not confuse an **altar** with to **alter** meaning 'to change'.

alter *VERB* **alters, altering, altered**
To alter something is to change it.

alternate *(say* ol-**ter**-nat*) ADJECTIVE*
happening on every other one
In the Doldrums, laughter is frowned upon and smiling is permitted only on alternate Thursdays.—THE PHANTOM TOLLBOOTH, Norton Juster

alternate *(say* ol-**ter**-nayt*) VERB* **alternates, alternating, alternated**
To alternate is to happen in turns.

alternately *ADVERB*
one after the other in turn • *The weather was alternately fine and wet.*

> ⚠ **WATCH OUT!**
> Do not confuse with **alternatively** meaning 'instead'.

alternative *(say* ol-**ter**-nat-iv*) NOUN*
alternatives
An alternative is something you can choose instead of something else.

alternative *(say* ol-**ter**-nat-iv*) ADJECTIVE*
that you can choose instead of something else
• *Here's an alternative idea.*
➤ **alternatively** *ADVERB* • *Alternatively, you could use butter.*

although *CONJUNCTION*
in spite of the fact that • *Although it was morning, the sky was still dark.*

altitude *NOUN* **altitudes**
the height of something, especially above sea level

altogether *ADVERB*
❶ in total • *How many people are there altogether?*
❷ completely • *He slowed down, then stopped altogether.*

aluminium *NOUN*
a silver-coloured metal that is light in weight

> ⚙ **BUILD YOUR VOCABULARY**
> Aluminium is an **element**.

always *ADVERB*
all the time or every time • *Always look before crossing the road.*

am *(present form of* **be** *used with 'I')*
• *I am thirsty.*

a.m. *ABBREVIATION*
in the morning • *Be here at 9 a.m.*

> ✳ **WORD STORY**
> **a.m.** is short for Latin *ante meridiem*, meaning 'before midday'.

> ⚙ **BUILD YOUR VOCABULARY**
> Look at **p.m.**

amateur *(say* **am**-at-er*) NOUN* **amateurs**
someone who does something without being paid for it

> ✳ **WORD STORY**
> The word **amateur** is from a French word meaning 'a person who loves something'.

> ⚙ **BUILD YOUR VOCABULARY**
> The opposite is **professional**.

amaze *VERB* **amazes, amazing, amazed**
to surprise someone very much
➤ **amazement** *NOUN* • *They stared in amazement.*

amazing *ADJECTIVE*
very surprising or remarkable • *We saw some amazing sights.*
➤ **amazingly** *ADVERB*

ambassador *NOUN* **ambassadors**
a person sent to a foreign country to represent their own government

amber *NOUN*
❶ a hard, clear, yellow substance used in jewellery, that comes from fossilised tree sap
❷ a yellow-orange colour used in traffic lights

ambiguity NOUN
If there is ambiguity, something is not clear because it could have more than one meaning.

ambiguous ADJECTIVE
having more than one possible meaning

ambition NOUN ambitions
❶ An ambition is something you want to do very much. • *His ambition is to play for his country.*
❷ Ambition is a strong desire to be successful.

ambitious ADJECTIVE
❶ An ambitious person wants very much to be successful. ❷ An ambitious plan is difficult or challenging.

amble VERB ambles, ambling, ambled
to walk slowly

ambulance NOUN ambulances
a vehicle for carrying sick or injured people

ambush NOUN ambushes
a surprise attack from a hidden place
ambush VERB ambushes, ambushing, ambushed
to attack someone suddenly from a hidden place

amid (also **amidst**) PREPOSITION
in the middle of, among • *Something moved amid the wreckage.*

ammonite (say am-mon-ite)
NOUN ammonites
a type of fossil with a spiral shape

ammunition NOUN
bullets, bombs and other explosive objects used in fighting

ammonite

amoeba (say a-mee-ba) NOUN amoebas
a tiny creature made of one cell

among (also **amongst**) PREPOSITION
❶ in the middle of • *Birds flew among the trees.*
❷ between several people or things • *Share the work among you.*

amount NOUN amounts
a quantity or total

ampersand NOUN ampersands
the sign '&', which means 'and'

amphibian NOUN
an animal that can live on land and in water, such as a frog
➤ **amphibious** ADJECTIVE

amphitheatre NOUN amphitheatres
a circular or oval building without a roof, with rows of seats around the sides

amphora (say am-fo-ra) NOUN amphoras
an ancient Greek or Roman vase with two handles

amplify VERB amplifies, amplifying, amplified
To amplify something is to make it louder or stronger.

amuse VERB amuses, amusing, amused
❶ If something amuses you, it makes you laugh or smile. ❷ To amuse yourself is to find pleasant things to do.
➤ **amusing** ADJECTIVE • *It was an amusing story.*

amusement NOUN amusements
❶ Amusement is the feeling of being made to laugh or smile.
I looked back at her, disconcerted to see a trace of amusement creeping into her eyes.—SIGRUN'S SECRET, Marie-Louise Jensen
❷ An amusement is a pleasant thing to do.

an DETERMINER
a word used instead of **a** when the next word begins with a vowel sound or a silent 'h' • *an apple* • *an hour*

BUILD YOUR VOCABULARY
The word **an** is an **indefinite article**.

anaemia (say a-nee-mee-a) NOUN
a condition in which someone's blood does not have enough red cells, making them feel tired and look pale
➤ **anaemic** ADJECTIVE

anaesthetic (say an-iss-thet-ik) NOUN anaesthetics
a drug or gas that makes you unable to feel pain

anagram NOUN anagrams
a word or phrase made by rearranging the letters of another word or phrase. For example *dream* is an anagram of *armed.*

a
b
c
d
e
f
g
h
i
j
k
l
m
n
o
p
q
r
s
t
u
v
w
x
y
z

A

analogue *ADJECTIVE*
An analogue clock or watch has hands and a dial with numbers or marks around it.

> **BUILD YOUR VOCABULARY**
> The other type of clock or watch is **digital**.

analogy *NOUN* **analogies**
a comparison between two things that are similar in some ways • *He makes an **analogy** between the brain and a computer.*

analyse *VERB* **analyses, analysing, analysed**
To analyse something is to examine it carefully.

analysis *NOUN* **analyses**
a detailed study or examination of something

anatomy *NOUN*
the study of the parts of the body
➤ **anatomical** *ADJECTIVE*

ancestor *NOUN* **ancestors**
Your ancestors are people in your family who lived in the past, before you.

anchor *NOUN* **anchors**
a heavy object joined to a ship by a chain or rope and dropped to the bottom of the sea to stop the ship from moving

ancient *ADJECTIVE*
existing or happening very long ago

and *CONJUNCTION*
a word used to link words and phrases that are connected • *We had cakes **and** lemonade.*
• *Go upstairs **and** lie down.*

anecdote *NOUN* **anecdotes**
a short amusing or interesting story about a real person or thing

anemone *(say* a-**nem**-on-ee*)*
NOUN **anemones**
a small flower shaped like a cup

angel *NOUN* **angels**
❶ a human-like being with wings that some people believe is a messenger from God ❷ someone who is perfectly behaved or very kind
➤ **angelic** *ADJECTIVE*

> ✳ **WORD STORY**
> The word **angel** comes from a Greek word meaning 'messenger'.

anger *NOUN*
a feeling of being very annoyed

angle *NOUN* **angles**
❶ the space between two lines or surfaces that meet

> **BUILD YOUR VOCABULARY**
> Look at **acute**, **obtuse**, **reflex** and **right angle**.

❷ a direction or point of view • *They looked at it from all **angles**.*
angle *VERB* **angles, angling, angled**
to put something in a slanting position

Anglo-Saxon *NOUN* **Anglo-Saxons**
❶ an English person, especially from the time before the Norman Conquest in 1066 ❷ the old form of English spoken before 1066

angry *ADJECTIVE* **angrier, angriest**
very annoyed
➤ **angrily** *ADVERB* • *'What now?' he snapped angrily.*

anguish *NOUN*
great suffering or unhappiness

animal *NOUN* **animals**
An animal is a living thing that can move and feel. This word is normally used to mean creatures that are not humans.

animated *ADJECTIVE*
❶ lively and excited ❷ An animated film is one made using lots of drawings or computer images that appear to move.

animation *NOUN*
❶ liveliness or excitement ❷ a way of making films from still images so they appear to move

ankle NOUN ankles
the part of your leg where it is joined to your foot

annihilate *(say an-eye-il-ate)* VERB
annihilates, annihilating, annihilated
to destroy something completely
➤ **annihilation** NOUN

anniversary NOUN anniversaries
a day when you remember something special that
happened on the same date in an earlier year

announce VERB announces, announcing,
announced
to say something publicly
'I refuse to go!' announced Grandpa George.—CHARLIE AND
THE CHOCOLATE FACTORY, Roald Dahl
➤ **announcement** NOUN

annoy VERB annoys, annoying, annoyed
to make someone feel slightly angry
➤ **annoyance** NOUN • *A look of annoyance
crossed his face.*
➤ **annoyed** ADJECTIVE • *What are you so annoyed
about?*

annual ADJECTIVE
happening or coming every year • *the annual school
book sale*
➤ **annually** ADVERB
annual NOUN annuals
a book for children that comes out once a year

anonymous ADJECTIVE
An anonymous book or letter is written by someone
who does not give their name.
➤ **anonymously** ADVERB • *The story was
published anonymously.*

anorak NOUN anoraks
a waterproof jacket with a hood

WORD STORY

The word **anorak** comes from an Inuit word meaning
'waterproof coat'.

anorexia *(say an-er-reks-ee-a)* NOUN
an illness which makes someone not want to eat
➤ **anorexic** ADJECTIVE

another DETERMINER, PRONOUN
a different person or thing • *Have another look.*
• *Show me another.*

answer NOUN answers
❶ An answer is something you say or write when
someone asks you a question. ❷ The answer to a
problem is something that solves it.
answer VERB answers, answering,
answered
❶ to give an answer • *I asked his name, but he
didn't answer.* ❷ If you answer the phone or the
door, you speak to the person who is calling or
knocking.

ant NOUN ants
a tiny insect that lives with others

BUILD YOUR VOCABULARY

A group of ants living together is called a **colony**.

antagonise *(also* **antagonize***)* VERB
antagonises, antagonising, antagonised
to make someone feel angry or unfriendly

Antarctic *or* **Antarctica** NOUN
The Antarctic is the area around the South Pole.
➤ **Antarctic** ADJECTIVE • an **Antarctic** expedition

BUILD YOUR VOCABULARY

Look at **polar**.

anteater NOUN anteaters
an animal with a long tongue that eats ants

antelope NOUN antelope, antelopes
an animal like a deer, that lives in Africa and parts
of Asia

a b c d e f g h i j k l m n o p q r s t u v w x y z

antenna NOUN

❶ a long thin feeler on the head of an insect or shellfish

> ⚠ **WATCH OUT!**
>
> The plural of this meaning is **antennae**.

❷ an aerial

> ⚠ **WATCH OUT!**
>
> The plural of this meaning is **antennas**.

anthem NOUN anthems

a religious or patriotic song

anther NOUN anthers

the part of a flower that contains pollen

> ⚙ **BUILD** YOUR VOCABULARY
>
> Look at **pistil** and **stamen**.

anthology NOUN anthologies

a collection of poems, stories or songs in one book

antibiotic NOUN antibiotics

a drug that kills bacteria, used to cure infections

> ⚙ **BUILD** YOUR VOCABULARY
>
> Look at **penicillin**.

anticipate VERB anticipates, anticipating, anticipated

to expect something and be prepared for it

I had not anticipated this pitch black, where there were no visible markers to guide me.–VIKING GIRL, Pauline Chandler

anticipation NOUN

a feeling of looking forward to something

anticlimax NOUN anticlimaxes

a disappointing ending or result after something exciting

anticlockwise ADVERB, ADJECTIVE

moving round in the opposite direction to the hands of a clock

> ⚙ **BUILD** YOUR VOCABULARY
>
> Look at **clockwise**.

antidote NOUN antidotes

something which takes away the bad effects of a poison

antique (say an-**teek**) NOUN antiques

something that is valuable because it is very old

antiseptic NOUN antiseptics

a chemical that kills germs

antler NOUN antlers

a male deer's horn, which has several branches

> ⚙ **BUILD** YOUR VOCABULARY
>
> A male deer is called a **stag**.

antonym NOUN antonyms

a word that is opposite in meaning to another

• *'Soft' is an **antonym** of 'hard'.*

anxiety (say ang-zy-it-ee) NOUN

a feeling of being worried or nervous

anxious ADJECTIVE

❶ worried and nervous ❷ If you are anxious to do something, you want to do it. • *He was **anxious** to help.*

any DETERMINER

❶ one or some • *Have you **any** spare paper?*
❷ no matter which • *Come **any** day you like.*

any PRONOUN

one or some • *I don't have **any** left.*

any ADVERB

at all; in some way • *Is the cake **any** good?*

anybody PRONOUN

anyone

anyhow ADVERB

❶ anyway ❷ carelessly, without thinking • *You can't put them away just **anyhow**.*

anyone PRONOUN

any person • *Don't tell **anyone**!*

anything PRONOUN

any object, situation, idea, etc. • *I can't hear **anything**.*

anyway ADVERB

whatever happens; in any situation • *If it rains, we'll go **anyway**.*

anywhere ADVERB

in any place or to any place • *I couldn't see her **anywhere**.*

apart ADVERB

❶ away from each other; separately • *The male lion and cubs are kept **apart**.* ❷ into pieces • *The book was beginning to fall **apart**.*

apartment *NOUN* apartments
a set of rooms for living in

> **BUILD YOUR VOCABULARY**
>
> An **apartment** is the usual word in American English for a **flat**.

ape *NOUN* apes
a monkey without a tail, such as a gorilla or a chimpanzee

> **BUILD YOUR VOCABULARY**
>
> Look at **primate**.

apex *NOUN* apices
the highest point of something pointed, such as a cone or triangle

aphid *NOUN* aphids
a tiny insect that sucks sap from plants

apologise *(also* **apologize***) VERB*
apologises, apologising, apologised
To apologise to someone is to tell them you are sorry.

apology *NOUN* apologies
a statement that you are sorry for doing something wrong

apostrophe *(say* a-**poss**-trof-ee*) NOUN*
apostrophes
An apostrophe is a punctuation mark (') used to show that letters have been left out, as in *can't* and *we'll*. It is also used with s to show who owns something, as in *the cat's paws* (one cat), or *the cats' paws* (more than one cat).

app *NOUN* apps
a computer program for doing a particular thing, especially one that you download on to a mobile phone

appalling *ADJECTIVE*
dreadful, shocking

apparatus *NOUN*
Apparatus is special equipment you use for something. • *gym* **apparatus**

apparent *ADJECTIVE*
❶ clear, obvious • *He laughed for no* **apparent** *reason.* ❷ appearing to be true • *She spoke with* **apparent** *calm.*
➤ **apparently** *ADVERB*

appeal *VERB* appeals, appealing, appealed
❶ To appeal to someone for something is to ask for it when you need it badly.
'Is there nothing we can do?' asked the Ladybird, appealing to James.—JAMES AND THE GIANT PEACH, Roald Dahl
❷ If something appeals to you, it interests or attracts you.

appeal *NOUN* appeals
An appeal is asking for something you need badly.

appear *VERB* appears, appearing, appeared
❶ To appear is to start to be seen or exist. • *A face* **appeared** *at the window.*

> **BUILD YOUR VOCABULARY**
>
> The opposite of this meaning is **disappear**.

❷ To appear to be something is to seem it.
• *She* **appeared** *upset.*

appearance *NOUN* appearances
❶ the fact of starting to be seen or to exist
• *the* **appearance** *of a new species*

> **BUILD YOUR VOCABULARY**
>
> The opposite of this meaning is **disappearance**.

❷ Someone's appearance is what they look like.

appendicitis *NOUN*
a painful infection in someone's appendix

appendix *NOUN*
❶ a small tube leading off from the intestines in the body

> ⚠ **WATCH OUT!**
>
> The plural of this meaning is **appendixes**.

❷ an extra section at the end of a book

> ⚠ **WATCH OUT!**
>
> The plural of this meaning is **appendices**.

appetite *NOUN* appetites
a feeling of hunger

appetizing *ADJECTIVE*
looking or smelling good to eat

> **BUILD YOUR VOCABULARY**
>
> An opposite is **unappetizing**.

applaud *VERB* applauds, applauding, applauded
to show that you like someone or something by clapping

a
b
c
d
e
f
g
h
i
j
k
l
m
n
o
p
q
r
s
t
u
v
w
x
y
z

applause NOUN
clapping or cheering after someone has given a speech or performance • *We gave her a round of applause.*

apple NOUN apples
a round fruit with skin that is red, green or yellow

appliance NOUN appliances
a device or gadget • *a kitchen appliance*

applicable ADJECTIVE
that applies to someone • *This rule is applicable to everybody.*

application NOUN applications
❶ a letter or form asking for something important, such as a job ❷ a program on a computer or mobile phone for performing a particular activity

apply VERB applies, applying, applied
❶ To apply for a job is to write formally and ask for it.

> **BUILD** YOUR VOCABULARY
Look at **application**.

❷ To apply to someone is to concern them. • *These rules apply to everybody.*

> **BUILD** YOUR VOCABULARY
Look at **applicable**.

❸ To apply something is to put it on to a surface. • *Don't forget to apply sunscreen.*

appoint VERB appoints, appointing, appointed
To appoint someone is to choose them for a job.

appointment NOUN appointments
an arrangement to meet or visit someone • *I have an appointment at the dentist's.*

appreciate VERB appreciates, appreciating, appreciated
To appreciate something is to enjoy it or be grateful for it.
➤ **appreciation** NOUN • *Let's show our appreciation.*

apprehensive ADJECTIVE
nervous or worried about something that is going to happen

apprentice NOUN apprentices
someone who is learning a trade or craft
• *a plumber's apprentice*

approach VERB approaches, approaching, approached
to come near or nearer • *He approached the dog nervously.* • *The big day approached.*

approach NOUN approaches
❶ the fact of coming near or nearer • *They heard the approach of a truck.* ❷ a way of tackling a problem
• *Let's try a new approach.*

appropriate ADJECTIVE
suitable

> **BUILD** YOUR VOCABULARY
The opposite is **inappropriate**.

approve VERB approves, approving, approved
To approve of someone or something is to think they are good or suitable.
➤ **approval** NOUN • *They want her approval.*

> **BUILD** YOUR VOCABULARY
The opposite is **disapprove**.

approximate ADJECTIVE
roughly correct but not exact • *What is your approximate height?*
➤ **approximately** ADVERB

apricot NOUN apricots
a juicy orange-coloured fruit like a small peach, with a stone in it

April Fool's Day NOUN
1 April, when it is traditional to play tricks on people

apron NOUN aprons
a piece of clothing worn over the front of your clothes to protect them

aptitude NOUN aptitudes
a talent • *She has an aptitude for music.*

aquarium NOUN aquariums
a tank or building for keeping live fish

aquatic ADJECTIVE
living or happening in water • *aquatic plants*

aqueduct NOUN aqueducts
a bridge that carries water across a valley

Arab *NOUN* Arabs
a member of a people living in parts of the Middle East and North Africa

Arabic *NOUN*
the language spoken by Arabs

 WORD STORY
The words **algebra**, **monsoon** and **zero** come from Arabic.

Arabic numeral *NOUN* Arabic numerals
one of the figures 1, 2, 3, 4 and so on, that we use to represent numbers

BUILD YOUR VOCABULARY
Look at **Roman numeral**.

arable *ADJECTIVE*
to do with growing crops

arc *NOUN* arcs
❶ a curving line
Sara tossed the book in a high arc over her shoulder.
—THE DAY OF THE PSYCHIC SOCK, Steve Cole
❷ part of the circumference of a circle

⚠ **WATCH OUT!**
Don't confuse with **ark** meaning 'Noah's ship'.

arcade *NOUN* arcades
a covered place to walk, with shops down each side

arch *NOUN* arches
a curved structure that helps to support a bridge or building
arch *VERB* arches, arching, arched
to curve
The wind itself had ceased and a brilliant, deep blue sky arched high over the moorland.—THE SECRET GARDEN, Frances Hodgson Burnett

archaeology *(say ar-kee-ol-oj-ee)* *NOUN*
the study of ancient people from the remains of their buildings and possessions
➤ **archaeologist** *NOUN*

⚠ **WATCH OUT!**
Archaeology has three vowels in a row, aeo. The a is silent.

archbishop *NOUN* archbishops
the chief bishop of a region

archer *NOUN* archers
someone who shoots with a bow and arrows

archery *NOUN*
the sport of shooting with a bow and arrows

architect *(say ar-kee-tekt)* *NOUN* architects
someone whose job is to design buildings

architecture *NOUN*
❶ the work of designing buildings ❷ a style of building • *ancient Roman architecture*

Arctic *NOUN*
The Arctic is the area around the North Pole.
➤ **Arctic** *ADJECTIVE* • *a famous Arctic explorer*

BUILD YOUR VOCABULARY
Look at **polar**.

are *(present form of be used with 'you', 'we' and 'they')*
• *You are late.* • *The children are playing.*

area *NOUN* areas
❶ part of a country, place, etc. ❷ the space something takes up • *The area of this room is 20 square metres.*

arena *(say a-ree-na)* *NOUN* arenas
a place where a big sports event or concert takes place

argue *VERB* argues, arguing, argued
❶ To argue with someone is to quarrel with them.
❷ To argue is to give reasons for something.
• *She argued that it was wrong to eat meat.*

argument *NOUN* arguments
a quarrel

arid *ADJECTIVE*
Arid land is very dry so nothing grows.

arise *VERB* arises, arising, arose, arisen
❶ to appear or start existing • *A problem arose.*
❷ *(old use)* to get up; to stand up • *'Arise, Sir Lancelot.'*

arithmetic *NOUN*
mathematics that involves working things out with numbers

ark *NOUN* arks
a ship built by Noah in the Bible to escape the flood

⚠ **WATCH OUT!**
Don't confuse with **arc** meaning 'a curved line'.

a
b
c
d
e
f
g
h
i
j
k
l
m
n
o
p
q
r
s
t
u
v
w
x
y
z

arm NOUN arms
① the part of your body between your shoulder and your hand ② Arms are weapons.

arm VERB arms, arming, armed
To arm people is to give them weapons.

armada *(say ar-mah-da)* NOUN armadas
a fleet of warships, especially the Spanish Armada which attacked England in 1588

armadillo NOUN armadillos
a South American animal whose body is covered with a shell of bony plates

armchair NOUN armchairs
a chair with parts on either side to rest your arms on

armed forces NOUN
a country's army, navy and air force

armful NOUN armfuls
as much of something as you can hold in your arms
• *She carried an **armful** of books.*

armour NOUN
metal covering to protect people or things in battle
➤ **armoured** ADJECTIVE

armpit NOUN armpits
the hollow part under your arm at your shoulder

army NOUN armies
a large number of soldiers ready to fight

aroma *(say a-roh-ma)* NOUN aromas
a pleasant smell • *delicious **aromas***

arose VERB *(past tense of **arise**)*
• *A problem **arose**.*

around ADVERB, PREPOSITION
① in various places or in a circle • *People sat **around** the room.* ② from one place to another • *Stop running **around**.* ③ approximately • *It takes **around** half an hour.*

arrange VERB arranges, arranging, arranged
① To arrange things is to put them in the position you want. ② To arrange a meeting or event is to organise it. ③ To arrange to do something is to make sure that it happens.

arrangement NOUN arrangements
① an agreement or plan • *We made an **arrangement** to meet.* ② The way things are displayed or organised.
• *We changed the **arrangement** of the desks.*

array NOUN arrays
① a large number of things on display • *There was a huge **array** of pots and pans.* ② in mathematics, a way of representing numbers in rows and columns

arrest VERB arrests, arresting, arrested
If the police arrest someone, they take them to the police station because they think they have committed a crime.

arrest NOUN arrests
An arrest is when the police arrest someone.
➤ **under arrest** taken and held by the police

arrival NOUN arrivals
① a time when someone or something arrives at a place ② Someone who is new or has just arrived.
• *Have you met the new **arrivals**?*

arrive VERB arrives, arriving, arrived
① to get to a place at the end of a journey
② When a day arrives, it comes. • *The great day finally **arrived**.*

arrogant ADJECTIVE
thinking you are better or more important than other people
➤ **arrogance** NOUN

arrow NOUN arrows
① a pointed stick shot from a bow ② a sign used to show direction or position

arrows

arsenic NOUN
a deadly poison

arson NOUN
the crime of deliberately setting fire to a building

art NOUN arts
① Art is activities like drawing, painting and sculpture and the things created by them. ② An art is a skill. • *the **art** of baking*

artefact NOUN artefacts
an object made by humans, especially one from the past

artery NOUN arteries
Your arteries are tubes that carry blood from your heart to other parts of your body.

BUILD YOUR VOCABULARY
Look at **vein**.

arthritis *(say* arth-**ry**-tiss*)* *NOUN*
a disease that makes joints in the body painful
and stiff

article *NOUN* articles
❶ an object or thing ❷ a piece of writing in a
newspaper or magazine ❸ *(in grammar)* the word
a or *an* (the **indefinite article**) or the word *the* (the
definite article)

artificial *ADJECTIVE*
made by human beings and not by nature
➤ **artificially** *ADVERB*

artist *NOUN* artists
❶ someone who creates art, especially a painter
❷ an entertainer

artistic *ADJECTIVE*
❶ to do with art and artists ❷ showing skill and
beauty • *an **artistic** flower arrangement*
➤ **artistically** *ADVERB*

as *CONJUNCTION, ADVERB, PREPOSITION*
❶ because • *As it was late, I went home.* ❷ when,
while • *She sang **as** she worked.* ❸ used to make
comparisons • *It is not **as** easy **as** you think.*
• *as cold as ice*

⚙ **BUILD YOUR VOCABULARY**
Look at **simile**.

ascend *VERB* ascends, ascending,
ascended
to go up something, such as a hill or a staircase

⚙ **BUILD YOUR VOCABULARY**
The opposite is **descend**.

ascent *NOUN* ascents
a climb up something • *the **ascent** of Everest*

⚠ **WATCH OUT!**
Do not confuse an **ascent** (which means 'a climb' and
has a silent c) with **assent** meaning 'agreement'.

ash *NOUN* ashes
❶ Ash is the powder that is left after something
burns. ❷ An ash or ash tree is a tree with
smooth grey bark and seeds that have parts
like wings.

ashamed *ADJECTIVE*
feeling shame • *I was **ashamed** of my behaviour.*

ashen *ADJECTIVE*
very pale • *Her face was **ashen**.*

ashore *ADVERB*
on or on to the shore • *The sailors came **ashore**.*

aside *ADVERB*
to or at one side • *Step **aside** and let them pass.*

ask *VERB* asks, asking, asked
❶ If you ask someone something, you speak
to them in order to get them to tell you
something or do something. • *He **asked** me
my name.* • *She **asked** us to help.* ❷ To ask
someone to an event is to invite them. • *Did you
ask her to the party?* ❸ To ask for something
is to say that you want it. • *He **asked** for
two tickets.*

askew *(say* a-**skew***)* *ADJECTIVE*
not straight or level • *His glasses were **askew**.*

asleep *ADVERB, ADJECTIVE*
sleeping

aspect *NOUN* aspects
one part or feature of a situation • *We will study
different **aspects** of Roman Britain.*

aspirin *NOUN* aspirins
a drug used to reduce pain or fever

ass *NOUN* asses
a donkey

assassinate *VERB* assassinates,
assassinating, assassinated
to murder a ruler or leader
➤ **assassination** *NOUN*

assault *NOUN* assaults
a violent attack

assemble *VERB* assembles, assembling,
assembled
❶ If people assemble or if they are assembled,
they come together in one place. • *Please **assemble**
in the playground.* ❷ To assemble something is to
put its parts together. • *The cars are **assembled** by
robots.*

assembly *NOUN* assemblies
a time when people come together and someone
speaks to them, for example in a school

a
b
c
d
e
f
g
h
i
j
k
l
m
n
o
p
q
r
s
t
u
v
w
x
y
z

A

assent *NOUN*
Assent is agreement or permission to do something.

> ! **WATCH OUT!**
> Do not confuse with an **ascent** meaning 'a climb'.

assess *VERB* **assesses, assessing, assessed**
To assess something is to decide how good it is or make a judgement about it. • *We have to assess our writing.*
➤ **assessment** *NOUN*

asset *NOUN* **assets**
❶ something useful or valuable • *Katie is a real asset to the team.* ❷ A person's or company's assets are the things they own that they could sell to raise money.

assign *VERB* **assigns, assigning, assigned**
To assign a task to someone is to give it to them. • *We were all assigned homework.*

assignment *NOUN* **assignments**
a piece of work that someone is given to do

assist *VERB* **assists, assisting, assisted**
to help someone

assistance *NOUN*
help

assistant *NOUN* **assistants**
❶ someone whose job is to help another person in their work ❷ someone who serves in a shop

> ! **WATCH OUT!**
> Remember that **assistant** and **assistance** end in -ant and -ance.

associate *VERB* **associates, associating, associated**
To associate one thing with another is to connect or link them. • *Robins are often associated with Christmas.*

association *NOUN* **associations**
❶ an organisation for people with the same interest or work • *the local athletics association* ❷ a connection between things

assorted *ADJECTIVE*
of various kinds
A large wooden trunk stood open at the foot of his bed, revealing a cauldron, broomstick, black robes and assorted spellbooks.—HARRY POTTER AND THE GOBLET OF FIRE, J. K. Rowling

assortment *NOUN* **assortments**
a mixture of different things or people

assume *VERB* **assumes, assuming, assumed**
to believe something is true or likely, although you do not know for certain • *I assumed the girl was his sister.*

assumption *NOUN* **assumptions**
Something you believe is true or likely, although you do not know for certain.
• *My assumption that he would help turned out to be wrong.*

assure *VERB* **assures, assuring, assured**
to tell someone something to make them less worried • *He assured us the ride was safe.*
➤ **assurance** *NOUN* • *She gave us an assurance she'd be on time.*

asterisk *NOUN* **asterisks**
a star-shaped sign (*) used to draw attention to something in a text

asteroid *NOUN* **asteroids**
a very small rocky planet that orbits the sun

> ⬤ **BUILD** YOUR VOCABULARY
> Look at **meteor** and **meteorite**.

asthma *(say* ass-ma*) NOUN*
a disease which makes breathing difficult

astonish *VERB* **astonishes, astonishing, astonished**
to surprise someone very much
➤ **astonishment** *NOUN*

astound *VERB* **astounds, astounding, astounded**
to surprise or shock someone very much

astrology *NOUN*
the belief that the position of the planets and stars affect people's lives and personalities

> ⬤ **BUILD** YOUR VOCABULARY
> Do not confuse with **astronomy** meaning 'the scientific study of planets and stars'.

astronaut *NOUN* **astronauts**
someone who travels in a spacecraft

✳ **WORD STORY**
The word **astronaut** comes from Greek words meaning 'star sailor'.

astronomical *ADJECTIVE*
to do with astronomy

astronomy *NOUN*
the scientific study of the sun, moon, planets and stars
➤ **astronomer** *NOUN*

at *PREPOSITION*
❶ used for showing where someone or something is • *The children are at school.* • *My house is at the top of the hill.* ❷ used for giving a time when something happens • *The match starts at 3 o'clock.*

ate *VERB (past tense of **eat**)*
• *She ate a banana.*

atheist *NOUN* **atheists**
someone who does not believe in a God

athlete *NOUN* **athletes**
someone who does athletics

athletic *ADJECTIVE*
❶ to do with athletics • *an athletic competition*
❷ physically fit and good at sports

athletics *NOUN*
sports in which people compete at running, jumping or throwing

atlas *NOUN* **atlases**
a book of maps

✳ **WORD STORY**
Atlases are named after *Atlas*, a character in Greek mythology who was made to carry the universe on his shoulders.

atmosphere *NOUN* **atmospheres**
❶ The earth's atmosphere is the gases surrounding it. ❷ An atmosphere is a feeling you get in a place. • *The classroom has a busy atmosphere.*

atom *NOUN* **atoms**
the smallest possible part of a chemical element

⚙ **BUILD YOUR VOCABULARY**
Look at **molecule**

at once *ADVERB*
immediately • *Come here at once!*

attach *VERB* **attaches, attaching, attached**
To attach one thing to another is to fix or join them together.

attachment *NOUN* **attachments**
❶ an extra part you can fix to a device • *The tap has a shower attachment.* ❷ something such as a file or photograph that you send with an electronic message • *I opened the attachment.*

attack *VERB* **attacks, attacking, attacked**
to try to hurt someone using violence
attack *NOUN* **attacks**
a violent attempt to hurt someone

attempt *VERB* **attempts, attempting, attempted**
To attempt to do something is to try to do it.
attempt *NOUN* **attempts**
an effort to do something • *My first attempt failed.*

attend *VERB* **attends, attending, attended**
❶ to be present at an event • *100 people attended the wedding.* ❷ to go somewhere regularly • *You must attend school.* ❸ To attend to something is to deal with it. • *She had some business to attend to.*

attendance *NOUN* **attendances**
❶ Attendance is being somewhere where you are supposed to be. • *His attendance at school is good.* ❷ the number of people who are present at an event

a
b
c
d
e
f
g
h
i
j
k
l
m
n
o
s
t
u
v
w
x
y
z

attendant *NOUN* attendants
someone whose job is to help another person or to help people in a public place • *a car park attendant*

attention *NOUN*
care or thought given to someone or something

attic *NOUN* attics
a room or space under the roof of a house

✱ WORD STORY

The word **attic** comes from *Attica*, an area in ancient Greece which was famous for the special design of its buildings.

attitude *NOUN* attitudes
Your attitude is the way you think, feel or behave in relation to something.

attract *VERB* attracts, attracting, attracted
❶ If someone or something attracts you, you are interested in them and like them. ❷ to make someone or something come • *The city attracts a lot of tourists.* ❸ to pull something by a physical force like magnetism • *Magnets attract metal pins.*

⚙ BUILD YOUR VOCABULARY
The opposite is **repel**.

attraction *NOUN* attractions
❶ Attraction is a feeling of liking or interest. ❷ An attraction is something that people like to come and see. ❸ Attraction is the power of something like a magnet to pull things towards it.

attractive *ADJECTIVE*
❶ good-looking • *an attractive face*
❷ interesting to look at • *The shop windows looked very attractive.*

aubergine *NOUN*
a dark purple vegetable with a stalk at one end

⚙ BUILD YOUR VOCABULARY
In American English this vegetable is called an **eggplant**.

auburn *ADJECTIVE*
Auburn hair is a reddish-brown colour.

auction *NOUN* auctions
A sale at which things are sold to the person who offers the most money for them.

audible *ADJECTIVE*
loud enough to be heard • *an audible whisper*

⚙ BUILD YOUR VOCABULARY
The opposite is **inaudible**.

audience *NOUN* audiences
❶ the people who have come to see or hear an event like a concert or film ❷ a formal interview with an important person • *an audience with the Queen*

audiobook *NOUN* audiobooks
a spoken recorded version of a printed book

audition *NOUN* auditions
a test to see if an actor or musician is suitable for a part

auditorium *(say* aw-dit-or-ree-um*) NOUN* auditoriums, auditoria
the part of a building where the audience sits

auk *(say* awk*) NOUN* auks
a northern seabird with a black head and short wings

aunt *(also* **auntie**, **aunty** *informal) NOUN* aunts, aunties
your mother's or father's sister or your uncle or aunt's wife

authentic *ADJECTIVE*
real, genuine

author *NOUN* authors
the writer of a book, poem, story, etc.

authorise *(also* **authorize***) VERB* authorises, authorising, authorised
to give official permission for something to be done

authority *NOUN* authorities
❶ Authority is the power to give orders to other people. ❷ The authorities are the people in charge, for example the government or police.

autism *ADJECTIVE*
a condition that can make it difficult for someone to communicate with other people

autobiography *NOUN* autobiographies
a story of someone's own life that they have written
➤ **autobiographical** *ADJECTIVE* • *The story is autobiographical.*

⚙ BUILD YOUR VOCABULARY
Look at **biography**.

autograph *NOUN* autographs
the signature of a famous person

automatic *ADJECTIVE*
An automatic process is one that works on its own, without needing attention or control by anyone.
➤ **automatically** *ADVERB* • *The heating comes on automatically.*

autumn *(say* aw-tum*) NOUN* autumns
the season when leaves fall off the trees, between summer and winter

⚠ WATCH OUT!
There is a silent **n** at the end of **autumn.**

auxiliary verb *NOUN* auxiliary verbs
a type of verb like *be*, *have* or *do* that is used with other verbs to make questions, negatives and tenses • *In 'I have finished', the auxiliary verb is 'have'.*

⚙ BUILD YOUR VOCABULARY
Look at **modal verb**.

available *ADJECTIVE*
able to be found or used • *There are lots of free maths games available on the Internet.*

avalanche *(say* av-a-lahnsh*) NOUN* avalanches
a sudden fall of a large amount of snow down the side of a mountain

avenue *NOUN* avenues
a wide street, usually with trees along each side

average *NOUN* averages
the number you get by adding several amounts together and dividing the total by the number of amounts • *The average of 2, 4, 6 and 8 is 5.*

average *ADJECTIVE*
ordinary or usual; not special in any way
Hiccup was just absolutely average, the kind of unremarkable, skinny, freckled boy who was easy to overlook in a crowd.—HOW TO BE A PIRATE, Cressida Cowell

aviary *NOUN* aviaries
a large cage where birds are kept

avid *ADJECTIVE*
keen, eager • *Matilda is an avid reader.*

avocado *NOUN* avocados
a green pear-shaped fruit with soft light-green flesh and a large stone

avoid *VERB* avoids, avoiding, avoided
❶ to keep away from someone or something
• *I avoid her when she's in a bad mood.* **❷** If you avoid doing something, you try not to do it. • *He was careful to avoid touching the hot pan.*

await *VERB* awaits, awaiting, awaited
To await someone or something is to wait for them.

a
b
c
d
e
f
g
h
i
j
k
l
m
n
o
p
q
r
s
t
u
v
w
x
y
z

awake ADJECTIVE
not sleeping
awake VERB awakes, awaking, awoke, awoken
To awake is to wake up.

awaken VERB awakens, awakening, awakened
to wake up

award NOUN awards
something such as a prize given for doing something well
award VERB awards, awarding, awarded
To award something to someone is to give it to them for doing well. • *He was awarded first prize.*

aware ADJECTIVE
To be aware of something is to know about it or realise it is there. • *They were not aware of the danger.*
➤ **awareness** NOUN

away ADVERB
❶ at a distance or somewhere else • *The shop is half a mile away.* • *The bird flew away.* • *My friend is away.* ❷ doing something with a lot of effort or energy • *She was knitting away.*

awe NOUN
fear and wonder • *The mountains filled him with awe.*

awesome ADJECTIVE
❶ very impressive and powerful
For a brief moment, the terrible Red-Hot Smoke-Belching Gruncher made the lake boil and smoke like a volcano, then the fire went out and the awesome beast disappeared under the waves.–BILLY AND THE MINPINS, Roald Dahl
❷ *(informal)* excellent • *That new game is awesome!*

awful ADJECTIVE
very bad • *They got some awful news.*

awfully ADVERB *(informal)*
very, extremely • *It's awfully difficult.*

awkward ADJECTIVE
❶ difficult to use or cope with • *The box was an awkward shape.* ❷ embarrassed, uncomfortable • *I felt awkward asking them.*

awoke VERB *(past tense of awake)*
• *She awoke early.*

awoken VERB *(past participle of awake)*
• *The giant had awoken.*

axe NOUN axes
a tool for chopping

axis *(say aks-iss)* NOUN axes *(say aks-eez)*
❶ an imaginary line through the centre of a spinning object • *The earth spins on its axis.* ❷ a horizontal or vertical line on a grid or graph from which points on the grid or graph can be measured • *Label the axes.*

BUILD YOUR VOCABULARY
Look at **coordinate**.

axle NOUN axles
the rod through the centre of a wheel, on which it turns

azalea *(say a-zay-lee-a)* NOUN azaleas
a flowering shrub with bright flowers

azure ADJECTIVE
sky-blue

B is a letter name that also sounds like a word: **be** or **bee**.

Can you think of other letter names that sound like words? There are lots!

babble VERB babbles, babbling, babbled
to talk quickly, without making much sense

baboon NOUN baboons
a large kind of monkey with a long pointed face

baby NOUN babies
❶ a very young child ❷ A baby animal is a very young animal. • *a baby elephant*

babyish ADJECTIVE
silly and childish

babysit VERB babysits, babysitting, babysat
To babysit is to look after a child while its parents are out.
➤ **babysitter** NOUN

bachelor NOUN bachelors
a man who has not married

back NOUN backs
❶ the part of your body between your shoulders and your bottom ❷ the upper part of a four-legged animal's body ❸ the part of a thing that is furthest away from the front • *the back of the house*
back ADJECTIVE
at or near the back • *I sat in the back row.*
back ADVERB
❶ backwards or towards the back • *She fell back.*
❷ to where or how someone or something was before • *Come back soon.* • *I went back to sleep.*
back VERB backs, backing, backed
to move backwards • *He nervously backed away.*
➤ **To back someone up** is to give someone support or help.
➤ **To back something up** is to make a spare copy of a computer file for safety.

backbone NOUN backbones
Your backbone is your spine.

background NOUN backgrounds
❶ the part of a scene or view that is furthest away from you
⚙ **BUILD** YOUR VOCABULARY
The opposite of this meaning is **foreground**.
❷ The background to an event or situation is all the things that help to explain why it happened.
❸ A person's background is their family, education and experience.

backing NOUN
Backing is support or help.

backpack NOUN backpacks
a bag you carry on your back
⚙ **BUILD** YOUR VOCABULARY
A synonym is **rucksack**.

backside NOUN backsides (informal)
Your backside is your bottom.

backstroke NOUN
a stroke you use when swimming on your back

backup NOUN backups
a spare copy of a computer file kept in case the original is lost or damaged

backward ADJECTIVE
looking towards the back • *She walked away without a backward glance.*

backwards ADVERB
❶ towards the back • *She stepped backwards.*
❷ in the opposite order to the usual one • *Can you say the alphabet backwards?*

bacon NOUN
smoked or salted meat from a pig

bacteria NOUN
tiny organisms that can cause diseases

bad ADJECTIVE worse, worst
❶ not good or well done • *I had a bad dream.*
• *The food tasted really bad.* ❷ A bad person is evil or naughty. ❸ serious or unpleasant • *He had a bad accident.* ❹ harmful to your health • *Eating junk food is bad for you.*

a
b
c
d
e
f
g
h
i
j
k
l
m
n
o
p
q
r
s
t
u
v
w
x
y
z

badge NOUN badges
a small piece of metal, plastic or cloth that you pin or sew on your clothes to tell people something about you

badger NOUN badgers
a grey animal with a black and white head, which lives underground and comes out at night to feed
badger VERB badgers, badgering, badgered
To badger someone is to keep asking them to do something. • *He kept **badgering** his mother for his pocket money.*

badly ADVERB
❶ not well • *They did the work **badly**.* ❷ seriously
• *He was **badly** wounded.*

badminton NOUN
a game in which players use rackets to hit a light object called a **shuttlecock** backwards and forwards across a high net

bad-tempered ADJECTIVE
often becoming angry

baffle VERB baffles, baffling, baffled
to confuse someone or puzzle them completely

bag NOUN bags
a container made of soft material, for holding or carrying things

bagel NOUN bagels
a hard ring-shaped bread roll

baggage NOUN
the suitcases and bags you take on a journey

BUILD YOUR VOCABULARY
A synonym is **luggage**.

baggy ADJECTIVE baggier, baggiest
baggy clothes hang loosely from your body
➤ **bagginess** NOUN

bagpipes PLURAL NOUN
Bagpipes are a musical instrument you play by squeezing air out of a bag into a set of pipes.

bail NOUN bails
❶ Bail is money paid so that an accused person can be allowed to stay out of prison until their trial.
❷ In cricket, bails are the two small pieces of wood placed on top of the stumps.

BUILD YOUR VOCABULARY
Look at **stump** and **wicket**.

bail VERB bails, bailing, bailed
To bail water out of a boat is to scoop it over the side.

Bairam (*say* by-**rahm**) NOUN Bairams
either of two Muslim festivals, one in the tenth month and one in the twelfth month of the Islamic year

Baisakhi (*say* by-**sah-kee**) NOUN
a Sikh festival held in April

bait NOUN
Bait is a small amount of food put on a hook or in a trap to catch fish or animals.
bait VERB baits, baiting, baited
To bait a hook or trap is to put bait on it to catch fish or animals.

bake VERB bakes, baking, baked
❶ to cook food, especially bread or cakes, in an oven ❷ To bake clay or earth is to make it hard by heating it.

baker NOUN bakers
someone who makes or sells bread and cakes

bakery NOUN bakeries
a place where bread is made or sold

baking powder NOUN
a special powder used in baking to make cakes rise

balance NOUN balances
❶ A person's balance is their feeling of being steady.
• *I lost my **balance** and fell.* ❷ A balance is a pair of scales for weighing things. ❸ The balance of a bank account is the amount of money in it.
balance VERB balances, balancing, balanced
❶ To balance is to keep yourself steady. • *We balanced on a beam.* ❷ To balance something is to keep it steady. • *He **balanced** the ball on his foot.*

balcony NOUN balconies
❶ a platform on the outside wall of a building, with railings round it ❷ the upstairs part of a cinema or theatre

bald ADJECTIVE balder, baldest
A bald person does not have much or any hair on their head.

bale *NOUN* bales
a large bundle of something like hay or straw, tied up tightly

bale *VERB* bales, baling, baled
another spelling of **bail**

ball *NOUN* balls
❶ a round object used in games ❷ a grand or formal party where people dance

⚪ **BUILD YOUR VOCABULARY**
A room for this type of party is called a **ballroom**.

ballad *NOUN* ballads
a simple song or poem that tells a story

ballerina *(say* bal-er-ree-na*) NOUN* ballerinas
a female ballet dancer

ballet *(say* bal-ay*) NOUN* ballets
a form of dancing with special steps, often on the tips of the toes

balloon *NOUN* balloons
❶ a colourful bag filled with air or gas, used for celebrations • *party balloons* ❷ a large object filled with light gas or hot air, often used with a basket to carry passengers • *a hot-air balloon*

bamboo *NOUN* bamboos
a tall tropical plant with hard hollow stems, used for making furniture

ban *VERB* bans, banning, banned
to forbid something, usually by law

banana *NOUN* bananas
a long curved fruit with a yellow skin

band *NOUN* bands
❶ a group of people who play music together
❷ a group of people doing something together
• *a band of robbers* ❸ a circular strip of something
• *an elastic band*

bandage *(say* ban-dij*) NOUN* bandages
a strip of material that you wrap round a wound to protect it

bandit *NOUN* bandits
a member of a gang of robbers who attack travellers

bang *NOUN* bangs
❶ a sudden loud noise ❷ a heavy blow or knock
bang *VERB* bangs, banging, banged
❶ to hit something hard against something
• *I banged my head.* ❷ to make a sudden loud noise
• *The door banged shut.*

banish *VERB* banishes, banishing, banished
to punish someone by sending them away
The wicked witch Duchess shall be banished for seven years to the tiny Isle of Stones where nothing grows and the sea-current is strong.—THE BRAVE WHALE, Alan Temperley
➤ **banishment** *NOUN*

banister *NOUN* banisters
a handrail on posts at the side of a staircase

banjo *NOUN* banjos
a musical instrument like a small round guitar

banjo

bank *NOUN* banks
❶ a business which looks after people's money
❷ a piece of raised or sloping ground, usually by a river or lake

bank *VERB* banks, banking, banked
to lean over while changing direction • *The plane banked sharply.*

bank holiday *NOUN* bank holidays
a public holiday, when the banks are closed

a b c d e f g h i j k l m n o p q r s t u v w x y z

bankrupt *ADJECTIVE*
not able to pay the money you owe

banner *NOUN* banners
a long flag with a message carried in a procession or demonstration

banquet *(say* bank-wit*) NOUN* banquets
a large formal dinner, often with speeches

banshee *(say* ban-shee*) NOUN* banshees
In Celtic mythology, a banshee is a female spirit who wails to warn of someone's death.

banyan *NOUN* banyans
an Indian fig tree with roots which hang down from its branches

baobab *(say* bay-o-bab*) NOUN* baobabs
a tropical tree with a thick trunk and edible fruit

baptise *(also* **baptize***) VERB* baptises, baptising, baptised
to sprinkle someone with water or dip them in water, in a ceremony that shows they have become a Christian

baptism *NOUN* baptisms
the ceremony of baptising someone

bar *NOUN* bars
❶ a long piece of something hard • *an iron* **bar**
❷ a block of soap or chocolate ❸ a counter or room where drinks are served
bar *VERB* bars, barring, barred
To bar someone's way is to stop them getting past.

barbarian *NOUN* barbarians
an uncivilised or savage person

barbecue *NOUN* barbecues
❶ a metal frame used for grilling food over a charcoal fire outdoors ❷ a party at which food is cooked outdoors on a barbecue

barbed wire *NOUN*
wire with sharp twisted spikes on it, used to make fences

barber *NOUN* barbers
someone whose job is to cut men's hair

bar chart *(also* **bar graph***) NOUN* bar charts, bar graphs
a graph showing amounts as bars of different heights

barcode *NOUN* barcodes
a set of black lines printed on goods so that a computer can read the price or other information

ISBN 978-0-19-276845-2

9 780192 768452

bard *NOUN* bards *(old use)*
a poet

bare *ADJECTIVE* barer, barest
❶ not covered with anything • *The trees were* **bare**.
❷ empty or almost empty • *The cupboard was* **bare**.
❸ only just enough • *Just bring the* **bare** *minimum*.

barely *ADVERB*
only just; with difficulty • *I could* **barely** *hear him*.

bargain *NOUN* bargains
❶ something that you buy cheaply ❷ an agreement between two people to do something for each other • *I will keep my side of the* **bargain**.

bargain *VERB* bargains, bargaining, bargained
to discuss a price or agreement • *I'm not* **bargaining** *with you*.

barge *NOUN* barges
a long flat-bottomed boat used especially on canals
barge *VERB* barges, barging, barged
To barge into something or someone is to push into them clumsily and rudely.

bark *NOUN* barks
❶ A bark is the sound made by a dog. ❷ Bark is the outer covering of a tree.
bark *VERB* barks, barking, barked
When a dog barks, it makes its special sound.

barley *NOUN*
a kind of grain which is used for food and to make beer

bar mitzvah *NOUN* bar mitzvahs
a religious ceremony for Jewish boys who have reached the age of 13

⚙ **BUILD YOUR VOCABULARY**
Look at **bat mitzvah**.

barn NOUN barns
a building on a farm used to store things such as grain or hay

barnacle NOUN barnacles
a shellfish that attaches itself to rocks and the bottoms of ships

barometer (say ba-**rom**-it-er) NOUN barometers
an instrument that measures air pressure, used in forecasting the weather

baron NOUN barons
a member of the lowest rank of noblemen

baroness NOUN baronesses
a female baron or a baron's wife

barracks NOUN barracks
the buildings where soldiers live

barrage (say ba-rahzh) NOUN barrages
❶ a large number of shots, missiles or bombs aimed at a place ❷ a large amount of something • *He was asked a barrage of questions.*

barrel NOUN barrels
❶ a large container for liquids, with curved sides and flat ends ❷ The long tube of a gun, through which bullets are fired.

barren ADJECTIVE
Barren land or plants cannot produce any crops or fruit.

barricade NOUN barricades
a barrier, especially one put up quickly to block a place
barricade VERB barricades, barricading, barricaded
to block or defend a place with a barrier

barrier NOUN barriers
❶ a fence or wall that stops people getting past ❷ something that stops you doing something • *Her shyness was a barrier to friendship.*

barrister NOUN barristers
a lawyer who presents legal cases in the higher courts

barrow NOUN barrows
❶ a small cart ❷ an ancient mound of earth over a grave

base NOUN bases
❶ the lowest part of something or the part on which something stands ❷ A place from which an organisation like an army or business is controlled.
base VERB bases, basing, based
To base one thing on another thing is to use the second thing as the starting point for the first.
• *I based the story on something that happened to me.*

baseball NOUN
a game similar to rounders that is popular in America

basement NOUN basements
a room or part of a building below ground level

bash VERB bashes, bashing, bashed (informal)
to hit someone or something hard

bashful ADJECTIVE
shy
➤ **bashfully** ADVERB ➤ **bashfulness** NOUN

basic ADJECTIVE
most simple and necessary • *We learned some basic things about computers.*
• *Food is a basic human need.*

basically ADVERB
in the most important ways; essentially
• *The new system is basically the same.*

basil NOUN
a Mediterranean herb used in cooking

basilisk

basilisk NOUN basilisks
a mythological creature like a snake which could kill people just by looking at them

basin NOUN basins
❶ a deep, wide bowl or container ❷ A river basin is the area of land where the river's water comes from.

basis NOUN bases
the starting point or main idea that is used to create something • *Her work as a detective was the basis for her first book.*

bask VERB basks, basking, basked
to lie or sit comfortably warming yourself in the sun

basket NOUN baskets
a container woven from strips of wood, cane or wire

basketball NOUN
a team game in which players try to throw a large ball through a high net hanging from a hoop

bass (say bayss) ADJECTIVE
❶ A bass instrument or voice has a very low sound. ❷ In music, a bass clef is a symbol to show the notes in it are low.

> **BUILD** YOUR VOCABULARY
Look at **treble**.

bassoon NOUN bassoons
a woodwind instrument that plays low notes

bat NOUN bats
❶ a shaped piece of wood used to hit the ball in cricket, rounders and other games ❷ a flying mammal that looks like a mouse with wings. Bats come out at night to feed.
bat VERB bats, batting, batted
The team that is batting in cricket or rounders is the team whose turn it is to use the bat.

batch NOUN batches
a set of things made at one time or dealt with together

bath NOUN baths
a large container you fill with water and get into to wash yourself

bathe (say bayth) VERB bathes, bathing, bathed
❶ to go swimming or wash yourself, especially in a sea, lake or river ❷ to wash a sore part of your body

bathroom NOUN bathrooms
a room for having a bath or wash in

bat mitzvah NOUN bat mitzvahs
a religious ceremony for Jewish girls who have reached the age of 12

> **BUILD** YOUR VOCABULARY
Look at **bar mitzvah**.

baton NOUN batons
a short stick, especially one used to conduct an orchestra or in a relay race

batsman NOUN batsmen
a player who tries to hit the ball with a bat in cricket

battalion NOUN battalions
a large group of soldiers who fight together

batter VERB batters, battering, battered
to hit something or someone hard many times • *Huge waves battered the rocks.*
batter NOUN
Batter is a mixture of flour, eggs and milk used to make pancakes or to coat food before you fry it.

battery NOUN batteries
a device for storing and supplying electricity

battle NOUN battles
❶ a fight between two armies ❷ a struggle
Harald stifled a yawn, in a desperate battle to stay awake, then slumped backwards and emitted a huge snore.—OLAF THE VIKING, Martin Conway

battlefield NOUN battlefields
a place where a battle is or was fought

battlements NOUN
the top of a castle wall, usually with gaps through which people defending the castle could fire arrows

battleship NOUN battleships
a large warship armed with powerful guns

bauble NOUN baubles
a colourful ornament, especially one hung on a Christmas tree

bawl VERB bawls, bawling, bawled
to shout or cry loudly

bay NOUN bays
a place by the sea or a lake where the shore curves inwards
➤ **To keep someone at bay** is to prevent them from coming near you.

bayonet *NOUN* **bayonets**
a steel blade that can be fixed to the end of a rifle and used for stabbing

bazaar *NOUN* **bazaars**
❶ a market in a Middle Eastern country ❷ a sale held to raise money for charity

✳ **WORD STORY**
The word **bazaar** comes from a Persian word meaning 'market'.

BC *ABBREVIATION*
short for *before Christ*, used with dates that come before the birth of Jesus Christ • *Julius Caesar came to Britain in 55 **BC**.*

⚙ **BUILD** YOUR VOCABULARY
Look at **AD**.

be *VERB* **I am, you/we/they are, he/she/it is; I/he/she/it was, you/we/they were; I/you/we/they have been, he/she/it has been**
❶ used before a noun or adjective to say something about someone or something • *She **is** my teacher.* • *You **are** very tall.* • *The game **was** boring.* • *Don't **be** silly.* ❷ to exist • *There **are** no dinosaurs now.* • *There **were** a lot of people.* • *There **have been** some problems.* ❸ The verb **be** can be used with other verbs to make tenses. • *They **are** playing football.* • *A window **was** broken.*

⚙ **BUILD** YOUR VOCABULARY
A verb that can be used with other verbs in this way is called an **auxiliary verb**.

beach *NOUN* **beaches**
the strip of sand or pebbles close to the sea

⚠ **WATCH OUT!**
Do not confuse with a **beech**, which is a tree and which is spelt with two 'ee's' like tree.

beacon *NOUN* **beacons**
a light or fire used as a warning signal

bead *NOUN* **beads**
❶ a small piece of glass, wood or plastic with a hole through it, threaded on a string or wire to make jewellery or decorate something ❷ a small drop of liquid • *She had **beads** of sweat on her face.*

beady *ADJECTIVE* **beadier, beadiest**
Beady eyes are small and bright.

beagle *NOUN* **beagles**
a type of dog with long ears

beak *NOUN* **beaks**
the hard pointed part of a bird's mouth

beaker *NOUN* **beakers**
❶ a drinking cup without a handle ❷ a glass container used for pouring liquids in a laboratory

beam *NOUN* **beams**
❶ a long thick bar of wood or metal ❷ a ray of light
beam *VERB* **beams, beaming, beamed**
to smile very happily

bean *NOUN* **beans**
a kind of plant with seeds growing in pods. The seeds or the pods can be eaten as food.

⚙ **BUILD** YOUR VOCABULARY
Look at **broad bean**, **runner bean** and **soya bean**.

bear *NOUN* **bears**
a large heavy animal with thick fur and sharp hooked claws
bear *VERB* **bears, bearing, bore, born** or **borne**
❶ To bear something is to carry or support it. ❷ To bear a mark or signature is to have or show it. • *The letter **bore** her signature.* ❸ To bear something is to put up with it. • *I can't **bear** all this noise.*

beard *NOUN* **beards**
hair on the lower part of a man's face

bearing *NOUN* **bearings**
❶ Someone's bearing is their manner and the way they stand. • *She had a noble **bearing**.* ❷ the position of something in relation to other things
➤ **To get your bearings** is to work out where you are in relation to other things.

beast *NOUN* **beasts**
❶ any large, usually wild, animal ❷ (*informal*) a person you think is cruel or unkind

beastly *ADJECTIVE* **beastlier, beastliest** (*informal*)
cruel or unkind
Mrs Twit may have been ugly and she may have been beastly, but she was not stupid.—THE TWITS, Roald Dahl

beat VERB beats, beating, beat, beaten
❶ to hit someone or something many times, especially with a stick ❷ To beat someone in a game or competition is to do better than them or defeat them. ❸ To beat a mixture is to stir it quickly. ❹ When your heart beats, it makes regular movements.

beat NOUN beats
❶ a strong rhythm in music or poetry ❷ the regular movement of your heart

beautiful ADJECTIVE
very attractive or pleasing
➤ **beautifully** ADVERB • He sang **beautifully**.

⚠ **WATCH OUT!**
The word **beautiful** has three vowels in the middle. Think of the phrase *every ancient unicorn is beautiful* to help you remember!

beauty NOUN beauties
❶ Beauty is the quality of being beautiful or pleasing. • They enjoyed the **beauty** of the sunset.
❷ A beauty is a beautiful or pleasing person or thing. *'Did you ever taste such beauties?' said Dodder with his mouth full.*—THE LITTLE GREY MEN, BB

beaver NOUN beavers
a brown furry animal with strong teeth and a long flat tail, which builds dams in rivers

became VERB (past tense of **become**)
• The dark passageway **became** completely black.

because CONJUNCTION
for the reason that • I was happy **because** we won.
➤ **because of** used before a noun to give a reason
• He was late **because of** the traffic.

beckon VERB beckons, beckoning, beckoned
to make a hand signal asking someone to come to you

become VERB becomes, becoming, became, become
❶ to start being something • It was **becoming** dark. • He **became** upset. ❷ to start doing a job or being a particular type of person • She wanted to **become** a doctor.
➤ **What becomes of someone** or **something** is what happens to them in the end. • What will **become** of us?

bed NOUN beds
❶ A bed is a piece of furniture for sleeping on.
❷ Bed is the place where you sleep. • I'm going to **bed**. ❸ The bed of the sea or of a river is the bottom of it.

bedclothes PLURAL NOUN
sheets, blankets or duvets for using on a bed

bedding NOUN
things for making a bed, such as sheets, blankets and duvets

bedraggled (say be-**drag**-uld) ADJECTIVE
wet and dirty

bedridden (say **bed**-rid-en) ADJECTIVE
too ill or injured to get out of bed

bedroom NOUN bedrooms
a room where you sleep

bedstead NOUN bedsteads
the frame of a bed

bedtime NOUN
the time when you are supposed to go to bed

bee NOUN bees
a stinging insect that makes honey

beech NOUN beeches
a tree with smooth bark and glossy leaves

⚠ **WATCH OUT!**
Do not confuse with a **beach**, which is by the sea and is spelt like sea.

beef NOUN
the meat of an ox, bull or cow

beehive NOUN beehives
a container that bees are kept in so that their honey can be collected

beekeeper NOUN beekeepers
someone who owns bees and collects their honey
➤ **beekeeping** NOUN

been VERB (past participle of **be**)
• I have **been** feeling poorly for a while.

beer NOUN beers
an alcoholic drink

beet NOUN beets
a plant used as a vegetable or for making sugar

beetle NOUN beetles
an insect with hard shiny covers over its wings

beetroot NOUN beetroots
a dark red root used as a vegetable

before ADVERB, PREPOSITION
❶ earlier or earlier than • Have you seen this before? • She arrived **before** me. ❷ in front of
• He vanished **before** my eyes.

beforehand ADVERB
earlier or before something else happens • Let me know **beforehand** if you want to come.

beg VERB begs, begging, begged
❶ to ask people to give you money or food ❷ To beg someone is to ask them seriously or desperately.
• He **begged** us to hurry.

began VERB (past tense of **begin**)
• The ground beneath them **began** to shake.

beggar NOUN beggars
someone who lives by begging in the street

begin VERB begins, beginning, began, begun
to start doing something • She **began** to cry.
• I'll **begin** my story. • The game has already **begun**.

beginner NOUN beginners
Someone who is just starting to learn something.

beginning NOUN beginnings
the start of something

begun VERB (past participle of **begin**)
• Tears had **begun** to run down Emily's face.

behalf NOUN
➤ **On behalf of someone** or **something** means for them or in their name. • Will you say something **on behalf of** the class?

behave VERB behaves, behaving, behaved
❶ To behave in a particular way is to act in that way.
• I **behaved** stupidly. ❷ to show good behaviour
• Why can't you **behave?**

behaviour NOUN
❶ Your behaviour is the way you behave. ❷ Animal behaviour is the things animals normally do.

behind PREPOSITION
❶ at or to the back of • She hid **behind** a tree.
❷ supporting someone • We're all **behind** you.
behind ADVERB
❶ still in a place • You have to stay **behind** after school. ❷ not as fast or as advanced as others
• I was a long way **behind** in the race.

behold VERB beholds, beholding, beheld
(old use) to see something in front of you

beige (say bayzh) NOUN, ADJECTIVE
a light yellow-brown colour

being NOUN beings
a person or creature of any kind • There were no living **beings.**

belch VERB belches, belching, belched
❶ to make a noise by letting air come up from your stomach through your mouth

🔵 **BUILD YOUR VOCABULARY**
A synonym is **burp**.

❷ to send out a lot of smoke • The bus **belched** black fumes.

belief NOUN beliefs
❶ A belief is something you believe. • He has strong religious **beliefs**. ❷ Belief is when you believe something.

believe VERB believes, believing, believed
❶ To believe something is to think that it is true. ❷ To believe someone is to think that they are telling the truth. ❸ To believe in something is to think it is real or important. • *Do you believe in ghosts?*
➤ **believable** ADJECTIVE • *a believable story*

bell NOUN bells
a device that makes a ringing sound

bellow VERB bellows, bellowing, bellowed
To bellow is to roar or shout loudly and deeply.

bellows PLURAL NOUN
Bellows are a device for blowing out air, especially to make a fire burn more strongly.

belly NOUN bellies
your abdomen or stomach

belong VERB belongs, belonging, belonged
❶ To belong to someone is to be their property. • *That book belongs to me.* ❷ To belong to a club or group is to be a member of it. • *We belong to the tennis club.* ❸ To belong somewhere is to have a special place where it goes. • *Put the box back where it belongs.*

belongings PLURAL NOUN
Your belongings are the things that you own.

beloved (*say* be-**luvd** *or* be-**luv**-id) ADJECTIVE
greatly loved

below PREPOSITION, ADVERB
❶ at or to a lower place • *They live in the flat below us.* • *We looked down at the valley below.* ❷ less than • *If you score below 5 you have to try again.*

belt NOUN belts
a strip of material that you wear round your waist

bench NOUN benches
❶ a long seat ❷ a long table for working at

bend VERB bends, bending, bent
❶ To bend something is to make it curved or crooked. ❷ To bend is to become curved or crooked. • *The trees bent in the wind.* ❸ to move the top of your body downwards • *She bent down to fasten her shoe.*

bend NOUN bends
a part where something curves or turns • *There is a bend in the road.*

beneath PREPOSITION, ADVERB
under or underneath • *The ground beneath our feet was wet.* • *The ice has water flowing beneath.*

benefit NOUN benefits
something that is useful or helpful • *A big benefit of exercise is that it makes you feel good.*

benefit VERB benefits, benefiting, benefited
If you benefit from something or it benefits you, it helps you.

bent ADJECTIVE
curved or crooked
➤ **To be bent on something** is to be determined to do it. • *They were bent on destruction.*

bereaved ADJECTIVE
A bereaved person is someone with a close relative who has recently died.

beret (*say* bair-ay) NOUN berets
a soft round flat cap

berry NOUN berries
a small juicy fruit

⚙ **BUILD YOUR VOCABULARY**
Look at **blackberry**, **blueberry**, **cranberry**, **mulberry**, **raspberry** and **strawberry**.

berserk ADJECTIVE
To go berserk is to become extremely angry or lose control.

✳ **WORD STORY**
The word **berserk** comes from the *Berserkers*, Viking warriors who wore bear skins and went into a mad frenzy during battle.

berth NOUN berths
❶ a sleeping place on a ship or train or in a caravan ❷ a place where a ship is tied up

beside PREPOSITION
next to • *Come sit beside me.*
➤ **beside yourself** very upset, angry or emotional • *Her parents were beside themselves with worry.*

besides PREPOSITION
in addition to • *Who is on the team besides you?*

besides ADVERB
also, in addition • *I don't want to do it. Besides, I haven't got time.*

besiege (say be-**seej**) VERB besieges, besieging, besieged
to surround a place until the people inside surrender

best ADJECTIVE
most excellent • *She is the best swimmer in the class.*

best ADVERB
❶ most • *Which one do you like best?* ❷ in the best way • *I think you described it best.*

best NOUN
the best person or thing • *This film is the best I've ever seen.*

bet VERB bets, betting, bet, betted
To bet on something is to risk money on the result, so that you will win money if you are right about what happens.

betray VERB betrays, betraying, betrayed
To betray someone who trusts you is to harm them or tell their secrets.
➤ **betrayal** NOUN • *She was shocked by her brother's betrayal.*

BUILD YOUR VOCABULARY
Look at **treacherous** and **treachery**.

better ADJECTIVE
❶ more excellent • *This bike is better than my last one.* ❷ well again after an illness • *I'm much better now.*
➤ **To get the better of someone** is to defeat or outwit them.

better ADVERB
in a better way • *You played better today.*

between PREPOSITION, ADVERB
❶ in a place or time that is within two or more things • *I sat between my two friends.* • *He left between 2 and 2.30.* • *There are two hills with a river between.* ❷ among • *Divide the sweets between you.*

beware VERB (only used in the form beware)
be careful • *Beware of pickpockets.*

bewilder VERB bewilders, bewildering, bewildered
To bewilder someone is to puzzle them completely.
➤ **bewildered** ADJECTIVE
➤ **bewilderment** NOUN • *He scratched his head in bewilderment.*

bewitch VERB bewitches, bewitching, bewitched
to put a spell on someone

beyond PREPOSITION, ADVERB
further than • *Don't go beyond the end of the street.*

bib NOUN bibs
a piece of cloth or plastic that you put under a baby's chin during meals to protect its clothes

Bible NOUN Bibles
the holy book of Christianity

bibliography (say bib-lee-**og**-raf-ee) NOUN bibliographies
a list of books about a subject or by a particular author

bicycle NOUN bicycles
a two-wheeled vehicle that you ride by pushing pedals with your feet

WORD STORY
From *bi*, the Greek word for 'two', + *cycle* meaning 'wheel'.

bid VERB bids, bidding, bid
If you bid an amount of money, you offer it for something.

big ADJECTIVE bigger, biggest
❶ large in size • *That's a big pizza!* ❷ important • *This is a big decision.* ❸ elder • *My big sister is 15.*

bike NOUN bikes (informal)
a bicycle or motorcycle

bikini NOUN bikinis
a girl's or woman's two-piece swimsuit

bilingual ADJECTIVE
speaking two languages well

bill NOUN bills
❶ a piece of paper that tells you how much money you owe for something ❷ a plan for a new law in parliament ❸ a bird's beak

a b c d e f g h i j k l m n o p q r s t u v w x y z

billion *NOUN* **billions**
the number 1,000,000,000 (one thousand million)
➤ **billionth** *ADJECTIVE, NOUN* • *You must be the billionth person to ask that question!*

billionaire *NOUN* **billionaires**
Someone who has at least a billion pounds or dollars.

billow *VERB* **billows, billowing, billowed**
to rise, float up or spread in a shape like a cloud
As she floated gently down, Mrs Twit's petticoat billowed out like a parachute, showing her long knickers.
—THE TWITS, Roald Dahl

billy goat *NOUN* **billy goats**
a male goat

⚙ **BUILD** YOUR VOCABULARY
A female goat is a **nanny goat**.

bin *NOUN* **bins**
a container, especially one that you put rubbish in

binary *ADJECTIVE*
The binary system or a binary number, is one that uses only the digits 0 and 1. The binary system is used in computer programming.

bind *VERB* **binds, binding, bound**
❶ to tie someone or something up • *They bound his hands with rope.* ❷ to commit someone to something or someone • *She was bound by a solemn promise.*

bingo *NOUN*
a game in which you have to match numbers or words that are called out with numbers or words you have on squares on a card

binoculars *NOUN*
a device with two tubes with lenses, which you look through to see things far away

biodegradable *ADJECTIVE*
able to break down and decay naturally • *Most plastic is not biodegradable, so it pollutes the oceans.*

biography *NOUN* **biographies**
the story of a person's life written by someone else
➤ **biographical** *ADJECTIVE*

⚙ **BUILD** YOUR VOCABULARY
Look at **autobiography**.

biology *NOUN*
the science or study of living things
➤ **biologist** *NOUN* • *She is a marine biologist who studies dolphins.*

birch *NOUN* **birches**
a thin tree with shiny bark and slender branches

bird *NOUN* **birds**
an animal with feathers, two wings, two legs and a beak

bird of prey *NOUN* **birds of prey**
a bird that kills and eats other animals

⚙ **BUILD** YOUR VOCABULARY
Look at **talon**, **buzzard**, **eagle**, **hawk**, **falcon**, **kestrel**, **osprey** and **owl**.

bird's-eye view *NOUN*
a view of something seen from above

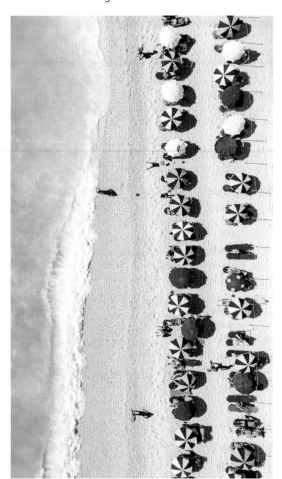

birth *NOUN* births
the beginning of a person's or animal's life, when they come out of their mother

birthday *NOUN* birthdays
the anniversary of the day on which you were born

birthmark *NOUN* birthmarks
a coloured mark that has been on someone's skin since they were born

birthplace *NOUN* birthplaces
the place where someone was born

biscuit *NOUN* biscuits
a small flat kind of cake that has been baked until it is hard

★ **WORD STORY**
From French words *bis* meaning 'twice' + *cuit* meaning 'cooked'.

bishop *NOUN* bishops
a senior priest in some Christian churches

bison *NOUN* bison
a wild ox with shaggy hair

bit *VERB (past tense of* **bite***)*
• *The cat* **bit** *me.*

bit *NOUN* bits
❶ a small piece or amount of something ❷ the part of a horse's bridle that is put into its mouth

bitch *NOUN* bitches
a female dog, fox or wolf

bite *VERB* bites, biting, bit, bitten
❶ to cut or hold something with your teeth
❷ to sting or hurt • *a* **biting** *wind*

bite *NOUN* bites
an act of biting something or someone • *She took a* **bite** *out of her apple.*

bitter *ADJECTIVE*
❶ tasting strong and unpleasant ❷ extremely cold
Much rain fell in the night; and the next morning there blew a bitter wintry wind out of the northwest, driving scattered clouds.—KIDNAPPED, Robert Louis Stevenson
❸ feeling angry and resentful
➤ **bitterly** *ADVERB*

bizarre *ADJECTIVE*
very strange or unusual • *We saw a* **bizarre** *creature.*
➤ **bizarrely** *ADVERB*

black *ADJECTIVE* blacker, blackest
❶ of the colour of coal or a very dark night sky
❷ Black people are people with dark skin, especially those whose families originally come from Africa or Aboriginal Australia.

black *NOUN* blacks
a black colour

blackberry *NOUN* blackberries
a soft dark-purple or black berry made up of lots of small round parts, that often grows wild

⚙ **BUILD YOUR VOCABULARY**
Look at **bramble**.

blackbird *NOUN* blackbirds
a dark European songbird. The male bird has a yellow beak.

blackboard *NOUN* blackboards
a dark board for writing on with chalk

blackcurrant *NOUN* blackcurrants
❶ Blackcurrants are small, round, black berries that grow in bunches. ❷ Blackcurrant is a drink made from the juice of blackcurrants.

blacken *VERB* blackens, blackening, blackened
to make something black

black eye *NOUN* black eyes
an eye with bruises round it

black hole *NOUN* black holes
a region in space with such strong gravity that no light escapes

blackmail *VERB* blackmails, blackmailing, blackmailed
to get money from someone by threatening to tell people something that they want to keep secret

blacksmith *NOUN* blacksmiths
someone who makes things out of iron and fits shoes on horses

bladder *NOUN* bladders
a part inside the body like a bag, where urine collects

blade *NOUN* blades
❶ the sharp part of a knife or sword ❷ A blade of grass is one leaf of it.

a
b
c
d
e
f
i
j
k
l
m
n
o
p
q
r
s
t
u
v
w
x
y
z

blame VERB blames, blaming, blamed
To blame someone is to say that they have done something wrong. • *They **blamed** me for something that was not my fault.*
blame NOUN
To get the blame for something is to be blamed for it.
➤ **To be to blame** is to be the person who has done something wrong.

blancmange *(say* bla-**monj***)* NOUN blancmanges
a pudding like a jelly made with milk

bland ADJECTIVE
not strong or interesting • *The food tasted **bland**.*

blank ADJECTIVE
❶ A blank piece of paper has nothing written or drawn on it. ❷ A blank expression shows no interest or emotion.
blank NOUN blanks
an empty space

blanket NOUN blankets
❶ a thick, warm cover for a bed ❷ a layer covering a surface • *A **blanket** of snow lay on the ground.*

blare VERB blares, blaring, blared
to make a loud unpleasant sound

blast NOUN blasts
❶ an explosion ❷ a very strong rush of wind, air or liquid
blast VERB blasts, blasting, blasted
❶ to blow something up with an explosion ❷ If wind or water blasts someone, it hits them with a lot of force.

blatant *(say* blay-tant*)* ADJECTIVE
clear and obvious • *a **blatant** lie*
➤ **blatantly** ADVERB

blaze NOUN blazes
❶ a very bright fire ❷ a very bright colour or light
blaze VERB blazes, blazing, blazed
to burn or shine brightly

blazer NOUN blazers
a kind of jacket, often with a badge on the front

bleach VERB bleaches, bleaching, bleached
to make something white

bleach NOUN
a substance used to clean things or make clothes white

bleak ADJECTIVE bleaker, bleakest
❶ bare and cold • *a **bleak** and barren landscape*
❷ miserable or hopeless • *The future looked **bleak**.*

bleary ADJECTIVE blearier, bleariest
Bleary eyes are tired and do not see clearly.

bleat VERB bleats, bleating, bleated
When a sheep or goat bleats, it makes a high sound.
bleat NOUN bleats
the cry of a sheep or goat

bleed VERB bleeds, bleeding, bled
to lose blood from your body, for example if you are injured

bleep NOUN bleeps
a short high sound made by an electronic device
bleep VERB bleeps, bleeping, bleeped
to make a short high sound • *The robot **bleeped**.*

blend VERB blends, blending, blended
❶ to mix things together smoothly or easily ❷ to put letter sounds together when making words
blend NOUN blends
❶ a smooth mixture ❷ two or more letter sounds that are used together, for example 'sp' at the beginning of *spell*

blender NOUN blenders
a kitchen device for mixing food or turning it into liquid

bless VERB blesses, blessing, blessed
❶ to ask God to look after someone or something ❷ to bring someone happiness
➤ **blessing** NOUN

blew VERB *(past tense of* **blow***)*
• *The wind **blew** the candles out.*

blind ADJECTIVE blinder, blindest
❶ not able to see ❷ without thought or understanding • *He expected **blind** obedience.*
blind VERB blinds, blinding, blinded
❶ to make someone unable to see ❷ to make someone unable to understand or think clearly

blind *NOUN* **blinds**
a screen to cover a window

blindfold *NOUN* **blindfolds**
a piece of cloth used to cover someone's eyes so that they cannot see

blindfold *VERB* **blindfolds, blindfolding, blindfolded**
to cover someone's eyes with a blindfold

blink *VERB* **blinks, blinking, blinked**
to shut and open your eyes quickly

bliss *NOUN*
great happiness

blister *NOUN* **blisters**
a swelling like a bubble on your skin

blizzard *NOUN* **blizzards**
a very bad snowstorm

bloated *ADJECTIVE*
swollen or puffed out

blob *NOUN* **blobs**
a small round lump of something like paint or ice cream

block *NOUN* **blocks**
❶ a solid piece of something hard such as wood
❷ a large building containing offices or flats
❸ an area of a city with streets on all sides

block *VERB* **blocks, blocking, blocked**
to be across something or in the way, so that something can not get through • *Something is blocking the pipe.*

block capitals *(also* **block letters***)* *NOUN*
large capital letters

○ **BUILD YOUR VOCABULARY**
Look at **upper case**.

block graph *(also* **block diagram***)* *NOUN*
block graphs, block diagrams
a graph showing amounts as columns of blocks at different heights

blog *NOUN* **blogs**
a website on which someone writes regularly about something

blog *VERB* **blogs, blogging, blogged**
to write about something in a blog
➤ **blogger** *NOUN* ➤ **blogging** *NOUN*

blond *(also* **blonde***)* *ADJECTIVE* **blonder, blondest**
fair-haired

blood *NOUN*
❶ the red liquid that your heart pumps around your body ❷ Someone's blood is their family. • *She is of royal blood.*

blood-curdling *ADJECTIVE*
terrifying • *a blood-curdling scream*

bloodhound *NOUN* **bloodhounds**
a large breed of dog which can track people by following their scent

bloodshed *NOUN*
Bloodshed is the killing and injuring of people.

bloodshot *ADJECTIVE*
Bloodshot eyes are streaked with red.

bloodstream *NOUN*
Your bloodstream is the blood flowing round your body.

bloodthirsty *ADJECTIVE* **bloodthirstier, bloodthirstiest**
enjoying killing and violence

bloody *ADJECTIVE* **bloodier, bloodiest**
covered in or involving a lot of blood

bloom *VERB* **blooms, blooming, bloomed**
to produce flowers
bloom *NOUN* **blooms**
A bloom is a flower.
➤ **in bloom** producing flowers
• *The bushes are in bloom.*

blossom *NOUN* **blossoms**
❶ Blossom is a mass of flowers on a tree, especially a fruit tree.
❷ A blossom is a flower, especially on a fruit tree.
blossom *VERB* **blossoms, blossoming, blossomed**
to produce flowers

blot *VERB* **blots, blotting, blotted**
➤ **To blot something out** is to cover something so that it cannot be seen. • *A dark cloud **blotted out** the sun.*
blot *NOUN* **blots**
a spot or a blob of ink

blouse *NOUN* **blouses**
a woman's loose shirt

blow *VERB* **blows, blowing, blew, blown**
❶ to force out air from your mouth or nose • *She **blew** on the hot soup.* ❷ When the wind blows, it can be felt.
➤ **to blow up** to explode
➤ **To blow something up** ❶ is to fill a balloon or tyre with air. ❷ is to destroy it with an explosion.
blow *NOUN* **blows**
a hard knock or hit

blue *ADJECTIVE* **bluer, bluest**
of the colour of a bright cloudless sky
blue *NOUN* **blues**
a blue colour

bluebell *NOUN* **bluebells**
a blue bell-shaped wild flower

blueberry *NOUN* **blueberries**
a round, dark bluish-purple berry

bluebottle *NOUN* **bluebottles**
a large fly that makes a loud buzz

bluff *VERB* **bluffs, bluffing, bluffed**
to make someone think that you will do something that you don't intend to do or that you know something that you don't really know
bluff *NOUN* **bluffs**
❶ something such as a threat or claim that is an attempt to bluff someone ❷ a steep cliff or bank

blunder *NOUN* **blunders**
a careless mistake
blunder *VERB* **blunders, blundering, blundered**
❶ to make a careless mistake ❷ to move in a clumsy way • *He **blundered** into a door.*

blunt *ADJECTIVE* **blunter, bluntest**
❶ having an edge that is not sharp or pointed
❷ saying what you mean without trying to be polite or tactful

blur *NOUN* **blurs**
an unclear shape with no definite outline • *Without her glasses, everything was a **blur**.*
blur *VERB* **blurs, blurring, blurred**
to make something look unclear • *Tears **blurred** his vision.*

blurb *NOUN* **blurbs**
a short description of a book printed on its cover

blurry *ADJECTIVE* **blurrier, blurriest**
not able to be seen clearly • *a **blurry** photograph*

blurt *VERB* **blurt, blurting, blurted**
To blurt something out is to say it suddenly, without thinking.

blush *VERB* **blushes, blushing, blushed**
to have a red face because you are embarrassed or ashamed

bluster *VERB* **blusters, blustering, blustered**
to boast or make threats that do not mean very much

boa (also **boa constrictor**) *NOUN* **boas, boa constrictors**
a large snake that coils round its prey and crushes it

boar *NOUN* **boars**
❶ a wild pig ❷ a male pig

⬤ **BUILD YOUR VOCABULARY**
A female pig is a **sow**.

board *NOUN* **boards**
❶ a flat piece of wood, used in building ❷ a flat piece of wood, plastic or other material, used for a particular activity • *a chess board* • *a chopping board*
➤ **on board** on a ship

⚠ **WATCH OUT!**
Do not confuse with **bored** meaning 'not interested'.

board *VERB* **boards, boarding, boarded**
To board a ship or train or aircraft is to get on it.

board game *NOUN* **board games**
a game played on a board, such as chess or draughts

boarding school *NOUN* **boarding schools**
a school in which the pupils live during the term

boast *VERB* **boasts, boasting, boasted**
to talk too proudly about something you can do or something you own
➤ **boastful** *ADJECTIVE* • *He was very boastful about his success.*

boat *NOUN* **boats**
a vehicle that floats and travels on water

bob *VERB* **bobs, bobbing, bobbed**
to move gently up and down, like something floating on water

bobble *NOUN* **bobbles**
a small round ball of something soft, used as a decoration

bodice *NOUN* **bodices**
the upper part of a woman's dress

body *NOUN* **bodies**
❶ A person's or animal's body is all its physical parts. • *We drew a diagram of the human body.* ❷ a dead person

⚙ **BUILD YOUR VOCABULARY**
A synonym is **corpse**.

❸ an object or piece of matter in space • *A moon is a body that orbits a planet.*

bodyguard *NOUN* **bodyguards**
a guard who protects someone from attack

bog *NOUN* **bogs**
an area of wet spongy ground
➤ **boggy** *ADJECTIVE*

boil *VERB* **boils, boiling, boiled**
❶ If liquid boils or if you boil it, it is heated until it starts to bubble and give off vapour. ❷ To boil food is to cook it in boiling water. • *I boiled an egg.*

boiler *NOUN* **boilers**
a container for heating water or making steam

boisterous *ADJECTIVE*
noisy and lively

bold *ADJECTIVE* **bolder, boldest**
❶ brave and daring ❷ clear and easy to see • *bold colours*
bold *NOUN*
thick dark printed letters • *The title is in bold.*

bolt *NOUN* **bolts**
❶ a sliding bar for fastening a door or window ❷ a thick metal pin for screwing things together ❸ a flash of lightning
bolt *VERB* **bolts, bolting, bolted**
❶ to suddenly run somewhere • *She bolted for the door.* ❷ to fasten something with a bolt • *bolt the window*

bomb *NOUN* **bombs**
an object filled with explosives, which can be made to blow up
bomb *VERB* **bombs, bombing, bombed**
To bomb a place is to attack it with bombs.

bombard *VERB* **bombards, bombarding, bombarded**
❶ To bombard a place is to attack it with a lot of bullets or bombs. ❷ To bombard someone is to ask them a lot of questions.

bond *NOUN* **bonds**
❶ a shared experience or feeling that brings people close together ❷ Bonds are ropes or chains used to tie people up.

bone *NOUN* **bones**
one of the hard white parts inside a person's or animal's body. • *He broke a bone in his foot.*

⚙ **BUILD YOUR VOCABULARY**
Look at **skeleton**.

bonfire NOUN bonfires
a large fire lit out of doors

WORD STORY
From *bone* + *fire*, because they used to be used for burning bones.

bonnet NOUN bonnets
❶ the part of a car that covers the engine ❷ a baby's or woman's hat that ties under the chin

bonus NOUN bonuses
❶ an extra payment that someone gets for their work ❷ an extra advantage or reward

bony ADJECTIVE bonier, boniest
thin, without much flesh

boo VERB boos, booing, booed
to make loud noises that show disapproval

book NOUN books
an object made of pieces of paper, usually with printing or writing on, fastened together inside a cover

book VERB books, booking, booked
to arrange for something such as a seat on a train, a room in a hotel or a table at a restaurant to be kept for you to use

bookcase NOUN bookcases
a piece of furniture with shelves for holding books

booklet NOUN booklets
a small book with paper covers

bookmark NOUN bookmarks
❶ something you use to keep your place in a book ❷ a link you save on a computer to a website or file

bookmark VERB bookmarks, bookmarking, bookmarked
to save a link to a website or file

boom NOUN booms
❶ a deep hollow sound • *We heard the **boom** of thunder.* ❷ a long pole at the bottom of a sail to keep it stretched

boom VERB booms, booming, boomed
to make a loud deep sound
'Hello hello hello!' a loud voice boomed out and from behind the door stepped a short, chubby man with a round red face.–THE REPTILE ROOM, Lemony Snicket

boomerang NOUN boomerangs
a curved stick which returns to you when you throw it

WORD STORY
From an Australian Aboriginal language, as **boomerangs** were originally used for hunting by Aborigines.

boost VERB boosts, boosting, boosted
to improve or increase something • *Lots of practice at the game will **boost** your score.*

booster NOUN boosters
❶ something that increases the power of something • *a signal **booster*** ❷ part of a rocket or spacecraft used to give it extra speed when it first takes off

boot NOUN boots
❶ a shoe that covers your ankle and sometimes part of your leg ❷ the space for luggage at the back of a car

boot VERB boots, booting, booted
❶ *(informal)* to kick someone or something ❷ To boot up a computer is to switch it on and start it.

booth NOUN booths
a small compartment for a special purpose • *a ticket booth*

border NOUN borders
❶ The border between two countries is the line where they meet. ❷ an edge • *The cloth has a red border.* ❸ a flower bed

bore VERB *(past tense of **bear**)*
• *The chair **bore** his weight.*

bore VERB bores, boring, bored
❶ If something bores you, it is dull and uninteresting. ❷ To bore a hole is to drill it through something.

bore NOUN bores
a dull or uninteresting person or thing

bored ADJECTIVE
feeling tired and without any interest in something • *I was really **bored** because I had nothing to do.*

WATCH OUT!
Do not confuse with a **board** meaning 'a flat object'.

boredom NOUN
a feeling of tiredness and lack of interest

boring ADJECTIVE
dull and uninteresting • *The book was really boring.*

born or **borne** VERB (*past participle of* **bear**)
• *I couldn't have borne it.*

born ADJECTIVE
➤ **To be born** is to start to live when you come out of your mother. • *He was born in May.*

borough (*say* buh-ruh) NOUN **boroughs**
a town or district with its own local council

> ⚠ **WATCH OUT!**
> Borough is spelt like **thorough** and it sounds the same.

borrow VERB **borrows, borrowing, borrowed**
to use something that belongs to someone else for a while before giving it back to them • *Can I borrow your pen?*

boss NOUN **bosses**
A person who is in charge of a business or group of workers.
boss VERB **bosses, bossing, bossed** (*informal*)
To boss someone around is to tell them what to do.

bossy ADJECTIVE **bossier, bossiest**
a bossy person likes to tell other people what to do
➤ **bossiness** NOUN

botany NOUN
the study of plants
➤ **botanist** NOUN

both DETERMINER, PRONOUN
two things or people, not just one • *I like them both.*
• *Use both hands.*

bother VERB **bothers, bothering, bothered**
❶ To bother someone is to annoy or worry them.
❷ To be bothered to do something is to make the effort to do it.
bother NOUN
Bother is trouble or worry.

bottle NOUN **bottles**
a glass or plastic container with a narrow neck for holding liquids
bottle VERB **bottles, bottling, bottled**
To bottle something is to put it in a bottle.

bottom NOUN **bottoms**
❶ The bottom of something is its lowest point.
❷ Your bottom is the part of your body that you sit on.

bottomless ADJECTIVE
very deep or not seeming to have any bottom

bough NOUN **boughs**
a large branch of a tree

> ⚠ **WATCH OUT!**
> In **bough** and **plough**, the letters *ough* sound like 'ow' in the word 'how'.

bought VERB (*past tense and past participle of* **buy**)
• *My parents bought me a new bike.* • *I've bought some sweets.*

> ⚠ **WATCH OUT!**
> In **bought**, **brought**, **ought** and **thought**, the letters *ough* sound like 'aw' in the word 'saw'.

boulder NOUN **boulders**
a very large smooth stone

bounce VERB **bounces, bouncing, bounced**
❶ If something bounces, it springs back when it hits a surface. ❷ To bounce a ball is to throw it so that it bounces.
bounce NOUN **bounces**
A bounce is the action of bouncing.
➤ **bouncy** ADJECTIVE • *a bouncy ball*

bound VERB (*past tense and past participle of* **bind**)
• *They bound the logs together with ropes.*
• *We've bound the sticks into bundles.*
bound ADJECTIVE
➤ **To be bound for a place** is to be travelling towards it. • *The Titanic was bound for New York.*
➤ **To be bound to do something** is to be certain to do it. • *She is bound to agree.*
bound VERB **bounds, bounding, bounded**
To bound is to leap or to run with leaping steps.
bound NOUN **bounds**
a leaping movement

boundary NOUN **boundaries**
a limit or line at the edge of something • *the boundary between the two farms*

bouquet (*say* boo-**kay** *or* boh-**kay**) NOUN **bouquets**
a bunch of flowers

bout *NOUN* **bouts**
a fight

boutique *(say* boo-**teek***) NOUN* **boutiques**
a small shop, especially one that sells fashionable clothes

bovine *ADJECTIVE*
to do with cows or like a cow

bow *(rhymes with* **go***) NOUN* **bows**
❶ a knot made with two loops and two loose ends
❷ the stick used for playing a stringed instrument such as a violin ❸ a long curved piece of wood used for shooting arrows

bow *(rhymes with* **cow***) VERB* **bows, bowing, bowed**
to bend your body forwards to show respect or say thank you

bow *(rhymes with* **cow***) NOUN* **bows**
❶ the action of bowing • *The actors took a* **bow***.*
❷ the front part of a ship

bowel *NOUN*
Your bowel is the tube through which waste passes from the stomach before leaving your body.

bowl *NOUN* **bowls**
a deep round dish • *a* **bowl** *of porridge*

bowl *VERB* **bowls, bowling, bowled**
In cricket or rounders, to throw the ball towards someone who is trying to hit it.

bowler *NOUN* **bowlers**
❶ bowler hat; a hat with a rounded top and a narrow brim ❷ someone who bowls in cricket or rounders

bowling *NOUN*
A game in which you have to knock down wooden objects with a heavy ball you roll down a track.

box *NOUN* **boxes**
❶ a container made of wood or cardboard, often with a lid ❷ a small square or rectangle that you fill in on a form or computer screen

box *VERB* **boxes, boxing, boxed**
to fight with your fists

boxer *NOUN* **boxers**
❶ someone who boxes ❷ a breed of dog with a smooth coat and a flat face

Boxing Day *NOUN* **Boxing Days**
the day after Christmas Day

✳ **WORD STORY**

In the past, it was traditional to give servants or people who did jobs for you a box containing money or presents on **Boxing Day**.

boy *NOUN* **boys**
a male child
➤ **boyish** *ADJECTIVE* • *He had a young* **boyish** *face.*

boyfriend *NOUN* **boyfriends**
Someone's boyfriend is a man or boy they have a romantic relationship with.

bra *NOUN* **bras**
a piece of underwear women wear to support their breasts

brace *NOUN* **braces**
❶ a device for straightening or supporting something, such as your teeth ❷ Braces are straps worn over the shoulders to hold trousers up.

bracelet *NOUN* **bracelets**
a piece of jewellery you wear round your wrist

bracken *NOUN*
Bracken is a large feathery plant that grows on moors.

bracket *NOUN* **brackets**
a punctuation mark used in pairs around words or figures to separate them from what comes before and after. Brackets are round ( ) or square [ ].

brag *VERB* **brags, bragging, bragged**
To brag is to boast.

braid *NOUN* **braids**
a plait

braid *VERB* **braids, braiding, braided**
to plait hair

Braille NOUN
Braille is a system of writing or printing using raised dots, which blind people can read by touch.

✴ **WORD STORY**
Braille is named after its inventor, a blind French teacher called Louis Braille (1809–1852).

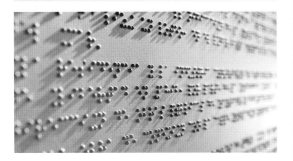

brain NOUN brains
Your brain is the part inside the top of your head that controls your body.

brainy ADJECTIVE brainier, brainiest (informal)
clever, intelligent • *She's really brainy.*

brake NOUN brakes
a device for making a vehicle stop or slow down

⚠ **WATCH OUT!**
Do not confuse a **brake** with a **break**, which means 'a rest' or 'a gap'.

brake VERB brakes, braking, braked
to use a brake to stop or slow down

bramble NOUN brambles
A bramble is a prickly bush, especially a blackberry bush.

branch NOUN branches
❶ a part that sticks out from the trunk of a tree
❷ one of the shops or offices that are part of a large organisation • *The store has branches all over the world.*
branch VERB branches, branching, branched
If a tree or path branches, it separates into parts that stick out or lead in different directions.

brand NOUN brands
a particular make or kind of something • *What brand of toothpaste do you use?*

brandish VERB brandishes, brandishing, brandished
to wave something about
In a fury, he brandished his sword.—VIKING GIRL, Pauline Chandler

brandy NOUN brandies
Brandy is a kind of strong alcoholic drink.

brass NOUN
a metal made from copper and zinc

brass instrument NOUN
brass instruments
a musical instrument made of brass, such as a trumpet or trombone

🔵 **BUILD YOUR VOCABULARY**
Look at **percussion**, **stringed instrument**, **wind instrument** and **woodwind instrument**.

brave ADJECTIVE braver, bravest
ready to face danger or suffering
➤ **bravely** ADVERB ➤ **bravery** NOUN

bray VERB brays, braying, brayed
to make a noise like a donkey

brazen ADJECTIVE
shameless or cheeky

brazier (say bray-zee-er) NOUN braziers
a metal container holding hot coal

bread NOUN
food made by baking flour and water, usually with yeast

breadth NOUN breadths
the width of something from side to side

break VERB breaks, breaking, broke, broken
❶ If you break something or it breaks, it becomes damaged or separates into pieces. • *I dropped my phone and it broke.* ❷ To break a law, rule or promise is to do something that goes against it. ❸ To break a record is to do better than the previous best result. ❹ Waves break when they fall and make foam. ❺ A boy's voice breaks when it starts to go deeper at about the age of 14.
➤ **To break down** is to fail or stop working.
➤ **To break off** is to stop talking or doing something. • *She broke off to stare at him.*
➤ **To break out** is to start happening. • *A fight broke out.*

a
b
c
d
e
f
g
h
i
j
k
l
m
n
o
p
q
r
s
t
u
v
w
x
y
z

break NOUN breaks
❶ a short rest or pause • *We worked all morning without a break.* ❷ a gap • *The sun appeared through a break in the clouds.*

⚠ **WATCH OUT!**
Do not confuse a **break** with a **brake**, which is a device for slowing down.

breakdown NOUN breakdowns
a sudden failure, especially by a car • *We had a breakdown on the motorway.*

breaker NOUN breakers
a wave breaking on the shore

breakfast NOUN breakfasts
the first meal of the day

breakthrough NOUN breakthroughs
an important piece of progress, for example in scientific research

breast NOUN breasts
❶ one of the two parts on the front of a woman's body that can produce milk to feed a baby
❷ a person's or animal's chest

breaststroke NOUN
a stroke you use when swimming on your front, pushing your arms forward and bringing them round and back

breath (say breth) NOUN breaths
air that you bring into your lungs and send out again • *Take a deep breath.*
➤ **To be out of breath** is to be breathing fast or with difficulty after exercise.
➤ **To take someone's breath away** is to surprise or delight them.

⚠ **WATCH OUT!**
Breath is a noun and **breathe** is a verb, as in *I can't breathe.*

breathe (say bree*th*) VERB breathes, breathing, breathed
To breathe is to bring air into your lungs through your nose or mouth and send it out again. • *Relax and breathe slowly.*

breathless ADJECTIVE
finding it hard to breathe, because of exercise or because you are excited
➤ **breathlessly** ADVERB

breathtaking ADJECTIVE
extremely beautiful or delightful

bred VERB (past tense and past participle of **breed**)
➤ **born and bred** having lived in a particular place or a particular way since birth • *She's a country girl born and bred.*

breeches (say brich-iz) NOUN
short trousers that fit tightly at the knee

breed VERB breeds, breeding, bred
❶ To breed is to produce offspring. • *Locusts breed very quickly.* ❷ To breed animals is to get young animals from them. • *He bred ponies.*

breed NOUN breeds
a particular type of an animal • *A corgi is a breed of dog.*

breeze NOUN breezes
a gentle wind
➤ **breezy** ADJECTIVE • *a breezy day*

brethren NOUN (old use)
brothers

brew VERB brews, brewing, brewed
To brew beer or tea is to make it.

brewery NOUN breweries
a place where beer is made

briar NOUN briars
a thorny bush, especially a wild rose bush

bribe NOUN bribes
a gift or money offered to someone to persuade them to do something
bribe VERB bribes, bribing, bribed
To bribe someone is to give them a bribe.

brick NOUN bricks
a small hard block of baked clay used in building

bridal ADJECTIVE
to do with a bride • *a bridal gown*

⚠ **WATCH OUT!**
Do not confuse the adjective **bridal** with a **bridle**, which is part of a horse's harness. Adjectives often end in '-al' and rarely in '-le', for example *central, global* or *natural.*

bride *NOUN* brides
a woman on her wedding day

bridegroom *NOUN* bridegrooms
a man on his wedding day

bridesmaid *NOUN* bridesmaids
a girl or woman who helps the bride at her wedding

bridge *NOUN* bridges
❶ a structure built over a river, railway or road, to allow people to cross it ❷ The bridge of a ship is the platform from where it is controlled.

bridle *NOUN* bridles
the part of a horse's harness that fits over its head

⚠ **WATCH OUT!**
Do not confuse with **bridal**, which means 'to do with a bride'.

brief *ADJECTIVE* briefer, briefest
lasting a short time or using only a few words
➤ **briefly** *ADVERB*

briefcase *NOUN* briefcases
a flat case for papers

briefs *NOUN*
short underpants

brigade *NOUN* brigades
❶ an army unit usually consisting of three battalions ❷ a group of people in uniform, for example the fire brigade

brigand *NOUN* brigands
an old word for a robber or outlaw

bright *ADJECTIVE* brighter, brightest
❶ shining strongly ❷ A bright colour is strong and vivid. ❸ clever
➤ **brightly** *ADVERB* ➤ **brightness** *NOUN*

brighten *or* **brighten up** *VERB* brightens, brightening, brightened
to become brighter or more cheerful
She looked discouraged for a moment, but she soon brightened up.—PIPPI IN THE SOUTH SEAS, Astrid Lindgren

brilliant *ADJECTIVE*
❶ very clever • *a brilliant idea* ❷ very bright and sparkling • *a brilliant light* ❸ (informal) really good or enjoyable
➤ **brilliance** *NOUN* ➤ **brilliantly** *ADVERB*

brim *NOUN* brims
❶ the edge round the top of a container ❷ the wide bottom edge of a hat

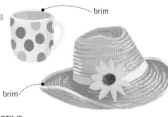

brim

brim

brimming *ADJECTIVE*
completely full • *a brimming bucket*

bring *VERB* brings, bringing, brought
to take someone or something with you to a place
➤ **To bring something about** is to make it happen.
➤ **To bring someone up** is to look after them as a child.

brink *NOUN*
the edge of a steep or dangerous place

brisk *ADJECTIVE* brisker, briskest
quick and lively
➤ **briskly** *ADVERB*

bristle *NOUN* bristles
a short stiff hair

Briton *NOUN* Britons
a member of the Celtic peoples who lived in southern Britain at the time of the Romans

brittle *ADJECTIVE* brittler, brittlest
hard but likely to break or snap

broad *ADJECTIVE* broader, broadest
❶ wide and open • *a broad avenue* ❷ Broad daylight is clear and full daylight. ❸ general, not detailed • *a broad outline*
➤ **broaden** *VERB* • *His smile broadened.*

broadband *NOUN*
a system for sending information quickly over the Internet

broad bean *NOUN* broad beans
a type of large flat bean with seeds that can be eaten

broadcast *NOUN* broadcasts
a radio or television programme
broadcast *VERB* broadcasts, broadcasting, broadcast
To broadcast a radio or television programme is to transmit or show it.

a b c d e f g h i j k l m n o p q r s t u v w x y z

broccoli NOUN
a vegetable with green or purple buds on green stalks

brochure NOUN brochures
a booklet containing information, especially about a place

broke VERB (past tense of **break**)
• Chloe **broke** her leg last year.

broke ADJECTIVE (informal)
having no money • I'm completely **broke**.

broken VERB (past participle of **break**)
• Poor Chloe has just **broken** her leg again!

bronchitis (say brong-**ky**-tiss) NOUN
a disease of the lungs

bronze NOUN
a metal made from copper and tin

brooch (rhymes with **coach**) NOUN brooches
a piece of jewellery that is pinned on to clothes

brood NOUN broods
a number of young birds hatched together
brood VERB broods, brooding, brooded
To brood over something is to keep on thinking and worrying about it.

brook NOUN brooks
a small stream

broom NOUN brooms
❶ a brush with a long handle, for sweeping floors
❷ Broom is a shrub with yellow, white or pink flowers.

broth NOUN broths
thin soup

brother NOUN brothers
Your brother is a man or boy who has the same parents as you.
➤ **brotherly** ADJECTIVE • **brotherly** love

brother-in-law NOUN brothers-in-law
A person's brother-in-law is the brother of their husband or wife or the husband of their sister or brother.

brought VERB (past tense and past participle of **bring**)
• They **brought** their friends. • Have you **brought** a picnic?

⚠ **WATCH OUT!**
In **brought**, **bought**, **ought** and **thought**, the letters ough sound like 'aw' in the word 'saw'.

brow NOUN brows
❶ Your brow is your forehead. ❷ Your brows are your eyebrows. ❸ The brow of a hill is the top of it.

brown ADJECTIVE browner, brownest
❶ of the colour of earth, wood or chocolate
❷ Brown bread or rice contains all parts of the grain.

⚙ **BUILD YOUR VOCABULARY**
The opposite of the second meaning is **white** and a synonym is **wholemeal**.

brown NOUN
a brown colour

browse VERB browses, browsing, browsed
to read or look through books, magazines or web pages

browser NOUN browsers
a computer program that allows you to look at different websites

bruise NOUN bruises
A dark mark that appears on your skin when it is hit or hurt.
bruise VERB bruises, bruising, bruised
To bruise someone is to cause a bruise.

⚠ **WATCH OUT!**
Remember **bruise** has an 'i' in it!

brunch NOUN brunches
a meal in the late morning instead of breakfast and lunch

brush NOUN brushes
an object with hairs or bristles. Brushes are used for sweeping and cleaning, for tidying hair and for painting.
brush VERB brushes, brushing, brushed
❶ to use a brush on something • **brush** your teeth
❷ to touch something lightly as it passes • Cobwebs **brushed** against his face.

Brussels sprout NOUN Brussels sprouts
a green vegetable like a tiny cabbage

brutal ADJECTIVE
savage and cruel
➤ **brutality** NOUN ➤ **brutally** ADVERB

brute NOUN brutes
❶ a cruel person ❷ an animal

bubble NOUN bubbles
a ball of air or gas in a liquid
bubble VERB bubbles, bubbling, bubbled
to produce bubbles • *a bubbling cauldron*

buccaneer NOUN buccaneers
an old word for a pirate

buck NOUN bucks
a male deer, rabbit or hare

○ BUILD YOUR VOCABULARY
The female is a **doe**.

buck VERB bucks, bucking, bucked
If a horse bucks, it jumps with its back arched.

bucket NOUN buckets
a container with a handle, for carrying liquids
or sand

buckle NOUN buckles
a clip at the end of a belt or strap for fastening it
buckle VERB buckles, buckling, buckled
❶ To buckle something is to fasten it with a buckle.
❷ To buckle is to bend or give way. • *His knees
buckled under the weight.*

bud NOUN buds
a flower or leaf
before it has
opened

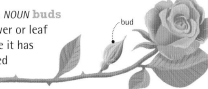
bud

Buddhist NOUN
someone who believes in **Buddhism**, a religion that
started in Asia and follows the teachings of Buddha
➤ **Buddhist** ADJECTIVE

budge VERB budges, budging, budged
to move • *The door was stuck and wouldn't budge.*

budgerigar (also **budgie** informal) NOUN
budgerigars, budgies
a small brightly coloured bird often kept as a pet in
a cage

 WORD STORY
The word **budgerigar** comes from an Australian
Aboriginal word.

budget NOUN budgets
a plan for how much money will be spent on
different things
budget VERB budgets, budgeting, budgeted
To budget is to plan how much you are going to spend.

buffalo NOUN buffalo, buffaloes
a wild ox with long curved horns

buffet (say buh-fay or boof-ay) NOUN buffets
❶ a cafe or place for buying drinks and snacks
❷ a meal where guests serve themselves

bug NOUN bugs
❶ a small insect ❷ (informal) a germ that causes
illness • *I had a tummy bug.* ❸ a fault or problem in
a computer program
bug VERB bugs, bugging, bugged
to put a hidden microphone somewhere • *The room
was bugged.*

buggy NOUN buggies
❶ a folding pram for small children ❷ a small vehicle
with an open top • *a beach buggy*

bugle NOUN bugles
a brass instrument like a small trumpet

build VERB builds, building, built
to make something by putting the parts together
➤ **To build up** is to gradually increase. • *The
excitement was building up.*

builder NOUN builders
someone who puts up buildings

building NOUN buildings
A building is a structure that someone has built, such
as a house.

bulb NOUN bulbs
❶ the glass part of a light that shines ❷ an
onion-shaped root of a plant or flower, such as
a daffodil

bulge VERB bulges, bulging, bulged
to stick out or swell • *His eyes bulged in shock.*
bulge NOUN bulges
a lump or a part that sticks out

bulk NOUN
A thing's bulk is its size, especially when it is large.

bulky ADJECTIVE bulkier, bulkiest
taking up a lot of space

bull NOUN bulls
a male cow, seal, whale or elephant

bulldog NOUN bulldogs
a breed of dog with a short thick neck

bulldozer NOUN bulldozers
a heavy vehicle with a wide metal blade in front, used to clear or flatten land
➤ **bulldoze** VERB

bullet NOUN bullets
a piece of shaped metal shot from a gun

bulletin NOUN bulletins
a short news announcement

bullet point NOUN bullet points
an item in a list, printed with a black dot in front of it • *List your information as bullet points.*

bullion NOUN
gold or silver in the form of bars

bullock NOUN bullocks
a young bull

bullseye NOUN bullseyes
the centre of a target

bully VERB bullies, bullying, bullied
to hurt or frighten someone weaker
bully NOUN bullies
someone who bullies people

bulrush NOUN bulrushes
a tall reed that grows in water

bulwark NOUN
a ship's side above the level of the deck

bumblebee NOUN bumblebees
a large bee with a loud buzz

bump VERB bumps, bumping, bumped
to knock something accidentally • *I bumped my head.*
bump NOUN bumps
❶ the noise of something knocking or falling somewhere • *He fell with a bump.* ❷ a lump or swelling • *a bump in the road*
➤ **bumpy** ADJECTIVE • *a bumpy road*

bumper NOUN bumpers
a bar along the front or back of a vehicle to protect it if it hits anything

bun NOUN buns
❶ a small, round cake or bread roll ❷ a round bunch of hair at the back of the head

bunch NOUN bunches
a number of things joined together, such as fruit, flowers or keys • *a bunch of grapes*

bundle NOUN bundles
a number of things tied or wrapped together
• *a bundle of rags*
bundle VERB bundles, bundling, bundled
❶ To bundle things is to tie or wrap them together. ❷ To bundle someone somewhere is to push them there hurriedly.

bungalow NOUN bungalows
a house with all the rooms on one floor

✴ **WORD STORY**

The word **bungalow** comes from a Hindi word for a type of cottage.

bunk NOUN bunks
a narrow bed fixed to a wall, for example on a ship

bunk bed NOUN bunk beds
a single bed with another bed above it or below it

bunker NOUN bunkers
an underground shelter

buoy (say boy) NOUN buoys
a floating object fixed to the bottom of the sea, used as a marker

buoyant ADJECTIVE
❶ able to float ❷ lively and cheerful • *He was in a buoyant mood.*
➤ **buoyancy** NOUN

⚠ **WATCH OUT!**
Buoyant (meaning 'able to float') contains the word buoy (meaning 'floating object') and they both have a silent 'u'.

burble VERB burbles, burbling, burbled
❶ to make a light bubbling sound, like water in a stream ❷ to talk in a rambling way

✳ **WORD STORY**
Burble is an old word that was made popular by the writer Lewis Carroll.

burden NOUN burdens
❶ a heavy load ❷ a problem or difficult responsibility

burger NOUN burgers
a flat round fried food made from meat or vegetables

burglar NOUN burglars
someone who breaks into a building to steal things
➤ **burglary** NOUN
➤ **burgle** VERB • *Their house was burgled.*

burial NOUN burials
the act of putting a dead body in a grave

burly ADJECTIVE burlier, burliest
big and strong

burn VERB burns, burning, burnt or burned
❶ If something burns, it catches fire or is destroyed by fire or heat. ❷ If you burn something, you damage or destroy it using fire or heat.

burn NOUN burns
an injury or mark caused by fire or strong heat

burning ADJECTIVE
A burning desire is very strong.

burp VERB burps, burping, burped
To burp is to make a noise through your mouth by letting air come up from your stomach.

burp NOUN burps
the act or sound of burping

burr NOUN burrs
part of a plant that clings to your clothes or hair

burrow NOUN burrows
a hole dug by an animal such as a rabbit or fox

burrow VERB burrows, burrowing, burrowed
❶ to dig a hole or burrow ❷ to feel or go deep inside something • *She burrowed in her pocket for the key.*

burst VERB bursts, bursting, burst
If something bursts or you burst it, it breaks apart suddenly.
➤ **To burst in** is to rush in suddenly and noisily.
➤ **To burst into something** is to suddenly start doing it.
The next moment he burst into a peal of joyous laughter.
—RINKITINK IN OZ, L. Frank Baum
➤ **To be bursting with something** is to feel something very strongly. • *I was bursting with curiosity.*

burst NOUN bursts
a sudden short period of noise • *a burst of gunfire*

bury VERB buries, burying, buried
❶ To bury something is to put it under the ground.
❷ To bury someone is to put them in a grave when they are dead.

⭘ **BUILD YOUR VOCABULARY**
Look at **burial**.

bus NOUN buses
a large road vehicle for carrying passengers

✳ **WORD STORY**
A **bus** used to be called an *omnibus*, which comes from a Latin word meaning 'for everyone'.

bush NOUN bushes
❶ A bush is a plant like a small tree with a lot of stems or branches. ❷ The bush is wild land, especially in Australia or Africa.

bushy ADJECTIVE bushier, bushiest
thick and hairy • *His dad has bushy eyebrows.*

busily ADVERB
in a busy way

business (say biz-niss) NOUN businesses
❶ A business is an organisation that makes money by selling something. ❷ Business is work related to buying or selling something. ❸ Your business is what concerns you and no one else.

✳ **WORD STORY**
The word **business** comes from 'being **busy**', which might help you to remember how to spell it.

bus stop *NOUN* **bus stops**
a place where a bus regularly stops

bustle *VERB* **bustles, bustling, bustled**
to rush about in a busy way
Mum bustled into the kitchen, stuffing papers into her briefcase.—GRANNY NOTHING, Catherine MacPhail

busy *ADJECTIVE* **busier, busiest**
❶ A busy person is one with a lot to do. ❷ A busy place is one with a lot going on.

but *CONJUNCTION*
You use **but** to join two words or statements that say different or opposite things.
• *I wanted to go **but** I couldn't.*

but *PREPOSITION*
except • *There's no one here **but** me.*

butcher *NOUN* **butchers**
someone who has a shop where meat is cut and sold

butler *NOUN* **butlers**
a male servant in charge of other servants in a large house

butt *NOUN* **butts**
the thicker end of a weapon or tool

butter *NOUN*
a soft yellow food made from cream

buttercup *NOUN* **buttercups**
a yellow wild flower

butterfly *NOUN* **butterflies**
❶ an insect with large white or brightly coloured wings ❷ a stroke you use when swimming on your front, raising both arms together over your head

WORD STORY
The name **butterfly** may have come from their creamy yellow colour or the belief that they stole butter.

buttocks *NOUN*
Your buttocks are the part of your body which you sit on.

button *NOUN* **buttons**
❶ a flat plastic or metal disc sewn on clothes and used to fasten them ❷ a small knob you press to work equipment

button *VERB* **buttons, buttoning, buttoned**
To button clothes or to button them up is to fasten them with buttons.

buy *VERB* **buys, buying, bought**
To buy something is to get it by paying for it.
• *I **bought** a book.*

buzz *NOUN* **buzzes**
a humming sound, like bees make

buzz *VERB* **buzzes, buzzing, buzzed**
To buzz is to make a buzzing sound.

buzzard *NOUN* **buzzards**
a bird of prey like a large hawk

buzzard

buzzer *NOUN* **buzzers**
a device that makes a buzzing noise • *I heard the door **buzzer** go.*

by *PREPOSITION*
❶ used to say who or what does something • *This photo was taken **by** my mum.* ❷ used to say how something is done • *I found it **by** looking on the Internet.* ❸ next to or near • *Sit here **by** me.* ❹ before • *You need to leave **by** 8.30.*

by *ADVERB*
past • *A car went **by**.*

bye-bye *EXCLAMATION* (informal)
goodbye

byte *NOUN* **bytes**
a unit that measures computer data or memory

Cc

🔧 **C** is for **cent** and **centimetre**, which come from the Latin word for 'hundred'.

🔧 Can you find any more words containing *cent* that have 'hundred' as part of their meaning?

C *ABBREVIATION*
❶ the abbreviation for **Celsius** ❷ 100 in Roman numerals

cab *NOUN* cabs
❶ a taxi ❷ the place for the driver in a lorry, bus, train or crane

cabbage *NOUN* cabbages
a large green leafy vegetable

cabin *NOUN* cabins
❶ a hut or shelter ❷ a small room on a ship for sleeping in ❸ the part of an aircraft where the passengers sit

cabinet *NOUN* cabinets
❶ a small cupboard ❷ the group of ministers who help the prime minister to run the government

cable *NOUN* cables
❶ a thick rope, wire or chain ❷ a tube with a bundle of electrical wires inside

cable television (*also* **cable TV**) *NOUN*
television programmes that are sent into people's homes using underground cables

cackle *VERB* cackles, cackling, cackled
to give a loud harsh laugh • *The witch cackled as she stirred the pot.*

cackle *NOUN* cackles
a loud harsh laugh

cacophony (*say* ka-**kof**-on-ee) *NOUN*
a loud unpleasant noise of clashing sounds

cactus *NOUN* cacti
a fleshy plant covered in spikes, that grows in hot dry places

⚠ **WATCH OUT!**
The word **cactus** has a Latin plural: *some cacti* (not *cactuses*).

cadet *NOUN* cadets
a young person being trained for the armed forces or the police

cafe (*say* **kaf**-ay) *NOUN* cafes
a place that sells hot and cold drinks and small meals

caffeine *NOUN*
a substance in coffee and some other drinks, that makes you feel more awake

⚠ **WATCH OUT!**
The word **caffeine** is an exception to the spelling rule 'i before e except after c'.

cage *NOUN* cages
a box or room made of bars or wires, for keeping birds or animals in

cake *NOUN* cakes
❶ a sweet food made from a baked mixture of flour, eggs, fat and sugar ❷ a block of a hard substance such as soap

caked *ADJECTIVE*
covered with something that has dried hard • *Her legs were **caked** with mud.*

calamity *NOUN* calamities
a disaster

calcium *NOUN*
a white chemical found in teeth, bones and chalk and foods such as milk and cheese

calculate *VERB* calculates, calculating, calculated
to work something out, using numbers or other information

calculation *NOUN* calculations
something you work out, using numbers or other information
It was taking a long time. Maybe he'd got the calculation wrong.—LIFEGAME, Alison Allen-Gray

calculator *NOUN* **calculators**
a small machine for doing calculations with numbers

calendar *NOUN* **calendars**
a chart or display that shows the days of the year

calf *NOUN* **calves**
❶ a young cow ❷ a young seal, whale or elephant
❸ Your calf is the back part of your leg below your knee.

call *VERB* **calls, calling, called**
❶ To call is to shout out. • *'Bye!' she* **called**. ❷ To call someone or something a name is to give them that name. • *They* **called** *the baby Lisa.* • *This is* **called** *a protractor.* ❸ To call someone is to ask them to come. • *The headteacher* **called** *me to her office.* ❹ To call someone is to telephone them.

call *NOUN* **calls**
❶ a shout or cry • *They heard a* **call** *for help.*
❷ a telephone conversation

callous *ADJECTIVE*
unkind and uncaring about other people's feelings

calm *ADJECTIVE* **calmer, calmest**
❶ not excited, worried or angry • *Please try to keep* **calm**. ❷ The sea or the weather is calm when it is quiet and still.
➤ **calmly** *ADVERB* ➤ **calmness** *NOUN*

calorie *NOUN* **calories**
a unit for measuring the amount of heat or the energy produced by food

calves *NOUN (plural of* **calf***)*

came *VERB (past tense of* **come***)*
• *The truck* **came** *to a stop.*

camel *NOUN* **camels**
a large animal with a long neck and one or two humps on its back • *Arabian* **camels** *have one hump and Bactrian* **camels** *have two.*

camera *NOUN* **cameras**
a device for taking photographs, films or television pictures

✳ **WORD STORY**
The word **camera** comes from a Latin word meaning 'chamber' or 'room'.

camouflage *(say* **kam**-o-flah*zh) NOUN*
❶ clothes or coverings that make people or things look like part of their surroundings ❷ markings on an animal that allow it to blend in with its surroundings

camouflage *(say* **kam**-o-flah*zh) VERB*
camouflages, camouflaging, camouflaged
to hide something by blending it in with the surroundings • *The insect* **camouflages** *itself.*

camp *NOUN* **camps**
a place where people live in tents, huts or caravans for a short time

camp *VERB* **camps, camping, camped**
To camp is to stay in a tent.
➤ **camper** *NOUN* ➤ **camping** *NOUN*

campaign *NOUN* **campaigns**
a planned series of actions in order to achieve something • *a* **campaign** *for human rights*

campaign *VERB* **campaigns, campaigning, campaigned**
to carry out a plan of action in order to achieve something • *They are* **campaigning** *against plastic pollution.*

campsite *NOUN* **campsites**
a place for camping

can *VERB*
❶ to be able to do something or to know how to do it • *Can you see him?* • *She* **could** *swim when she was 3.*
❷ to be allowed to do something • *Can I go now?*

⭘ **BUILD YOUR VOCABULARY**
Can is a **modal verb**.

can *NOUN* **cans**
a metal container holding food or drink

canal *NOUN* **canals**
a long narrow waterway created by people

canary NOUN canaries
a small yellow bird that sings

cancel VERB cancels,
cancelling, cancelled
To cancel something planned
is to say that it will not
happen. • *The match was
cancelled because of snow.*

canary

cancer NOUN cancers
a serious disease in which a harmful growth forms in
the body

candidate NOUN candidates
someone who is being considered to get something
• *Each candidate gave a speech.*

candle NOUN candles
a stick of wax with a wick through the middle, that is
lit to give light

candlestick NOUN candlesticks
a holder for a candle or candles

candy NOUN candies
❶ Candy is crystallised sugar. ❷ *(North American)*
a sweet or chocolate

cane NOUN canes
a stick made from the hollow stem of a plant

canine ADJECTIVE
to do with dogs or like a dog
canine or **canine tooth** NOUN canines,
canine teeth
a pointed tooth at the front of the mouth, used for
tearing food. Humans have four canines.

BUILD YOUR VOCABULARY
Look at **incisor** and **molar**.

cannibal NOUN cannibals
a person who eats human flesh

cannon NOUN cannon, cannons
a large gun that fires heavy balls made of metal
or stone

cannot
can not • *I cannot understand what you are saying.*

canoe NOUN canoes
a light narrow boat that you paddle

canoe VERB canoes, canoeing, canoed
to travel in a canoe

Canopic jar NOUN Canopic jars
a covered jar used in ancient Egypt to hold the
organs from a mummified body

canopy NOUN canopies
❶ a covering that hangs over something ❷ the top
branches of trees in a rainforest

can't
short for *can not*

BUILD YOUR VOCABULARY
Look at **cannot**.

canteen NOUN canteens
a restaurant in a school, office or factory

canter VERB canters, cantering, cantered
When a horse canters, it runs fairly fast.

BUILD YOUR VOCABULARY
Look at **trot** and **gallop**.

canvas NOUN canvases
❶ Canvas is strong coarse cloth. ❷ A canvas is a
piece of this cloth used for painting on.

canyon NOUN canyons
a deep valley with a river running through it

cap NOUN caps
❶ a soft hat without a brim but often with a peak
❷ a cover or top

capable ADJECTIVE
able to do something • *Bats are the only mammals
capable of flight.*
➤ **capability** NOUN

capacity NOUN capacities
the amount that something can hold • *Can you find
the capacity of this jar in millilitres?*

cape NOUN capes
❶ A cape is a cloak. ❷ a piece of high land sticking
out into the sea • *They sailed around the cape.*

capital NOUN capitals
❶ (**capital city**) the most important city in a
country ❷ (**capital letter**) a large letter used at
the start of a name or a sentence, such as A, B, C
• *Write it in capitals.*

a b c d e f g h i j k l m n o p q r s t u v w x y z

A B C D E F G H I J K L M N O P Q R S T U V W X Y Z

capsize VERB capsizes, capsizing, capsized
If a boat capsizes, it overturns in the water.

capsule NOUN capsules
❶ a hollow pill containing medicine ❷ a small spacecraft or the part of a spacecraft in which the crew travel

captain NOUN captains
❶ the officer in charge of a ship or aircraft ❷ an officer in the army or navy ❸ the leader of a sports team

caption NOUN captions
the words printed beside a picture to describe it

captive ADJECTIVE
imprisoned or unable to escape
captive NOUN captives
a prisoner

captivity NOUN
❶ Captivity is being held prisoner. ❷ An animal in captivity is one that does not live in the wild but is kept in a zoo or park.

capture VERB captures, capturing, captured
To capture an animal or person is to catch or imprison them.
capture NOUN
the act of catching or imprisoning an animal or person

car NOUN cars
a vehicle with four wheels and space for the driver and a few passengers

caramel NOUN caramels
Caramel is a sweet brown substance made by burning sugar.

caravan NOUN caravans
❶ a vehicle towed by a car and used for holidays or for living in ❷ a group of people travelling together, especially across a desert

carbohydrate NOUN carbohydrates
a substance found in foods such as bread, potatoes and pasta, that gives your body energy

carbon NOUN
Carbon is a chemical found in charcoal, diamonds and graphite and in all living things.

BUILD YOUR VOCABULARY
Carbon is an **element**.

carbon dioxide NOUN
A gas that is breathed out by humans and animals and produced when carbon is burnt.

BUILD YOUR VOCABULARY
Carbon dioxide is a **greenhouse gas**—look at **greenhouse effect**.

carbon footprint NOUN
Your carbon footprint is the amount of carbon dioxide produced by your activities, which affects the environment. • *The school is trying to reduce its carbon footprint by using renewable energy.*

carcass NOUN carcasses
a dead body, usually of an animal

card NOUN cards
❶ Card is thick, stiff paper. ❷ A card is a piece of thick paper with information or greetings on. • *I sent her a birthday card.* ❸ Cards is a game played using cards called playing cards . ❹ A card is a small piece of plastic used to pay for things.

cardboard NOUN
Cardboard is thick, stiff paper.

cardigan NOUN cardigans
a knitted jumper fastened down the front

WORD STORY
The **cardigan** is named after the Earl of Cardigan, a commander in the Crimean War whose soldiers wore a kind of woollen jacket.

care VERB cares, caring, cared
To care is to feel interested or concerned. • *I care a lot about my sister.* • *I don't care what he thinks.*
➤ **To care for someone** is to look after them.
care NOUN cares
❶ Care is serious thought or attention. • *He took a lot of care over his work.* ❷ worry or trouble • *I forgot all my cares.*
➤ **To take care of someone** or **something** is to look after them. • *Will you take care of my rabbit?*

career NOUN careers
A person's career is the work they do in life. • *I'd love
a career as a teacher.*

carefree ADJECTIVE
with no worries or responsibilities

careful ADJECTIVE
making sure that you do something in a sensible or
safe way or without any mistakes
➤ **carefully** ADVERB

careless ADJECTIVE
not taking enough care • *You made some careless
mistakes.*
➤ **carelessly** ADVERB ➤ **carelessness** NOUN

carer NOUN carers
someone who looks after a person who is ill or
elderly

caress VERB caresses, caressing, caressed
to touch something gently or lovingly

caretaker NOUN caretakers
someone who looks after a large building

cargo NOUN cargoes
the goods carried in a ship or aircraft

Caribbean (*say* ka-rib-ee-an) ADJECTIVE
to do with the Caribbean Sea or the islands of the
West Indies

carnation NOUN carnations
a garden flower with a sweet smell

carnival NOUN carnivals
a festival or celebration with a procession of people
in fancy dress

carnivore NOUN carnivores
an animal that eats meat
➤ **carnivorous** ADJECTIVE

BUILD YOUR VOCABULARY
Look at **herbivore** and **omnivore**.

carol NOUN carols
a hymn or song that you sing at Christmas

carp NOUN carp
a freshwater fish

carpenter NOUN carpenters
someone who makes things out of wood
➤ **carpentry** NOUN

carpet NOUN carpets
a thick soft covering for a floor
carpet VERB carpets, carpeting, carpeted
to cover something with a carpet or other thick layer
*The floor of the sitting-room was carpeted with deep red
blotting-paper, which was warm and cosy and soaked up
the spills.*—THE BORROWERS, Mary Norton

carriage NOUN carriages
❶ one of the sections of a train where passengers
sit ❷ a passenger vehicle pulled by horses

carrot NOUN carrots
a long thin orange-coloured vegetable

carry VERB carries, carrying, carried
❶ to hold and take something or someone
somewhere ❷ If a sound carries, it can be heard a
long way away.
➤ **To carry on** is to continue. • *They carried on
chatting.*
➤ **To carry something out** is to do it. • *We
carried out an experiment.*

cart NOUN carts
a small vehicle for carrying loads

carthorse NOUN carthorses
a large heavy horse

carton NOUN cartons
a cardboard container • *a carton of juice*

cartoon NOUN cartoons
❶ a drawing that is funny or tells a joke ❷ a series of
drawings that tell a story ❸ an animated film
➤ **cartoonist** NOUN

cartridge NOUN **cartridges**
❶ a container holding a bullet and explosive that is put into a gun ❷ a container holding ink that is put into a pen or printer

cartwheel NOUN **cartwheels**
a somersault done sideways, with your arms and legs spread wide

carve VERB **carves, carving, carved**
❶ To carve something is to shape it out of wood or stone by cutting. ❷ To carve cooked meat is to cut slices from it.

cascade NOUN **cascades**
a waterfall or a series of waterfalls

cascade VERB **cascades, cascading, cascaded**
If things cascade, they fall or run down like water.
• Rubble **cascaded** down on us.

case NOUN **cases**
❶ a container • a pencil **case** ❷ a suitcase
❸ a situation or example of something • He had a bad **case** of flu. ❹ an incident being investigated by the police or authorities • She was working on a murder **case**.
➤ **in case** because something may happen • Take a hat **in case** it's cold.

cash NOUN
Cash is coins and banknotes.

cashew NOUN **cashews**
a small edible nut with a curved shape

cashier NOUN **cashiers**
someone in charge of the money in a bank, office or shop

cash register NOUN **cash registers**
a machine that records and stores money received in a shop

cask NOUN **casks**
a barrel

cast VERB **casts, casting, cast**
❶ To cast something somewhere is to throw or direct it there. • The TV **cast** a blue glow over the room.
• He **cast** a glance at the clock. ❷ To cast a shadow is to make it appear by blocking light. ❸ To cast a spell is to say or make a magic spell.
➤ **To cast off** is to untie a boat and start sailing in it.

cast NOUN **casts**
❶ something made by pouring a liquid such as plaster into a mould ❷ The cast of a play or film is all the performers in it.

castaway NOUN **castaways**
someone who has been left in a deserted place, especially after a shipwreck

castle NOUN **castles**
a large old building with heavy stone walls, built to protect people from attack

casual ADJECTIVE
❶ not deliberate or planned • It was just a **casual** remark. ❷ Casual clothes are informal clothes suitable for leisure time.
➤ **casually** ADVERB

casualty NOUN **casualties**
someone killed or injured in an accident or a war

cat NOUN **cats**
❶ a small furry animal, often kept as a pet and known for catching mice ❷ a larger member of the same family, for example a lion, tiger or leopard

🔵 **BUILD YOUR VOCABULARY**
Look at **feline**.

catalogue NOUN **catalogues**
a list of goods for sale or of books in a library

catapult NOUN **catapults**
❶ a small weapon for firing small stones, made from a forked stick with elastic attached ❷ in the past, a machine that could throw large rocks at an enemy

catastrophe (say ka-**tass**-trof-ee) NOUN **catastrophes**
a great disaster

catch VERB **catches, catching, caught**
❶ To catch something, for example a ball in the air, is to get hold of it. ❷ To catch a person or animal is to capture them. • Did you **catch** any fish? ❸ To catch someone is to discover them doing something wrong. • He was **caught** cheating. ❹ To catch an

illness is to get it from someone else. **❺** To catch a bus or train is to get on it.
➤ **To catch fire** is to start burning.

catch *NOUN* catches
a device for fastening a door or window

catching *ADJECTIVE*
If a disease is catching, people catch it easily.

category *NOUN* categories
a group of similar things • *Put the books into the right* **category**: *fiction or non-fiction.*

caterpillar *NOUN* caterpillars
a long creeping creature that turns into a butterfly or moth

 WORD STORY
The word **caterpillar** is thought to come from an Old French word meaning 'hairy cat'.

BUILD YOUR VOCABULARY
Look at **larva**.

cathedral *NOUN* cathedrals
a large and important church, with a bishop in charge of it

Catholic *NOUN* Catholics
a member of the Roman Catholic Church
➤ **Catholic** *ADJECTIVE*

catkin *NOUN* catkins
a tiny flower hanging down from a willow or hazel

cattle *NOUN*
Cattle are cows and bulls and other large grass-eating animals.

caught *VERB (past tense and past participle of* catch*)*
• *I caught Hannah looking at me.* • *I think you've caught a cold.*

cauldron *NOUN* cauldrons
a large round metal cooking pot, especially one used by witches in stories

cauliflower *NOUN* cauliflowers
a large round vegetable with a head of white flowers and green leaves around it

cause *VERB* causes, causing, caused
To cause something is to make it happen.

cause *NOUN* causes
The cause of something is what makes it happen.
• *What was the* **cause** *of the problem?*

caution *NOUN* cautions
❶ Caution is care to avoid danger or mistakes.
❷ A caution is a warning.

cautious *ADJECTIVE*
careful to avoid a risk or difficulty
➤ **cautiously** *ADVERB*

cavalry *NOUN*
soldiers who fight on horseback or in armoured vehicles

cave *NOUN* caves
a large hole in the side of a hill or cliff or under the ground
cave *VERB* caves, caving, caved
➤ **To cave in** is to collapse.

caveman or **cavewoman** *NOUN* cavemen, cavewomen
a person who lived in a cave in prehistoric times

cavern *NOUN* caverns
a cave, especially a deep or dark one

cavity *NOUN* cavities
a hollow or hole

CD *NOUN* CDs
short for *compact disc*, a small plastic disc on which music or computer information is stored

CD-ROM *NOUN* CD-ROMs
a small plastic disc on which computer information is stored, short for *compact disc read-only memory*

cease *VERB* ceases, ceasing, ceased
To cease doing something is to stop doing it.

cedar *NOUN* cedars
an evergreen tree with hard sweet-smelling wood

ceiling *(say* see*-ling) NOUN* ceilings
the flat surface along the top of a room

 WATCH OUT!
The word **ceiling** follows the rule 'i before e except after c'.

celebrate *VERB* celebrates, celebrating, celebrated
To celebrate a day or event is to do something special to show that it is important.

celebration *NOUN* celebrations
A celebration is a party or other special event to celebrate something.

celebrity *NOUN* celebrities
a famous person, especially in show business or on television

celery *NOUN*
a vegetable with crisp white or green stems

cell *NOUN* cells
❶ a small room, especially in a prison ❷ a tiny part of a living creature or plant ❸ a device for producing electric current using chemicals

cellar *NOUN* cellars
an underground room for storing things

cello *(say* chel-oh*) NOUN* cellos
a large musical instrument with four strings, which you stand between your knees and play with a bow

⚙ **BUILD** YOUR VOCABULARY
A **cello** is a **stringed instrument**.

Celsius *NOUN*
a scale for measuring temperature in which water freezes at 0 degrees and boils at 100 degrees • *The oven is set to 180 degrees* **Celsius** *or 180°C.*

Celt *(say* kelt*) NOUN* Celts
a member of the ancient peoples who lived in Britain and parts of Europe before the Romans came
➤ **Celtic** *ADJECTIVE* • *Celtic peoples*

cement *NOUN*
a grey mixture used in building to make floors and join bricks together

cemetery *(say* sem-et-ree*) NOUN* cemeteries
a place where dead people are buried

census *NOUN* censuses
an official count of the number of people in a place

cent *NOUN* cents
a unit of money in Europe and the US. There are 100 cents in 1 euro or 1 dollar.

centaur *(say* sen-tor*)*
NOUN centaurs
in mythology, a creature with the head and upper body of a man and the lower body and legs of a horse

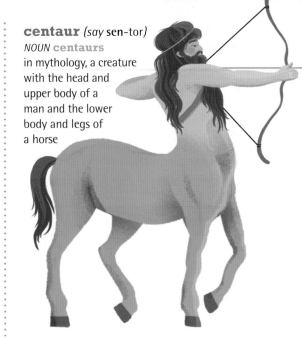

centenary *NOUN* centenaries
the hundredth anniversary of something special or important

centigrade *NOUN*
another word for **Celsius**

centimetre *NOUN* centimetres
a measurement of length. There are 100 centimetres in a metre and 10 millimetres in a centimetre. • *The line is 25* **centimetres** *long.*

⚙ **BUILD** YOUR VOCABULARY
The abbreviation is **cm**.

centipede *NOUN* centipedes
a small long creature with many pairs of legs

✳ **WORD STORY**
The word **centipede** means 'hundred feet', but most centipedes have fewer than a hundred legs.

central *ADJECTIVE*
at or near the centre of something

central heating *NOUN*
a system of heating a building by sending hot water or hot air around it in pipes

centre *NOUN* centres
❶ the middle of something • *They live in the* **centre** *of town.* ❷ a building or place for a particular purpose • *a shopping* **centre** • *a sports* **centre**

centurion *NOUN* centurions
an officer in the ancient Roman army

century *NOUN* centuries
a period of a hundred years

WORD STORY

The word **century** comes from the Latin word for 'a hundred'.

ceramics *NOUN*
Ceramics is the art of making pottery.

cereal *NOUN* cereals
❶ A cereal is a plant such as wheat, rye or barley, whose seeds are used as food. ❷ Cereal is a breakfast food made from seeds like this.

WORD STORY

The word **cereal** comes from *Ceres*, the Roman goddess of farming and agriculture.

⚠ **WATCH OUT!**

Do not confuse with a **serial**, which means 'a story in parts'.

ceremonial *ADJECTIVE*
to do with a ceremony or used in a ceremony
• *ceremonial robes*

ceremony *NOUN* ceremonies
A ceremony is a formal event such as a wedding or funeral.

certain *ADJECTIVE*
❶ If something is certain, it is definitely true or going to happen. • *He is **certain** to win.* ❷ If you are certain, you are sure. • *I'm quite **certain** you're wrong.* ❸ Certain things are particular things.
• *There are **certain** foods she won't eat.*

certainly *ADVERB*
definitely, without any doubt • *We will **certainly** help.*

certainty *NOUN* certainties
❶ Certainty is being sure. ❷ A certainty is something that is sure to happen.

certificate *NOUN* certificates
an official document that records and proves something • *a birth **certificate***

CGI *ABBREVIATION*
CGI is special effects created by a computer. It is short for *computer generated imagery*.

chaffinch *NOUN* chaffinches
a small bird with blue and pink feathers

chain *NOUN* chains
❶ a row of metal rings fastened together
❷ a connected series of things • *The story told of a strange **chain** of events.*

chair *NOUN* chairs
a seat with a back, for one person

chalet *(say* shal-ay*) NOUN* chalets
a small house, usually built of wood, with a sloping roof

chalk *NOUN* chalks
❶ a kind of soft white rock

⚙ **BUILD** YOUR VOCABULARY

Chalk is **permeable**.

❷ a soft white or coloured stick used for writing on blackboards
➤ **chalky** *ADJECTIVE*

challenge *VERB* challenges, challenging, challenged
To challenge someone is to ask them to compete, fight or do something difficult.
'Why don't we just challenge him to a fair fight?' Egil asked. 'Because we'd lose, idiot,' said Grimnir.—OLAF THE VIKING, Martin Conway
➤ **challenger** *NOUN*

challenge *NOUN* challenges
something difficult that someone has to do • *This task is a real **challenge**.*

chamber *NOUN* chambers *(old use)*
a room

chameleon
(say ka-**mee**-lee-on*)*
NOUN chameleons
a small lizard that can change the colour of its skin to match its surroundings

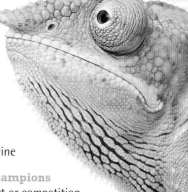

champagne
(say sham-**payn***) NOUN*
a bubbly white French wine

champion *NOUN* champions
the best person in a sport or competition or a member of the best team

a b **c** d e f g h i j k l m n o p q r s

championship *NOUN* **championships**
a contest to find the best player or team

chance *NOUN* **chances**
❶ A chance is a possibility or opportunity. • *This is a chance to try something new.* ❷ A chance is how likely something is to happen. • *There is no chance she will agree.* ❸ Chance is the way things happen accidentally. • *We met by chance.*

chancellor *NOUN* **chancellors**
an important government or legal official

chandelier *(say* shan-dil-**eer***) NOUN*
chandeliers
a light fitting with a lot of bulbs or candles that hangs from the ceiling

change *VERB* **changes, changing, changed**
❶ To change something or someone is to make them different. • *I changed the ending of my story.*
❷ To change is to become different. • *Tadpoles change into frogs.* ❸ To change something is to exchange it. • *Will you change seats with me?*
❹ To change or get changed is to put on different clothes. • *We changed into our swimming costumes.*
change *NOUN* **changes**
❶ Change or a change is something that changes.
❷ Your change is the money you get back when you give too much money to pay for something.

channel *NOUN* **channels**
❶ a way for water to flow along ❷ The Channel is the stretch of water between England and France.
❸ a broadcasting station for TV or radio

chant *NOUN* **chants**
a repeated set of words that you say or sing with a particular rhythm

chaos *(say* kay-oss*) NOUN*
complete disorder or confusion • *The room was in chaos.*

chaotic *(say* kay-ot-ik*) ADJECTIVE*
completely confused or in a mess

chapel *NOUN* **chapels**
a small church or part of a large church

chapter *NOUN* **chapters**
a section of a book

character *NOUN* **characters**
❶ the special qualities of a person or thing • *She has a strong character.* ❷ a person in a story, film or play
• *Who is the main character?*

characteristic *NOUN* **characteristics**
A special quality that someone or something has.
• *Kindness is one of his main characteristics.*
characteristic *ADJECTIVE*
typical of someone or something

charades *(say* sha-**rahdz***) NOUN*
Charades is a game in which people have to guess a word, phrase or title when other people act it out.

charcoal *NOUN*
burnt wood, used as fuel or for drawing

charge *NOUN* **charges**
a payment asked for something • *There is no charge for using the library.*
➤ **to be in charge** is to be in control of or responsible for something or someone • *The referee is in charge of the game.*
charge *VERB* **charges, charging, charged**
❶ To charge a price for something is to ask people to pay it. ❷ to suddenly run towards someone or something • *The rhino charged at us.* ❸ To charge a device is to put more power into its battery.

charger *NOUN* **chargers**
❶ a horse ridden by a knight ❷ a device for putting more power in the battery of a phone, laptop, etc.

chariot *NOUN* **chariots**
a horse-drawn vehicle with two wheels, used in ancient times

charity *NOUN* **charities**
❶ A charity is an organisation that helps people in need. ❷ Charity is money or help given to people in need.

charm *NOUN* **charms**
❶ Charm is being pleasant and attractive. ❷ A charm is a magic spell. ❸ A charm is something small worn or carried for luck.
charm *VERB* **charms, charming, charmed**
To charm someone is to give them pleasure or delight.
➤ **charming** *ADJECTIVE*

charred *ADJECTIVE*
burnt or blackened with fire • *a charred stick*

chart NOUN **charts**
❶ a diagram or table showing information ❷ a large plan or map

chase VERB **chases, chasing, chased**
to go quickly after someone in order to catch them
chase NOUN **chases**
A chase is when you chase someone.

chasm *(say* kaz-um*)* NOUN **chasms**
a deep opening in the ground
The ice bridge . . . was a mighty structure stretching the entire length between two sides of a deep, yawning chasm.—THE POLAR BEAR EXPLORERS' CLUB, Alex Bell

chat NOUN **chats**
a friendly or informal talk with someone
chat VERB **chats, chatting, chatted**
to talk to someone in a friendly or informal way

chatter VERB **chatters, chattering, chattered**
❶ to talk quickly or too much ❷ If your teeth chatter, they make a rattling noise because you are cold.

chauffeur *(say* shoh-fer*)* NOUN **chauffeurs**
a person whose job is to drive someone around in a car

cheap ADJECTIVE **cheaper, cheapest**
not costing much
➤ **cheaply** ADVERB

cheat VERB **cheats, cheating, cheated**
❶ To cheat in a game or test is to break the rules in order to do well. ❷ To cheat someone is to get something from them by tricking them.
cheat NOUN **cheats**
someone who cheats

check VERB **checks, checking, checked**
To make sure that something is correct or all right.
• *Remember to* **check** *your spellings.*
check NOUN **checks**
A check is when you check something.

checkmate NOUN **checkmates**
In chess, checkmate is when one side wins by trapping the other side's king.

✳ **WORD STORY**
The word **checkmate** comes from Persian words that mean 'the king is dead'.

checkout NOUN **checkouts**
the place where you pay for your shopping in a supermarket

cheek NOUN **cheeks**
❶ Your cheeks are the sides of your face below your eyes. ❷ Cheek is cheeky or rude behaviour.

cheeky ADJECTIVE **cheekier, cheekiest**
rude or disrespectful, without being nasty
➤ **cheekily** ADVERB

cheer NOUN **cheers**
a shout of praise or support
cheer VERB **cheers, cheering, cheered**
to shout to show support or pleasure
➤ **To cheer someone up** is to make them more cheerful.
➤ **To cheer up** is to become more cheerful.

cheerful ADJECTIVE
happy
Dr Mead . . . was a tall, broad-shouldered man with kind grey eyes and a cheerful smile. Pollyanna liked him at once.—POLLYANNA, Eleanor Porter
➤ **cheerfulness** NOUN

cheese NOUN **cheeses**
a white or yellow food made from milk, which can be either hard like Cheddar or soft like cream cheese
➤ **cheesy** ADJECTIVE • *a **cheesy** pizza*

cheetah NOUN **cheetahs**
a large spotted animal of the cat family, which can run very fast

chef *(say* shef*)*
NOUN **chefs**
the chief cook in a hotel or restaurant

chemical
NOUN **chemicals**
a substance used in or made by chemistry
chemical
ADJECTIVE
to do with chemistry or made by chemistry

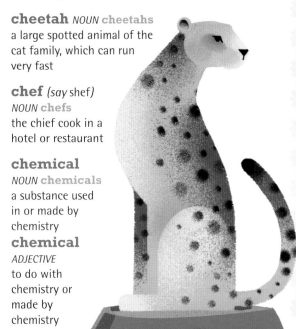

a
b
c
d
e
f
g
h
i
j
k
l
m
n
o
p
q
r
s
t
u
v
w
x
y
z

chemist NOUN chemists
1. someone who makes or sells medicines
2. an expert in chemistry

chemistry NOUN
the study of the way substances combine and react with one another

chequered ADJECTIVE
marked with a pattern of squares

cherish VERB cherishes, cherishing, cherished
to treasure something or keep it lovingly

cherry NOUN cherries
a small bright red fruit with a large stone

chess NOUN
a game for two players played with 16 pieces each on a board of 64 squares

> **BUILD** YOUR VOCABULARY
> The pieces are called **chessmen** and the board is called a **chessboard**.

chest NOUN chests
1. a large strong box
2. Your chest is the front part of your body between your neck and your waist.

chestnut NOUN chestnuts
a brown nut with a prickly brown case or the tree that produces this nut

> **BUILD** YOUR VOCABULARY
> Look at **horse chestnut**.

chest of drawers NOUN chests of drawers
a piece of furniture with drawers

chew VERB chews, chewing, chewed
To chew food is to grind it between your teeth.
> **chewy** ADJECTIVE • This meat is a bit **chewy**.

chick NOUN chicks
a young bird

chicken NOUN chickens
1. A chicken is a young hen.
2. Chicken is the meat of a chicken used as food.

chickenpox NOUN
a disease that produces red itchy spots on your skin

chickpea NOUN chickpeas
a round yellow seed that you can eat

chief NOUN chiefs
a leader or ruler

chief ADJECTIVE
1. having the highest rank or power • the king's **chief** adviser
2. main, most important • Our **chief** problem was lack of money.
> **chiefly** ADVERB • They feed **chiefly** on insects.

chieftain NOUN chieftains
the chief of a tribe or clan

child NOUN children
1. a young person; a boy or girl
2. Someone's child is their son or daughter.

childhood NOUN childhoods
Your childhood is the time when you are a child.

childish ADJECTIVE
silly and immature

childminder NOUN childminders
A person who is paid to look after children while their parents are at work.

chill VERB chills, chilling, chilled
to make something cold
chill NOUN chills
1. Chill is an unpleasant feeling of being cold.
2. A chill is a cold that makes you shiver.

chilli NOUN chillies
a hot-tasting pod of a type of pepper, used in cooking

chilly ADJECTIVE chillier, chilliest
1. cold • a grey **chilly** day
2. unfriendly • Her voice was **chilly**.

chime NOUN chimes
a ringing sound made by a bell
chime VERB chimes, chiming, chimed
to ring • The clock **chimes** every half-hour.

chimney NOUN chimneys
a tall pipe that carries away smoke from a fire

chimpanzee NOUN chimpanzees
a small African ape with black fur and large eyes

chin *NOUN* **chins**
Your chin is the part of your face under your mouth.

china *NOUN*
China is thin and delicate pottery.

 WORD STORY
> The word **china** originally meant 'from China', because the pottery was first made there.

chink *NOUN* **chinks**
❶ a narrow opening • *I looked through a **chink** in the wall.* ❷ a clinking sound

chip *NOUN* **chips**
❶ a small piece of fried potato ❷ a small piece of something • *wood **chips*** ❸ a place where a small piece has been knocked off something ❹ a small electronic part of a computer
chip *VERB* **chips, chipping, chipped**
to knock a small piece off something by accident

chipmunk *NOUN* **chipmunks**
a North American animal like a squirrel, with cheek pouches and stripes along its body

chirp *VERB* **chirps, chirping, chirped**
to make short sharp sounds like a small bird

chisel *NOUN* **chisels**
a tool with a sharp end for shaping wood or stone
chisel *VERB* **chisels, chiselling, chiselled**
to shape or cut something with a chisel

chivalry *NOUN*
help and protection towards someone weaker

chlorine *(say* klor-een*) NOUN*
a yellow-green chemical used to disinfect water

 WORD STORY
> **Chlorine** was named after *khloros*, the Greek word for 'green'. Words where the spelling *ch* is pronounced 'k' usually come from Greek.

chocolate *NOUN* **chocolates**
❶ Chocolate is a sweet food made from roasted cocoa beans. ❷ A chocolate is a sweet made of chocolate.
➤ **chocolatey** *ADJECTIVE*

 WORD STORY
> The word **chocolate** comes from the Nahuatl (Mexican) word *chocolatl*.

choice *NOUN* **choices**
❶ a number of things that you can choose from • *There is a **choice** of flavours.* ❷ Your choice is what you choose. • *You've made a good **choice**.*

choir *NOUN* **choirs**
a group of singers, especially in a church

choke *VERB* **chokes, choking, choked**
to be unable to breathe properly because something is blocking your throat

cholesterol *(say* kol-**est**-er-rol*) NOUN*
a substance found in fat and in animal body cells and blood

chomp *VERB* **chomps, chomping, chomped**
to chew on something

choose *VERB* **chooses, choosing, chose, chosen**
to decide which of a range of things you want to have or do • *I've **chosen** a new book.* • *There are two colours, so you can **choose**.*

chop *VERB* **chops, chopping, chopped**
❶ to cut something into small pieces • ***Chop** the onions.* ❷ to cut something with a quick heavy blow • *He was **chopping** wood.*
chop *NOUN* **chops**
a small thick slice of meat

choppy *ADJECTIVE* **choppier, choppiest**
A choppy sea is fairly rough with lots of small waves.

chopsticks *NOUN*
a pair of thin sticks used for eating Chinese or Japanese food

choral *(say* kor-al*) ADJECTIVE*
for a choir or chorus

chord *(say* kord*) NOUN* **chords**
a number of musical notes sounded together

⚠ **WATCH OUT!**
> A musical **chord** starts with **ch-**, like a **choir** or a **chorus**, but **cord** meaning 'rope' has no **h**.

chore *NOUN* **chores**
a boring task that has to be done

a
b
c
d
e
f
g
h
i
j
k
l
m
n
o
p
q
r
s
t
u
v
w
x
y
z

chortle VERB chortles, chortling, chortled
to laugh loudly and happily

chorus (say kor-us) NOUN choruses
❶ The chorus of a song or poem is the part repeated after every verse. ❷ a large group of singers

chose VERB (past tense of **choose**)
• Everyone **chose** a partner.

chosen VERB (past participle of **choose**)
• Has everyone **chosen** a partner?

christen VERB christens, christening, christened
to pour water on someone and give them a name as part of a ceremony making them part of the Christian church
➤ **christening** NOUN

Christian NOUN Christians
someone who believes in Jesus Christ and follows his teachings
➤ **Christian** ADJECTIVE

Christianity NOUN
the religion of Christians

Christmas NOUN Christmases
25 December or the time around it, when people celebrate Jesus's birth

chrome or **chromium** NOUN
a shiny silvery metal

chronic ADJECTIVE
A chronic illness or problem is one that lasts for a long time.

chronicle NOUN chronicles
a list of events with their dates

chronological ADJECTIVE
in the order in which things happened • *Put these historical events in **chronological** order.*
➤ **chronologically** ADVERB

chrysalis (say kriss-a-liss) NOUN chrysalises
a butterfly or moth at the stage when it is transforming from a larva into an adult

butterfly

egg

pupa

larva

chrysanthemum NOUN chrysanthemums
a garden flower that blooms in autumn

chubby ADJECTIVE chubbier, chubbiest
plump and rounded
➤ **chubbiness** NOUN

chuckle VERB chuckles, chuckling, chuckled
to laugh quietly
chuckle NOUN chuckles
a quiet laugh

chug VERB chugs, chugging, chugged
to move with the sound of a slow-running engine

chunk NOUN chunks
a thick lump of something
➤ **chunky** ADJECTIVE

church NOUN churches
a building where Christians worship

churchyard NOUN churchyards
the ground round a church, used as a graveyard

churn NOUN churns
❶ a large container for milk ❷ a machine for making butter

churn *VERB* **churns, churning, churned**
to stir something vigorously, for example milk when making butter

chute *(say* shoot*) NOUN* **chutes**
a steep channel for people or things to slide down • *a rubbish* **chute**

cider *NOUN* **ciders**
an alcoholic drink made from apples

cigar *NOUN* **cigars**
a roll of dried tobacco leaves for smoking

cigarette *NOUN* **cigarettes**
a small paper tube containing shredded tobacco for smoking

cinder *NOUN* **cinders**
a small piece of partly burned coal or wood

cinema *NOUN* **cinemas**
a place where people go to see films

cinnamon *NOUN*
a light-brown sweet spice

circle *NOUN* **circles**
a round flat shape, the shape of a coin or wheel
circle *VERB* **circles, circling, circled**
❶ To circle is to move in a circle. • *Vultures* **circled** *overhead.* ❷ To circle a place is to go round it.
• *The space probe* **circled** *Mars.*

circuit *(say* ser-kit*) NOUN* **circuits**
❶ a circular line or journey ❷ the path of an electric current

circular *ADJECTIVE*
round like a circle

circulate *VERB* **circulates, circulating, circulated**
To circulate is to move around and come back to the beginning. • *Blood* **circulates** *in the body.*
➤ **circulation** *NOUN* • *the* **circulation** *of the blood*

circumference *NOUN* **circumferences**
the line or distance round a circle

🔵 **BUILD YOUR VOCABULARY**
Look at **diameter** and **radius**.

circumstance *NOUN* **circumstances**
Circumstances are facts or situations that affect what happens. • *He won under difficult* **circumstances**.

circus *NOUN* **circuses**
an entertainment with clowns and acrobats, usually taking place in a large tent

citizen *NOUN* **citizens**
A citizen of a place is someone who lives there and legally belongs there.

citrus fruit *NOUN* **citrus fruits**
Citrus fruits are juicy fruits with a thick skin and a sharp taste, such as oranges, lemons, limes and grapefruit.

city *NOUN* **cities**
a large and important town

civil *ADJECTIVE*
❶ polite ❷ to do with the citizens of a place
• *civil* rights

civilian *NOUN* **civilians**
an ordinary person who is not in the armed forces

civilisation *(also* **civilization***) NOUN* **civilisations**
❶ A civilisation is a society or culture at a particular time in history. • *ancient* **civilisations** ❷ Civilisation is a well-developed and organised way of life.

civilised *(also* **civilized***) ADJECTIVE*
❶ A civilised society is considered to be advanced and well-organised. ❷ A civilised person has good manners.

civil war *NOUN* **civil wars**
a war fought between people of the same country

clad *ADJECTIVE (old use)*
clothed or covered • *He was* **clad** *in filthy rags.*

claim *VERB* **claims, claiming, claimed**
❶ to state that something is true • *She* **claims** *she wasn't there.* ❷ to ask for something that you think belongs to you • *He had come to* **claim** *his throne.*
claim *NOUN* **claims**
something someone says is true • *He made false* **claims**.

a
b
c
d
e
f
g
h
i
j
k
l
m
n
o
p
q
r
s
t
u
v
w
x
y
z

clam NOUN clams
a shellfish with a smooth shell

○ **BUILD** YOUR VOCABULARY
A **clam** is a **mollusc**.

clamber VERB
clambers, clambering, clambered
to climb somewhere using your hands and feet • We **clambered** over the rocks.

clammy ADJECTIVE clammier, clammiest
unpleasantly damp • Her hands were **clammy** with sweat.

clamp NOUN clamps
a device for holding things together
clamp VERB clamps, clamping, clamped
to hold something in place using a clamp

clan NOUN clans
a number of families with the same ancestor

clang VERB clangs, clanging, clanged
to make a loud ringing sound

clank VERB clanks, clanking, clanked
to make a loud sound like heavy pieces of metal banging together
clank NOUN clanks
a clanking sound

clap VERB claps, clapping, clapped
to make a noise by hitting the palms of your hands together, especially to show you like something
clap NOUN claps
❶ an act of clapping, especially to show you like something • Let's give the winners a **clap**. ❷ A clap of thunder is a sudden sound of loud thunder.

clarinet NOUN clarinets
a musical instrument shaped like a tube with a wide end, that you play by blowing into it

○ **BUILD** YOUR VOCABULARY
A **clarinet** is a **woodwind instrument**.

clarity NOUN
Clarity is a clear quality. • I saw everything with total **clarity**.

clash VERB clashes, clashing, clashed
❶ to make a loud sound like cymbals banging together ❷ to fight or argue • The two armies **clashed**.
clash NOUN clashes
❶ a clashing sound • the **clash** of swords ❷ a fight or argument

clasp VERB clasps, clasping, clasped
to hold someone or something tightly
clasp NOUN clasps
a device for fastening things

class NOUN classes
❶ a group of children who are taught together ❷ a group of similar people, animals or things • Reptiles are a large **class** of animals.
class VERB classes, classing, classed
To class things is to put them in classes or groups.

classic NOUN classics
a book, film or story that is well known and thought to be very good
classic ADJECTIVE
known about and thought to be very good by most people • a **classic** film

classical ADJECTIVE
❶ to do with ancient Greece or Rome • a **classical** statue ❷ Classical music is serious music, often written in the past.

classify VERB classifies, classifying, classified
To classify things is to put them in classes or groups.
➤ **classification** NOUN

classmate NOUN classmates
Your classmates are the people in the same class as you at school.

classroom NOUN classrooms
a room where lessons are given at a school

clatter VERB clatters, clattering, clattered
to make a loud rattling or banging sound
clatter NOUN
a loud noise of things being rattled or banged

clause NOUN clauses
a group of words that includes a verb and can be a whole sentence or part of a sentence

BUILD YOUR VOCABULARY
Look at **main clause**, **relative clause** and **subordinate clause**.

claw NOUN claws
a hard sharp nail on a bird's or animal's foot
claw VERB claws, clawing, clawed
to grasp or scratch something with a claw or hand
• The beast **clawed** at the net.

clay NOUN
a sticky kind of earth, used for making bricks and pottery

clean ADJECTIVE cleaner, cleanest
without any dirt, stains or marks
clean VERB cleans, cleaning, cleaned
to make something clean

cleaner NOUN cleaners
❶ someone who cleans rooms or offices as a job
❷ something used for cleaning

cleanly ADVERB
neatly, exactly • He cut the brick **cleanly** in two.

cleanse (say klenz) VERB cleanses, cleansing, cleansed
to make something clean or pure

clear ADJECTIVE clearer, clearest
❶ easy to see, hear or understand • He spoke with a **clear** voice. ❷ Clear glass or water is easy to see through. • a **clear** liquid ❸ not blocked or covered by anything • The sky is **clear**.
clear VERB clears, clearing, cleared
❶ To clear something is to take away things that are blocking or covering it. • Will you **clear** the table?
❷ To clear is to become clearer or brighter. • The mist **cleared** and we could see the view. ❸ To clear something is to pass over it without touching it.
• The horse **cleared** the fence by half a metre.

clearing NOUN clearings
an open space in a wood or forest

clearly ADVERB
❶ in a clear way • We could see him **clearly**.
❷ obviously • This one is **clearly** the best.

clef NOUN clefs
a symbol written at the start of a line of music that shows whether the notes are low or high

BUILD YOUR VOCABULARY
Look at **bass** and **treble**.

clench VERB clenches, clenching, clenched
To clench your teeth or fingers is to close them tightly.

clergyman or **clergywoman** NOUN clergymen, clergywomen
a man or woman who is a priest in the Christian church

clerk (say klark) NOUN clerks
someone who works in an office keeping records or accounts

clever ADJECTIVE cleverer, cleverest
❶ quick to learn and understand ❷ skilful or effective • a **clever** idea
➤ **cleverly** ADVERB

cliché (say klee-shay) NOUN clichés
a phrase that people use a lot, so that it is not very interesting or meaningful, for example at the end of the day or at this moment in time

click NOUN clicks
a short sharp sound • She heard the **click** of a light switch.
click VERB clicks, clicking, clicked
❶ to make a short sharp sound ❷ to press a mouse button to select something on a screen • **Click** to exit.

client NOUN clients
a customer of a professional person such as a lawyer or architect

cliff NOUN cliffs
a steep rock face, especially on the coast

cliffhanger NOUN cliffhangers
A story or situation that is exciting because you do not know what will happen next.

climate NOUN climates
the usual sort of weather in a particular area • the warm humid **climate** of the rainforest

a b c d e f g h i j k l m n o p q r s t u v w x y z

climax NOUN **climaxes**
the most important or exciting part of a story or series of events

climb VERB **climbs, climbing, climbed**
❶ to move towards the top of a hill, a ladder, stairs, etc. • *The cat* **climbed** *a tree.* ❷ to move across something using your feet and hands • *She* **climbed** *over the rocks.*
➤ **climber** NOUN • *a mountain* **climber**

climb NOUN **climbs**
an act of climbing • *It's a long* **climb** *to the top.*

cling VERB **clings, clinging, clung**
to hold on tightly to someone or something • *The child* **clung** *to its mother.*

clinic NOUN **clinics**
a place where people see doctors for treatment or advice

clink VERB **clinks, clinking, clinked**
to make a short ringing sound • *I heard the* **clink** *of cutlery.*

clip NOUN **clips**
a fastener for keeping things together

clip VERB **clips, clipping, clipped**
❶ to fasten something with a clip ❷ to cut something with shears or scissors

clipboard NOUN **clipboards**
a board that you can carry around, with a clip at the top to hold papers

cloak NOUN **cloaks**
a wide coat, usually without sleeves, that hangs loosely from your shoulders

cloakroom NOUN **cloakrooms**
❶ a place where you can leave coats and bags in a building ❷ a toilet

clock NOUN **clocks**
an instrument that shows what the time is

clockwise ADVERB, ADJECTIVE
moving round in the same direction as the hands of a clock

BUILD YOUR VOCABULARY
The opposite is **anticlockwise**.

clockwork ADJECTIVE
worked by a spring which you wind up

clog NOUN **clogs**
a shoe with a wooden sole

clog VERB **clogs, clogging, clogged**
to block something accidentally

clone NOUN **clones**
an animal or plant made from the cells of another animal or plant

close (*say* klohss) ADJECTIVE **closer, closest**
❶ near, either in time or place • *We live* **close** *to the bus stop.* • *It's getting* **close** *to my birthday.*
❷ careful • *Pay* **close** *attention.* ❸ A close race or competition is one in which people are nearly equal.

close (*say* klohss) ADVERB **closer, closest**
at a close distance • *The police were* **close** *behind.*

close (*say* klohss) NOUN **closes**
a street that is closed at one end • *They live in Beech* **Close.**

close (*say* klohz) VERB **closes, closing, closed**
❶ to move something so that it is shut • **Close** *the door.* ❷ If a shop or place closes, you cannot go into it. • *What time does the library* **close**?

closely *(say* klohss-lee*) ADVERB*
❶ carefully, with attention • *Look **closely** at this picture.* ❷ at a close distance • *The bus was **closely** followed by another.*

close-up *(say* klohss-up*) NOUN* close-ups
a photograph or film taken at short range

cloth *NOUN* cloths
❶ Cloth is material woven from wool, cotton or some other fabric. ❷ A cloth is a piece of this material.

clothe *(say* klohth*) VERB* clothes, clothing, clothed
to put clothes on someone

clothes *(say* klohthz*) PLURAL NOUN*
Clothes are the things you wear to cover your body. • *My **clothes** were wet.*

clothing *NOUN*
clothes

cloud *NOUN* clouds
❶ a mass of water vapour floating in the air ❷ A cloud of smoke or dust is a mass of it.
cloud *VERB* clouds, clouding, clouded
To cloud or cloud over is to become full of clouds. • *The sky **clouded** over.*
➤ **cloudless** *ADJECTIVE* • *a **cloudless** sky*

cloudy *ADJECTIVE* cloudier, cloudiest
❶ with a lot of clouds • *a **cloudy** day* ❷ hard to see through • *a **cloudy** liquid*

clover *NOUN*
a small wild plant whose leaves have three parts

clown *NOUN* clowns
a performer who wears bright face paint and funny clothes and does silly things to make people laugh

club *NOUN* clubs
❶ a group of people who meet regularly because they are interested in the same thing • *I'm in the dance **club**.* ❷ a heavy stick used as a weapon or a stick for playing golf

cluck *VERB* clucks, clucking, clucked
to make a noise like a hen

clue *NOUN* clues
something that helps you to solve a puzzle or a mystery

clump *NOUN* clumps
a small thick group or lump, especially of plants • *a **clump** of seaweed*

clumsy *ADJECTIVE* clumsier, clumsiest
awkward and likely to break or drop things
➤ **clumsily** *ADVERB* ➤ **clumsiness** *NOUN*

clung *VERB (past tense and past participle of* **cling***)*
• *The child **clung** to its mother's arms.*

cluster *NOUN* clusters
a group of people or things close together

clutch *VERB* clutches, clutching, clutched
To clutch something or clutch at something is to grab or hold it tightly. • *She **clutched** my arm.*
clutch *NOUN* clutches
a tight grasp

clutter *VERB* clutters, cluttering, cluttered
To clutter a place is to make it untidy or messy.
clutter *NOUN*
Clutter is a lot of things left around untidily.

cm *ABBREVIATION*
the abbreviation for **centimetre**

Co. *ABBREVIATION*
short for **company**

coach *NOUN* coaches
❶ a comfortable bus used for long journeys ❷ a carriage of a railway train ❸ a carriage pulled by horses ❹ a person who trains people in a sport or skill
coach *VERB* coaches, coaching, coached
to train someone in a sport or skill

coal *NOUN*
a hard black mineral used as fuel

coarse *ADJECTIVE* coarser, coarsest
rough, not delicate or smooth

coast *NOUN* coasts
the seashore and the land close to it
➤ **coastal** *ADJECTIVE* • *coastal areas*

a
b
c
d
e
f
g
h
i
j
k
l
m
n
o
p
q
r
s
t
u
v
w
x
y
z

coastguard NOUN coastguards
someone whose job is to watch coasts to prevent smuggling or help sailors in trouble

coat NOUN coats
❶ a piece of clothing with sleeves, worn outdoors over other clothes ❷ A coat of paint is a layer.
coat VERB coats, coating, coated
to cover something with a coating

coating NOUN coatings
a layer that covers something • *raisins with a chocolate* **coating**

coat of arms NOUN coats of arms
a design on a shield or building that represents an old family or town

coax VERB coaxes, coaxing, coaxed
to persuade someone gently or patiently • *I coaxed the rabbit out with some food.*

cobble (also **cobblestone**) NOUN
a rounded stone used to make the surface of roads in the past
➤ **cobbled** ADJECTIVE • *an old town with* **cobbled** *streets*

cobbler NOUN cobblers
someone whose job is to mend shoes

cobra (say koh-bra) NOUN cobras
a large poisonous snake

cobweb NOUN cobwebs
a thin sticky net that a spider spins to catch insects

✳ WORD STORY
The first part of **cobweb** comes from an old word *coppe* meaning 'spider'.

cock NOUN cocks
a male bird, especially a male chicken

cockerel NOUN cockerels
a young male chicken

cocker spaniel NOUN cocker spaniels
a kind of small spaniel often with a golden brown coat and long hanging ears

cockle NOUN cockles
a small edible shellfish

cockpit NOUN cockpits
the place in an aircraft where the pilot sits

cockroach NOUN cockroaches
a dark brown insect with a hard shell

cocky ADJECTIVE cockier, cockiest (informal)
very confident, often in a cheeky way

cocoa NOUN cocoas
❶ powdered chocolate used in baking or to make hot drinks made from roasted cocoa beans ❷ a hot drink made from cocoa powder and milk

coconut NOUN coconuts
a large hard nut that grows on palm trees, with a brown hairy shell, white flesh and milky juice

cocoon NOUN cocoons
the silk case that a moth or butterfly larva spins around itself before turning into an adult insect

⚙ BUILD YOUR VOCABULARY
Look at **chrysalis** and **larva**.

cod NOUN cod
a large edible sea fish

code NOUN codes
❶ a set of signs and letters for sending messages secretly • *The note was in* **code**. ❷ computer program instructions
code VERB codes, coding, coded
to write programs for a computer

coffee NOUN coffees
❶ a powder made from the roasted and crushed beans of a tropical plant ❷ a hot drink made from this powder

coffin NOUN coffins
a long box in which a dead body is buried or cremated

cog NOUN cogs
a wheel with teeth around the edge, that drives another wheel

for words beginning with
a k sound, try also ch–

cohesion *NOUN*
the quality a piece of writing has when it is clear
how the ideas and words in it relate to each other

coil *NOUN* coils
a circle or spiral of rope or wire
coil *VERB* coils, coiling, coiled
to wind something into circles or spirals • *The snake
coiled itself around his leg.*

coin *NOUN* coins
a piece of metal money

coincidence *NOUN* coincidences
Coincidence, or a coincidence, is when two things
happen by chance at the same time.

colander *(say* kul-an-der*) NOUN* colanders
a bowl with holes, for draining water from food

cold *ADJECTIVE* colder, coldest
❶ low in temperature; not hot or warm • *a cold
drink* ❷ unfriendly • *a cold expression*
➤ **coldly** *ADVERB* • *She looked at me coldly.*
➤ **coldness** *NOUN*
cold *NOUN* colds
❶ The cold is cold weather. • *I don't like the cold.*
❷ A cold is a minor illness that makes your nose run.

cold-blooded *ADJECTIVE*
❶ A cold-blooded animal has blood that changes
temperature according to the surroundings. • *Lizards
are cold-blooded.* ❷ cruel and without pity
• *a cold-blooded killer*

coleslaw *NOUN*
a salad made of chopped cabbage covered in
mayonnaise

collaborate *VERB* collaborates,
collaborating, collaborated
to work together or share information
➤ **collaboration** *NOUN*
➤ **collaborator** *NOUN* • *The book is the work of
several collaborators.*

collage *(say* kol-ahzh*) NOUN*
a picture made by sticking scraps of paper and other
things on a surface

collapse *VERB* collapses, collapsing, collapsed
❶ to fall down or break apart because of too
much weight • *The table collapsed.* ❷ If someone
collapses, they fall because they are very weak or ill.

collar *NOUN* collars
❶ the part of a piece of clothing that goes round
your neck ❷ a band that goes round an animal's neck

collate *VERB* collates, collating, collated
to collect and organise information • *We collated
the results in the form of a graph.*

colleague *NOUN* colleagues
Someone's colleague is a person they work with.

collect *VERB* collects, collecting, collected
❶ to get things together from various places,
especially as a hobby • *She collects stickers.*
❷ To collect someone or something is to go and get
them. • *Dad's collecting me.*
➤ **collector** *NOUN*

collection *NOUN* collections
❶ Your collection is things you have collected as
a hobby. ❷ A collection is money collected from
people for charity.

collective noun *NOUN* collective nouns
a noun that is a name for a group of things, people
or animals, for example a *flock* (of birds) or a *class*
(of children)

college *NOUN* colleges
a place where students study after they have left
school

collide *VERB* collides, colliding, collided
If things or people collide, they hit each other while
moving. • *The two ships almost collided.*

collie *NOUN* collies
a breed of dog with a long pointed muzzle and
long hair

collision *NOUN* collisions
a crash between two moving things

colon *NOUN* colons
a punctuation mark (:) used before a list or between
two clauses that could stand on their own

colonel *(say* ker-nel*) NOUN* colonels
a senior army officer

colony *NOUN* colonies
a group of people or animals living together
• *a colony of seals*

a b **c** d e f g h i j k l m n o p q r s t u v w x y z

A B C D E F G H I J K L M N O P Q R S T U V W X Y Z

colossal *ADJECTIVE*
huge, enormous
The monster did not laugh. He set off, up from the earth, beating his colossal wings.—THE IRON MAN, Ted Hughes

colour *NOUN* colours
❶ red, green, yellow, blue and so on • *What colour are his eyes?* • *My favourite colour is pink.*
❷ the use of all colours, not just black and white • *I printed it in colour.*
colour *VERB* colours, colouring, coloured
to give something a colour
➤ **coloured** *ADJECTIVE* • *a bunch of coloured balloons*

colour-blind *ADJECTIVE*
not able to see the difference between some colours, usually red and green • *If you are colour-blind, you may not see the 5 in the circle below.*

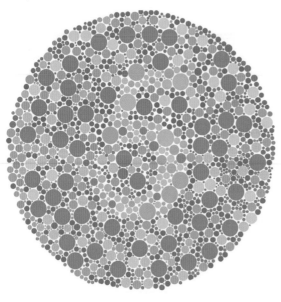

colourful *ADJECTIVE*
❶ with a lot of bright colours ❷ lively and exciting
• *a very colourful story*

colouring *NOUN*
A person's colouring is the colour of their skin and hair. • *She had the same colouring as her mother.*

colourless *ADJECTIVE*
without any colour • *a colourl-blind liquid*

colt *NOUN* colts
a young male horse

column *NOUN* columns
❶ a stone pillar ❷ something long and narrow
• *a column of smoke* ❸ a line of numbers or words one underneath the other • *Write the names in the first column.* ❹ a strip of printing in a book or newspaper

coma *(say koh-ma) NOUN* comas
If someone is in a coma, they are unconscious for a long time.

comb *NOUN* combs
a strip of plastic or metal with a row of thin teeth along it for making your hair tidy
comb *VERB* combs, combing, combed
To comb your hair is to tidy it with a comb.

combat *NOUN* combats
a fight or battle • *He was killed in combat.*
combat *VERB* combats, combating, combated
To combat something is to try to stop it from happening. • *The superhero combats crime.*

combination *NOUN* combinations
❶ a mixture of things • *He felt a combination of fear and excitement.* ❷ a way of arranging a set of numbers, letters or words to open a lock or form a message • *I tried every combination but nothing worked.*

combine *VERB* combines, combining, combined
To combine things is to join them or mix them together.

combustion *NOUN*
burning

come *VERB* comes, coming, came, come
❶ to move towards a person or place • *You can come to my house.* • *There's a bus coming.* ❷ to arrive at or reach a place • *A card came for you.*
• *Her hair comes to her waist.* ❸ to happen
• *Christmas comes once a year.*

comedian *NOUN* comedians
someone who entertains people with humour and jokes

comedy *NOUN* comedies
❶ A comedy is a play or film that makes people laugh.
❷ Comedy is using humour to make people laugh.

comet *NOUN* comets
a bright moving object in space with a core of ice
and a tail of dust particles behind it

✳ **WORD STORY**

The word **comet** comes from a Greek word meaning
'long-haired star'.

comfort *NOUN*
a feeling of relief from worry or pain
comfort *VERB* comforts, comforting,
comforted
to make someone feel happier when they are sad or
worried

comfortable *ADJECTIVE*
❶ Something that is comfortable is pleasant to use
or wear. • *a comfortable chair* ❷ Someone who is
comfortable is relaxed and not worried or in pain.
➤ **comfortably** *ADVERB*

comic *NOUN* comics
❶ A children's magazine that has stories with
pictures. ❷ a comedian
comic (also **comical**) *ADJECTIVE*
funny; making people laugh
➤ **comically** *ADVERB*

comma *NOUN* commas
a punctuation mark (,) used to mark a pause in a
sentence or between items in a list

command *NOUN* commands
❶ A command is an instruction telling someone to
do something. ❷ Command is authority or control.
• *Who is in **command**?*
command *VERB* commands, commanding,
commanded
❶ To command someone to do something is to order
them to do it. ❷ To command a group of people is to
be in charge of them.
➤ **commander** *NOUN*

commemorate *VERB* commemorates,
commemorating, commemorated
To commemorate a past event is to do something
special so that people remember it.
➤ **commemoration** *NOUN*

commence *VERB* commences,
commencing, commenced
to begin • *Let the battle **commence**!*

commend *VERB* commends, commending,
commended
to praise someone or something
➤ **commendable** *ADJECTIVE* • *They acted with
commendable speed.*
➤ **commendation** *NOUN* • *She received a
commendation for bravery.*

comment *NOUN* comments
a remark or opinion

commentary *NOUN* commentaries
a description of an event by someone who is
watching it, especially for radio or television

commentator *NOUN* commentators
a person who gives a commentary, especially of a
sports event

commerce *NOUN*
Commerce is buying and selling goods.

commercial *ADJECTIVE*
connected with buying, selling and making money
commercial *NOUN* commercials
an advertisement, especially on television or radio

commit *VERB* commits, committing,
committed
To commit a crime or bad act is to do it. • *He had
committed murder.*
➤ **To commit yourself to something** is to
decide or promise that you will do it.

commitment *NOUN* commitments
❶ Commitment is determination to do something.
❷ A commitment is a promise to do something.

committee *NOUN* committees
a group of people who meet to organise or discuss
something

common *ADJECTIVE* commoner, commonest
❶ ordinary or usual • *The robin is a **common** bird.*
• *These problems are **common**.* ❷ shared by two or
more people • *They have a **common** interest.*
common *NOUN* commons
a piece of open land that anyone can use
➤ **To have something in common** is to share a
quality or interest with one or more other people.
• *We **have** so much **in common**.*

commonplace *ADJECTIVE*
ordinary, familiar

Commonwealth NOUN
The Commonwealth is an association of Britain and other countries that used to be part of the British Empire.

commotion NOUN commotions
a noisy uproar
Shutters were thrown open by the townsfolk to see what all the commotion was.—CHEESE GALORE!, Alan Snow

communal ADJECTIVE
shared by several people

communicate VERB communicates, communicating, communicated
to talk or write to someone in order to give them information

communication NOUN communications
❶ Communication is giving people information by talking or writing to them. ❷ Communications are links such as radios that allow people to exchange information.

community NOUN communities
the people living in one area

commute NOUN commutes, commuting, commuted
to travel from home to work and back again every day
➤ **commuter** NOUN

compact ADJECTIVE
taking up only a little space

companion NOUN companions
a person or animal who spends a lot of time with you
➤ **companionship** NOUN • *They travelled together for* **companionship**.

company NOUN companies
❶ A company is a business that sells or provides something. • *a travel* **company** ❷ Company is having people with you. • *I was lonely and needed some* **company**.

comparative NOUN comparatives
the form of an adjective or adverb that expresses 'more' • *The* **comparative** *of 'big' is 'bigger' and the* **comparative** *of 'bad' is 'worse'.*
comparative ADJECTIVE
The comparative form is the same as the comparative.

compare VERB compares, comparing, compared
To compare two or more things is to see or say how they are similar. • *Compare your answers.*
➤ **compared with** or **to** in comparison to • *This is a palace* **compared with** *our house.*

comparison NOUN comparisons
To make a comparison is to think about two or more things and say how they are similar or different.

compartment NOUN compartments
a special place or section where you can put something • *the freezer* **compartment** *of the fridge*

compass NOUN compasses
❶ an instrument with a magnetised needle that shows which direction you are facing • *North, south, east and west are all points of a* **compass**.
❷ A compass or a pair of compasses is a device for drawing circles.

compassion NOUN
pity or mercy you show to people who are suffering
➤ **compassionate** ADJECTIVE

compel VERB compels, compelling, compelled
To compel someone to do something is to force them to do it.

compete VERB competes, competing, competed
to try to do better than other people in a competition or activity

competent ADJECTIVE
able to do something well • *She is a very* **competent** *driver.*
➤ **competence** NOUN

⚙ **BUILD YOUR VOCABULARY**
The opposite is **incompetent**.

competition NOUN competitions
a game or race in which you try to do better than other people

competitive ADJECTIVE
❶ a competitive person enjoys competing and likes to win ❷ A competitive situation is one where people compete.

competitor NOUN competitors
someone who competes in a game, race or activity

compile VERB compiles, compiling, compiled
To compile a list or book is to put it together.
• We **compiled** a list of questions.
➤ **compilation** NOUN • a **compilation** of poems

complain VERB complains, complaining, complained
to say that you are not pleased about something
'I wish you'd said before we started,' complains Mikkel.
—BETWEEN TWO SEAS, Marie-Louise Jensen

complaint NOUN complaints
If you make a complaint, you say you are not pleased about something.

complement VERB complements, complementing, complemented
to complete or go with something else • Her jewellery **complemented** her clothes.

> ⚠ **WATCH OUT!**
> **Complement** is related to the word **complete**, which might help you remember how to spell it (with an 'e'). Do not confuse with **compliment** meaning 'say something nice to someone'.

complete ADJECTIVE
❶ with nothing missing • a **complete** set of stickers
❷ finished • Now our mission is **complete**.

> ⚙ **BUILD YOUR VOCABULARY**
> The opposite of both meanings is **incomplete**.

❸ utter, total • It was a **complete** surprise.

complete VERB completes, completing, completed
to finish something or make it complete
➤ **completion** NOUN • The work is nearing **completion**.

completely ADVERB
totally, utterly • It was **completely** dark.

complex ADJECTIVE
difficult and complicated

complex NOUN complexes
a group of buildings, such as a sports centre

complexion NOUN complexions
the appearance of your skin on your face • She had a rosy **complexion**.

complicate VERB complicates, complicating, complicated
to make something difficult or awkward

complicated ADJECTIVE
difficult to understand or cope with

complication NOUN complications
something that makes a situation difficult or awkward

compliment NOUN compliments
something nice that you say to someone about them
• She paid me a **compliment** about my dancing.

compliment VERB compliment, complimenting, complimented
to say something nice to someone about them
• She **complimented** my shoes.

> ⚠ **WATCH OUT!**
> Do not confuse with **complement** which means 'to go with or complete something'.

component NOUN components
one of the parts that something is made of

compose VERB composes, composing, composed
❶ To compose music or poetry is to write it. ❷ To be composed of something is to be made up of it.
• Clouds are **composed** of water vapour.
➤ **composer** NOUN • Bach was a famous **composer**.

composition NOUN compositions
❶ a piece of music or writing ❷ The composition of something is the things it is made up of.

compost NOUN
a mixture of rotted plants, for example waste food and cut grass, used as a fertiliser

compound NOUN compounds
❶ (**compound word**) a word that is made from two or more other words, such as *bathroom* or *newspaper* ❷ a substance made of two or more elements or ingredients

comprehend VERB comprehends, comprehending, comprehended
to understand something

comprehension NOUN comprehensions
❶ understanding ❷ an exercise to see if you understand something you have read or listened to

a
b
c
d
e
f
g
h
i
j
k
l
m
n
o
p
q
r
s
t
u
v
w
x
y
z

comprehensive *ADJECTIVE*
including everything or everyone • *a comprehensive list*

comprehensive (also **comprehensive school**) *NOUN* comprehensives, comprehensive schools
a secondary school for children of all abilities

compress *VERB* compresses, compressing, compressed
to squeeze or press something into a small space

comprise *VERB* comprises, comprising, comprised
To comprise several people or things is to include them. • *The fleet comprised 20 ships.*

compromise (say com-pro-mise) *VERB* compromises, compromising, compromised
to accept something that is not exactly what you wanted

compromise (say com-pro-mise) *NOUN* compromises
an agreement in which you accept something that is not exactly what you wanted

compulsory *ADJECTIVE*
If something is compulsory, you have to do it.
• *School uniform is compulsory.*

computer *NOUN* computers
an electronic machine that sorts data and does rapid calculations

computing *NOUN*
the activity of using computers

comrade *NOUN* comrades
a friend, especially a fellow soldier

con *VERB* cons, conning, conned *(informal)*
to trick someone into doing or buying something

concave *ADJECTIVE*
curving inwards

> **BUILD** YOUR VOCABULARY
> To remember this, think of the shape inside a **cave**. The opposite is **convex**.

conceal *VERB* conceals, concealing, concealed
to hide something

conceited *ADJECTIVE*
Someone who is conceited has a high opinion of themselves.

conceive *VERB* conceives, conceiving, conceived
❶ To conceive of something is to think of it. ❷ If a woman conceives, she becomes pregnant.

> **BUILD** YOUR VOCABULARY
> Look at **conception**.

concentrate *VERB* concentrates, concentrating, concentrated
to give something all your attention • *I need to concentrate on what I'm doing.*

concentrated *ADJECTIVE*
A concentrated liquid is strong because water has been removed from it.

concentration *NOUN*
Concentration is giving something all your attention.

concentric *ADJECTIVE*
Concentric circles are placed one inside another and have the same centre.

concept *NOUN* concepts
an idea • *the concept of right and wrong*

conception *NOUN* conceptions
❶ an idea ❷ the time when a woman becomes pregnant

concern *VERB* concerns, concerning, concerned
❶ to worry someone ❷ to be important to someone or relate to someone • *This doesn't concern you.*

concern *NOUN* concerns
❶ a worry • *His teacher had some concerns.*
❷ someone's business • *What I do is not your concern.*

concerned *ADJECTIVE*
worried about something • *When he was late home, they became very concerned.*

concerning PREPOSITION
on the subject of; about • *a report concerning the crime*

concert NOUN concerts
a performance of music

concerto (*say* kon-**cher**-toh) NOUN concertos
a piece of music for a solo instrument and an orchestra • *a violin concerto*

concession NOUN concessions
To make a concession is to allow someone to have or to do something in order be helpful.

concise ADJECTIVE
giving a lot of information in a few words

conclude VERB concludes, concluding, concluded
❶ to form an opinion based on evidence
• *I concluded that nobody was at home.*
❷ to end something • *He concluded his speech with a joke.*

conclusion NOUN conclusions
❶ a decision that you reach after a lot of thought
❷ the ending of something

concrete NOUN
cement mixed with water and gravel or sand and used in building

concussion NOUN
a temporary brain injury caused by a hard knock, that makes you dizzy or unconscious

condemn VERB condemns, condemning, condemned
❶ To condemn something is to say that you strongly disapprove of it. ❷ If someone is condemned to a punishment, they are given that punishment.

condensation NOUN
drops of liquid formed from vapour that has condensed

condense VERB condenses, condensing, condensed
When a vapour condenses, it changes to a liquid.
• *Steam condenses on cold windows.*

condition NOUN conditions
❶ the state of a person or thing • *This bike is in good condition.* ❷ The conditions around a person, animal or plant are the things around them that affect them, for example the temperature. • *They were living in very poor conditions.* ❸ Something that must happen if something else is to happen.
• *You can come on condition that you help.*

conduct (*say* con-**duct**) VERB conducts, conducting, conducted
❶ To conduct something is to organise it or carry it out. • *We conducted an experiment.* ❷ To conduct an orchestra or a band is to direct it. ❸ To conduct electricity or heat is to allow it to pass along.

conduct (*say* **con**-duct) NOUN
A person's conduct is their behaviour.

conductor NOUN conductors
❶ someone who directs an orchestra or a band
❷ something that conducts electricity or heat
• *Metals are good conductors.*

cone NOUN cones
❶ an object which is circular at one end and pointed at the other ❷ the fruit of a pine, fir or cedar tree

conference NOUN conferences
a large meeting or set of meetings where people discuss a topic

confess VERB confesses, confessing, confessed
To confess to something is to admit it.

confession NOUN confessions
If you make a confession, you admit you have done something wrong.

confetti NOUN
tiny bits of coloured paper thrown at the bride and bridegroom after a wedding

confide VERB confides, confiding, confided
To confide in someone is to tell them a secret.

confidence NOUN
❶ the feeling that you can do something well or that you are right ❷ Confidence in someone is trusting or believing them.

confident ADJECTIVE
❶ sure of your own abilities • *She's a very* **confident** *girl.* ❷ sure that something will happen • *I am* **confident** *you'll like it.*
➤ **confidently** ADVERB

confidential ADJECTIVE
Confidential information has to be kept secret.
➤ **confidentially** ADVERB

confine VERB confines, confining, confined
❶ To confine something is to restrict or limit it.
• *He* **confined** *his visit to two days.* ❷ To confine someone is to keep them or lock them in a place.
• *His grandmother was* **confined** *to her bed through illness.*

confirm VERB confirms, confirming, confirmed
❶ To confirm something is to say or show that it is true. • *What I saw* **confirmed** *my suspicions.* ❷ To confirm an arrangement is to make it definite.

confirmation NOUN
something that shows something is true or has happened • *She gave a nod of* **confirmation**

confiscate VERB confiscates, confiscating, confiscated
to take something away from someone as a punishment
➤ **confiscation** NOUN

conflict (say con-flict) NOUN conflicts
fighting or serious disagreement

conflict (say con-**flict**) VERB conflicts, conflicting, conflicted
If things conflict, they contradict or disagree with one another. • *I was filled with* **conflicting** *emotions.*

confront VERB confronts, confronting, confronted
❶ to challenge someone so they have to argue or fight • *I decided to* **confront** *him with the accusation.* ❷ If you are confronted with a situation, you have to deal with it.

confrontation NOUN
a serious face-to-face disagreement or a fight

confuse VERB confuses, confusing, confused
❶ If something confuses you, it puzzles you and you cannot understand it. ❷ To confuse things is to mistake one thing for another. • *A lot of people confuse 'there' and 'their'.*
➤ **confused** ADJECTIVE • *I'm really* **confused** *now.*
➤ **confusing** ADJECTIVE • *His explanation was* **confusing**.
➤ **confusion** NOUN • *I stared at them in* **confusion**.

congratulate VERB congratulates, congratulating, congratulated
To tell someone that you are happy for them about something they have done.
➤ **congratulations** NOUN

congregation NOUN congregations
the people who attend a church service

conical ADJECTIVE
shaped like a cone

conifer (say con-if-er) NOUN conifers
an evergreen tree with cones
➤ **coniferous** ADJECTIVE

conjunction NOUN conjunctions
a word that joins other words and parts of a sentence, for example *and*, *but* and *whether*

⚙ **BUILD** YOUR VOCABULARY
Conjunction is a **word class**.

conjure VERB conjures, conjuring, conjured
❶ To conjure something or to conjure something up is to make it appear as if by magic. ❷ To conjure an idea or conjure it up is to make someone think of it.
• *Her words* **conjured** *up a strange vision.*

conker NOUN conkers
a hard and shiny
reddish-brown nut that
grows on a horse chestnut
tree, used to play a game
called **conkers**

⚠ **WATCH OUT!**

Do not confuse a **conker** with to **conquer**, meaning
'to defeat'.

✱ **WORD STORY**

Conker comes from an English dialect word meaning
'snail shell', because the game was first played with
snail shells.

connect VERB connects, connecting,
connected
❶ To connect things is to join them together. ❷ To
connect things or people is to link them. • *What
connects the two crimes?*

connection NOUN connections
a link between people or things • *We have a family
connection.* • *There's no Internet connection.*

connective NOUN connectives
a word or phrase that links clauses or sentences, for
example *because, however* or *on the other hand*

conquer VERB conquers, conquering,
conquered
❶ to defeat the people in a place and take it over
• *William I conquered England.* ❷ to succeed in
overcoming or controlling something • *You must
conquer your fears.*
➤ **conqueror** NOUN

conquest NOUN conquests
a victory over another country or people

conscience (*say* **kon**-shens) NOUN
your feeling of knowing what is right and wrong

⚠ **WATCH OUT!**

Conscience contains the word **science** (from the
Latin word meaning 'know'), which might help you
remember how to spell it.

conscientious (*say* kon-shee-en-shus)
ADJECTIVE
careful and hard-working
➤ **conscientiously** ADVERB

conscious (*say* **kon**-shus) ADJECTIVE
❶ awake and knowing what is happening ❷ aware
of something • *I was conscious of a strange smell.*
➤ **consciously** ADVERB ➤ **consciousness** NOUN

⚠ **WATCH OUT!**

Remember that **conscious** has **sci** in the middle, as in
science.

consecutive ADJECTIVE
consecutive things come one after another

consent NOUN
agreement or permission
consent VERB consents, consenting,
consented
To consent to something is to agree to it or permit it.

consequence NOUN consequences
something that happens because of an event or
action • *Think about the consequences of your
actions.*

conservation NOUN
taking care of nature, animals and plants • *I'm
interested in wildlife conservation.*

conservatory NOUN conservatories
a room with glass walls and a glass roof

conserve VERB conserves, conserving,
conserved
❶ to protect nature, animals or plants • *You can
help to conserve these insects' habitat.* ❷ to not use
too much of something • *She tried to conserve her
strength.*

consider VERB considers, considering,
considered
❶ to think carefully about something ❷ to believe
something • *Some people consider it wrong to eat
meat.*

considerable ADJECTIVE
large or a lot of • *We had considerable difficulty.*

considerate ADJECTIVE
kind and thoughtful towards other people

⬤ **BUILD YOUR VOCABULARY**

An opposite is **inconsiderate**.

consideration NOUN considerations
thought or attention

considering *PREPOSITION*
if you consider • *I could see quite well, **considering** how dark it was.*

consist *VERB* **consists, consisting, consisted**
To consist of something is to be made up of it. • *The meal **consisted** of bread and cheese.*

consistent *ADJECTIVE*
always the same, not changing

BUILD YOUR VOCABULARY
An opposite is **inconsistent**.

consolation *NOUN* **consolations**
something that gives someone comfort or cheers them up

console *(say con-**sole**) VERB* **consoles, consoling, consoled**
to give someone comfort or cheer them up

console *(say con-**sole**) (also **games console**) NOUN* **consoles, games consoles**
a small machine for playing computer games

consonant *NOUN* **consonants**
a letter that is not a vowel

conspicuous *ADJECTIVE*
Something conspicuous is easy to notice.

BUILD YOUR VOCABULARY
An opposite is **inconspicuous**.

conspiracy *NOUN* **conspiracies**
a plot to do something bad or illegal

constable *NOUN* **constables**
an ordinary member of the police

constant *ADJECTIVE*
happening or existing all the time and not changing • *They need a **constant** supply of wood.*
➤ **constantly** *ADVERB* • *We argue **constantly**.*

constellation *NOUN* **constellations**
a group of stars

constitution *NOUN* **constitutions**
❶ A country's constitution is a set of laws or principles for governing it. ❷ Your constitution is your state of health.

construct *VERB* **constructs, constructing, constructed**
to build something

construction *NOUN* **constructions**
❶ Construction is the process of building.
❷ A construction is something that has been built.

constructive *ADJECTIVE*
helpful and positive • *I like **constructive** criticism.*

consult *VERB* **consults, consulting, consulted**
❶ To consult someone is to ask them for advice.
❷ To consult a book or website is to look at it for information.

consume *VERB* **consumes, consuming, consumed**
❶ to eat or drink something ❷ to use up or destroy something • *The stove **consumes** a lot of fuel.*

consumer *NOUN* **consumers**
someone who buys goods or services

consumption *NOUN*
the using up of food or fuel • *They tried to reduce their oil **consumption**.*

contact *NOUN* **contacts**
❶ Contact is touching someone or something.
❷ Contact is communication. • *I've lost **contact** with my uncle.*

contact *VERB* **contacts, contacting, contacted**
To contact someone is to get in touch with them.

contact lens *NOUN* **contact lenses**
a small plastic lens worn against the eyeball instead of glasses

contagious *(say kon-**tay**-jus) ADJECTIVE*
A contagious disease is one you catch by touching someone or something infected with it.

contain *VERB* **contains, containing, contained**
To contain something is to have it inside. • *This book **contains** a lot of information.*

container *NOUN* **containers**
something that is designed to contain things

contaminate *VERB* **contaminates, contaminating, contaminated**
to make something dirty in a way that is harmful
➤ **contamination** *NOUN*

contemplate *VERB* contemplates,
contemplating, contemplated
❶ To contemplate doing something is to plan or
intend to do it. ❷ To contemplate something is to
look at and think about it.

contempt *NOUN*
a feeling of dislike and no respect at all for someone
or something • *She looked at him with utter
contempt.*

contemptuous *ADJECTIVE*
showing dislike and no respect • *I could hear their
contemptuous laughter.*
➤ **contemptuously** *ADVERB*

contend *VERB* contends, contending,
contended
➤ **To contend with something** is to have to deal
with it.

content *(say con-tent) NOUN*
❶ The contents of a box or other container are what
is inside it. ❷ The content or contents of a book are
what is written in it.

content *(say con-tent) ADJECTIVE*
happy and willing • *Are you content to stay behind?*

contented *ADJECTIVE*
happy and satisfied
➤ **contentedly** *ADVERB* • *The baby fell to sleep
contentedly.*

contest *NOUN* contests
a competition

contestant *NOUN* contestants
someone who takes part in a contest or
competition

context *NOUN* contexts
The context of a word or phrase is the words that
come before or after it and help you to understand
what it means.

continent *NOUN* continents
The continents are the main masses of land
in the world, which are Africa, Antarctica,
Asia, Oceania, Europe, North America and
South America.
➤ **continental** *ADJECTIVE*

continual *ADJECTIVE*
happening repeatedly • *I'm sick of his continual
complaints.*
➤ **continually** *ADVERB* • *He complains
continually.*

⚙ **BUILD YOUR VOCABULARY**
Do not confuse **continual** with **continuous**,
meaning 'without stopping'.

continue *VERB* continues, continuing,
continued
to go on doing something • *She continued talking.*
• *He continued to cry.* • *Continue with your work.*
• *The rain continued all day.*
➤ **continuation** *NOUN*

continuous *ADJECTIVE*
continuing without stopping • *There was a
continuous noise.*
➤ **continuously** *ADVERB* • *The bell rang
continuously for 5 minutes.*

⚙ **BUILD YOUR VOCABULARY**
Look at **continual**.

contour *NOUN* contours
❶ The contour of something is its shape or outline.
❷ A line on a map joining points that are the same
height above sea level.

contract *(say con-tract) NOUN* contracts
a legal agreement
contract *(say con-tract) VERB* contracts,
contracting, contracted
To contract is to become smaller. • *Metal contracts
as it cools.*

contraction *NOUN* contractions
a shortened form, often marked by an apostrophe,
for example *don't* or *I'm* • *'It's' is a contraction of
'it is'.*

contradict *VERB* contradicts, contradicting,
contradicted
To contradict someone or something is to say they
are wrong or that it is untrue.
➤ **contradiction** *NOUN*

contraption *NOUN* contraptions
a clumsy or strange-looking device or machine

contrary ADJECTIVE
❶ *(say* kon-tra-ree*)* If one thing is contrary to another, they are opposites or contradict one another. • *Contrary to popular belief, having wet hair cannot make you catch a cold.* ❷ *(say* con-trair-ree*)* Someone who is contrary is obstinate and difficult to deal with. • *Mary, Mary, quite contrary.*
➤ **on the contrary** *(say* kon-tra-ree*)* The opposite is true.

contrast *(say* con-**trast***)* VERB contrasts, contrasting, contrasted
❶ To contrast two things is to show they are different. ❷ If one thing contrasts with another, it is clearly different.
contrast *(say* con-trast*)* NOUN contrasts
a great or clear difference

contribute VERB contributes, contributing, contributed
❶ To contribute to something is to give money to help it. ❷ To contribute to a result is to help cause it. • *His tiredness* **contributed** *to the accident.*
➤ **contribution** NOUN

contrive VERB contrives, contriving, contrived
❶ To contrive something is to cleverly plan or invent it. ❷ To contrive to do something is to manage to do it.

control NOUN controls
❶ Control is the power to make someone or something do what you want. ❷ The controls of a machine are the switches or knobs that make it work.
control VERB controls, controlling, controlled
❶ If you control something, you have power to decide what happens there. ❷ to use the controls of a machine to make it do something • *This knob* **controls** *the temperature.*
➤ **controller** NOUN

convenience NOUN conveniences
❶ Convenience is usefulness and comfort.
❷ A convenience is something that helps make life easy.

convenient ADJECTIVE
causing little trouble or effort for someone
• *Is Monday* **convenient***?*
➤ **conveniently** ADVERB • *Our house is* **conveniently** *near the bus stop.*

◉ BUILD YOUR VOCABULARY
The opposite is **inconvenient**.

convent NOUN convents
a place where nuns live and work

conventional ADJECTIVE
usual; ordinary or traditional • *It travels much faster than a* **conventional** *plane.*

converge VERB converges, converging, converged
to come together at a point • *People* **converged** *on him from all sides.*

conversation NOUN conversations
If you have a conversation, you talk with someone for a while.

converse VERB converses, conversing, conversed
To converse is to talk together. • *They* **conversed** *in whispers.*

convert VERB converts, converting, converted
❶ to change something into something new • *You can* **convert** *a noun into an adjective by adding -y, for example 'hairy'.* ❷ to change a number from one form to another • *Convert the time from hours into minutes.* • *Do you know how to* **convert** *miles to kilometres?*

convex ADJECTIVE
curving outwards like the outside of a ball

◉ BUILD YOUR VOCABULARY
The opposite is **concave**.

convey *VERB* conveys, conveying, conveyed
To convey a message or idea is to get someone to understand it.

conveyor belt *NOUN* conveyor belts
a long belt or chain for carrying goods in a factory

convict *(say con-**vict**) VERB* convicts, convicting, convicted
If a court convicts someone, it finds them guilty of a crime. • *He was **convicted** of spying.*

convict *(say **con**-vict) NOUN* convicts
a prisoner who has been found guilty of a crime

conviction *NOUN* convictions
a strong belief that you are right • *She spoke with conviction.*

convince *VERB* convinces, convincing, convinced
To convince someone is to persuade them about something.

convoy *NOUN* convoys
a group of ships or vehicles travelling together

cook *VERB* cooks, cooking, cooked
To cook food is to make it ready to eat by heating it.
cook *NOUN* cooks
someone who cooks, especially as their job

cooker *NOUN* cookers
a device with an oven and hot surfaces for cooking food

cookery *NOUN*
the art or skill of cooking food

cookie *NOUN* cookies *(North American)*
a sweet biscuit

cool *ADJECTIVE* cooler, coolest
❶ quite cold; not very warm • *The air was fresh and cool.* ❷ calm and not easily excited • *She stayed cool.* ❸ *(informal)* good • *That's so cool!*
➤ **coolly** *ADVERB* ➤ **coolness** *NOUN*
cool *VERB* cools, cooling, cooled
If something cools or if you cool it, it becomes cool.

cooperate *VERB* cooperates, cooperating, cooperated
To cooperate with people is to work helpfully with them.
➤ **cooperation** *NOUN*

cooperative *ADJECTIVE*
willing to help or to work with someone

coordinate *NOUN* coordinates
two numbers or letters used to show the position of something on a graph or map • *The **coordinates** of point P are (4,2).*

coot *NOUN* coots
a water bird with a white patch on its forehead

cop *NOUN* cops *(informal)*
a police officer

cope *VERB* copes, coping, coped
To cope with something difficult is to deal with it successfully.

copper *NOUN* coppers
a reddish-brown metal used for making wire and pipes

🔧 **BUILD YOUR VOCABULARY**
Copper is an **element**.

copy *VERB* copies, copying, copied
❶ To copy something is to make something that looks like it. ❷ To copy someone is to do the same as them. ❸ To copy a computer file, program or piece of text is to create another one exactly the same.
copy *NOUN* copies
❶ something made to look like something else ❷ a computer file, program or piece of text you create that is exactly the same as another one ❸ one newspaper, magazine or book • *I have my own **copy** of the dictionary.*

coral *NOUN*
a hard substance made of the skeletons of tiny sea creatures

cord *NOUN* cords
❶ a thin rope ❷ a length of electrical wire covered in plastic

cordial *NOUN* cordials
a sweet fruit-flavoured drink

corduroy *(say **kor**-der-oi) NOUN*
heavy cotton cloth with raised ridges

core *NOUN* cores
the part in the middle of something

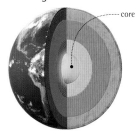
core

a
b
c
d
e
f
g
h
i
j
k
l
m
n
o
p
q
r
s
t
u
v
w
x
y
z

A
B
C
D
E
F
G
H
I
J
K
L
M
N
O
P
Q
R
S
T
U
V
W
X
Y
Z

corgi NOUN corgis
a small breed of dog with short legs and large upright ears

cork NOUN corks
❶ Cork is a light substance made from the bark of a tree. ❷ A cork is a piece of cork used to close a bottle.

corkscrew NOUN corkscrews
❶ a device for removing corks from bottles ❷ a spiral

cormorant NOUN cormorants
a large black seabird

corn NOUN corns
Corn is grain. • *a field of corn*

corner NOUN corners
the point where two lines, roads or walls meet
corner VERB corners, cornering, cornered
To corner someone is to trap them. • *They had me cornered and I could not escape.*

cornet NOUN cornets
a musical instrument like a small trumpet

cornflower NOUN cornflowers
a blue wild flower

coronation NOUN coronations
the ceremony of crowning a king or queen

corporal NOUN corporals
an army officer of low rank

corps *(say* kor*)* NOUN corps
an army unit with special duties • *She is in the Medical Corps.*

corpse NOUN corpses
a dead body

corral *(say* kor-ahl*)* NOUN corrals
a fenced area for horses or cattle

correct ADJECTIVE
❶ true or accurate; without mistakes • *That's the correct spelling.*

> **BUILD** YOUR VOCABULARY
> An opposite is **incorrect**.

❷ proper, suitable • *Make sure you use the correct equipment.*
➤ **correctly** ADVERB • *She answered correctly.*

correct VERB corrects, correcting, corrected
To correct a piece of work is to put right the mistakes in it.
➤ **correction** NOUN • *I have to make a few corrections.*

correspond VERB corresponds, corresponding, corresponded
❶ To correspond with something is to match it or go together with it. • *Each colour corresponds with a different reading level.* ❷ To correspond is to write letters to someone.

correspondence NOUN
letters or writing letters

correspondent NOUN correspondents
a news reporter

corridor NOUN corridors
a long narrow passage with rooms leading off it

corrode VERB corrodes, corroding, corroded
to wear away by rust or be eaten away by a chemical • *Stainless steel does not corrode easily.*

> **BUILD** YOUR VOCABULARY
> The process of corroding is called **corrosion**.

corrugated ADJECTIVE
shaped into parallel ridges • *a corrugated iron roof*

corrupt ADJECTIVE
a corrupt person uses their power dishonestly, for example in exchange for money
corrupt VERB
❶ to make someone dishonest, for example by offering them money or power ❷ To corrupt computer data is to add errors that change it or make it impossible to use.
➤ **corruption** NOUN

corset NOUN corsets
a tight piece of underwear worn round the hips and waist

cosmetics NOUN
make-up and beauty products such as lipstick and skin cream

cosmic ADJECTIVE
relating to space or the universe

cost VERB **costs, costing, cost**
If something costs an amount, that is what you have
to pay for it. • *The drinks cost £3 each.*

cost NOUN **costs**
The cost of something is what you have to pay for it.
• *The cost of a bus ticket has gone up.*

costly ADJECTIVE **costlier, costliest**
expensive

costume NOUN **costumes**
clothes, especially worn to look like someone else
or worn at a particular time in history

cosy ADJECTIVE **cosier, cosiest**
warm and comfortable • *a pair of cosy pyjamas*

cot NOUN **cots**
a baby's bed with high sides

cottage NOUN **cottages**
a small house, especially in the country

cotton NOUN
❶ soft thread or cloth made from a plant called
cotton ❷ any thread used for sewing

couch NOUN **couches**
a sofa or a long seat

cough (say kof) VERB **coughs, coughing,
coughed**
to push air suddenly out of your lungs with a harsh
noise

cough (say kof) NOUN **coughs**
❶ the action or sound of coughing ❷ an illness
which makes you cough a lot

> ⚠ **WATCH OUT!**
> In **cough** and **trough**, the letters *ough* sound like
> 'off'.

could VERB
used in polite questions or requests • *Could I come
with you?*

> ⚙ **BUILD** YOUR VOCABULARY
> **Could** is a **modal verb**.

council NOUN **councils**
a group of people chosen to discuss and make
decisions about something on behalf of other people
• *the school council*
➤ **councillor** NOUN • *She's a town councillor.*

> ⚠ **WATCH OUT!**
> Do not confuse with **counsel** which means 'advice'
> and **counsellor** which means 'someone who gives
> advice'.

counsel NOUN **counsels**
advice

counsel VERB **counsels, counselling,
counselled**
to give someone advice
➤ **counsellor** NOUN • *He talked to a counsellor
about his problems.*

> ⚠ **WATCH OUT!**
> Do not confuse with **council** which means 'a group
> of people chosen to make decisions' and **councillor**
> which is 'one of these people'.

count VERB **counts,
counting, counted**
❶ To count things or people
is to use numbers to find out
how many there are. ❷ To
count is to say numbers in
order. • *Count to 10 before you
open your eyes.*
❸ To count is to matter or be
important. • *A goal scored by cheating doesn't count.*
➤ **To count on someone** or **something** is to
rely on them.

count NOUN **counts**
If you keep count of things, you keep recording or
remembering how many there are.

a b c d e f g h i j k l m n o p q r s t u v w x y z

countable ADJECTIVE *(in grammar)*
A countable noun can be counted and have a plural.
• *'Car' is a **countable** noun.*

> ⚙ **BUILD** YOUR VOCABULARY
> Look at **non-countable**.

countdown NOUN countdowns
the act of counting backwards to zero before
something happens, such as a rocket launch

counter NOUN counters
❶ a long table where customers are served in a shop
or cafe ❷ a small plastic disc used in board games

counterfeit *(say* count-er-fit*)* ADJECTIVE
fake and intended to trick people • *They were using
counterfeit money.*

countless ADJECTIVE
too many to count

country NOUN countries
❶ a nation • *What **country** are you from?*
❷ The country is the countryside.

countryman or **countrywoman** NOUN
countrymen, countrywomen
Your fellow countryman or countrywoman is
someone who comes from the same country
as you.

countryside NOUN
an area away from towns, with fields, woods
and villages

county NOUN counties
one of the areas that a country is divided into, for
example Kent in England, Fife in Scotland or Powys
in Wales

couple NOUN couples
❶ two people who are in a relationship ❷ A couple
of things or people is two or a small number of them.
• *I've been there a **couple** of times.*

coupon NOUN coupons
a piece of paper that you can use to pay for
something

courage NOUN
the quality of being brave enough to do something
dangerous or difficult

courageous ADJECTIVE
willing to do something dangerous or difficult

> ⚠ **WATCH OUT!**
> Don't forget the **e** in **courageous**.

courgette NOUN courgettes
a long vegetable with dark green skin that is usually
eaten cooked

> ⚙ **BUILD** YOUR VOCABULARY
> In North America courgettes are known as *zucchini*.

courier *(say* koor-ee-er*)* NOUN couriers
❶ someone who carries a message ❷ someone whose
job is to look after people on holiday

course NOUN courses
❶ a series of lessons for learning something
• *She went on a computer **course**.* ❷ the direction
in which something travels • *The pilot changed
course.* ❸ one part of a meal • *For my main **course**
I had chicken.* ❹ a piece of land for races or
playing golf
➤ **of course** certainly

court NOUN courts
❶ an area for games like tennis or netball ❷ a place
where legal matters are decided or the people that
make decisions there • *He was found guilty by the
court.* ❸ the place where a king or queen lives and
rules

court VERB courts, courting, courted
to try to get someone's love or support

courteous *(say* ker-tee-us*)* ADJECTIVE
polite and thoughtful
➤ **courteously** ADVERB

> ✴ **WORD STORY**
> The word **courteous** comes from an old word meaning
> 'having manners good enough for a royal court'.

courtyard NOUN courtyards
a paved area surrounded by walls or buildings

cousin NOUN cousins
Your cousin is a child of your uncle or aunt.

cove NOUN coves
a small bay

cover VERB covers, covering, covered
1 To cover something is to put something over it
or form a layer over it. • *Cover the dish with a plate.*
• *Snow **covered** the ground.* **2** To cover a distance is
to travel over it. • *He **covered** ten miles a day.*
3 To cover a subject is to deal with it or discuss it.
• *We haven't **covered** the Vikings at school yet.*

cover NOUN covers
1 A cover is a piece of material that goes over
something. **2** The cover of a book or magazine is the
outside of it. **3** Cover is a place where you can hide
or take shelter.

cow NOUN cows
a large female animal kept for its milk and beef

🔧 **BUILD** YOUR VOCABULARY
Look at **bovine** and **cattle**.

coward NOUN cowards
someone who is not brave and runs away from
danger or difficulties
➤ **cowardly** ADJECTIVE

cowboy NOUN cowboys
a man who looks after cattle on a large farm,
especially in North America

cower VERB cowers, cowering, cowered
to crouch because you are afraid
*The pair fell to the floor and cowered there, their heads
buried in their arms.*—THE PITS OF PERIL!, Ian Ogilvy

cowslip NOUN cowslips
a wild plant that has yellow flowers in spring

crab NOUN crabs
a shellfish with ten legs and two claws

🔧 **BUILD** YOUR VOCABULARY
A **crab** is a **crustacean**.

crab apple NOUN crab apples
a small sour apple

crack NOUN cracks
1 a line on something where it has nearly broken
• *There's a **crack** in the glass.* **2** a narrow gap
• *I peeped through a **crack** in the door.* **3** a sudden
sharp noise • *There was a loud **crack**.*

crack VERB cracks, cracking, cracked
1 If something cracks or you crack it, a line or split
appears on its surface. • *The plate has **cracked**.* **2** to
make a sudden sharp noise

cracker NOUN crackers
1 a thin biscuit **2** a decorated paper object used
at celebrations which bangs when two people pull
it apart

crackle VERB crackles, crackling, crackled
to make small cracking sounds, like a fire

cradle NOUN cradles
a cot for a baby

craft NOUN crafts
1 an activity which needs skill with the hands
2 a boat

craftsman or **craftswoman** NOUN
craftsmen, craftswomen
someone who is skilled at making things with their
hands
➤ **craftsmanship** NOUN

crafty ADJECTIVE craftier, craftiest
cunning and clever
➤ **craftily** ADVERB ➤ **craftiness** NOUN

crag NOUN crags
a steep piece of rough rock
➤ **craggy** ADJECTIVE

cram VERB crams, cramming, crammed
To cram things into something is to push them there
when they do not easily fit.

cramp NOUN cramps
pain caused by a muscle tightening suddenly

cramped ADJECTIVE
with not enough space • *The small house was
cramped.*

cranberry NOUN cranberries
a sour red berry used to make juice

crane NOUN cranes
1 a large machine for lifting and moving heavy
objects **2** a large bird with long legs and neck
crane VERB cranes, craning, craned
To crane your neck is to stretch it so that you can see
or hear something.

cranefly NOUN craneflies
an insect with long thin legs and a thin body

🔧 **BUILD** YOUR VOCABULARY
A synonym is **daddy-long-legs**.

a
b
c
d
e
f
g
h
i
j
k
l
m
n
o
p
q
r
s
t
u
v
w
x
y
z

A B C D E F G H I J K L M N O P Q R S T U V W X Y Z

crank NOUN cranks
an L-shaped rod used to turn or control something

cranny NOUN crannies
a narrow hole or space

BUILD YOUR VOCABULARY
A synonym is **crevice**.

crash NOUN crashes
❶ the loud noise of something falling or breaking
❷ an accident in which a vehicle hits something
crash VERB crashes, crashing, crashed
❶ to fall or bump into something violently
❷ To crash a vehicle is to have a crash while driving it. ❸ If a computer crashes, it stops working suddenly.

crate NOUN crates
a container in which goods are transported

crater NOUN craters
❶ the mouth of a volcano ❷ a hole in the ground made by a bomb

crave VERB craves, craving, craved
to want something very much

crawl VERB crawls, crawling, crawled
❶ to move on your hands and knees • He **crawled** out of the tent. ❷ to move along very slowly • The traffic was **crawling** along.
crawl NOUN
a fast swimming stroke in which the arms hit the water alternately

crayon NOUN crayons
a coloured pencil or coloured stick of wax

craze NOUN crazes
something that is very popular for a short time

crazy ADJECTIVE crazier, craziest
mad or strange
➤ **crazily** ADVERB ➤ **craziness** NOUN

creak NOUN creaks
a sound like the noise made by a stiff door opening
creak VERB creaks, creaking, creaked
to make a creak
The door creaked open slowly and the Baudelaire orphans held their breath as they peered into the dark entryway.
—THE REPTILE ROOM, Lemony Snicket
➤ **creaky** ADJECTIVE • **creaky** floorboards

cream NOUN creams
❶ a thick fatty liquid that comes from milk
❷ a yellow-white colour
➤ **creamy** ADJECTIVE

crease NOUN creases
❶ a line made in paper or cloth by folding or pressing it ❷ a wrinkle in the skin • He had **creases** around his eyes.
crease VERB creases, creasing, creased
to make a crease in something

create VERB creates, creating, created
To create something is to make it exist.
➤ **creation** NOUN
➤ **creator** NOUN • She is the **creator** of Harry Potter.

creative ADJECTIVE
showing imagination in thinking of new ideas
• We had some **creative** ideas.

creature NOUN creatures
a living animal or person

crèche (say kresh) NOUN crèches
a place where babies or small children are looked after while their parents are busy

credit NOUN
❶ praise or approval • She deserves **credit** for trying. ❷ a system of paying for something later or in small amounts • We bought a new car on **credit**. ❸ The credits in a film or TV programme are the names of the people who helped make it.

credit card NOUN credit cards
a plastic card allowing someone to buy goods on credit

creek NOUN creeks
a narrow inlet or stream

creep VERB creeps, creeping, crept
❶ to move quietly or secretly • He **crept** downstairs in the middle of the night. ❷ to move along with the body close to the ground
creep NOUN creeps (informal)
a nasty or unpleasant person
➤ **the creeps** (informal) a feeling of fear or disgust

creeper NOUN creepers
a plant that grows along the ground or up trees or walls

creepy ADJECTIVE creepier, creepiest
(informal)
strange and slightly frightening

cremate VERB cremates, cremating,
cremated
If a dead body is cremated, it is burned rather than
buried.

crept VERB (past tense and past participle of **creep**)
• He got up and **crept** down the stairs.

crescendo (say krish-**en**-doh) NOUN
crescendos
a gradual increase in the loudness of a sound

crescent NOUN crescents
a narrow curved shape that is pointed at both ends,
like a new moon

crest NOUN crests
❶ a tuft of hair, feathers or skin on an animal's
head ❷ the top of a hill or wave

crevice NOUN crevices
a crack in rock or in a wall

crew NOUN crews
❶ the people who work on a ship or aircraft
❷ a team of people who work together
• an ambulance **crew**

crib NOUN cribs
❶ a baby's cot ❷ a frame containing hay for animals

cricket NOUN crickets
❶ Cricket is a sport played by two teams with a ball,
bats and wickets. ❷ A cricket is a brown insect like a
grasshopper.

cried VERB (past tense and past participle of **cry**)
• 'Look out!' **cried** Tom.

crime NOUN crimes
an act that breaks the law • He has committed a **crime**.

criminal NOUN criminals
someone who has done something that is a crime
criminal ADJECTIVE
to do with crime or criminals • a **criminal** trial

crimson NOUN, ADJECTIVE
a dark red colour

cringe VERB cringes, cringing, cringed
to move away or shiver slightly because you are
afraid or embarrassed • He **cringed** as if he expected
to be hit.

crinkle VERB crinkles, crinkling, crinkled
to crease or wrinkle • Her eyes **crinkled** as
she smiled.
➤ **crinkly** ADJECTIVE

cripple VERB cripples, crippling, crippled
❶ to make someone unable to walk properly
❷ to damage something so it will not work properly

crisis (say **kry**-sis) NOUN crises
a serious or dangerous situation

crisp ADJECTIVE crisper, crispest
❶ very dry so that it breaks easily • **crisp** autumn
leaves ❷ firm and fresh • a nice **crisp** apple
crisp NOUN crisps
a thin fried slice of potato, sold in packets

critic NOUN critics
❶ a person who criticises someone or something
❷ someone whose job is to give opinions on books,
plays, films or music

critical ADJECTIVE
❶ saying what something's or someone's faults are
• She was **critical** of his work. ❷ very important and
serious • The situation is **critical**.
➤ **critically** ADVERB • He was **critically** ill.

a
b
c
d
e
f
g
h
i
j
k
l
m
n
o
p
q
r
s
t
u
v
w
x
y
z

criticise (also **criticize**) VERB criticises, criticising, criticised
to say what you think someone's or something's faults are

⚠ **WATCH OUT!**
The word **criticise** contains the word **critic** + '-ise'.

criticism (say krit-iss-iz-um) NOUN criticisms
a judgement about something, usually pointing out its faults

croak NOUN croaks
a rough sound like a frog makes
croak VERB croaks, croaking, croaked
to make a rough sound like a frog

crochet (say kroh-shay) NOUN
a way of making things out of wool with a hooked needle

crockery NOUN
dishes, plates, and cups and saucers used for eating

crocodile NOUN crocodiles
a large reptile that lives near rivers in tropical countries, with thick skin, a long tail and big jaws

✳ **WORD STORY**
The word **crocodile** comes from a Greek word meaning 'worm of the stones'.

⚙ **BUILD YOUR VOCABULARY**
Look at **alligator**.

crocus NOUN crocuses
a small spring flower that is yellow, purple or white

crook NOUN crooks
❶ (informal) a criminal ❷ a shepherd's stick with a curved end

crooked (say crook-id) ADJECTIVE
❶ bent or twisted ❷ (informal) dishonest or criminal

croon VERB croons, crooning, crooned
to sing softly or lovingly

crop NOUN crops
❶ a type of plant grown as food • *Wheat is a cereal crop.* ❷ the amount of a food plant that is harvested • *We had a good crop of potatoes.*

crop VERB crops, cropping, cropped
to cut something short • *They cropped his hair.*

cross NOUN crosses
a mark or shape like + or x

cross VERB crosses, crossing, crossed
❶ To cross something is to go across it. • *We crossed the ocean.* ❷ To cross one breed of animal with another is to produce a new animal from them. • *When you cross a horse with a donkey you get a mule.* ❸ To cross your fingers or legs is to put one over the other.
➤ **To cross something out** is to put a line through it because it is unwanted or wrong.

cross ADJECTIVE
annoyed
➤ **crossly** ADVERB ➤ **crossness** NOUN

crossbow NOUN crossbows
a kind of bow for shooting arrows, held and shot like a gun

cross-country NOUN
the sport of racing through fields and paths rather than on a track

crossing NOUN crossings
❶ a place where you can cross a road or railway
❷ a journey by ship across a sea

crossroads NOUN crossroads
a place where two or more roads cross one another

cross-section NOUN cross-sections
a view of something that has been cut through • *The picture shows a cross-section of the earth.*

crossword NOUN crosswords
a puzzle with blank squares in which you put the answers to clues

crotchet (say kroch-it) NOUN crotchets
a musical note equal to half a minim, written ♩

⚙ **BUILD YOUR VOCABULARY**
Look at **minim**, **quaver** and **semibreve**.

crouch VERB crouches, crouching, crouched
to lower your body, with arms and legs bent

crow NOUN crows
a large black bird

crow VERB crows, crowing, crowed
When a cock crows, it makes a loud sound.

crowbar NOUN crowbars
an iron bar used as a lever

crowd NOUN crowds
a large number of people in one place

crowd VERB crowds, crowding, crowded
To crowd round is to form a crowd around someone
or something.

crowded ADJECTIVE
with a lot of people in a place • *The shops were very
crowded.*

crown NOUN crowns
A crown is a special headdress worn by a king or
queen.

crown VERB crowns, crowning, crowned
To crown someone is to make them king or queen.

crow's nest NOUN crow's nests
a lookout position at the top of a ship's mast

crucial (say kroo-shal) ADJECTIVE
extremely important

crucify VERB crucifies, crucifying,
crucified
to execute someone by fixing their hands and feet to
a cross and leaving them to die

⚙ **BUILD YOUR VOCABULARY**
Execution by this method is called **crucifixion** and was
used by the ancient Romans.

crude ADJECTIVE cruder, crudest
❶ rough and simple • *We built a crude shelter.*
❷ rude or vulgar • *crude language* ❸ in a natural
state; not purified • *crude oil*

cruel ADJECTIVE crueller, cruellest
deliberately causing pain and suffering • *They were
ruled by a cruel tyrant.*
➤ **cruelly** ADVERB ➤ **cruelty** NOUN

cruise NOUN cruises
a holiday on a ship, usually visiting different places

cruise VERB cruises, cruising, cruised
to sail or travel at a gentle speed

crumb NOUN crumbs
a tiny piece of bread or cake

crumble VERB crumbles, crumbling,
crumbled
If something crumbles or you crumble it, it breaks
into small pieces.
➤ **crumbly** ADJECTIVE

crumpet NOUN crumpets
a small cake made with yeast that you toast and eat
with butter

crumple VERB crumples, crumpling,
crumpled
If you crumple something or it crumples, it becomes
creased.

crunch NOUN crunches
the noise made by chewing hard food or walking on
gravel or snow
Behind him, he heard the crunch of feet on gravel.
—THE MONSTER OF MUCUS!, Ian Ogilvy

crunch VERB crunches, crunching,
crunched
to chew or crush something with a crunch
➤ **crunchy** ADJECTIVE • *a crunchy biscuit*

crusade NOUN crusades
❶ a Christian military expedition to Palestine in
the Middle Ages ❷ a determined campaign against
something
➤ **crusader** NOUN

crush VERB crushes, crushing, crushed
❶ to press something hard so that it gets broken or
squashed ❷ to completely defeat someone

crust NOUN crusts
❶ the hard outside part of bread ❷ the rocky outer
part of a planet

crustacean (say krus-tay-shan) NOUN
crustaceans
a shellfish, for example a crab, prawn or lobster

✳ **WORD STORY**
The word **crustacean** comes from a Latin word *crusta*
meaning 'shell'.

crutch NOUN crutches
a stick that fits under your arm, used to help you
walk

a b **c** d e f g h i j k l m n o p q r s t u v w x y z

cry VERB cries, crying, cried
❶ to shout • *'Help!' he* **cried**. ❷ to let tears fall from
your eyes • *I* **cried** *at the end of the film.*
cry NOUN cries
a loud shout • *We heard* **cries** *of joy.*

crypt NOUN crypts
an underground room beneath a church, usually used
for burials

crystal NOUN crystals
❶ a small symmetrical piece of a substance, for
example snow or salt ❷ a clear substance similar to
glass

crystallise (*also* **crystallize**) VERB
crystallises, crystallising, crystallised
to form into crystals

cub NOUN cubs
a young animal, especially a lion, tiger, fox or bear

cube NOUN cubes
❶ an object with six square faces,
for example a dice ❷ (*also* **cube
number**) the result of multiplying
something by itself twice • *The
cube of 3 is 3 x 3 x 3 = 27.*

🔵 **BUILD** YOUR VOCABULARY
Look at **square**.

cubed ADJECTIVE
If a number is cubed it is multiplied by itself twice. It
can be written as ^{3}. • *3* **cubed** *or 3^3 = 3 x 3 x 3 = 27.*

🔵 **BUILD** YOUR VOCABULARY
Look at **squared**.

cubic ADJECTIVE
❶ shaped like a cube ❷ used for measurements of
volume. A cubic centimetre is written as cm^3 and a
cubic metre is written as m^3. • *The volume of the box
is 32* **cubic** *centimetres.*

cubicle NOUN cubicles
a small enclosed area, for example for getting
changed

cuboid NOUN cuboids
an object with six rectangular sides

cuckoo NOUN cuckoos
a bird that makes a sound like 'cuck-oo' and lays its
eggs in other birds' nests

cucumber NOUN cucumbers
a long green vegetable that is eaten raw

cud NOUN
half-digested food that a cow brings back from its
first stomach to chew again

cuddle VERB cuddles, cuddling, cuddled
to put your arms around someone and hold them in
a loving way
➤ **cuddly** ADJECTIVE

cue NOUN cues
something that tells an actor when to speak or do
something

⚠ **WATCH OUT!**
Do not confuse with **queue** meaning 'a line waiting
for something'.

cuff NOUN cuffs
the end of a sleeve that fits round your wrist
cuff VERB cuffs, cuffing, cuffed
to hit someone with your hand

culprit NOUN culprits
someone who is to blame for something

cult NOUN cults
a religion, especially one that is small and considered
strange

cultivate VERB cultivates, cultivating,
cultivated
To cultivate land is to grow crops on it.
➤ **cultivation** NOUN

culture NOUN cultures
the ideas, art and customs of a group of people • *I'm
interested in ancient* **cultures**.
➤ **cultural** ADJECTIVE • *The museum is full of
cultural treasures.*

cunning ADJECTIVE
clever, especially at deceiving people

cup NOUN cups
❶ a small container with a handle, for holding a drink
❷ a prize in the form of a metal cup with two
handles
➤ **cupful** NOUN • *Add two* **cupfuls** *of milk.*

cup VERB cups, cupping, cupped
To cup your hands is to form them into the shape of a cup.
John lifted up one of the eggs, cupping it carefully in his hands.—AKIMBO AND THE CROCODILE MAN, Alexander McCall Smith

cupboard (say kub-erd) NOUN cupboards
a compartment or piece of furniture with a door, for storing things

> ⚠ **WATCH OUT!**
> Remember that the word **cupboard** is spelt *cup + board*, although it is not pronounced that way.

cupcake NOUN cupcakes
a small sponge cake, often topped with icing or a mix of butter and icing sugar

curator (say kewr-ay-ter) NOUN curators
someone in charge of the objects in a museum or art gallery

curd NOUN curds
a thick substance formed from milk, used when making cheese

curdle VERB curdles, curdling, curdled
If milk curdles, it thickens and turns sour.

cure VERB cures, curing, cured
❶ To cure someone is to make them better from an illness. ❷ To cure meat or fish is to preserve it, usually with smoke.
cure NOUN cures
something that cures a person or an illness

curfew NOUN curfews
an order to stay indoors after a particular time

curiosity NOUN curiosities
❶ Curiosity is wanting to find out about something.
❷ A curiosity is something unusual and interesting.

curious ADJECTIVE
❶ wanting to find out about things ❷ strange or unusual • *a curious incident*
➤ **curiously** ADVERB

curl NOUN curls
❶ Curls are curly hair. ❷ A curl of something is a curved or coiled shape. • *curls of steam*
curl VERB curls, curling, curled
to form into curls

curly ADJECTIVE curlier, curliest
Curly hair is not straight.

currant NOUN currants
❶ a small black dried fruit made from a grape
❷ a small juicy berry or the bush that produces it

> ⚠ **WATCH OUT!**
> Do not confuse with a **current** meaning 'a flow'.
> A **currant** is a food and is spelt with an 'a', so it might help to think 'I ate a **currant**'.

currency NOUN currencies
A country's currency is the money used there.

current NOUN currents
a flow of water, air or electricity

> ⚠ **WATCH OUT!**
> Do not confuse with a **currant** meaning 'a fruit'. A **current** of water or electricity is spelt with an 'e', so it might help to think of electricity starting with an 'e'.

current ADJECTIVE
happening or existing now • *Who is your current teacher?*
➤ **currently** ADVERB • *The fare into town is currently £1.50.*

curriculum NOUN curriculums, curricula
all the subjects that you study at school

curry NOUN curries
a dish of meat or vegetables cooked with hot spices

> ✳ **WORD STORY**
> The word **curry** comes from a Tamil (Indian language) word *kari* meaning 'hot sauce'.

curse NOUN curses
a spell or wish for someone to be harmed or killed
curse VERB curses, cursing, cursed
❶ to put a harmful spell on someone or something
❷ to use swear words

cursor NOUN cursors
a moving flashing sign on a computer screen, that shows where you are typing

curtain NOUN curtains
a piece of material hung at a window or door or at the front of a stage

curtsy NOUN curtsies
a bend of the knees to show respect

a
b
c
d
e
f
g
h
i
j
k
l
m
n
o
p
q
r
s
t
u
v
w
x
y
z

curtsy *VERB* **curtsies, curtsying, curtsied**
to bend your knees to show respect

curve *NOUN* **curves**
a line that bends smoothly

curve *VERB* **curves, curving, curved**
to bend smoothly

cushion *NOUN* **cushions**
a piece of comfortable soft material covered with fabric

cushion *VERB* **cushions, cushioning, cushioned**
To cushion a fall is to make it less damaging.
• *The mat will* **cushion** *your fall.*

custard *NOUN*
a sweet yellow sauce

custom *NOUN* **customs**
a tradition or a usual way of behaving
• *It is a* **custom** *to eat chocolate at Easter.*

customary *ADJECTIVE*
usual • *She sat in her* **customary** *place.*

customer *NOUN* **customers**
someone who uses a shop, bank or business

cut *VERB* **cuts, cutting, cut**
❶ To cut something is to divide or damage it with something sharp, such as a knife. • *Cut the pizza into eight pieces.* • *I've* **cut** *my finger.*
❷ To cut something is to reduce it.
• *We want to* **cut** *the amount of plastic we use.*
❸ To cut something from a computer document is to remove it. • *I* **cut** *the picture and pasted it on the next page.*

cut *NOUN* **cuts**
a mark or wound made by something sharp • *I've got a* **cut** *on my knee.*

cute *ADJECTIVE* **cuter, cutest**
pretty, attractive or lovable

cutlass *NOUN* **cutlasses**
a short sword with a wide curved blade

cutlery *NOUN*
knives, forks and spoons used for eating

cyberman *NOUN* **cybermen**
In stories, a cyberman is a creature that is part-human and part-robot.

cycle *NOUN* **cycles**
❶ a bicycle ❷ a series of events that are regularly repeated • *Rainfall is part of the water* **cycle**.

cycle *VERB* **cycles, cycling, cycled**
To cycle is to ride a bicycle.
➤ **cyclist** *NOUN*

cyclone *NOUN* **cyclones**
a strong wind that blows in a spiral

Cyclops (*say* **sy**-klops) *NOUN*
a monster in Greek mythology with one eye

cygnet (*say* **sig**-nit) *NOUN* **cygnets**
a young swan

cylinder *NOUN* **cylinders**
an object with straight sides and circular ends

cylindrical *ADJECTIVE*
shaped like a cylinder

cymbal *NOUN* **cymbals**
a metal plate that you hit to make a ringing sound in music

BUILD YOUR VOCABULARY
A **cymbal** is a **percussion** instrument.

cypress *NOUN* **cypresses**
an evergreen tree with dark leaves

Cyclops

D is for **dream**, which has two past tenses: *dreamt* (pronounced /dremt/) and *dreamed*. Both are correct, but British people are more likely to use **dreamt** and Americans are more likely to use **dreamed**.

For more UK/US differences, look at the back of the dictionary.

D *ABBREVIATION*
500 in Roman numerals

dab *VERB* **dabs, dabbing, dabbed**
to touch something gently • *I dabbed my eyes with a tissue.*

dachshund *(say* daks-hund*) NOUN* **dachshunds**
a small dog with a long body and short legs

dad *(also* **daddy***) NOUN* **dads, daddies** *(informal)*
father

daddy-long-legs *NOUN* **daddy-long-legs**
another name for a **cranefly**

daffodil *NOUN* **daffodils**
a yellow flower that grows from a bulb

daft *ADJECTIVE* **dafter, daftest**
silly or stupid

dagger *NOUN* **daggers**
a short pointed knife, used as a weapon

dahlia *(say* day-lee-a*) NOUN* **dahlias**
a garden plant with brightly coloured flowers

daily *ADJECTIVE, ADVERB*
something that happens daily happens every day

dainty *ADJECTIVE* **daintier, daintiest**
small and delicate
➤ **daintily** *ADVERB* ➤ **daintiness** *NOUN*

dairy *NOUN* **dairies**
a place where milk, butter, cream and cheese are made or sold
dairy *ADJECTIVE*
Dairy foods are made from milk.

daisy *NOUN* **daisies**
a small flower with white petals and a yellow centre

✱ **WORD STORY**
The word **daisy** comes from Old English words meaning 'day's eye', because the petals open in the morning and close at night.

daisy chain *NOUN* **daisy chains**
a string of daisies linked together by their stems

dale *NOUN* **dales**
a valley

Dalmatian *NOUN* **Dalmatians**
a large dog that is white with black or brown spots

dam *NOUN* **dams**
a wall built across a river to hold the water back
dam *VERB* **dams, damming, dammed**
To dam a river is to build a dam across it.

damage *VERB* **damages, damaging, damaged**
To damage something is to harm or break it.
damage *NOUN*
Damage is injury or harm. • *The storm caused a lot of damage.*

damp *ADJECTIVE* **damper, dampest**
slightly wet
damp *NOUN*
Damp, or the damp, is wetness in the air or on something.
➤ **dampness** *NOUN*

dampen *VERB* **dampens, dampening, dampened**
❶ To dampen something is to make it damp.
❷ To dampen a feeling is to make it less strong.

damson *NOUN* **damsons**
a small purple plum or the tree it grows on

a
b
c
d
e
f
g
h
i
j
k
l
m
n
o
p
q
r
s
t
u
v
w
x
y
z

dance VERB dances, dancing, danced
to move about in time to music
➤ **dancer** NOUN

dance NOUN dances
❶ a set of dancing movements • *She did a little dance.* ❷ a party where people dance

dandelion NOUN dandelions
a wild plant with bright yellow flowers that turn into fluffy seeds

✳ **WORD STORY**

The word **dandelion** comes from French words meaning 'lion's tooth', because of its jagged leaves.

danger NOUN dangers
a dangerous situation or thing

dangerous ADJECTIVE
likely to harm you • *It is **dangerous** to climb on the roof.*
➤ **dangerously** ADVERB

dangle VERB dangles, dangling, dangled
to swing or hang down loosely

dank ADJECTIVE danker, dankest
A dank place is damp and cold.

dappled ADJECTIVE
marked with patches of different colours

dare VERB dares, daring, dared
❶ To dare to do something is to be brave enough to do it. • *I didn't **dare** say anything.* ❷ To dare someone to do something is to challenge them to do it. • *I **dare** you to ring the doorbell.*
➤ **daring** ADJECTIVE • *her **daring** adventures*

dark ADJECTIVE darker, darkest
❶ with little or no light • *a **dark** room*
❷ A dark colour is near to black. • *a **dark** green coat*

dark NOUN
Dark, or the dark, is when there is no light. • *Cats can see in the **dark**.*
➤ **darkness** NOUN • *They peered into the **darkness**.*

darken VERB darkens, darkening, darkened
❶ To darken something is to make it dark.
❷ To darken is to become dark. • *The sky suddenly darkened.*

darling NOUN darlings
a word for someone you love

darn VERB darns, darning, darned
To darn a hole is to mend it by sewing across it.

dart NOUN darts
an object with a sharp point that you throw at a dartboard in the game of **darts**

dart VERB darts, darting, darted
to run very quickly and lightly
Daniel Holmes darted through the Saturday shopping crowds in Glasgow, pushing and twisting and weaving.—THE NOWHERE EMPORIUM, Ross MacKenzie

dash VERB dashes, dashing, dashed
to run or rush somewhere
dash NOUN dashes
❶ a quick run or rush • *They made a **dash** for the door.* ❷ a short line (–) that is sometimes used instead of brackets

dashboard NOUN dashboards
a panel with dials and controls in a car

data (say **day**-ta) NOUN
information, for example numbers or facts
• *Record your **data** in a graph.*

database NOUN databases
a store of information held in a computer

date NOUN dates
❶ the day or year when something happens or happened ❷ an arrangement to go out with someone ❸ a sweet brown fruit that grows on a palm tree

date VERB dates, dating, dated
❶ To date something is to put the date on it.
• *The letter was dated 5th May.* ❷ To date from a time is to have existed from then. • *The church dates from the 15th century.*

daughter NOUN daughters
Someone's daughter is their female child.

dawdle VERB dawdles, dawdling, dawdled
to walk or do something too slowly

dawn NOUN dawns
the time of day when the sun rises
dawn VERB dawns, dawning, dawned
❶ When day dawns, it becomes light. ❷ If something dawns on you, you begin to realise it.

day NOUN days
❶ a period of 24 hours between midnight and the next midnight ❷ the light part of the day
❸ a period in time • *In Grandma's day they didn't have computers.*

daybreak NOUN
the time when it becomes light

⚙ **BUILD YOUR VOCABULARY**
A synonym is **dawn**.

daydream VERB daydreams, daydreaming, daydreamed
to have pleasant thoughts about things you would like to happen

daylight NOUN
❶ the light of day ❷ dawn • *They left before daylight.*

⚙ **BUILD YOUR VOCABULARY**
A synonym is **daybreak**.

daytime NOUN
the time between sunrise and sunset

daze NOUN
➤ **in a daze** unable to think or see clearly

dazed ADJECTIVE
unable to think or see clearly

dazzle VERB dazzles, dazzling, dazzled
If light dazzles you, it is so bright that you cannot see for a while.
➤ **dazzling** ADJECTIVE

dead ADJECTIVE
❶ no longer alive ❷ no longer working or active
• *The engine was dead.*

deaden VERB deadens, deadening, deadened
To deaden pain or noise is to make it weaker.

dead end NOUN dead ends
a road or passage that is closed at one end

deadline NOUN deadlines
the time by which you must finish doing something

deadly ADJECTIVE deadlier, deadliest
likely to kill • *The bottle contained a deadly poison.*

deaf ADJECTIVE deafer, deafest
unable to hear
➤ **deafness** NOUN

deafen VERB deafens, deafening, deafened
If noise deafens you, it is so loud that you cannot hear for a while.
The buzzing was so loud now that Dinah was almost deafened by it.—REVENGE OF THE DEMON HEADMASTER, Gillian Cross

deal VERB deals, dealing, dealt
To deal things is to hand them out. • *Deal the cards.*
➤ **To deal with something** is to do what must be done to sort it out. • *She dealt with the problem.*
deal NOUN deals
an agreement or bargain
➤ **a good deal** or **a great deal** a large amount
• *They lost a great deal of money.*

dear ADJECTIVE dearer, dearest
❶ 'Dear' is the usual way to begin a letter.
• *Dear Auntie Fran* ❷ expensive
dear NOUN dears
a word for someone you like or love • *Thank you, dear.*

dearly ADVERB
very much • *I would dearly love to know.*

death NOUN deaths
the end of life, when someone or something dies

deathly ADJECTIVE, ADVERB
as quiet, as pale or as cold as death • *The silence was deathly.* • *He looked deathly pale.*

a b c d e f g h i j k l m n o p q r s t u v w x y z

debate *NOUN* **debates**
a formal discussion about a subject

debate *VERB* **debates, debating, debated**
to discuss or argue about something

debris *(say* **deb**-ree*)* *NOUN*
scattered pieces that are left after something has been destroyed

debt *(say* det*)* *NOUN* **debts**
something that someone owes
➤ **in debt** owing money

debut *(say* **day**-bew *or* **day**-boo*)* *NOUN* **debuts**
someone's first public appearance or performance

decade *NOUN* **decades**
a period of ten years

⁕ **WORD STORY**
Decade comes from the Latin *deca-* meaning 'ten'.

decay *VERB* **decays, decaying, decayed**
to rot or go bad
decay *NOUN*
the process of going bad or rotting

deceased *(say* de-**seest***)* *ADJECTIVE (formal)*
A deceased person has died.

deceit *(say* de-**seet***)* *NOUN*
Deceit is telling lies or doing something dishonest.
➤ **deceitful** *ADJECTIVE*

deceive *(say* de-**seev***)* *VERB* **deceives, deceiving, deceived**
to make someone believe something that is not true

○ **BUILD** YOUR **VOCABULARY**
Look at **deception**.

decency *NOUN*
respectable and honest behaviour

decent *ADJECTIVE*
❶ respectable and honest • *He's a **decent** man.*
❷ fairly good • *The food was **decent**.*
➤ **decently** *ADVERB*

deception *NOUN* **deceptions**
❶ Deception is making someone believe something that is not true. ❷ A deception is a trick or a lie.

decibel *NOUN* **decibels**
a unit for measuring how loud a sound is

decide *VERB* **decides, deciding, decided**
❶ to make up your mind about something or make a choice • *I **decided** to go.* ❷ To decide a contest or argument is to settle it.

decidedly *ADVERB*
very or definitely • *He felt **decidedly** odd.*

deciduous *ADJECTIVE*
a deciduous tree loses its leaves in autumn

○ **BUILD** YOUR **VOCABULARY**
Look at **evergreen**.

decimal *ADJECTIVE*
a decimal system uses tens or tenths to count things
decimal *NOUN* **decimals**
a decimal fraction

decimal fraction *NOUN* **decimal fractions**
a number with tenths shown as numbers after a dot, for example is 0.5 (the same as $\frac{1}{2}$) or 1.25 (the same as $1\frac{1}{4}$)

decimal point *NOUN* **decimal points**
the dot in a decimal fraction

decipher *(say* de-**sy**-fer*)* *VERB* **deciphers, deciphering, deciphered**
to work out the meaning of something that is difficult to read

decision *NOUN* **decisions**
something that someone has decided

decisive *ADJECTIVE*
❶ A decisive person makes quick and firm decisions. ❷ A decisive event ends or decides something important. • *It was a **decisive** victory.*

deck *NOUN* **decks**
a floor on a ship or bus

declare *VERB* **declares, declaring, declared**
to say something clearly and openly
➤ **declaration** *NOUN*

decline *VERB* **declines, declining, declined**
❶ to become weaker or smaller ❷ To decline an offer is to refuse it politely.

decode *VERB* **decodes, decoding, decoded**
to work out the meaning of something, especially something that is written in code

decompose VERB decomposes, decomposing, decomposed
to decay or rot
➤ **decomposition** NOUN

decorate VERB decorates, decorating, decorated
❶ to make something look more beautiful or colourful ❷ To decorate a room is to put new paint or paper on the walls.
➤ **decoration** NOUN

decorative ADJECTIVE
used to make something look pretty or more colourful

decoy NOUN decoys
something used to tempt a person or animal into a trap

decrease (say de-**crease**) VERB decreases, decreasing, decreased
If something decreases or you decrease it, it becomes smaller or less.

BUILD YOUR VOCABULARY
An opposite is **increase**.

decrease (say de-**crease**) NOUN decreases
the act of decreasing • There has been a **decrease** in crime.

BUILD YOUR VOCABULARY
An opposite is **increase**.

decree NOUN decrees
an official order or decision

decree VERB decrees, decreeing, decreed
to give an official order that something must happen

dedicate VERB dedicates, dedicating, dedicated
❶ If you dedicate yourself or your life to something, you give your time to it. • He **dedicated** his life to helping animals.

BUILD YOUR VOCABULARY
A synonym is **devote**.

❷ To dedicate a book to someone is write at the beginning that it is written for them.
➤ **dedication** NOUN

deduce VERB deduces, deducing, deduced
to work out a fact or answer from what you already know is true • I **deduced** that she was his sister.

deduction NOUN deductions
something that you work out by deducing • We can make a **deduction** about the size of the missing angle.

deed NOUN deeds
❶ something that someone has done • a brave **deed** ❷ a legal document that shows who owns something

deep ADJECTIVE deeper, deepest
❶ going down a long way • a **deep** river ❷ measured from top to bottom • The water is 2cm **deep**. ❸ intense or strong • **deep** sorrow ❹ low in pitch • a **deep** voice
➤ **deepen** VERB • The pool **deepens** here.
➤ **deeply** ADVERB • She was **deeply** upset.

deer NOUN deer
a wild animal with hooves that can run fast

BUILD YOUR VOCABULARY
A male deer is called a **stag** and has **antlers**. A female deer is called a **doe**.

defeat VERB defeats, defeating, defeated
to beat someone in a game or battle

defeat NOUN defeats
❶ Defeat is losing a game or battle. ❷ A defeat is a lost game or battle.

defect NOUN defects
a flaw or fault

defence NOUN defences
❶ A defence is something that protects you. • High walls were built as a **defence** against the enemy. ❷ the act of defending someone or something against attack or criticism • My friend came to my **defence**.

defend VERB defends, defending, defended
❶ to protect someone or something from an attack ❷ to argue in support of a person or an idea
➤ **defender** NOUN

defiant ADJECTIVE
openly showing that you refuse to obey
➤ **defiance** NOUN ➤ **defiantly** ADVERB

a b c d e f g h i j k l m n o p q r s t u v w x y z

define VERB defines, defining, defined
to say exactly what something means or what
it is

definite ADJECTIVE
certain or clear • We can't give a **definite** answer
yet.

> ⚠ **WATCH OUT!**
> There are two 'i's in **definite**. Think of the word
> *finished* to help you remember.

definite article NOUN definite articles
the word *the*

> ⚙ **BUILD** YOUR VOCABULARY
> Look at **indefinite article**.

definitely ADVERB
certainly, without doubt • I'll **definitely** be
there!

definition NOUN definitions
an explanation of what a word means

deflate VERB deflates, deflating, deflated
to let air out of something such as a tyre
or ball

> ⚙ **BUILD** YOUR VOCABULARY
> The opposite is **inflate**.

deflect VERB deflects, deflecting, deflected
To deflect something that is moving is to make it go
in a different direction.
➤ **deflection** NOUN

deforestation NOUN
the cutting down of a large number of trees in an
area

deformed ADJECTIVE
not properly shaped

deft ADJECTIVE defter, deftest
skilful and quick
➤ **deftly** ADVERB

defy VERB defies, defying, defied
To defy someone or something is to refuse to
obey them.

> ⚙ **BUILD** YOUR VOCABULARY
> Look at **defiant**.

degree NOUN degrees
❶ a unit for measuring temperature • Water boils at
100 **degrees** Celsius or 100°C. ❷ a unit for measuring
angles • There are 90 **degrees** (90°) in a right angle.
❸ an amount of something • They showed varying
degrees of enthusiasm. ❹ a qualification gained
after studying at university

dehydrated ADJECTIVE
weak or ill from lack of water

deity (say **day**-it-ee) NOUN deities
a god or goddess

dejected ADJECTIVE
sad or depressed
➤ **dejection** NOUN

delay VERB delays, delaying, delayed
❶ to make someone late or slow something down
• The train has been **delayed**. ❷ to wait before doing
something • Don't **delay**!

delay NOUN delays
If there is a delay, something happens after a wait
or pause. • There was a 10-minute **delay** before the
match started.

delete VERB deletes, deleting, deleted
to cross something out or remove it
➤ **deletion** NOUN

deliberate ADJECTIVE
❶ done on purpose • It was a **deliberate** lie.
❷ slow and careful • He has a **deliberate** way
of talking.
➤ **deliberately** ADVERB

delicacy NOUN delicacies
❶ A delicacy is something small and tasty to eat.
❷ Delicacy is being delicate.

delicate ADJECTIVE
❶ fine and graceful or easily damaged • **delicate**
china cups ❷ a delicate situation needs great care
➤ **delicately** ADVERB

delicatessen NOUN delicatessens
a shop that sells cooked meats, cheeses, salads, etc.

delicious ADJECTIVE
tasting or smelling very pleasant

delight VERB delights, delighting, delighted
to please someone a lot

delight NOUN delights
great pleasure
➤ **delighted** ADJECTIVE

delightful ADJECTIVE
giving great pleasure • *What a delightful surprise!*
➤ **delightfully** ADVERB

delirious ADJECTIVE
in a confused state of mind because you are ill or have a high fever
➤ **deliriously** ADVERB

deliver VERB delivers, delivering, delivered
❶ to take and give something to someone
• *I delivered a message for him.* ❷ To deliver a speech is to give it.

delivery NOUN deliveries
A delivery is when letters, goods, etc. are brought and given to someone.

delta NOUN deltas
a triangular area at the mouth of a river where it spreads into branches

deluge NOUN deluges
❶ a very heavy fall of rain ❷ something coming in great numbers • *There was a deluge of questions.*

demand VERB demands, demanding, demanded
to ask for something or ask a question in a forceful way

demand NOUN demands
❶ a very firm request ❷ If there is demand for something, people want to buy or use it.
• *Demand for electricity is lower at night.*

democracy NOUN democracies
a system of government in which the people elect their leaders
➤ **democratic** ADJECTIVE

demolish VERB demolishes, demolishing, demolished
To demolish a building is to knock it down.
➤ **demolition** NOUN

demon NOUN demons
a devil or evil spirit

demonstrate VERB demonstrates, demonstrating, demonstrated
❶ To demonstrate something is to show it or show how it works. ❷ To demonstrate is to take part in a protest.
➤ **demonstrator** NOUN

demonstration NOUN demonstrations
❶ If you give a demonstration, you show how to do or work something. ❷ a march or meeting to protest about something

den NOUN dens
❶ the home of a wild animal • *a lion's den*
❷ a hiding place, especially for children

denial NOUN denials
❶ a statement that something is not true
❷ the denial of a request is a refusal

denim NOUN
strong cotton cloth, used to make jeans

denominator NOUN denominators
the number below the line in a fraction. In $\frac{1}{4}$ the denominator is the number 4.

BUILD YOUR VOCABULARY
Look at **numerator**.

dense ADJECTIVE **denser, densest**
❶ with a lot of people or things in a small area
• *a dense forest* ❷ thick • *There was a dense fog.*
➤ **densely** ADVERB • *a densely populated area*

density NOUN **densities**
how many or how much of something there is in a space

dent NOUN **dents**
a hollow in a surface made by hitting or pressing
dent VERB **dents, denting, dented**
to make a dent in something

dental ADJECTIVE
to do with teeth

dentist NOUN **dentists**
a person who is qualified to care for teeth

deny VERB **denies, denying, denied**
❶ To deny something is to say that it is not true.
❷ To deny a request is to refuse it.

BUILD YOUR VOCABULARY
Look at **denial**.

deodorant NOUN **deodorants**
a substance for hiding or preventing unpleasant smells

depart VERB **departs, departing, departed**
to go away or leave
➤ **departure** NOUN

department NOUN **departments**
one part of a large organisation or shop

department store NOUN **department stores**
a large shop that sells many different kinds of goods

depend VERB **depends, depending, depended**
➤ **To depend on someone** or **something** is to need them. • *They depend on the river for their water.*
➤ **To depend on something** is to be decided or controlled by it. • *How long it takes depends on how fast you can type.*

dependable ADJECTIVE
reliable

dependent ADJECTIVE
needing someone to help you or provide something
• *Many baby animals are dependent on their mothers.*

BUILD YOUR VOCABULARY
The opposite is **independent**.

depict VERB **depicts, depicting, depicted**
to show something in a picture or describe it in a story

deposit NOUN **deposits**
an amount of money you pay as the first part of a bigger payment

depot (say dep-oh) NOUN **depots**
❶ a place where things are stored ❷ a place where buses or trains are kept and repaired

depressed ADJECTIVE
feeling very sad and without hope

depression NOUN **depressions**
❶ a feeling of great sadness and lack of hope
❷ a shallow hollow or dip in the ground

deprive VERB **deprives, depriving, deprived**
To deprive someone of something is to take it away from them. • *Prisoners are deprived of their freedom.*

depth NOUN **depths**
The depth of something is how deep it is. • *What is the depth of the river here?*
➤ **in depth** thoroughly
➤ **out of your depth** ❶ You are **out of your depth** if you are in water that is too deep to stand in.
❷ You are **out of your depth** if you are trying to do something that is too difficult for you.

deputy NOUN **deputies**
a person who helps someone in their work and does their job when they are away

derail VERB **derails, derailing, derailed**
If a train is derailed, something causes it to leave the track.

derelict (say deh-rel-ikt) ADJECTIVE
abandoned and falling into ruin • *The factory is completely derelict.*

derision NOUN
scorn or ridicule • *She gave a snort of derision.*

derive *VERB* **derives, deriving, derived**
To derive something from somewhere is to get it from there. • *The word 'photography' is **derived** from the Greek words for light and writing.*

descend *VERB* **descends, descending, descended**
to go down something • *He **descended** the ladder.*
➤ **To be descended from someone** is to be in the same family as them but living at a later time.

descendant *NOUN* **descendants**
A person's descendants are the people who are descended from them.

descent *NOUN* **descents**
A descent is a climb down, usually a hard or long one.

⚠ **WATCH OUT!**
Descent is related to **descend** and is spelt in the same way.

describe *VERB* **describes, describing, described**
to say what someone or something is like

description *NOUN* **descriptions**
an account of what someone or something is like • *He gave the police a **description** of the man.*

desert *(say* dez-ert*) NOUN* **deserts**
a large area of very dry, often sandy, land
desert *(say* diz-ert*) VERB* **deserts, deserting, deserted**
to leave someone who needs you

⚠ **WATCH OUT!**
Do not confuse the verb **desert** with the noun **dessert** meaning 'pudding', which is pronounced the same but spelt with double 's'.

deserted *ADJECTIVE*
If a place is deserted, there is nobody there.

desert island *NOUN* **desert islands**
a tropical island where nobody lives

deserve *VERB* **deserves, deserving, deserved**
to be worthy of something or have a right to it
• *You **deserve** a treat after all that work.*

design *NOUN* **designs**
❶ the way that something is made or arranged • *The car has a very clever **design**.* ❷ a drawing that shows how something is to be made ❸ a pattern of lines and shapes • *a pretty floral **design***
design *VERB* **designs, designing, designed**
to make a design or plan for something
➤ **designer** *NOUN* • *a clothes **designer***

desirable *ADJECTIVE*
worth having or doing • *It's a very **desirable** bike.*

desire *NOUN* **desires**
a feeling of wanting something very much
desire *VERB* **desires, desiring, desired**
to want something

desk *NOUN* **desks**
❶ a table for writing or working at ❷ a counter where you go for information

desktop *NOUN* **desktops**
❶ the main screen of a computer • *Click the icon on your **desktop**.* ❷ a computer designed to be used on a desk and not carried around

desolate *ADJECTIVE*
❶ feeling lonely and sad ❷ A desolate place is empty and bleak.
They had come to the edge of a clearing in the wood, a desolate place like a quarry strewn with boulders.
—THE LITTLE WHITE HORSE, Elizabeth Goudge

a b c d e f g h i j k l m n o p q r s t u v w x y z

despair *NOUN*
complete loss of hope

despair *VERB* despairs, despairing, despaired
To despair is to lose hope completely.

despatch *NOUN, VERB*
another spelling of **dispatch**

desperate *ADJECTIVE*
❶ ready to do anything to get out of a difficulty
• *I was so **desperate** I asked everyone to help.*
❷ A desperate situation is extremely serious or hopeless. ❸ needing or wanting something very much • *I'm **desperate** for some chocolate.*
➤ **desperately** *ADVERB* • *'Please don't go,' he said **desperately**.*

despicable *ADJECTIVE*
very unpleasant or evil
➤ **despicably** *ADVERB*

despise *VERB* despises, despising, despised
to hate someone or something and have no respect for them

despite *PREPOSITION*
in spite of • *They went out **despite** the rain.*

dessert *(say diz-ert)* *NOUN* desserts
fruit or a sweet food eaten at the end of a meal

⚠ **WATCH OUT!**
Dessert meaning 'sweet food' has a double 's'. Think of a double helping of dessert to help you remember!

destination *NOUN* destinations
the place you are travelling to

destined *ADJECTIVE*
intended by fate • *He felt he was **destined** to succeed.*

destiny *NOUN* destinies
Your destiny is what is intended for you by fate.
• *It was their **destiny** to meet.*

destroy *VERB* destroys, destroying, destroyed
to completely ruin something or put an end to it

destruction *NOUN*
Destruction is completely destroying something.
• *the **destruction** of the rainforests*

destructive *ADJECTIVE*
causing a lot of damage

detach *VERB* detaches, detaching, detached
to remove or separate something • *A leaf **detached** itself from the tree.*

⚙ **BUILD YOUR VOCABULARY**
The opposite is **attach**.

detached *ADJECTIVE*
not emotionally involved in a situation • *She watched with a **detached** air.*

detail *NOUN* details
a small, particular fact or feature • *I don't need to know all the **details**.*
➤ **in detail** describing or dealing with everything fully

detailed *ADJECTIVE*
including a lot of small exact facts or features
• *It was a very **detailed** description.*

detain *VERB* detains, detaining, detained
to make someone stay in a place

detect *VERB* detects, detecting, detected
to discover or notice something

detective *NOUN* detectives
a person, especially a police officer, who investigates crimes

detector *NOUN* detectors
a device that can tell you if something is there
• *a smoke **detector***

detention *NOUN* detentions
❶ the punishment of being made to stay late at school ❷ being made to stay somewhere, for example because you are under arrest

deter *VERB* deters, deterring, deterred
to put someone off doing something • *The alarm **deters** burglars.*

detergent *NOUN* detergents
a substance for washing or cleaning something

deteriorate *VERB* deteriorates, deteriorating, deteriorated
To deteriorate is to become worse. • *The weather started to **deteriorate**.*
➤ **deterioration** *NOUN*

determination *NOUN*
a firm intention to do something, even if it is difficult

determined *ADJECTIVE*
firmly intending to do something even if it is difficult

determiner *NOUN* determiners
a word that goes before a noun and any adjectives, for example *a*, *the*, *some* and *many*

BUILD YOUR VOCABULARY
Determiner is a **word class**.

detest *VERB* detests, detesting, detested
to dislike someone or something very much
➤ **detestable** *ADJECTIVE*

detonate *VERB* detonates, detonating, detonated
To detonate a bomb is to make it explode.

detour *NOUN* detours
a roundabout route you use instead of the normal route

devastate *VERB* devastates, devastating, devastated
① to destroy or very severely damage a place
② to make someone extremely upset
➤ **devastation** *NOUN*

develop *VERB* develops, developing, developed
① To develop something is to create it or make it more advanced. • *He developed a new type of camera.* ② To develop is to grow or become more advanced. • *A friendship developed between them.*

development *NOUN* developments
a change or advance • *new developments in computing*

device *NOUN* devices
a piece of equipment • *You plug the device in here.*

devil *NOUN* devils
an evil spirit or person

devious *ADJECTIVE*
dishonest, secretive and clever in an unpleasant way

devise *VERB* devises, devising, devised
To devise a plan or idea is to think it up.

devote *VERB* devotes, devoting, devoted
If you devote yourself or your life to something, you give your time to it. • *He devoted his life to caring for others.*

BUILD YOUR VOCABULARY
A synonym is **dedicate**.

devoted *ADJECTIVE*
loving and loyal • *They are devoted parents.*
➤ **devotion** *NOUN*

devour *VERB* devours, devouring, devoured
to eat something greedily

devout *ADJECTIVE*
very religious

dew *NOUN*
tiny drops of water that form on the ground at night
➤ **dewy** *ADJECTIVE*

diabetes (*say* dy-a-bee-teez) *NOUN*
a disease in which there is too much sugar in a person's blood because their body does not have enough of a chemical called insulin

diabetic (*say* dy-a-bet-ik) *NOUN* diabetics
a person suffering from diabetes
➤ **diabetic** *ADJECTIVE*

diabolical *ADJECTIVE*
very wicked or like a devil

diagnose *VERB* diagnoses, diagnosing, diagnosed
to find out what disease someone has

diagonal *NOUN* diagonals
a straight line joining opposite corners
diagonal *ADJECTIVE*
slanting or going from one corner to an opposite corner
➤ **diagonally** *ADVERB*

diagram *NOUN* diagrams
a drawing or picture that shows the parts of something or how it works

dial *NOUN* dials
a circular part of a machine with numbers or letters round it
dial *VERB* dials, dialling, dialled
To dial a number is to call it on a phone.

dialect NOUN dialects
the form of a language used by people in one area of a country

dialogue NOUN dialogues
talk between people, especially in a play, film or book

diameter NOUN diameters
a straight line or the distance from one side of a circle to the other, passing through the centre

BUILD YOUR VOCABULARY
Look at **circumference** and **radius**.

diamond NOUN diamonds
❶ a very hard jewel that looks like clear glass ❷ A shape which has four equal sides but is not a square.

BUILD YOUR VOCABULARY
Look at **rhombus**.

diarrhoea (say dy-a-ree-a) NOUN
an illness that affects your bowels and makes the waste matter from them watery

diary NOUN diaries
a book or electronic resource in which you write down what happens each day or what you have to do on future days

dice NOUN dice
a small cube marked with one to six dots on each side, used for playing games

dictate VERB dictates, dictating, dictated
❶ To dictate something is to speak or read it aloud for someone else to write down. ❷ To dictate to someone is to give them orders in a bossy way.

dictator NOUN dictators
a single ruler who has complete power

dictionary NOUN dictionaries
a book or electronic resource with words listed in alphabetical order with their meanings

did VERB (past tense of **do**)
• She **did** a little dance.

die VERB dies, dying, died
to stop living
➤ **To die down** is to become less strong. • The wind died down at last.
➤ **To die out** is to disappear completely. • Why did dinosaurs **die out**?

diet NOUN diets
❶ If someone is on a diet, they eat special foods or less food to be healthy or to lose weight. • He had to go on a **diet**. ❷ Someone's diet is the food they normally eat.

differ VERB differs, differing, differed
to be different • Opinions **differ** about why this happens.

difference NOUN differences
❶ the way in which something is different from something else • What is the **difference** between a frog and a toad? ❷ the number you get when you take one number away from another • The **difference** between 23 and 40 is 17.

different ADJECTIVE
If one person or thing is different from another, they are not the same. • The brothers are completely **different**.
➤ **differently** ADVERB

difficult ADJECTIVE
not easy to do, deal with or understand

difficulty NOUN difficulties
❶ A difficulty is a problem. ❷ Difficulty is trouble. • I had **difficulty** standing on the ice.

dig VERB digs, digging, dug
❶ to make a hole in earth or sand • We **dug** a tunnel. ❷ to poke something or push something into it • He **dug** his toes into the sand.

dig NOUN digs
❶ a hard push or poke • She gave me a **dig** in the ribs. ❷ a place where archaeologists dig to look for ancient remains

digest VERB digests, digesting, digested
To digest food is to break it down in the body so it can be absorbed.
➤ **digestion** NOUN

digestive ADJECTIVE
to do with digesting food • *the digestive system*

digit *(say* dij-it*)* NOUN **digits**
❶ any of the numbers from 0 to 9 ❷ a finger or toe

digital ADJECTIVE
❶ A digital camera, television or other device stores and produces images or sound in an electronic way, using binary digits. ❷ A digital clock or watch shows time with a row of numbers, not hands pointing around a circle.

BUILD YOUR VOCABULARY
The other type of clock, watch or device is **analogue**.

dignified ADJECTIVE
calm and serious in a way that makes people feel respect

dignity NOUN
a quality that makes people feel respect

dilemma NOUN **dilemmas**
a difficult situation in which there is a choice between two bad options

dilute VERB **dilutes, diluting, diluted**
To dilute a liquid is to make it weaker by mixing it with water.

dim ADJECTIVE **dimmer, dimmest**
faint or not bright, so it is difficult to see
➤ **dimly** ADVERB • *a dimly lit hall*
dim VERB **dims, dimming, dimmed**
If a light dims or you dim it, it becomes less bright.

dimension NOUN **dimensions**
a measurement such as length, width, area or volume • *What are the dimensions of the box?*

diminish VERB **diminishes, diminishing, diminished**
To diminish or to be diminished is to become smaller.

dimple NOUN **dimples**
a small hollow place on a person's cheek or chin

din NOUN
a loud noise
The din of the machines was nearly deafening.
—LYDIA'S TIN LID DRUM, Neale Osborne

dine VERB **dines, dining, dined**
To dine is to have dinner.

dinghy *(say* ding-ee*)* NOUN **dinghies**
a kind of small boat

dingy *(say* din-jee*)* ADJECTIVE **dingier, dingiest**
shabby and dirty-looking

dinner NOUN **dinners**
the main meal of the day, eaten either in the evening or in the middle of the day

dinosaur NOUN **dinosaurs**
a large prehistoric reptile

WORD STORY
The word **dinosaur** comes from Greek words meaning 'terrible lizard'.

dip VERB **dips, dipping, dipped**
❶ To dip something into a liquid is to put it in and then take it out again.
• *I dipped my brush in the paint.*
❷ To dip is to go or slope downwards.
• *The ground dipped suddenly.*
dip NOUN **dips**
❶ a hollow or downward slope
• *They bumped over a dip in the track.* ❷ a quick swim
• *I had a dip in the pool.*

diplodocus *(say* dip-lo-**do**-cus *or* dip-**lod**-oc-us*)* NOUN
a large plant-eating dinosaur with a long slender neck and tail

diploma NOUN **diplomas**
a certificate awarded for completing a course of study

a b c d e f g h i j k l m n o p q r s t u v w x y z

diplomatic *ADJECTIVE*
❶ related to the official work of keeping friendly relations between countries ❷ tactful and polite, so people are not upset • *I was trying to be **diplomatic**.*

dire *ADJECTIVE* **direr, direst**
very bad or serious • *They are in **dire** need of help.*

direct *ADJECTIVE*
❶ as straight or quick as possible • *We took the **direct** route.* ❷ frank and honest
➤ **directly** *ADVERB* • *She went **directly** home.*

> **BUILD YOUR VOCABULARY**
> An opposite is **indirect**.

direct *VERB* **directs, directing, directed**
❶ To direct someone is to show them the way.
❷ To direct a film or play is to decide how it should be made and performed.

direction *NOUN* **directions**
❶ the way someone or something is going • *He went in that **direction**.* ❷ Directions are information on how to get somewhere or how to do something. • *She gave us **directions** to the train station.*

director *NOUN* **directors**
❶ a person who is in charge of a company
❷ a person who decides how a film or play should be made and performed

directory *NOUN* **directories**
a book or website that lists names, addresses and telephone numbers

direct speech *NOUN*
someone's words written down exactly in the way they were said using inverted commas, for example *'I want to go home,' said Josh*

> **BUILD YOUR VOCABULARY**
> Look at **indirect speech** and **inverted commas**.

dirt *NOUN*
❶ A substance that is not clean. ❷ earth or soil

dirty *ADJECTIVE* **dirtier, dirtiest**
❶ covered with dirt ❷ unfair or unpleasant
• *That was a **dirty** trick.*

disability *NOUN* **disabilities**
something that prevents someone from using their body in the way most people can

disabled *ADJECTIVE*
having a disease or injury that makes it harder for someone to do something

disadvantage *NOUN* **disadvantages**
a bad feature or something that makes things difficult

disagree *VERB* **disagrees, disagreeing, disagreed**
to have or express a different opinion from someone else
➤ **disagreement** *NOUN*

disagreeable *ADJECTIVE*
unpleasant

> **BUILD YOUR VOCABULARY**
> An opposite is **agreeable**.

disappear *VERB* **disappears, disappearing, disappeared**
❶ to become impossible to see; to vanish
• *He **disappeared** into the darkness.*
❷ to stop happening or existing • *My fears **disappeared**.*
➤ **disappearance** *NOUN*

> ⚠ **WATCH OUT!**
> Remember that there is a double **p** in **disappear** and **disappoint** (but only one **s**)!

disappoint *VERB* **disappoints, disappointing, disappointed**
To disappoint someone is to fail to do what they want.
➤ **disappointing** *ADJECTIVE*
➤ **disappointment** *NOUN*

disapprove *VERB* **disapproves, disapproving, disapproved**
To disapprove of someone or something is to have a bad opinion of them.
➤ **disapproval** *NOUN*

> **BUILD YOUR VOCABULARY**
> The opposite is **approve**.

disaster *NOUN* **disasters**
❶ a very bad accident or event, such as an earthquake or big fire ❷ a complete failure
• *The party was a **disaster**.*

disastrous *ADJECTIVE*
very bad • It was a **disastrous** defeat.

⚠ **WATCH OUT!**
There is no e in **disastrous**.

disc *NOUN* discs
❶ a round flat object ❷ a round, flat piece of plastic on which sound, pictures or other data is recorded

discard *VERB* discards, discarding, discarded
to throw something away

discharge *VERB* discharges, discharging, discharged
❶ to let someone leave hospital ❷ to send out or release something • He **discharged** an arrow.

disciple *NOUN* disciples
a follower of a political or religious leader

discipline *NOUN*
❶ training to obey rules and punishment if people do not obey • The school had strict **discipline**. ❷ self-control • The team needs to show more **discipline**.

✳ **WORD STORY**
Disciple and **discipline** both come from a Latin word meaning 'learner'.

disclose *VERB* discloses, disclosing, disclosed
to tell someone information or a secret

disco *NOUN* discos
a place or party where you dance to pop music

discomfort *NOUN*
a feeling of slight pain or worry

disconnect *VERB* disconnects, disconnecting, disconnected
to detach or unplug something from something else • **Disconnect** the printer.

discontented *ADJECTIVE*
unhappy and not satisfied
➤ **discontent** *NOUN*

discount *NOUN* discounts
an amount by which a price is reduced

discourage *VERB* discourages, discouraging, discouraged
❶ To discourage someone is to make them less enthusiastic or confident. ❷ To discourage someone from doing something is to try to persuade them not to do it.
➤ **discouragement** *NOUN*

⚙ **BUILD YOUR VOCABULARY**
The opposite is **encourage**.

discover *VERB* discovers, discovering, discovered
to find something or learn about it for the first time

discovery *NOUN* discoveries
something that is found or learned about for the first time • She made an important scientific **discovery**.

discreet *ADJECTIVE*
careful in what you say and do, especially in order to keep a secret
➤ **discreetly** *ADVERB*

discriminate *VERB* discriminates, discriminating, discriminated
❶ to treat people differently or unfairly because of their race, sex or religion ❷ To discriminate between things is to notice the differences between them.
➤ **discrimination** *NOUN*

discus (say **dis**-cus) *NOUN* discuses
a thick heavy disc thrown in an athletic contest

discuss (say dis-**cuss**) *VERB* discusses, discussing, discussed
to talk in detail about a subject with other people

discussion *NOUN* discussions
a detailed conversation about a subject

disease *NOUN* diseases
an illness or a sickness

disembark *VERB* disembarks, disembarking, disembarked
to get out of a boat or an aircraft

⚙ **BUILD YOUR VOCABULARY**
An opposite is **embark**.

a b c **d** e f g h i j k l m n o p q r s t u v w x y z

disgrace NOUN
❶ something or someone that is shamefully bad
• *This room is a **disgrace**.* ❷ Disgrace is shame.
• *He brought **disgrace** on his family.*
➤ **disgraceful** ADJECTIVE
➤ **disgracefully** ADVERB

disgrace VERB disgraces, disgracing, disgraced
To disgrace someone or something is to bring them shame.

disguise VERB disguises, disguising, disguised
to make someone or something look different so that people will not recognise them

disguise NOUN disguises
clothes or make-up you put on so that people will not recognise you

disgust NOUN
a strong feeling of dislike or contempt

disgust VERB disgusts, disgusting, disgusted
to make someone feel disgust
➤ **disgusted** ADJECTIVE ➤ **disgusting** ADJECTIVE

dish NOUN dishes
❶ a plate or bowl for food ❷ food that has been prepared for eating • *Curry is my favourite **dish**.*

dishevelled ADJECTIVE
untidy in appearance

dishonest ADJECTIVE
not honest or truthful
➤ **dishonesty** NOUN ➤ **dishonestly** ADVERB

dishwasher NOUN dishwashers
a machine for washing dishes automatically

disinfectant NOUN disinfectants
a substance that kills germs

disintegrate VERB disintegrates, disintegrating, disintegrated
to break up into small pieces

disk NOUN disks
a disc, especially one used to store computer data

dislike VERB dislikes, disliking, disliked
to not like someone or something

dislike NOUN dislikes
a feeling of not liking someone or something

dislodge VERB dislodges, dislodging, dislodged
to move something from its place

disloyal ADJECTIVE
not loyal

dismal ADJECTIVE
gloomy or making you feel gloomy • *a **dismal** lonely place*

dismantle VERB dismantles, dismantling, dismantled
to take something to pieces

dismay NOUN
a feeling of shock and worry
➤ **dismayed** ADJECTIVE

dismiss VERB dismisses, dismissing, dismissed
❶ To dismiss someone is to tell them they have to leave a place or their job. ❷ To dismiss an idea is to reject it.

dismount VERB dismounts, dismounting, dismounted
to get off a horse or bicycle

disobedient ADJECTIVE
refusing to obey rules or instructions
➤ **disobedience** NOUN
➤ **disobediently** ADVERB

disobey VERB disobeys, disobeying, disobeyed
to refuse to obey rules or instructions

disorder NOUN disorders
❶ a confused or untidy state ❷ an illness
• *a skin disorder*

dispatch NOUN dispatches
a report or message

dispatch VERB dispatches, dispatching, dispatched
to send someone or something somewhere
• *A messenger was dispatched.*

dispense VERB dispenses, dispensing, dispensed
To dispense something is to give it out to people.
➤ **To dispense with something** is to do without it.

disperse VERB disperses, dispersing, dispersed
If people disperse or someone disperses them, they go away in various directions.

displace VERB displaces, displacing, displaced
❶ To displace something is to move it from its place. ❷ To displace someone is to take their place.

display VERB displays, displaying, displayed
to arrange something so that it can be clearly seen

display NOUN displays
❶ a show or exhibition ❷ the showing of information on a computer screen

displease VERB displeases, displeasing, displeased
to annoy someone

disposable ADJECTIVE
made to be thrown away after using • *disposable cups*

disposal NOUN
Disposal is throwing something away.
➤ **at your disposal** available for you to use

dispose VERB disposes, disposing, disposed
➤ **To dispose of something** is to throw it away.

disposition NOUN dispositions
a person's nature • *He has a cheerful disposition.*

disprove VERB disproves, disproving, disproved
to prove that something is not true

dispute NOUN disputes
a quarrel or disagreement

disqualify VERB disqualifies, disqualifying, disqualified
to remove someone from a competition because they have broken the rules

disregard VERB disregards, disregarding, disregarded
to take no notice of something

disrespect NOUN
lack of respect; rudeness
➤ **disrespectful** ADJECTIVE
➤ **disrespectfully** ADVERB

disrupt VERB disrupts, disrupting, disrupted
to create interruptions or confusion in something
• *You must not disrupt the lesson.*
➤ **disruption** NOUN

dissatisfied ADJECTIVE
not satisfied or pleased
➤ **dissatisfaction** NOUN

dissect VERB dissects, dissecting, dissected
to cut something up so that you can examine it

dissolve VERB dissolves, dissolving, dissolved
❶ to mix something with a liquid so that it becomes part of the liquid ❷ To dissolve is to melt or become liquid.
As the book sank into the green sea the ink dissolved from its pages. And as each page washed blank, the spell written upon it was broken.
—THE BRAVE WHALE, Alan Temperley

🄾 **BUILD YOUR VOCABULARY**
Look at **insoluble, soluble, solution** and **solvent**.

a
b
c
d
e
f
g
h
i
j
k
l
m
n
o
p
q
r
s
t
u
v
w
x
y
z

dissuade VERB dissuades, dissuading, dissuaded
to persuade someone not to do something

distance NOUN distances
the amount of space between two places or things
➤ **in the distance** a long way off but able to be seen

distant ADJECTIVE
far away • *distant lands* • *Their voices grew distant.*

distinct ADJECTIVE
❶ clear or easy to notice • *There was a distinct smell of gas.* ❷ having a clear or important difference • *The word has two distinct meanings.*
➤ **distinctly** ADVERB • *I distinctly saw him smile.*

⚙ **BUILD YOUR VOCABULARY**
An opposite is **indistinct**.

distinction NOUN distinctions
❶ a clear difference between two things
❷ excellence or honour • *She is a writer of distinction.*

distinctive ADJECTIVE
easy to recognise • *A robin has a distinctive red chest.*

distinguish VERB distinguishes, distinguishing, distinguished
❶ To distinguish one thing from another is to see or make the difference between them. • *What distinguishes humans from other animals?*
❷ To distinguish something is to see or hear it.
• *I could distinguish a shape in the fog.*

distinguished ADJECTIVE
famous, successful and admired

distort VERB distorts, distorting, distorted
to change the shape or form of something to make it strange • *The mirror distorts your image.*

distract VERB distracts, distracting, distracted
to take someone's attention away from what they are doing • *Don't distract the driver.*
➤ **distraction** NOUN

distress NOUN
great sorrow, suffering or trouble
➤ **in distress** in difficulty and needing help

distress VERB distresses, distressing, distressed
to make someone feel very upset or worried

distribute VERB distributes, distributing, distributed
to give or send things out • *They distributed food to the crowd.*
➤ **distribution** NOUN

district NOUN districts
part of a town or country

distrust NOUN
lack of trust; suspicion

distrust VERB distrusts, distrusting, distrusted
to think that someone or something cannot be trusted

disturb VERB disturbs, disturbing, disturbed
❶ to interrupt someone or spoil their peace
• *Sorry to disturb you.* ❷ to worry or upset someone • *The news report disturbed me.*

disused ADJECTIVE
no longer used • *a disused quarry*

ditch NOUN ditches
a narrow trench to hold or carry away water

dither VERB dithers, dithering, dithered
to hesitate because you cannot decide

dive VERB dives, diving, dived
❶ to go into water head first ❷ to move downwards quickly • *The plane dived.*

diver NOUN divers
❶ someone who dives into water ❷ someone who goes under water using special breathing equipment ❸ a bird that dives for its food

diverse ADJECTIVE
of many different kinds • *The habitat supports a diverse range of wildlife.*
➤ **diversity** NOUN

diversion NOUN diversions
❶ a different way for traffic to go when the usual road is closed ❷ something amusing or entertaining

divert VERB diverts, diverting, diverted
❶ to distract or entertain someone ❷ to make something change the direction it is moving in

divide VERB divides, dividing, divided
❶ to separate something into smaller parts or shares • *The teacher divided the class into teams.* ❷ To divide a number by a smaller number is to find out how many times the smaller number is contained in it. • *Twelve divided by four is three (12 ÷ 4 = 3).*

divine ADJECTIVE
coming from or like God or a god • *divine power*

division NOUN divisions
❶ the process of dividing numbers or things ❷ one of the parts or sections into which something is divided • *The teams are in different divisions.*

divorce NOUN divorces
the legal ending of a marriage
divorce VERB divorces, divorcing, divorced
When two people divorce, they end their marriage by law.

Diwali (*say* de-**wah**-lee*) NOUN
a Hindu festival held in October or November

dizzy ADJECTIVE dizzier, dizziest
feeling as if things are spinning around you
➤ **dizzily** ADVERB ➤ **dizziness** NOUN

do VERB does, doing, did, done
❶ To do something is to perform an action or task.
• *We did an experiment.* • *I'll do the washing-up.*
• *I'm doing some painting.* • *What have you done today?* ❷ The verb **do** is also used with other verbs to make questions and negatives. • *Does she like it?*
• *He did not understand.*
➤ **To do without something** is to manage without it.

⚙ **BUILD** YOUR VOCABULARY
A verb that can be used with other verbs in this way is called an **auxiliary verb**.

dock NOUN docks
a part of a harbour where ships are loaded, unloaded or repaired
dock VERB docks, docking, docked
to come into a dock

doctor NOUN doctors
a person who has been trained to heal sick or injured people

document NOUN documents
❶ an important written or printed piece of paper ❷ something stored in a computer, such as a piece of text or a picture

documentary NOUN documentaries
a film or programme that tells you about real events

dodge VERB dodges, dodging, dodged
to move quickly to avoid something

dodgy ADJECTIVE dodgier, dodgiest (*informal*)
risky or not reliable • *The whole plan sounded dodgy.*

dodo NOUN dodos
a large bird that was unable to fly and is now extinct

doe NOUN does
a female deer, rabbit or hare
⚙ **BUILD** YOUR VOCABULARY
The male is a **buck**.

does VERB (*3rd singular present tense of* **do**)
• *Ranjit does his homework before he has his tea.*

dog NOUN dogs
a four-legged animal that barks, often kept as a pet
⚙ **BUILD** YOUR VOCABULARY
Look at **canine**.

doll NOUN dolls
a toy that looks like a baby or person

dollar NOUN dollars
the unit of money in the USA, Canada, Australia and some other countries

dollop NOUN dollops
a soft pile or scoop of something • *a dollop of ice cream*

dolphin NOUN dolphins
a sea mammal like a small whale that has a snout

domain NOUN domains
an area that is ruled or controlled by someone

dome NOUN domes
a roof shaped like half of a ball

domestic ADJECTIVE
❶ to do with the home ❷ A domestic animal is tame and kept at home.

domesticated ADJECTIVE
A domesticated animal is trained to live with people.

dominant ADJECTIVE
most powerful or important
➤ **dominance** NOUN

dominate VERB dominates, dominating, dominated
to be the most powerful or noticeable person or thing • *A large table dominated the room.*

dominion NOUN dominions
an area ruled by one ruler

domino NOUN dominoes
a small block marked with groups of dots, used in the game of **dominoes**

donate VERB donates, donating, donated
to give something, especially to charity
➤ **donation** NOUN

done VERB (past participle of do)
• *I've done the washing-up.*

donkey NOUN donkeys
an animal that looks like a small horse with long ears

BUILD YOUR VOCABULARY
Look at **bray**.

doodle NOUN doodles
a drawing or scribble done when you are thinking about something else
doodle VERB doodles, doodling, doodled
to draw a doodle

doomed ADJECTIVE
certain to suffer a bad fate

door NOUN doors
a panel that opens and closes the entrance to a room, building or cupboard

doorstep NOUN doorsteps
the step or piece of ground outside a door

doorway NOUN doorways
the opening into which a door fits

dormant ADJECTIVE
A dormant volcano is not erupting or not likely to erupt soon.

BUILD YOUR VOCABULARY
Look at **active** and **extinct**.

dormitory NOUN dormitories
a room for several people to sleep in, especially in a school

dormouse NOUN dormice
an animal like a large mouse that hibernates in winter

dorsal ADJECTIVE
A dorsal fin or spine is on the back of an animal.

dose NOUN doses
the amount of a medicine that you are meant to take at one time

dot NOUN dots
a tiny spot
dot VERB dots, dotting, dotted
To dot something is to mark it with dots.

dotty ADJECTIVE dottier, dottiest (informal)
crazy or silly

double ADJECTIVE
❶ twice as much or twice as many • *a double helping* ❷ having two of something
• *double doors* ❸ suitable for two people
• *a double room*

BUILD YOUR VOCABULARY
The opposite is **single**.

double *NOUN* doubles
twice the amount or cost • *The big one costs* **double**.

double *VERB* doubles, doubling, doubled
If you double something or it doubles, it becomes twice as big. • *The price has* **doubled**.

double bass *NOUN* double basses
a musical instrument with strings, like a large cello

doubly *ADVERB*
twice as much or much more • *The job was* **doubly** *difficult on my own.*

doubt *NOUN* doubts
a feeling of not being sure about something

doubt *VERB* doubts, doubting, doubted
to feel that something is probably not true • *I* **doubt** *he will come.*

doubtful *ADJECTIVE*
❶ unsure • *She looked* **doubtful**. ❷ unlikely • *Victory is* **doubtful**.

doubtless *ADVERB*
certainly, of course

dough (*rhymes with* **go**) *NOUN*
a thick mixture of flour and water used for making bread or pastry

⚠ **WATCH OUT!**
In **dough** and **though**, the letters *ough* sound like 'ow' in the word 'flow'.

doughnut *NOUN* doughnuts
a fried sweet round or ring-shaped bun

dove *NOUN* doves
a kind of pigeon, often used as a symbol of peace

down *ADVERB, PREPOSITION*
❶ to or in a lower place • *The rain came* **down**. • *He ran* **down** *the stairs.* ❷ along • *I was walking* **down** *the road.*

down *NOUN*
❶ very soft feathers or hair ❷ **Downs** are grass-covered hills.

downcast *ADJECTIVE*
❶ looking downward • *She stood with* **downcast** *eyes.* ❷ sad and gloomy • *He looked* **downcast**.

downfall *NOUN* downfalls
A person's downfall is their ruin or fall from power.

downhill *ADVERB*
down a slope

download *VERB* downloads, downloading, downloaded
To download something is to transfer it from the Internet to your computer or phone.

download *NOUN* downloads
something that has been downloaded

downpour *NOUN* downpours
a heavy fall of rain

downright *ADJECTIVE, ADVERB*
complete or completely • *a* **downright** *lie*

downstairs *ADVERB, ADJECTIVE*
to or on a lower floor

downstream *ADVERB*
in the direction that a river or stream flows

⚙ **BUILD** YOUR VOCABULARY
The opposite is **upstream**.

downward (*also* **downwards**) *ADJECTIVE, ADVERB*
going towards what is lower

⚙ **BUILD** YOUR VOCABULARY
The opposite is **upward** or **upwards**.

doze *VERB* dozes, dozing, dozed
To doze is to sleep lightly. • *A cat was* **dozing** *in the sun.*

dozen *NOUN* dozens
a set or group of twelve • *a* **dozen** *eggs*

Dr *ABBREVIATION*
short for *Doctor* in titles, for example *Dr Watson*

drab *ADJECTIVE* drabber, drabbest
dull and dreary or without colour

draft *NOUN* drafts
a first attempt at writing something

draft VERB drafts, drafting, drafted
to make a first attempt at writing something

⚠ **WATCH OUT!**
Do not confuse with a **draught** meaning 'a current of air'.

drag VERB drags, dragging, dragged
to pull something along with difficulty

dragon NOUN dragons
in stories, a monster like a large
lizard with wings that
breathes fire

dragon

dragonfly NOUN dragonflies
an insect with a long body and two pairs
of transparent wings

dragonfly

drain NOUN drains
a pipe or ditch for taking away water
or sewage

drain VERB drains, draining,
drained
If water drains or is drained, it flows or trickles away.

drake NOUN drakes
a male duck

drama NOUN dramas
❶ Drama is writing or performing plays. ❷ A drama
is a play. ❸ Drama is a series of exciting events.

dramatic ADJECTIVE
exciting and impressive • *The change was dramatic.*
➤ **dramatically** ADVERB

drank VERB (past tense of drink)
• *I drank my water.*

drape VERB drapes, draping, draped
to hang cloth loosely over something

drastic ADJECTIVE
having a strong or severe effect
➤ **drastically** ADVERB

draught (rhymes with **craft**) NOUN draughts
❶ a current of air indoors

⚠ **WATCH OUT!**
Do not confuse with a **draft** meaning 'a first attempt at writing something'.

❷ **Draughts** is a game played with 24 round pieces
on a board with black and white squares.

draw VERB draws, drawing, drew,
drawn
❶ To draw something is to make a picture
of it with a pencil or pen. ❷ to end a game or
contest with the same score on both sides
• *They drew 2-2.* ❸ To draw the curtains is
to open or close them. ❹ To draw near is to
come nearer.

draw NOUN draws
a game that ends with the same score on
both sides

drawback NOUN drawbacks
a disadvantage

drawbridge NOUN drawbridges
a bridge over a moat with hinges at one end so that
it can be raised or lowered

drawer NOUN drawers
part of a piece of furniture that slides out, for
keeping things in

drawing NOUN drawings
something drawn with a pencil or pen

drawl VERB drawls, drawling, drawled
to speak very slowly or lazily

dread VERB dreads, dreading, dreaded
to feel worried or frightened about something

dreadful ADJECTIVE
very bad • We've had **dreadful** weather.
➤ **dreadfully** ADVERB

dream NOUN dreams
❶ things you seem to see while you are sleeping
❷ an ambition or ideal • My **dream** is to be an artist.
dream VERB dreams, dreaming, dreamt or dreamed
to have a dream • I was so hungry I **dreamt** about food.

dreary ADJECTIVE drearier, dreariest
dull or gloomy
➤ **dreariness** NOUN

drench VERB drenches, drenching, drenched
to soak someone or something

dress NOUN dresses
❶ a woman's or girl's piece of clothing, with a top and skirt joined together ❷ Dress is clothes or costume. • They are wearing traditional **dress**.
dress VERB dresses, dressing, dressed
❶ To dress is to put clothes on. ❷ To dress a wound is to put a bandage or plaster on it.

dresser NOUN dressers
a piece of furniture with cupboards and drawers underneath and shelves at the top

dressing NOUN dressings
❶ a sauce made of oil, vinegar or lemon and other ingredients for a salad ❷ a bandage or plaster for a wound

dressing gown NOUN dressing gowns
a long loose garment you wear indoors over night clothes

dressmaker NOUN dressmakers
a person whose job is to make clothes for women

drew VERB (past tense of **draw**)
• I **drew** a picture of a tiger.

dribble VERB dribbles, dribbling, dribbled
❶ to let saliva trickle out of your mouth
❷ to kick a ball gently in front of you as you run forward

dried VERB (past tense and past participle of **dry**)
• I **dried** the dog. • Have you **dried** your hair?

drift VERB drifts, drifting, drifted
to be carried gently along by water or air
drift NOUN drifts
a mass of snow or sand piled up by the wind

driftwood NOUN
wood floating on the sea or washed ashore

drill NOUN drills
❶ a tool for making holes ❷ repeated exercises in military training or sport
drill VERB drills, drilling, drilled
To drill a hole is to make one with a drill.

drink VERB drinks, drinking, drank, drunk
to swallow liquid • I **drank** my water. • Who has **drunk** all the milk?
drink NOUN drinks
a liquid for drinking

drip VERB drips, dripping, dripped
to fall or let liquid fall in drops • The tap was **dripping**.
drip NOUN drips
a falling drop of liquid

drive VERB drives, driving, drove, driven
❶ To drive a vehicle is to operate it.
❷ To drive animals is to make them move.
➤ **driver** NOUN
drive NOUN drives
❶ a journey in a vehicle ❷ a private road leading to a house

drizzle NOUN
gentle rain
drizzle VERB drizzles, drizzling, drizzled
to rain gently

a b c **d** e f g h i j k l m n o p q r s t u v w x y z

drone *VERB* **drones, droning, droned**
to make a low humming sound

drone *NOUN* **drones**
❶ a low humming sound ❷ a male bee
❸ a remote-controlled aircraft

drool *VERB* **drools, drooling, drooled**
to drop a lot of saliva from the mouth

droop *VERB* **droops, drooping, drooped**
to hang down loosely

drop *NOUN* **drops**
❶ a tiny amount of liquid ❷ a fall or decrease
• *There was a **drop** in temperature.*

drop *VERB* **drops, dropping, dropped**
❶ If you drop something or it drops, it falls to
the ground. ❷ To drop is to become less or lower.
• *Prices have **dropped**.*

droplet *NOUN* **droplets**
a small drop

drought *(rhymes with* **out***) NOUN* **droughts**
a long period of dry weather

drove *VERB (past tense of* **drive***)*
• *Mum **drove** us to the concert.*

drown *VERB* **drowns, drowning, drowned**
❶ If someone drowns or is drowned, they die from
being under water and unable to breathe.
❷ To drown sounds is to make so much noise that
they cannot be heard.

drowsy *ADJECTIVE* **drowsier, drowsiest**
sleepy
➤ **drowsily** *ADVERB* ➤ **drowsiness** *NOUN*

drug *NOUN* **drugs**
❶ a substance that kills pain or cures a disease
❷ a substance that people take because it makes
them feel a certain way. Many drugs cause harm and
are illegal.

Druid *NOUN* **Druids**
a priest of an ancient religion in Britain and
France

drum *NOUN* **drums**
❶ a hollow musical instrument with a thin
skin stretched over one end, that you play by
hitting it

🔵 **BUILD** YOUR VOCABULARY
A **drum** is a **percussion** instrument.

❷ a cylindrical container • *an oil **drum***

drum *VERB* **drums, drumming, drummed**
❶ to play a drum ❷ to tap repeatedly on something
• *Rain **drummed** on the roof.*
➤ **drummer** *NOUN*

drunk *VERB (past participle of* **drink***)*
• *Somebody has **drunk** all the juice.*

drunk *ADJECTIVE*
having drunk too much alcohol

dry *ADJECTIVE* **drier, driest**
not wet or damp • *a **dry** towel*
➤ **dryness** *NOUN*

dry *VERB* **dries, drying, dried**
If something dries or you dry it, it becomes dry.
• *I **dried** my hair.*

dubious *ADJECTIVE*
❶ feeling doubtful or unsure • *She looked **dubious**.*
❷ not completely honest or good • *His story
sounded rather **dubious**.*

duchess *NOUN* **duchesses**
a woman who has the same rank as a duke or is
married to a duke

duck *NOUN* **ducks**
a web-footed water bird with a flat beak

🔵 **BUILD** YOUR VOCABULARY
A male duck is a **drake**.

duck *VERB* **ducks, ducking, ducked**
❶ to bend down quickly to avoid something
❷ To duck someone is to push them under water
quickly.

duckling *NOUN* **ducklings**
a young duck

duct *NOUN* **ducts**
a tube or pipe

due *ADJECTIVE*
❶ expected to arrive • *When is the next bus* **due**? ❷ needing to be given in or paid • *Your homework is* **due** *tomorrow.*

duel *NOUN* **duels**
a fight between two people, especially with pistols or swords

duet *NOUN* **duets**
a piece of music for two players or two singers

duffel coat *NOUN* **duffel coats**
a thick overcoat with a hood

dug *VERB* *(past tense and past participle of* **dig***)*
• *We* **dug** *a big hole in the garden.*

duke *NOUN* **dukes**
a member of the highest rank of noblemen

dull *ADJECTIVE* **duller, dullest**
❶ boring • *What a* **dull** *programme.* ❷ not bright, clear or sharp • *It was a* **dull** *day.*

duly *ADVERB*
as expected after something else • *The letter was sent and* **duly** *arrived.*

dumb *ADJECTIVE* **dumber, dumbest**
❶ unable to speak ❷ *(informal)* stupid

dumbfounded *ADJECTIVE*
unable to speak because you are so surprised

dummy *NOUN* **dummies**
❶ a display model made to look like a person or thing • *a shop* **dummy** ❷ a rubber or plastic object for a baby to suck

dump *NOUN* **dumps**
❶ a place where something, especially rubbish, is left or stored ❷ *(informal)* an unattractive or dirty place
dump *VERB* **dumps, dumping, dumped**
❶ to throw something away ❷ to put something down carelessly

dumpling *NOUN* **dumplings**
a lump of boiled or baked dough

dune *NOUN* **dunes**
a hill of loose sand formed by the wind

dung *NOUN*
solid waste matter from an animal

dungeon *(say* **dun**-jun*) NOUN* **dungeons**
an underground prison cell

dunk *VERB* **dunks, dunking, dunked**
to dip something into a liquid

duplicate *(say* **dew**-plik-at*) NOUN* **duplicates**
something that is exactly the same as something else or an exact copy
duplicate *(say* **dew**-plik-ayt*) VERB* **duplicates, duplicating, duplicated**
to make an exact copy of something
➤ **duplication** *NOUN*

during *PREPOSITION*
while a period of time is happening
• *I had fun* **during** *the holidays.*

dusk *NOUN*
the time just after sunset, when it starts to get dark

BUILD YOUR VOCABULARY
A synonym is **twilight**.

dust *NOUN*
a fine powder made up of tiny pieces of dry dirt
• *The horse kicked up clouds of* **dust**.
dust *VERB* **dusts, dusting, dusted**
to clear dust or small pieces off something
• *She* **dusted** *the crumbs off her skirt.*

dustbin *NOUN* **dustbins**
a bin for household rubbish

duster *NOUN* **dusters**
a cloth for dusting things

a b c **d** e f g h i j k l m n o p q r s t u v w x y z

dustpan *NOUN* dustpans
a pan into which you brush dust

dusty *ADJECTIVE* dustier, dustiest
covered with or full of dust • *dusty* old
books

dutiful *ADJECTIVE*
doing your duty

duty *NOUN* duties
Your duty is what you have to do, for example as
part of your job.

duvet *(say* doo-vay*) NOUN* duvets
a thick quilt used instead of sheets and blankets

DVD *NOUN* DVDs
a disc on which film, pictures or music can be stored;
short for *digital versatile disc*

dwarf *NOUN* dwarfs, dwarves
a very small person or thing

dwarf *VERB* dwarfs, dwarfing, dwarfed
To dwarf something is to make it seem very small.
• *The skyscraper **dwarfs** all the buildings round it.*

dwell *VERB* dwells, dwelling, dwelt
to live somewhere

dwelling *NOUN* dwellings
a house or other place to live in

dwindle *VERB* dwindles, dwindling,
dwindled
to gradually get smaller or less
*As the last rays of daylight dwindled and disappeared,
absolute blackness settled down on Treasure Island.*
—TREASURE ISLAND, Robert Louis Stevenson

dye *VERB* dyes, dyeing, dyed
to change the colour of something by putting it in
a special liquid
dye *NOUN* dyes
a substance used to dye things

dying *VERB (present participle of* die*)*

dyke *NOUN* dykes
a wall, bank or barrier that stops water from flooding
an area of land

dynamite *NOUN*
a powerful explosive

dynamo *NOUN* dynamos
a machine that makes electricity

dynasty *(say* din-a-stee*) NOUN* dynasties
a series of rulers from the same family

dyslexia *(say* dis-**leks**-ee-a*) NOUN*
a condition that makes it difficult to learn to read
and spell words

dyslexic *(say* dis-**lek**-sik*) ADJECTIVE*
Someone who is dyslexic has dyslexia.
➤ **dyslexic** *NOUN*

E is the most frequently used letter in the English language. It is difficult to write a sentence without using a single e—try it!

However, **e** is not the most common letter at the start of words. Can you guess what is?

CLUE Which letter takes up the most pages in this dictionary?

each *DETERMINER, PRONOUN*
Each person or thing in a group is every one of them when you think of them separately. • *Each film lasts an hour.* • *She gave a present to **each** of the children.*

eager *ADJECTIVE*
wanting very much to do something or to have something • *He was **eager** to play the game.*
➤ **eagerly** *ADVERB* ➤ **eagerness** *NOUN*

eagle *NOUN* **eagles**
a large bird of prey with a hooked beak

ear *NOUN* **ears**
❶ Your ears are the parts of your body that you hear with. ❷ An ear of corn or wheat is the spike of seeds at the top of the stalk.

earache *NOUN*
a pain inside your ear

eardrum *NOUN* **eardrums**
a membrane in the ear that vibrates when sound reaches it

early *ADVERB, ADJECTIVE* **earlier, earliest**
❶ arriving or happening before the usual or expected time • *School finishes **early** today.* ❷ happening near the beginning • *They meet **early** in the story.* • *It was **early** morning.*

earn *VERB* **earns, earning, earned**
❶ To earn money is to get it by working for it.
❷ To earn a reward or praise is to do something good so that you deserve it.

earnest *ADJECTIVE*
serious about something
➤ **earnestly** *ADVERB*

earnings *NOUN*
money that someone earns • *What will you buy with your **earnings**?*

earphones *NOUN*
small speakers that fit over your ears

earring *NOUN* **earrings**
a piece of jewellery that you wear on your ear

earshot *NOUN*
If a sound is in earshot, it is close enough to hear.

earth *NOUN* **earths**
❶ The earth is the planet that we live on. ❷ Earth is soil or the ground. ❸ An earth is a connection to the ground to complete an electric circuit. ❹ An earth is a hole where a fox or badger lives.
➤ **earthy** *ADJECTIVE* • *an **earthy** smell*

earthly *ADJECTIVE*
living or belonging on earth

earthquake *NOUN* **earthquakes**
a violent movement of the ground caused by pressure under the earth's surface

a b c d e f g h i j k l m n o p q r s t u v w x y z

earthworm NOUN **earthworms**
a worm that lives in soil

earwig NOUN **earwigs**
a crawling garden insect with pincers at the end of its body

> ✳ **WORD STORY**
> The word **earwig** means 'ear insect', because people used to believe that earwigs crawled into their ears.

ease NOUN
If you do something with ease, you do it without any trouble.
➤ **at ease** comfortable and relaxed • *I feel at ease with him.*
ease VERB **eases, easing, eased**
❶ to become or make something become less severe or unpleasant • *The wind eased.* • *Her words eased his pain.* ❷ to move something gently and slowly • *She eased her feet out of the boots.*

easel NOUN **easels**
a frame for holding a painting that an artist is working on

easily ADVERB
without difficulty • *He won the race easily.*

east NOUN
the direction in which the sun rises or a place that is in this direction. • *The city is in the east.*
east ADVERB
towards the east • *They travelled east.*
east ADJECTIVE
coming from the east • *an east wind*

Easter NOUN
a Christian festival in spring, celebrating Christ's rising from the dead

Easter egg NOUN **Easter eggs**
a chocolate or painted egg given at Easter

eastern ADJECTIVE
coming from or to do with the east

easy ADJECTIVE **easier, easiest**
not difficult to do or understand • *It was an easy question.* • *The game is easy to play.*

eat VERB **eats, eating, ate, eaten**
To eat food is to chew it and swallow it. • *Pandas eat bamboo.* • *I ate my breakfast.*

eaves NOUN
the overhanging edges of a roof

eavesdrop VERB **eavesdrops, eavesdropping, eavesdropped**
To eavesdrop on someone is to listen to their conversation in secret.

ebb VERB **ebbs, ebbing, ebbed**
When the tide ebbs, it goes away from the land.

ebony NOUN
a hard black wood

eccentric (*say* ik-**sen**-trik) ADJECTIVE
with slightly strange behaviour or ideas

echidna (*say* e-**kid**-na) NOUN **echidnas**
an Australian animal like an anteater with sharp spines

echo NOUN **echoes**
a repeated sound that you hear when sound is reflected off a hard surface
echo VERB **echoes, echoing, echoed**
to make an echo • *Their voices echoed around the cave.*

eclipse NOUN **eclipses**
a time when the sun is partly hidden for a short time because the moon comes between it and the earth *or* when the moon is hidden because the earth comes between it and the sun

ecology (*say* ee-**kol**-oj-ee) NOUN
the study of living creatures and plants in their environment

economical (*say* e-con-om-**ic**-al *or* ec-on-om-**ic**-al) ADJECTIVE
using money or resources carefully
➤ **economically** ADVERB

economy (say ik-**on**-om-ee) NOUN economies
❶ A country's economy is the way money is made and spent there by businesses, banks and people.
❷ Economy is being careful with money or resources.
➤ **economic** ADJECTIVE • *economic problems*

ecstasy NOUN ecstasies
great happiness or joy
➤ **ecstatic** ADJECTIVE

eczema (say eks-ma) NOUN
a skin condition that causes rough itchy patches

edge NOUN edges
the part along the side or end of something • *They were at the edge of a cliff.* • *Put tape around the edges.*

edible ADJECTIVE
safe to eat • *Are those mushrooms edible?*

edit VERB edits, editing, edited
❶ to correct a piece of writing or make it ready to publish ❷ To edit a film or recording is to choose parts of it and put them in order.
➤ **editor** NOUN

edition NOUN editions
a copy or all the copies of a newspaper, magazine or book printed at a particular time • *A new edition of the dictionary is coming out.*

educate VERB educates, educating, educated
to teach someone and give them knowledge

education NOUN
the process of teaching people and giving them knowledge
➤ **educational** ADJECTIVE • *an educational film*

eel NOUN eels
a long thin fish that looks like a snake

eerie ADJECTIVE eerier, eeriest
strange and frightening • *There was an eerie silence.*
➤ **eerily** ADVERB ➤ **eeriness** NOUN

effect NOUN effects
something that happens because of something else
• *The drink had a strange effect on Alice.*

⚠ **WATCH OUT!**
Do not confuse the noun **effect** with the verb **affect**, meaning 'have an effect on': *How did the drink affect Alice?*

effective ADJECTIVE
successful in getting the result you want
• *The medicine was very effective.*
➤ **effectively** ADVERB ➤ **effectiveness** NOUN

efficient ADJECTIVE
working well without wasting time or energy
• *She was very efficient and finished quickly.*
➤ **efficiency** NOUN ➤ **efficiently** ADVERB

effort NOUN efforts
❶ the use of physical or mental energy ❷ An effort is an attempt. • *This was my first effort.*

e.g. ABBREVIATION
for example • *Eat lots of fruit, e.g. apples, oranges and berries.*

✴ **WORD STORY**
e.g. is short for Latin *exempli gratia*, meaning 'for the sake of example'.

egg NOUN eggs
❶ an oval or round object produced by a female bird, reptile, fish or insect, in which her young develop
❷ a hen's egg used as food • *I had a fried egg.*

reptile eggs

bird eggs

fish eggs

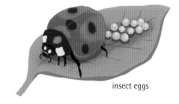

insect eggs

Egyptian (say ee-jip-shan) ADJECTIVE
from or to do with Egypt • *the tomb of an Egyptian pharaoh*
➤ **Egyptian** NOUN • *ancient Egyptians*

Eid (say eed) NOUN
a Muslim festival that marks the end of the fast of Ramadan

either DETERMINER
❶ one or the other of two people or things • *Either bag will do.* • *You can have either rice or chips.*
❷ both • *There were hills on either side.*

either PRONOUN
one or the other of two people or things • *You can take either of them.*

either ADVERB
used at the end of a negative sentence to mean 'also' • *Lisa's not going and I'm not either.*

eject VERB ejects, ejecting, ejected
to send or force something or someone out of a place • *Eject the disc.*

elaborate ADJECTIVE
complicated or detailed

elastic NOUN
material with rubber in it so that it can stretch

elated ADJECTIVE
very happy and pleased

elbow NOUN elbows
the joint in the middle of your arm, where it bends

elbow VERB elbows, elbowing, elbowed
to push or prod someone with your elbow

elder ADJECTIVE
older • *She has an elder brother.*

elder NOUN elders
a tree with white flowers and black berries

elderberry NOUN elderberries
a small black berry that grows on an elder tree

elderly ADJECTIVE
rather old

eldest ADJECTIVE
oldest • *I am the eldest in our family.*

elect VERB elects, electing, elected
to choose someone by voting

election NOUN elections
the process of voting for people to represent you

electric, electrical ADJECTIVE
to do with electricity or worked by electricity
➤ **electrically** ADVERB

electrician NOUN electricians
someone whose job is to fit and repair electrical equipment

electricity NOUN
energy used to produce light and heat and to make machines work

electrify VERB electrifies, electrifying, electrified
to make someone suddenly very excited or interested

electronic ADJECTIVE
electronic equipment uses transistors and silicon chips
➤ **electronically** ADVERB

elegant ADJECTIVE
graceful and smart
➤ **elegance** NOUN ➤ **elegantly** ADVERB

element NOUN elements
❶ a chemical substance that cannot be split up into simpler substances

⚙ **BUILD YOUR VOCABULARY**

Some elements are **carbon, oxygen, hydrogen, nitrogen, copper** and **gold**.

❷ a part of something • *Luck and skill are both elements of the game.* ❸ The elements are the weather, especially bad weather. • *He was out in the elements with no shelter.*

elementary ADJECTIVE
easy or basic

elephant NOUN elephants
a very large animal found in Africa and India, with a thick grey skin, large ears, a trunk and tusks

elevator NOUN elevators (North American)
a lift

elf NOUN elves
in stories, a tiny mischievous fairy

eligible *ADJECTIVE*
qualified or suitable for something

eliminate *VERB* eliminates, eliminating, eliminated
to get rid of something or someone

elixir *(say* il-**iks**-er*) NOUN* elixirs
a magic liquid
*The Stone will transform any metal into pure gold. It also produces the elixir of Life, which will make the drinker immortal.—*HARRY POTTER AND THE PHILOSOPHER'S STONE, J. K. Rowling

elk *NOUN* elk, elks
a large kind of deer

BUILD YOUR VOCABULARY
Look at **moose**.

ellipse *NOUN* ellipses
an oval shape

elm *NOUN* elms
a tall tree with large rough leaves

eloquent *ADJECTIVE*
speaking well and expressing ideas clearly
➤ **eloquence** *NOUN*

else *ADJECTIVE, ADVERB*
different; besides • *Let's do something else.*
• *Who else knows?*
➤ **or else** otherwise • *Run or else you'll be late.*

elsewhere *ADVERB*
somewhere else

elude *VERB* eludes, eluding, eluded
to escape from or avoid someone

elusive *ADJECTIVE*
difficult to find or catch • *Deer are elusive animals.*

elves *NOUN (plural of* elf*)*

email *NOUN* emails
❶ a system of sending messages from one computer to another. Email is short for *electronic mail.*
❷ a message sent by email

email *VERB* emails, emailing, emailed
to send someone a message by email

embankment *NOUN* embankments
a long bank of earth that holds back water or supports a road or railway

embark *VERB* embarks, embarking, embarked
to go on board a ship or plane
➤ **To embark on something** is to begin something important.

BUILD YOUR VOCABULARY
To get off a ship or plane is to **disembark**.

embarrass *VERB* embarrasses, embarrassing, embarrassed
to make someone feel shy or awkward
➤ **embarrassment** *NOUN*

⚠ **WATCH OUT!**
There is a double **r** and a double **s** in **embarrass**.

embers *NOUN*
small pieces of coal or wood that keep glowing when a fire is going out

emblem *NOUN* emblems
a symbol • *The dove is an emblem of peace.*

embrace *VERB* embraces, embracing, embraced
to hold someone closely in your arms

embroider
VERB embroiders, embroidering, embroidered
to decorate cloth by stitching designs
➤ **embroidery** *NOUN*

embryo *NOUN* embryos
a baby or young animal that is growing in the womb

embroidery

emerald *NOUN* emeralds
❶ a green precious stone ❷ a bright green colour

emerge *VERB* emerges, emerging, emerged
to come out or appear
➤ **emergence** *NOUN*

emergency *NOUN* emergencies
a sudden dangerous event that needs to be dealt with very quickly

emigrate VERB emigrates, emigrating, emigrated
to leave your own country and go and live in another country
➤ **emigration** NOUN

BUILD YOUR VOCABULARY
Look at **immigrate** and **migrate**.

emit VERB emits, emitting, emitted
To emit something such as smoke or a sound is to send it out.

emoji NOUN emojis
a small digital image, such as a smiling face, used to express an idea or emotion

※ WORD STORY
The word **emoji** comes from a Japanese word meaning 'picture letter'.

emotion NOUN emotions
a feeling such as love or sadness
➤ **emotional** ADJECTIVE • I felt very **emotional**.

emperor NOUN emperors
the ruler of an empire

emphasis NOUN emphases
special importance given to something or stress put on something
emphasise (also **emphasize**) VERB
emphasises, emphasising, emphasised
to give something special importance or put stress on it • Underline the words you want to **emphasise**.

empire NOUN empires
a group of countries under one ruler • the Roman empire

employ VERB employs, employing, employed
to pay someone to work for you

employee NOUN employees
someone who works for another person or a company

employer NOUN employers
a person or company that has people working for them

employment NOUN
paid work

empress NOUN empresses
a female emperor or the wife of an emperor

empty ADJECTIVE emptier, emptiest
An empty place or container has nothing or no one in it. • He stood in an **empty** hall. • My cup is **empty**.
➤ **emptiness** NOUN

empty VERB empties, emptying, emptied
If you empty something, you take out the contents. • I'll **empty** the bin.

emu NOUN emus
a large Australian bird that cannot fly, like a small ostrich

enable VERB enables, enabling, enabled
To enable someone to do something is to make it possible. • The Internet **enables** us to find and share information.

enamel NOUN enamels
❶ a shiny glassy substance baked on to metal or pottery ❷ the hard shiny surface of teeth

encampment NOUN encampments
a military camp

enchanted ADJECTIVE
under a magic spell

encircle VERB encircles, encircling, encircled
to completely surround something or someone
• Walls **encircled** the town.

enclose *VERB* **encloses, enclosing, enclosed**
❶ to put a fence or wall around an area
❷ to send something with a letter inside an envelope or packet
➤ **enclosure** *NOUN* • *an enclosure for cattle*

encore *(say on-kor) NOUN* **encores**
an extra item performed after an audience has applauded at the end of a show

encounter *VERB* **encounters, encountering, encountered**
❶ to meet someone unexpectedly ❷ to experience or come across something • *Did you encounter any difficulties?*

encourage *VERB* **encourages, encouraging, encouraged**
to try to persuade and give someone confidence to do something • *My parents always encourage me to try new things.*
➤ **encouragement** *NOUN*

BUILD YOUR VOCABULARY
The opposite is **discourage**.

encrusted *ADJECTIVE*
covered with a hard layer of something

encyclopedia *NOUN* **encyclopedias**
a book or set of books giving information about different topics

✳ **WORD STORY**
The word **encyclopedia** comes from Greek words meaning 'complete education'.

end *NOUN* **ends**
❶ the furthest away part of something • *There's a shop at the end of the road.* ❷ the time when something finishes • *It was the end of the holidays.*
end *VERB* **ends, ending, ended**
To end is to finish. • *I liked the way the film ended.*

endanger *VERB* **endangers, endangering, endangered**
to put someone or something in danger

endeavour *VERB* **endeavours, endeavouring, endeavoured**
to try to do something

ending *NOUN* **endings**
the way that something finishes • *The story has a happy ending.*

endless *ADJECTIVE*
never stopping • *I'm sick of this endless rain.*
➤ **endlessly** *ADVERB*

endure *VERB* **endures, enduring, endured**
to put up with something • *They had to endure blazing heat.*

enemy *NOUN* **enemies**
someone who is opposed to you and wants to harm you

energetic *ADJECTIVE*
having or using a lot of energy • *energetic dancing*
➤ **energetically** *ADVERB*

energy *NOUN* **energies**
❶ power from electricity or a fuel, that makes something work • *We can get energy from the sun.*
❷ strength and fitness to do things • *I don't have much energy today.*

enforce *VERB* **enforces, enforcing, enforced**
To enforce a law or rule is to make people obey it.

engage *VERB* **engages, engaging, engaged**
To engage in or be engaged in an activity is to take part in it.

engaged *ADJECTIVE*
❶ having promised to marry someone • *My sister got engaged.* ❷ busy or being used • *The phone number was engaged.*

engagement *NOUN* **engagements**
❶ a promise to marry someone ❷ an appointment

engine *NOUN* **engines**
❶ a machine that turns energy into motion
❷ a vehicle that pulls a railway train

engineer *NOUN* **engineers**
a person who designs and builds machines, roads and bridges
➤ **engineering** *NOUN*

engrave *VERB* **engraves, engraving, engraved**
to carve figures or words on something

engrossed ADJECTIVE
giving all your attention to something, so you do not notice other things • *She was engrossed in a book.*

engulf VERB engulfs, engulfing, engulfed
to completely cover something • *Flames engulfed the building.*

enhance VERB enhances, enhancing, enhanced
to make something better • *The victory enhanced his reputation.*

enjoy VERB enjoys, enjoying, enjoyed
❶ To enjoy something is to get pleasure from it.
❷ To enjoy yourself is to have a good time.
➤ **enjoyable** ADJECTIVE ➤ **enjoyment** NOUN

enlarge VERB enlarges, enlarging, enlarged
to make something larger

enlist VERB enlists, enlisting, enlisted
❶ to join the armed forces ❷ To enlist someone's help is to ask them to help you.

enormous ADJECTIVE
very large in size or amount
➤ **enormously** ADVERB • *I enjoyed the party enormously.*

enough DETERMINER, NOUN, ADVERB
as much or as many as you need or can cope with
• *Have you got enough paper?* • *I've eaten enough.*
• *I'm not tall enough to reach.*

> ⚠ **WATCH OUT!**
> In **enough**, **rough** and **tough**, the letters *ough* sound like 'uff'.

enquire VERB enquires, enquiring, enquired
to ask for information about something • *'Who's this?' she enquired.*

enquiry NOUN enquiries
❶ a question you ask to find out information
• *She made some enquiries about the school.*
❷ an official investigation • *There will be an enquiry into the accident.*

enrage VERB enrages, enraging, enraged
to make someone very angry

ensue VERB ensues, ensuing, ensued
to happen after something else

ensure VERB ensures, ensuring, ensured
to make sure of something • *Please ensure that you lock the door.*

entangled ADJECTIVE
tangled or caught up in something • *A bird had become entangled in the net.*

enter VERB enters, entering, entered
❶ to come or go into a place • *The teacher entered.*
❷ to write down or type in information • *Enter your password.* ❸ To enter a competition is to take part in it.

enterprise NOUN enterprises
❶ a new or difficult task that you undertake
❷ a business or company

entertain VERB entertains, entertaining, entertained
to amuse someone or give them pleasure
➤ **entertainer** NOUN
➤ **entertainment** NOUN

enthusiasm NOUN enthusiasms
a feeling of excitement and interest

> ✳ **WORD STORY**
> The word **enthusiasm** comes from a Greek word meaning 'possessed by a god'.

enthusiastic ADJECTIVE
full of enthusiasm • *She is very enthusiastic about science.*
➤ **enthusiastically** ADVERB

entire ADJECTIVE
whole or complete • *My entire family came.*
➤ **entirely** ADVERB • *That's not entirely true.*

entitle VERB entitles, entitling, entitled
❶ To entitle someone to something is to give them a right to it. • *We are all entitled to a share of the money.* ❷ To entitle something is to give it a title.
• *a book entitled 'Monsters'*

entrance (say en-trance) NOUN entrances
the way into a place

entrance (say en-**trance**) VERB entrances, entrancing, entranced
to delight or enchant someone

entreat VERB entreats, entreating, entreated
to ask someone very urgently for something

entrust VERB entrusts, entrusting, entrusted
To entrust someone with something or to entrust something to someone, is to give it to them to look after.

entry NOUN entries
❶ an entrance ❷ something written in a list or diary ❸ something you enter in a competition • *the winning entry*

envelop *(say* en-vel-op*)* VERB envelops, enveloping, enveloped
to cover something completely • *The ship was enveloped in fog.*

envelope *(say* en-vel-ohp *or* on-vel-ohp*)* NOUN envelopes
a covering for a letter

envious ADJECTIVE
If you are envious of someone, you want something that they have got.
➤ **enviously** ADVERB

environment NOUN environments
❶ The environment is the natural world of the land and sea and air. • *We need to care for the environment.* ❷ the conditions that are around someone or something • *This is not a good environment for learning.*

⚠ **WATCH OUT!**
Don't forget to write the second **n** in **environment**, which some people do not pronounce.

envy NOUN
the unhappy feeling of wanting something that someone else has got

envy VERB envies, envying, envied
to feel envy about someone or something

epic NOUN epics
an exciting, long story about heroes

epic ADJECTIVE
heroic or grand in scale • *an epic journey to the South Pole*

epidemic NOUN epidemics
a disease that spreads quickly

epilepsy NOUN
a disease that causes someone to become unconscious for short periods and to make uncontrolled body movements

episode NOUN episodes
❶ one programme in a radio or television serial ❷ an event in a series of happenings or period of time • *There was an unfortunate episode.*

equal ADJECTIVE
If things are equal, they are the same in amount, size or value. • *Cut the pie into three equal parts.* • *0.5 is equal to 50%.*
➤ **equally** ADVERB • *We shared the sweets equally.*

equal VERB equals, equalling, equalled
To equal something is to be the same in amount, size or value. • *Four times seven equals 28 (4 x 7 = 28).*

equality NOUN
Equality is being treated in the same way or having the same rights.

equals sign NOUN
the symbol (=) used in maths to mean that two amounts are the same

equation NOUN equations
In maths, a statement that two amounts are equal, for example 3 + 4 = 2 + 5.

equator NOUN
an imaginary line round the earth at an equal distance from the North and South Poles

🔵 **BUILD YOUR VOCABULARY**
Look at **tropic**.

equilateral triangle *(say* ee-kwil-lat-er-al*)* NOUN equilateral triangles
a triangle whose sides are all the same length

🔵 **BUILD YOUR VOCABULARY**
Look at **isosceles triangle** and **scalene triangle**.

equinox NOUN equinoxes
a time of year when day and night are equal in length (about 20 March and 22 September)

a b c d e f g h i j k l m n o p q r s t u v w x y z

equipment NOUN
a set of things needed for doing something

equipped ADJECTIVE
having equipment for doing something • *They were equipped with ropes and hooks.*

equivalent ADJECTIVE
If things are equivalent, they are the same in value, importance or meaning.

equivalent NOUN equivalents
something that has the same value, importance or meaning as something else • *50mm is the equivalent of 5cm.*

equivalent fraction NOUN equivalent fractions
Equivalent fractions are ones that look different but have the same value, for example $\frac{1}{3}$, $\frac{2}{6}$ and $\frac{4}{12}$.

era (*say* eer-a) NOUN eras
a long period of history • *the Jurassic era*

erase VERB erases, erasing, erased
❶ to rub something out ❷ to wipe out a recording

erect ADJECTIVE
standing straight up

erect VERB erects, erecting, erected
to set up or build something • *They erected a fence.*

erode VERB erodes, eroding, eroded
to wear something away • *Water has eroded the rocks.*
➤ **erosion** NOUN • *the erosion of the coast*

errand NOUN errands
a short journey to take a message or fetch something

erratic ADJECTIVE
not reliable or regular
➤ **erratically** ADVERB

error NOUN errors
a mistake

erupt VERB erupts, erupting, erupted
❶ When a volcano erupts, it shoots out lava.
❷ If a situation or noise erupts, it suddenly happens.
• *The class erupted into laughter.*

escalator NOUN escalators
a moving staircase

escapade (*say* ess-kap-**ayd** *or* ess-kap-ayd)
NOUN escapades
a daring adventure • *He told everyone about his escapades.*

escape VERB escapes, escaping, escaped
❶ to get free or get away • *A monkey escaped from the zoo.* ❷ To escape something is to avoid it.
• *They were lucky to escape injury.*

escape NOUN escapes
an act of escaping • *They made their escape.*

escort (*say* ess-kort) NOUN escorts
a person or group who goes somewhere with someone to protect or guide them

escort (*say* iss-kort) VERB escorts, escorting, escorted
to go somewhere with someone, as an escort

Eskimo NOUN Eskimos, Eskimo
a member of a group of people who live in the Arctic, that includes the Inuit

especially ADVERB
more than anything else • *I love sport, especially football.*

essay NOUN essays
a short piece of writing on one subject

essence NOUN essences
a concentrated liquid that smells or tastes of something • *vanilla essence*

essential ADJECTIVE
very important and necessary • *It is essential to wear a helmet.*

essential NOUN essentials
something important and necessary • *I packed a few essentials.*

establish VERB establishes, establishing, established
❶ to start something such as an organisation or a friendship and make it successful ❷ To establish a fact is to show that it is true. • *We must establish what really happened.*

establishment NOUN establishments
an organisation or business • *an educational establishment*

estate NOUN estates
❶ an area of land with houses or factories on it
❷ a large area of land belonging to one person

estate agent NOUN estate agents
someone whose job is selling houses

estimate *(say* ess-tim-at*)* NOUN estimates
a rough calculation or guess
estimate *(say* ess-tim-ayt*)* VERB estimates, estimating, estimated
to guess or roughly calculate an amount • *Can you estimate the area of this room?*

estuary *(say* ess-tew-er-ee*)* NOUN estuaries
the wide part of a river where it joins the sea

etc. *(say* et-**set**-er-a*)* ABBREVIATION
used after a list to mean 'and so on' • *We study maths, English, science, etc.*

⭐ **WORD STORY**
etc. is short for Latin *et cetera*, meaning 'and the rest'.

etch VERB etches, etching, etched
to scratch, cut or create fine lines across something

eternal ADJECTIVE
lasting or seeming to last forever
➤ **eternally** ADVERB

ethnic ADJECTIVE
relating to a particular national or racial group

EU ABBREVIATION
the *European Union*, a group of countries in Europe that work together

eucalyptus *(say* yoo-kal-**ip**-tus*)* NOUN eucalyptuses
a tree whose oil has a strong pleasant smell

euro NOUN euros, euro
the unit of money in many countries in the European Union

evacuate VERB evacuates, evacuating, evacuated
to remove people from a dangerous place
➤ **evacuation** NOUN

evacuee *(say* e-vac-u-**ee***)* NOUN evacuees
someone who is removed from the place where they live because of war or danger

evade VERB evades, evading, evaded
to make an effort to avoid someone or something
• *He evaded capture.*

evaporate VERB evaporates, evaporating, evaporated
to change from liquid into steam or vapour
➤ **evaporation** NOUN

eve NOUN eves
the day or evening before an important day • *on the eve of battle*

even ADJECTIVE
❶ An even number can be divided by two with no remainders. • *5 is odd and 6 is even.*

⚙ **BUILD YOUR VOCABULARY**
The opposite is **odd**.

❷ level and smooth • *Work on an even surface.*
❸ equal • *The scores were even at half-time.*
➤ **evenly** ADVERB • *Spread the butter evenly.*

a b c d e f g h i j k l m n o p q r s t u v w x y z

even ADVERB
used to emphasise something • *You haven't even started!* • *I ran fast, but she ran even faster.* • *Even if it rains, I'd rather play outside.*

evening NOUN evenings
the time at the end of the day before night time

event NOUN events
❶ something that happens, especially something important • *an unexpected event* ❷ an organised activity • *an athletics event*

eventually ADVERB
finally, in the end • *We eventually gave up.*

ever ADVERB
at any time • *It's the biggest dog I've ever seen.*

evergreen ADJECTIVE
an evergreen tree keeps its leaves all through the year

BUILD YOUR VOCABULARY
Look at **deciduous**.

evergreen NOUN evergreens
an evergreen tree

everlasting ADJECTIVE
lasting forever or for a long time

every DETERMINER
all the people or things of a particular kind
• *Every child in the school was there.*
• *I go swimming every Monday.*
➤ **every other** every second one • *I see my Grandma every other week.*

everybody PRONOUN
everyone

everyday ADJECTIVE
ordinary • *Just wear your everyday clothes.*

everyone PRONOUN
every person; all people • *Everyone likes chocolate.*

everything PRONOUN
all things; all • *Have you got everything you need?*

everywhere ADVERB
in all places

evidence NOUN
facts and information that help to prove something is true or exists

evident ADJECTIVE
obvious or clear • *It was evident that they had left.*
➤ **evidently** ADVERB

evil ADJECTIVE
wicked and harmful
evil NOUN evils
Evil, or an evil, is something wicked or harmful.

evolution (say ee-vol-oo-shun) NOUN
the process by which animals and plants slowly develop from earlier or simpler forms of life

evolve VERB evolves, evolving, evolved
to gradually change or develop

ewe (say yoo) NOUN ewes
a female sheep

BUILD YOUR VOCABULARY
A male sheep is a **ram**.

exact ADJECTIVE
completely correct and accurate • *I don't know the exact amount.*
➤ **exactly** ADVERB

exaggerate VERB exaggerates, exaggerating, exaggerated
to say that something is bigger, better or worse than it really is
➤ **exaggeration** NOUN

exam NOUN exams
an important test to find out what someone knows about a subject

examination NOUN examinations
❶ the full word for an *exam* ❷ a close inspection of something

examine VERB examines, examining, examined
to carefully check or look at something or someone
• *The doctor examined my ears.*

example NOUN examples
❶ something that belongs in a group of things and shows what they are like • *Can you give an example of a reptile?* ❷ a person or thing that you should copy
➤ **for example** as an example

excavate VERB excavates, excavating, excavated
to dig in an area or dig something up there
• They **excavated** some ancient statues.

exceed VERB exceeds, exceeding, exceeded
to be more or bigger than something • Its speed can **exceed** 100 miles per hour.

exceedingly ADVERB
extremely • He felt **exceedingly** proud.

excel VERB excels, excelling, excelled
To excel at something is to be very good at it.

excellent ADJECTIVE
extremely good
➤ **excellence** NOUN

except PREPOSITION
not including; apart from • Everyone got a prize **except** me.

exception NOUN exceptions
something or someone that is not included in a general statement or rule

exceptional ADJECTIVE
unusual or remarkable
➤ **exceptionally** ADVERB • an **exceptionally** large fish

excess NOUN excesses
too much of something • We have an **excess** of food.

excessive ADJECTIVE
more than is wanted or allowed
➤ **excessively** ADVERB

exchange VERB exchanges, exchanging, exchanged
To exchange something is to give it and receive something else for it.

excite VERB excites, exciting, excited
to make someone feel eager and enthusiastic
• The thought of getting a new bike **excited** him.
➤ **excitement** NOUN • We were full of **excitement**.
➤ **exciting** ADJECTIVE • The story was so **exciting**.

excited ADJECTIVE
feeling eager and enthusiastic • I was too **excited** to sleep.
➤ **excitedly** ADVERB

exclaim VERB exclaims, exclaiming, exclaimed
To exclaim is to shout or cry out. • 'Wow!' she **exclaimed**.

exclamation NOUN exclamations
a word or phrase you say out loud that expresses a strong feeling such as surprise

exclamation mark NOUN exclamation marks
the punctuation mark (!) used in writing after an exclamation

exclude VERB excludes, excluding, excluded
To exclude someone or something is to leave them out or keep them out.

exclusive *ADJECTIVE*
only for one person or group • *She gave the magazine an **exclusive** interview.*

excursion *NOUN* excursions
a short trip for pleasure

excuse (*say* iks-kewss) *NOUN* excuses
a reason someone gives to explain something they have done wrong

excuse (*say* iks-kewz) *VERB* excuses, excusing, excused
❶ To excuse someone is to forgive them. ❷ If you are excused from something, you are allowed not to do it.
➤ **excuse me** a way of politely getting someone's attention

execute *VERB* executes, executing, executed
❶ to kill someone as a punishment ❷ to do something or put it into practice • *Now he needed to execute his plan.*
➤ **execution** *NOUN*

executive *NOUN* executives
a senior person in a company

exercise *NOUN* exercises
❶ activity to make your body strong and healthy ❷ a piece of work done for practice • *a writing exercise*

exercise *VERB* exercises, exercising, exercised
to do activities to make your body strong and healthy

exert *VERB* exerts, exerting, exerted
to use your strength with a lot of effort • *He exerted all his strength to bend the bar.*

exhale *VERB* exhales, exhaling, exhaled
to breathe out

BUILD YOUR VOCABULARY
The opposite is **inhale**.

exhaust *VERB* exhausts, exhausting, exhausted
❶ to make someone very tired ❷ To exhaust a supply is to use it all up.
➤ **exhausted** *ADJECTIVE* • *I'm absolutely exhausted.*

exhaust *NOUN* exhausts
waste gases from an engine

exhibit *VERB* exhibits, exhibiting, exhibited
to show something in public, especially in a gallery or museum

exhibit *NOUN* exhibits
something displayed in a gallery or museum

exhibition *NOUN* exhibitions
a collection of things put on display for people to look at

exile *VERB* exiles, exiling, exiled
to send someone away from their country as a punishment

exile *NOUN* exiles
❶ If someone is in exile, they are not allowed to live in their own country. ❷ A person who is not allowed to live in their own country.

exist *VERB* exists, existing, existed
❶ to be real • *Do ghosts exist?* ❷ to stay alive • *Plants need water to exist.*
➤ **existence** *NOUN*

exit *NOUN* exits
❶ the way out of a place ❷ To make an exit is to leave a place.

exit *VERB* exits, exiting, exited
To exit a place is to leave it.

exotic *ADJECTIVE*
unusual and colourful, especially because of coming from far away

expand *VERB* expands, expanding, expanded
If something expands or if you expand it, it becomes larger.
➤ **expansion** *NOUN* • *the expansion of water as it freezes*

expanse *NOUN* expanses
a wide area

expect *VERB* expects, expecting, expected
❶ to think that something will probably happen • *No one expected him to win.* ❷ To be expecting someone is to be waiting for them to arrive.
❸ To expect something is to think that it ought to happen. • *I expect you to pay attention.*

expectant ADJECTIVE
expecting something to happen • *I looked at their expectant faces.*

expectation NOUN expectations
❶ Expectation is expecting something to happen.
• *an air of expectation* ❷ An expectation is something you expect to have.

expedition NOUN expeditions
a journey to do something • *They went on an expedition to the South Pole.*

expel VERB expels, expelling, expelled
❶ to send or force something out • *The fan expels stale air.* ❷ to make someone leave a school • *He was expelled for bullying.*

expense NOUN expenses
the cost of doing something

expensive ADJECTIVE
costing a lot of money

BUILD YOUR VOCABULARY
The opposite is **inexpensive**.

experience NOUN experiences
❶ Experience is what you learn from doing things.
• *She has a lot of experience of using computers.*
❷ An experience is something that happens to you.
• *I had a strange experience.*

experience VERB experiences, experiencing, experienced
to have something happen to you

experiment NOUN experiments
a scientific test to find out something
experiment VERB experiments, experimenting, experimented
to carry out experiments
➤ **experimentation** NOUN

experimental ADJECTIVE
being tried out to see how successful it is
• *an experimental new design*

expert NOUN experts
someone who has skill or special knowledge in something
expert ADJECTIVE
having great knowledge or skill

expire VERB expires, expiring, expired
to come to an end or to stop being usable
• *Your library card has expired.*

explain VERB explains, explaining, explained
to help someone to understand something
• *She explained the problem to me.*

explanation NOUN explanations
a statement that helps you to understand something
• *He gave a clear explanation of how the machine works.*

explode VERB explodes, exploding, exploded
to burst or blow up with great force

exploit (*say* ex-ploit) NOUN exploits
a brave or exciting action

exploit (*say* ex-ploit) VERB exploits, exploiting, exploited
to make use of something or someone
• *They exploited his ignorance.*

explore VERB explores, exploring, explored
to travel around a place to find out more about it
• *They explored the island.*
➤ **exploration** NOUN ➤ **explorer** NOUN

explosion NOUN explosions
the exploding of a bomb or other weapon

explosive NOUN explosives
a substance that can explode
explosive ADJECTIVE
likely to explode

export (*say* ex-port) VERB exports, exporting, exported
To export goods is to sell or send them to another country.

BUILD YOUR VOCABULARY
The opposite is **import**.

export (*say* ex-port) NOUN exports
something that is sold or sent to another country

BUILD YOUR VOCABULARY
The opposite is **import**.

expose VERB exposes, exposing, exposed
to reveal or uncover something

A
B
C
D
E
F
G
H
I
J
K
L
M
N
O
P
Q
R
S
T
U
V
W
X
Y
Z

exposure *NOUN* exposures
Exposure to something is not being protected or sheltered from it. • *Skin can be harmed by* **exposure** *to the sun.*

express *VERB* expresses, expressing, expressed
to put an idea or feeling into words • *I couldn't* **express** *how I was feeling.*

express *ADJECTIVE*
going quickly • *an* **express** *train*

express *NOUN* expresses
a fast train

expression *NOUN* expressions
❶ a look on a person's face that shows what they are feeling ❷ a word or phrase ❸ the act of expressing feelings
➤ **expressive** *ADJECTIVE* • *Her face is very* **expressive**.

expressly *ADVERB*
clearly or specifically • *I* **expressly** *forbade you to go there.*

exquisite *ADJECTIVE*
very delicate or beautiful
Next came a tall, beautiful woman clothed in a splendid trailing gown, trimmed with exquisite lace as fine as cobweb.—THE ROAD TO OZ, L. Frank Baum
➤ **exquisitely** *ADVERB*

extend *VERB* extends, extending, extended
to make something longer or to stretch it out • *She* **extended** *one arm.*

extension *NOUN* extensions
a part added on, especially to a building

extensive *ADJECTIVE*
covering a large area or including many things • *The bomb caused* **extensive** *damage.*
➤ **extensively** *ADVERB*

extent *NOUN* extents
❶ the area or length of something ❷ an amount or level • *I agree with you to some* **extent**.

exterior *NOUN* exteriors
the outside of something

exterminate *VERB* exterminates, exterminating, exterminated
to kill all of a group of animals or people
➤ **extermination** *NOUN*

external *ADJECTIVE*
outside
➤ **externally** *ADVERB*

extinct *ADJECTIVE*
❶ If a species of animal or plant is extinct, it no longer exists. ❷ An extinct volcano is no longer likely to erupt.

dodo

➤ **extinction** *NOUN*

BUILD YOUR VOCABULARY
Look at **active** and **dormant**.

extinguish *VERB* extinguishes, extinguishing, extinguished
To extinguish a fire or light is to put it out.
➤ **extinguisher** *NOUN*

extra *ADJECTIVE*
more than usual; added • *I had* **extra** *chips.*

extract (*say* ex-tract) *NOUN* extracts
a small section from a book, play or film
extract (*say* ex-**tract**) *VERB* extracts, extracting, extracted
to remove something or take it out of something else

extraordinary *ADJECTIVE*
very unusual or remarkable
➤ **extraordinarily** *ADVERB*

extraterrestrial *NOUN* extraterrestrials
a living thing from another planet, especially in science fiction
➤ **extraterrestrial** *ADJECTIVE*

extravagant *ADJECTIVE*
spending or using too much of something
➤ **extravagance** *NOUN*
➤ **extravagantly** *ADVERB*

extreme *ADJECTIVE*
❶ very great or intense • *He was in extreme danger.*
❷ farthest away • *They stood at the extreme end of the wall.*

extreme *NOUN* extremes
the highest or lowest point or the most intense point of something • *Desert creatures survive extremes of heat and cold.*

extremely *ADVERB*
to a very great degree; very • *They are extremely pleased.*

extremity *(say iks-trem-it-ee) NOUN*
extremities
❶ an extreme point ❷ Your extremities are your hands and feet.

eye *NOUN* eyes
Your eyes are the parts of your body that you see with.

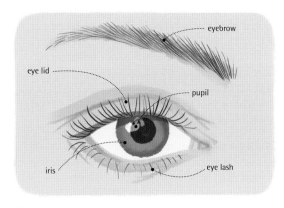

eyebrow
eye lid
pupil
iris
eye lash

⚙ **BUILD** YOUR VOCABULARY
Look at **iris**, **lens**, **pupil** and **retina**.

eye *VERB* eyes, eyeing, eyed
to look at someone or something • *She eyed the food greedily.*

eyeball *NOUN* eyeballs
the ball-shaped part of your eye, inside your eyelids

eyebrow *NOUN* eyebrows
the line of hair growing above each eye

eyelash *NOUN* eyelashes
one of the short hairs that grow on your eyelids

eyelid *NOUN* eyelids
the upper or lower fold of skin that can close over your eyeball

eyesight *NOUN*
Your eyesight is your ability to see.

eyewitness *NOUN* eyewitnesses
someone who saw something happen, especially an accident or a crime

a
b
c
d
e
f
g
h
i
j
k
l
m
n
o
p
q
r
s
t
u
v
w
x
y
z

⚙ **F** is for **French**. Lots of English words to do with food come from French. For example, we say **sheep** for an animal, but mutton (from the French word for 'sheep', *mouton*) is a sheep's meat.

⚙ For another example, look at **biscuit**!

F *ABBREVIATION*
the abbreviation for **Fahrenheit**

fable *NOUN* **fables**
a short story, often with animals as characters, that teaches a moral lesson

fabric *NOUN* **fabrics**
cloth

fabulous *ADJECTIVE*
❶ wonderful; amazing ❷ Fabulous creatures are found in stories, not in real life.

face *NOUN* **faces**
❶ the front part of your head, where your eyes, nose and mouth are ❷ a person's look or expression • *I saw his shocked face.* ❸ one of the flat surfaces of something • *A cube has six faces.* ❹ the front of a clock or watch

face *VERB* **faces, facing, faced**
❶ To face in a certain direction is to look there or have the front in that direction. • *Please face the board.* • *The house faces north.* ❷ To face a problem or danger is to have to deal with it.

facility *(say* fass-il-it-tee*) NOUN* **facilities**
a place or set of equipment that allows you to take part in an activity • *The school has good sports facilities.*

fact *NOUN* **facts**
something that we know is true
➤ **as a matter of fact** or **in fact** really; actually • *I'm leaving this morning. Now, **in fact**.*

factor *NOUN* **factors**
❶ something that affects a situation or event • *They had forgotten one important **factor**: the weather.* ❷ a number by which a larger number can be divided exactly • *2 and 3 are **factors** of 6.*

factory *NOUN* **factories**
a building where things are made with machines in large amounts

fade *VERB* **fades, fading, faded**
to become less bright, less strong or less loud

Fahrenheit *(say* fa-ren-hyt*) NOUN*
a scale for measuring temperature in which water freezes at 32 degrees and boils at 212 degrees

⚙ **BUILD** YOUR VOCABULARY
Look at **Celsius**.

fail *VERB* **fails, failing, failed**
❶ to not succeed in doing something • *I tried, but I **failed**.* ❷ to stop working • *The engine **failed**.* ❸ To fail a test is not to pass it. ❹ To fail to do something is not to do it. • *The light **failed** to come on.*

fail *NOUN*
➤ **without fail** definitely or always • *He calls every day **without fail**.*

failure *NOUN* **failures**
❶ Failure is lack of success. ❷ A failure is someone or something who has not had any success. • *The experiment was a **failure**.* ❸ A failure is when something stops working. • *The storm caused a power **failure**.*

faint *ADJECTIVE* **fainter, faintest**
❶ not strong or clear • *I heard a **faint** tapping sound.* ❷ feeling very weak • *I was **faint** with hunger.*

faint *VERB* **faints, fainting, fainted**
To faint is to become unconscious for a short time.
➤ **faintly** *ADVERB* ➤ **faintness** *NOUN*

fair *ADJECTIVE* **fairer, fairest**
❶ right or reasonable • *It's not **fair** if he gets more.*
❷ Fair hair is light in colour. ❸ Fair weather is fine and dry. ❹ quite good • *We've got a **fair** chance of winning.*
➤ **fairness** *NOUN*

fair *NOUN* **fairs**
an outdoor entertainment with stalls and games or amusements

fairground *NOUN* **fairgrounds**
a place where a fair is held

fairly *ADVERB*
❶ quite or rather • *The cake is **fairly** easy to make.*
❷ reasonably or equally • *He treats everyone **fairly**.*

fairy *NOUN* **fairies**
an imaginary small magical creature with wings

fairyland *NOUN*
an imaginary place where fairies live

fairy tale (*also* **fairy story**) *NOUN* **fairy tales, fairy stories**
a story, usually a traditional one, about magic

faith *NOUN* **faiths**
❶ strong belief or trust • *We have a lot of **faith** in her.* ❷ a religion

faithful *ADJECTIVE*
loyal to someone
➤ **faithfully** *ADVERB* ➤ **faithfulness** *NOUN*

fake *NOUN* **fakes**
a copy of something made to deceive people into thinking it is real
fake *ADJECTIVE*
not real or genuine • *fake fur* • *a **fake** laugh*
fake *VERB* **fakes, faking, faked**
to make something look real or pretend something, in order to deceive people • *The photographs had been **faked**.*

falcon *NOUN* **falcons**
a bird of prey that is a small kind of hawk

fall *VERB* **falls, falling, fell, fallen**
❶ to drop down towards the ground • *A tree had **fallen** across the path.* • *My key **fell** out of my pocket.* ❷ to decrease • *The temperature **fell** to zero.* ❸ If you fall asleep, fall ill or fall in love, you start to sleep, to be ill or to be in love.

➤ **To fall for something** is to be tricked into believing it.
➤ **To fall out** is to quarrel and stop being friends.

fall *NOUN* **falls**
If someone has a fall, they fall and hurt themselves.

false *ADJECTIVE*
❶ untrue or incorrect • *What he said about me was **false**.* ❷ fake; not genuine • *a **false** passport*

falsehood *NOUN* **falsehoods**
a lie

falter *VERB* **falters, faltering, faltered**
to hesitate or weaken because you are unsure

fame *NOUN*
the state of being famous

familiar *ADJECTIVE*
❶ that you know about or recognise • *I saw a **familiar** face.* ❷ To be familiar with something is to know about or understand it.

family *NOUN* **families**
❶ Your family is the people who are related to you, for example your parents, brothers or sisters.
❷ a group of animals or plants that are closely related • *The tiger is a member of the cat **family**.*

family tree *NOUN* **family trees**
a diagram showing how people in a family are related

famine *NOUN* **famines**
a severe shortage of food that causes many people to die

famished *ADJECTIVE*
extremely hungry

famous *ADJECTIVE*
known to a lot of people • *Her aunt is a **famous** artist.*

fan *NOUN* **fans**
❶ a device that moves air to cool people or things
❷ an enthusiastic supporter of someone or something

fan VERB fans, fanning, fanned
to direct air onto something • *She **fanned** her face with a book.*
➤ **To fan out** is to spread out in the shape of a fan.
Lloyd could see the men in brown overalls fanning out across the Dome, like hounds searching for a scent.
—THE REVENGE OF THE DEMON HEADMASTER, Gillian Cross

fanatic NOUN fanatics
someone who is too enthusiastic about something

fanciful ADJECTIVE
imaginative and not realistic • *That's a rather **fanciful** idea.*

fancy ADJECTIVE fancier, fanciest
decorated or special; not plain

fancy VERB fancies, fancying, fancied
❶ to want or feel like something • *I **fancy** a swim.*
❷ to imagine something • *I **fancied** I heard a voice.*
fancy NOUN fancies
❶ something you imagine • *His head was filled with strange **fancies**.* ❷ a liking or desire

fancy dress NOUN
clothes you wear to a party or an event that make you look like someone or something else

fang NOUN fangs
a long sharp tooth

✱ **WORD STORY**

The word **fang** comes from an Old Norse word meaning 'catch' or 'grasp', because fangs can catch hold of things.

fantastic ADJECTIVE
❶ excellent, wonderful ❷ strange or unusual
• *fantastic beasts*
➤ **fantastically** ADVERB

fantasy NOUN fantasies
an imaginative story or dream that is not realistic

far ADVERB farther, farthest
❶ a long way • *My house isn't **far**.* ❷ much; by a large amount • *This one is **far** better.*
➤ **so far** up to now
far ADJECTIVE farther, farthest
distant; opposite • *My grandma lives on the **far** side of town.*

faraway ADJECTIVE
distant or remote • *faraway lands*

fare NOUN fares
the money you pay to travel on a bus, train, boat or aircraft

farewell EXCLAMATION
goodbye

far-fetched ADJECTIVE
unlikely to be true

farm NOUN farms
an area of land and buildings where someone grows crops and keeps animals for food
farm VERB farms, farming, farmed
to grow crops and raise animals for food
➤ **farmer** NOUN

farmhouse NOUN farmhouses
the house where a farmer lives

farmyard NOUN farmyards
an area surrounded by farm buildings

farther ADVERB, ADJECTIVE
at or to a greater distance • *The town lies **farther** west.*

❗ **WATCH OUT!**

Farther contains the word *far*. Do not confuse with **father** meaning 'male parent'.

farthest ADVERB, ADJECTIVE
at or to the greatest distance • *Which planet is the **farthest** from the sun?*

farthing NOUN farthings
an old British coin of very low value

fascinate VERB fascinates, fascinating, fascinated
If something fascinates you, it interests you very much.
➤ **fascination** NOUN

> ⚠ **WATCH OUT!**
> Don't forget that the s sound in **fascinate** is spelt **sc** with a silent 'c', as in 'science'.

fashion NOUN fashions
the style of clothes or other things that is popular at a particular time • *a blog about the latest fashions*

fashionable ADJECTIVE
following a style that is popular at a particular time

fast ADJECTIVE faster, fastest
❶ quick, speedy • *Cheetahs are fast runners.* ❷ If a watch or clock is fast, it shows a time later than the correct time.

fast ADVERB
❶ quickly • *She talks too fast.* ❷ firmly or securely • *The lid was stuck fast.*
➤ **fast asleep** deeply asleep

fast VERB fasts, fasting, fasted
To fast is to eat no food. • *He's fasting for Ramadan.*

fast NOUN fasts
a time when you go without food

fasten VERB fastens, fastening, fastened
to join something firmly to something else
➤ **fastener** NOUN

fat NOUN fats
❶ the white greasy substance under an animal's or a person's skin or in meat ❷ oil or grease used in cooking

fat ADJECTIVE fatter, fattest
having a body with a lot of fat

fatal ADJECTIVE
causing someone's death • *There was a fatal accident.*
➤ **fatally** ADVERB • *He was fatally wounded.*

fate NOUN fates
❶ a power that is thought to control what happens ❷ Someone's fate is what happens to them.

father NOUN fathers
a male parent

> ⚙ **BUILD YOUR VOCABULARY**
> Look at **paternal**.

father-in-law NOUN fathers-in-law
the father of someone's husband or wife

Father's Day NOUN
a day of the year on which fathers are celebrated

fathom NOUN fathoms
a unit used for measuring the depth of water, equal to 1.83 metres

fathom VERB fathoms, fathoming, fathomed
to work out or understand something • *I can't fathom why he did it.*

fatigue (*say* fat-**eeg**) NOUN
extreme tiredness

fatten VERB fattens, fattening, fattened
to make someone or something fat

fatty ADJECTIVE fattier, fattiest
fatty food contains a lot of fat

fault NOUN faults
❶ If something is your fault, you are to blame for it. • *It's my fault we're late.* ❷ a flaw or problem in someone or something

fault VERB faults, faulting, faulted
To fault something is to find something wrong with it.

faulty ADJECTIVE faultier, faultiest
having something wrong with it

favour NOUN favours
❶ If you do someone a favour, you do something to help them. ❷ Favour is approval. • *The Queen looked on him with favour.*
➤ **To be in favour of someone** or **something** is to support them or be on their side.

favour VERB favours, favouring, favoured
to like and support or prefer someone or something

favourable ADJECTIVE
helpful or positive • *a favourable response*

favourite ADJECTIVE
liked more than others • *Purple is my favourite colour.*

a b c d e f g h i j k l m n o p q r s t u v w x y z

A
B
C
D
E
F
G
H
I
J
K
L
M
N
O
P
Q
R
S
T
U
V
W
X
Y
Z

favourite *NOUN* **favourites**
the person or thing that you like best • *This song is my favourite.*

fawn *NOUN* **fawns**
❶ a young deer ❷ a light brown colour

fear *NOUN* **fears**
a feeling that something unpleasant may happen
fear *VERB* **fears, fearing, feared**
to be afraid of something or someone • *There's nothing to fear.*

fearful *ADJECTIVE*
❶ afraid ❷ frightening, dreadful • *It was a fearful sight.*

fearless *ADJECTIVE*
brave and without fear
➤ **fearlessly** *ADVERB*

fearsome *ADJECTIVE*
frightening • *a fearsome beast*

feast *NOUN* **feasts**
a large and special meal for a lot of people
feast *VERB* **feasts, feasting, feasted**
to have a feast

feat *NOUN* **feats**
a brave or clever deed

feather *NOUN* **feathers**
A bird's feathers are the light soft parts that cover its body.
➤ **feathery** *ADJECTIVE*

feature *NOUN* **features**
❶ Your features are the parts of your face.
❷ an aspect of something; a characteristic
❸ an article about something in a newspaper, magazine or programme

fed *VERB* (*past tense and past participle of* **feed**)
• *She fed us soup and bread.* • *Have you fed the cat?*

fed up *ADJECTIVE* (*informal*)
bored or unhappy

fee *NOUN* **fees**
a payment or charge

feeble *ADJECTIVE* **feebler, feeblest**
weak • *He was too feeble to stand.*
➤ **feebly** *ADVERB*

feed *VERB* **feeds, feeding, fed**
❶ To feed a person or an animal is to give them food. • *Have you fed the cat?* ❷ To feed is to eat. • *Sheep feed on grass.* ❸ To feed something into a machine is to put it in.

feel *VERB* **feels, feeling, felt**
❶ to experience a feeling or emotion • *I felt sorry for him.* • *She felt a sharp pain.* ❷ to touch something to find out what it is like • *Feel this smooth rock.* ❸ to have a particular quality that you can feel • *The water feels warm.* ❹ to believe or think something • *I feel we should help them.*
➤ **To feel like something** is to want it.

feeler *NOUN* **feelers**
An insect's feelers are the long thin parts it uses for feeling.

 BUILD YOUR VOCABULARY
A synonym is **antenna**.

feeling *NOUN* **feelings**
❶ Your feelings are your emotions. • *I have hurt her feelings.* ❷ a physical sensation • *I had a funny feeling in my stomach.*

feet *NOUN* (*plural of* **foot**)

feline *ADJECTIVE*
to do with cats or like a cat

fell *VERB* (*past tense of* **fall**)
• *He was so tired he fell asleep instantly.*
fell *VERB* **fells, felling, felled**
❶ To fell a tree is to cut it down. ❷ To fell someone is to knock them down.

fell *NOUN* **fells**
Fells are wild hilly country.

fellow *NOUN* **fellows**
❶ (*informal*) a man or boy ❷ a friend or companion

fellow *ADJECTIVE*
belonging to the same group • *She talked to some of her fellow teachers.*

felt VERB (past tense and past participle of **feel**)
• He **felt** a sharp pain in his leg. • I had **felt** sorry
for her.

felt NOUN
thick cloth made from threads pressed together

female ADJECTIVE
belonging to the sex that can have babies or young
female NOUN females
a female person or animal

feminine ADJECTIVE
to do with women or like a woman
➤ **femininity** NOUN

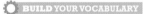 **BUILD YOUR VOCABULARY**
Look at **masculine**.

fence NOUN fences
a wooden or metal barrier round an area of land

fend VERB fends, fending, fended
➤ **To fend for yourself** is to take care of yourself.
➤ **To fend someone** or **something off** is to
keep them away when they are attacking you.

fern NOUN ferns
a plant with feathery leaves and no flowers

ferocious ADJECTIVE
fierce and dangerous
➤ **ferociously** ADVERB

ferret NOUN ferrets
a small animal with a long thin body, used for
catching rabbits and rats

ferry NOUN ferries
a boat that takes people or things across a short
stretch of water
ferry VERB ferries, ferrying, ferried
to take people or things back and forth from one
place to another

fertile ADJECTIVE
❶ Fertile land is good for growing plants. ❷ People
or animals that are fertile can produce babies or
young.
➤ **fertility** NOUN

BUILD YOUR VOCABULARY
An opposite is **infertile**.

fertilise (also **fertilize**) VERB fertilises,
fertilising, fertilised
❶ To fertilise an egg is to put male cells into it so
that reproduction begins. ❷ To fertilise soil is to add
chemicals or manure to it so that plants grow better.
➤ **fertilisation** NOUN

fervent ADJECTIVE
very enthusiastic or sincere • He made a **fervent**
promise.
➤ **fervently** ADVERB

festival NOUN festivals
❶ an organised set of events and performances
• a music **festival** ❷ a special celebration, especially
a religious one

festive ADJECTIVE
to do with joyful celebrating

festivities NOUN
parties and celebrations

festoon VERB festoons, festooning,
festooned
to decorate a place by hanging strips of cloth or
strings of flowers or lights

fetch VERB fetches, fetching, fetched
to go and get someone or something • Will you **fetch**
me my glasses?

fete (say fayt) NOUN fetes
an outdoor event with stalls and games, often held
to raise money

feud (say fewd) NOUN **feuds**
a bitter quarrel between people or families that lasts a long time
feud (say fewd) VERB **feuds, feuding, feuded**
to keep up a quarrel for a long time

fever NOUN **fevers**
If you have a fever, your body temperature is high because you are ill.

feverish ADJECTIVE
❶ having a high body temperature because of illness
❷ excited or frantic • *feverish activity*

few DETERMINER, PRONOUN **fewer, fewest**
not many • *Few people went there.* • *Few went there.*
➤ **a few** several; more than two but not a large number • *I've been there a few times.* • *'Have you got any games?'—'A few.'*
➤ **fewer** not as many • *Try to make fewer mistakes.*

fiancé (say fee-ahn-say) NOUN **fiancés**
Someone's fiancé is the man they are engaged to marry.

fiancée (say fee-ahn-say) NOUN **fiancées**
Someone's fiancée is the woman they are engaged to marry.

fiasco (say fee-ass-koh) NOUN **fiascos**
a complete failure • *The party turned into a fiasco.*

fib NOUN **fibs**
a lie about something unimportant
fib VERB **fibs, fibbing, fibbed**
to tell a lie about something unimportant

fibre (say fy-ber) NOUN **fibres**
❶ a thin thread ❷ part of plants that your body cannot digest, that helps you digest other food properly

fickle ADJECTIVE
often changing your mind; not staying loyal

fiction NOUN **fictions**
writing, such as stories and novels, about imaginary events
➤ **fictional** ADJECTIVE • *a fictional character*

⚙ **BUILD** YOUR VOCABULARY
The opposite is **non-fiction**.

fiddle VERB **fiddles, fiddling, fiddled**
to keep touching or playing with something
• *Stop fiddling with your phone!*
fiddle NOUN **fiddles** (informal)
a violin

fidget VERB **fidgets, fidgeting, fidgeted**
to make small restless movements because you are bored or nervous
➤ **fidgety** ADJECTIVE

field NOUN **fields**
❶ a piece of land with crops or grass growing on it
❷ an area of interest or study • *Biology is an interesting field.*

fiend (say feend) NOUN **fiends**
❶ a devil or evil spirit ❷ a wicked or cruel person
➤ **fiendish** ADJECTIVE

fierce ADJECTIVE **fiercer, fiercest**
❶ aggressive and violent • *a fierce animal* ❷ strong or intense • *The heat was fierce.*
➤ **fiercely** ADVERB ➤ **fierceness** NOUN

fiery ADJECTIVE **fierier, fieriest**
❶ full of flames or heat • *a fiery furnace* ❷ bright red • *fiery red hair* ❸ passionate or easily made angry • *a fiery temper*

fig NOUN **figs**
a soft fruit full of small seeds

fight NOUN **fights**
❶ a physical struggle using hands or weapons
❷ an attempt to achieve or stop something
• *Recycling is part of the fight against waste.*
fight VERB **fights, fighting, fought**
❶ To fight someone is to have a fight with them.
❷ To fight something is to try to stop it.
• *Firefighters fought the blaze.* ❸ To fight is to try hard to make something happen. • *Women fought for the right to vote.*

figurative ADJECTIVE
Figurative language uses words for special effect and not with their usual meaning. For example 'a flood of emails' is a figurative use of the word 'flood'.

 **BUILD** YOUR VOCABULARY
Look at **metaphor** and **simile**.

figure *NOUN* **figures**
❶ a written number • *We added up all the* **figures**.
❷ a person or the shape of a person • *I saw a* **figure** *through the window.*

figure of speech *NOUN* **figures of speech**
a way of using words for special effect and not with their usual meaning • *'You make me sick' is just a* **figure of speech**.

🔧 **BUILD YOUR VOCABULARY**
Look at **figurative**, **metaphor** and **simile**.

filament *NOUN* **filaments**
a thread or thin wire

file *NOUN* **files**
❶ a box or folder for keeping papers in ❷ a set of information stored under one name in a computer ❸ a tool with a rough surface for shaping things or making them smooth
➤ **To walk in single file** is to walk one behind the other.

file *VERB* **files, filing, filed**
❶ to put a document in a box or folder ❷ to shape or smooth something with a file ❸ To file somewhere is to walk there one behind the other.

fill *VERB* **fills, filling, filled**
❶ If something fills or you fill it, it becomes full.
• *The room was* **filling** *quickly.* • *I* **filled** *the bucket with water.* ❷ To fill something is to take up all the space in it.
➤ **To fill in a form** is to write information in the spaces on it.

fillet *NOUN* **fillets**
a piece of fish or meat without bones

filling *NOUN* **fillings**
❶ food you put inside a pie, sandwich or cake
❷ a piece of metal or plastic put in your tooth by a dentist to fill a hole in it

film *NOUN* **films**
❶ a series of moving pictures that tells a story, shown in a cinema or on television ❷ a roll of thin plastic that you put in some types of camera to record images
film *VERB* **films, filming, filmed**
To film something is to make a film of it.

filter *NOUN* **filters**
a device that allows some substances or light to pass through it but stops others
filter *VERB* **filters, filtering, filtered**
To filter a liquid or gas is to pass it through a filter.

filth *NOUN*
disgusting dirt
➤ **filthy** *ADJECTIVE*

fin *NOUN* **fins**
a thin flat part that sticks out from a fish's body

final *ADJECTIVE*
❶ coming at the end; last • *We read the* **final** *chapter.* ❷ not possible to change or argue with
• *The teacher's decision is* **final**.
final *NOUN* **finals**
the last of a series of contests, that decides the overall winner

finalist *NOUN* **finalists**
a person or team taking part in a final

finally *ADVERB*
❶ after a long time; at last • *The door* **finally** *opened.* ❷ as the last thing • **Finally**, *decorate the cake with berries.*

finance *NOUN*
Finance is money or things relating to it.
finance *VERB* **finances, financing, financed**
To finance something is to provide money for it.

financial *ADJECTIVE*
to do with money

a b c d e f g h i j k l m n o p q r s t u v w x y z

A B C D E F G H I J K L M N O P Q R S T U V W X Y Z

finch *NOUN* finches
a small bird with a short thick beak

find *VERB* finds, finding, found
① to see or get something by chance or by looking for it • *I found this coin on the floor.* ② to learn something by experience • *She has found that she loves science.*
➤ **To find something out** is to get information.

findings *NOUN*
Your findings are things you have found out from an investigation or experiment.

fine *ADJECTIVE* finer, finest
① well or unharmed • *Don't worry, I'm fine.*
② satisfactory; acceptable • *It's fine if you want to leave early.* ③ thin • *There was a fine mist.*
④ excellent • *This is a fine example of a fossil.*
⑤ Fine weather is dry and sunny.

fine *NOUN* fines
money that someone must pay as a punishment
fine *VERB* fines, fining, fined
to make someone pay money as a punishment

finger *NOUN* fingers
one of the long thin parts that stick out on your hand

fingernail *NOUN* fingernails
the hard covering at the end of your finger

fingerprint *NOUN* fingerprints
a mark made by the pattern of curved lines on the tip of your finger

finish *VERB* finishes, finishing, finished
① To finish something is to complete it. • *I've finished my book.* ② To finish is to come to an end. • *What time does school finish?*
finish *NOUN* finishes
the end of something

fir *NOUN* firs
an evergreen tree with leaves like needles

fire *NOUN* fires
① flames, heat and light from something that is burning • *They tried to put out the fire.* ② a piece of equipment that uses wood, coal, electricity or gas to heat a place
➤ **To be on fire** is to be burning.
➤ **To set fire to something** is to start it burning.

fire *VERB* fires, firing, fired
① To fire a gun is to shoot it. ② *(informal)* To fire someone is to dismiss them from their job.

fire brigade *NOUN* fire brigades
a team of people whose job is to put out fires and rescue people from fires

fire engine *NOUN* fire engines
a large vehicle that carries firefighters and their equipment

fire extinguisher *NOUN* fire extinguishers
a cylinder containing water or foam for spraying over a fire to put it out

firefighter *NOUN* firefighters
a member of a fire brigade

fireplace *NOUN* fireplaces
an open space for a fire in the wall of a room

firework NOUN fireworks
an object that produces coloured lights and loud bangs when lit, used for celebrations

firm ADJECTIVE firmer, firmest
❶ fixed or solid • *The ground is firm.* ❷ quite strict and not likely to change your mind • *You have to be firm with the dog.*
➤ **firmly** ADVERB • *'We stay together,' I said firmly.*
➤ **firmness** NOUN

firm NOUN firms
a company • *She runs a small firm.*

first ADJECTIVE
❶ coming before all others • *January is the first month.* ❷ the most important • *I won first prize.*
first ADVERB
before everything else • *Finish your homework first.*
first NOUN
a person or thing that is first
➤ **at first** at the beginning; to start with

first aid NOUN
simple medical treatment given to an injured person before a doctor comes

first-class ADJECTIVE
of the best category or quality

first floor NOUN first floors
the next floor above the ground floor

firstly ADVERB
as the first thing • *Firstly, let me explain the rules.*

first name NOUN
the name that your parents gave you and that people usually call you
🔧 **BUILD** YOUR VOCABULARY
Look at **surname**.

first person NOUN
the use of the words 'I' and 'me' and the verbs that go with them, for example when writing a story • *A diary is usually written in the first person.*
🔧 **BUILD** YOUR VOCABULARY
Look at **second person** and **third person**.

firth NOUN firths
an estuary or a river mouth in Scotland

fish NOUN fish, fishes
a cold-blooded animal with fins that lives and breathes in water
fish VERB fishes, fishing, fished
to try to catch fish

fisherman NOUN fishermen
someone who catches fish, either as a job or sport

fishmonger NOUN fishmongers
a shopkeeper who sells fish

fishy ADJECTIVE fishier, fishiest
❶ like a fish • *fishy eyes*
❷ (informal) suspicious or strange • *There's something fishy going on.*

fissure NOUN fissures
a narrow opening or crack • *There was a fissure in the rock.*

fist NOUN fists
your hand when it is tightly closed with your fingers bent into your palm

fit ADJECTIVE fitter, fittest
❶ healthy and strong through exercise • *I'm trying to get fit.* ❷ suitable or good enough • *This food is not fit to eat.*
➤ **fitness** NOUN

fit VERB fits, fitting, fitted
❶ to be the right size and shape for a person or place • *These shoes fit me.* • *The lid doesn't fit.*
❷ to put something into place • *We fitted a lock on the door.* ❸ to be suitable for something • *The music fitted the film perfectly.*

fit NOUN fits
❶ a sudden illness in which someone becomes unconscious and makes uncontrolled movements
❷ a sudden outburst or attack • *He had a coughing fit.*

fix VERB fixes, fixing, fixed
❶ to join something firmly to something else • *She fixed a shelf to the wall.* ❷ to mend something • *Can you fix my computer?*
➤ **To fix something up** is to arrange or organise it.

fizz VERB fizzes, fizzing, fizzed,
❶ to make a hissing or spluttering sound
❷ to produce a lot of small bubbles

fizzle VERB fizzles, fizzling, fizzled
to make a hissing or crackling sound

fizzy ADJECTIVE fizzier, fizziest
A fizzy drink has a lot of bubbles.

fjord (say fee-ord) NOUN fjords
a long narrow sea inlet, especially in Norway

flabbergasted ADJECTIVE (informal)
completely astonished

flabby ADJECTIVE flabbier, flabbiest
fat and soft

flag NOUN flags
a piece of material with a coloured pattern or shape
on it, used as the symbol of a country or group

flake NOUN flakes
a light thin piece of something • *Flakes of paint
came off the wall.*
➤ **flaky** ADJECTIVE

flake VERB flakes, flaking, flaked
To flake is to come off in light thin pieces.

flame NOUN flames
a bright flickering strip of fire

flame VERB flames, flaming, flamed
to produce flames • *a piece of flaming
coal*

flamingo NOUN flamingos
a large, pale pink wading
bird with long legs and
a long neck

flammable
ADJECTIVE
able to catch
fire easily

! WATCH OUT!
The words **flammable** and
inflammable are synonyms,
not opposites.

flank NOUN flanks
the side of something, especially an animal's
body, a hill or an army

flannel NOUN flannels
❶ a small piece of towel you use to wash yourself
❷ Flannel is a soft woollen material.

flap NOUN flaps
a loose piece hanging down, for example to cover
an opening

flap VERB flaps, flapping, flapped
❶ To flap something is to move it up and down or
from side to side. • *The bird flapped its wings.*
❷ To flap is to wave about. • *The sails were flapping
in the breeze.*

flare VERB flares, flaring, flared
❶ to burn with a sudden bright flame • *A match
flared in the darkness.* ❷ to widen • *His nostrils flared.*

flare NOUN flares
❶ a sudden bright light or flame • *the flare of a
torch* ❷ an emergency signalling device that fires a
bright light into the sky

flash NOUN flashes
a sudden bright burst of light • *a flash of lightning*

flash VERB flashes, flashing, flashed
❶ to make a sudden bright burst of light
• *Lightning flashed.* ❷ If something flashes or
you flash it, it shines quickly on and off. • *Why is
that light flashing?*

flask NOUN flasks
❶ a drink container with a narrow
neck • *a leather flask* ❷ a special
bottle for keeping drinks hot
or cold

flat ADJECTIVE flatter, flattest
❶ smooth and level with no curves
or bumps • *We sat on a flat rock.*
❷ A flat tyre or ball has lost its air.
❸ A flat battery has no power left in it.
➤ **flatness** NOUN

flat NOUN flats
a set of rooms for living in, usually on one
floor of a building

flatly ADVERB
❶ very definitely and firmly • *He flatly refused to
go.* ❷ without emotion • *'I see,' he said flatly.*

flatten VERB flattens, flattening, flattened
to make something flat • *The monster flattened
everything in its path.*

flatter VERB flatters, flattering, flattered
to praise someone more than they deserve because you want to please them
➤ **flattery** NOUN

flaunt VERB flaunts, flaunting, flaunted
to show something off

flavour NOUN flavours
the taste and smell of a food or drink
flavour VERB flavours, flavouring, flavoured
To flavour food or drink is to give it a particular taste and smell.

flaw NOUN flaws
a fault that stops a person or thing from being perfect • *There was a major flaw in their escape plan.*
➤ **flawless** ADJECTIVE

flax NOUN
a plant whose fibres are used to make a cloth called linen

flea NOUN fleas
a small jumping insect that sucks blood

fleck NOUN flecks
a small piece or speck • *There were flecks of paint on the desk.*

flee VERB flees, fleeing, fled
To flee is to run away from something. • *The villagers fled in terror.*

fleece NOUN fleeces
A sheep's fleece is its wool.

fleet NOUN fleets
a number of ships or vehicles owned by one country or company

fleeting ADJECTIVE
very brief • *I caught a fleeting glimpse of a fox.*

flesh NOUN
the soft part of the bodies of people and animals

flew VERB (past tense of **fly**)
• *The bird flew away.*

flex VERB flexes, flexing, flexed
to bend or stretch something • *She flexed her fingers.*

flexible ADJECTIVE
easy to bend or stretch
➤ **flexibility** NOUN

⚙ **BUILD YOUR VOCABULARY**
An opposite is **rigid**.

flick NOUN flicks
a quick light hit or movement
flick VERB flicks, flicking, flicked
to hit or move something with a flick • *The horse flicked its tail.*

flicker VERB flickers, flickering, flickered
to burn or shine unsteadily
The sky was quite black and the big stars flickered as if they were alive.—COMET IN MOOMINLAND, Tove Jansson

flight NOUN flights
❶ A flight is a journey in an aircraft or a rocket. ❷ Flight is the action of flying. • *the history of space flight* ❸ Flight is the action of running away. • *He saw us and took flight.* ❹ A flight of stairs is one set of stairs.

flimsy ADJECTIVE flimsier, flimsiest
light and thin or fragile • *a flimsy wooden hut*

flinch VERB flinches, flinching, flinched
to make a sudden movement because of fear or pain

fling VERB flings, flinging, flung
to throw something hard or carelessly • *He flung his pen down.*

flint NOUN flints
a very hard kind of stone, used for starting fires and making weapons

flip VERB flips, flipping, flipped
to turn something over quickly • *Flip the pancake.*

flipper NOUN flippers
❶ a limb that a water animal such as a seal uses for swimming ❷ a flat rubber shoe that you wear to help you swim

flit VERB flits, flitting, flitted
to fly or move lightly and quickly • *Butterflies flitted around.*

float VERB floats, floating, floated
to stay or move on the surface of a liquid or in the air

a
b
c
d
e
f
g
h
i
j
k
l
m
n
o
p
q
r
s
t
u
v
w
x
y
z

float *NOUN* floats
a device designed to float • *A fishing line has a float.*

flock *NOUN* flocks
a group of sheep, goats or birds
flock *VERB* flocks, flocking, flocked
to gather or move in a crowd • *People flocked to the fair.*

flood *NOUN* floods
❶ a large amount of water spreading over a place that is usually dry ❷ a great amount of something • *We got a flood of calls.*
flood *VERB* floods, flooding, flooded
❶ To flood something or to flood is to cover an area with a lot of water. • *The fields were flooded.* • *The river sometimes floods.* ❷ to fill something with light or with a sound, smell or feeling • *Sunlight flooded the room.* • *He was flooded with relief.*

floodlight *NOUN* floodlights
a large bright lamp used to light a public building or a sports ground at night

floor *NOUN* floors
❶ the part of a room that people walk on ❷ all the rooms on the same level in a building • *My room is on the top floor.*

flop *VERB* flops, flopping, flopped
❶ to fall or sit down heavily • *I flopped into a chair.*
❷ to hang loosely • *His hair flops over his eyes.*

floppy *ADJECTIVE* floppier, floppiest
soft or hanging loosely • *Our dog has floppy ears.*

floral *ADJECTIVE*
made of or decorated with flowers

flounder *VERB* flounders, floundering, floundered
to move clumsily or struggle

flour *NOUN*
a powder made from corn or wheat, used for making bread, cakes and pastry
➤ **floury** *ADJECTIVE*

flourish *VERB* flourishes, flourishing, flourished
to grow or develop successfully

flourish *NOUN* flourishes
a dramatic waving movement • *He produced the papers with a flourish.*

flow *VERB* flows, flowing, flowed
❶ to move along smoothly ❷ to hang loosely
• *She had long flowing hair.*

flow *NOUN* flows
a continuous steady movement of something

flow chart *NOUN* flow charts
a diagram that shows the different stages of how something happens

flower *NOUN* flowers
the part of a plant from which the seed or fruit develops
➤ **flowery** *ADJECTIVE*

BUILD YOUR VOCABULARY
Look at **floral**.

flower *VERB* flowers, flowering, flowered
When a plant flowers, it produces flowers.

flown *VERB* (past participle of **fly**)
• *Have you ever flown in a plane?*

flu *NOUN*
a disease like a very bad cold, that causes fever and aching and can be very serious

fluent *ADJECTIVE*
If you are fluent in a language, you can speak it very easily.

fluff NOUN
small soft bits of wool or fibres

fluffy ADJECTIVE fluffier, fluffiest
soft like fluff • *a fluffy cloud*

fluid NOUN fluids
a substance that flows easily; a liquid or gas

fluke NOUN flukes
a success caused by unexpected good luck

flung VERB (past tense and past participle of **fling**)
• She **flung** her bag on a chair. • He was **flung** backwards by the blast.

fluorescent ADJECTIVE
❶ A fluorescent colour or object is very bright and gives out light. ❷ A fluorescent light produces a harsh, bright light.

fluoride NOUN
a chemical that helps prevent tooth decay

flurry NOUN flurries
a sudden gust of wind, rain or snow

flush VERB flushes, flushing, flushed
❶ to go slightly red in the face ❷ To flush something is to clean or remove it with a fast flow of liquid.

flustered ADJECTIVE
nervous and stressed

flute NOUN flutes
a musical instrument like a long pipe, that you play by holding it to one side and blowing across a hole in it

BUILD YOUR VOCABULARY
A **flute** is a **wind instrument**.

flutter VERB flutters, fluttering, fluttered
to flap or move quickly and lightly • *Flags **fluttered** in the breeze.*

fly VERB flies, flying, flew, flown
❶ to move through the air with wings or in an aircraft ❷ to move or pass quickly • *The door **flew** open.* • *The holidays have **flown** by.*

fly NOUN flies
a small flying insect with two wings

foal NOUN foals
a young horse

foam NOUN
❶ a mass of tiny bubbles on top of a liquid
❷ a spongy material used to fill cushions and mattresses

foam VERB foams, foaming, foamed
to form a mass of tiny bubbles

focus VERB focuses, focusing, focused
❶ To focus your eye or a camera lens is to adjust it so that objects appear clearly. ❷ To focus on something is to concentrate on it.

focus NOUN focuses or foci
➤ **To be in focus** is to appear clearly and not blurred.
➤ **To be out of focus** is to appear blurred.

fodder NOUN
food for horses and farm animals

foe NOUN foes
Your foe is your enemy.

foetus (say **fee**-tus) NOUN foetuses
an unborn animal in the womb, especially a human that has been developing for at least 8 weeks

BUILD YOUR VOCABULARY
Look at **embryo**.

fog NOUN fogs
thick mist which makes it difficult to see
➤ **foggy** ADJECTIVE

foil NOUN foils
very thin sheets of metal, used to wrap food

foil VERB foils, foiling, foiled
To foil an attempt or a plan is to stop it from succeeding.

fold VERB folds, folding, folded
to bend something so that one part lies over another part • *Fold the paper in the middle.*

fold NOUN folds
a line where something has been folded

folder NOUN folders
❶ a piece of folded cardboard or plastic to keep papers in ❷ a set of files kept together in a computer

foliage NOUN
the leaves of a tree or plant

folk NOUN
people

a
b
c
d
e
f
g
h
i
j
k
l
m
n
o
p
q
r
s
t
u
v
w
x
y
z

follow VERB follows, following, followed
❶ To follow someone or something is to go or come after them. ❷ To follow a road or path is to go along it. ❸ To follow instructions is to obey them. ❹ To follow something is to understand it. • *I couldn't follow the story.*

follower NOUN followers
someone who supports or believes in someone or something • *He had many loyal followers.*

fond ADJECTIVE fonder, fondest
➤ **To be fond of someone** or **something** is to like them very much.
➤ **fondly** ADVERB ➤ **fondness** NOUN

font NOUN fonts
❶ a style of writing on a computer • *I used a large font for the title.* ❷ a large stone basin in a church, that holds water for baptism

food NOUN foods
anything that you can eat to make you grow or give you energy

food chain NOUN food chains
a series of plants and animals that are linked because each one eats the thing below it in the chain

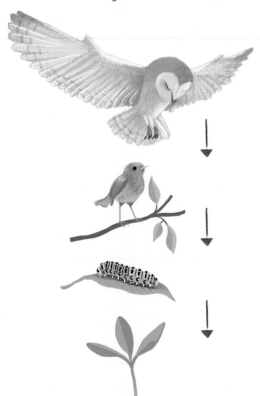

fool NOUN fools
a silly or stupid person
fool VERB fools, fooling, fooled
to trick or deceive someone

foolish ADJECTIVE
stupid
➤ **foolishly** ADVERB ➤ **foolishness** NOUN

foolproof ADJECTIVE
A foolproof plan is easy to follow and unlikely to fail.

foot NOUN feet
❶ the lower part of your leg below your ankle ❷ the lowest part of something • *They met at the foot of the hill.* ❸ a measurement of length. There are 12 inches in 1 foot and it is about the same as 30 centimetres.
➤ **on foot** walking

football NOUN footballs
❶ a game played by two teams who try to kick a ball into their opponents' goal ❷ the ball used in this game
➤ **footballer** NOUN

foothill NOUN foothills
a low hill near the bottom of a mountain or range of mountains

foothold NOUN footholds
a place where you can put your foot when you are climbing

footing NOUN
Your footing is the position of your feet when you are standing firmly on something. • *He lost his footing and slipped.*

footpath NOUN footpaths
a path for people to walk along, especially one in the countryside

footprint NOUN footprints
a mark made by a feet or shoe

footstep NOUN footsteps
a sound made by the feet of someone walking • *I heard footsteps coming up the path.*

for PREPOSITION
❶ If something is for someone, it is to be given to them or used by them. • *This letter is for you.* • *It's a website for children.* ❷ If something is for

something, that is its purpose or reason. • *You need eggs* **for** *this recipe.* • *This is just* **for** *fun.* • *What did you say that* **for**? ❸ used to show length of time or distance • *We've been waiting* **for** *hours.* • *They walked* **for** *three miles.* ❹ used to show price or cost • *She bought it* **for** *£2.* ❺ If you are **for** something, you agree with or support it.

⚙ **BUILD** YOUR VOCABULARY
The opposite of this last meaning is **against**.

forbid *VERB* forbids, forbidding, forbade, forbidden
❶ To forbid someone to do something is to tell them that they must not do it. ❷ To forbid something is not to allow it. • *Running in the corridor is* **forbidden**.

forbidding *ADJECTIVE*
looking threatening • *The sky was dark and* **forbidding**.

force *NOUN* forces
❶ strength or violence • *They had to use* **force** *to open the door.* ❷ in science, something that pushes or pulls an object • *magnetic* **forces** ❸ an organised team of soldiers or police
force *VERB* forces, forcing, forced
❶ to use power or violence to make someone do something • *She was* **forced** *to sign the letter.* ❷ If you force something open, you use a lot of strength to open it.

forcibly *ADVERB*
using force • *He was* **forcibly** *removed.*

ford *NOUN* fords
a shallow place where you can wade or drive across a river

fore *ADJECTIVE*
front • *The horse lifted one* **fore** *foot.*

⚙ **BUILD** YOUR VOCABULARY
Look at **hind**.

forecast *NOUN* forecasts
a statement about what is likely to happen
forecast *VERB* forecasts, forecasting, forecast, forecasted
To forecast something is to say it is likely to happen. • *They are* **forecasting** *snow for tomorrow.*

forefinger *NOUN* forefingers
the finger next to the thumb

⚙ **BUILD** YOUR VOCABULARY
Look at **index finger**.

foreground *NOUN* foregrounds
the part of a scene or view that is nearest to you

⚙ **BUILD** YOUR VOCABULARY
The opposite is **background**.

forehead *NOUN* foreheads
the part of your face above your eyes

foreign *ADJECTIVE*
belonging to or coming from another country
• *Do you speak any* **foreign** *languages?*
➤ **foreigner** *NOUN*

⚠ **WATCH OUT!**
The word **foreign** has a difficult spelling. Think of '*a foreign king reigns*' to help you remember.

foremost *ADJECTIVE*
first or nearest the front

foresee *VERB* foresees, foreseeing, foresaw, foreseen
to realise that something is likely to happen

forest *NOUN* forests
a large area of trees growing close together

a
b
c
d
e
f
g
h
i
j
k
l
m
n
o
p
q
r
s
t
u
v
w
x
y
z

foretell VERB foretells, foretelling, foretold
To foretell the future is to say what will happen.

forever ADVERB
always

forgave VERB (past tense of **forgive**)
• He **forgave** my rudeness.

forge NOUN forges
a place where a blacksmith heats and shapes metal
forge VERB forges, forging, forged
To forge metal is to shape it by heating and
hammering.

forget VERB forgets, forgetting, forgot,
forgotten
to not remember something • I **forgot** how to spell it.

forgetful ADJECTIVE
tending to forget things

forget-me-not NOUN forget-me-nots
a plant with small blue flowers

forgive VERB forgives, forgiving, forgave,
forgiven
to stop being angry with someone for something
they have done • He said sorry, so I **forgave** him.
➤ **forgiveness** NOUN

fork NOUN forks
❶ an instrument with prongs, used for eating or
digging ❷ a place where a road or river divides into
two or more parts

forlorn ADJECTIVE
sad and lonely

form NOUN forms
❶ a type of something • Do you do any **form** of
exercise? ❷ a shape • The witch took the **form** of a
snake. ❸ a class in a school ❹ a piece of paper with
printed questions and spaces for the answers
form VERB forms, forming, formed
❶ To form something is to shape or make it. • We all
formed a line. ❷ To form is to develop or come into
being. • Ice **formed** on the window.

formal ADJECTIVE
❶ Formal events or clothes are very smart and not
relaxed. • People usually wear something quite
formal for weddings. ❷ Formal language is correct
and suitable for serious or official contexts, rather
than talking to friends. • 'Request' is a more **formal**
way to say 'ask for'.
➤ **formally** ADVERB

 **BUILD** YOUR VOCABULARY
The opposite is **informal**.

format NOUN formats
the way something such as information is arranged
or presented • The file is in PDF **format**.

formation
❶ the creation or development of something • the
formation of ice crystals ❷ a pattern or shape
• They flew in a V **formation**.

former ADJECTIVE
past; earlier • She's a **former** world champion.
➤ **the former** the first of two people or things just
mentioned • If it's a choice between a picnic or a
swim I prefer **the former**.
➤ **formerly** ADVERB • This was **formerly** a school.

BUILD YOUR VOCABULARY
Look at **latter**.

formidable (say **for**-mid-a-bul) ADJECTIVE
impressive and slightly frightening

formula NOUN formulas, formulae
❶ in maths, a rule or problem shown as a sequence
of symbols and numbers • Do you know the **formula**
to calculate the area of a triangle? ❷ a set of
chemical symbols showing what a substance consists
of • H_2O is the **formula** for water.

forsake VERB forsakes, forsaking, forsook,
forsaken
to abandon someone

fort NOUN forts
a building that has been strongly built against attack

forth ADVERB
forwards or onwards

fortify VERB fortifies, fortifying, fortified
to make a place strong against attack

fortnight NOUN fortnights
a period of two weeks
➤ **fortnightly** ADVERB

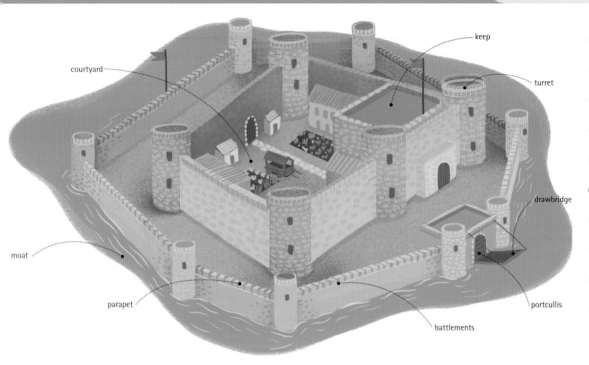

courtyard

keep

turret

drawbridge

moat

parapet

portcullis

battlements

a
b
c
d
e
f
g
h
i
j
k
l
m
n
o
p
q
r
s
t
u
v
w
x
y
z

fortress NOUN fortresses
a castle or town that has been strongly built against attack

fortunate ADJECTIVE
lucky
➤ **fortunately** ADVERB • *Fortunately no one was hurt.*

fortune NOUN fortunes
❶ Fortune is luck or chance. ❷ A fortune is a large amount of money.

forward ADJECTIVE
going towards the front • *a forward jump*
forward ADVERB
forwards • *They rushed forward.*
forward NOUN forwards
a player in an attacking position in a team

forwards ADVERB
to or towards the front • *Lean forwards.*

fossil NOUN fossils
the remains of a prehistoric animal or plant that has become hardened in rock
➤ **fossilised** (or **fossilized**) ADJECTIVE
• *a fossilised fern*

⚙ **BUILD** YOUR VOCABULARY
Look at **ammonite** and **trilobite**.

foster VERB fosters, fostering, fostered
to look after someone else's child as if they were your own, but without adopting them

foster child NOUN foster children
a child who is being brought up by foster parents

foster parent NOUN foster parents
a parent who is fostering a child

fought VERB (past tense and past participle of **fight**)
• *They **fought** over the money.* • *They have **fought** for their rights.*

foul ADJECTIVE fouler, foulest
disgusting or very unpleasant

foul NOUN fouls
an action that breaks the rules of a sport
• *He committed a **foul** and was sent off.*

found VERB (past tense and past participle of **find**)
• *They suddenly **found** themselves surrounded by tigers.* • *I have **found** the book I had lost.*
found VERB founds, founding, founded
To found an organisation is to start it or set it up.
• *The school was **founded** in 1901.*
➤ **founder** NOUN • *Guru Nanak was the **founder** of the Sikh religion.*

159

foundation NOUN foundations
❶ A building's foundations are the solid base on which it is built. ❷ an organisation that has been set up to do something • *a charitable* **foundation** ❸ the act of founding something • *the* **foundation** *of Rome*

fountain NOUN fountains
a structure with jets of water, used to decorate a park or garden

fountain pen NOUN fountain pens
a pen that can be filled with ink that flows through its nib

fowl NOUN fowl, fowls
a bird, such as a chicken or duck, that is kept for its eggs or meat

fox NOUN foxes
a wild animal similar to a dog with red-brown fur and a long furry tail

⚙ **BUILD** YOUR VOCABULARY
A female **fox** is a **vixen**.

foxglove NOUN foxgloves
a tall plant with long bell-shaped flowers

foyer (say **foy-ay**) NOUN foyers
the entrance hall of a public building or hotel

fraction NOUN fractions
❶ a number that is not a whole number, for example $\frac{1}{2}$ or 0.5

⚙ **BUILD** YOUR VOCABULARY
Look at **decimal fraction**, **equivalent fraction**, **improper fraction**, **mixed fraction** and **proper fraction**.
Also look at **denominator** and **numerator**.

❷ a tiny part or amount of something

fracture VERB fractures, fracturing, fractured
to break or crack something, especially a bone

fracture NOUN fractures
a crack or break, especially in a bone

fragile (say **fraj-ile**) ADJECTIVE
easy to break or damage

fragment NOUN fragments
a small broken piece of something • *fragments of pottery*

fragrance (say **fray-granss**) NOUN fragrances
a sweet or pleasant smell

fragrant (say **fray-grant**) ADJECTIVE
smelling sweet or pleasant

frail ADJECTIVE frailer, frailest
weak or fragile

frame NOUN frames
the part around the outside of a picture, mirror or pair of glasses that holds and supports it • *a picture in a gold* **frame**
frame VERB frames, framing, framed
To frame a picture is to put a frame round it.

framework NOUN frameworks
a structure that supports something

frank ADJECTIVE franker, frankest
honest, open • *She was* **frank** *in her criticism.*
➤ **frankly** ADVERB

frantic ADJECTIVE
wildly anxious or excited
➤ **frantically** ADVERB

fraud NOUN frauds
❶ Fraud or a fraud is a dishonest trick to get money. ❷ someone who is not what they pretend to be

frayed ADJECTIVE
Frayed material is worn and ragged at the edge.

freak NOUN freaks
a very strange or abnormal person, animal or thing

freckle NOUN freckles
a small brown spot on someone's skin
'It isn't sunny enough for my freckles to thrive here,' said Pippi. 'And I do think it's nice having freckles.'
—PIPPI LONGSTOCKING, Astrid Lindgren
➤ **freckled** ADJECTIVE

free ADJECTIVE freer, freest
❶ able to do what you want to do or go where you want to go ❷ not costing any money • *Entrance to*

the museum is **free**. ❸ not busy or being used
• Is this seat **free**?

free VERB frees, freeing, freed
to set someone or something free • They **freed** the
prisoners.

freedom NOUN
the right to go where you like or do what you like

freeze VERB freezes, freezing, froze, frozen
❶ to turn into ice or to become covered with ice
• The pond had **frozen** in the night. ❷ To be freezing
is to be very cold. • My hands are **freezing**.
❸ to store food at a very low temperature to
preserve it ❹ To suddenly stand still because there is
a danger. • We all **froze** on the spot.

freezer NOUN freezers
a large container for keeping food frozen

freight (say frayt) NOUN
goods carried by road or in a ship or an aircraft

frenzy NOUN frenzies
➤ **To be in a frenzy** is to be wildly excited or
angry about something.
➤ **frenzied** ADJECTIVE

frequency NOUN frequencies
❶ The frequency of something is how often it
happens. ❷ The frequency of a sound wave or light
wave is the number of vibrations it makes each
second.

frequent ADJECTIVE
happening often
➤ **frequently** ADVERB

fresh ADJECTIVE fresher, freshest
❶ newly made, clean or not used • Is the bread
fresh? • I put **fresh** sheets on the bed. ❷ not tinned
or preserved • Eat lots of **fresh** fruit. ❸ Fresh air is
outside and feels cool and clean. • I need some **fresh**
air. ❹ Fresh water is water that is not salty.
➤ **freshly** ADVERB • **freshly** baked bread

freshwater ADJECTIVE
freshwater fish live in rivers or lakes and not the sea

fret VERB frets, fretting, fretted
to worry or be upset about something

fretful ADJECTIVE
worried and upset

friction NOUN
the force which is produced when one thing rubs
against another

fridge NOUN fridges
a short word for **refrigerator**

friend NOUN friends
Your friend is someone you know and like and who
knows and likes you.

friendless ADJECTIVE
with no friends

friendly ADJECTIVE friendlier, friendliest
kind and pleasant
➤ **friendliness** NOUN

friendship NOUN friendships
being friends with someone • Your **friendship** means
a lot to me.

frieze (say freez) NOUN friezes
a strip of designs or pictures on a wall

! WATCH OUT!
The noun **frieze**, meaning 'picture', has an **i** in it. Don't
confuse it with the verb to **freeze**.

fright NOUN frights
a sudden feeling of fear

frighten VERB frightens, frightening,
frightened
to make someone afraid

frightful ADJECTIVE
awful • We heard a **frightful** shriek.

frill NOUN frills
a strip of pleated material used to decorate
something
➤ **frilly** ADJECTIVE

fringe NOUN fringes
❶ short hair that hangs down over your forehead
❷ a decorative edge of hanging threads

frisk VERB frisks, frisking, frisked
to skip or leap playfully

a
b
c
d
e
f
g
h
i
j
k
l
m
n
o
p
q
r
s
t
u
v
w
x
y
z

frisky ADJECTIVE friskier, friskiest
playful or lively

frivolous ADJECTIVE
light-hearted, not serious

frizzy ADJECTIVE frizzier, frizziest
Frizzy hair has tight short curls.

fro ADVERB
➤ **to and fro** backwards and forwards

frock NOUN frocks
a dress

frog NOUN frogs
a small jumping animal that can live both in water
and on land

BUILD YOUR VOCABULARY
A **frog** is an **amphibian**.

frolic VERB frolics, frolicking, frolicked
to play in a lively and cheerful way

from PREPOSITION
❶ From is used to show where something or someone
started or where you get something. • My dad is **from**
Spain. • School is two miles **from** here. • Get some
water **from** the tap. • I got cards **from** all my friends.
❷ From is used to give the earliest time or smallest
number in a range. • The library is open **from** 9.
• The book is aimed at children **from** 8 to 10.

frond NOUN fronds
a leaf-like part of a fern or similar plant

front NOUN fronts
❶ the part of something that faces forwards • What
is on the **front** of the box? ❷ the part of something
that is furthest forward • Sit at the **front** of the
class.
➤ **in front** at or near the front

front ADJECTIVE
placed at or near the front • We sat in the **front** row.

frontier NOUN frontiers
the boundary between two countries or regions

frost NOUN frosts
powdery ice that forms on things in freezing weather
➤ **frosty** ADJECTIVE • a **frosty** day

froth NOUN
a white mass of tiny bubbles on or in a liquid
➤ **frothy** ADJECTIVE • **frothy** milk

froth VERB froths, frothing, frothed
to form a froth

frown VERB frowns, frowning, frowned
to wrinkle your forehead because you are angry or
worried

frown NOUN frowns
an expression in which you wrinkle your forehead

froze VERB (past tense of **freeze**)
• The lake **froze** last winter.

frozen VERB (past participle of **freeze**)
• I've **frozen** the leftovers to eat another time.

frozen ADJECTIVE
very cold • I'm **frozen**. Can we go inside?

fruit NOUN fruit, fruits
the part of a plant that contains the seed and is
often good to eat. Apples, oranges and bananas are
all types of fruit.
➤ **fruity** ADJECTIVE • a **fruity** flavour

fruitless ADJECTIVE
not having any good result • It was a **fruitless**
attempt.

frustrating ADJECTIVE
making you feel annoyed because you cannot do
something

frustration NOUN
a feeling of annoyance when you cannot do
something

fry VERB fries, frying, fried
to cook food in hot fat

fuchsia (say few-sha) NOUN fuchsias
a plant with bright red, pink or purple hanging
flowers

fudge NOUN
a soft sweet made with milk, sugar and butter

fuel NOUN fuels
something that is burnt to give heat or power, such
as coal or oil

fugitive (say few-jit-iv) NOUN fugitives
a person who is running away, especially from the
police

fulfil *VERB* **fulfils, fulfilling, fulfilled**
to fulfil something is to carry it out. • *I will **fulfil** my promise.*

> **! WATCH OUT!**
> To **fulfil** has no double l! You only double the last l when you are adding *-ing* or *-ed*.

fulfilment *NOUN*
a feeling of satisfaction at achieving something important

> **! WATCH OUT!**
> Fulfilment has no double l!

full *ADJECTIVE*
❶ containing as much or as many of something as is possible • *The cinema was **full**.* ❷ complete • *I want to hear the **full** story.* ❸ the greatest possible • *They drove at **full** speed.*
➤ **fully** *ADVERB*

full moon *NOUN* **full moons**
the moon when you can see the whole of it as a bright disc

> **⊙ BUILD YOUR VOCABULARY**
> Look at **new moon**.

full stop *NOUN* **full stops**
the dot (.) used as a punctuation mark at the end of a sentence or after an abbreviation

full-time *ADJECTIVE, ADVERB*
doing something for all the normal working hours of the day • *She has a **full-time** job.* • *He works full-time.*

fumble *VERB* **fumbles, fumbling, fumbled**
to feel for or handle something clumsily
• *He **fumbled** for the light switch.*

fume *VERB* **fumes, fuming, fumed**
to be very angry; to say something very angrily
• *'It's ridiculous,' she **fumed**.*

fumes *NOUN*
strong-smelling smoke or gas produced by something
• *They had breathed in poisonous **fumes**.*

fun *NOUN*
amusement or enjoyment
➤ **To make fun of someone** or **something** is to make them look silly or make people laugh at them.

function *NOUN* **functions**
❶ the purpose or job of something or someone
• *What is the **function** of this tool?* ❷ something that a computer, calculator or other device is able to do • *My phone has a stopwatch **function**.*

function *VERB* **functions, functioning, functioned**
to work or operate • *The engine does not **function** well at low temperatures.*

fund *NOUN* **funds**
an amount of money collected for a special purpose
• *The school has a **fund** for sports equipment.*

funeral *NOUN* **funerals**
the ceremony where a person who has died is buried or cremated

fungus *NOUN*
fungi
a plant without leaves or flowers, such as a mushroom or toadstool

> **! WATCH OUT!**
> The word **fungus** has a Latin plural: *some poisonous fungi.*

funnel *NOUN* **funnels**
❶ a tube with a wide top, for pouring things into containers ❷ a chimney on a ship or steam engine

funny *ADJECTIVE* **funnier, funniest**
❶ making you laugh or smile • *We heard a **funny** joke.* ❷ strange or odd • *There's a **funny** smell in here.*

fur *NOUN* **furs**
the soft hair that covers some animals • *Rabbit **fur** is so soft.*

furious *ADJECTIVE*
very angry
➤ **furiously** *ADVERB* • *'Get out!' she said **furiously**.*

furl *VERB* **furls, furling, furled**
To furl a sail, flag or umbrella is to roll it up and fasten it.

furnace *NOUN* **furnaces**
a very hot oven for making glass or heating metals

a
b
c
d
e
f
g
h
i
j
k
l
m
n
o
p
q
r
s
t
u
v
w
x
y
z

furnish *VERB* **furnishes, furnishing, furnished**
To furnish a room or building is to put furniture in it.

furniture *NOUN*
tables, chairs, beds and other movable objects that you need inside a building

furrow *NOUN* **furrows**
❶ a long cut in the ground made by a plough
❷ a deep wrinkle on the skin
➤ **furrowed** *ADJECTIVE* • *his furrowed brow*

furry *ADJECTIVE* **furrier, furriest**
like fur or covered with fur

further *ADVERB, ADJECTIVE*
❶ at or to a greater distance • *I can't walk any further.* ❷ more • *There are further details on our website.*

furthermore *ADVERB*
also; in addition

furthest *ADVERB, ADJECTIVE*
at or to the greatest distance • *an expedition to the furthest corners of the earth*

furtive *ADJECTIVE*
secretive, cautious
➤ **furtively** *ADVERB* • *He glanced furtively at his watch.*

fury *NOUN* **furies**
violent or extreme anger

fuse *NOUN* **fuses**
❶ a safety device containing a piece of wire that melts if too much electricity passes through it
❷ a device that is lit to set off an explosive

fuse *VERB* **fuses, fusing, fused**
If electrical equipment fuses or something fuses it, it stops working because a fuse has melted.

fuselage *(say* few-zel-ah*zh) NOUN* **fuselages**
the main body of an aircraft

fuss *NOUN* **fusses**
unnecessary excitement or worry about something
fuss *VERB* **fusses, fussing, fussed**
to be excited or worried about something that is not important

fussy *ADJECTIVE* **fussier, fussiest**
difficult to please • *He's so fussy about what he eats.*
➤ **fussily** *ADVERB* ➤ **fussiness** *NOUN*

futile *(say* few-tile*) ADJECTIVE*
useless; without purpose • *It was futile to argue.*

future *NOUN*
the time that will come or things that will happen
• *Nobody can predict the future.*
➤ **in future** from now onwards
future *ADJECTIVE*
happening in or relating to the future • *She met her future husband at school.* • *We can use 'will' to talk about future time.*

fuzzy *ADJECTIVE* **fuzzier, fuzziest**
❶ blurred or not clear ❷ soft and fluffy

⚙ G is for **global language**. There are many different varieties of English, such as Australian English, Indian English and South African English. They each have some different words, spellings, pronunciations and even grammar rules.

⚙ Do you know any words that are different in other varieties of English?

g *ABBREVIATION*
the abbreviation for **gram**

gabble *VERB* **gabbles, gabbling, gabbled**
to talk so quickly that it is difficult to hear the words

gable *NOUN* **gables**
a triangular part of a wall between two sloping roofs

gadget *(say* **gaj**-it*)* *NOUN* **gadgets**
a small device or tool

Gaelic *NOUN*
❶ *(say* **gal**-ik*)* a language spoken in the Highlands and western islands of Scotland ❷ *(say* **gay**-lik*)* the Irish language

✳ **WORD STORY**
The word **slogan** comes from Gaelic.

gag *NOUN* **gags**
something put over someone's mouth to stop them from speaking
gag *VERB* **gags, gagging, gagged**
To gag someone is to put a gag over their mouth.

gain *VERB* **gains, gaining, gained**
to get something that you did not have before
• *She* **gained** *some useful experience.*

gala *(say* **gah**-la*)* *NOUN* **galas**
a special contest, celebration or performance

galaxy *(say* **gal**-ak-see*)* *NOUN* **galaxies**
a very large group of stars, for example the Milky Way

✳ **WORD STORY**
The word **galaxy** comes from a Greek word meaning 'milky'.

gale *NOUN* **gales**
a very strong wind

gallant *ADJECTIVE*
brave or polite, especially to women
➤ **gallantly** *ADVERB*

galleon *NOUN* **galleons**
a large Spanish sailing ship used in the 16th and 17th centuries

gallery *NOUN* **galleries**
❶ a building or room for showing works of art
❷ the highest set of seats in a cinema or theatre

galley *NOUN* **galleys**
❶ the kitchen in a ship ❷ an ancient type of long ship driven by oars

gallon *NOUN* **gallons**
a measurement of the volume of liquid. There are 8 pints in 1 gallon, which is about 4.5 litres

a b c d e f **g** h i j k l m n o p q r s t u v w x y z

gallop VERB gallops, galloping, galloped
When a horse gallops, it runs very fast.

> **BUILD YOUR VOCABULARY**
> Look at **canter** and **trot**.

gallop NOUN gallops
the fastest pace that a horse can go

gamble NOUN gambles
a risk • *He had to take a gamble and trust her.*

gamble VERB gambles, gambling, gambled
❶ to play a betting game for money ❷ to take a risk
• *We gambled that it wouldn't rain.*
➤ **gambler** NOUN

game NOUN games
❶ something that you play for fun, usually with rules
❷ wild animals or birds hunted for sport or food

gamekeeper NOUN gamekeepers
someone who protects game birds and animals from poachers

gaming NOUN
the activity of playing computer or video games

gander NOUN ganders
a male goose

gang NOUN gangs
❶ a group of people who do things together
❷ a group of criminals

gangplank NOUN gangplanks
a plank for walking on to or off a ship

gangster NOUN gangsters
a member of a gang of violent criminals

gangway NOUN gangways
❶ a gap between rows of seats for people to walk through ❷ a movable bridge for getting on or off a ship

gannet NOUN gannets
a large seabird which catches fish by diving into the sea

gap NOUN gaps
an opening or space in something

gape VERB gapes, gaping, gaped
❶ to stare with your mouth wide open
❷ If something gapes, it is wide open. • *There was a gaping hole in the roof.*

garage (*say* ga-rahzh *or* ga-rij) NOUN garages
❶ a building for keeping a car in ❷ a place where vehicles are repaired and petrol is sold

garbage NOUN (North American)
rubbish; household waste

garden NOUN gardens
an area outside a house for growing flowers or plants
• *We played in the garden.*

gardener NOUN gardeners
someone who looks after a garden, especially as a job
➤ **gardening** NOUN

gargoyle NOUN gargoyles
an ugly or comical carving of a face on a building

garland NOUN garlands
a wreath of flowers used as a decoration

garlic NOUN
a small white plant bulb with separate sections, used in cooking for its strong taste and smell

garment NOUN garments
a piece of clothing

garrison NOUN garrisons
troops who stay in a town or fort to defend it

gas NOUN gases
❶ a substance, such as oxygen, that can move freely and is not liquid or solid ❷ a type of gas that burns, used for heating or cooking

> ✱ **WORD STORY**
> **Gas** is an invented word based on the Greek word *chaos.*

gash NOUN gashes
a long deep cut or wound

gasp VERB gasps, gasping, gasped
❶ to breathe in suddenly when you are shocked or surprised ❷ to struggle to breathe or speak
• *'We made it!' she gasped.*

gate NOUN gates
a barrier that can be opened and closed in a wall or fence

gateau (*say* gat-oh) NOUN gateaux
a rich cream cake

gather *VERB* **gathers, gathering, gathered**
❶ to come together • *A crowd **gathered**.*
❷ to collect things or bring them together
• *We **gathered** some materials to make our model.*

gathering *NOUN* **gatherings**
a group of people gathered together

gaudy *ADJECTIVE* **gaudier, gaudiest**
very showy and bright

gauge (*say* gayj) *NOUN* **gauges**
a measuring instrument • *The fuel **gauge** showed the tank was empty.*
gauge (*say* gayj) *VERB* **gauges, gauging, gauged**
to estimate or assess something • *It's difficult to **gauge** how much paint is left.*

gaunt *ADJECTIVE*
thin and tired-looking

gauntlet *NOUN* **gauntlets**
a glove with a wide covering for the wrist

gauze *NOUN*
thin transparent material

gave *VERB* (*past tense of* **give**)
• *Mum **gave** me a present.*

gaze *VERB* **gazes, gazing, gazed**
to look at someone or something for a long time
• *She **gazed** into the distance.*
gaze *NOUN* **gazes**
a long steady look

gazelle *NOUN* **gazelles**
a type of small antelope

gear *NOUN* **gears**
❶ The gears in a car or bicycle are a set of cogs working together to control the speed of the wheels.
❷ Gear is equipment or clothes. • *He forgot his sports **gear**.*

gecko *NOUN*
geckos
a small tropical lizard with sticky pads on its feet

geek *NOUN* **geeks** (*informal*)
someone with an obsessive interest in something

geese *NOUN* (*plural of* **goose**)

gel *NOUN* **gels**
a substance like soft jelly

gem *NOUN* **gems**
a precious stone or jewel

gender (*say* jen-der) *NOUN* **genders**
the fact of being male or female

gene (*say* jeen) *NOUN* **genes**
part of a living cell that you inherit from your parents and that controls characteristics such as eye colour

general *ADJECTIVE*
❶ including most people or things • *The **general** public are not allowed in.* ❷ not detailed • *She gave a **general** description.*
➤ **in general** mostly; in most cases • *She likes animals **in general**.* • ***In general**, I agree.*

general *NOUN* **generals**
an army officer of high rank

generally *ADVERB*
usually; in most cases • *People **generally** enjoy music.*

generate *VERB* **generates, generating, generated**
to produce or create something • *The machine **generates** a lot of heat.*

generation *NOUN* **generations**
❶ a single stage in a family • *Three **generations** of my family are in the photo.* ❷ all the people born about the same time • *Her **generation** lived through the war.*

generator *NOUN* **generators**
a machine for producing electricity

generosity *NOUN*
generous giving

generous *ADJECTIVE*
kind and ready to give or share what you have
➤ **generously** *ADVERB*

genie (*say* jee-nee) NOUN **genies**
in stories, a magical being who grants wishes

genius NOUN **geniuses**
someone who is unusually intelligent or creative

gentle ADJECTIVE **gentler, gentlest**
not rough; careful or mild • Be **gentle** with the baby.
• a **gentle** breeze
➤ **gentleness** NOUN ➤ **gently** ADVERB

gentleman NOUN **gentlemen**
❶ a man ❷ a well-mannered or honest man • He's a
real **gentleman**.

genuine ADJECTIVE
❶ Something genuine is real and not fake.
❷ A genuine person is honest and sincere.
➤ **genuinely** ADVERB

geography NOUN
the study of the earth, its natural features and its
countries, cities and people
➤ **geographical** ADJECTIVE

✷ **WORD STORY**
The word **geography** comes from Greek words
meaning 'earth writing'.

geology (*say* jee-ol-o-jee) NOUN
the study of the earth's crust and its layers of rock
➤ **geological** ADJECTIVE

geometry NOUN
the study of lines, angles and shapes

geranium (*say* je-ray-nee-um) NOUN **geraniums**
a plant with red, pink or white flowers

gerbil (*say* jer-bil) NOUN **gerbils**
a small rodent with long back legs, often kept as
a pet

germ NOUN **germs**
a tiny organism, especially one that causes a disease

germinate VERB **germinates, germinating,
germinated**
If a seed germinates, it starts growing and
developing.
➤ **germination** NOUN

gesture (*say* jes-cher) NOUN **gestures**
a movement or an action that expresses something

get VERB **gets, getting, got**
❶ To get something is to obtain, receive or fetch it.
• I **got** a bike for my birthday. • We **got** some good
ideas from the website. • Will you **get** me a drink?
❷ To get angry, upset, bigger, etc. is to become that
thing. • I'm **getting** tired. • It **gets** dark early.
❸ To get somewhere is to reach a place. • We **got**
home late. ❹ To get a bus, train or plane is to travel
on it. • We had to **get** a taxi. ❺ To get something to
happen is to succeed in making it happen. • I can't
get the lid off. • I **got** my mum to agree. ❻ To get
something is to understand it. • I didn't **get** the joke.
➤ **To get on** is to make progress or to be friendly
with someone.
➤ **To get out of something** is to avoid having to
do it.

getaway NOUN **getaways**
an escape • They made a fast **getaway**.

geyser (*say* gee-zer *or* gy-zer) NOUN **geysers**
a natural spring that shoots up columns of hot water

ghastly ADJECTIVE **ghastlier, ghastliest**
horrible; awful

ghost NOUN **ghosts**
the spirit of a dead person seen by a living person
➤ **ghostly** ADJECTIVE • The moon gave a **ghostly**
light.

ghoul (*say* gool) NOUN **ghouls**
an evil spirit

giant NOUN **giants**
in stories, a creature like a huge human being
giant ADJECTIVE
huge • a **giant** box of chocolates

giddy ADJECTIVE **giddier, giddiest**
feeling dizzy and unsteady
➤ **giddily** ADVERB ➤ **giddiness** NOUN

gift NOUN **gifts**
❶ a present ❷ a special talent or ability • She has a
special **gift** for drawing.
➤ **gifted** ADJECTIVE • He is a **gifted** musician.

gigantic ADJECTIVE
huge; enormous
*Suddenly the boy let out a gigantic belch which rolled
around the Assembly Hall like thunder.*–MATILDA,
Roald Dahl

A B C D E F G H I J K L M N O P Q R S T U V W X Y Z

giggle VERB giggles, giggling, giggled
to laugh in a silly way
giggle NOUN giggles
a silly laugh

gild VERB gilds, gilding, gilded
to cover something with a thin layer of gold

gills PLURAL NOUN
A fish's gills are the part of its body that it breathes through.

ginger NOUN
❶ a hot-tasting tropical root or a powder made from it, used in cooking ❷ a reddish-yellow colour • *He has* **ginger** *hair.*

gingerbread NOUN
a cake or biscuit flavoured with ginger

gingerly ADVERB
carefully and cautiously • *Gingerly, she lifted the lid.*

gipsy
another spelling of **Gypsy**

giraffe NOUN giraffes
a tall African mammal that is yellow with brown patches and has a very long neck

✳ WORD STORY

An old word for a **giraffe** is *camelopard*, which means 'camel leopard'.

girder NOUN girders
a metal beam supporting part of a building or bridge

girdle NOUN girdles
a belt or cord worn around the waist

girl NOUN girls
a female child or young woman
➤ **girlish** ADJECTIVE • *She looked young and* **girlish.**

girlfriend NOUN girlfriends
❶ a female romantic partner ❷ a female friend

girth NOUN girths
❶ the measurement round something • *The tree's* **girth** *showed its age.* ❷ a band fastened round a horse's belly to keep its saddle on

give VERB gives, giving, gave, given
❶ To give someone something is to let them have it or cause them to have it. • *She* **gave** *me a sweet.* • *That noise has* **given** *me a headache.* ❷ To give a laugh, yell, smile, etc. is to make that sound or do that action. • *He* **gave** *a shrug.* ❸ To give a performance, speech, etc. is to perform or present something. • *We're* **giving** *a concert.*
➤ **To give in** is to surrender.
➤ **To give up** is to stop doing or trying something.
➤ **To give way** is to break or collapse.

glacier (say **glass**-ee-er *or* **glay**-see-er) NOUN glaciers
a mass of ice moving slowly along a valley

glad ADJECTIVE gladder, gladdest
happy and pleased
➤ **gladly** ADVERB ➤ **gladness** NOUN

gladiator NOUN gladiators
in ancient Rome, a man who fought in arenas as a public entertainment

glamorous ADJECTIVE
attractive and exciting

glamour NOUN
the quality of being attractive or exciting

✳ WORD STORY

The word **glamour** originally meant 'magic' or 'enchantment'.

glance VERB glances, glancing, glanced
to look at something quickly
She glanced over the first pages and was soon eagerly reading.—A GIRL OF THE LIMBERLOST, Gene Stratton-Porter
glance NOUN glances
a quick look

gland NOUN glands
an organ in the body that produces a substance for a special purpose • *sweat* **glands**

glare VERB glares, glaring, glared
❶ to look angrily at someone
The bald man glared down at the children and spoke to them in a frightening whisper.—THE HOSTILE HOSPITAL, Lemony Snicket
❷ to shine with a bright or dazzling light
glare NOUN glares
an angry stare

glass NOUN **glasses**
1 the hard transparent substance used in windows
2 a container made of glass, for drinking
➤ **glassful** NOUN • *a glassful of milk*

glasses PLURAL NOUN
A pair of glasses is a frame with two lenses in it, worn over your eyes to help you see.

glassy ADJECTIVE **glassier, glassiest**
1 like glass • *the water's glassy surface* 2 Glassy eyes are without expression. • *He gave a glassy stare.*

glaze VERB **glazes, glazing, glazed**
1 If your eyes glaze over, you look bored or without expression. 2 to cover something with a shiny surface • *a glazed doughnut* 3 To glaze a window is to put glass in it.
glaze NOUN **glazes**
a shiny surface

gleam NOUN **gleams**
a soft shining light
gleam VERB **gleams, gleaming, gleamed**
to shine with a soft light

glee NOUN
a happy and excited feeling

glen NOUN **glens**
a narrow valley, especially in Scotland

glide VERB **glides, gliding, glided**
1 to move smoothly • *The canoe glided across the lake.* 2 to fly supported by air currents

glider NOUN **gliders**
an aircraft without an engine

glimmer NOUN **glimmers**
a faint unsteady light
glimmer VERB **glimmers, glimmering, glimmered**
to shine with a faint unsteady light

glimpse VERB **glimpses, glimpsing, glimpsed**
to see something briefly
glimpse NOUN **glimpses**
a brief view of something • *I caught a glimpse of the sea.*

glint VERB **glints, glinting, glinted**
to shine with a brief flash of light
High upon the slope to our right, in among the trees, a little frozen waterfall glinted brilliantly.—COUNT KARLSTEIN, Philip Pullman

glint NOUN **glints**
a brief flash of light

glisten VERB **glistens, glistening, glistened**
to shine like something wet or oily

glitter VERB **glitters, glittering, glittered**
to shine with tiny flashes of light • *The gold glittered in the sun.*

gloat VERB **gloats, gloating, gloated**
to show pleasure in an unkind way because you have done well and someone else has done badly

global ADJECTIVE
to do with the whole world • *the global effects of climate change*
➤ **globally** ADVERB

global warming NOUN
the gradual increase in the temperature of the earth's atmosphere, thought to be caused by pollution

globe NOUN **globes**
1 something shaped like a ball, especially one with a map of the world on it 2 the earth

gloom NOUN
a feeling of being sad or depressed

gloomy ADJECTIVE **gloomier, gloomiest**
1 not well lit; dark • *a gloomy corridor* 2 sad or depressed • *I felt gloomy.*
➤ **gloomily** ADVERB

glorious ADJECTIVE
splendid or magnificent
➤ **gloriously** ADVERB • *It was gloriously sunny.*

glory NOUN **glories**
1 fame and honour • *He wanted glory and riches.*
2 splendour or beauty

gloss NOUN **glosses**
the shine on a smooth surface
➤ **glossy** ADJECTIVE • *her smooth glossy hair*

glossary *NOUN* glossaries
a list of words with their meanings explained
• *a **glossary** of computing terms*

glove *NOUN* gloves
You wear **gloves** on your hands to keep them warm or protect them.

glow *NOUN*
❶ a soft steady warm light • *the **glow** of the lamp*
❷ a warm or cheerful feeling • *She felt a **glow** of pleasure at the compliment.*
glow *VERB* glows, glowing, glowed
to shine with a soft steady light

glower (rhymes with **flower**) *VERB* glowers, glowering, glowered
to stare with an angry look

glow-worm *NOUN* glow-worms
an insect with a tail that gives out a green light

glucose *NOUN*
a type of sugar found in fruit and honey

glue *NOUN* glues
a substance for sticking things together
glue *VERB* glues, gluing, glued
to stick something with glue

glum *ADJECTIVE* glummer, glummest
sad or depressed
➤ **glumly** *ADVERB*

gnarled (say narld) *ADJECTIVE*
twisted and knobbly, like an old tree

gnash (say nash) *VERB* gnashes, gnashing, gnashed
To gnash your teeth is to grind them together.

⚠ WATCH OUT!
The g is silent in words that start with **gn-**, like **gnash**, **gnaw** and **gnome**.

gnat (say nat) *NOUN* gnats
a tiny fly that bites

gnaw (say naw) *VERB* gnaws, gnawing, gnawed
to repeatedly bite something hard

gnome (say nohm) *NOUN* gnomes
in stories, a tiny old man

go *VERB* goes, going, went, gone
❶ To go somewhere is to move, travel or lead there.
• *I **went** out with my friends.* • *He's **gone** to work.*
• *A path **goes** through the wood.* ❷ If something goes, it works or operates. • *The engine won't **go**.*
• *Start your watch **going**.* ❸ to happen or pass in a particular way • *The party **went** well.* • *The holidays **go** so fast.* ❹ To go red, go bad, etc. is to become that thing. • *The milk **went** sour.* • *My tea has **gone** cold.* ❺ to disappear • *All the food has **gone**.*
➤ **To be going to do something** is to be planning to do it or about to do it.
➤ **To go on** is to happen or continue. • *What's going on?*

a b c d e f g h i j k l m n o p q r s t u v w x y z

177

go NOUN goes
A go is a turn or try. • *May I have a go?*

goal NOUN goals
❶ the place where the ball must go to score a point in football, hockey and other games ❷ a point scored in football, hockey and other games ❸ something that you hope to achieve • *Our goal is to help you learn.*

goalkeeper NOUN goalkeepers
the player who guards the goal in football and hockey

goat NOUN goats
an animal with horns, belonging to the same family as sheep

BUILD YOUR VOCABULARY
Look at **billy goat**, **kid** and **nanny goat**.

gobble VERB gobbles, gobbling, gobbled
to eat something quickly and greedily

goblet NOUN goblets
a drinking cup with a long stem and a base

goblin NOUN goblins
in stories, an evil or mischievous fairy

god NOUN gods
❶ a being or thing that people worship • *Thor was the Norse god of thunder.* ❷ God is the supreme being worshipped in many religions.

goddess NOUN goddesses
a female being that people worship

goggles NOUN
special glasses that you wear to protect your eyes • *swimming goggles*

go-kart NOUN go-karts
a type of small car used for racing

gold NOUN
❶ a valuable, shiny yellow metal

BUILD YOUR VOCABULARY
Gold is an **element**.

❷ a bright yellow colour

golden ADJECTIVE
❶ made of gold • *a golden ring* ❷ gold in colour • *golden hair*

goldfinch NOUN goldfinches
a small bird with yellow feathers in its wings

goldfish NOUN goldfish
a small red or orange fish, often kept as a pet

golf NOUN
a game which you play by hitting a small white ball with a stick called a **club** into small holes in a grassy area
➤ **golfer** NOUN ➤ **golfing** NOUN

gone VERB (past participle of **go**)
• *He has gone out.*

gong NOUN gongs
a large metal disc that you hit to make a deep hollow sound

goo NOUN (informal)
a sticky or slimy substance
• *The ditch was full of smelly green goo.*
➤ **gooey** ADJECTIVE

good ADJECTIVE better, best
❶ pleasant or enjoyable • *Did you have a good time?*
• *The weather wasn't very good.* ❷ high in quality
• *Your work is good.* • *She's a good singer.* ❸ kind or honest • *He was always good to me.* ❹ well behaved
• *Be good while I'm out.* ❺ healthy • *Carrots are good for you.*
➤ **goodness** NOUN

good NOUN
benefit or advantage • *I'm telling you for your own good.*
➤ **for good** forever

goodbye EXCLAMATION
a word you say when you leave someone or at the end of a telephone call

Good Friday NOUN
the Friday before Easter, when Christians remember Christ's death on the Cross

good-looking ADJECTIVE
attractive or handsome

good-natured ADJECTIVE
kind

goods NOUN
things that people buy and sell

goose *NOUN* geese
a water bird with webbed feet, larger than a duck

BUILD YOUR VOCABULARY
Look at **gander** and **gosling**.

gooseberry *NOUN* gooseberries
a small green fruit that grows on a prickly bush

gore *NOUN*
blood • *The creature's fangs were dripping gore.*

gorge *NOUN* gorges
a narrow valley with steep sides

gorgeous *ADJECTIVE*
very beautiful

gorilla *NOUN* gorillas
a large strong African ape with black or grey fur

gorse *NOUN*
a prickly bush with small yellow flowers

gory *ADJECTIVE* gorier, goriest
involving a lot of blood or killing

gosling *NOUN* goslings
a young goose

gospel *NOUN* gospels
one of the four books in the New Testament that describe the life and teachings of Jesus Christ

gossip *VERB* gossips, gossiping, gossiped
to talk about other people's private lives
gossip *NOUN* gossips
talk or rumours about people's private lives

got *VERB* (past tense and past participle of **get**)
• *I got a bike for my birthday.* • *It has got very cold.*

gouge *VERB* gouges, gouging, gouged
to scoop something out with a lot of force
• *He gouged a hole in the wood.*

govern *VERB* governs, governing, governed
to rule or be in charge of something, especially a country

government *NOUN* governments
the group of people who are in charge of a country

BUILD YOUR VOCABULARY
Remember **government** contains the word **govern**, so it has an **n** in it.

gown *NOUN* gowns
a long dress or loose flowing garment

GP *NOUN* GPs
a doctor who treats all kinds of diseases and sends people to specialists if necessary; short for *general practitioner*

grab *VERB* grabs, grabbing, grabbed
to take hold of something firmly or suddenly

grace *NOUN* graces
❶ beautiful and elegant movement ❷ a kind and pleasant way of behaving
➤ **graceful** *ADJECTIVE* ➤ **gracefully** *ADVERB*

gracious *ADJECTIVE*
kind, pleasant and generous
➤ **graciously** *ADVERB* • *He graciously gave up his seat.*

grade *NOUN* grades
a level or mark that shows quality • *He got the top grade in his exam.*
grade *VERB* grades, grading, graded
to give something a grade

gradient *(say* **gray**-dee-ent*) NOUN* gradients
a slope or the steepness of a slope

gradual *ADJECTIVE*
happening slowly but steadily
➤ **gradually** *ADVERB* • *Gradually it became easier.*

graffiti *(say* gra-**fee**-tee*) NOUN*
words or images painted or drawn on a wall

✳ WORD STORY
The word **graffiti** comes from an Italian word meaning 'scratches'.

grain *NOUN* grains
❶ cereals that are growing or harvested • *fields of grain* ❷ A grain is the hard seed of a cereal.
• *Eat plenty of whole grains.* ❸ a small amount of something • *a grain of salt*

gram *NOUN* grams
a measurement of weight. There are 1000 grams in a kilogram.

BUILD YOUR VOCABULARY
The abbreviation is **g**.

a
b
c
d
e
f
g
h
i
j
k
l
m
n
o
p
q
r
s
t
u
v
w
x
y
z

grammar NOUN grammars
the rules of a language, which say how words can be put together

✱ **WORD STORY**
The word **grammar** comes from a Latin word *grammatica* which could mean 'witchcraft' as well as 'learning'.

grand ADJECTIVE grander, grandest
very big and splendid • *a grand palace*
➤ **grandly** ADVERB

grandad NOUN grandads (informal)
grandfather

grandchild NOUN grandchildren
Someone's grandchild is their son's or daughter's child. A girl is a granddaughter and a boy is a grandson.

grandfather NOUN grandfathers
Your grandfather is your mother's or father's father.

grandfather clock NOUN grandfather clocks
a clock in a tall wooden case

grandma NOUN grandmas (informal)
grandmother

grandmother NOUN grandmothers
Your grandmother is your mother's or father's mother.

grandpa NOUN grandpas (informal)
grandfather

grandparent NOUN grandparents
a grandmother or grandfather

granite NOUN
a very hard kind of rock

⚙ **BUILD YOUR VOCABULARY**
Granite is **impermeable**.

granny NOUN grannies (informal)
grandmother

grant VERB grants, granting, granted
To grant someone something is to allow them to have it. • *The genie will grant you three wishes.*
➤ **To take something for granted** is to assume that it is true or will happen.

grape NOUN grapes
a small green or purple fruit that grows in bunches on a vine

grapefruit NOUN grapefruit
a large round yellow citrus fruit with soft juicy flesh

graph NOUN graphs
a diagram that shows how two amounts are related

graphics NOUN
pictures, designs and diagrams, especially ones produced by a computer

grapple VERB grapples, grappling, grappled
❶ to fight or struggle with someone ❷ To grapple with a problem is to try to deal with it.

grasp VERB grasps, grasping, grasped
❶ to hold something or someone tightly
❷ to understand something • *He couldn't grasp what was happening.*
grasp NOUN
a firm hold • *He had the magic wand in his grasp.*

grass NOUN grasses
a green plant that grows over lawns and fields
➤ **grassy** ADJECTIVE • *a grassy bank*

grasshopper NOUN grasshoppers
a jumping insect that makes a shrill noise

grate NOUN grates
a metal framework in a fireplace for holding fuel
grate VERB grates, grating, grated
to shred something into small pieces • *Grate the cheese.*

grateful *ADJECTIVE*
feeling thankful that someone has done something
for you • *I was really grateful for her help.*
➤ **gratefully** *ADVERB*

gratitude *NOUN*
the feeling of being grateful or thankful • *He didn't
show any gratitude for what we'd done.*

grave *NOUN* graves
a place where a dead body is buried
grave *ADJECTIVE* graver, gravest
very serious • *He looked grave.*
➤ **gravely** *ADVERB* • *She was gravely ill.*

gravel *NOUN*
small stones used to make paths

graveyard *NOUN* graveyards
a place where dead bodies are buried

gravity *NOUN*
the force that pulls all objects in the universe
towards each other and pulls things down to earth

gravy *NOUN*
a hot brown sauce made from meat juices

graze *VERB* grazes, grazing, grazed
❶ to feed on growing grass • *Sheep grazed in the
meadow.* ❷ To graze something is to scrape it lightly,
sometimes causing a scratch.
graze *NOUN* grazes
a sore place where skin has been scraped

grease *NOUN*
thick fat or oil
➤ **greasy** *ADJECTIVE*

great *ADJECTIVE* greater, greatest
❶ very large • *We heard a great crash.* ❷ very
important • *She was a great artist.* ❸ very good or
enjoyable • *It's great to see you.*
➤ **greatly** *ADJECTIVE* ➤ **greatness** *NOUN*

greed *NOUN*
the bad quality of wanting more food or money than
you need

greedy *ADJECTIVE* greedier, greediest
wanting more food or money than you need
➤ **greedily** *ADVERB*

green *ADJECTIVE* greener, greenest
of the colour of grass and leaves
green *NOUN* greens
a green colour

greenery *NOUN*
green leaves or plants

greengrocer *NOUN* greengrocers
someone who keeps a shop that sells fruit and
vegetables

greenhouse *NOUN* greenhouses
a glass building for growing plants that need to be
kept warm

greenhouse effect *NOUN*
the warming of the earth's surface by gases called
greenhouse gases, which trap heat in the atmosphere

⚙ **BUILD YOUR VOCABULARY**
Look at **carbon dioxide** and **methane**.

greet *VERB* greets, greeting, greeted
to welcome someone when they arrive • *His cat
greeted him with a miaow.*

greeting *NOUN* greetings
words or actions used to greet someone • *She called
out a friendly greeting.*

grew *VERB* (past tense of **grow**)
• *The flowers grew tall.*

grey *ADJECTIVE* greyer, greyest
of the colour between black and white, like ashes
or dark clouds
grey *NOUN*
a grey colour

a b c d e f **g** h i j k l m n o p q r s t u v w x y z

greyhound NOUN greyhounds
a slim dog with smooth hair, used in racing

grid NOUN grids
a framework or pattern of bars or lines crossing each other

grief NOUN
deep sadness, especially when someone has died

grievance NOUN grievances
a reason to feel angry or unhappy

grieve VERB grieves, grieving, grieved
to feel very sad, especially when someone has died

grievous ADJECTIVE
very sad or serious • *a grievous misfortune*

grill NOUN grills
a hot part on a cooker that cooks food from above
grill VERB grills, grilling, grilled
To grill food is to cook it under a grill.

grim ADJECTIVE grimmer, grimmest
very serious or unpleasant • *His expression was grim.*
➤ **grimly** ADVERB

grimace NOUN grimaces
a twisted expression on your face

grime NOUN
a layer of dirt on a surface
➤ **grimy** ADJECTIVE • *a grimy floor*

grin NOUN grins
a smile showing your teeth
grin VERB grins, grinning, grinned
to smile showing your teeth

grind VERB grinds, grinding, ground
❶ to crush something into a powder • *They ground the corn.* ❷ to rub something or be rubbed forcefully against a hard surface • *The ship ground against the rocks.*

grip VERB grips, gripping, gripped
to hold something tightly
grip NOUN grips
❶ a firm hold on something • *Keep a grip on the rope.* ❷ a handle

grisly ADJECTIVE grislier, grisliest
horrifying or disgusting • *They saw a grisly sight.*

grit NOUN
tiny pieces of stone or sand
➤ **gritty** ADJECTIVE
grit VERB grits, gritting, gritted
To grit your teeth is to clench them tightly to get through pain or difficulty.

grizzly bear NOUN grizzly bears
a large brown bear found in North America

groan VERB groans, groaning, groaned
to make a long deep sound of pain or distress
groan NOUN groans
the sound of someone groaning

grocer NOUN grocers
someone who keeps a shop that sells food, drink and household goods

grocery NOUN groceries
❶ a grocer's shop ❷ Groceries are goods sold by a grocer.

groom NOUN grooms
someone whose job is to look after horses
groom VERB grooms, grooming, groomed
to clean and brush a horse

groove NOUN **grooves**
a long narrow channel cut into a surface

grope VERB **gropes, groping, groped**
to feel about for something that you cannot see

gross ADJECTIVE **grosser, grossest**
❶ disgusting ❷ very bad • *an example of* **gross** *stupidity*

grotesque *(say* groh-**tesk***)* ADJECTIVE
strange and ugly or ridiculous
➤ **grotesquely** ADVERB

ground VERB *(past tense and past participle of* **grind***)* • *The witch scowled and* **ground** *her teeth.* • *The traffic had* **ground** *to a halt.*

ground NOUN **grounds**
❶ The ground is the surface of the earth.
❷ A ground is a sports field. ❸ Grounds are the gardens and land around a large building. • *Bikes are not allowed on school* **grounds**. ❹ Grounds for something are reasons for it. • *They have no* **grounds** *for complaint.*

group NOUN **groups**
a number of people, animals or things that belong together in some way

group VERB **groups, grouping, grouped**
to get into a group or put people or things into a group • *They were* **grouped** *around a table.*

grouse NOUN **grouse**
a large game bird with feathered legs

grove NOUN **groves**
a group of trees, especially fruit trees • *an olive* **grove**

grovel VERB **grovels, grovelling, grovelled**
❶ to be excessively humble and obedient towards someone ❷ to crawl on the ground

grow VERB **grows, growing, grew, grown**
❶ to become bigger or increase • *My grandma said I'd* **grown**. • *The flowers have started to* **grow**.
❷ To grow something is to plant it and look after it. • *She* **grows** *vegetables.* ❸ To grow is to become. • *It was* **growing** *dark.* • *He* **grew** *impatient.*
➤ **To grow up** is to become an adult.

growl VERB **growls, growling, growled**
to make a deep rough sound, like an angry dog

growl NOUN **growls**
the sound of an animal or person growling

grown-up NOUN **grown-ups**
an adult

growth NOUN **growths**
the process of growing or increasing

grub NOUN **grubs**
❶ a tiny creature like a worm, that will become an insect

⚙ **BUILD YOUR VOCABULARY**
Look at **larva**.

❷ *(informal)* food • *Lovely* **grub***!*

grubby ADJECTIVE **grubbier, grubbiest**
dirty

grudge NOUN **grudges**
If you have a grudge against someone, you dislike them because of something they did in the past.

grudge VERB **grudges, grudging, grudged**
To grudge someone something is to feel annoyed that they have it.

gruesome ADJECTIVE
shocking and horrible • *a* **gruesome** *tale*

gruff ADJECTIVE **gruffer, gruffest**
A gruff voice or manner is rough and unfriendly.
➤ **gruffly** ADVERB

grumble VERB **grumbles, grumbling, grumbled**
to complain in a bad-tempered way

grumpy ADJECTIVE **grumpier, grumpiest**
bad-tempered
➤ **grumpily** ADVERB ➤ **grumpiness** NOUN

grunt VERB **grunts, grunting, grunted**
to make a snorting sound like a pig

grunt NOUN **grunts**
a snort like that of a pig

guarantee NOUN **guarantees**
a formal promise, especially to repair something if it goes wrong

guarantee VERB **guarantees, guaranteeing, guaranteed**
to promise something • *I* **guarantee** *he'll be there.*

a
b
c
d
e
f
g
h
i
j
k
l
m
n
o
p
q
r
s
t
u
v
w
x
y
z

guard VERB guards, guarding, guarded
to watch someone or something carefully to keep them safe or stop them getting away

guard NOUN guards
someone who protects a person or place or guards a prisoner

⚠ WATCH OUT!
The **u** is silent in words that start with **gu–**, like **guard**, **guess** and **guide**.

guardian NOUN guardians
❶ someone who is legally in charge of a child instead of the child's parents ❷ someone who protects something

guess VERB guesses, guessing, guessed
to say what you think something is without knowing for sure or without working it out carefully • *Can you guess what's in the box?*

guess NOUN guesses
an opinion or answer that you give when you guess • *Amazingly, my guess was right.*

guest NOUN guests
a person who has been invited to someone's house or to an event

guide NOUN guides
someone who shows people the way or points out interesting sights in a place

guide VERB guides, guiding, guided
to show someone the way or help them do something • *He guided them across the desert.*

guide dog NOUN guide dogs
a dog that has been specially trained to lead a blind person

guild (*say* gild) NOUN guilds
a society of people with similar skills or interests

guilt
❶ an unhappy feeling when you know you have done something wrong • *You shouldn't feel any guilt over the accident.* ❷ A person's guilt is the fact that they have done something wrong. • *Everyone was sure of his guilt.*

guilty ADJECTIVE guiltier, guiltiest
❶ If someone is guilty, they have done something wrong. ❷ If you feel guilty, you know you have done wrong.

guinea NOUN guineas
an old British gold coin of high value

guinea pig NOUN guinea pigs
a small furry animal without a tail, kept as a pet

guitar NOUN guitars
a musical instrument with a long neck and six strings that you play with your fingers
➤ **guitarist** NOUN

guitar

gulf NOUN gulfs
a large area of sea partly surrounded by land

gull NOUN gulls
a seagull

gullet NOUN gullets
the tube from the throat to the stomach

gully NOUN gullies
a narrow channel that carries water

gulp VERB gulps, gulping, gulped
❶ to swallow something quickly or greedily ❷ to make a loud swallowing noise, especially out of fear

gulp NOUN gulps
a loud swallow • *He took a gulp of water.*

gum NOUN gums
❶ Your gums are the firm fleshy parts in your mouth that hold your teeth. ❷ Gum is a sweet that you chew but do not swallow.

gun NOUN guns
a weapon that fires bullets or shells

gunpowder NOUN
a type of explosive

gurdwara NOUN gurdwaras
a Sikh temple

gurgle VERB gurgles, gurgling, gurgled
to make a bubbling sound • *Water gurgled down the drain.*

guru *NOUN* gurus
a Hindu religious teacher

Guru Granth Sahib *NOUN*
the holy book of the Sikh religion

gush *VERB* gushes, gushing, gushed
to flow quickly and in large amounts

gust *NOUN* gusts
a sudden rush of wind
➤ **gusty** *ADJECTIVE*

gut *NOUN* guts
Someone's gut or guts means their digestive system, especially their stomach and intestines.

gutter *NOUN* gutters
a pipe or channel along a roof or street, for carrying away rainwater

guzzle *VERB* guzzles, guzzling, guzzled
to eat or drink something greedily

gym *(say* jim*) NOUN* gyms
a large room for exercise and indoor sports; short for *gymnasium*

gymnasium *NOUN* gymnasiums
a **gym**

gymnast *NOUN* gymnasts
someone who does gymnastics

gymnastics *NOUN*
exercises and movements that show the body's agility and strength

Gypsy *NOUN* Gypsies
a member of a group of people who usually travel from place to place living in caravans or similar vehicles and who speak a language called **Romany**

🔧 **BUILD** YOUR VOCABULARY
Gypsies are also called **travellers**.

a
b
c
d
e
f
g
h
i
j
k
l
m
n
o
p
q
r
s
t
u
v
w
x
y
z

⚙ **H** is for **happy**. Evidence shows that the word *happy* is used at least three times as often in English as the word *sad*!

habit *NOUN* **habits**
something that you do often and without thinking

habitat *NOUN* **habitats**
An animal's or plant's habitat is the place where it naturally lives or grows.

hack *VERB* **hacks, hacking, hacked**
❶ to chop or cut something roughly ❷ to get access to someone's computer or computer system without permission

had *VERB (past tense and past participle of* **have***)*
• We **had** a nice time. • Have you **had** lunch?

haddock *NOUN* **haddock**
a sea fish used for food

hag *NOUN* **hags**
an ugly old woman

haggard *ADJECTIVE*
looking ill or very tired

haggis *NOUN* **haggises**
a Scottish food made from some inner parts of a sheep mixed with oatmeal and spices

haggle *VERB* **haggles, haggling, haggled**
to argue about a price or agreement

haiku *(say* hy-koo*) NOUN* **haiku**
a Japanese short poem, with three lines and seventeen syllables in the pattern 5, 7, 5

hail *NOUN*
frozen drops of rain

hail *VERB* **hails, hailing, hailed**
❶ When it hails, hail falls. ❷ To hail a taxi or other vehicle is to signal that you want it to stop.

hailstone *NOUN* **hailstones**
a piece of hail

hair *NOUN* **hairs**
Hair is the fine threads, called **hairs**, that grow on your head and body or on an animal's body.
➤ **hairy** *ADJECTIVE* • Dad has **hairy** arms.

haircut *NOUN* **haircuts**
the act of cutting someone's hair or the style into which it is cut

hairdresser *NOUN* **hairdressers**
someone whose job is to cut people's hair

hairstyle *NOUN* **hairstyles**
the way someone's hair is cut and arranged

Hajj *NOUN*
the pilgrimage to Mecca that all Muslims try to make at least once in their lives

hake NOUN hake
a sea fish used for food

halal ADJECTIVE
Halal food is prepared according to Islamic law.

half NOUN halves
one of two equal parts that something is divided into. It can be written as $\frac{1}{2}$.

half ADVERB
partly; not completely • *Don't leave the job half done.*

➤ **half past** a time thirty minutes past the hour • *Half past two is 2.30.*

half-time NOUN half-times
a short break in the middle of a match

halfway ADVERB, ADJECTIVE
at a middle point between two places or times

halibut NOUN halibut
a large flat sea fish used for food

hall NOUN halls
❶ a space or passage inside the front door of a house ❷ a large room or building for public events

hallo
another spelling of **hello**

Halloween NOUN
the night of 31 October, when ghosts and witches are supposed to appear

✳ **WORD STORY**
The word **Halloween** is a short form of *All Hallow Even*, meaning the evening before All Saints' Day.

halo NOUN haloes
a circle of light, especially one shown round the head of a saint or angel

halt VERB halts, halting, halted
to stop
halt NOUN
➤ **To come to a halt** is to stop.

halter NOUN halters
a strap put round a horse's head so it can be led

halve VERB halves, halving, halved
to divide something into two halves

halves NOUN (plural of **half**)

ham NOUN hams
meat from a pig's leg

hamburger NOUN hamburgers
a flat round cake of minced meat, often grilled and served in a bread roll

hammer NOUN hammers
a tool with a heavy metal head on a handle, used for hitting in nails
hammer VERB hammers, hammering, hammered
❶ to hit something with a hammer ❷ to knock very loudly • *He hammered on the door.*

hammock NOUN hammocks
a bed made of net or cloth hung between two points

hamper NOUN hampers
a large basket with a lid

hamper VERB hampers, hampering, hampered
to make it difficult for someone to do something • *The rescue was hampered by bad weather.*

hamster NOUN hamsters
a small furry animal with cheek pouches, often kept as a pet

a b c d e f g h i j k l m n o p q r s t u v w x y z

hand NOUN hands
❶ Your hands are the parts of your body at the end of your arms. ❷ The hands on a clock or watch are the pointers that point to the numbers. ❸ A hand is some help. • *Do you need a hand with those bags?*
➤ **at hand** near or close by
➤ **by hand** using your hands rather than a machine
➤ **on hand** ready and available or nearby

hand VERB hands, handing, handed
to give or pass something to someone • *Hand me a cloth.*

handbag NOUN handbags
a small bag for holding money, keys and other personal items

handcuffs NOUN
a pair of metal rings used for locking a prisoner's wrists together
➤ **handcuffed** ADJECTIVE

handful NOUN handfuls
❶ as much as you can carry in one hand ❷ a small number • *Only a handful of people came.*

handiwork NOUN
Someone's handiwork is something they have made or done.

handkerchief NOUN handkerchiefs
a square piece of material or paper for wiping your nose

handle NOUN handles
the part of a thing that you hold to use it or pick it up

handle VERB handles, handling, handled
❶ to touch or feel something with your hands ❷ To handle a task or problem is to deal with it. • *I thought you handled the situation very well.*

handlebars NOUN
The handlebars on a bike are the bars that you use to steer it.

handsome ADJECTIVE handsomer, handsomest
attractive or good-looking

handwriting NOUN
Your handwriting is the way you write with your hand. • *The note was in my mum's handwriting.*

handy ADJECTIVE handier, handiest
useful or convenient

hang VERB hangs, hanging, hung
❶ to put something on a hook or nail • *Hang your coat on a peg.* ❷ If something hangs, it is attached at the top and does not touch the ground. • *Fruit hung from the trees.*
➤ **To hang around** is to stay or wait somewhere not doing anything.
➤ **To hang on** (informal) is to wait. • *Hang on! I'm not ready yet.*
➤ **To hang on to something** is to keep it or hold it tightly.
➤ **To hang up** is to end a phone call.

hangar NOUN hangars
a large shed where aircraft are kept

⚠ **WATCH OUT!**
Hangar is spelt with two a's, like aircraft. Do not confuse with a **hanger**, which is an object for hanging up clothes.

hanger NOUN hangers
a wooden, plastic or wire object with a hook at the top, that you use for hanging up clothes

hank NOUN hanks
a thick coil of wool, thread or hair

Hanukkah NOUN
a Jewish festival held in December

happen VERB happens, happening, happened
to take place or occur
➤ **To happen to do something** is to do it by chance without planning it. • *I happened to see him in the street.*

happily ADVERB
❶ in a happy way • *They played happily.* ❷ willingly • *I will happily save you a seat.* ❸ used to say that something is fortunate • *Happily, no one was hurt.*

happiness NOUN
the feeling of being happy • *Her eyes shone with happiness.*

happy ADJECTIVE happier, happiest
❶ pleased or joyful • *I'm so happy we won.* • *a happy face* ❷ satisfied with something • *Are you happy with your picture?* ❸ willing to do something • *I'm happy to help in any way I can.*

A B C D E F G H I J K L M N O P Q R S T U V W X Y Z

harass (say ha-rass or ha-**rass**) VERB **harasses, harassing, harassed**
If someone harasses another person, they keep bothering or upsetting them.

harbour NOUN **harbours**
a sheltered place where ships can be tied up

hard ADJECTIVE **harder, hardest**
❶ firm or solid; not soft • The ground was **hard**.
❷ difficult; not easy • The sums were **hard**.
• This is **hard** work. ❸ using a lot of force
• a **hard** kick
➤ **hardness** NOUN
hard ADVERB **harder, hardest**
❶ with great effort • We tried really **hard**. ❷ with a lot of force • It was raining **hard**.

hard disk (also **hard drive**) NOUN **hard disks, hard drives**
the part inside a computer that is able to store large amounts of data

harden VERB **hardens, hardening, hardened**
to become hard • Wait for the varnish to **harden**.

hardly ADVERB
only just; almost not • She could **hardly** walk.

hardship NOUN **hardships**
suffering or difficulty

hardware NOUN
❶ tools and other pieces of equipment you use in the house and garden ❷ the machinery and electronic parts of a computer, not the programs
⚙ **BUILD YOUR VOCABULARY**
Look at **software**.

hardy ADJECTIVE **hardier, hardiest**
able to endure cold or difficult conditions

hare NOUN **hares**
a fast-running animal like a large rabbit

hark VERB **harks, harking, harked** (old use)
to listen

harm VERB **harms, harming, harmed**
to hurt or damage someone or something • Plastic is **harming** the environment.

harm NOUN
injury or damage • They do not mean you any **harm**.
➤ **harmful** ADJECTIVE • **harmful** chemicals
➤ **harmless** ADJECTIVE • The snake is **harmless**.

harmony NOUN **harmonies**
❶ a pleasant combination of musical notes played or sung at the same time ❷ agreement or friendship
• They live in perfect **harmony**.

harness NOUN **harnesses**
straps put over a horse's head and round its neck to control it
harness VERB **harnesses, harnessing, harnessed**
❶ To harness a horse is to put a harness on it.
❷ To harness something is to control it and make use of it. • They **harness** the power of wind to make electricity.

harp NOUN **harps**
a musical instrument made of a frame with strings stretched across it that you pluck with your fingers
➤ **harpist** NOUN

harpoon NOUN **harpoons**
a spear attached to a rope, fired from a gun to catch whales and large fish

harsh ADJECTIVE **harsher, harshest**
❶ rough and unpleasant to hear, see, feel or experience • a **harsh** climate ❷ cruel or severe
• a **harsh** punishment
➤ **harshly** ADVERB ➤ **harshness** NOUN

harvest NOUN **harvests**
the time when crops are gathered in or the crop itself
harvest VERB **harvests, harvesting, harvested**
To harvest crops is to gather them in.

has VERB (3rd person singular of **have**)
• She **has** two brothers.

hashtag NOUN **hashtags**
the symbol #, used in messages on social media

hassle NOUN **hassles** (informal)
difficulty or problems or something that causes this
hassle VERB **hassles, hassling, hassled** (informal)
to bother or pester someone

a
b
c
d
e
f
g
h
i
j
k
l
m
n
o
p
q
r
s
t
u
v
w
x
y
z

haste NOUN
hurry or speed
➤ **To make haste** is to hurry.

hasten VERB hastens, hastening, hastened
❶ to hurry ❷ To hasten something is to speed it up.

hasty ADJECTIVE hastier, hastiest
hurried; done too quickly • a **hasty** decision
➤ **hastily** ADVERB

hat NOUN hats
a covering for your head

hatch VERB hatches, hatching, hatched
If an egg or a young bird or reptile hatches, the egg breaks and the young bird or reptile comes out.
• The chicks **hatched** this morning.

hatch NOUN hatches
an opening in a floor, wall or door, usually with a covering

hatchet NOUN hatchets
a small axe

hate VERB hates, hating, hated
to dislike someone or something very strongly

hate NOUN hates
a strong feeling of great dislike

hateful ADJECTIVE
very nasty

hatred (say **hay**-trid) NOUN
a strong feeling of great dislike

haughty (say **haw**-tee) ADJECTIVE haughtier, haughtiest
too proud and looking down on other people
➤ **haughtily** ADVERB ➤ **haughtiness** NOUN

haul VERB hauls, hauling, hauled
to pull something using a lot of effort • They **hauled** the boat out of the water.

haunt VERB haunts, haunting, haunted
If a ghost haunts a place, it appears there often.
➤ **haunted** ADJECTIVE • a **haunted** castle

have VERB has, having, had
❶ If you **have** or **have got** something, it belongs to you or you possess it. • She **has** brown eyes. • I **have** no money. • The book **has** got a red cover. • I **have** got two brothers. ❷ If you have an experience, it happens to you. • She **had** an accident. • I'm **having** a nice time. ❸ If you have a meal or drink, you eat or drink it. • **Have** you **had** breakfast? • We're **having** fish and chips. ❹ To have something done is to get someone to do it. • I **had** my hair cut. ❺ If you **have to** or **have got to** do something, you are obliged or forced to do it. • I **had** to tidy up. • We **have** got to go now. ❻ The verb **have** can be used with other verbs to make tenses. • They **have** finished now.
• **Has** he replied yet? • I **had** not seen him before.

BUILD YOUR VOCABULARY
A verb that can be used with other verbs in this way is called an **auxiliary verb**.

hatch

haven (say **hay**-ven) NOUN havens
a safe place

havoc NOUN
great destruction or disorder
• The storm wreaked **havoc**.

hawk NOUN hawks
a bird of prey with a hooked beak and a long tail

hawthorn NOUN hawthorns
a thorny tree with white flowers and small red berries

hay NOUN
cut grass that is dried and used to feed animals

hay fever NOUN
an allergy to pollen that makes you sneeze and makes your eyes water or itch

haystack NOUN haystacks
a large neat pile of stored hay

hazard NOUN hazards
a risk or danger
➤ **hazardous** ADJECTIVE • a **hazardous** mission

haze NOUN hazes
thin mist

hazel NOUN **hazels**
❶ a type of small nut tree or a nut from this tree ❷ a light brown colour

hazy ADJECTIVE **hazier, haziest**
❶ misty • *hazy* sunshine ❷ vague and unclear • *I have a hazy memory of that day.*
➤ **hazily** ADVERB ➤ **haziness** NOUN

he PRONOUN, NOUN
a male person or animal who does something

BUILD YOUR VOCABULARY
He is used as the **subject** of a verb.

head NOUN **heads**
❶ the part of your body containing your brain, eyes and mouth ❷ the person in charge • *She's the head of this school.* ❸ the top or front of something • *an arrow head* ❹ the side of a coin on which someone's head is shown

BUILD YOUR VOCABULARY
In sense 4, the other side is **tails**.

head VERB **heads, heading, headed**
❶ To head something is to lead it or be the person in charge. ❷ To head somewhere is to start going there. • *We headed home.* ❸ To head a ball is to hit it with your head.

headache NOUN **headaches**
If you have a headache, your head hurts.

headdress NOUN **headdresses**
a decorative covering for the head

heading NOUN **headings**
a word or words written as a title • *I wrote the heading 'Jobs'.*

headland NOUN **headlands**
a piece of high land sticking out into the sea

headlight NOUN **headlights**
a powerful light at the front of a vehicle

headline NOUN **headlines**
words printed in large type as the title of a newspaper story

headlong ADVERB, ADJECTIVE
fast and without taking care, especially with the head first • *He ran headlong down the slope.* • *a headlong fall into a ditch*

headmaster NOUN **headmasters**
a male head teacher

headmistress NOUN **headmistresses**
a female head teacher

headphones NOUN
a pair of small speakers that you wear over your ears

headquarters NOUN
headquarters
the place from which an organisation is controlled

head teacher NOUN **head teachers**
the person in charge of a school

heal VERB **heals, healing, healed**
❶ If a wound or an injury heals, it gets better. • *The cut soon healed.* ❷ To heal a person or disease is to cure them.

heal

health NOUN
❶ Your health is how healthy you are. • *His health is bad.* ❷ Health is being healthy. • *We wished them health and happiness.*

⚠ **WATCH OUT!**
Remember **health** and **healthy** contain the word *heal*, so they have an **a** in them.

healthy ADJECTIVE **healthier, healthiest**
❶ strong and not ill; well ❷ good for you • *Eat lots of healthy foods.*
➤ **healthily** ADVERB ➤ **healthiness** NOUN

heap NOUN **heaps**
a pile, especially an untidy pile
heap VERB **heaps, heaping, heaped**
To heap things somewhere is to pile them up.

hear VERB **hears, hearing, heard**
❶ to notice a sound through your ears • *Speak up, I can't hear.* • *He heard footsteps.* ❷ To hear news or information is to receive it. • *Have you heard about the fire?*

a
b
c
d
e
f
g
h
i
j
k
l
n
o
p
q
r
s
t
u
v
w
x
y
z

hearing NOUN **hearings**
the ability to hear

heart NOUN **hearts**
❶ the part of the body inside your chest that pumps blood around your body ❷ a person's feelings or emotions
'I will honour Christmas in my heart and try to keep it all the year.'—A CHRISTMAS CAROL, Charles Dickens
❸ a curved shape representing a heart, used as a symbol of love ❹ the middle of something • *She was lost in the* **heart** *of the forest.*
➤ **by heart** from memory

hearth (*say* harth) NOUN **hearths**
the floor of a fireplace or the area near it

heartless ADJECTIVE
cruel; without pity • *How could you be so* **heartless?**

hearty ADJECTIVE **heartier, heartiest**
❶ strong and energetic • *a* **hearty** *handshake*
❷ A hearty meal is large and filling.
➤ **heartily** ADVERB

heat NOUN **heats**
great warmth; a hot feeling • *The* **heat** *of the sun was too much.*
heat VERB **heats, heating, heated**
to make something hot or warm • *A stove* **heats** *the house.*
➤ **heater** NOUN • *an electric* **heater**

heath NOUN **heaths**
wild flat land, often covered with heather or bushes

heathen NOUN **heathens** (*old use*)
someone who does not believe in one of the main world religions

heather NOUN
a low bush with small purple, pink or white flowers

heave VERB **heaves, heaving, heaved**
to lift or move something somewhere with great effort • *She* **heaved** *herself out of the hole.*
➤ **To heave a sigh** is to sigh deeply.
heave NOUN **heaves**
a strong pull or shove

heaven NOUN
in some religions, the place where good people are thought to go when they die and where God is thought to live
➤ **the heavens** the sky

heavenly ADJECTIVE
❶ to do with the sky or heaven ❷ very pleasant

heavy ADJECTIVE **heavier, heaviest**
❶ weighing a lot; hard to lift ❷ used to talk about how much something weighs • *How* **heavy** *is the bottle when it's full of water?* ❸ strong or forceful • *Heavy rain was falling.*
➤ **heavily** ADVERB • *He fell* **heavily** *to the ground.*

Hebrew NOUN
the language of the ancient Jewish people or a modern form of the language used in Israel

hectare (*say* hek-tar) NOUN **hectares**
a unit of area equal to 10,000 square metres or just over 2 acres

he'd
short for *he had* or *he would* • *He'd (= he had) already gone.* • *He'd (= he would) like that.*

hedge NOUN **hedges**
a row of bushes along the edge of a garden or field

hedgehog NOUN **hedgehogs**
a small animal covered with prickles

hedgerow NOUN **hedgerows**
a long hedge, especially along a field or road

heed VERB **heeds, heeding, heeded**
to listen or pay attention to something • *He had not* **heeded** *the warnings.*
heed NOUN
attention or notice • *She paid no* **heed** *to what they said.*

heel NOUN **heels**
❶ the back part of your foot ❷ the back bottom part of a sock or shoe

hefty ADJECTIVE **heftier, heftiest**
big, heavy or forceful • *He gave the door a* **hefty** *kick.*

height NOUN heights
① how high someone or something is • *Let me measure your height.* ② a high place • *My dog is afraid of heights.*
➤ **The height of something** is right in the middle of it. • *It was the height of the summer.*

WATCH OUT!
Height is pronounced 'hight' but it is spelt like **weight**, with an e in it.

heir (*say* air) NOUN heirs
someone who inherits money or property

held VERB (*past tense and past participle of* **hold**)
• *The box held some tools.* • *Have you held the baby?*

helicopter NOUN helicopters
a kind of aircraft with a large propeller on top instead of wings

WORD STORY
The word **helicopter** comes from Greek words meaning 'spiral wing'.

helium (*say* hee-lee-um) NOUN
a colourless gas that is lighter than air and is sometimes used in balloons

BUILD YOUR VOCABULARY
Look at **element**.

hell NOUN
① in some religions, a place where wicked people are thought to be punished after they die and where the Devil is thought to live ② a very unpleasant place or situation

hello EXCLAMATION
a word you say to greet someone or to attract their attention

helm NOUN helms
the handle or wheel used to steer a ship

helmet NOUN helmets
a strong covering that you wear to protect your head

help VERB helps, helping, helped
① to do something useful for someone or make things easier for them ② If you cannot help doing something, you cannot avoid doing it. • *I can't help coughing.* ③ To help yourself to food is to take some.
➤ **helper** NOUN
help NOUN
something you do to help someone

helpful ADJECTIVE
giving help; useful • *a very helpful suggestion*
➤ **helpfully** ADVERB

helping NOUN helpings
a portion of food at a meal

helpless ADJECTIVE
unable to do anything or unable to look after yourself
➤ **helplessly** ADVERB

hem NOUN hems
the bottom or edge of fabric, where it has been folded and sewn down
hem VERB hems, hemming, hemmed
➤ **To hem someone in** is to surround them so they cannot move.

hemisphere NOUN hemispheres
half the earth • *Australia is in the southern hemisphere.*

hen NOUN hens
a female bird, especially a chicken

hence ADVERB
① therefore • *A bus broke down, hence the delay.*
② from now • *People will remember this 100 years hence.*

heptagon NOUN heptagons
a shape with seven straight sides
➤ **heptagonal** (*say* hept-**ag**-on-al) ADJECTIVE

WORD STORY
Heptagon comes from the Greek *hept-* meaning 'seven'.

a
b
c
d
e
f
g
h
i
j
k
l
m
n
o
p
q
r
s
t
u
v
w
x
y
z

her PRONOUN

a word used instead of *she* when it comes after a verb or preposition • *Can you see **her**?* • *I got a present from **her**.*

BUILD YOUR VOCABULARY

Her is used as the **object** of a verb.

her DETERMINER

belonging to her • *I think that is **her** book.*

herald NOUN heralds

in the past, an official who made announcements or carried messages for a king or queen

herald VERB heralds, heralding, heralded

To herald something is to show that it is coming.

heraldry NOUN

the study of coats of arms

herb NOUN herbs

a plant used for flavouring food or making medicines ➤ **herbal** ADJECTIVE • *herbal* tea

herbivore NOUN herbivores

an animal that only eats plants

BUILD YOUR VOCABULARY

Look at **carnivore** and **omnivore**.

herd NOUN herds

a large group of animals, especially cattle

herd VERB herds, herding, herded

to get people or animals to move together in a large group

here ADVERB

in or to this place

hereditary ADJECTIVE

passed down to a child from a parent

heritage NOUN heritages

things such as customs and traditions that have been passed from one generation to another

hermit NOUN hermits

someone who lives alone and keeps away from people, often for religious reasons

hero NOUN heroes

❶ someone who has done something very brave ❷ the most important male character in a story, film or play • *The **hero** is called Harry.*

WATCH OUT!

Remember to put an **e** in the plural: *tales of ancient heroes.*

heroic (say he-ro-ic) ADJECTIVE

like a hero; very brave • *a **heroic** rescue*

heroine NOUN heroines

❶ a woman or girl who has done something very brave ❷ the most important female character in a story, film or play • *Sophie is the **heroine** of 'The BFG'.*

heron NOUN herons

a wading bird with long legs and a long neck

herring NOUN herring, herrings

a sea fish that swims in large groups and is used for food

hers PRONOUN

belonging to her • *Those books are **hers**.*

herself PRONOUN

❶ used instead of 'her' when the same girl or woman does something and is affected by it • *She saw **herself** in the mirror.* ❷ on her own; without help • *She wrote the poem **herself**.* ➤ **by herself** on her own; alone • *She sat **by herself**.*

he's

short for *he is* or (before a verb in the past tense) *he has* • *He's (= he is) coming.* • *He's (= he has) finished now.*

hesitant *ADJECTIVE*
slow and uncertain when you speak or move
➤ **hesitantly** *ADVERB*

hesitate *VERB* hesitates, hesitating, hesitated
to be slow and uncertain when you speak or move

hesitation *NOUN*
pausing or a pause • *She answered without hesitation.*

hexagon *NOUN* hexagons
a flat shape with six sides
➤ **hexagonal** (*say* hex-**ag**-on-al) *ADJECTIVE*

WORD STORY

Hexagon comes from the Greek and Latin *hex-* meaning 'six'.

hibernate
VERB hibernates, hibernating, hibernated
If animals hibernate, they sleep for a long time during cold weather.
➤ **hibernation** *NOUN*

hiccup *NOUN*
hiccups
Hiccups are short gasps that you cannot control, sometimes caused by drinking too fast.

hiccup *VERB* hiccups, hiccupping, hiccupped
If you hiccup, you are affected by hiccups.

hide *VERB* hides, hiding, hid, hidden
❶ to get into a place where you cannot be seen or found • *I hid behind a tree.* ❷ To hide someone or something is to keep them from being seen or discovered. • *The gold was hidden in a cave.*

hideous *ADJECTIVE*
very ugly or unpleasant
➤ **hideously** *ADVERB*

hideout *NOUN* hideouts
a place where someone hides

hiding *NOUN* hidings
To be in hiding is to keep yourself hidden.
• *The outlaws went into hiding.*

hieroglyphics (*say* hy-ro-**glif**-iks) *PLURAL NOUN*
pictures or symbols used in ancient Egypt to represent words

high *ADJECTIVE* higher, highest
❶ very tall • *They came to a high wall.* ❷ far above the ground or sea • *I saw a bird high in the sky.* ❸ used to talk about how tall or far up something is • *a little creature only three inches high* ❹ A high voice or sound is not deep or low. ❺ large in amount or importance • *Prices are high.* • *They are people of a high rank.*

high jump *NOUN*
an athletic contest in which competitors jump over a high bar

highlands *PLURAL NOUN*
mountainous country, especially in Scotland

BUILD YOUR VOCABULARY
Look at **lowlands** and **uplands**.

highlight *NOUN* highlights
the best or most interesting part of something
• *The highlight of the trip was going canoeing.*
highlight *VERB* highlights, highlighting, highlighted
to draw attention to something

highly *ADVERB*
extremely • *It is highly unlikely that we will win.*

Highness *NOUN* Highnesses
a title of a prince or princess

high-pitched *ADJECTIVE*
high in sound

highwayman *NOUN* highwaymen
in the past, a man who robbed travellers

hijab *NOUN* hijabs
a head covering worn in public by some Muslim women

hijack *VERB* hijacks, hijacking, hijacked
To hijack an aircraft or a vehicle is to take control of it by force.
➤ **hijacker** *NOUN*

hike *NOUN* hikes
a long walk in the countryside

a b c d e f g h i j k l m n o p q r s t u v w x y z

hike VERB hikes, hiking, hiked
to go for a long walk in the countryside
➤ **hiker** NOUN

hilarious ADJECTIVE
very funny
➤ **hilariously** ADVERB

hill NOUN hills
a high rounded area of ground
➤ **hilly** ADJECTIVE

hillside NOUN hillsides
the side of a hill

hilt NOUN hilts
the handle of a sword or dagger

him PRONOUN
a word used instead of *he* when it comes after a verb or preposition • *Do you like* **him**? • *I gave the money to* **him**.

> **BUILD YOUR VOCABULARY**
> **Him** is used as the **object** of a verb.

himself PRONOUN
❶ used instead of *him* when the same boy or man does something and is affected by it • *He saw* **himself** *in the mirror.* ❷ on his own; without help • *He made the cake* **himself**.
➤ **by himself** on his own; alone • *He sat* **by** **himself**.

hind (*rhymes with* **find**) ADJECTIVE
back • *The dog stood on its* **hind** *legs.*

> **BUILD YOUR VOCABULARY**
> Look at **fore**.

hinder (*say* hin-der) VERB hinders, hindering, hindered
to get in someone's way or make it difficult for them to do something
➤ **hindrance** NOUN

Hindi NOUN
the main language of northern India

> ✳ **WORD STORY**
> The words **bungalow** and **shampoo** come from Hindi.

Hindu NOUN Hindus
someone who believes in *Hinduism*, an Indian religion with many gods
➤ **Hindu** ADJECTIVE

hinge NOUN hinges
a piece of metal fixed to a door, gate or lid, which allows it to open and shut

hint NOUN hints
❶ a suggestion or tip • *The website has helpful* **hints** *for improving your spelling.* ❷ a small amount of a quality • *There was a* **hint** *of sarcasm in her voice.*

hint VERB hints, hinting, hinted
to suggest something without actually saying it
• *She* **hinted** *that she'd like to come.*

hip NOUN hips
Your hips are the bony parts at the side of your body between your waist and your thighs.

hippo NOUN hippos
a short word for **hippopotamus**

hippopotamus NOUN hippopotamuses
a very large heavy African mammal that lives near water

> ✳ **WORD STORY**
> The word **hippopotamus** comes from Greek words meaning 'river horse'.

hire VERB hires, hiring, hired
To hire something is to pay to use it for a time.
• *On holiday we* **hired** *bikes.*
hire NOUN
➤ **for hire** available for people to hire

his DETERMINER, PRONOUN
belonging to him • **His** *mum is a doctor.* • *That bike is* **his**.

hiss VERB hisses, hissing, hissed
to make a long s sound, like a snake

historian NOUN historians
someone who writes about or studies history

historic ADJECTIVE
famous or important enough to be part of history
• *This is a historic occasion.*

⚠ **WATCH OUT!**
Do not confuse with **historical**.

historical ADJECTIVE
from or happening in the past, in history • *The story is based on historical events.*

⚠ **WATCH OUT!**
Do not confuse with **historic**.

history NOUN **histories**
❶ the study of the past • *I like history.* ❷ a list or description of past events • *Do you know the history of this house?*

hit VERB **hits, hitting, hit**
❶ To hit someone or something is to bang or crash into them or to strike or knock them. • *I hit my head on the shelf.* • *She hit the tennis ball hard.*
❷ If something hits you, you suddenly realise or feel it. • *The answer suddenly hit me.*

hit NOUN **hits**
❶ the action of hitting something ❷ something or someone that is very successful • *The book was a big hit.*

hitch VERB **hitches, hitching, hitched**
to tie something to something • *She hitched her horse to a post.*

hitch NOUN **hitches**
a slight problem

hither ADVERB (old use)
to or towards this place
➤ **hither and thither** here and there

hive NOUN **hives**
a beehive
➤ **a hive of activity** a very busy place

hoard NOUN **hoards**
a hidden store • *a hoard of pirate treasure*

⚠ **WATCH OUT!**
Don't confuse a **hoard** meaning 'a hidden store' with a **horde** which means 'a large crowd'.

hoard VERB **hoards, hoarding, hoarded**
to collect things and store them away

hoarse ADJECTIVE **hoarser, hoarsest**
a hoarse voice sounds rough or croaking

⚠ **WATCH OUT!**
Don't forget that **hoarse** has an **a** in it, unlike **horse** (an animal).

hoax NOUN **hoaxes**
a trick in which people are made to believe something that is not true • *The fire alarm was a hoax.*

hobble VERB **hobbles, hobbling, hobbled**
to walk with unsteady steps, especially because your feet are sore

hobby NOUN **hobbies**
something that you enjoy doing in your spare time

hockey NOUN
an outdoor game played by two teams with long curved sticks and a small hard ball

hoe NOUN **hoes**
a long gardening tool with a small blade, used for scraping up weeds and making soil loose
hoe VERB **hoes, hoeing, hoed**
to scrape or dig with a hoe

hog NOUN **hogs**
a pig, usually a male

Hogmanay NOUN
New Year's Eve in Scotland

hoist VERB **hoists, hoisting, hoisted**
to lift something up using ropes or pulleys

hold VERB **holds, holding, held**
❶ to have something in your hands or arms • *She was holding a stick.* • *Can I hold the baby?* ❷ to contain something • *The frame held a photograph.*
• *This jug holds a litre.* ❸ to organise an event
• *A banquet was held in their honour.* ❹ to possess or own something • *She holds the world record.*
➤ **To hold someone** or **something up** is to delay them. • *We were held up by the traffic.*
➤ **holder** NOUN

hold NOUN **holds**
❶ the act of holding something • *Keep hold of the railing.* ❷ the part of a ship or an aircraft where cargo is stored

a
b
c
d
e
f
g
h
i
j
k
l
m
n
o
p
q
r
s
t
u
v
w
x
y
z

hole NOUN holes
❶ a gap or opening made in something • *My pocket has a hole in it.* ❷ an animal's burrow • *a rabbit hole*

⚠ WATCH OUT!
Don't confuse a **hole** with **whole** meaning 'entire'.

Holi NOUN
a Hindu festival held in the spring

holiday NOUN holidays
❶ a day when you do not go to work or school • *Next Monday is a holiday.* ❷ a time when you go away to enjoy yourself • *We went on holiday to the seaside.*

hollow ADJECTIVE
having an empty space inside; not solid • *a hollow tree*

hollow NOUN hollows
a hollow or sunken place • *a small hollow in the ground*

holly NOUN
an evergreen bush with shiny prickly leaves and red berries

hologram NOUN holograms
a laser image that appears as three-dimensional

holy ADJECTIVE holier, holiest
related to God or a religion
➤ **holiness** NOUN

home NOUN homes
❶ the place where a person or animal lives • *Welcome to our home.* ❷ the place where you were born or where you feel you belong • *London is my home.* ❸ a place where people are looked after • *a home for the elderly*

home ADVERB
to or at the place where someone lives • *I'm going home now.*

home VERB homes, homing, homed
➤ **To home in on something** is to aim for it.

homeless ADJECTIVE
without a place to live

homesick ADJECTIVE
sad because you miss your home
➤ **homesickness** NOUN

homeward or **homewards** ADVERB, ADJECTIVE
going or leading towards home

homework NOUN
school work that you have to do at home

homograph NOUN homographs
Homographs are words with the same spelling but with a different meaning and sometimes a different pronunciation, for example *bow* (for shooting arrows) and *bow* (to bend forwards).

homonym NOUN homonyms
a **homograph** or **homophone**

homophone NOUN homophones
Homophones are words with the same sound but with a different spelling and meaning, such as *son* and *sun*.

honest ADJECTIVE
❶ not stealing, cheating or telling lies • *an honest man* ❷ truthful • *an honest answer*
➤ **honestly** ADVERB ➤ **honesty** NOUN

honey NOUN
a sweet sticky food made by bees

honeycomb NOUN honeycombs
a wax framework made by bees to hold their honey

honeymoon NOUN honeymoons
a holiday that a newly married couple spend together

honeysuckle NOUN
a climbing plant with sweet-smelling yellow or pink flowers

honk NOUN honks
a loud sound like the one made by a car horn or a goose
honk VERB honks, honking, honked
to make a honking sound

honour NOUN honours
❶ Honour is respect or a good reputation. • *They insulted his family* **honour**. ❷ An honour is an award or medal. ❸ An honour is something you are proud to do. • *It is an* **honour** *to meet you.*
honour VERB honours, honouring, honoured
to show someone respect or give them an honour

honourable ADJECTIVE
able to be trusted; worthy of respect
➤ **honourably** ADVERB

hood NOUN hoods
a part of a coat or top that you can put over your head

hoof NOUN hoofs, hooves
the hard bony part of the foot of horses, cattle or deer

hook NOUN hooks
a bent metal or plastic object for hanging things on or catching something
hook VERB hooks, hooking, hooked
to attach or catch something with a hook

hoop NOUN hoops
a large ring made of metal, wood or plastic

hooray
another spelling of **hurray**

hoot NOUN hoots
a sound like the one made by an owl or a car horn
hoot VERB hoots, hooting, hooted
to make a sound like an owl or a car horn

hop VERB hops, hopping, hopped
❶ to jump on one foot ❷ If an animal hops, it moves in jumps.

hope VERB hopes, hoping, hoped
to want or expect something to happen • *I hope he comes.*

hope NOUN hopes
❶ the wish or expectation that something good will happen ❷ something that gives you hope • *You're our only* **hope**.

hopeful ADJECTIVE
❶ feeling that something will go well • *I felt* **hopeful** *about the match.* ❷ likely to be good or successful • *The future is* **hopeful**.
➤ **hopefulness** NOUN

hopefully ADVERB
❶ in a hopeful way ❷ used for saying you hope something will happen • *Hopefully, she'll like it.*

hopeless ADJECTIVE
❶ without hope ❷ very bad at something • *I'm* **hopeless** *at singing.*
➤ **hopelessly** ADVERB

horde NOUN hordes
a large group or crowd • *hordes of enemy warriors*

⚠ **WATCH OUT!**
Don't confuse a **horde** meaning 'a large crowd' with a **hoard** meaning 'a hidden store'.

horizon NOUN horizons
the line where the sky appears to meet the land or sea

horizontal (*say* hor-iz-**on**-tal) ADJECTIVE
level or flat; going sideways rather than up or down
➤ **horizontally** ADVERB

hormone NOUN hormones
a substance made in your body that controls something such as development or growth

horn NOUN horns
❶ The horns of a cow, goat or other animal are bony parts that grow on its head. ❷ a brass musical instrument that you blow ❸ a device for making a warning sound

hornet NOUN hornets
a large kind of wasp

horoscope NOUN **horoscopes**
a prediction about what will happen to someone based on the belief that this is influenced by the position of the stars and planets

BUILD YOUR VOCABULARY
Look at **astrology**.

horrible ADJECTIVE
very unpleasant or nasty
➤ **horribly** ADVERB

horrid ADJECTIVE
very unpleasant

horrific ADJECTIVE
shocking or terrifying
➤ **horrifically** ADVERB

horrify VERB **horrifies, horrifying, horrified**
to make someone feel shocked and disgusted

horror NOUN **horrors**
great fear or disgust

horse NOUN **horses**
a four-legged animal used for riding on or pulling carts

BUILD YOUR VOCABULARY
Look at **foal**, **mare** and **stallion**.

WATCH OUT!
Don't confuse with **hoarse** meaning 'croaky'.

horseback NOUN
➤ **To be on horseback** is to be riding a horse.

horse chestnut NOUN **horse chestnuts**
a large tree that produces shiny reddish-brown nuts with spiky green cases

BUILD YOUR VOCABULARY
Look at **conker**.

horsepower NOUN **horsepower**
a unit for measuring the power of an engine

horseshoe NOUN **horseshoes**
a U-shaped piece of metal nailed to a horse's hoof or something shaped like this • *a horseshoe magnet*

hose NOUN **hoses**
a long flexible tube through which liquids or gases can travel

hospitable ADJECTIVE
welcoming to people and making them feel at home

hospital NOUN **hospitals**
a place where sick or injured people are given medical treatment

hospitality NOUN
food, drink and entertainment given to guests

host NOUN **hosts**
❶ someone who has guests and looks after them
❷ a large number of people or things • *We saw a **host** of faces.*

host VERB **hosts, hosting, hosted**
to give a party or organise an event • *London **hosted** the Olympic games in 2012.*

hostage NOUN **hostages**
someone who is held prisoner until the people who are holding them get what they want

hostile ADJECTIVE
unfriendly and angry
In the bedroom, the children were grouped in two corners of the room, regarding each other in hostile silence.
—NANNY MCPHEE AND THE BIG BANG, Emma Thompson
➤ **hostility** NOUN

hot ADJECTIVE **hotter, hottest**
❶ having a high temperature; very warm ❷ having a spicy warm taste • *hot chillies*

hotel NOUN **hotels**
a building where people pay to stay for the night

hotly ADVERB
strongly or angrily • *He **hotly** denied that he'd done it.*

hound NOUN **hounds**
a dog used for hunting or racing

hour NOUN **hours**
❶ one of the twenty-four parts into which a day is divided ❷ a particular time • *Why are you up at this **hour**?*

house (say howss) NOUN **houses**
a building where people live
house (say howz) VERB **houses, housing, housed**
to provide someone with somewhere to live

houseboat NOUN houseboats
a boat for living in

household NOUN households
all the people who live together in the same house

housewife, househusband NOUN
housewives, househusbands
a woman or man who looks after the children and does housework, rather than having a paid job

housework NOUN
the work of cooking and cleaning that has to be done in a house

hover VERB hovers, hovering, hovered
to stay in one place in the air

hovercraft NOUN hovercraft
a vehicle that travels just above the surface of water or land supported by a cushion of air

how ADVERB
❶ used for asking or talking about the way something is done • *How did you hurt your leg?* • *I'll show you how to print the document.* ❷ used for asking or talking about quantity • *How much do you want?* • *I don't know how long it will take.* ❸ used for asking or talking about the condition of something • *How are you?* • *Let me know how it goes.*

however ADVERB
❶ nevertheless; but • *I was very disappointed. However, I did not complain.* ❷ no matter how • *I couldn't do it, however hard I tried.*

however CONJUNCTION
in any way • *You can do it however you like.*

howl VERB howls, howling, howled
to make a long loud high sound like a dog or a crying baby • *The wind howled.*

howl NOUN howls
a long loud cry like a dog or a crying baby

hub NOUN hubs
the centre of a wheel

hubbub NOUN
a noisy mixture of voices from a crowd of people

huddle VERB huddles, huddling, huddled
to crowd together for warmth or comfort

hue NOUN hues
a colour or shade • *His face had a greenish hue.*

hug VERB hugs, hugging, hugged
to clasp someone tightly in your arms
hug NOUN hugs
If you give someone a hug, you hug them.

huge ADJECTIVE huger, hugest
very big or great • *We had huge problems.*
➤ **hugely** ADVERB • *She was hugely successful.*

hulk NOUN hulks
❶ the remains of an old ship ❷ a large clumsy person or thing

hull NOUN hulls
the main part or framework of a ship

hullo
another spelling of **hello**

hum VERB hums, humming, hummed
❶ to sing a tune with your lips closed ❷ to make a low continuous sound like a bee
hum NOUN hums
a humming sound

human NOUN humans
a person; a human being
human ADJECTIVE
to do with humans • *the human body*

human being NOUN human beings
a person; a human

humanity NOUN
all people; the human race • *We risk destroying all humanity.*

humble ADJECTIVE humbler, humblest
modest and not proud
➤ **humbly** ADVERB

a b c d e f g h i j k l m n o p q r s t u v w x y z

humid (*say* hew-mid) *ADJECTIVE*
If the air is humid, it is damp and warm.
➤ **humidity** *NOUN*

humiliate *VERB* **humiliates, humiliating, humiliated**
to make someone feel ashamed or foolish in front of other people
➤ **humiliation** *NOUN*

humility *NOUN*
the quality of being humble

hummingbird *NOUN* **hummingbirds**
a small tropical bird that beats its wings rapidly

humorous *ADJECTIVE*
amusing or funny

> **⚠ WATCH OUT!**
>
> The word **humour** loses a **u** when it becomes humorous.

humour *NOUN*
❶ things that are amusing or make people laugh ❷ the ability to enjoy things that are funny • *He has a good sense of **humour**.*

hump *NOUN* **humps**
a rounded lump or mound

hunch *VERB* **hunches, hunching, hunched**
To hunch your shoulders is to bring them up and forward.
hunch *NOUN* **hunches**
a feeling or instinct about what will happen • *I have a **hunch** that this is a lucky ticket.*

hung *VERB* (*past tense and past participle of* **hang**) • *I **hung** up my coat.* • *Lanterns were **hung** around the hall.*

hunger *NOUN*
the feeling of wanting or needing to eat

hungry *ADJECTIVE* **hungrier, hungriest**
If you are hungry, you want or need to eat.
➤ **hungrily** *ADVERB*

hunk *NOUN* **hunks**
a large piece or chunk • *a **hunk** of cheese*

hunt *VERB* **hunts, hunting, hunted**
❶ To hunt animals is to chase and kill them for food or sport. ❷ To hunt for something is to look hard for it.

hunt *NOUN* **hunts**
❶ an act of chasing and killing animals for sport or food ❷ a search for something • *Let's have a **hunt** for that book.*

hunter (*also* **huntsman**) *NOUN* **hunters, huntsmen**
someone who hunts for sport

hurdle *NOUN* **hurdles**
❶ a barrier that runners have to jump over in a race ❷ a problem or difficulty

hurl *VERB* **hurls, hurling, hurled**
to throw something as far as you can

hurray (*also* **hurrah**) *EXCLAMATION*
a word you shout when you are very happy • *We won! **Hurray!***

hurricane *NOUN* **hurricanes**
a severe storm with a strong wind

hurry *VERB* **hurries, hurrying, hurried**
❶ to move or act quickly; to rush ❷ To hurry someone is to try to make them be quick.
➤ **hurried** *ADJECTIVE* • *We ate a **hurried** meal.*
➤ **hurriedly** *ADVERB* • *He dressed **hurriedly**.*
hurry *NOUN*
quick rushed movement or action • *What's all the **hurry**?*
➤ **in a hurry** hurrying or impatient • *They were **in a hurry** to leave.*

hurt *VERB* **hurts, hurting, hurt**
❶ To hurt a person or an animal is to cause them pain. ❷ If part of your body hurts, you feel pain there. ❸ To hurt someone or hurt their feelings is to upset them.
hurt *ADJECTIVE*
❶ injured • *He was badly **hurt** in the crash.* ❷ upset • *I felt very **hurt** that I wasn't invited.*

hurtle *VERB* **hurtles, hurtling, hurtled**
to move quickly or dangerously • *A cart came **hurtling** along the track towards them.*

husband *NOUN* **husbands**
the man that someone is married to

hush *EXCLAMATION*
used to tell someone to be quiet • ***Hush!** You'll wake the baby.*

hush *VERB* hushes, hushing, hushed
If someone hushes or you hush them, they become quiet.
➤ **hushed** *ADJECTIVE* • *They spoke in **hushed** voices.*

hush *NOUN*
silence or quiet • *A **hush** fell over the room.*

husk *NOUN* husks
the dry outer covering of a seed

husky *ADJECTIVE* huskier, huskiest
a husky voice sounds deep and rough

husky *NOUN* huskies
a large strong dog used for pulling sledges over snow

hustle *VERB* hustles, hustling, hustled
To hustle someone is to push them somewhere.
• *I was **hustled** out of the room.*

hut *NOUN* huts
a small roughly made house or shelter

hutch *NOUN* hutches
a cage for a pet rabbit

hyacinth *(say* hy-a-sinth*)* *NOUN* hyacinths
a sweet-smelling flower that grows from a bulb

hydrangea *(say* hy-**drayn**-ja*)* *NOUN* hydrangeas
a shrub with large pink, blue or white flowers

hydraulic *ADJECTIVE*
worked by the movement of water or other liquid

hydroelectric *ADJECTIVE*
Hydroelectric power is electricity made using the power of water.

hydrogen *NOUN*
a very light flammable gas which is the most common element in the universe

> **BUILD** YOUR VOCABULARY
Hydrogen is an **element**.

hyena *(say* hy-ee-na*)* *NOUN* hyenas
a wild animal that looks similar to a wolf with long front legs and a small mane

hygiene *(say* hy-jeen*)* *NOUN*
the state of being clean and free of germs
➤ **hygienic** *ADJECTIVE* • *It's not **hygienic** to put your dirty shoes on the table.*

hymn *NOUN* hymns
a Christian religious song that praises God

hyphen *NOUN* hyphens
a punctuation mark (-) used to join words or parts of words together, for example in *good-looking* and *re-enter*
➤ **hyphenated** *ADJECTIVE* • *a **hyphenated** word*

hypnotise *(also* **hypnotize***)* *VERB*
hypnotises, hypnotising, hypnotised
to put someone into a state similar to sleep in which they will do things that are suggested to them

hysteria *NOUN*
wild uncontrollable excitement or emotion

hysterical *ADJECTIVE*
❶ very excited or emotional • *The crowd were **hysterical**.* ❷ *(informal)* very funny • *Have you seen the film? It's **hysterical**!*
➤ **hysterically** *ADVERB*

a b c d e f g h i j k l m n o p q r s t u v w x y z

⚙ **I** is the most commonly used word in spoken English.

⚙ How many other one-letter words can you think of? There are not very many!

I PRONOUN
used when you are talking or writing about things you do yourself

⚙ **BUILD YOUR VOCABULARY**
I is used as the **subject** of a verb.

I ABBREVIATION
1 in Roman numerals

ice NOUN
frozen water

ice VERB ices, icing, iced
To ice a cake is to put icing on it.

ice age NOUN
a time in the past when ice covered large areas of the earth

iceberg NOUN icebergs
a large mass of ice floating in the sea, with most of it under water

ice cream NOUN ice creams
a sweet creamy frozen food

ice skate NOUN ice skates
a boot with a blade attached to the sole, for sliding over ice
➤ **ice skater** NOUN ➤ **ice skating** NOUN

icicle NOUN icicles
a thin pointed piece of hanging ice

icing NOUN
a sugary paste for decorating cakes and biscuits

icon NOUN icons
❶ a small picture or symbol on a computer screen
❷ a painting of a holy person

ICT ABBREVIATION
a name for the subject in which you learn to use computers; short for *information and communication technology*

icy ADJECTIVE icier, iciest
❶ with ice on it • *Careful—the path is icy.* ❷ very cold • *an icy wind*

I'd
short for *I had* or *I would* • *I'd (= I had) already finished.* • *I'd (= I would) like that.*

idea NOUN ideas
❶ something that you have thought of; a plan • *I had a great idea.* ❷ a picture of something in your mind • *This is my idea of a perfect day.*

ideal ADJECTIVE
perfect • *This is an ideal place for a picnic.*

identical ADJECTIVE
exactly the same • *Liam and Finn are identical twins.*

identification NOUN
a document that proves who you are

identify VERB identifies, identifying, identified
to be able to say who someone is or what something is • *They identified the ship by its sails.*

identity NOUN identities
who someone is or what something is • *Can you guess the identity of our mystery guest?*

idiom NOUN idioms
a group of words that have a special meaning when used together, for example *lose your temper*

idiot NOUN idiots (informal)
a stupid or foolish person

idiotic ADJECTIVE (informal)
stupid or foolish • *That was an idiotic thing to do.*

idle ADJECTIVE idler, idlest
❶ If someone is idle, they are lazy or doing nothing.
❷ If a machine is idle, it is not being used.
➤ **idly** ADVERB ➤ **idleness** NOUN

idol NOUN idols
a famous person who is admired by a lot of people

i.e. ABBREVIATION
used to explain or name something • *Someone, i.e. you, will have to clear up this mess.*

✳ **WORD STORY**
i.e. is short for *id est*, which is Latin for 'that is'.

if CONJUNCTION
❶ used to talk about something that might happen • *If you see him, say hello.* ❷ on condition that • *You can come if you help carry the bags.*
❸ whether • *Do you know if lunch is ready?*
➤ **if only . . .** I wish . . . • *If only animals could talk!*

igloo NOUN igloos
a small round house made of blocks of hard snow

✳ **WORD STORY**
The word **igloo** comes from the Inuit word *iglu* which means 'house'.

igneous (*say* ig-nee-us) ADJECTIVE
Igneous rocks are formed by the action of a volcano.

ignite VERB ignites, igniting, ignited
If something ignites or you ignite it, it catches fire.

ignorant ADJECTIVE
not knowing about something
➤ **ignorance** NOUN • *I was shocked by their ignorance.*

ignore VERB ignores, ignoring, ignored
to take no notice of someone or something

ill ADJECTIVE
❶ not well; suffering from an illness ❷ bad or harmful • *Fortunately there were no ill effects.*

I'll
short for *I will* or *I shall*

illegal ADJECTIVE
not allowed by law
➤ **illegally** ADVERB • *The car was parked illegally.*

⚙ **BUILD YOUR VOCABULARY**
The opposite is **legal**.

illegible (*say* il-**lej**-ib-ul) ADJECTIVE
not clear enough to read

⚙ **BUILD YOUR VOCABULARY**
The opposite is **legible**.

illiterate (*say* il-**lit**-er-at) ADJECTIVE
unable to read or write

⚙ **BUILD YOUR VOCABULARY**
The opposite is **literate**.

illness NOUN illnesses
❶ something that makes people ill; a disease • *Flu is a serious illness.* ❷ Illness is being ill. • *She couldn't come because of illness.*

illogical ADJECTIVE
not reasonable; not thought through using logic

⚙ **BUILD YOUR VOCABULARY**
The opposite is **logical**.

illuminate VERB illuminates, illuminating, illuminated
to light up a place or decorate it with lights
➤ **illumination** NOUN

illusion NOUN illusions
❶ a false idea or belief • *They were under the illusion that he was a king.* ❷ something that you seem to see but that does not really exist

illustrate VERB illustrates, illustrating, illustrated
❶ To illustrate a book is to put pictures in it.
❷ to show something using examples • *Let me illustrate what I mean.*

illustration NOUN illustrations
a picture in a book

illustrator NOUN illustrators
a person who produces illustrations for a book

illustrious (*say* il-**luss**-tree-us) ADJECTIVE
famous

image NOUN images
❶ a picture or photograph ❷ the reputation someone or something has • *The star is very concerned about his image.*

a
b
c
d
e
f
g
h
i
j
k
l
m
n
o
p
q
r
s
t
u
v
w
x
y
z

imagery *NOUN*
the use of words to produce pictures in a reader's mind

⚙ **BUILD** YOUR VOCABULARY
Examples of **imagery** are **metaphors** and **similes**.

imaginary *ADJECTIVE*
existing only in your mind or in stories • *A unicorn is an* ***imaginary*** *creature.*

imagination *NOUN*
imaginations
your ability to form pictures and ideas in your mind

imaginative *ADJECTIVE*
having new and exciting ideas • *Her stories are always* ***imaginative***.

imagine *VERB* imagines, imagining, imagined
to form a picture of something or someone in your mind • ***Imagine*** *you lived in Roman times.*

imam *NOUN* imams
a Muslim religious leader

imbecile *(say* im-biss-eel*) NOUN* imbeciles
(informal)
a very stupid person

imitate *VERB* imitates, imitating, imitated
to copy or do the same as someone or something
➤ **imitation** *NOUN*

immaculate *ADJECTIVE*
perfectly neat and clean • *Her room is always* ***immaculate***.

immature *ADJECTIVE*
❶ not fully grown or developed ❷ silly or childish
➤ **immaturity** *NOUN*

⚙ **BUILD** YOUR VOCABULARY
An opposite is **mature**.

immediate *ADJECTIVE*
happening now or at once • *There is no* ***immediate*** *danger.*

immediately *ADVERB*
at once • *We must leave* ***immediately***.

immense *ADJECTIVE*
extremely large; huge
The largest of the trees was immense: its trunk was as thick and tall as the column in Trafalgar Square.
—THE EXPLORER, Katherine Rundell
➤ **immensity** *NOUN*

immensely *ADVERB*
extremely; very much • *We enjoyed ourselves* ***immensely***.

immerse *VERB* immerses, immersing, immersed
❶ To immerse something is to put it completely into a liquid. ❷ To be immersed in something or to immerse yourself in it is to be very interested or involved in it.
➤ **immersion** *NOUN*

immigrant *NOUN* immigrants
someone who has come into a country to live there

immigrate VERB immigrates, immigrating, immigrated
to come into a country to live there
➤ **immigration** NOUN

immoral ADJECTIVE
morally wrong; against accepted rules of good behaviour
➤ **immorality** NOUN

BUILD YOUR VOCABULARY
The opposite is **moral**.

immortal ADJECTIVE
Someone who is immortal lives forever and never dies.
➤ **immortality** NOUN

immune ADJECTIVE
If someone is immune to a disease, they cannot catch it.
➤ **immunity** NOUN

immunise (also **immunize**) VERB
immunises, immunising, immunised
to make someone safe from a disease, usually by giving them an injection
➤ **immunisation** NOUN

imp NOUN imps
in stories, a small devil or sprite

impact NOUN impacts
❶ the force of one thing hitting another ❷ a strong influence or effect • *The Internet has had a big impact on our lives.*

impartial ADJECTIVE
fair and not supporting any side • *A referee must be impartial.*

impatient ADJECTIVE
annoyed with waiting for something to happen
➤ **impatience** NOUN ➤ **impatiently** ADVERB

imperfect ADJECTIVE
not perfect

imperial ADJECTIVE
❶ relating to an empire, emperor or empress
❷ An imperial unit is a non-metric one, for example **inch** or **ounce**.

impermeable ADJECTIVE
not letting water soak through it • *Granite is an impermeable rock.*

BUILD YOUR VOCABULARY
The opposite is **permeable**.

impertinent ADJECTIVE
not showing respect; rude
➤ **impertinence** NOUN

implement (say im-ple-ment) NOUN
implements
a tool or device for doing something • *gardening implements*

implication NOUN implications
The implications of something are its possible effects.

implore VERB implores, imploring, implored
to beg someone to do something • *'Please come back,' he implored.*

imply VERB implies, implying, implied
to suggest something without actually saying it
• *Are you implying that I'm lazy?*

impolite ADJECTIVE
rude or disrespectful

import (say im-**port**) VERB imports, importing, imported
To import goods is to buy or bring them in from another country.

BUILD YOUR VOCABULARY
The opposite is **export**.

import (say im-port) NOUN imports
something bought or brought in from another country

BUILD YOUR VOCABULARY
The opposite is **export**.

important ADJECTIVE
❶ very serious or necessary; having a great effect or meaning • *This is an important decision.*
• *It's important to use the right equipment.*
❷ An important person is powerful or well known.
➤ **importance** NOUN
➤ **importantly** ADVERB
• *Don't forget your towel or, more importantly, your swimming trunks.*

a
b
c
d
e
f
g
h
i
j
k
l
m
n
o
p
q
r
s
t
u
v
w
x
y
z

impose VERB imposes, imposing, imposed
to make someone have or do something; to force something on someone • *The invaders **imposed** a new system of government.*

imposing ADJECTIVE
looking important and impressive

impossible ADJECTIVE
If something is impossible, it cannot be done or cannot happen.
➤ **impossibility** NOUN ➤ **impossibly** ADVERB

impostor NOUN impostors
someone who is not what he or she pretends to be

impress VERB impresses, impressing, impressed
❶ If something or someone impresses you, you admire them. ❷ To impress something on someone is to make them realise or remember it.

impression NOUN impressions
❶ an idea or feeling that you have about something or someone • *I had the **impression** that he wanted something.* ❷ an imitation of a person or animal • *This is my **impression** of an elephant.*

impressive ADJECTIVE
making you feel admiration
➤ **impressively** ADVERB

imprison VERB imprisons, imprisoning, imprisoned
to put someone in prison or lock them somewhere
➤ **imprisonment** NOUN

improbable ADJECTIVE
unlikely to be true or to happen

improper fraction NOUN improper fractions
a fraction in which the numerator (the top number) is larger than the denominator (the bottom number), for example $\frac{3}{2}$

⬤ BUILD YOUR VOCABULARY
Look at **proper fraction**.

improve VERB improves, improving, improved
If something improves or you improve it, it becomes better. • *I hope the weather **improves**.*
➤ **improvement** NOUN • *There's been a big **improvement** in your work.*

improvise VERB improvises, improvising, improvised
❶ to play or perform without using music or a script written in advance ❷ To improvise something is to make it quickly using whatever you have.
➤ **improvisation** NOUN
➤ **improvised** ADJECTIVE • *an **improvised** shelter*

impudent ADJECTIVE
not respectful; rude
➤ **impudence** NOUN

impulse NOUN impulses
a sudden desire to do something

impulsive ADJECTIVE
doing things suddenly without much thought
➤ **impulsively** ADVERB

in PREPOSITION, ADVERB
❶ at or inside something • *They live **in** York.* • *She got in the car.* • *We all jumped **in**.* ❷ during • *My birthday is **in** May.* • *I'll see you **in** the morning.* ❸ wearing something • *I was **in** my pyjamas.* • *a man **in** black*

inability NOUN
Someone's inability to do something is the fact that they cannot do it.

inaccurate ADJECTIVE
not correct • *What he said was **inaccurate**.*
➤ **inaccuracy** NOUN ➤ **inaccurately** ADVERB

inactive ADJECTIVE
not busy, moving or doing anything
➤ **inactivity** NOUN

inaudible ADJECTIVE
not able to be heard

incapable ADJECTIVE
unable to do something • *They are **incapable** of understanding.*

incense NOUN
a substance that makes a spicy smell when it is burnt

incense sticks

incessant ADJECTIVE
continuing without stopping • *He hated the incessant noise.*
➤ **incessantly** ADVERB

inch NOUN inches
a measurement of length. There are 12 inches in 1 foot and 1 inch is about 2.5 centimetres.

incident NOUN incidents
an event, especially a strange or unusual one

incisor *(say* in-**size**-er*)* NOUN incisors
one of the sharp teeth at the front of your mouth, used for biting off pieces of food

BUILD YOUR VOCABULARY
Look at **canine** and **molar**.

inclination NOUN inclinations
a feeling that you want to do something • *He had no inclination to help them.*

incline *(say* in-**cline***)* VERB inclines, inclining, inclined
To incline your head is to bend it to one side.
➤ **To be inclined to do something** is to want to do it or often do it. • *I am inclined to agree with you.*

incline *(say* in-**cline***)* NOUN inclines
a slope • *a steep incline*

include VERB includes, including, included
If you include someone or something, you count them as part of a group. • *Who shall we include on the list?* • *A drink is included in the price.*

income NOUN incomes
money that a person receives regularly

incomplete ADJECTIVE
not complete or finished

incomprehensible ADJECTIVE
not able to be understood

inconvenient ADJECTIVE
causing trouble or effort for someone; awkward
➤ **inconvenience** NOUN

incorrect ADJECTIVE
not accurate; wrong
➤ **incorrectly** ADVERB wrongly • *You've spelt my name incorrectly.*

increase *(say* in-**crease***)* VERB increases, increasing, increased
If something increases or you increase it, it becomes bigger. • *The amount of traffic has increased.*
➤ **increasingly** ADVERB • *I became increasingly annoyed.*

BUILD YOUR VOCABULARY
The opposite is **decrease**.

increase *(say* in-**crease***)* NOUN increases
the act of increasing • *There has been a big increase in prices.*

BUILD YOUR VOCABULARY
The opposite is **decrease**.

incredible ADJECTIVE
unbelievable; amazing • *It's an incredible story.*
➤ **incredibly** ADVERB • *She's incredibly clever.*

incredulous ADJECTIVE
finding it difficult to believe something
➤ **incredulously** ADVERB • *'How much?' she asked incredulously.*

incubate VERB incubates, incubating, incubated
To incubate eggs is to hatch them by keeping them warm.

indeed ADVERB
used for emphasis • *The dog was very wet indeed.*

indefinite article NOUN indefinite articles
the word *a* or *an*

BUILD YOUR VOCABULARY
Look at **definite article**.

independent ADJECTIVE
❶ free from the control of another person or country ❷ not needing help from other people
➤ **independence** NOUN
➤ **independently** ADVERB • *The children work independently.*

WATCH OUT!
Remember that **independent** and **independence** end in **-ent** and **-ence**, like **confident** and **confidence**.

index NOUN indexes
a list of names or topics, usually in alphabetical order at the end of a book

index finger *NOUN* **index fingers**
the finger next to the thumb

> **BUILD** YOUR VOCABULARY
> A synonym is **forefinger**.

indicate *VERB* **indicates, indicating, indicated**
to point something out or show that it exists
➤ **indication** *NOUN* • *There was no indication that he was upset.*

indifferent *ADJECTIVE*
If you are indifferent, you do not care about something at all. • *He seemed indifferent to what was happening.*
➤ **indifference** *NOUN*

indigestion *NOUN*
pain caused by difficulty in digesting food

indignant *ADJECTIVE*
angry at something that seems unfair
'Stupid things!' Alice began in a loud, indignant voice.—ALICE'S ADVENTURES IN WONDERLAND, Lewis Carroll
➤ **indignantly** *ADVERB* ➤ **indignation** *NOUN*

indigo *NOUN*
a deep blue colour

indirect speech *NOUN*
someone's words reported by someone else, without inverted commas and with changed tenses, as in *He said that he would come* (reporting the words 'I will come')

> **BUILD** YOUR VOCABULARY
> Look at **direct speech** and **inverted commas**.

indistinct *ADJECTIVE*
not clear • *She saw an indistinct shape.*

individual *ADJECTIVE*
❶ of or for one person • *She was having individual music lessons.* ❷ single or separate • *With the microscope we can see individual cells.*
➤ **individually** *ADVERB*
individual *NOUN* **individuals**
one person • *Who is that individual?*

indoor *ADJECTIVE*
done or placed inside a building • *Basketball is a popular indoor sport.*

indoors *ADVERB*
inside a building • *Let's go indoors.*

induce *VERB* **induces, inducing, induced**
To induce someone to do something is to persuade them to do it.

indulge *VERB* **indulges, indulging, indulged**
To indulge someone is to let them have or do what they want.
➤ **To indulge in something** is to have or do something that you really like.

industrious *ADJECTIVE*
hard-working
➤ **industriously** *ADVERB*

industry *NOUN* **industries**
❶ Industry is producing goods to sell, especially in factories. ❷ all the people, factories and work involved in one type of industry • *the car industry*
➤ **industrial** *ADJECTIVE*

inevitable *ADJECTIVE*
If something is inevitable, it cannot be avoided.
➤ **inevitability** *NOUN* ➤ **inevitably** *ADVERB*

infamous *(say* in-fam-us*) ADJECTIVE*
well known for something bad

> **BUILD** YOUR VOCABULARY
> A synonym is **notorious**.

infant *NOUN* **infants**
a baby or very young child

> ✳ **WORD STORY**
> The word **infant** comes from a Latin word meaning 'unable to speak'.

infantry *NOUN*
soldiers trained to fight on foot

infect *VERB* **infects, infecting, infected**
to pass a disease on to someone

infection *NOUN* **infections**
a disease caused by germs

infectious *ADJECTIVE*
❶ an infectious disease can spread from one person to another ❷ If a feeling is infectious, it easily spreads to other people.

infer VERB infers, inferring, inferred
To infer something is to work it out from the details you have. • *I infer from the coats in the hall that we have visitors.*
➤ **inference** NOUN

⚠ WATCH OUT!
Do not confuse **infer** with **imply**, which means 'to suggest something without saying it'.

inferior ADJECTIVE
less good or important than something else
➤ **inferiority** NOUN

⚙ BUILD YOUR VOCABULARY
The opposite is **superior**.

infernal ADJECTIVE
like hell or to do with hell

inferno (say in-fer-no) NOUN infernos
a large fierce fire

infested ADJECTIVE
If a place is infested with unpleasant things, it is full of them.

infiltrate VERB infiltrates, infiltrating, infiltrated
to get into a place or an organisation without being noticed

infinite (say in-fin-it) ADJECTIVE
❶ with no end or limit • *A circle has an infinite number of sides.* ❷ extremely great • *She lifted the cup with infinite care.*
➤ **infinitely** ADVERB

infinitive (say in-fin-it-iv) NOUN infinitives
the basic form of a verb, often used after *to* or after a **modal verb** such as *can* or *will*. You can talk about possibility using 'might' followed by an **infinitive**, for example 'It might rain.'

⚙ BUILD YOUR VOCABULARY
Look at **modal verb**.

infinity (say in-fin-it-ee) NOUN
an infinite number or distance

inflame VERB inflames, inflaming, inflamed
If a part of the body is inflamed, it is red and sore.

inflammable ADJECTIVE
able to catch fire easily

⚠ WATCH OUT!
The words **flammable** and **inflammable** are synonyms, not opposites.

inflate VERB inflates, inflating, inflated
to fill something with air or gas so that it swells up
• *I inflated my bicycle tyres.*
➤ **inflatable** ADJECTIVE • *an inflatable bed*

⚙ BUILD YOUR VOCABULARY
The opposite is **deflate**.

inflict VERB inflicts, inflicting, inflicted
To inflict something on someone is to make them suffer it. • *He could inflict serious wounds with his sword.*

influence NOUN influences
the power to affect someone or something
influence VERB influences, influencing, influenced
To influence someone or something is to have an effect on what they are or do. • *The tides are influenced by the moon.*

influential ADJECTIVE
having a big influence; important

influenza (say in-flu-en-za) NOUN
the full name of the disease **flu**

inform VERB informs, informing, informed
to tell someone about something

a b c d e f g h i j k l m n o p q r s t u v w x y z

informal ADJECTIVE
❶ Informal events or clothes are casual and relaxed.
❷ Informal language is suitable for talking to friends, not for serious or official contexts. • *'Hi' is an informal way to start a letter.*
➤ **informally** ADVERB

BUILD YOUR VOCABULARY
An opposite is **formal**.

information NOUN
facts about something • *Where would you get information about bus services?*

information technology NOUN
technology for storing and communicating information, especially computers

BUILD YOUR VOCABULARY
The abbreviation for **information technology** is **IT**.

infuriate VERB infuriates, infuriating, infuriated
to make someone very angry

ingenious ADJECTIVE
very clever • *an ingenious idea*
➤ **ingeniously** ADVERB

ingot NOUN ingots
a lump of gold or silver in the form of a brick

ingredient (*say* in-**gree**-dee-ent) NOUN ingredients
one of the foods or substances in a recipe or mixture • *We have all the ingredients for pancakes.*

ingot

inhabit VERB inhabits, inhabiting, inhabited
To inhabit a place is to live in it.

inhabitant NOUN inhabitants
An inhabitant of a place is someone who lives there.

inhale VERB inhales, inhaling, inhaled
to breathe in

BUILD YOUR VOCABULARY
The opposite is **exhale**.

inhaler NOUN inhalers
a device that helps you breathe, especially if you have asthma

inherit VERB inherits, inheriting, inherited
❶ To inherit money or property is to receive it from someone when they die. ❷ To inherit qualities or characteristics is to get them from your parents or ancestors.
➤ **inheritance** NOUN

BUILD YOUR VOCABULARY
Look at **heir**.

inhospitable ADJECTIVE
unpleasant and difficult to live in • *an inhospitable climate*

inhuman ADJECTIVE
❶ cruel and without pity • *What they are doing is inhuman.* ❷ not human • *I heard an inhuman cry.*

initial NOUN initials
the first letter of a name • *It was signed with the initials 'E. B.'*
initial ADJECTIVE
first; happening at first • *She soon got over her initial shock.*
➤ **initially** ADVERB • *Initially I didn't understand.*

initiate (*say* in-**ish**-ee-ate) VERB initiates, initiating, initiated
❶ to start something • *This button initiates a video chat.* ❷ to let someone become a member of a group and know its secrets • *They had initiated her into the mysteries of the Society.*

initiative (*say* in-**ish**-a-tiv) NOUN
the ability to start things or to get them done on your own
➤ **To take the initiative** is to start something happening.

inject VERB injects, injecting, injected
to put a medicine or drug into someone's body using a hollow needle
➤ **injection** NOUN

injure VERB injures, injuring, injured
to harm or hurt someone

injury NOUN injuries
harm or damage done to someone

injustice NOUN injustices
unfair action or treatment

ink NOUN inks
a black or coloured liquid used for writing and
printing
➤ **inky** ADJECTIVE

inkling NOUN
a slight idea or suspicion • *I had no **inkling** of what
was happening.*

inland ADVERB
away from the coast

inlet NOUN inlets
a strip of water reaching into the land from a sea
or lake

inn NOUN inns
a hotel or pub, especially in the country

inner ADJECTIVE
inside; near the centre • *the **inner** surface of
the box*

BUILD YOUR VOCABULARY
The opposite is **outer**.

innings NOUN innings
the time when a cricket team or player is batting

innocent ADJECTIVE
❶ not guilty of doing something wrong • *He claims
he's **innocent**.* ❷ without much experience of the
world or the bad things in it • *an **innocent** child*
➤ **innocence** NOUN ➤ **innocently** ADVERB

innumerable ADJECTIVE
too many to be counted • *The sky was filled with
innumerable birds.*

input NOUN inputs
information or instructions put into a computer

inquire VERB inquires, inquiring, inquired
another spelling of **enquire**

inquiry NOUN inquiries
another spelling of **enquiry**

inquisitive ADJECTIVE
always trying to find out things

insane ADJECTIVE
mad • *Who came up with this **insane** plan?*

inscribe VERB inscribes, inscribing,
inscribed
to write or carve something on a surface

inscription NOUN inscriptions
words written or carved on a surface or written in
the front of a book

insect NOUN insects
a small animal, such as an ant, fly or beetle, with six
legs and no backbone

✳ WORD STORY
The word **insect** comes from a Latin word meaning
'cut up', because of its divided body.

⚙ BUILD YOUR VOCABULARY
The three parts of an insect's body are its **head**, its
thorax and its **abdomen**. Look at **invertebrate**.

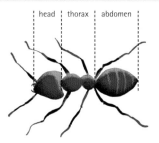

head ┆ thorax ┆ abdomen

insecure ADJECTIVE
❶ not safe or protected properly ❷ not feeling safe
or confident

insert VERB inserts, inserting, inserted
to put something into something else • ***Insert** the
card into the machine.*

inshore ADJECTIVE, ADVERB
at sea near the shore • *These fish are caught in
inshore waters.*

inside NOUN insides
❶ the inner side, surface or part • *There was ice on
the **inside** of the window.* ❷ Your insides are your
stomach or abdomen. • *My **insides** were churning
with fear.*
➤ **inside out** with the inside facing outwards
inside ADVERB, PREPOSITION
in or to the inside of something • *Come **inside**.*
• *What's **inside** the box?*

a
b
c
d
e
f
g
h
i
j
k
l
m
n
o
p
q
r
s
t
u
v
w
x
y
z

inside *ADJECTIVE*
on the inside of something • *Check the inside pocket.*

insight *NOUN* insights
an understanding or idea

insignificant *ADJECTIVE*
not important
➤ **insignificance** *NOUN*

insist *VERB* insists, insisting, insisted
to say or ask for something in a very firm and determined way • *I insist that you sit down.*

insistent *ADJECTIVE*
saying or asking for something in a very firm or determined way • *He was so insistent that in the end we agreed.*
➤ **insistence** *NOUN*

insolent *ADJECTIVE*
very rude and insulting
Malfoy gave Professor Lupin an insolent stare.—HARRY POTTER AND THE PRISONER OF AZKABAN, J. K. Rowling
➤ **insolence** *NOUN*

insoluble *ADJECTIVE*
❶ unable to dissolve • *Some chemicals are insoluble.* ❷ impossible to solve • *It is an insoluble problem.*

inspect *VERB* inspects, inspecting, inspected
to look carefully at someone or something in order to check them
➤ **inspection** *NOUN*

inspector *NOUN* inspectors
❶ someone with the official job of inspecting something • *a school inspector* ❷ a police officer above a sergeant in rank

inspiration *NOUN* inspirations
❶ new ideas and enthusiasm • *Her speech filled us with inspiration.* ❷ something that gives you a new creative idea • *What was your inspiration for this picture?*

inspire *VERB* inspires, inspiring, inspired
To inspire someone is to fill them with ideas or enthusiasm.

install *VERB* installs, installing, installed
to put something in place ready for use
• *They installed a new computer system.*

instalment *NOUN* instalments
one part of a story that is told in parts

⚠ **WATCH OUT!**
The word **instalment** only has one **l**.

instance *NOUN* instances
an example
➤ **for instance** for example

instant *ADJECTIVE*
happening immediately • *It was an instant success.*
instant *NOUN* instants
a moment • *It was over in an instant.*

instantly *ADVERB*
without any delay

instead *ADVERB*
in place of something else • *You can have rice instead of chips.*

instinct *NOUN* instincts
a natural tendency to do or feel something without being taught • *Spiders spin webs by instinct.*
➤ **instinctive** *ADJECTIVE*
➤ **instinctively** *ADVERB* • *He knew instinctively that something was wrong.*

institution *NOUN* institutions
a large organisation

instruct *VERB* instructs, instructing, instructed
❶ to tell someone what to do • *We were instructed to wait.* ❷ to teach someone a subject or skill
➤ **instructor** *NOUN* • *a swimming instructor*

instruction *NOUN* instructions
Instructions are orders or information about what to do. • *Follow the instructions carefully.*

instrument *NOUN* instruments
❶ a device for making music • *Do you play an instrument?* ❷ a tool • *measuring instruments*

insufficient *ADJECTIVE*
not enough

insulate VERB insulates, insulating, insulated
to cover something to stop heat, cold or electricity from passing in or out
➤ **insulation** NOUN

insulin NOUN
a chemical that controls how much sugar there is in your blood

insult (say in-sult) VERB insults, insulting, insulted
to speak or behave in a rude way that offends someone
insult (say in-sult) NOUN insults
a rude remark or action that offends someone

insurance NOUN
an arrangement in which you make regular payments in exchange for getting money if you suffer a loss or an injury

intact ADJECTIVE
complete and not damaged • *Despite the storm our tent was still intact.*

intellectual ADJECTIVE
❶ intelligent and enjoying thinking about ideas
❷ involving intelligence, thought and understanding

intelligence NOUN
❶ the ability to think and learn ❷ secret information, especially about an enemy's activities

intelligent ADJECTIVE
good at thinking and learning
➤ **intelligently** ADVERB

intend VERB intends, intending, intended
To intend to do something is to have it in mind as a plan. • *I never intended to upset you.*

intense ADJECTIVE
very strong or great • *The heat was intense.*
➤ **intensely** ADVERB ➤ **intensity** NOUN

intensify VERB intensifies, intensifying, intensified
If something intensifies or you intensify it, it becomes stronger. • *The wind intensified.*

intensive ADJECTIVE
using a lot of effort over a short time or area
• *The training is intensive.*
➤ **intensively** ADVERB

intent ADJECTIVE
very focused on doing something or determined to do it • *She was intent on solving the problem.*
➤ **intently** ADVERB • *He listened intently.*

intent NOUN intents
A person's intent is what they intend to do.

intention NOUN intentions
something that you plan or mean to happen

intentional ADJECTIVE
done on purpose; deliberate
➤ **intentionally** ADVERB • *He would never intentionally hurt anyone.*

interact VERB interacts, interacting, interacted
If people or things interact, they have an effect on one another. • *We watch how the characters interact.*
➤ **interaction** NOUN

interactive ADJECTIVE
allowing the user to change and control things by entering information • *an interactive whiteboard*

intercept VERB intercepts, intercepting, intercepted
to stop something or someone before they get to their destination • *The message was intercepted.*

interest VERB interests, interesting, interested
to make someone want to look at, listen to or take part in something • *Sport doesn't interest me at all.*

a b c d e f g h i j k l m n o p q r s t u v w x y z

interest NOUN interests
❶ the feeling of being interested • *He showed no interest in my story.* ❷ Your *interests* are things that you enjoy doing.

interfere VERB interferes, interfering, interfered
to get involved in something when it has nothing to do with you
➤ **interference** NOUN

interior NOUN interiors
the inside of something

interjection NOUN interjections
an exclamation, such as *ow!* or *oh dear!*

internal ADJECTIVE
happening or found inside something • *Vertebrates have internal skeletons.*
➤ **internally** ADVERB

international ADJECTIVE
involving more than one country • *an international football match*

Internet NOUN
The Internet is the computer network that allows people all over the world to share information and send messages.

interpret VERB interprets, interpreting, interpreted
❶ to explain what something means • *Can you interpret these symbols?* ❷ to translate what someone is saying into another language • *Her son interpreted for her.*
➤ **interpreter** NOUN

interrogate VERB interrogates, interrogating, interrogated
to question someone closely in order to get information
➤ **interrogation** NOUN ➤ **interrogator** NOUN

interrupt VERB interrupts, interrupting, interrupted
❶ To interrupt someone is to stop them talking.
❷ To interrupt something is to stop it continuing.
➤ **interruption** NOUN

⚠ **WATCH OUT!**
Interrupt has two rs.

interval NOUN intervals
a time between two events or between two parts of a play or concert

intervene VERB intervenes, intervening, intervened
to get involved in a situation, often in order to stop an argument or fight

interview VERB interviews, interviewing, interviewed
to ask someone questions to find out what they are like, what they can do, etc.
➤ **interviewer** NOUN

interview NOUN interviews
a meeting in which you ask someone questions

intestine NOUN (or **intestines**) PLURAL NOUN
the long folded tube inside your body that carries food from your stomach

intimate ADJECTIVE
❶ very friendly or close • *They were intimate friends.* ❷ private or personal • *He shared his intimate thoughts.*

intimidate VERB intimidates, intimidating, intimidated
to frighten a person into doing something
➤ **intimidation** NOUN

into PREPOSITION
in or inside • *He went into the kitchen.*

intolerable ADJECTIVE
unbearable • *His behaviour was intolerable.*

intransitive ADJECTIVE
An intransitive verb is used without an object, for example *wait* in *they waited.*

🔧 **BUILD YOUR VOCABULARY**
Look at **transitive**.

intrepid ADJECTIVE
brave or fearless

intricate ADJECTIVE
detailed and complicated
➤ **intricately** ADVERB

intrigue (say in-treeg) VERB intrigues, intriguing, intrigued
to interest someone very much and make them curious
➤ **intriguing** ADJECTIVE

introduce VERB introduces, introducing, introduced
❶ To introduce someone is to tell other people their name. ❷ To introduce something is to start it being used.

introduction NOUN introductions
❶ the act of introducing someone or something
❷ a section at the start of a book saying what it is about

intrude VERB intrudes, intruding, intruded
to come in or join in without being wanted
➤ **intrusion** NOUN • *Please forgive my intrusion.*

intruder NOUN intruders
someone who forces their way into a place where they are not supposed to be

intuition (say in-tew-**ish**-un) NOUN
the ability to know something by instinct rather than by thinking or reason

Inuit NOUN Inuit, Inuits
❶ a member of a group of people living in northern Canada and Greenland ❷ the language of Inuits

 WORD STORY
The words **igloo** and **kayak** come from Inuit.

invade VERB invades, invading, invaded
to attack and enter a country or place
➤ **invader** NOUN ➤ **invasion** NOUN

invalid (say in-val-id) NOUN invalids
someone who is ill for a long time and needs looking after

invalid (say in-**val**-id) ADJECTIVE
If a document is invalid, it cannot be accepted.

invaluable ADJECTIVE
very useful

invariably ADVERB
always

invent VERB invents, inventing, invented
❶ to be the first person to make or think of something new • *Who invented the telescope?*
❷ To invent a story or excuse is to make it up.
➤ **inventor** NOUN • *the inventor of the light bulb*

invention NOUN inventions
something that has been invented • *His latest invention was a kind of flying car.*

inventive ADJECTIVE
good at thinking of new ideas
➤ **inventiveness** NOUN

inverse NOUN
the opposite of something • *Multiplication is the inverse of division.*

invert VERB inverts, inverting, inverted
to turn something upside down • *He sat on an inverted bucket.*

invertebrate
(say in-**vert**-rat) NOUN
invertebrates
an animal without a backbone

snail

🔵 **BUILD YOUR VOCABULARY**
The opposite is **vertebrate**.

inverted commas NOUN
punctuation marks (" " or ' ') that you put around spoken words and quotations

invest VERB invests, investing, invested
to put money into something that you hope will make a profit • *He invested in his nephew's business.*
➤ **investment** NOUN

investigate VERB investigates, investigating, investigated
to find out as much as you can about something or someone • *Police are investigating the crime.*
➤ **investigation** NOUN ➤ **investigator** NOUN

invincible ADJECTIVE
impossible to defeat

invisible ADJECTIVE
impossible to see
➤ **invisibility** NOUN

invitation NOUN invitations
a message asking someone to do something, such as come to a party

invite VERB invites, inviting, invited
to ask someone to come to an event or to go somewhere with you

a b c d e f g h i j k l m n o p q r s t u v w x y z

inviting ADJECTIVE
attractive or tempting
The two little white beds on the remainder of the floor looked soft and inviting.—THE WIND IN THE WILLOWS, Kenneth Grahame

involuntary ADJECTIVE
not deliberate • *She gave an involuntary shudder.*

involve VERB involves, involving, involved
❶ To involve something is to need it or result in it. • *The job involved a lot of work.* ❷ To be involved in something is to take part in it. • *I was not involved in the argument.*
➤ **involvement** NOUN

inwardly ADVERB
in your mind • *He inwardly groaned.*

inwards (also **inward**) ADVERB
towards the inside • *The door opens inwards.*

irate (say eye-rayt) ADJECTIVE
very angry
➤ **irately** ADVERB

iridescent ADJECTIVE
shining with rainbow colours • *an iridescent beetle*

iris NOUN irises
❶ the coloured part of your eye

> ⚙ **BUILD** YOUR VOCABULARY
> Look at **pupil**.

iris

❷ a flower with long pointed leaves

iron NOUN irons
❶ a strong heavy metal

> ⚙ **BUILD** YOUR VOCABULARY
> Iron is an **element**.

❷ An iron is a device that you heat and press on clothes to make them smooth.

iron VERB irons, ironing, ironed
to smooth clothes with an iron

ironic (say eye-ron-ik) ADJECTIVE
funny because the opposite happens to what you might expect

irony (say eye-ron-ee) NOUN ironies
a funny quality or situation because something is the opposite of what you might expect • *'Boiled cabbage is my favourite!' he said with irony.*

irregular ADJECTIVE
❶ not even or symmetrical • *an irregular shape* ❷ happening at different or unexpected times • *Their mealtimes are irregular.* ❸ not usual; not following normal rules • *The word 'child' has an irregular plural, 'children'.*
➤ **irregularly** ADVERB

irrelevant ADJECTIVE
not related to what is being discussed • *I ignored his irrelevant comments.*
➤ **irrelevance** NOUN

> ⚙ **BUILD** YOUR VOCABULARY
> The opposite is **relevant**.

> ⚠ **WATCH OUT!**
> Irrelevant ends in -ant.

irresistible ADJECTIVE
too strong or tempting to resist

irresponsible ADJECTIVE
not sensible; not thinking enough about the results of your actions

irrigate VERB irrigates, irrigating, irrigated
To irrigate land is to supply it with water so that crops can grow.
➤ **irrigation** NOUN

irritable ADJECTIVE
bad-tempered; annoyed
➤ **irritability** NOUN ➤ **irritably** ADVERB

irritate VERB irritates, irritating, irritated
to annoy someone
➤ **irritated** ADJECTIVE ➤ **irritating** ADJECTIVE
➤ **irritation** NOUN

is VERB (present form of **be** used with 'he', 'she' and 'it')
• *Her name is Mia.*

Islam (say iz-lahm) NOUN
Islam is the religion of Muslims.
➤ **Islamic** ADJECTIVE

island *NOUN* islands
a piece of land surrounded by water

> **WATCH OUT!**
> Island has a silent **s**.

islander *NOUN* islanders
someone who lives on an island

isle *NOUN* isles
an island

> **WATCH OUT!**
> Do not confuse **isle** with **aisle** meaning 'passage', which sounds the same.

isolated *ADJECTIVE*
far from other places or people • *They lived on an isolated farm.*

isosceles triangle *(say* eye-**soss**-il-eez)*
NOUN isosceles triangles
a triangle with two sides the same length

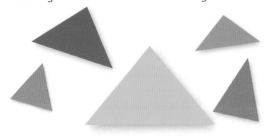

> **BUILD YOUR VOCABULARY**
> Look at **equilateral triangle** and **scalene triangle**.

ISP *NOUN*
a company that connects you to the Internet; short for *Internet service provider*

issue *VERB* issues, issuing, issued
❶ to give something or send it out • *He **issued** a challenge to his rival.* ❷ to come out of something • *Fire **issued** from the dragon's mouth.*

issue *NOUN* issues
a subject or problem • *We care about environmental issues.*

IT *(say* eye-**tea***) NOUN*
computers and work connected with them; short for *information technology*

it *PRONOUN*
❶ the thing being talked about • *I dropped **it** and **it** broke.* ❷ used for talking about the weather • *It is raining.*

> **BUILD YOUR VOCABULARY**
> It can be used as the **subject** or **object** of a verb.

italics *(say* it-**al**-ics*) NOUN*
letters printed with a slant, *like this*

> **BUILD YOUR VOCABULARY**
> Look at **bold**.

itch *VERB* itches, itching, itched
If part of your body itches, it tickles so that you want to scratch it.

itch NOUN itches
a tickling feeling that makes you want to scratch
➤ **itchy** ADJECTIVE

item NOUN items
one thing in a list or group

its DETERMINER
belonging to it • *The cat licked its paw.*

⚠ **WATCH OUT!**
Do not confuse **its** with **it's**, which means 'it is' or 'it has'.

it's
short for *it is* or (before a verb in the past tense) *it has.* • *It's (= it is) raining.* • *It's (= it has) been raining all day.*

⚠ **WATCH OUT!**
Do not confuse **it's** with **its**, which means 'belonging to it'.

itself PRONOUN
Used when the same thing or animal does something and is affected by it. • *The cat was cleaning itself.*
➤ **by itself** on its own; alone • *The house stands by itself in a wood.*

ivory NOUN
❶ the hard creamy-white substance that forms elephants' tusks
❷ a creamy-white colour

ivy NOUN
a climbing evergreen plant with shiny leaves

Jj

⚙ J is for **jump**. This word probably started to be used because it sounded like feet hitting the ground.

⚙ Do you know what you call a word that sounds like the thing it describes?

CLUE Look at letter **O** in this dictionary.

jab *VERB* jabs, jabbing, jabbed
to poke someone or something roughly • *Someone jabbed me in the back.*

jab *NOUN* jabs
❶ a sudden sharp poke or hit ❷ *(informal)* an injection

jabber *VERB* jabbers, jabbering, jabbered
to speak fast, in a way that is not clear

jackal *NOUN* jackals
a wild animal similar to a dog

jackdaw *NOUN* jackdaws
a bird like a small crow

jacket *NOUN* jackets
❶ a short coat ❷ a paper cover for a book

jade *NOUN*
a hard green stone which is carved to make ornaments

jagged *(say* jag-id*)* *ADJECTIVE*
A jagged rock or edge is uneven, with sharp points.

jaguar *NOUN* jaguars
a South American big cat, similar to a leopard

jail *NOUN* jails
a prison

jail *VERB* jails, jailing, jailed
To jail someone is to put them in prison.
➤ **jailer** *NOUN*

jam *NOUN* jams
❶ a sweet food made of fruit boiled with sugar until it is thick ❷ a lot of people or cars or other things crowded together so that it is difficult to move

jam *VERB* jams, jamming, jammed
❶ If something jams or you jam it, it becomes stuck. • *The door has jammed.* ❷ to force or push something hard somewhere • *She jammed her foot down on the brake.*

jangle *VERB* jangles, jangling, jangled
to make a harsh ringing sound

jar *NOUN* jars
a glass container for food

jar *VERB* jars, jarring, jarred
to jolt something painfully • *Every time I hop, it jars my knee.*

jaunty *ADJECTIVE* jauntier, jauntiest
lively and cheerful

javelin *NOUN* javelins
a light spear thrown in an athletics contest

jaw *NOUN* jaws
❶ Your jaws are the bones that hold your teeth.
❷ the mouth and teeth of a person or animal
• *The crocodile had a big fish in its jaws.*

jay *NOUN* jays
a noisy brightly coloured bird

jazz *NOUN*
a kind of music with a strong rhythm

a
b
c
d
e
f
g
h
i
j
k
l
m
n
o
p
q
r
s
t
u
v
w
x
y
z

jealous (*say* jel-us) ADJECTIVE
unhappy because you want what someone else has or want to be like them
➤ **jealously** ADVERB ➤ **jealousy** NOUN

jeans NOUN
casual trousers made of denim

✴ WORD STORY
The word **jeans** comes from the Italian city *Genoa*, where heavy cotton cloth used to be made.

Jeep NOUN Jeeps (*trademark*)
a small strong car that can be driven over rough ground

✴ WORD STORY
The name **Jeep** comes from the initals *GP*, standing for *general purpose*.

jeer VERB jeers, jeering, jeered
to laugh rudely at someone and insult them

jelly NOUN jellies
a soft wobbly sweet food with a fruit flavour

jellyfish NOUN jellyfish
a sea animal with a clear soft body and tentacles that can sting

jerk VERB jerks, jerking, jerked
❶ to pull something suddenly or make a sudden sharp movement with it • *She **jerked** her hand away.*
❷ to make a sudden sharp movement • *The car **jerked** forward.*

jerk NOUN jerks
a sudden sharp movement
➤ **jerky** ADJECTIVE • *The robot moved with short jerky steps.*

jersey NOUN jerseys
a jumper

jester NOUN jesters
in medieval times, a professional entertainer at a royal court

jet NOUN jets
❶ a stream of liquid, gas or flame forced out of a narrow opening ❷ a fast aircraft

jetty NOUN jetties
a small platform for boats to stop or be tied up

Jew NOUN Jews
someone who follows the religion of **Judaism** or who is descended from the ancient Hebrews
➤ **Jewish** ADJECTIVE

jewel NOUN jewels
a precious stone
➤ **jewelled** ADJECTIVE • *a **jewelled** box*

jeweller NOUN jewellers
someone who sells or makes jewellery

jewellery NOUN
jewels or ornaments that people wear, such as rings or necklaces

jib NOUN jibs
a triangular sail of a ship

jiffy NOUN (*informal*)
a moment • *I'll be back in a **jiffy**.*

jig NOUN jigs
a lively jumping dance

jigsaw puzzle (*also* **jigsaw**) NOUN jigsaw puzzles, jigsaws
a puzzle made of differently shaped pieces that you fit together to make a picture

jingle VERB jingles, jingling, jingled
to make a tinkling or clinking sound
jingle NOUN jingles
❶ a tinkling or clinking sound ❷ a short tune or song used in an advertisement

job *NOUN* jobs
❶ work that someone does to earn money • *She has a babysitting job.* ❷ a task that needs to be done • *Mum gave me some jobs to do.*

jog *VERB* jogs, jogging, jogged
❶ to run slowly ❷ to knock or push something so that it moves slightly • *I accidentally jogged his elbow.*

join *VERB* joins, joining, joined
❶ If two things join or you join them, they combine or are connected or fastened together. • *Join the two ends of the rope.* • *This is where the road joins the motorway.* ❷ To join a club or group is to become a member of it.
➤ **To join in** is to take part in something.
join *NOUN* joins
a place where things join

joint *NOUN* joints
❶ the place where two bones fit together • *your elbow joint* ❷ a large piece of meat
joint *ADJECTIVE*
shared or done by two or more people or groups • *The project was a joint effort.*

joke *NOUN* jokes
something that you say or do to make people laugh
joke *VERB* jokes, joking, joked
to say funny things or to talk in a way that is not serious
➤ **joker** *NOUN*

jolly *ADJECTIVE* jollier, jolliest
happy and cheerful

Jolly Roger *NOUN*
a pirate's flag with a white skull and crossbones on a black background

jolt *VERB* jolts, jolting, jolted
❶ to make a sudden sharp movement • *The bus jolted to a halt.* ❷ to make someone or something move suddenly and sharply • *A crash jolted me awake.*
jolt *NOUN* jolts
❶ a sudden sharp movement • *The plane landed with a jolt.* ❷ a surprise or shock

jostle *VERB* jostles, jostling, jostled
to push someone roughly or from many sides

journal *NOUN* journals
❶ a newspaper or magazine ❷ a diary

journalist *NOUN* journalists
someone whose job is to write news stories for a newspaper or for a news programme or website
➤ **journalism** *NOUN*

journey *NOUN* journeys
If you go on a journey, you travel from one place to another.

joust *VERB* jousts, jousting, jousted
to fight on horseback with lances, as knights did in medieval times

jovial *ADJECTIVE*
cheerful and jolly

a
b
c
d
e
f
g
h
i
j
k
l
m
n
o
p
q
r
s
t
u
v
w
x
y
z

joy NOUN joys
❶ great happiness ❷ A joy is something that gives happiness.

joyful ADJECTIVE
very happy
➤ **joyfully** ADVERB

joyous ADJECTIVE
full of joy or making you feel joy
The following days were some of the most joyous that Clara had spent on the mountain.
—HEIDI, Johanna Spyri
➤ **joyously** ADVERB

joystick NOUN joysticks
❶ a lever that controls the movement of an aircraft ❷ a lever for controlling a computer cursor or game

jubilant (*say* ju-bil-ant) ADJECTIVE
very happy because you have won or succeeded

jubilee NOUN jubilees
a special anniversary of an important event

Judaism (*say* ju-day-izm) NOUN
the religion that Jewish people follow

judge NOUN judges
❶ someone who hears cases in a law court and decides what should be done ❷ someone who decides who has won a competition
judge VERB judges, judging, judged
❶ to form an opinion about something • *Judging by the dust, no one had opened the book in years.* ❷ to act as a judge in a law case or competition

judgement (*also* **judgment**) NOUN
judgements, judgments
❶ an opinion of something • *I haven't had time to form a judgement yet.* ❷ the ability to make decisions wisely

judo NOUN
a sport that is a Japanese form of unarmed combat

✳ **WORD STORY**
The word **judo** comes from Japanese words meaning 'gentle way'.

jug NOUN jugs
a container for pouring liquids, with a handle and lip

juggle VERB juggles, juggling, juggled
to throw and catch several objects, keeping one or more always in the air
➤ **juggler** NOUN

juice NOUN juices
the liquid from fruit, vegetables or other food
➤ **juicy** ADJECTIVE • *a juicy orange*

jumble NOUN
a confused or untidy mixture • *There was a jumble of clothes on the floor.*
jumble VERB jumbles, jumbling, jumbled
to mix things up in a confused way • *The days were jumbled in my memory.*

jump VERB jumps, jumping, jumped
❶ to push yourself up from the ground into the air • *Can you jump across the stream?* ❷ to make a quick sudden movement • *He jumped out of his seat.*
jump NOUN jumps
a sudden movement into the air

🔘 **BUILD YOUR VOCABULARY**
A synonym is **leap**.

jumper NOUN jumpers
a warm top with sleeves

jumpy ADJECTIVE jumpier, jumpiest
nervous and anxious

junction NOUN junctions
a place where roads or railway lines join

jungle NOUN jungles
a thick tropical forest

junior ADJECTIVE
❶ for younger children • *She plays for the junior team.* ❷ less important or experienced • *He was a junior employee.*

🔘 **BUILD YOUR VOCABULARY**
Look at **senior**.

junk NOUN junks
❶ worthless or unwanted things • *The garage is full of old junk*. ❷ A junk is a Chinese sailing boat.

jury NOUN juries
a group of people chosen to make a decision in a law court about whether someone is guilty

just ADVERB
❶ exactly • *It's just what I wanted*. ❷ only; simply • *I was just trying to help*. ❸ barely; by a small amount • *We just made it in time*. ❹ a short time ago • *He has just left*.
just ADJECTIVE
fair and right

justice NOUN justices
❶ Fair treatment; what is fair and right. • *We want justice*. ❷ the system of laws and activities to do with the law

justify VERB justifies, justifying, justified
to show that something is reasonable or necessary • *Their fears were justified*.

jut VERB juts, jutting, jutted
to stick out • *A rock jutted out over the river*.

juvenile *(say* ju-ven-ile*)* ADJECTIVE
❶ relating to or done by young people
❷ childish and silly
juvenile NOUN juveniles
a young person who is not yet an adult

a
b
c
d
e
f
g
h
i
j
k
l
m
n
o
p
q
r
s
t
u
v
w
x
y
z

⚙ K is for **kilogram** (1000 grams) and **kilometre** (1000 metres). These come from the Greek word meaning 'thousand'.

⚙ Do you know which letter was the Roman numeral for 1000?

CLUE The word meaning '1000 years' and the word for 1000th of a metre begin with this letter.

kaleidoscope *(say* kal-**eye**-dos-kohp*) NOUN* **kaleidoscopes**
a tube you look through to see coloured patterns which change as you turn the end of the tube

kangaroo *NOUN* **kangaroos**
an Australian animal that moves by jumping on its strong back legs and carries its babies in a pouch

⚙ **BUILD YOUR VOCABULARY**
A **kangaroo** is a **marsupial**.

karate *(say* ka-**rah**-tee*) NOUN*
a sport that is a Japanese method of self-defence using the hands, arms and feet

✴ **WORD STORY**
The word **karate** comes from Japanese words meaning 'empty hand'.

kayak *(say* **ky**-ak*) NOUN* **kayaks**
a small covered canoe

keel *NOUN* **keels**
the long piece of wood or metal along the bottom of a boat
keel *VERB* **keels, keeling, keeled**
➤ **To keel over** is to fall sideways or overturn.

keen *ADJECTIVE* **keener, keenest**
❶ enthusiastic or eager • *We are **keen** to go.* • *I'm not **keen** on swimming.* ❷ strong or sharp • *Dogs have a **keen** sense of smell.*
➤ **keenly** *ADVERB* • *He watched them **keenly**.*

keep *VERB* **keeps, keeping, kept**
❶ To keep something is to have it and not get rid of it. • *We **kept** a few toys and gave the rest away.*
❷ to store something somewhere • *Where do you **keep** the key?* ❸ to make something or yourself stay a certain way • *He **kept** his room tidy.* • *Try to **keep** warm.* ❹ To keep animals is to have them and look after them. ❺ To keep doing something is to do it repeatedly or continue doing it. • *She **keeps** staring at me.* • *I just **kept** walking.* ❻ To keep a promise is to do what you have said you will do.

keep *NOUN* **keeps**
a strong tower in a castle

keeper *NOUN* **keepers**
❶ someone who looks after animals in a zoo
❷ a goalkeeper

kelp *NOUN*
a large brown type of seaweed

kennel *NOUN* **kennels**
a shelter for a dog

kept *VERB (past tense and past participle of* **keep***)*
• *He **kept** asking questions.* • *I have **kept** some sweets for myself.*

kerb *NOUN* **kerbs**
the edge of a pavement

kernel *NOUN* **kernels**
the part inside the shell of a nut

kestrel *NOUN* **kestrels**
a bird of prey that is a kind of small falcon

ketchup *NOUN*
a thick spicy sauce made from tomatoes and vinegar

kettle *NOUN* **kettles**
a container with a spout and handle, used for boiling water in

key *NOUN* **keys**
❶ a piece of metal shaped so that it opens a lock
❷ The keys on a piano or computer are the parts that

you press when you use it. ❸ a table of information showing what things mean • *The key shows what the symbols on the map represent.*

keyboard NOUN keyboards
a set of keys that you press to work a computer or play a piano

keyhole NOUN keyholes
the hole through which you put a key into a lock

key word or **key phrase** NOUN key words, key phrases
an important word or phrase in a text

kg ABBREVIATION
the abbreviation for **kilogram**

khaki *(say kah-kee)* NOUN
a dull yellow-brown colour, often used for army uniforms

 WORD STORY

The word **khaki** comes from a Persian or Urdu word meaning 'dust'.

kick VERB kicks, kicking, kicked
❶ to hit something or someone with your foot
❷ to move your legs and feet energetically
kick NOUN kicks
a kicking movement

kick-off NOUN kick-offs
the start of a football match

kid NOUN kids
❶ a young goat ❷ *(informal)* a child
kid VERB kids, kidding, kidded *(informal)*
to say something that is not true, as a joke or trick

kidnap VERB kidnaps, kidnapping, kidnapped
to capture someone by force, usually to get a ransom
➤ **kidnapper** NOUN

kidney NOUN kidneys
Your kidneys are the two organs in your body that remove waste products from your blood and make urine.

kill VERB kills, killing, killed
To kill a person or animal is to cause them to die.
➤ **killer** NOUN

killer whale NOUN killer whales
a whale with black and white markings

kiln NOUN kilns
an oven for baking pottery or bricks

kilo NOUN kilos
a **kilogram**

WORD STORY

Words beginning **kilo–** are based on the Greek word *chilioi* meaning 'thousand'.

kilobyte NOUN kilobytes
a unit that measures computer data or memory, equal to 1024 bytes

kilogram NOUN kilograms
a measurement of weight. There are 1000 grams in 1 kilogram, which is about 2.2 pounds.

BUILD YOUR VOCABULARY

The abbreviation is **kg**.

kilometre *(say kil-om-it-er or kil-o-mee-ter)* NOUN kilometres
a measurement of length. There are 1000 metres in 1 kilometre, which is about $\frac{5}{8}$ of a mile.

BUILD YOUR VOCABULARY

The abbreviation is **km**.

kilowatt NOUN kilowatts
a measurement of electrical power. There are 1000 watts in 1 kilowatt.

BUILD YOUR VOCABULARY

The abbreviation is **kW**.

kilt NOUN kilts
a pleated tartan skirt, sometimes worn by men as part of traditional Scottish dress

kimono NOUN kimonos
a traditional Japanese robe, worn by both men and women

kin NOUN
Your kin are your relatives.

kind NOUN kinds
a type or sort of something • *What kind of music do you like?*
kind ADJECTIVE kinder, kindest
helpful and friendly • *It was kind of you to call.*
➤ **kindness** NOUN

a
b
c
d
e
f
g
h
i
j
k
l
m
n
o
p
q
r
s
t
u
v
w
x
y
z

kindergarten *NOUN* **kindergartens**
a school or class for very young children

kindle *VERB* **kindles, kindling, kindled**
If you kindle something or it kindles, it starts burning.

kindling *NOUN*
small pieces of wood for lighting fires

kindly *ADVERB*
❶ in a kind way • *She smiled kindly.* ❷ please • *Kindly close the door.*
kindly *ADJECTIVE* **kindlier, kindliest**
kind • *He was a kindly old man.*
➤ **kindliness** *NOUN*

kinetic energy *(say kin-et-ic) ADJECTIVE*
the kind of energy that something has when it moves

king *NOUN* **kings**
a man who has been crowned as the ruler of a country

kingdom *NOUN* **kingdoms**
a country that is ruled by a king or queen

kingfisher *NOUN* **kingfishers**
a brightly coloured bird that lives near water and eats fish

kiosk *(say kee-osk) NOUN* **kiosks**
a small hut or stall where you can buy newspapers, sweets and drinks

kipper *NOUN* **kippers**
a smoked herring

kiss *NOUN* **kisses**
the act of touching someone with your lips to show affection
kiss *VERB* **kisses, kissing, kissed**
To kiss someone is to give them a kiss.

kit *NOUN* **kits**
❶ equipment or clothes that you need to do a sport or activity • *I forgot my gym kit.* ❷ a set of parts that you fit together to make something • *a model aircraft kit*

kitchen *NOUN* **kitchens**
a room where food is prepared and cooked

kite *NOUN* **kites**
a light frame covered with cloth or paper that you fly in the wind at the end of a long string

kitten *NOUN* **kittens**
a very young cat

kiwi *(say kee-wee) NOUN* **kiwis**
❶ a fruit with thin hairy skin, soft green flesh and black seeds ❷ a New Zealand bird that cannot fly

kiwi fruit *NOUN* **kiwi fruits**
a fruit with thin hairy skin, soft green flesh and black seeds

km *ABBREVIATION*
the abbreviation for **kilometre**

knack *NOUN*
a special skill or ability • *There's a knack to opening this lock.*

⚠ **WATCH OUT!**
The **k** is silent in words that start with kn-, like **knack**, **know** and **knock**.

knave *NOUN* **knaves** *(old use)*
a dishonest man; a rascal

knead *VERB* **kneads, kneading, kneaded**
To knead dough is to press and stretch it with your hands.

⚠ **WATCH OUT!**
Do not confuse 'to **knead** the dough' with 'to **need** something' meaning that it is necessary.

knee *NOUN* **knees**
the joint in the middle of your leg

kneel *VERB* **kneels, kneeling, knelt**
to bend your legs so you are resting on your knees

knew *VERB (past tense of **know**)*
• *Nobody knew the answer.*

knickers *NOUN*
underpants worn by women or girls

knife *NOUN* **knives**
a tool for cutting, with a short blade and a handle

knight NOUN **knights**
a nobleman, especially one in medieval times who fought for his king or lord

knight VERB **knights, knighting, knighted**
To knight someone is to make them a knight.

knit VERB **knits, knitting, knitted**
to make something by looping together threads of wool, using long needles or a machine

knitting NOUN
❶ Knitting is the activity of making things by knitting. ❷ Someone's knitting is something that they are making by knitting.

knives NOUN (plural of **knife**)

knob NOUN **knobs**
❶ the round handle of a door or drawer ❷ a round switch for controlling something

knobbly ADJECTIVE **knobblier, knobbliest**
with many lumps and bumps
His head was made of a great knobbly turnip, with a broad crack for a mouth and a long thin sprout for a nose.—THE SCARECROW AND HIS SERVANT, Philip Pullman

knock VERB **knocks, knocking, knocked**
❶ To knock is to tap something to make a noise. • *Knock before you come in.* ❷ to hit someone or something hard or bump into them • *The wind knocked the bins over.*
➤ **To knock someone out** is to hit them so that they become unconscious.

knock NOUN **knocks**
the act or sound of hitting something • *I heard a knock on the wall.*

knocker NOUN **knockers**
an object for knocking on a door

knot NOUN **knots**
❶ a fastening made by tying or twisting ends of string or cloth together ❷ a round spot on a piece of wood where a branch joined it ❸ a unit for measuring the speed of ships and aircraft

figure-eight knot

knot VERB **knots, knotting, knotted**
to tie or fasten something with a knot

know VERB **knows, knowing, knew, known**
❶ To have learnt something or have some information. • *Do you know any Spanish?* • *Nobody knew where he was.* ❷ to recognise or be familiar with a person or place • *I've known him for years.*

knowingly ADVERB
❶ in a way that suggests you know something • *He winked at me knowingly.* ❷ deliberately • *She would never knowingly hurt anyone.*

knowledge (say nol-ij) NOUN
information or facts that someone knows • *She has a good knowledge of history.*

knuckle NOUN **knuckles**
a joint in your finger

koala (say koh-ah-la) NOUN **koalas**
a furry Australian animal that looks like a small bear

🔹 **BUILD YOUR VOCABULARY**
A **koala** is a **marsupial**.

kookaburra NOUN **kookaburras**
a large Australian kingfisher that makes a sound like a loud laugh

Koran (say kor-ahn) NOUN
the holy book of Islam

kosher (say koh-sher) ADJECTIVE
Kosher food is prepared according to Jewish religious law.

kraken NOUN **krakens**
a sea monster in Norse myth

a b c d e f g h i j k l m n o p q r s t u v w x y z

⚙ **L** is for **long**. The longest words in English that have only one syllable (one single beat) are nine letters long. One example is screeched. There are a few more—can you find any?

CLUE Look at words starting **scr-** and **str-**.

L ABBREVIATION
50 in Roman numerals

l ABBREVIATION
the abbreviation for **litre**

label NOUN **labels**
❶ a piece of paper, cloth or plastic put on something to give information about it • *Read the ingredients on the label.* ❷ words written next to part of a diagram saying what it is
label VERB **labels, labelling, labelled**
to put a label on something • *Remember to label the axes of your graph.*

laboratory NOUN **laboratories**
a room or building with equipment for scientific experiments

labour NOUN
hard or physical work
➤ **labourer** NOUN

Labrador NOUN **Labradors**
a large black, golden or dark brown dog

laburnum NOUN **laburnums**
a tree with hanging yellow flowers

labyrinth NOUN **labyrinths**
a complicated set of passages or paths; a maze

✳ **WORD STORY**
The **Labyrinth** was the name of the maze in Greek mythology where the Minotaur lived.

lace NOUN **laces**
❶ thin material with decorative patterns of holes
❷ A lace is a piece of thin cord used to tie a shoe.
➤ **lacy** ADJECTIVE
lace VERB **laces, lacing, laced**
To lace up a shoe or boot is to fasten it with a lace.

lack NOUN
If there is a lack of something, there is not enough of it or there is none. • *I was frustrated by my lack of success.*
lack VERB **lacks, lacking, lacked**
To lack something is to be without it. • *He lacks courage.*

lacquer NOUN
a thin clear hard varnish for wood
➤ **lacquered** ADJECTIVE • *a lacquered box*

lad NOUN **lads** *(informal)*
a boy or young man

ladder NOUN **ladders**
a tall frame for climbing up made of wood, metal or rope, with bars across it

⬤ **BUILD YOUR VOCABULARY**
Look at **rung**.

laden ADJECTIVE
carrying or weighed down by a heavy load

ladle NOUN **ladles**
a large deep spoon with a long handle, for serving soup

lady NOUN **ladies**
❶ a polite name for a woman ❷ a woman of high social status, especially one who is allowed to use the title 'Lady'

ladybird NOUN **ladybirds**
a small flying beetle, usually red with black spots

lag VERB **lags, lagging, lagged**
to go too slowly and not keep up with others • *My little brother was lagging behind.*

lagoon NOUN **lagoons**
a lake separated from the sea by banks of sand or reefs

laid *VERB (past tense and past participle of* **lay***)*
• *She* **laid** *the map on the ground.* • *I have* **laid** *the table.*

lain *VERB (past participle of* **lie***)*
• *The treasure had* **lain** *there for centuries.*

lair *NOUN* lairs
the place where a wild animal lives

lake *NOUN* lakes
a large area of water completely surrounded by land

lamb *NOUN* lambs
❶ a young sheep ❷ Lamb is the meat from young sheep.

lame *ADJECTIVE* lamer, lamest
❶ unable to walk well because of an injured leg
❷ weak; not very convincing or good • *What a* **lame** *excuse.*
➤ **lamely** *ADVERB* • *'Sorry,' I said* **lamely***.*

lament *VERB* laments, lamenting, lamented
to express grief or disappointment about something
➤ **lamentation** *NOUN*

lamp *NOUN* lamps
a device for producing light from electricity, gas or oil

lamp-post *NOUN* lamp-posts
a tall post with a lamp at the top in a street or public place

lance *NOUN* lances
a long spear with a wooden shaft, used by medieval knights

land *NOUN* lands
❶ Land is an area of ground. • *This* **land** *is good for growing crops.* ❷ Land is all the dry parts of the world's surface. • *Does it live on* **land** *or in the water?* ❸ A land is a country.

land *VERB* lands, landing, landed
to come down to the ground from the air • *The bird* **landed** *on a branch.* • *What time does their plane* **land***?*

landing *NOUN* landings
the floor at the top of a flight of stairs

landlady *NOUN* landladies
❶ a woman who owns a room or house that she rents to someone ❷ a woman who runs a pub

landlord *NOUN* landlords
❶ a person who owns a room, a house or some land that is rented to someone ❷ a person who runs a pub

landmark *NOUN* landmarks
a natural feature or structure that is easy to see and that you can use to work out where you are • *Mist covered everything, so there were no* **landmarks***.*

landowner *NOUN* landowners
a person who owns a large amount of land

landscape *NOUN* landscapes
a view of a particular area of land

landslide *NOUN* landslides
a fall of earth or rocks down the side of a hill

lane *NOUN* lanes
❶ a narrow road, especially in the country ❷ one of the single strips that a road, race track or swimming pool is divided into

language *NOUN* languages
❶ the use of words in speech and writing
❷ A language is the words used in a particular country or by a particular group. • *She speaks three* **languages***.*

lantern *NOUN* lanterns
a transparent case for holding a light and shielding it from the wind

a
b
c
d
e
f
g
h
i
j
k
l
m
n
o
p
q
r
s
t
u
v
w
x
y
z

lap NOUN laps
❶ Your lap is the flat area above your knees formed when you are sitting down. ❷ A lap is one time around a race track.

lap VERB laps, lapping, lapped
❶ If water laps somewhere, it splashes gently against it. • *Waves lapped the side of the boat.* ❷ If an animal laps a liquid, it drinks it with its tongue.

lapel (*say* lap-**el**) NOUN lapels
the part of a coat or jacket that is folded back at the front

lapse VERB lapses, lapsing, lapsed
To lapse into a state is to pass gradually into it.
• *They lapsed into silence.*

lapse NOUN lapses
an amount of time that passes • *After a lapse of five years he saw her again.*

laptop NOUN laptops
a computer small enough to be carried and used on your lap

lapwing NOUN lapwings
a black and white bird with a loud cry

larch NOUN larches
a tall deciduous tree that produces small cones

lard NOUN
solid white fat from pigs, used in cooking

larder NOUN larders
a cupboard or small room for storing food
In Aunt Gwen's larder there were two cold pork chops, half a trifle, some bananas and some buns and cakes.
—TOM'S MIDNIGHT GARDEN, Philippa Pearce

large ADJECTIVE larger, largest
big; bigger than usual
➤ **at large** ❶ free and dangerous • *A tiger was at large.* ❷ in general • *'Go away!' she shouted to the room at large.*
➤ **largeness** NOUN

largely ADVERB
mainly; mostly • *They succeeded, largely thanks to her.*

lark NOUN larks
a small brown bird with a beautiful song

larva NOUN larvae
an insect in the first stage of its life, after it comes out of the egg. A caterpillar is the larva of a butterfly or moth and a maggot is the larva of a fly.

🞉 **BUILD** YOUR VOCABULARY
Look at **chrysalis**, **cocoon** and **pupa**.

lasagne (*say* laz-**an**-ya) NOUN
sheets of pasta cooked in layers with meat or vegetables and sauce

laser (*say* **lay**-zer) NOUN lasers
a device that makes a very strong narrow beam of light

lash NOUN lashes
an eyelash

lash VERB lashes, lashing, lashed
❶ to hit something or someone with a whip or like a whip • *Rain lashed the window.* ❷ to tie something tightly • *They lashed the sail to the mast.*
➤ **To lash out** is to speak or hit out angrily.

lass NOUN lasses (*informal*)
a girl or young woman

lasso (*say* lass-**oo**) NOUN lassos
a rope with a loop at the end, used for catching cattle or horses

last ADJECTIVE
❶ coming after all the others; final • *The last bus goes at midnight.* ❷ most recent or latest • *I saw her last week.*

last NOUN
a person or thing that is last • *She was the last to arrive.*
➤ **at last** finally; after a long time

last *VERB* lasts, lasting, lasted
❶ to continue for an amount of time • *The show lasts for two hours.* ❷ to go on without being used up • *How long will our food last?*

lastly *ADVERB*
finally

latch *NOUN* latches
a small bar fastening a gate or door

late *ADJECTIVE, ADVERB*
❶ after the proper or expected time • *The bus was ten minutes late.* • *We had a late breakfast.* ❷ near the end of a period of time • *It was late in the afternoon.*
➤ **lateness** *NOUN*

lately *ADVERB*
recently • *I've been reading a lot lately.*

later *ADVERB*
at a time in the future; afterwards • *I'll see you later.* • *Ten minutes later, he left.*

latest *ADJECTIVE*
most recent or up to date • *Check our website for the latest news.*

lather *NOUN* lathers
the thick foam you get when you mix soap with water

Latin *NOUN*
the language of the ancient Romans

latitude *NOUN* latitudes
the distance of a place north or south of the equator, measured in degrees

BUILD YOUR VOCABULARY
Look at **longitude**.

latter *ADJECTIVE*
The latter part of something is the last or latest part.
• *He lived here in the latter years of his life.*
➤ **the latter** the second of two people or things just mentioned • *If it's a choice between a picnic or a swim I prefer the latter.*

BUILD YOUR VOCABULARY
Look at **former**.

laugh *VERB* laughs, laughing, laughed
to make sounds that show you are happy or that you think something is funny

laugh *NOUN* laughs
the sound you make when you laugh

laughter *NOUN*
laughing or the sound of laughing

launch *VERB* launches, launching, launched
❶ To launch a ship is to put it into the water.
❷ To launch a rocket is to send it into space.

laundry *NOUN* laundries
❶ Laundry is clothes to be washed. ❷ A laundry is a place where clothes are washed.

laurel *NOUN* laurels
an evergreen bush with smooth shiny leaves

lava *NOUN*
the molten rock that flows from a volcano

⚠ WATCH OUT!
Don't confuse **lava** meaning 'molten rock', which has no **r** in it, with a **larva** meaning 'a young insect'.

lavatory *NOUN* lavatories
a toilet

lavender *NOUN*
❶ a shrub with pale purple flowers that smell sweet
❷ a pale purple colour

lavish *ADJECTIVE*
plentiful; generous • *The table was spread with a lavish banquet.*

law *NOUN* laws
a rule or the system of rules that everyone in a country must obey

lawful *ADJECTIVE*
allowed or accepted by the law
➤ **lawfully** *ADVERB*

lawn *NOUN* lawns
an area of grass in a garden

lawyer *NOUN* lawyers
a person whose job is to help people with the law

lay *VERB (past tense of lie)*
• *I lay down and went to sleep.*

a b c d e f g h i j k l m n o p q r s t u v w x y z

lay *VERB* lays, laying, laid
❶ To lay something somewhere is to put it down there. • *Lay the map out on the table.* • *She laid her hand on my arm.* ❷ To lay a table is to put things such as knives and forks on it for a meal. ❸ To lay an egg is to produce it.

> ⚠ **WATCH OUT!**
> Don't confuse **lay** and **lie**. **Lay** is either a past tense or means 'to put something down'. In the sentence *I need to lay down*—this should be **lie**.

layer *NOUN* layers
a flat part on top of, below or between other flat parts • *The cake had a layer of jam inside.*

layout *NOUN* layouts
the arrangement or design of something

lazy *ADJECTIVE* lazier, laziest
not wanting to work or to make any effort
➤ **lazily** *ADVERB* ➤ **laziness** *NOUN*

lb *ABBREVIATION*
short for **pound** *(in weight)*

lead *VERB (rhymes with* seed*)* leads, leading, led
❶ to take a person or animal somewhere by going in front • *He led us to the gate.* ❷ If a road or path leads somewhere, it goes there. • *This road leads to town.* ❸ to be in charge of something or someone • *The captain leads the team.* ❹ To lead in a race or contest is to be winning it.
➤ **To lead to something** is to cause it. • *What has led to this situation?*

lead *NOUN (rhymes with* seed*)* leads
❶ the first or winning place • *Who's in the lead now?* ❷ a strap or cord for leading a dog ❸ an electric wire

lead *NOUN (rhymes with* bed*)*
a soft heavy grey metal

> ⚙ **BUILD YOUR VOCABULARY**
> Lead is an **element**.

leader *NOUN* leaders
someone who leads or is in charge
➤ **leadership** *NOUN*

leaf *NOUN* leaves
❶ a flat, usually green part that grows on a tree or plant ❷ a page of a book
➤ **leafy** *ADJECTIVE*

leaflet *NOUN* leaflets
a piece of paper printed with information

league *(say* leeg*) NOUN* leagues
a group of teams that play matches against each other

> ⚠ **WATCH OUT!**
> The 'g' sound is spelt **-gue** in **league** and **tongue**. Both these words come from French.

leak *NOUN* leaks
a hole or crack through which liquid or gas escapes
➤ **leaky** *ADJECTIVE*

leak *VERB* leaks, leaking, leaked
❶ If something leaks, it lets liquid or gas out through a hole or crack. • *The bottle was leaking.* ❷ If liquid or gas leaks out, it escapes.

lean *VERB* leans, leaning, leaned, leant
❶ to bend your body towards something or over it • *She leaned over to look at my book.* ❷ to rest yourself or rest something against something • *He leant on his stick.* • *Do not lean bikes against the window.*

lean *ADJECTIVE* leaner, leanest
Lean meat has little fat.

leap *NOUN* leaps
a high or long jump

leap *VERB* leaps, leaping, leapt, leaped
❶ to jump high or a long way ❷ to suddenly move somewhere • *She leapt to her feet.*

leap year *NOUN* leap years
a year with an extra day in it, on 29 February. Leap years come every 4 years and can be divided by four, for example 2016 and 2020.

> ✳ **WORD STORY**
> It is probably called **leap year** because the dates from March onwards 'leap' one day forward because of the extra day.

learn *VERB* learns, learning, learnt, learned
to gain knowledge or a skill • *We learnt about Rosa Parks today.* • *She's learning to swim.*
➤ **learner** *NOUN* ➤ **learning** *NOUN*

lease *NOUN* leases
an agreement to let someone use a building, land or machine in return for payment

leash *NOUN* leashes
a dog's lead

least *DETERMINER, ADVERB*
less than all the others • *I get the **least** pocket money.* • *I like this one **least**.*

least *PRONOUN*
the smallest amount • *I ate the **least**.*
➤ **at least** not less and perhaps more than something • *It will cost **at least** £50.*

leather *NOUN* leathers
a strong material made from animals' skins

leave *VERB* leaves, leaving, left
① to go away from a place or person • *We **left** the house early.* • *The bus has already **left**.* ② To let something stay where it is or remain as it is. • *Leave your shoes here.* • *You've **left** the door open.*

leave *NOUN*
permission • *The guard had gone away without **leave**.*

leaves *NOUN (plural of leaf)*

lecture *NOUN* lectures
a formal talk about a subject to an audience

led *VERB (past tense and past participle of lead)*
• *She **led** us into the garden.* • *She has **led** her team well.*

ledge *NOUN* ledges
a narrow shelf

lee *NOUN*
the sheltered side of something, away from the wind

leaves

leek *NOUN* leeks
a long vegetable that is white at one end and green at the other and tastes similar to an onion

leer *VERB* leers, leering, leered
to smile unpleasantly

left *VERB (past tense and past participle of leave)*
• *Nan **left** today.* • *We've **left** the dog at home.*

left *ADJECTIVE, ADVERB*
on or towards the west if you are facing north
• *I write with my **left** hand.* • *Turn **left** here.*

BUILD YOUR VOCABULARY
The opposite is **right**.

left *NOUN*
the left side • *Our house is on the **left**.*

left-hand *ADJECTIVE*
on the left side of something

BUILD YOUR VOCABULARY
The opposite is **right-hand**.

leftovers *NOUN*
food that has not been eaten by the end of a meal

leg *NOUN* legs
① one of the parts of a human's or an animal's body on which they stand or an move ② one of the parts of a pair of trousers that cover your legs ③ one of the parts that supports a table or chair

legal *ADJECTIVE*
① allowed by the law

BUILD YOUR VOCABULARY
The opposite is **illegal**.

② to do with the law or lawyers
➤ **legally** *ADVERB* • *Legally, you are allowed on this land.*

legend *(say lej-end) NOUN* legends
an old story handed down from the past

legendary *ADJECTIVE*
mentioned in legends or very famous
• *This was the palace of a **legendary** king.*

legible *ADJECTIVE*
clear enough to read • *Make sure your writing is **legible**.*
➤ **legibly** *ADVERB* ➤ **legibility** *NOUN*

BUILD YOUR VOCABULARY
The opposite is **illegible**.

legion *NOUN* legions
a group of soldiers, especially a division of the ancient Roman army

legitimate *(say lij-it-im-at) ADJECTIVE*
allowed by a law or rule

leisure *NOUN*
free time, when you can do what you like

leisurely *ADJECTIVE*
done with plenty of time, without hurrying
• *We went for a **leisurely** walk.*

a b c d e f g h i j k l m n o p q r s t u v w x y z

lemon NOUN lemons
❶ a yellow citrus fruit with a sour taste ❷ a pale yellow colour

lemonade NOUN lemonades
a sweet, usually fizzy drink with a lemon flavour

lend VERB lends, lending, lent
❶ to let someone have something of yours to use for a short time • *I've lent my game to Sara.* ❷ to give someone money to use which they must pay back • *My sister lent me £5.*

length NOUN lengths
how long something is or lasts • *Find the length of the line.*

⚠ **WATCH OUT!**
The word **length** has a **g** in it, like the related adjective **long**.

lengthen VERB lengthens, lengthening, lengthened
If something lengthens or you lengthen it, it becomes longer.

lengthy ADJECTIVE lengthier, lengthiest
long • *He gave a lengthy speech.*

lens NOUN lenses
❶ a curved piece of glass or plastic used to make something look bigger, smaller or clearer ❷ the transparent part of the eye, behind the pupil

✳ **WORD STORY**
The word **lens** comes from a Latin word meaning 'lentil', because of its round shape.

Lent NOUN
a period of about 6 weeks before Easter when some Christians give up something they enjoy

lent VERB (past tense and past participle of **lend**)
• *My friend lent me her pen.*
• *The bank had lent them some money.*

lentil NOUN lentils
a kind of small flat bean

leopard (say lep-erd) NOUN leopards
a large spotted wild animal of the cat family

leprechaun NOUN leprechauns
in Irish mythology, a mischievous creature that looks like a little old man

less DETERMINER, ADVERB
not so much or not so • *Please make less noise.*
• *This one is less difficult.*
less PRONOUN
a smaller amount • *The bus costs less than the train.*

lessen VERB lessens, lessening, lessened
If something lessens or you lessen it, it becomes smaller or not so much.

lesser ADJECTIVE
less great or important • *The high king ruled over the lesser kings.*

lesson NOUN lessons
❶ a time during which you are taught something • *It's my swimming lesson today.* ❷ something that you learn

lest CONJUNCTION (old use)
so that something does not happen; in case • *He ran away lest he should be seen.*

let VERB lets, letting, let
❶ To let someone do something is to allow them to do it. • *He let me watch him practise.* ❷ To let something happen is to cause it or not prevent it. • *You've let your books get wet.*

lethal ADJECTIVE
able to kill you

let's VERB
used to suggest what you should do; short for *let us* • *Let's go.*

letter NOUN letters
❶ one of the symbols used for writing words, such as *a, b* or *c.* There are 26 letters in the English alphabet ❷ a message written on paper and sent to someone

letter box NOUN letter boxes
a box or slot into which letters are delivered or posted

lettering NOUN
drawn or painted letters

lettuce *NOUN* lettuces
a green vegetable with crisp leaves used in salads

leukaemia *(say* lew-**kee**-mee-a*)* *NOUN*
a disease in which there are too many white cells in the blood

WORD STORY

Leukaemia has a difficult spelling. The **leuk–** part comes from a Greek word meaning 'white'. The **–aemia** part comes from a Greek word meaning 'blood' and is also found in the word **anaemia**.

level *NOUN* levels
❶ a height or position • *The lines show the level of the water.* ❷ a standard or grade • *She has reached level 3 in gymnastics.*

level *ADJECTIVE*
❶ flat or horizontal • *The ground is level near the house.* ❷ at the same height or position • *Are these pictures level?*

level *VERB* levels, levelling, levelled
to make something flat or horizontal

lever *NOUN* levers
a bar that is pushed or pulled to lift something heavy, force something open or make a machine work

liable *ADJECTIVE*
likely to do something • *He is liable to lose his temper.*

liar *NOUN* liars
someone who tells lies

liberal *ADJECTIVE*
❶ tolerant of other people's opinions or behaviour
❷ generous • *She is liberal with her money.*

liberate *VERB* liberates, liberating, liberated
to set someone free
➤ **liberation** *NOUN*

liberty *NOUN* liberties
freedom

librarian *NOUN* librarians
someone who looks after a library or works in one

library *NOUN* libraries
a place where books are kept for people to use or borrow

lice *NOUN* (plural of **louse**)

licence *NOUN* licences
an official document allowing someone to do, use or own something • *You need a TV licence.*

WATCH OUT!

Don't confuse a **licence** (a noun, spelt **–ence**) with to **license** (a verb, spelt **–ense**).

license *VERB* licenses, licensing, licensed
to give someone official permission to do something
• *The ship was licensed to carry passengers.*

lichen *(say* **ly**-ken*)* *NOUN* lichens
a dry-looking plant that grows on rocks, walls and trees

lick *VERB* licks, licking, licked
to move your tongue over something

lid *NOUN* lids
❶ a cover for a box or jar ❷ an eyelid

lie *VERB* lies, lying, lay, lain
❶ to be or get into a flat position • *We can lie on the grass.* • *The cat had lain there all night.* ❷ to be in a certain position or condition • *The valley lay before us.* • *The castle was lying in ruins.*

WATCH OUT!

Lay is the past tense of **lie**, but it is also a verb with a separate meaning, 'to put something down': *Lay a blanket on the floor.*

lie *VERB* lies, lying, lied
to say something that you know is not true • *I could tell he was lying.*
lie *NOUN* lies
something you say that you know is not true
• *That's a lie!*

lieutenant *(say* lef-**ten**-ant*)* *NOUN* lieutenants
an officer in the army or navy

a
b
c
d
e
f
g
h
i
j
k
l
m
n
o
p
q
r
s
t
u
v
w
x
y
z

life NOUN lives
❶ Someone's life is the time when they are alive.
• *I've never been so tired in my life.* ❷ the state of being alive and able to grow • *Water is necessary for life.*

lifeboat NOUN lifeboats
a boat for rescuing people at sea

life cycle NOUN life cycles
the series of changes in the life of a living thing
• *The diagram shows the life cycle of a frog.*

life jacket NOUN life jackets
a jacket of material that will float, used to support a person in water

lifeless ADJECTIVE
not alive or not appearing to be alive • *a lifeless body*

lifelike ADJECTIVE
looking exactly like a real person or thing

lifelong ADJECTIVE
lasting throughout someone's life

lifestyle NOUN lifestyles
the way someone lives • *They have a very healthy lifestyle.*

lifetime NOUN lifetimes
the period of time during which someone is alive

lift VERB lifts, lifting, lifted
to pick something up or move it to a higher position
lift NOUN lifts
❶ a device for taking people or goods from one floor to another in a building ❷ a ride in someone's car
• *Can I have a lift to school?*

light NOUN lights
❶ brightness from the sun, a lamp or a fire that makes it possible to see things • *She read by the light of a candle.* ❷ a lamp or something that provides light • *Switch on the light.*
light ADJECTIVE lighter, lightest
❶ bright, so you can see well • *They left before it was light.* • *a light room*

🔧 **BUILD** YOUR VOCABULARY
The opposite of this meaning is **dark**.

❷ A light colour is pale. • *Her hair is light brown.*
🔧 **BUILD** YOUR VOCABULARY
The opposite of this meaning is **dark**.

❸ weighing little • *My bag is very light.*
🔧 **BUILD** YOUR VOCABULARY
The opposite of this meaning is **heavy**.

❹ not large or strong • *There is a light wind.*

light VERB lights, lighting, lit, lighted
❶ If you light something or it lights, it begins to burn. • *We lit a candle.* • *The fire won't light.*
❷ To light a place is to give it light. • *The streets were brightly lit.*
➤ **lightness** NOUN

light bulb NOUN light bulbs
the glass part of an electric light, that glows when you switch it on

lighten VERB lightens, lightening, lightened
If you lighten something or it lightens, it becomes lighter or brighter.

light-hearted ADJECTIVE
cheerful; not serious
➤ **light-heartedly** ADVERB
➤ **light-heartedness** NOUN

lighthouse NOUN lighthouses
a tower with a bright light at the top to guide ships

lighting NOUN
The lighting in a place is the way it is lit.

lightly ADVERB
gently • *She touched his cheek lightly.*

lightning NOUN
bright light in the sky during a thunderstorm • *I saw a flash of lightning.*

⚠ **WATCH OUT!**
There is no **e** in **lightning**!

light year NOUN light years
the distance that light travels in one year, which is about 6 million million miles

like VERB likes, liking, liked
to think someone or something is pleasant or good
• *I really like my teacher.* • *I don't like getting up early.*

like *PREPOSITION*
❶ similar to; in a similar way to • *Your hair is like mine.* • *He laughed like a hyena.* ❷ such as • *We need things like scissors and glue.*

likely *ADJECTIVE* **likelier, likeliest**
If something is likely, it will probably happen or is probably true. • *It's likely to rain today.*

likeness *NOUN* **likenesses**
something that looks similar to someone; a similar appearance

likewise *ADVERB*
similarly; in the same way

lilac *NOUN* **lilacs**
❶ a bush with sweet-smelling purple or white flowers ❷ a pale purple colour

lily *NOUN* **lilies**
a trumpet-shaped flower

limb *NOUN* **limbs**
a leg, arm or wing

lime *NOUN* **limes**
❶ a green citrus fruit like a small round lemon ❷ a tree with yellow blossom

limerick *(say* **lim-er-ick***) NOUN* **limericks**
a funny poem with five lines and a strong rhythm

limestone *NOUN*
a type of rock used in building and making cement

limit *NOUN* **limits**
a line, point or amount that you cannot go beyond • *You must obey the speed limit.*
limit *VERB* **limits, limiting, limited**
to keep something or someone within a limit • *You are limited to one free drink.*

limp *VERB* **limps, limping, limped**
to walk in an uneven way because something is wrong with your leg or foot
limp *ADJECTIVE* **limper, limpest**
floppy or weak • *My body felt limp.*
➤ **limply** *ADVERB*

limpet *NOUN* **limpets**
a small shellfish that attaches itself firmly to rocks

line *NOUN* **lines**
❶ a long thin mark made on a surface • *Draw a line joining the dots.* ❷ a row or series of people or things • *People waited in a long line.* • *a line of trees* ❸ a number of words together in a play, film, poem or song • *A limerick is a poem with five lines.* ❹ a railway or a section of railway track • *Something was blocking the line.* ❺ a piece of rope, string or wire • *a fishing line*
line *VERB* **lines, lining, lined**
to form an edge or border along something • *People lined the streets to watch the race.*
➤ **To line up** is to form a line. • *We lined up in the playground.*

line graph *NOUN* **line graphs**
a simple graph, using a line to show how two amounts are related

linen *NOUN*
cloth made from flax, used to make clothes, sheets and tablecloths

liner *NOUN* **liners**
a large ship or aircraft

linger *VERB* **lingers, lingering, lingered**
to stay for a long time • *The children lingered in front of the toy shop.*

lining *NOUN* **linings**
a layer of material covering the inside of something

link *NOUN* **links**
❶ one of the rings in a chain ❷ a connection between two things • *Is there a link between the two crimes?* ❸ a connection on a website that you can click to take you to another website
link *VERB* **links, linking, linked**
To link things is to join them together.

lion *NOUN* **lions**
a large strong light-brown animal from the cat family found in Africa and India. A male lion has a **mane.**

lioness *NOUN* **lionesses**
a female lion

a b c d e f g h i j k l m n o p q r s t u v w x y z

lip NOUN lips
❶ Your lips are the two fleshy edges of your mouth.
❷ the edge of something such as a jug or a crater

lipstick NOUN lipsticks
a type of make-up for colouring lips

liquid NOUN liquids
a substance that can flow but is not a gas, for example water or oil

liquorice (say lik-er-ish or lik-er-iss) NOUN
a black sweet with a strong taste, which comes from a plant root

liquorice

lisp NOUN lisps
If someone has a lisp, they pronounce s like th.

lisp VERB lisps, lisping, lisped
to speak with a lisp

list NOUN lists
a number of names or items written one after another

list VERB lists, listing, listed
to write or say things one after another

listen VERB listens, listening, listened
to pay attention to someone or something so that you can hear them • We **listened** to some music.
• Listen! I'm talking to you.
➤ **listener** NOUN

listless ADJECTIVE
too tired to be active or enthusiastic
➤ **listlessly** ADVERB

lit VERB (past tense and past participle of **light**)
• She **lit** a candle. • We have **lit** the fire.

literacy (say lit-er-a-see) NOUN
the ability to read and write

literally ADVERB
really; actually • The noise made me **literally** jump out of my seat.

literary (say lit-er-er-ee) ADJECTIVE
to do with literature

literate (say lit-er-at) ADJECTIVE
able to read and write

🔧 **BUILD** YOUR VOCABULARY
The opposite is **illiterate**.

literature NOUN
stories, plays and poetry, especially good or serious ones

litre (say lee-ter) NOUN litres
a measurement of the volume of liquid. There are 1000 millilitres in 1 litre, which is about 1.75 pints.
• The jug holds 2 **litres**.

🔧 **BUILD** YOUR VOCABULARY
The abbreviation is **l**.

litter NOUN litters
❶ rubbish or untidy things left lying about ❷ a number of young animals born to a mother at the same time

litter VERB litters, littering, littered
If things litter a place, they are scattered around it in an untidy way.

little ADJECTIVE
❶ small in size, amount or length • We saw a **little** kitten. • I had a **little** sleep. ❷ young or younger
• My **little** sister is 5.

little DETERMINER, PRONOUN less, least
not much • We have very **little** time. • There is **little** I can do.
➤ **a little** a bit • I felt a **little** sad. • Let's stay a **little** longer.

live VERB (rhymes with **give**) lives, living, lived
❶ To live is to be alive. ❷ To live somewhere is to have your home there. • She is **living** in France now.
❸ To live in a certain way is to have that kind of life.
• We try to **live** healthily.

live *ADJECTIVE (rhymes with* **five***)*
❶ A live animal is alive. ❷ A live programme is broadcast while it is actually happening, not recorded.

livelihood *NOUN* livelihoods
Someone's livelihood is the way they earn money to live.

lively *ADJECTIVE* livelier, liveliest
cheerful and full of energy
➤ **liveliness** *NOUN*

liver *NOUN* livers
a large organ in the body that helps keep the blood clean

lives *NOUN (plural of* **life***)*

livestock *NOUN*
farm animals

livid *ADJECTIVE*
❶ very angry ❷ dark blue-grey in colour • *a livid bruise*

living *NOUN* livings
a living is enough money to live • *She made a living selling eggs.*

living room *NOUN* living rooms
a room for sitting and relaxing in

lizard *NOUN* lizards
an animal with a scaly skin, four legs and a long tail

BUILD YOUR VOCABULARY
A lizard is a **reptile**.

llama *(say* lah-ma*) NOUN* llamas
a South American animal with woolly fur

load *NOUN* loads
❶ an amount of something that is being carried ❷ *(informal)* a large amount • *It's a load of nonsense.*
load *VERB* loads, loading, loaded
❶ To load a vehicle or load things into it is to put things into it. • *They loaded the boxes on to a truck.* ❷ To load a gun is to put a bullet into it. ❸ To load a program is to make it ready to use on a computer.

loaf *NOUN* loaves
a shaped mass of bread baked in one piece

loan *NOUN* loans
something that has been lent to someone, especially money
loan *VERB* loans, loaning, loaned
To loan something is to lend it.

loathe clothe *VERB* loathes, loathing, loathed
to dislike someone or something very much

loathsome *ADJECTIVE*
horrible; disgusting
'Now you've done it, you loathsome pest!' whispered the Earthworm to the Centipede.–JAMES AND THE GIANT PEACH, Roald Dahl

loaves *NOUN (plural of* **loaf***)*

lobby *NOUN* lobbies
an entrance hall

lobster *NOUN* lobsters
a large shellfish with eight legs and two claws

BUILD YOUR VOCABULARY
A lobster is a **crustacean**.

local *ADJECTIVE*
belonging to a particular place or area • *Where is your local library?*
local *NOUN* locals
someone who lives in a particular area • *The park is popular with both tourists and locals.*

locate *VERB* locates, locating, located
❶ to discover where something is • *They located his hiding place.* ❷ to be located somewhere is to be in that place • *The cinema is located in the High Street.*

location *NOUN* locations
the place where something is • *What is the exact location of the submarine?*

loch *NOUN* lochs
a lake in Scotland

lock *NOUN* locks
❶ a fastening that you open and close with a key ❷ A lock of hair is a few strands.
lock *VERB* locks, locking, locked
❶ to close something and fasten it with a lock • *Don't forget to lock the door.* ❷ to put something somewhere that can be fastened with a lock • *She locked the papers in a drawer.*

a
b
c
d
e
f
g
h
i
j
k
l
m
n
o
p
q
r
s
t
u
v
w
x
y
z

locker NOUN lockers
a small cupboard for keeping things safe, for example in a changing room

locket NOUN lockets
a necklace with a small case holding a photograph or lock of hair

locomotive NOUN locomotives
a railway engine

locust NOUN locusts
an insect like a large grasshopper, that flies in swarms eating all the plants in an area

lodge NOUN lodges
❶ a small house, sometimes one at the entrance to a large house ❷ a beaver's den

lodge VERB lodges, lodging, lodged
❶ to get stuck somewhere • The ball **lodged** in the branches. ❷ to stay in someone's house

loft NOUN lofts
the room or space under the roof of a house

lofty ADJECTIVE loftier, loftiest
high or tall

log NOUN logs
❶ a large piece of a tree that has fallen or been cut down ❷ a record of what happens each day, especially on a journey
log VERB logs, logging, logged
➤ **To log in** is to start using a computer.
➤ **To log out** is to finish using a computer.

logic NOUN
a system of thinking and working things out based on reason

logical ADJECTIVE
reasonable or worked out using logic
➤ **logically** ADVERB

BUILD YOUR VOCABULARY
The opposite is **illogical**.

logo NOUN logos
a symbol used by a company on its products

loiter VERB loiters, loitering, loitered
to wait around somewhere not doing anything

loll VERB lolls, lolling, lolled
to sit or lie in a very relaxed lazy way

lollipop NOUN lollipops
a hard sweet on the end of a stick

✳ **WORD STORY**
Lollipop may come from *lolly*, an old word for 'tongue' or from a Romany (Gypsy) word for a toffee apple, *lollipobbel*.

lolly NOUN lollies (informal)
❶ (or **ice lolly**) a piece of flavoured ice on a stick
❷ a lollipop

lone ADJECTIVE
on its own; solitary • a **lone** rider

lonely ADJECTIVE lonelier, loneliest
❶ unhappy because you are alone ❷ far from other places and people • a **lonely** village
➤ **loneliness** NOUN

long ADJECTIVE longer, longest
❶ big when measured from one end to the other
• We need a **long** cable. ❷ taking a lot of time
• It's a **long** film. ❸ used to talk about how much something measures or how much time it takes
• How **long** is the line? • The speech was not very **long**.
long ADVERB longer, longest
for a long time • Have you been waiting **long**?
➤ **no longer** or **not any longer** not any more; not now

long VERB longs, longing, longed
➤ **To long for something** is to want it very much.

long division NOUN
a method of dividing a large number by another number, in which you write down all the calculations

longitude NOUN longitudes
the distance of a place east or west of the Greenwich Meridian (an imaginary line that passes through London), measured in degrees

BUILD YOUR VOCABULARY
Look at **latitude**.

long jump NOUN
an athletics contest in which competitors jump as far along the ground as they can

longship *NOUN* longships
a long narrow Viking warship, with oars and a sail

look *VERB* looks, looking, looked
❶ to use your eyes to see something or to turn your eyes towards something • *We all **looked** at the screen.* ❷ If something or someone looks a certain way, they appear that way. • *You **look** tired.* • *That cake **looks** delicious.*
➤ **To look after something** or **someone** is to protect them or take care of them.
➤ **To look for something** or **someone** is to try to find them.
➤ **To look forward to something** is to be waiting eagerly for it to happen.
➤ **To look out** is to be careful.

look *NOUN* looks
❶ A look is the act of looking. • *Take a **look** at this.* ❷ the expression on someone's face • *She had an angry **look**.*

lookout *NOUN* lookouts
➤ **To be on the lookout** or **to keep a lookout for something** is to watch carefully in case it appears or happens.

loom *NOUN* looms
a machine for weaving cloth

loom *VERB* looms, looming, loomed
to appear large and threatening
A dark shadow blotted out the moonlight and loomed over Measle.—MEASLE AND THE SLITHERGHOUL, Ian Ogilvie

loop *NOUN* loops
a curved or circular shape, for example made by a piece of string

loop *VERB* loops, looping, looped
to make a loop with something • *I **looped** the rope over a post.*

loose *ADJECTIVE* looser, loosest
❶ not tight or firmly fixed • *This skirt is too **loose**.* • *a **loose** tooth* ❷ not tied up or shut in • *The dog got **loose**.*
➤ **loosely** *ADVERB* ➤ **looseness** *NOUN*

> ⚠ **WATCH OUT!**
> Don't confuse the adjective **loose**, pronounced 'looss', with the verb to **lose**, pronounced 'looz'.

loosen *VERB* loosens, loosening, loosened
If you loose something or it loosens, it becomes looser. • *I **loosened** my belt.*

loot *NOUN*
valuable things that have been stolen

loot *VERB* **loots, looting, looted**
to steal things from a place, especially during a war or riot

lopsided *ADJECTIVE*
uneven, with one side lower or larger than the other
• *a lopsided smile*

lord *NOUN* **lords**
a man of high social status, especially one who is allowed to use the title 'Lord'

lorry *NOUN* **lorries**
a large vehicle for carrying goods

lose *VERB* **loses, losing, lost**
❶ to no longer have something, especially because you cannot find it • *I've lost my hat.* ❷ To lose a contest, game or argument is to be beaten in it.
• *We lost the match 2-1.*
➤ **loser** *NOUN*

⚠ **WATCH OUT!**
Don't confuse the verb to **lose**, pronounced 'looz', with the adjective **loose**, pronounced 'looss'.

loss *PRONOUN, ADVERB*
The loss of something is losing it.

lost *VERB* (*past tense and past participle of* **lose**)
• *She lost her balance and fell backwards.*
• *She realised she had lost her purse.*

lost *ADJECTIVE*
❶ If you are lost, you do not know where you are.
• *I think we're lost.* ❷ If something is lost, it is missing. • *a lost dog*

lot *PRONOUN, ADVERB*
❶ A **lot** or **lots** is a large number of people or things.
• *A lot of people like this song.* • *We have lots of time.* ❷ A **lot** is very much. • *It's a lot warmer today.*
• *Thanks a lot!*

lotion *NOUN* **lotions**
a liquid that you put on your skin

lottery *NOUN* **lotteries**
a way of raising money by selling tickets and giving prizes to people who have the winning tickets

loud *ADJECTIVE* **louder, loudest**
noisy; producing a lot of sound
➤ **loudly** *ADVERB* ➤ **loudness** *NOUN*

loudspeaker *NOUN* **loudspeakers**
a piece of equipment for producing loud sound from a recording or voice

lounge *NOUN* **lounges**
a room for sitting in and relaxing

lounge *VERB* **lounges, lounging, lounged**
to sit or lean in a relaxed way
Sirius was lounging in his chair at his ease, tilting it back on two legs.—HARRY POTTER AND THE ORDER OF THE PHOENIX, J. K. Rowling

louse *NOUN* **lice**
a small insect that lives on people's or animal's bodies

love *NOUN* **loves**
a feeling of liking someone or something very much
➤ **To be in love** is to love another person in a romantic way.

love *VERB* **loves, loving, loved**
to like someone or something very much
➤ **lover** *NOUN* • *a music lover*
➤ **loving** *ADJECTIVE* • *a loving look*

lovely *ADJECTIVE* **lovelier, loveliest**
very pleasant or beautiful • *We had a lovely time.*
• *You look lovely.*
➤ **loveliness** *NOUN*

low *ADJECTIVE* **lower, lowest**
❶ only reaching a short way up; not high
• *I stepped over a low wall.* ❷ small in amount, level or importance • *Cook the soup at a low*

temperature. ❸ A low sound is deep. • *He played a low note.*
➤ **lowness** NOUN

> **BUILD YOUR VOCABULARY**
> The opposite is **high**.

lower VERB lowers, lowering, lowered
to move something down • *He lowered the blinds.*

lower case NOUN
small letters, not capitals

> **BUILD YOUR VOCABULARY**
> Look at **upper case**.

lowlands NOUN
flat low land, especially in Scotland

> **BUILD YOUR VOCABULARY**
> Look at **highlands** and **uplands**.

lowly ADJECTIVE lowlier, lowliest
humble • *He was a lowly peasant.*

loyal ADJECTIVE
always faithful and true to someone
➤ **loyally** ADVERB ➤ **loyalty** NOUN

> **BUILD YOUR VOCABULARY**
> The opposite is **disloyal**.

lozenge NOUN lozenges
❶ a sweet containing medicine for a sore throat
❷ a diamond shape

luck NOUN
❶ Luck is the way things happen by chance, without being planned. • *This game is mostly about luck, not skill.* ❷ Luck is good fortune. • *He wished me luck.*

lucky ADJECTIVE luckier, luckiest
having or bringing good luck
➤ **luckily** ADVERB • *Luckily, it didn't rain.*

ludicrous (say loo-dik-rus) ADJECTIVE
extremely silly or ridiculous
➤ **ludicrously** ADVERB

lug VERB lugs, lugging, lugged
to carry or drag something heavy

luggage NOUN
suitcases and bags taken on a journey

lull VERB lulls, lulling, lulled
to soothe or calm someone

lull NOUN lulls
a short period of quiet or calm • *There was a lull in the storm.*

lullaby NOUN lullabies
a song that you sing to send a baby to sleep

lumber VERB lumbers, lumbering, lumbered
to move clumsily and heavily
Conker howled as the ancient alligator lumbered up the deck past them.—THE MYSTIFYING MEDICINE SHOW, J. C. Bemis

lumber NOUN
❶ unwanted furniture or other things ❷ roughly cut wood; timber

luminous (say loo-min-us) ADJECTIVE
shining in the dark • *a jellyfish with luminous tentacles*

lump NOUN lumps
❶ a solid piece of something • *a lump of ice*
❷ a swelling or bump
➤ **lumpy** ADJECTIVE • *a lumpy bed*

lunar ADJECTIVE
to do with the moon • *a lunar eclipse*

lunatic (say lu-nat-ic) NOUN lunatics
a mad person

> ✳ **WORD STORY**
> From the Latin word *luna* meaning 'moon', because people used to believe that the moon could cause madness.

a
b
c
d
e
f
g
h
i
j
k
l
m
n
o
p
q
r
s
t
u
v
w
x
y
z

lunch NOUN lunches
a meal eaten in the middle of the day

lung NOUN lungs
Your lungs are the two organs in your chest, used for breathing.

lunge VERB lunges, lunging, lunged
to make a sudden movement forwards • *The monster lunged for him, but he dodged it.*

lunge NOUN lunges
a sudden movement forwards

lupin NOUN lupins
a garden plant with tall spikes of flowers

lurch VERB lurches, lurching, lurched
to stagger or move jerkily • *The truck **lurched** to a halt.*

lurch NOUN lurches
a sudden staggering or jerky movement • *My stomach gave a **lurch**.*

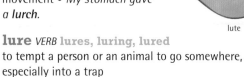
lute

lure VERB lures, luring, lured
to tempt a person or an animal to go somewhere, especially into a trap

lurk VERB lurks, lurking, lurked
to be present somewhere but not seen • *Danger seemed to **lurk** everywhere.*

luscious (say lush-us) ADJECTIVE
delicious
He would buy one luscious bar of chocolate and eat it all up, every bit of it, right then and there.—CHARLIE AND THE CHOCOLATE FACTORY, Roald Dahl

lush ADJECTIVE lusher, lushest
growing thickly and healthily • *We lay in the lush grass.*

lute NOUN lutes
a musical instrument similar to a small rounded guitar, which was popular in the Middle Ages

luxury NOUN luxuries
❶ A luxury is something expensive that you enjoy but do not really need. ❷ Luxury is great comfort and expense. • *They led a life of **luxury**.*
➤ **luxurious** ADJECTIVE • *a **luxurious** palace*

lying VERB (present participle of **lie**)
• *Dad was **lying** on the sofa.* • *I can tell you're **lying**.*

lynx (say links) NOUN lynxes
a wild animal like a very large cat

lyrics NOUN
the words of a song

⚙ M is for **month**. There is no commonly used word in English that rhymes with *month*.

⚙ Can you think of any more words that do not have a rhyme?

CLUE Think of colours.

M *ABBREVIATION*
1000 in Roman numerals

m *ABBREVIATION*
the abbreviation for **metre**

macaroni *NOUN*
pasta in the shape of short tubes

macaw *NOUN* macaws
a large parrot with brightly coloured feathers and a long tail

machine *NOUN* machines
a piece of equipment made of moving parts that work together to make or do something
• *a sewing machine*

machinery *NOUN*
machines • *She heard clanking machinery.*

mackerel *NOUN* mackerel
an edible sea fish with greenish-blue skin

mad *ADJECTIVE* madder, maddest
❶ very silly • *That's a mad idea!* ❷ mentally ill; insane ❸ *(informal)* If someone is mad about something, they like it a lot. ❹ *(informal)* angry
➤ **madness** *NOUN*

madam *NOUN*
a word used for speaking or writing politely to a woman • *Can I help you, madam?*

BUILD YOUR VOCABULARY
Look at **sir**.

madden *VERB* maddens, maddening, maddened
to make someone mad or angry

made *VERB (past tense and past participle of* **make***)*
• *My parents made me say sorry.* • *You've made a mess.*

madly *ADVERB*
with energy or enthusiasm
The birds were all pecking away madly at the raisins.
—DANNY THE CHAMPION OF THE WORLD, Roald Dahl

magazine *NOUN* magazines
a publication with pictures and articles or stories, that comes out every week or month

magenta *(say* maj-en-ta*)* *NOUN*
a reddish-purple colour

maggot *NOUN* maggots
the young worm-like form of a fly
➤ **maggoty** *ADJECTIVE*
• *maggoty apples*

BUILD YOUR VOCABULARY
Look at **larva**.

magic *NOUN*
❶ in stories, the power to make impossible things happen ❷ tricks performed to entertain people

magic *VERB* magicks, magicking, magicked
to make something happen using magic
'Abracadabra!' Winnie magicked herself a magnificent party dress.—WINNIE GOES FOR GOLD, Laura Owen

magical *ADJECTIVE*
having or using the power of magic • *a magical spell*
➤ **magically** *ADVERB*

magician *NOUN* magicians
❶ someone who does magic tricks
❷ in stories, a person with magic powers; a wizard

magistrate *NOUN* magistrates
a judge in a local court that deals with less serious cases

magma *NOUN*
the molten substance beneath the earth's crust

magnesium *NOUN*
a silver-white metal that burns with a very bright flame

BUILD YOUR VOCABULARY
Magnesium is an **element**.

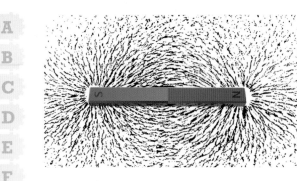

magnet NOUN magnets
a piece of metal that attracts iron or steel and can push away another magnet
➤ **magnetic** ADJECTIVE • *a magnetic object*
➤ **magnetism** NOUN • *Magnetism is a powerful force.*

BUILD YOUR VOCABULARY
Look at **attract** and **repel**.

magnificent ADJECTIVE
impressive or excellent • *a magnificent sight*
➤ **magnificence** NOUN
➤ **magnificently** ADVERB

magnify VERB magnifies, magnifying, magnified
to make something look bigger than it really is
➤ **magnification** NOUN

magnifying glass NOUN magnifying glasses
a lens that makes things look bigger

magnolia NOUN magnolias
a tree with large white or pale pink flowers

magpie NOUN magpies
a black and white bird, related to the crow

mahogany (say ma-**hog**-a-nee) NOUN
a hard brown wood used for making furniture

maid NOUN maids
❶ a female servant ❷ (or **maiden**) (old use) a girl

mail NOUN
letters and parcels sent by post or messages sent by email
mail VERB mails, mailing, mailed
to send something by post or by email

main ADJECTIVE
large or important • *They live near a busy main road.* • *The main thing to remember is to save your work.*

main (also **mains**) NOUN
the system of large pipes or cables that carries water, gas or electricity to a building

main clause NOUN main clauses
a clause which can form a complete sentence on its own

mainland NOUN
the large area of land that forms a country or continent, not including islands around it

mainly ADVERB
mostly or usually • *They worked mainly in silence.*

maintain VERB maintains, maintaining, maintained
❶ to keep something as it is • *We maintained a steady speed.* ❷ To maintain a machine or building is to keep it in good condition. ❸ to state or believe something firmly

maize NOUN
a tall plant with large yellow seeds that grow on cobs

majestic ADJECTIVE
very impressive or dignified
She sat there majestic in her armchair, filling every inch of it.—THE WITCHES, Roald Dahl
➤ **majestically** ADVERB

majesty NOUN majesties
the title of a king or queen • *Her majesty the Queen will be present.*

major ADJECTIVE
very important or serious • *There has been a major accident.*

BUILD YOUR VOCABULARY
An opposite is **minor**.

major NOUN majors
an army officer above a captain in rank

majority (say maj-or-rit-ee) NOUN majorities
the greatest part of a group; more than half
• *The majority of the class wanted a quiz.*

BUILD YOUR VOCABULARY
The opposite is **minority**.

make VERB makes, making, made
❶ to build, produce or create something • *They made a den out of boxes.* • *I'm making a cake.* ❷ To make something happen is to cause it. • *The story made us laugh.* ❸ To make someone do something is to force them. • *My parents made me go to bed.* ❹ To make money is to earn it. • *We made £10 washing cars.* ❺ To make a promise or comment is to say it. • *Can I make a suggestion?* ❻ You say numbers make a total when they are added together. • *4 and 6 make 10.*
➤ **To make something up** is to invent a false story or excuse.

make NOUN makes
the name of a product made by a particular company • *What make of car is that?*

make-believe NOUN
things that you pretend or imagine

makeshift ADJECTIVE
used because you have nothing better • *They slept under a makeshift shelter.*

make-up NOUN
creams and powders for making your face look beautiful or different

malaria *(say mal-air-ee-a)* NOUN
a tropical disease spread by mosquito bites

male ADJECTIVE
belonging to the sex that does not have babies or young, but fertilises egg cells

male NOUN males
a male person or animal

BUILD YOUR VOCABULARY
Look at **female**.

malevolent *(say mal-ev-ol-ent)* ADJECTIVE
wanting to cause harm; bad
'A bad idea, Professor Lockhart,' said Snape, gliding over like a large and malevolent bat.–HARRY POTTER AND THE CHAMBER OF SECRETS, J. K. Rowling
➤ **malevolently** ADVERB ➤ **malevolence** NOUN

malice *(say mal-iss)* NOUN
a desire to harm other people

malicious *(say ma-lish-us)* ADJECTIVE
intending to do harm
➤ **maliciously** ADVERB

mall NOUN malls
a large covered shopping centre

mallet NOUN mallets
a large wooden hammer

mamba NOUN mambas
a large poisonous African snake

mammal NOUN mammals
any animal of which the female gives birth to live young and can feed them with her own milk

mammoth NOUN mammoths
a kind of hairy elephant with long tusks that is now extinct

man NOUN men
a grown-up male human being

man VERB mans, manning, manned
to work at or operate something • *There was no one to man the stall.*

manage VERB manages, managing, managed
❶ to be able to do something although it is difficult • *I managed to finish in time.* ❷ to run or be in charge of something • *She manages a restaurant.*

management NOUN
❶ the job of being in charge of something ❷ people who are in charge in an organisation

manager NOUN managers
a person who is in charge of a business or team of people

manatee NOUN manatees
a large grey sea mammal with flippers and a flat tail

mane NOUN manes
the long hair along the back of the neck of a horse or lion

manger *(rhymes with danger)* NOUN mangers
a box for animal food in a stable

mangle VERB mangles, mangling, mangled
to crush or twist something so it is badly damaged

mango NOUN mangoes
a juicy yellow tropical fruit

maniac NOUN maniacs
someone who acts in a wild or crazy way

a b c d e f g h i j k l m n o p q r s t u v w x y z

manipulate VERB manipulates, manipulating, manipulated
❶ to handle or use something skilfully
❷ to get someone to do what you want in a clever and often unfair way

mankind NOUN
all human beings • *This discovery will help* **mankind**.

man-made ADJECTIVE
made by humans and not by nature
• *a* **man-made** *crater*

manner NOUN manners
❶ the way that something happens or is done
❷ Someone's **manners** are how they behave with others and whether they are polite.

manoeuvre (*say* man-oo-ver) NOUN manoeuvres
a skilful action or movement

manoeuvre (*say* man-oo-ver) VERB manoeuvres, manoeuvring, manoeuvred
If you manoeuvre something or manoeuvre, you move skilfully.
To your buttons, Charlie! You've got to help me manoeuvre!—CHARLIE AND THE GREAT GLASS ELEVATOR, Roald Dahl

manor NOUN manors
a large country house with land

mansion NOUN mansions
a very large house

mantelpiece NOUN mantelpieces
a shelf above a fireplace

mantle NOUN mantles (*old use*)
a cloak

manual ADJECTIVE
❶ done using your hands or physical strength
• *manual work* ❷ operated by hand rather than by machine or computer • *a* **manual** *typewriter*
➤ **manually** ADVERB
manual NOUN manuals
a book of instructions

manufacture VERB manufactures, manufacturing, manufactured
to make things with machines, usually in a factory
➤ **manufacturer** NOUN

manufacture NOUN
the process of making things with machines
• *chemicals used in the* **manufacture** *of paint*

manure NOUN
animal dung used as fertiliser

manuscript NOUN manuscripts
something written or typed before it has been printed

many DETERMINER, PRONOUN more, most
a large number • *Many people were injured.*
• *Many were injured.*
➤ **how many** used to ask about a quantity
• *How many pages did you write?*
➤ **not many** a small number • *Not many people know this.*

Maori (*rhymes with* **flowery**) NOUN Maoris
❶ one of the people whose ancestors were living in New Zealand before Europeans arrived
❷ the language of Maoris
➤ **Maori** ADJECTIVE

 WORD STORY
The word **kiwi** comes from Maori.

map NOUN maps
a diagram of a town, country or area, showing features such as roads and rivers
map VERB maps, mapping, mapped
to make a map of an area

maple NOUN maples
a tree with broad leaves

mar VERB mars, marring, marred
to spoil something

marathon NOUN marathons
a long running race on roads, usually 26 miles or 40 kilometres

WORD STORY
Marathon is a place near Athens where the Greeks defeated the Persians in 490 BC. A runner is said to have run from Marathon to Athens with news of the victory.

marble NOUN marbles
❶ a hard shiny stone used in buildings and sculptures
❷ a small coloured glass ball used in games

march VERB marches, marching, marched
to walk with regular steps, like a soldier

march NOUN marches
a protest by a large group of people walking together

mare NOUN mares
a female horse or donkey

margarine (say mar-ja-**reen**) NOUN
Margarine is a soft creamy substance used like butter, made from animal or vegetable fats.

margin NOUN margins
the empty space at the edge of a page

marigold NOUN marigolds
a yellow or orange garden flower

marine (say ma-**reen**) ADJECTIVE
to do with or living in the sea • marine animals

marine (say ma-**reen**) NOUN marines
a soldier trained to serve on land and sea

marionette NOUN marionettes
a puppet made to move by strings or wires

mark NOUN marks
❶ a spot, dot, line or stain on something ❷ a score or letter given to a piece of work to say how good it is

mark VERB marks, marking, marked
❶ to leave a mark on something • The hot dish has marked the table. ❷ To mark work is to correct it and usually give it a score or letter to say how good it is. ❸ To mark an opposing player in games like football, hockey or netball is to keep close to them to stop them getting the ball.

marker NOUN markers
❶ something used to show where a place is
❷ a thick felt-tip pen

market NOUN markets
a place where things are sold from stalls

market VERB markets, marketing, marketed
To market a product is to try to sell it.

marmalade NOUN
jam made from oranges or lemons

maroon VERB maroons, marooning, marooned
to leave someone trapped in a place far away
• Robinson Crusoe was **marooned** on a desert island.

maroon NOUN
a dark red colour

marriage NOUN marriages
❶ the relationship between two people who are married ❷ a wedding

marrow NOUN marrows
a large green or yellow vegetable with a hard skin

marry VERB marries, marrying, married
❶ To marry someone is to become their husband or wife. ❷ To marry two people is to perform a marriage ceremony.

marsh NOUN marshes
an area of low, very wet ground
➤ **marshy** ADJECTIVE

marshmallow NOUN marshmallows
a soft spongy sweet

marsupial (say mar-**soo**-pee-al) NOUN marsupials
an animal such as a kangaroo, wallaby or koala, that carries its young in a pouch

martial arts NOUN
fighting or self-defence sports, such as karate and judo

martin NOUN martins
a bird similar to a swallow

martyr (say **mar**-ter) NOUN martyrs
someone who dies or suffers for their beliefs

marvel NOUN marvels
a wonderful thing

marvel VERB marvels, marvelling, marvelled
To marvel at something is to be filled with wonder or surprise by it.

marvellous ADJECTIVE
wonderful
➤ **marvellously** ADVERB

marzipan NOUN
a soft sweet food made from almonds and sugar

mascot NOUN mascots
a person, animal or object that is believed to bring good luck

masculine ADJECTIVE
to do with men or like a man
➤ **masculinity** NOUN

BUILD YOUR VOCABULARY
Look at **feminine**.

mash VERB mashes, mashing, mashed
to crush something into a soft mass

mask NOUN masks
a covering that you wear over your face to disguise or protect it

mask VERB masks, masking, masked
❶ To mask your face is to cover it with a mask.
❷ To mask something is to hide it.

masonry NOUN
the stone parts of a building

mass NOUN masses
❶ a large amount or pile of something ❷ the amount of matter in an object, measured in grams

mass VERB masses, massing, massed
to collect into a mass • *Dark clouds were massing.*

massacre *(say* mass-a-ker*)* NOUN massacres
the killing of a large number of people

massacre *(say* mass-a-ker*)* VERB massacres, massacring, massacred
to kill a large number of people

massive ADJECTIVE
very big; large and heavy
➤ **massively** ADVERB

mast NOUN masts
a tall pole that holds up a ship's sails or a flag

master NOUN masters
❶ a man who is in charge of something • *The dog followed its master.* ❷ someone who is very skilled at something • *a master of invention*

master VERB masters, mastering, mastered
to learn completely how to do or control something
➤ **mastery** NOUN • *her mastery of painting*

mastermind NOUN masterminds
someone who cleverly plans something such as a crime

masterpiece NOUN masterpieces
an excellent piece of work

mat NOUN mats
❶ a piece of material that partly covers a floor
❷ a small piece of material to protect a surface

match NOUN matches
❶ a small thin stick that makes a flame when you rub it against a rough surface ❷ a game between two teams or players

match VERB matches, matching, matched
❶ to be the same colour or go well with something • *Your top matches your eyes.* ❷ to be equal to something • *Her speed matched his.* ❸ If you match two things, you put them together because they have a connection. • *Can you match each word to its definition?*

mate NOUN mates
❶ *(informal)* a friend ❷ one of a pair of animals that produce young together ❸ one of the officers on a ship

mate VERB mates, mating, mated
to come together in order to produce young

material NOUN materials
❶ cloth or fabric ❷ anything used for making something else • *Where do we keep the art materials?*

maternal ADJECTIVE
to do with a mother or like a mother

BUILD YOUR VOCABULARY
Look at **paternal**.

maternity ADJECTIVE
related to pregnancy and having a baby • *maternity clothes*

mathematical ADJECTIVE
related to or involving mathematics

mathematician (*say* math-em-a-**tish**-an)
NOUN mathematicians
an expert in mathematics

mathematics NOUN
the study of numbers, measurements and shapes

maths NOUN
a short word for **mathematics**

matted ADJECTIVE
tangled

matter NOUN matters
❶ something you need to discuss or deal with • *This is a serious matter.* ❷ a substance • *Matter can be solid, liquid or gas.*
➤ **What's the matter?** What is wrong?
matter VERB matters, mattering, mattered
To matter is to be important.

mattress NOUN mattresses
a thick layer of soft material or springs covered in cloth, for sleeping on

mature ADJECTIVE
❶ fully grown or developed ❷ sensible and grown-up
➤ **maturity** NOUN

BUILD YOUR VOCABULARY
The opposite is **immature**.

mature VERB matures, maturing, matured
to become fully grown or developed

mauve (*say* mohv) ADJECTIVE
pale purple in colour

maximum NOUN
the greatest number or amount possible • *You can borrow a maximum of five books.*
maximum ADJECTIVE
the greatest possible • *The maximum speed is 60 miles per hour.*

BUILD YOUR VOCABULARY
The opposite is **minimum**.

may VERB (past tense might)
❶ If you may do something, you are allowed to do it. • *May I go now?* ❷ If something may happen, it is possible. • *I may be late.*

BUILD YOUR VOCABULARY
May is a **modal verb**.

maybe ADVERB
perhaps

mayhem NOUN
great disorder or chaos
'The news,' twittered Munin, 'is that the giants are ranging all over the country, causing chaos and mayhem.'
—OLAF THE VIKING, Martin Conway

mayonnaise (*say* may-on-**ayz**) NOUN
a cold creamy sauce made from eggs and oil

mayor NOUN mayors
the person in charge of the council in a town or city

maze NOUN mazes
a complicated system of paths or lines which it is difficult to find your way through • *a maze of underground tunnels*

me PRONOUN

a word used instead of *I* when it comes after a verb or preposition • *I think she likes* **me**. • *She gave that book to* **me**.

> **BUILD YOUR VOCABULARY**
> **Me** is used as the **object** of a verb.

meadow NOUN
meadows
a field of grass

meagre
(*say* **meeg**-er)
ADJECTIVE
very little;
barely enough

meal NOUN **meals**
the food that you eat at one time, such as breakfast, lunch or dinner

mean VERB **means, meaning, meant**
❶ If a word or sign means a certain thing, that is what it signifies or expresses. • *What does 'quadrant' mean?* • *Red means stop.* ❷ If you mean to do something, you intend to do it. • *I meant to tell him, but I forgot.*

mean ADJECTIVE **meaner, meanest**
❶ not generous; selfish • *He was very mean with money.* ❷ unkind or spiteful
➤ **meanly** ADVERB ➤**meanness** NOUN

mean NOUN
(*in mathematics*) the average of a set of numbers

meander (*say* mee-an-der) VERB **meanders, meandering, meandered**
If a river or road meanders, it has a lot of bends.

> ☀ **WORD STORY**
> The word **meander** comes from the ancient river *Meander* in Asia Minor (now Turkey), which had a lot of bends.

meaning NOUN **meanings**
The meaning of something is what it signifies or expresses.

means NOUN
A means is a method. • *We need some* **means** *of transport.*

meantime NOUN
➤ **in the meantime** meanwhile

meanwhile ADVERB
while something else is happening

measles NOUN
an infectious disease that causes small red spots and a high temperature

measure VERB **measures, measuring, measured**
To measure something is to find out how big it is.

measure NOUN **measures**
❶ a unit used for measuring something • *A litre is a* **measure** *of volume.* ❷ a device used for measuring • *a tape* **measure**

> ⚠ **WATCH OUT!**
> Watch out for **measure**, **pleasure** and **treasure**, which rhyme and all end with the same spelling: **-easure**.

measurement NOUN **measurements**
a number that you get when you measure something

meat NOUN **meats**
animal flesh that is eaten as food

mechanic NOUN **mechanics**
someone whose job is to repair machines and engines

mechanical ADJECTIVE
❶ to do with or worked by a machine
The machine had a mechanical arm that shot out with tremendous force and grabbed hold of anything that had the slightest bit of gold inside it.—CHARLIE AND THE CHOCOLATE FACTORY, Roald Dahl
❷ done without thinking about it
➤ **mechanically** ADVERB

mechanism NOUN
mechanisms
a moving part of
a machine

medal NOUN
medals
a metal object shaped
like a coin, star or cross,
given for bravery or as a prize
• *He won a gold* **medal**.

meddle VERB meddles, meddling, meddled
to interfere in something

media NOUN
a plural of **medium**
➤ **the media** newspapers, radio, television and
the Internet

medical ADJECTIVE
to do with the treatment of disease
➤ **medically** ADVERB

medicine NOUN medicines
❶ a substance, usually swallowed, used to try to cure
an illness ❷ the treatment of disease and injuries

medieval (say med-ee-**ee**-val) ADJECTIVE
to do with the Middle Ages

mediocre (say meed-ee-oh-ker) ADJECTIVE
not very good
➤ **mediocrity** NOUN

meditate VERB meditates, meditating,
meditated
to think deeply and seriously, usually in silence
➤ **meditation** NOUN

medium ADJECTIVE
of middle size; average

medium NOUN
❶ (plural **media**) a way for something to be done,
communicated or expressed • Sound waves travel
through a **medium** such as air. ❷ (plural **mediums**)
someone who claims to communicate with the
dead

meek ADJECTIVE meeker, meekest
quiet and obedient
➤ **meekly** ADVERB ➤ **meekness** NOUN

meerkat NOUN meerkats
a small animal from southern Africa that often
stands on its back legs

meet VERB meets, meeting, met
❶ If people meet, they come together to the
same place. • We all **met** in the park. • I'll **meet** you
at the station. ❷ If lines or paths meet, they join.
• This is where the stream **meets** the river.
❸ to see and talk to someone for the first time
• Have you **met** Sally?

meeting NOUN meetings
a time when people come together, often to discuss
something

megabyte NOUN megabytes
a unit for measuring computer information, equal
to about one million bytes

melancholy (mel-an-kol-ee) ADJECTIVE
sad and gloomy

mellow ADJECTIVE mellower, mellowest
smooth, soft and rich • Her voice had a **mellow** sound.

melody NOUN melodies
a tune

melon NOUN melons
a large juicy fruit with hard yellow or green skin

melt VERB melts, melting, melted
❶ If you melt something solid or it melts, it becomes
liquid because of heat. ❷ to go away or disappear
• My fears **melted** away.

member NOUN members
someone who belongs to a society or group
➤ **membership** NOUN

membrane NOUN membranes
a very thin skin or covering

meme (say meem) NOUN memes
an image or short film with a caption that is shared
on social media

memorable ADJECTIVE
likely to be remembered • It was a **memorable** day.

memorial NOUN memorials
something built to remind people of a person or
an event

memorise (also **memorize**) VERB
memorises, memorising, memorised
to learn and remember something exactly
• I've **memorised** the whole poem.

memory NOUN memories
❶ Your memory is your ability to remember things.
❷ A memory is something that you remember.
• I have happy **memories** of that holiday.
❸ A computer's memory is the part where
information is stored.

a
b
c
d
e
f
g
h
i
j
k
l
m
n
o
p
q
r
s
t
u
v
w
x
y
z

men NOUN (plural of **man**)

menace NOUN menaces
something harmful or threatening

menace VERB menaces, menacing, menaced
to threaten to harm someone

menagerie (say min-aj-er-ee) NOUN menageries
a collection of different animals

mend VERB mends, mending, mended
to make something good again after it has been broken or damaged

menstruation NOUN
the natural flow of blood from a woman's womb, normally happening roughly every 28 days

mental ADJECTIVE
to do with or happening in the mind
• *mental* arithmetic
➤ **mentally** ADVERB • She **mentally** repeated the words.

mention VERB mentions, mentioning, mentioned
to speak or write briefly about someone or something

mention NOUN mentions
a time when someone or something is mentioned
• *Our school got a **mention** in the local paper.*

menu (say men-yoo) NOUN menus
❶ a list of the food that is served in a restaurant or at a meal ❷ (in computing) a list of possible actions to choose from on a computer screen

meow
another spelling of **miaow**

mercenary NOUN mercenaries
a soldier who can be paid to fight for any side

merchandise NOUN
goods for buying or selling

merchant NOUN merchants
someone involved in buying and selling goods

merciful ADJECTIVE
showing mercy
➤ **mercifully** ADVERB

merciless ADJECTIVE
showing no mercy; cruel
➤ **mercilessly** ADVERB

mercury NOUN
Mercury is a heavy silvery metal that is usually liquid, used in thermometers.

BUILD YOUR VOCABULARY
Mercury is an **element**.

mercy NOUN
kindness or pity, rather than punishing someone or being cruel

mere ADJECTIVE
no more than; just • *The **mere** thought of it made me sick.*
➤ **merely** ADVERB • *She said nothing, but **merely** smiled.*

merge VERB merges, merging, merged
to combine or be blended • *All the colours seemed to **merge**.*

meridian (say mer-**rid**-ee-an) NOUN meridians
a line on a map or globe from the North Pole to the South Pole

merit NOUN merits
a good quality

merit VERB merits, meriting, merited
to deserve something
• *This idea **merits** consideration.*

mermaid NOUN mermaids
in stories, a sea creature with a woman's body and a fish's tail instead of legs

merry ADJECTIVE merrier, merriest
happy and cheerful
➤ **merrily** ADVERB

mesh NOUN meshes
material like a net, with threads crossing each other and open spaces between

mesmerise (also **mesmerize**) VERB
mesmerises, mesmerising, mesmerised
to fascinate someone and hold their attention

mess NOUN messes
❶ something untidy or dirty ❷ a difficult or confused situation
➤ **messy** ADJECTIVE • *Your bedroom is so messy!*
mess VERB messes, messing, messed
➤ **To mess about** is to waste time behaving stupidly or doing things slowly.
➤ **To mess something up** is to do it very badly.

message NOUN messages
a piece of information or a question that one person sends to another

messenger NOUN messengers
someone who carries a message

met VERB (past tense and past participle of **meet**)
• *I met my friend in town.* • *I've never met him before.*

metal NOUN metals
a strong material that is good at conducting heat or electricity, such as copper, gold, iron or steel

⬤ BUILD YOUR VOCABULARY
Look at **conductor**.

metallic (say met-al-lic) ADJECTIVE
made of metal or like metal • *a metallic clanking sound*

metamorphosis NOUN metamorphoses
a complete physical change • *the metamorphosis of a caterpillar into a butterfly*

metaphor (say met-a-for) NOUN metaphors
a way of describing one thing as something else, for example 'His heart was a lump of ice.'
➤ **metaphorical** ADJECTIVE

⬤ BUILD YOUR VOCABULARY
Look at **imagery** and **simile**.

meteor NOUN meteors
a piece of rock or metal from outer space that burns up as it enters the earth's atmosphere, leaving a streak of light in the sky

⬤ BUILD YOUR VOCABULARY
A synonym is **shooting star**.

meteorite (say meet-ee-er-ryt) NOUN meteorites
a piece of rock from outer space that has landed on the earth

meteorology (say mee-tee-er-ol-oj-ee) NOUN
the study of the weather
➤ **meteorological** ADJECTIVE
➤ **meteorologist** NOUN

meter NOUN meters
a device for measuring something, such as how much gas or electricity has been used

methane NOUN
an inflammable gas produced when plants rot

⬤ BUILD YOUR VOCABULARY
Methane is a **greenhouse gas**—look at **greenhouse effect**.

method NOUN methods
a way of doing something

methodical (say meth-od-ic-al) ADJECTIVE
done carefully and in a logical way
➤ **methodically** ADVERB

metre (say meet-er) NOUN metres
a measurement of length. There are 100 centimetres in 1 metre and 1000 metres in 1 kilometre. • *The pool is 25 metres long.*

⬤ BUILD YOUR VOCABULARY
The abbreviation is **m**.

metric ADJECTIVE
using units of 10 and 100 • *The metric system uses millimetres, centimetres, metres and kilometres.*

mew VERB mews, mewing, mewed
to make a sound like a cat

mg ABBREVIATION
the abbreviation for **milligram**

miaow NOUN miaows
the high sound made by a cat

miaow VERB miaows, miaowing, miaowed
If a cat miaows, it makes a high sound.

mice NOUN (plural of **mouse**)

microbe (say **my**-krohb) NOUN microbes
a tiny organism that can only be seen with a microscope

microchip NOUN microchips
a very small piece of silicon with an electronic circuit, used in computers

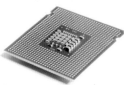

micro-habitat NOUN micro-habitats
a small **habitat** (a place where an animal or plant lives) that exists within a larger one

micro-organism NOUN micro-organisms
a living thing that can only be seen through a microscope

⚙ **BUILD** YOUR VOCABULARY
Some examples of **micro-organisms** are **bacteria**, a **fungus** and a **virus**.

microphone NOUN microphones
an electrical device that records sound or makes it louder

microscope NOUN microscopes
an instrument that makes tiny objects appear larger so you can study them

microscopic (say micro-**scop**-ic) ADJECTIVE
too small to be seen without a microscope

microwave NOUN microwaves
a kind of oven that heats things quickly using energy in very short waves

midday NOUN
the middle of the day; twelve o'clock in the day

⚙ **BUILD** YOUR VOCABULARY
A synonym is **noon**.

middle NOUN middles
❶ a part or place that is far from the ends, edges or sides of something • *Don't stop in the **middle***

of the road. ❷ a time that is after the first part and before the last part of something • *It's the **middle** of the night.*

middle ADJECTIVE
in the middle; not first or last • *I'm the **middle** child in our family.*

Middle Ages NOUN
the period in history from about AD 1100 to 1500

midge NOUN midges
a small biting insect like a gnat

midnight NOUN
twelve o'clock at night

midst NOUN
➤ **in the midst of something** in the middle

midsummer NOUN
the middle of summer, about 21 June in the northern hemisphere

midway ADVERB
halfway

midwife NOUN midwives
a person trained to look after a woman who is giving birth

might VERB
❶ If something might happen, it is possible.
• *The parcel **might** come today.* • *She **might** have forgotten.* ❷ (past tense of **may**) • *He said he **might** be late.*

⚙ **BUILD** YOUR VOCABULARY
Might is a **modal verb**.

might NOUN
great power or strength • *the **might** of the Roman army*

mighty ADJECTIVE mightier, mightiest
very strong or powerful • *They gave the door a **mighty** heave.*
➤ **mightily** ADVERB

migrant (say **my**-grant) NOUN migrants
❶ a person who moves from one place to another, usually to find work ❷ a bird or an animal that moves from one region to another

migrate *(say* my-**grayt***)* *VERB* migrates, migrating, migrated
❶ to move from one place to another, usually to find work ❷ When birds migrate, they fly to a different region for a part of the year.
➤ **migration** *NOUN*

mild *ADJECTIVE* milder, mildest
gentle; not severe or extreme
Miss Jennifer Honey was a mild and quiet person who never raised her voice.—MATILDA, Roald Dahl
➤ **mildly** *ADVERB* ➤ **mildness** *NOUN*

mile *NOUN* miles
a measure of distance. There are 1760 yards in 1 mile and it is about the same as 1.6 kilometres.

military *ADJECTIVE*
to do with soldiers or the armed forces

milk *NOUN*
a white liquid that female mammals produce to feed their young
➤ **milky** *ADJECTIVE* • *a **milky** liquid*
milk *VERB* milks, milking, milked
To milk a cow or other animal is to get milk from it.

Milky Way *NOUN*
the galaxy that earth is part of, that we see as a band of lights in the night sky

mill *NOUN* mills
❶ a building with machinery for grinding corn
• *a flour **mill*** ❷ a factory for making a material such as paper or steel • *a cotton **mill*** ❸ a small device for grinding something • *a pepper **mill***

millennium *NOUN* millenniums
a period of a thousand years

miller *NOUN* millers
someone who runs a flour mill

millet *NOUN*
a kind of cereal with tiny seeds

milligram *NOUN* milligrams
a measurement of weight. There are 1000 milligrams in 1 gram.

BUILD YOUR VOCABULARY
The abbreviation is **mg**.

millilitre *NOUN* millilitres
a measurement of volume. There are 1000 millilitres in 1 litre.

BUILD YOUR VOCABULARY
The abbreviation is **ml**.

millimetre *NOUN* millimetres
a measurement of length. There are 1000 millimetres in 1 metre and 10 millimetres in 1 centimetre.

BUILD YOUR VOCABULARY
The abbreviation is **mm**.

a
b
c
d
e
f
g
h
i
j
k
l
m
n
o
p
q
r
s
t
u
v
w
x
y
z

million NOUN millions
the number 1,000,000
➤ **millionth** ADJECTIVE, NOUN • the **millionth** visitor
• a **millionth** of a second

millionaire NOUN millionaires
someone who has at least a million pounds or dollars

millipede NOUN millipedes
a small crawling creature with many pairs of legs

mime VERB mimes, miming, mimed
to use movements and no words to express
something or tell a story • She **mimed** making a
phone call.
mime NOUN mimes
the use of movements and no words to express
something or tell a story

mimic VERB mimics, mimicking, mimicked
to imitate someone, especially to make people laugh
mimic NOUN mimics
a person who is good at imitating other people

minaret NOUN minarets
a tall tower on a mosque

mince NOUN
meat that has been cut up into very small pieces
mince VERB minces, mincing, minced
To mince food is to cut it up into very small pieces.

mincemeat NOUN
a sweet mixture of currants, raisins and chopped fruit

mind NOUN minds
Your mind is your ability to think and remember
and the thoughts and memories that you have.
➤ **To change your mind** is to change your
opinion or intention.
mind VERB minds, minding, minded
❶ If you do not mind something, you are not upset
or annoyed about it. • Mum doesn't **mind** a little bit
of mess. ❷ If you do not mind about something, you
don't have a preference or opinion. • I don't **mind**
where we sit. ❸ used to warn someone to be careful
about something • **Mind** the doors!

mine PRONOUN
belonging to me • That jacket is **mine**.

mine NOUN mines
❶ a place where coal, metal or precious stones
are dug out of the ground ❷ a bomb hidden under

the ground or sea, that explodes when anything
touches it

mine VERB mines, mining, mined
to dig something from a mine
➤ **miner** NOUN • a coal **miner**

mineral NOUN minerals
a solid substance that forms naturally in the ground,
such as coal or salt

mingle VERB mingles, mingling, mingled
If you mingle things or they mingle, they become
mixed together. • Smells from the kitchen **mingled**
deliciously.

miniature (say min-ich-er) ADJECTIVE
very small, especially copying something larger
• a dolls' house with **miniature** furniture

⚠ **WATCH OUT!**
The word **miniature** starts with **mini-**.

minibeast NOUN minibeasts
a very small creature such as an insect or spider

minibus NOUN minibuses
a small bus with seats for about ten people

minim NOUN minims
a musical note equal to two crotchets or half a
semibreve, written (♩)

⚙ **BUILD YOUR VOCABULARY**
Look at **crotchet**, **quaver** and **semibreve**.

minimum NOUN
the smallest number or amount possible
• You need a **minimum** of four players.
minimum ADJECTIVE
least or smallest • The **minimum** age for the ride is 8.

⚙ **BUILD YOUR VOCABULARY**
The opposite is **maximum**.

minion NOUN minions
a low-ranking assistant or helper

minister NOUN ministers
❶ a member of the government who is in charge
of a department ❷ a member of the clergy

ministry NOUN ministries
a government department • the **ministry** of
Education

mink *NOUN* minks
a small wild animal similar to a stoat, with brown fur

minnow *NOUN* minnows
a tiny freshwater fish

minor *ADJECTIVE*
not very important or serious • *We had a few minor problems.*

> ⚠ **WATCH OUT!**
> Minor ends in **-or**, like its opposite **major**. Don't confuse it with a **miner** meaning 'a mine worker'.

minority *(say my-nor-rit-ee) NOUN* minorities
the smaller part of a group of people or things; less than half • *Only a minority wanted to stay.*

> ⚙ **BUILD YOUR VOCABULARY**
> The opposite is **majority**.

Minotaur *NOUN*
in Greek myths, a creature that is part bull and part man

minstrel *NOUN* minstrels
a travelling singer and musician

mint *NOUN* mints
❶ a plant with sweet-smelling leaves used as a flavouring ❷ a sweet flavoured with a type of mint ❸ a place where a country's coins are made
> **in mint condition** in perfect condition; like new

minus *PREPOSITION*
❶ with the next number taken away; less
• *Eight minus two equals six (8 − 2 = 6).* ❷ less than zero • *The temperature is minus five degrees.*

minute *(say min-it) NOUN* minutes
❶ a measurement of time. There are 60 minutes in 1 hour and 60 seconds in 1 minute ❷ a short time
• *I'll come in a minute.*

minute *(say my-newt) ADJECTIVE*
tiny • *The baby mice are minute.*

miracle *NOUN* miracles
an unexpected and wonderful or magical event

miraculous *ADJECTIVE*
wonderful or magical
By lunchtime, the whole place was a seething mass of men, women and children all pushing and shoving to get

a glimpse of this miraculous fruit.—JAMES AND THE GIANT PEACH, Roald Dahl
> **miraculously** *ADVERB*

mirage *(say mirr-ahzh) NOUN* mirages
something that seems to be visible but is not really there, like a lake in a desert

mirror *NOUN* mirrors
a piece of glass or metal that reflects things clearly

mirth *NOUN*
laughter or fun

misbehave *VERB* misbehaves, misbehaving, misbehaved
to behave badly
> **misbehaviour** *NOUN*

mischief *NOUN*
behaviour that is naughty or causes trouble

mischievous *(say miss-chiv-us) ADJECTIVE*
naughty or liking to cause trouble
> **mischievously** *ADVERB*

> ⚠ **WATCH OUT!**
> The spelling of **mischievous** is tricky. There is an **ie** in the middle in **-chiev-** and it ends in **-vous**, NOT *-vious*.

miser *NOUN* misers
someone who stores money away and hates spending it
> **miserly** *ADJECTIVE*

miserable *ADJECTIVE*
❶ very unhappy • *He felt miserable.* ❷ unpleasant
• *What miserable weather!*
> **miserably** *ADVERB*

misery *NOUN* miseries
great unhappiness or suffering

misfire *VERB* misfires, misfiring, misfired
If a plan misfires, it goes wrong.

misfit *NOUN* misfits
someone who does not fit in well with other people

misfortune *NOUN* misfortunes
an unlucky event or an accident

mishap *(say mis-hap) NOUN* mishaps
an unfortunate accident

a b c d e f g h i j k l **m** n o p q r s t u v w x y z

misjudge *VERB* **misjudges, misjudging, misjudged**
to form a wrong idea or opinion about someone

mislay *VERB* **mislays, mislaying, mislaid**
to lose something for a short time

mislead *VERB* **misleads, misleading, misled**
to deliberately give someone a wrong idea
or impression

misprint *NOUN* **misprints**
a mistake in printing, such as a spelling mistake

miss *VERB* **misses, missing, missed**
❶ To miss something is to fail to hit or reach it.
• *The ball **missed** the basket.* ❷ If you miss someone
or something, you feel sad because they are not with
you. • *I **missed** my friend when she was away.*
❸ If you miss something, you do not go to it or see
it. • *He never **misses** school.* ❹ If you miss a bus,
train or plane, you fail to catch it.

miss *NOUN* **misses**
a failure to hit or reach something • *The shot was
a **miss**.*
➤ **Miss** a title for a girl or an unmarried woman

missile *NOUN* **missiles**
❶ a weapon that is fired a long distance and
explodes when it lands ❷ an object thrown at
someone

missing *ADJECTIVE*
lost or not in the proper place • *Some books are
missing.*

mission *NOUN* **missions**
an important task that someone is sent to do

missionary *NOUN* **missionaries**
someone who goes to another country to spread
a religious faith

misspell *VERB* **misspells, misspelling,
misspelt** or **misspelled**
to spell something wrongly

mist *NOUN* **mists**
damp cloudy air; a thin fog
➤ **misty** *ADJECTIVE* • *a **misty** day*

mistake *NOUN* **mistakes**
If you make a mistake, you do or say something wrong.

mistake *VERB* **mistakes, mistaking,
mistook, mistaken**
To mistake one person or thing for another is
to confuse them. • *I **mistook** him for his brother.*

mistaken *ADJECTIVE*
If you are mistaken, you are incorrect or wrong.
➤ **mistakenly** *ADVERB*

mister *NOUN*
❶ Mr ❷ *(informal)* sir • *Can you tell me the time,
mister?*

mistletoe
NOUN
a plant that
grows on trees
and has white
berries
in winter

mistreat *VERB* **mistreats, mistreating,
mistreated**
to treat someone badly or unfairly
➤ **mistreatment** *NOUN*

mistress *NOUN* **mistresses**
a woman who is in charge of something • *The dog
followed its **mistress**.*

mistrust *VERB* **mistrusts, mistrusting,
mistrusted**
not to trust someone
mistrust *NOUN*
a feeling of not trusting someone

misunderstand *VERB* **misunderstands,
misunderstanding, misunderstood**
to get a wrong idea or impression about something
• *I **misunderstood** the question.*
➤ **misunderstanding** *NOUN*

mite *NOUN* **mites**
❶ a small child ❷ a tiny insect
➤ **Not a mite** means not even a little bit.

mitten *NOUN* **mittens**
a glove without separate parts for the fingers

mix *VERB* **mixes, mixing, mixed**
to put, stir or shake things together to combine them
➤ **mixed** *ADJECTIVE* • *mixed nuts*

➤ **To mix up people** or **things** is to confuse them.

➤ **mixed up** ADJECTIVE • *I got their names **mixed up**.*

mixed fraction (also mixed number)

NOUN mixed fractions, mixed numbers
a number that contains a whole number and a fraction, for example $2\frac{1}{2}$

> **BUILD YOUR VOCABULARY**
> Look at **improper fraction**.

mixture NOUN mixtures

something made of different things mixed together • *Sleet is a **mixture** of rain and snow.*

ml ABBREVIATION

the abbreviation for **millilitre**

mm ABBREVIATION

the abbreviation for **millimetre**

moan VERB moans, moaning, moaned

❶ to make a low sound of pain or unhappiness ❷ to complain or grumble • *Stop **moaning** about the food.*

moan NOUN moans

a low sound of pain or unhappiness

moat NOUN moats

a deep ditch round a castle, usually filled with water

mob NOUN mobs

❶ a large disorderly crowd of people ❷ a gang

mob VERB mobs, mobbing, mobbed

people mob someone when they crowd round them • *The players were **mobbed** by fans wanting autographs.*

mobile ADJECTIVE

able to be moved or carried about easily
➤ **mobility** NOUN

mobile NOUN mobiles

❶ a mobile phone ❷ a hanging decoration which moves about in the air

mobile phone NOUN mobile phones

a telephone you can carry around with you

mock VERB mocks, mocking, mocked

to make fun of someone
➤ **mockery** NOUN

mock ADJECTIVE

not real or genuine • *She opened her mouth in **mock** surprise.*

modal verb NOUN modal verbs (in grammar)

a type of verb like *can, may, will* or *must* that is used with other verbs to express whether something is possible, certain or necessary • *A **modal verb** does not change its form: we say 'I can', 'she can' and 'they can'.*

> **BUILD YOUR VOCABULARY**
> Look at **auxiliary verb**.

mode NOUN modes

❶ a way of behaving or doing something • *Flying is the fastest **mode** of transport.* ❷ (in mathematics) the number in a set of numbers that appears the most

model NOUN models

❶ a small copy of an object • *a **model** of Big Ben* ❷ a particular version or design of something • *Your phone is like mine, but a newer **model**.* ❸ someone who displays clothes by wearing them or who poses for an artist or a photographer

model ADJECTIVE

❶ made as a small copy of something • *I built a **model** aeroplane.* ❷ perfect as an example for people to follow • *He's a **model** student.*

moderate ADJECTIVE

not too little and not too much; not extreme
➤ **moderately** ADVERB

modern ADJECTIVE

new and up to date • ***modern** equipment*

modest ADJECTIVE

❶ not boasting about how good you are ❷ fairly small or ordinary • *They lived in a **modest** house.*
➤ **modestly** ADVERB ➤ **modesty** NOUN

modify VERB modifies, modifying, modified

to change something slightly
➤ **modification** NOUN

module (say mod-yool) NOUN modules

a section of a spacecraft that can do something separately from the other parts

moist ADJECTIVE

slightly wet

moisten (say **moy**-sen) VERB moistens, moistening, moistened
to wet something slightly

moisture NOUN
tiny drops of water in the air or on a surface

molar (say **moh**-ler) NOUN molars
one of the wide teeth at the back of your mouth, used for crushing and grinding food

BUILD YOUR VOCABULARY
Look at **canine** and **incisor**.

mole NOUN moles
❶ a small furry animal that digs holes under the ground ❷ a small dark spot on the skin

molecule (say **mol**-ec-ule) NOUN molecules
the smallest part into which a substance can be divided without changing its chemical nature; a group of atoms
➤ **molecular** (say mol-ec-u-lar) ADJECTIVE

BUILD YOUR VOCABULARY
Look at **atom**.

mollusc NOUN molluscs
an animal with a soft body and no backbone, such as a snail or an oyster

BUILD YOUR VOCABULARY
A **mollusc** is an **invertebrate**.

molten ADJECTIVE
Molten rock or metal has been heated until it has melted.

moment NOUN moments
❶ a very short time • *Please wait a **moment**.*
❷ a point in time • *At that **moment**, all the lights went out.*
➤ **at the moment** now

momentary (say **moh**-men-ter-ee) ADJECTIVE
lasting for only a short time

momentum (say moh-**ment**-um) NOUN
the force and speed of something that is moving

monarch NOUN monarchs
a king or queen ruling a country

monarchy NOUN monarchies
a system in which a king or queen rules a country

monastery (say mon-a-**ster**-ee) NOUN monasteries
a place where monks live and work

money NOUN
coins and notes used to buy things

mongoose NOUN mongooses
a small animal like a large weasel that can kill snakes

mongrel (say **mung**-rel) NOUN mongrels
a dog of mixed breeds

monitor NOUN monitors
❶ a computer or television screen ❷ a device for checking something • *a heart **monitor*** ❸ a pupil who is given a special job to do at school

monitor VERB monitors, monitoring, monitored
to watch or test something to check it works properly

monk NOUN monks
a member of a religious community of men

monkey NOUN monkeys
an animal with hands and a long tail that can climb trees

BUILD YOUR VOCABULARY
Look at **ape** and **primate**.

monologue (say **mon**-o-log) NOUN monologues
a speech by one person or performer

monotonous (say mon-**ot**-on-us) ADJECTIVE
dull, boring and always staying the same
• *a **monotonous** voice*
➤ **monotonously** ADVERB

monsoon *NOUN* monsoons
a season of heavy rain and strong wind in south-east Asia

monster *NOUN* monsters
a huge frightening creature • *a terrifying sea monster*

monstrous *ADJECTIVE*
❶ huge, like a monster • *a monstrous spider*
❷ very shocking or bad • *a monstrous crime*

month *NOUN* months
one of the twelve parts into which a year is divided

WORD STORY
The word **month** is an Old English word related to **moon**, because time was measured by the phases of the moon.

monthly *ADJECTIVE, ADVERB*
happening every month • *a monthly magazine* • *The club meets monthly.*

monument *NOUN* monuments
something built to remind people of a person or event

moo *VERB* moos, mooing, mooed
to make the sound of a cow
moo *NOUN* moos
the sound a cow makes

mood *NOUN* moods
the way someone feels at a particular time • *I was in a good mood.*

moody *ADJECTIVE* moodier, moodiest
❶ gloomy or sulking • *He looked moody.*
❷ likely to have sudden changes of mood
➤ **moodily** *ADVERB* ➤ **moodiness** *NOUN*

moon *NOUN* moons
❶ the object that orbits the earth and shines at night ❷ a similar object that orbits another planet • *Titan is the largest of Saturn's moons.*

BUILD YOUR VOCABULARY
Look at **lunar**, **wane** and **wax**.

moonlight *NOUN*
light reflected from the moon

moor *NOUN* moors
an area of rough land covered with low plants

moor *VERB* moors, mooring, moored
To moor a boat is to tie it up to land.

moorhen *NOUN* moorhens
a small water bird with a red and yellow beak

mooring *NOUN* moorings
a place where a boat can be tied up

moose *NOUN* moose
a large North American deer

BUILD YOUR VOCABULARY
Look at **elk**.

mop *NOUN* mops
an object used for cleaning floors, with soft material on the end of a stick
mop *VERB* mops, mopping, mopped
to clean something with a mop

mope *VERB* mopes, moping, moped
to be miserable and not interested in doing anything

moral *ADJECTIVE*
❶ to do with what is right and wrong • *moral principles* ❷ good and right • *He was a very moral person.*
➤ **morally** *ADVERB*

BUILD YOUR VOCABULARY
The opposite of the second meaning is **immoral**.

moral *NOUN* morals
a lesson taught by a story or event • *The moral of the story is 'Help your friends'.*
➤ **Morals** are standards of behaviour.

more *DETERMINER*
greater in number or amount • *He had more sweets than I did.*
more *PRONOUN*
a larger number or amount • *Is there any more?*
more *ADVERB*
❶ to a greater extent • *Eat more slowly.* • *Try to exercise more.* ❷ again • *Let's try once more.*

moreover *ADVERB*
also; in addition

morning *NOUN* mornings
the early part of the day before noon

Morse code *NOUN*
a code for sending radio signals, using dots
(short sounds) and dashes (long sounds)

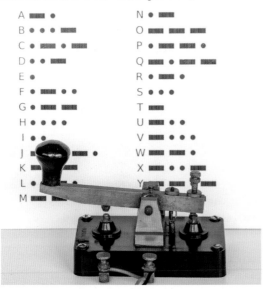

morsel *NOUN* morsels
a small piece of food

mortal *ADJECTIVE*
❶ unable to live forever • *All humans are **mortal**.*
❷ causing death • *a **mortal** wound*

> **BUILD** YOUR VOCABULARY
> Look at **fatal**.

mortal *NOUN* mortals
a human being or other mortal creature

mortar *NOUN*
a mixture used in building to stick bricks together

mosaic *(say* moh-**zay**-ik*) NOUN* mosaics
a design made from small coloured pieces of glass
or stone

mosque *(say* mosk*) NOUN* mosques
a building where Muslims worship

mosquito *(say* mosk-**kee**-toh*) NOUN* mosquitoes
an insect that sucks blood and carries disease

moss *NOUN* mosses
a plant that grows in damp places and has no flowers
➤ **mossy** *ADJECTIVE* • *a **mossy** stone*

most *DETERMINER*
greatest in number or amount • *Most people
like music.*

most *PRONOUN*
the greatest number or amount • *I ate **most** of
the food.*

most *ADVERB*
❶ more than any other • *I like this colour **most**.*
❷ very; extremely • *It was **most** unusual.*

mostly *ADVERB*
mainly

moth *NOUN* moths
an insect similar to a butterfly, that usually flies
at night

mother *NOUN* mothers
your female parent

> **BUILD** YOUR VOCABULARY
> Look at **maternal**.

mother-in-law *NOUN* mothers-in-law
the mother of someone's husband or wife

Mother's Day *NOUN*
a day of the year on which mothers are celebrated

motion *NOUN* motions
movement

motionless *ADJECTIVE*
not moving; still

motivate *VERB* motivates, motivating,
motivated
to make someone keen to achieve something

motive *NOUN* motives
A person's motive is what makes them do something.
• *What **motive** could he have for lying?*

motor *NOUN* motors
a machine that provides power to drive machinery

motorbike *(also* **motorcycle***) NOUN*
motorbikes, motorcycles
a vehicle with an engine, two wheels and a saddle
for the rider

motorway *NOUN* motorways
a wide road for fast long-distance traffic

mottled *ADJECTIVE*
marked with spots or patches of colour
• *a moth with **mottled** wings*

motto *NOUN* mottoes
a short saying used as a guide for behaviour
• *'Do your best' was his **motto**.*

mould *NOUN* moulds
❶ a container with a special shape, for making things like jelly ❷ a furry substance that grows on food when it goes bad
➤ **mouldy** *ADJECTIVE* • *This bread has gone **mouldy**.*
mould *VERB* moulds, moulding, moulded
to make something have a particular shape

moult *(say* molt *or* mohlt*) VERB* moults, moulting, moulted
When animals or birds moult, they lose hair or feathers.

mound *NOUN* mounds
a pile of earth or stones; a small hill

mount *VERB* mounts, mounting, mounted
❶ to climb up or get up onto something • *She **mounted** her horse.* ❷ to display something
• *A stuffed deer's head was **mounted** on the wall.*
mount *NOUN* mounts
❶ a mountain, especially in names such as *Mount Everest* ❷ a horse or other animal for someone to ride

mountain *NOUN* mountains
a very high hill
➤ **mountainous** *ADJECTIVE* • *Chile is very **mountainous**.*

mountaineer *NOUN* mountaineers
someone who climbs mountains as a sport
➤ **mountaineering** *NOUN*

mourn *VERB* mourns, mourning, mourned
to be sad, especially because someone has died
➤ **mourner** *NOUN*

mournful *ADJECTIVE*
sad and sorrowful • *I heard a **mournful** cry.*
➤ **mournfully** *ADVERB*

mouse *NOUN* mice
❶ a small animal with a long tail and a pointed nose

BUILD YOUR VOCABULARY
A **mouse** is a **rodent**.

❷ a small device that you move to control the movements of the cursor on a computer screen

moustache *(say* mus-**tahsh***) NOUN* moustaches
a strip of hair that a man grows above his upper lip

mouth *NOUN* mouths
❶ Your mouth is the part of your face you use for eating and speaking. ❷ The mouth of a river is the place where it flows into the sea. ❸ The mouth of a cave is its entrance.

mouthful *NOUN* mouthfuls
an amount of food you put in your mouth

move *VERB* moves, moving, moved
❶ To move something is to put it in a different place or position. • *Who **moved** my bag?*
❷ To move is to change place or position.
• *Don't **move!*** ❸ If something moves you, it makes you feel strong emotion. • *Their story **moved** us deeply.*
➤ **movable** *ADJECTIVE* • *a chair with **movable** arms*
move *NOUN* moves
❶ a movement ❷ a player's turn in a game

movement *NOUN* movements
an act of moving • *He made a sudden **movement**.*
• *the **movement** of the planets*

movie *NOUN* movies
a film

moving *ADJECTIVE*
making you feel strong emotion

a b c d e f g h i j k l m n o p q r s t u v w x y z

mow VERB mows, mowing, mowed, mown
To mow grass is to cut it.

Mr (say miss-ter) NOUN
a title used before a man's name

Mrs (say miss-iz) NOUN
a title used before a married woman's name

Ms (say miz) NOUN
a title used before a woman's name

much DETERMINER, PRONOUN more, most
a large amount • There was **much** excitement.
• Much remains to be done.
➤ how much used to ask about a quantity
• How much time do we have?
➤ not much a small amount • Not much happened.
• He didn't eat **much**.

much ADVERB
used in comparisons to mean 'a lot'
• This tastes **much** better.

muck NOUN
dirt, mud or manure

muck VERB mucks, mucking, mucked
(informal)
➤ To muck about or muck around is to waste
time behaving stupidly.

mud NOUN
wet soft earth

muddle VERB muddles, muddling, muddled
❶ To muddle things is to mix them up.
❷ To muddle someone is to confuse them.
➤ muddled ADJECTIVE

muddle NOUN muddles
a confused or messy state • I got in a **muddle**
with my maths.

muddy ADJECTIVE muddier, muddiest
covered in mud

muezzin NOUN muezzins
a man who calls Muslims to prayer from a minaret

muffin NOUN muffins
a small sponge cake
• a blueberry **muffin**

muffled ADJECTIVE
A muffled sound is quiet
and unclear.

mug NOUN mugs
a large cup

mulberry NOUN mulberries
a soft purple berry that grows on a tree

mule NOUN mules
an animal that is produced by a female horse
and a male donkey

multiple NOUN multiples
a number that can be divided exactly by another
number • 30 and 50 are **multiples** of 10.

multiple ADJECTIVE
having many parts

multiplication NOUN
the process of multiplying numbers

multiply VERB multiplies, multiplying,
multiplied
❶ If you multiply a number, you add it to itself a
certain number of times. • Five **multiplied** by four
equals twenty (5 x 4 = 20). ❷ To multiply is to
increase. • His doubts started to **multiply**.

multitude NOUN multitudes
a very large number of people or things

mum NOUN mums (informal)
mother

mumble VERB mumbles, mumbling,
mumbled
to speak softly and unclearly

mummify VERB mummifies, mummifying,
mummified
to prepare a dead body as a mummy
➤ mummification NOUN

mummy
NOUN mummies
❶ (informal) mother
❷ in ancient Egypt, a dead
body that was wrapped in cloth
and treated with oils to preserve it

mumps *NOUN*
an infectious disease that makes the neck swell painfully

munch *VERB* munches, munching, munched
to chew food noisily

mural *NOUN* murals
a picture painted on a wall

murder *VERB* murders, murdering, murdered
to kill someone deliberately
➤ **murderer** *NOUN*

murder *NOUN* murders
the deliberate killing of someone

murderous *ADJECTIVE*
seeming likely to kill someone
Who knows what murderous beasts lurk in there?
—JACK HOLBORN, Leon Garfield

murky *ADJECTIVE* murkier, murkiest
dark and gloomy • *a cold and murky cave*
➤ **murkiness** *NOUN*

murmur *NOUN* murmurs
a low continuous sound, especially of people speaking

murmur *VERB* murmurs, murmuring, murmured
to speak quietly

muscle *NOUN* muscles
Your muscles are the bundles of fibres that stretch to move your body.

⚠ **WATCH OUT!**
Don't confuse **muscles**, which are spelt with **-sc-** and **mussels**, which are shellfish and have double **s**.

muscular *(say* musk-yoo-ler*) ADJECTIVE*
having a lot of strong muscles

muse *VERB* muses, musing, mused
to think or wonder about something
• *'I wonder why?' she mused.*

museum *NOUN* museums
a place where interesting or valuable objects are displayed for people to see

mush *NOUN*
a thick soft mass • *The squashed cake had turned to mush.*

mushroom *NOUN* mushrooms
a plant with a short stem and a round top. Many mushrooms can be eaten.

⚙ **BUILD YOUR VOCABULARY**
A **mushroom** is a **fungus**.

music *NOUN*
❶ pleasant sounds made by instruments or by singing • *I heard music.* ❷ printed or written symbols representing musical sounds • *Here's the music for the song.*

musical *ADJECTIVE*
❶ to do with music • *a musical instrument*
❷ good at music or interested in it • *She's very musical.*
➤ **musically** *ADVERB*

musical *NOUN* musicals
a play or film with music and songs

musician *NOUN* musicians
someone who plays a musical instrument

musket *NOUN* muskets
an old type of gun with a long barrel

Muslim *(say* mooz-lim *or* muz-lim*) NOUN* Muslims
someone who follows the religion of Islam
➤ **Muslim** *ADJECTIVE*

muslin *NOUN*
a type of fine cotton cloth

✷ **WORD STORY**
Muslin comes from *Mosel*, a city in Iraq where the cloth was originally made.

mussel *NOUN* mussels
a shellfish with a black shell, often found sticking to rocks

⚙ **BUILD YOUR VOCABULARY**
A **mussel** is a **mollusc**.

must *VERB*
❶ If someone must do something, they have to do it.
• *You must be careful.* ❷ If something must be true, it is very likely. • *That must be his sister.*

⚙ **BUILD YOUR VOCABULARY**
Must is a **modal verb**.

mustard *NOUN*
a yellow sauce or powder with a hot taste

a
b
c
d
e
f
g
h
i
j
k
l
m
n
o
p
q
r
s
t
u
v
w
x
y
z

muster VERB musters, mustering, mustered
to manage to gather together or find something
'What . . . do you suppose . . . I am?' 'Um . . . a wolf?'
said Measle, with all the politeness he could muster.
—MEASLE: THE PITS OF PERIL!, Ian Ogilvy

musty ADJECTIVE mustier, mustiest
smelling or tasting mouldy or stale

mutant NOUN mutants
a living creature that is different from others of the
same type because of changes in its genes

mute ADJECTIVE
not speaking or not able to speak
➤ **mutely** ADVERB

mutiny (say **mew**-tin-ee) NOUN mutinies
a rebellion by sailors or soldiers against their officers
mutiny (say **mew**-tin-ee) VERB mutinies,
mutinying, mutinied
to take part in a rebellion against officers
➤ **mutineer** NOUN

mutter VERB mutters, muttering, muttered
to murmur or grumble in a low voice • *He muttered*
something under his breath.

mutton NOUN
meat from an adult sheep

mutual (say **mew**-tew-al) ADJECTIVE
true for both or all of the people involved
• *The deal was to their mutual advantage.*
➤ **mutually** ADVERB

muzzle NOUN muzzles
an animal's nose and mouth

my DETERMINER
belonging to me • *That's my bike over there.*

myriad ADJECTIVE
very many; countless • *the myriad stars in the*
night sky

myself PRONOUN
❶ used instead of 'me' when you do something and
are also affected by it • *I saw myself in the mirror.*
❷ on my own, without help • *I made the card*
myself.
➤ **by myself** on my own; alone • *They left me*
by myself.

mysterious ADJECTIVE
full of mystery; strange and puzzling
• *Mysterious noises came from inside the trunk.*
➤ **mysteriously** ADVERB • *He mysteriously*
vanished.

mystery NOUN mysteries
something strange or puzzling • *Why the ship sank*
is a mystery.

mystify VERB mystifies, mystifying,
mystified
to puzzle someone very much

myth (say mith) NOUN myths
❶ an ancient story, especially one about gods,
goddesses and heroes ❷ an untrue story or
belief • *It is a myth that carrots help you see in*
the dark.

mythical ADJECTIVE
imaginary; found in myths • *mythical creatures*

⚙ N is for **neologism**, which means 'new word'. In the early 20th century the word *television* was a neologism that described a new invention. In the 1970s the word *Internet* was invented to describe a computer network.

⚙ Can you think of any neologisms invented in the 21st century?

nag *VERB* **nags, nagging, nagged**
to keep criticising or complaining to someone

nail *NOUN* **nails**
❶ Your nails are the hard coverings on the end of your fingers or toes. ❷ a small sharp piece of metal used to fix things together
nail *VERB* **nails, nailing, nailed**
to fasten something somewhere with a nail

naive *(say* ny-**eev***) ADJECTIVE*
too trusting and innocent
➤ **naively** *ADVERB*

naked *(say* **nay**-kid*) ADJECTIVE*
without any clothes or coverings on
➤ **nakedness** *NOUN*

name *NOUN* **names**
Someone's or something's name is what they are called.
name *VERB* **names, naming, named**
to give something or someone a name • *We named the puppy Buster.*

nameless *ADJECTIVE*
not having a name or not identified

nanny *NOUN* **nannies**
a woman whose job is to look after someone else's children in their house

nanny goat *NOUN* **nanny goats**
a female goat

⚙ **BUILD YOUR VOCABULARY**
A male goat is a **billy goat**.

nap *NOUN* **naps**
a short sleep
nap *VERB* **naps, napping, napped**
to have a short sleep

napkin *NOUN* **napkins**
a piece of cloth or paper for wiping your hands and mouth at meals

nappy *NOUN* **nappies**
a piece of cloth or a paper pad put round a baby's bottom

narcissus *(say* nar-**sis**-us*) NOUN* **narcissi**
(say nar-**sis**-eye*)*
a garden flower that grows from a bulb in the spring

narrate *VERB* **narrates, narrating, narrated**
to tell a story to someone • *Sophie **narrated** her dream to the BFG.*

narrative *NOUN* **narratives**
a story or an account

narrator *NOUN* **narrators**
the person who is telling a story

narrow *ADJECTIVE* **narrower, narrowest**
not wide • *They squeezed through a **narrow** gap in the rocks.*

narrowly *ADVERB*
only just • *A rock fell, **narrowly** missing his foot.*

narwhal *NOUN* **narwhals**
a small Arctic whale with a long twisted tusk

a
b
c
d
e
f
g
h
i
j
k
l
m
n
p
q
r
s
t
u
v
w
x
y
z

nasturtium *(say* nast-**er**-shum*)* NOUN **nasturtiums**
a garden flower with round leaves and orange or yellow flowers

nasty ADJECTIVE **nastier, nastiest**
very unpleasant
➤ **nastily** ADVERB ➤ **nastiness** NOUN

nation NOUN **nations**
a country and the people who live there

national ADJECTIVE
to do with a whole country • *the national championships*

nationality NOUN **nationalities**
the nation someone belongs to • *His nationality is Canadian.*

native NOUN **natives**
a person born in a particular place • *He is a native of Sweden.*
native ADJECTIVE
related to the country where you were born
• *English is not her native language.*

Native American NOUN **Native Americans**
one of the people whose ancestors were living in North, Central or South America before Europeans arrived

nativity *(say* na-**tiv**-it-ee*)* NOUN **nativities**
someone's birth
➤ **the Nativity** the birth of Jesus Christ

natural ADJECTIVE
❶ existing in or made by nature, not made by people
• *natural materials such as wood* ❷ normal; not surprising • *It's natural to be upset when you lose.*
❸ A natural ability is one you were born with.

natural history NOUN
the study of plants and animals

naturally ADVERB
❶ as you would expect • *Naturally, we were worried.*
❷ in a way that comes from nature and is not made by people • *naturally curly hair* ❸ in a way that is part of the character you were born with • *She is naturally optimistic.*

nature NOUN **natures**
❶ everything in the world that was not made by people, such as plants and animals ❷ Someone's nature is the character they were born with.
• *She has a kind nature.*

nature reserve NOUN **nature reserves**
an area of land kept for wildlife

naughty ADJECTIVE **naughtier, naughtiest**
rude or disobedient
➤ **naughtily** ADVERB ➤ **naughtiness** NOUN

⚠ **WATCH OUT!**
Naughty has a tricky spelling! There is no **o** and it has a silent **gh**.

nausea NOUN
a feeling of sickness or disgust

nautical ADJECTIVE
connected with ships or sailors

naval ADJECTIVE
to do with a navy

navel NOUN **navels**
the small hollow on your stomach; your belly button

navigate VERB **navigates, navigating, navigated**
to make sure that an aircraft, ship or vehicle is going in the right direction
➤ **navigation** NOUN ➤ **navigator** NOUN

navy NOUN **navies**
❶ a fleet of ships and the people trained to use them ❷ (**navy blue**) very dark blue

near PREPOSITION
not far away from something • *She lives near the school.*
near ADVERB, ADJECTIVE **nearer, nearest**
not far away • *Come nearer.* • *Where is the nearest bus stop?*
➤ **near by** at a place not far away • *They live near by.*
near VERB **nears, nearing, neared**
to come close to a place or point • *They were nearing the end of their quest.*

nearby ADVERB, ADJECTIVE
near; not far away • *We live nearby.* • *a nearby town*

nearly ADVERB
almost • It was **nearly** midnight.

neat ADJECTIVE neater, neatest
tidy and carefully arranged • neat handwriting
➤ **neatly** ADVERB ➤ **neatness** NOUN

nebula NOUN nebulae
a cloud of gas and dust in outer space

necessarily ADVERB
for certain; definitely • It won't **necessarily** cost a lot.

necessary ADJECTIVE
needed • It is not **necessary** to apologise.

⚠ **WATCH OUT!**
There is a double **s** in **necessary** but only one **c**.

necessity NOUN necessities
❶ need • There is no **necessity** for you to come.
❷ A necessity is something needed. • She packed a few **necessities**.

neck NOUN necks
❶ Your neck is the part of your body that joins your head and shoulders. ❷ a narrow part of something, especially of a bottle

necklace NOUN necklaces
a piece of jewellery you wear round your neck

nectar NOUN
a sweet liquid collected by bees from flowers

nectarine NOUN nectarines
a kind of peach with a smooth skin

need VERB needs, needing, needed
If you need something or need to do something, it is necessary. • I **need** some help. • We **need** to leave now.

need NOUN needs
❶ A need is something that you need. ❷ Need is a situation in which something is necessary. • There's no **need** to shout.

needle NOUN needles
❶ a very thin pointed piece of metal used for sewing ❷ a long thin and sharp object • knitting needles • pine needles ❸ the pointer of a meter or compass

needy ADJECTIVE needier, neediest
very poor

negative ADJECTIVE
❶ A negative statement or answer is one that says 'no' or has 'no' or 'not' in it. ❷ A negative number is less than zero. ❸ bad or harmful • the **negative** effects of tourism
➤ **negatively** ADVERB

⬤ **BUILD YOUR VOCABULARY**
The opposite is **positive**.

negative NOUN negatives
❶ something that means 'no' • She replied in the **negative**. ❷ a disadvantage or bad thing

⬤ **BUILD YOUR VOCABULARY**
The opposite for the first meaning is **positive**.

neglect VERB neglects, neglecting, neglected
to fail to look after someone or something or deal with them
neglect NOUN
failure to look after someone or do something

negotiate (say nig-oh-shee-ate) VERB negotiates, negotiating, negotiated
to try to reach an agreement about something by discussing it
➤ **negotiation** NOUN

neigh VERB neighs, neighing, neighed
to make a high sound like a horse
neigh NOUN neighs
the high sound a horse makes

neighbour NOUN neighbours
someone who lives next door or near to you
➤ **neighbouring** ADJECTIVE

⚠ **WATCH OUT!**
Neighbour has a tricky spelling! It is one of the words in which the 'ey' sound is spelt eigh, like **weigh** and **weight**.

neighbourhood NOUN neighbourhoods
Your neighbourhood is the area around where you live.

a
b
c
d
e
f
g
h
i
j
k
l
m
n
o
p
q
r
s
t
u
v
w
x
y
z

neither *(say* ny-*ther or* nee-*ther)*
DETERMINER, PRONOUN
not either • *Neither boy can swim.* • *Neither of us wants to go.*

neither CONJUNCTION
and not; used to add another negative statement • *She can't do it and* **neither** *can I.*
➤ **neither . . . nor . . .** not one and not the other • *Neither mum* **nor** *dad said anything.*

neon *(say* nee-on*)* NOUN
a gas used to make glowing coloured lights and signs

nephew NOUN nephews
Someone's nephew is their brother's or sister's son.

nerve NOUN nerves
❶ one of the fibres inside your body that carry messages to and from your brain ❷ courage and calmness • *Don't lose your* **nerve**.
➤ **nerves** nervousness • *He was shaking with* **nerves** *before the play.*

nervous ADJECTIVE
feeling worried or easily worried
➤ **nervously** ADVERB ➤ **nervousness** NOUN

nest NOUN nests
❶ the place where a bird lays its eggs and feeds its young ❷ the home of a small animal or insect
nest VERB nests, nesting, nested
to make a nest somewhere • *Gulls* **nest** *on the cliffs.*

nestle VERB nestles, nestling, nestled
to curl up comfortably

net NOUN nets
❶ Net is material made of horizontal and vertical threads that cross each other with holes between.
❷ A net is a piece of this material, used for example for catching fish. ❸ The Net is the Internet.
❹ *(in mathematics)* A net is a drawing of a solid shape as it would look if it were opened out flat.

netball NOUN
a game in which two teams try to throw a ball through a high net hanging from a ring

nettle NOUN nettles
a wild plant with leaves that sting when you touch them

network NOUN networks
❶ a number of lines that cross each other
❷ a system with many parts that are connected to each other, such as a railway or computer system

neutral *(say* new-tral*)* ADJECTIVE
not supporting either side in a war or quarrel

never ADVERB
at no time; not ever

never-ending ADJECTIVE
lasting or seeming to last forever • *I walked along a* **never-ending** *corridor.*

nevertheless ADVERB
in spite of this; even so
He knows everyone and is well liked, but nevertheless, he's an outsider.—BETWEEN TWO SEAS, Marie-Louise Jensen

new ADJECTIVE newer, newest
❶ recently bought, made or received • *Is that a* **new** *top?* ❷ different • *I'm moving to a* **new** *school.*
➤ **newness** NOUN

newcomer NOUN newcomers
someone who has recently arrived in a place

newly ADVERB
recently • *the smell of* **newly** *cut grass*

new moon NOUN new moons
the moon when it appears as a thin crescent

BUILD YOUR VOCABULARY
Look at **full moon**.

news NOUN
❶ new information about people or recent events • *I've got some good* **news**. ❷ a radio or television report about important events

newsagent NOUN newsagents
a shopkeeper who sells newspapers and magazines

newspaper NOUN newspapers
a set of large folded sheets of paper printed with news reports and articles

newt NOUN newts
a small animal similar to a lizard, that lives near or in water

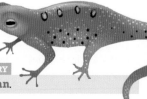

BUILD YOUR VOCABULARY
A **newt** is an **amphibian**.

next ADJECTIVE
❶ The next thing or person is the one that comes after this one. • *I'll see you next week.* ❷ The next place is the nearest one. • *They live in the next street.*
➤ **next to** in the nearest place to; to one side of • *Sit next to me.*

next ADVERB
immediately after something or someone • *What comes next?*

next door ADVERB, ADJECTIVE
in the next house or room • *Who lives next door?*
➤ **next-door** ADJECTIVE • *our next-door neighbours*

nib NOUN nibs
the part at the end of a pen where the ink comes out

nibble VERB nibbles, nibbling, nibbled
to take small or gentle bites at something
nibble NOUN nibbles
a small bite of something

nice ADJECTIVE nicer, nicest
pleasant • *It was a nice day.*
➤ **nicely** ADVERB ➤ **niceness** NOUN

nickname NOUN nicknames
an informal name for someone or something • *The pirate's nickname was 'Billy Two-Scars.'*

niece NOUN nieces
Someone's niece is their brother's or sister's daughter.

night NOUN nights
the dark part of the day, between sunset and sunrise

BUILD YOUR VOCABULARY
Look at **nocturnal**.

WATCH OUT!
Don't confuse **night** with a **knight** (a medieval fighter).

nightdress NOUN nightdresses
a loose light dress for a girl or woman to wear in bed

nightfall NOUN
the time when it becomes dark just after sunset

nightingale NOUN nightingales
a small brown bird that sings sweetly

nightly ADJECTIVE
happening every night

nightmare NOUN nightmares
❶ a frightening dream ❷ an unpleasant or frightening experience
➤ **nightmarish** ADJECTIVE terrifying

✳ **WORD STORY**
The *mare* in **nightmare** was an old word for a female evil spirit that was thought to cause bad dreams.

nightshirt NOUN nightshirts
a long shirt for wearing in bed

night-time NOUN
the time between evening and morning

nil NOUN
nothing • *We lost three-nil.*

nimble ADJECTIVE nimbler, nimblest
moving quickly and easily
➤ **nimbly** ADVERB

nip VERB nips, nipping, nipped
to pinch or bite someone sharply
nip NOUN nips
a quick pinch or bite

nitrogen (say **ny**-tro-jen) NOUN
a gas that makes up about 78% of the air

⚙ **BUILD YOUR VOCABULARY**
Nitrogen is an **element**.

no EXCLAMATION
a word you say when you disagree or when you refuse • *No, I don't want to go.*
no DETERMINER, ADVERB
not any • *There is no food left.* • *The creature was no bigger than my thumb.*

nobility NOUN
❶ people of high social rank ❷ the quality of being noble

noble ADJECTIVE nobler, noblest
❶ good and generous or brave • *It was a noble thing to do.* ❷ of high social rank • *She was of noble birth.*
➤ **nobly** ADVERB • *She nobly offered to give up her place.*
noble NOUN nobles
a person of high social rank

nobleman or **noblewoman** *NOUN*
noblemen, noblewomen
a man or woman of high social rank

nobody *PRONOUN*
no person; not anyone • *Nobody knows.*

> **BUILD YOUR VOCABULARY**
> A synonym is **no one**.

nocturnal *(say* noc-**turn**-al*) ADJECTIVE*
happening or active at night • *Badgers are **nocturnal** animals.*

nod *VERB* nods, nodding, nodded
If you nod or nod your head, you move your head up and down to show you agree.

noise *NOUN* noises
a sound, especially one that is loud or unpleasant

noisy *ADJECTIVE* noisier, noisiest
making a lot of noise
➤ **noisily** *ADVERB*

nomad *(say* no-mad*)* nomads *NOUN*
a person who does not have a permanent home but moves around, usually with their animals
➤ **nomadic** *ADJECTIVE*

nominate *VERB* nominates, nominating, nominated
to suggest someone should have a job, position or award
➤ **nomination** *NOUN*

non-countable *ADJECTIVE (in grammar)*
A non-countable noun cannot be counted and does not have a plural. • *'Traffic' is a **non-countable** noun.*

> **BUILD YOUR VOCABULARY**
> The opposite is **countable**.

none *PRONOUN*
not any; not one • *None of us went.*

nonetheless *ADVERB*
nevertheless

non-fiction *NOUN*
writing or books containing true information about real things and events

nonsense *NOUN*
❶ words that do not mean anything or make any sense ❷ very silly ideas or behaviour

non-stop *ADVERB, ADJECTIVE*
not stopping • *They talked **non-stop**.* • *a **non-stop** train*

noodles *NOUN*
pasta made in long thin strips

nook *NOUN* nooks
a quiet corner or place • *a hidden **nook** in the forest*

noon *NOUN*
twelve o'clock midday

no one *PRONOUN*
no person; not anyone

noose *NOUN* nooses
a loop in a rope that tightens when the rope is pulled

nor *CONJUNCTION*
and not; used to add another negative statement
• *She can't do it and **nor** can I.*

> **BUILD YOUR VOCABULARY**
> Look at **neither**.

normal *ADJECTIVE*
usual or ordinary • *It was just a **normal** day.*
➤ **normally** *ADVERB* • *We **normally** have lunch at 1.*

north *NOUN*
North is the direction to the left of a person facing east or a place that is in this direction. • *There are mountains in the **north**.*

north *ADVERB*
towards the north • *They sailed **north**.*

north *ADJECTIVE*
coming from the north • *a **north** wind*

north-east NOUN, ADJECTIVE, ADVERB
midway between north and east

northern ADJECTIVE
from or to do with the north • *a northern town*

north-west NOUN, ADJECTIVE, ADVERB
midway between north and west

nose NOUN noses
❶ Your nose is the part of your face that you use for breathing and smelling. ❷ the front part of a vehicle or aircraft

nose VERB noses, nosing, nosed
to move forward slowly or carefully • *The ship nosed through the ice.*

nostalgia *(say* nosss-tal-ja*)* NOUN
the feeling of remembering something that made you happy in the past
➤ **nostalgic** ADJECTIVE

nostril NOUN nostrils
Your nostrils are the two openings in your nose.

✳ **WORD STORY**
The word **nostril** comes from an Old English word meaning 'nose hole'.

nosy *(also* **nosey***)* ADJECTIVE nosier, nosiest *(informal)*
always wanting to know other people's business
➤ **nosiness** NOUN

not ADVERB
a word you use to make something mean the opposite • *'Easy' means 'not difficult.'* • *'You broke it.' —'I did not.'*

notable ADJECTIVE
famous or worth remembering • *a notable achievement*

notch NOUN notches
a small V-shaped cut or mark

note NOUN notes
❶ something you write down as a reminder • *I took some notes while she was speaking.* ❷ a short letter ❸ a single sound in music ❹ a piece of paper money • *a five-pound note*

note VERB notes, noting, noted
❶ to notice or pay attention to something
• *They noted landmarks along the way.* ❷ to write something down

notebook NOUN notebooks
❶ a book in which you write things down ❷ a small computer that you can carry around

nothing PRONOUN
not anything

notice NOUN notices
❶ a written or printed message put up for people to see ❷ attention that you pay to something • *I took no notice of him.*

notice VERB notices, noticing, noticed
to see or become aware of something • *Did you notice anything unusual?*

noticeable ADJECTIVE
easy to see or notice

notion NOUN notions
an idea, especially a strange or wrong one
• *Where did you get that notion?*

notorious ADJECTIVE
well known for doing something bad
• *a notorious criminal*

nought *(say* nawt*)* NOUN noughts
❶ the figure 0

⚙ **BUILD YOUR VOCABULARY**
A synonym is **zero**.

❷ nothing

noun NOUN nouns
a word that stands for a person, place or thing, for example *girl*, *sun*, *school* or *truth*. Most nouns can be used after *the*.

⚙ **BUILD YOUR VOCABULARY**
Noun is a **word class**.
Look at **collective noun** and **proper noun**.

noun phrase NOUN noun phrases *(in grammar)*
a group of words that has a noun in it and is used like a noun. In this sentence, the noun phrase is in bold: *Suddenly, a big brown bear with sharp claws appeared.*

nourish VERB nourishes, nourishing, nourished
to give someone enough good food
➤ **nourishment** NOUN • *They needed* ***nourishment***.

novel NOUN novels
a book that tells a long imaginary story

novel ADJECTIVE
new and unusual • *What a* ***novel*** *idea.*

novelist (*say* nov-el-ist) NOUN novelists
someone who writes novels

novelty NOUN novelties
❶ the quality of being new or unusual • *The* ***novelty*** *of living in a tent soon wore off.* ❷ something new and unusual

novice NOUN novices
a beginner

now ADVERB
at this time • *How tall are you* ***now***? • *We have to go* ***now***.
➤ **now and again** or **now and then** occasionally; sometimes

now CONJUNCTION
since or as • *Mum lets me stay up later* ***now*** *I'm 8.*

nowadays ADVERB
at the present time

nowhere ADVERB
not anywhere

nozzle NOUN nozzles
the end part of a hose or pipe

nuclear (*say* new-klee-er) ADJECTIVE
using the energy that is created by splitting atoms • ***nuclear*** *power*

nucleus (*say* new-klee-us) NOUN nuclei (*say* new-klee-eye)
the central part of an atom or cell

nude ADJECTIVE
not wearing any clothes

nudge VERB nudges, nudging, nudged
to touch or push someone with your elbow
nudge NOUN nudges
a gentle push with your elbow

nugget NOUN nuggets
a small rough lump of something, especially gold

nuisance NOUN nuisances
an annoying person or thing

numb ADJECTIVE
unable to feel anything
➤ **numbness** NOUN

number NOUN numbers
❶ a symbol or word that tells you how many of something there are • *He wrote the* ***number*** *3.* ❷ a quantity of things or people • *I disagree, for a* ***number*** *of reasons.* ❸ a telephone number • *I'll give you my* ***number***.

number VERB numbers, numbering, numbered
to mark things with numbers • ***Number*** *the items on the list.*

numeracy NOUN
the ability to understand and use numbers

numeral NOUN numerals
a symbol that represents a number

BUILD YOUR VOCABULARY
Look at **Arabic numeral** and **Roman numeral**.

numerator NOUN numerators
the number above the line in a fraction. In $\frac{1}{4}$ the numerator is the number 1.

BUILD YOUR VOCABULARY
Look at **denominator**.

numerous ADJECTIVE
many • *She is the author of* ***numerous*** *books.*

nun NOUN nuns
a member of a religious community of women

nurse NOUN nurses
a person trained to look after people who are ill or injured
nurse VERB nurses, nursing, nursed
to look after someone when they are ill or injured

nursery NOUN nurseries
❶ a place where young children are looked after
❷ a place where plants are grown and sold

nursery rhyme *NOUN* nursery rhymes
a simple poem or song for young children

nursery school *NOUN* nursery schools
a school for children aged 3 to 5

nurture *VERB* nurtures, nurturing, nurtured
to look after someone or something

nut *NOUN* nuts
❶ a fruit with a hard shell ❷ a small piece of metal for screwing on to a bolt

nutmeg *NOUN* nutmegs
a hard seed that is used as a spice

nutrient *(say* new-tree-ent*) NOUN* nutrients
a substance that a plant or animal needs to live and grow

nutrition *(say* new-**trish**-on*) NOUN*
the food someone needs to keep them alive and healthy

nutritious *(say* new-**trish**-us*) ADJECTIVE*
nutritious food helps you to grow and be healthy

nuzzle *VERB* nuzzles, nuzzling, nuzzled
to rub your nose gently against someone

nylon *NOUN*
a light strong artificial fibre used for making tents, ropes and some clothes

nymph *NOUN* nymphs
in myths, a young goddess living in trees, rivers or the sea

a
b
c
d
e
f
g
h
i
j
k
l
m
n
o
p
q
r
s
t
u
v
w
x
y
z

Oo

O is for **onomatopoeia**, which means using a word that sounds like the thing it describes, for example *buzz* or *plop*.

How many examples of *onomatopoeia* can you think of?

oak NOUN oaks
a large tree that produces seeds called acorns

oar NOUN oars
a pole with a flat blade at one end, used for rowing a boat

oasis *(say oh-ay-sis)* NOUN oases
a fertile place with water and trees in a desert

oath NOUN oaths
❶ a solemn promise ❷ a swear word

oatmeal NOUN
ground oats, used to make porridge

oats NOUN
a cereal used to make food for humans and animals

obedient ADJECTIVE
An obedient person does as they are told.
➤ **obedience** NOUN ➤ **obediently** ADVERB

⚠ **WATCH OUT!**
Remember that **obedient** and **obedience** end in **-ent** and **-ence**, like **innocent** and **innocence**.

obey VERB obeys, obeying, obeyed
If you obey a person or rule, you do what they say.

object *(say ob-ject)* NOUN objects
❶ a thing that can be seen or touched ❷ the purpose of something • *The object of the game is to match the cards.* ❸ *(in grammar)* the person or thing that is affected by the action of a verb in a sentence,

for example *the ball* in the sentence *The boy kicked the ball.*

⚙ **BUILD YOUR VOCABULARY**
Look at **subject**.

object *(say ob-ject)* VERB objects, objecting, objected
To object to something or someone is to say that you do not like them or do not agree.

objection NOUN objections
If you have an objection to something, you dislike or disagree with it.

objective NOUN objectives
an aim; something you are trying to achieve

obligation NOUN obligations
a duty

oblige VERB obliges, obliging, obliged
❶ If you are obliged to do something, you have to do it. • *As there were no chairs, we were obliged to stand.* ❷ If you are obliged, you are grateful to someone. • *I'd be obliged if you could make less noise.* ❸ to be helpful to someone • *I'd be happy to oblige you.*

oblong NOUN oblongs
a rectangle that is longer than it is wide
➤ **oblong** ADJECTIVE • *an oblong table*

oboe *(say oh-boh)* NOUN oboes
a musical instrument similar to a **clarinet** with a high sound

⚙ **BUILD YOUR VOCABULARY**
An **oboe** is a **woodwind instrument**.

obscure ADJECTIVE obscurer, obscurest
difficult to see or understand; unclear • *The meaning of the poem was obscure.*
➤ **obscurely** ADVERB ➤ **obscurity** NOUN

obscure VERB obscures, obscuring, obscured
to hide something; to make something difficult to see or understand • *Mist obscured the path.*

observant ADJECTIVE
quick to notice things
➤ **observantly** ADVERB

⚠ **WATCH OUT!**
Remember that **observant** has an a in its ending **-ant**, like 'observation'.

observation *NOUN* observations
1. the act of watching something carefully
2. An observation is a comment or remark.

observatory *(say ob-zerv-a-ter-ee) NOUN* observatories
a building with telescopes for looking at the stars or weather

observe *VERB* observes, observing, observed
1. to watch something or someone carefully
2. to notice something • *I observed footprints.*
➤ **observer** *NOUN*

obsessed *ADJECTIVE*
always thinking about something • *He is obsessed with football.*

obsession *NOUN* obsessions
something that someone thinks about too much

obstacle *NOUN* obstacles
something that gets in your way or makes it difficult for you to do something

obstinate *ADJECTIVE*
not willing to change your ideas or ways, even if they may be wrong
➤ **obstinacy** *NOUN* ➤ **obstinately** *ADVERB*

BUILD YOUR VOCABULARY
A synonym is **stubborn**.

obtain *VERB* obtains, obtaining, obtained
to get or be given something • *I've obtained some information.*

obtuse *ADJECTIVE*
An obtuse angle is between 90° and 180°.

BUILD YOUR VOCABULARY
Look at **acute**, **reflex** and **right angle**.

obvious *ADJECTIVE*
easy to see or understand; clear
➤ **obviously** *ADVERB* • *Obviously we want to win.*

occasion *NOUN* occasions
1. an important event • *You might wear this for a special occasion.* 2. a time when something happens • *I've seen her on a few occasions.*

occasional *ADJECTIVE*
happening sometimes but not often
➤ **occasionally** *ADVERB* • *We occasionally drive to school, but we usually walk.*

occupant *NOUN* occupants
someone who is living in or sitting in a place

occupation *NOUN* occupations
a job or task

occupy *VERB* occupies, occupying, occupied
1. To occupy a place is to be living in, sitting in or using it. • *The chair was already occupied.*
2. To occupy someone is to keep them busy.

occur *VERB* occurs, occurring, occurred
1. If something occurs, it happens. • *Something unexpected has occurred.* 2. If something occurs to you, you suddenly think of it. • *An idea occurred to me.*

occurrence *NOUN* occurrences
something that happens; an event

ocean *NOUN* oceans
one of the large areas of salt water on earth • *the Atlantic Ocean*

o'clock *ADVERB*
used after a number to say the time • *We'll start at nine o'clock.*

octagon *NOUN* octagons
a flat shape with eight sides
➤ **octagonal** *(say oct-ag-on-al) ADJECTIVE*

WORD STORY
Octagon comes from the Greek and Latin *oct-* meaning 'eight'.

octopus *NOUN* octopuses
a sea creature with a soft body and eight long arms

odd *ADJECTIVE* odder, oddest
1. strange or unusual • *What's that odd smell?*
2. an odd number cannot be divided exactly by 2
• *5 is odd and 6 is even.*

BUILD YOUR VOCABULARY
The opposite for this meaning is **even**.

3. left over or not matching • *She's wearing odd socks.*
➤ **oddly** *ADVERB* ➤ **oddness** *NOUN*

odds NOUN
the chance that something will happen

odour NOUN odours
a smell, usually an unpleasant one

of PREPOSITION
❶ belonging to or connected with • *the cover of the book* • *the end of the day* • *a friend of mine*
❷ consisting of or containing • *It's made of metal.*
• *a glass of water* • *a book of poems*

⚠ WATCH OUT!
Don't confuse of (pronounced 'ov' or 'uv') with **off** (pronounced 'off').

off ADVERB, ADJECTIVE
❶ not on; away • *His hat blew off.* • *She ran off.*
❷ not working or happening • *The heating went off.*
• *The match is off.* ❸ going bad • *I think the milk is off.*

off PREPOSITION
❶ not on; away or down from • *He fell off his chair.*
• *We got off the bus.* ❷ taken away from • *I got 10% off the normal price.*

offence NOUN offences
❶ a crime or an illegal action • *It is an offence to park here.* ❷ Offence is a feeling of hurt and anger.
• *I'm sorry if I caused offence.*

offend VERB offends, offending, offended
to make someone feel hurt and angry

offensive ADJECTIVE
rude, insulting and upsetting

offer VERB offers, offering, offered
to say that you will give someone something or do something for them, if they want • *He offered to do the washing-up.*

offer NOUN offers
something that you say you are willing to give or do for someone • *I accepted her offer of a lift home.*

office NOUN offices
❶ a room or building where people work at desks
❷ a place where you can go to get something such as tickets or information • *Go to the lost property office.*

officer NOUN officers
❶ someone who is in charge of other people, especially in the armed forces ❷ a policeman or policewoman

official ADJECTIVE
done by or relating to someone with authority
• *an official announcement*
➤ **officially** ADVERB

offline ADJECTIVE, ADVERB
not using or disconnected from the Internet
• *an offline computer* • *I'm working offline.*

⚙ BUILD YOUR VOCABULARY
The opposite is **online**.

offshore ADJECTIVE, ADVERB
in the sea • *an offshore wind farm*

offspring NOUN offspring
a child or young animal

often ADVERB
many times; in many cases

ogre NOUN ogres
in stories, a cruel giant

oh EXCLAMATION
a word you say when you are surprised, annoyed or pleased • *Oh, no!* • *Oh, how cute!*

oil NOUN oils
❶ a thick sticky liquid found underground, used as a fuel, for making machines run smoothly and for making plastic ❷ a thick greasy liquid made from plants, used in cooking • *sunflower oil*
➤ **oily** ADJECTIVE • *The food is very oily.*

oil VERB oils, oiling, oiled
to put oil on something

ointment NOUN ointments
a cream that you put on sore skin

OK *ADVERB, ADJECTIVE (informal)*
all right

old *ADJECTIVE* older, oldest
❶ bought, made or received a long time ago
• *She drives an old car.*

The opposite of this meaning is **new**.

❷ An old person has been alive for a long time.

BUILD YOUR VOCABULARY
The opposite of this meaning is **young**.

❸ used to talk about someone's age • *I'm 8 years old.*
• *How old is the baby?* ❹ previous; past • *My old school was nearer my house.*

BUILD YOUR VOCABULARY
The opposite of this meaning is **new**.

old-fashioned *ADJECTIVE*
out of date; not modern or fashionable

olive *NOUN* olives
a small evergreen tree or its small bitter fruit, used for eating or to make oil

Olympic Games *(also* **Olympics***) NOUN*
an international sports contest held every 4 years in different countries

omelette *(say* om-let*) NOUN* omelettes
eggs beaten together and fried

omen *NOUN* omens
an event that is believed to be a sign that something will happen

ominous *ADJECTIVE*
suggesting that something bad is going to happen
Dark, ominous clouds are rolling across the sky towards us.—BETWEEN TWO SEAS, Maire-Louise Jensen
➤ **ominously** *ADVERB*

omit *VERB* omits, omitting, omitted
to leave something out

omnivore *ADJECTIVE*
an animal that eats plants and meat
➤ **omnivorous** *ADJECTIVE*

BUILD YOUR VOCABULARY
Look at **carnivore** and **herbivore**.

on *PREPOSITION*
❶ at or over the top or surface of something • *Sit on the floor.* • *Do you want butter on your toast?*
❷ about; concerning • *a book on dinosaurs* ❸ used with days and dates • *Come on Monday.* ❹ using a device or machine • *I did it on the computer.*

on *ADVERB, ADJECTIVE*
❶ on top; over • *The lid is on.* • *Put some ketchup on.*
❷ forwards; continuing • *Move on.* • *I carried on.*
❸ on your body • *Put your shoes on.* • *He didn't have a coat on.* ❹ working or happening • *The lights came on.* • *Is the game on?*

once *ADVERB*
❶ one time only • *I've only met him once.* ❷ in the past • *A castle once stood here.*

once *CONJUNCTION*
as soon as • *You can play once you've finished your homework.*
➤ **at once** immediately

one *NOUN* ones
the number 1

one *ADJECTIVE*
a single • *There's one cookie left.*

one *PRONOUN*
a particular thing or person • *This is the best one.*
• *One of my friends is ill.*

onion *NOUN* onions
a round white vegetable with brown, red or white skin and a strong flavour

online *ADJECTIVE, ADVERB*
using or connected to the Internet • *online shopping*
• *Can you get online now?*

BUILD YOUR VOCABULARY
The opposite is **offline**.

onlooker *NOUN* onlookers
someone who watches an event or sees it happen

only *ADVERB*
❶ no more than; just • *We only have 5 minutes.*
• *He's only little.* ❷ used to make a condition • *You can only come if your parents agree.*

only *ADJECTIVE*
The only person or thing is the single one of a particular kind. • *He's the only person we can trust.*

only *CONJUNCTION*
but; except • *She's like her sister, only taller.*

a
b
c
d
e
f
g
h
i
j
k
l
m
n
o
p
q
r
s
t
u
v
w
x
y
z

onomatopoeia (say on-om-at-o-**pee**-a) NOUN
the use of words that sound like the thing they describe, such as *crunch*, *hiss* and *squelch*

onto PREPOSITION
to a position on • *They fell **onto** the sofa.*

⚠ **WATCH OUT!**
Onto is usually written as two words, on to, in British English.

onward (also **onwards**) ADVERB
forward or forwards

ooze VERB oozes, oozing, oozed
If a thick liquid oozes, it flows slowly. • *Mud **oozed** between my toes.*

opaque (say oh-**payk**) ADJECTIVE
impossible to see through

open ADJECTIVE
❶ If something is open, it is not closed, so things or people can get in or out. • *The box is **open**.* • *His mouth was **open**.* • *an **open** door* ❷ If a shop or place is open, you can go there and use it. • *Is the library **open** today?* ❸ not enclosed or covered • *There were miles of **open** land.*

open VERB opens, opening, opened
❶ If you open something or it opens, it becomes open. • ***Open** the window.* • *Her eyes **opened**.* ❷ To open is to start operating. • *The shop **opens** at 9.* • *A new swimming pool is **opening**.*

opening NOUN openings
❶ a space or gap ❷ the beginning of something

openly ADVERB
in a way that is clear to see; not secretly

opera NOUN operas
a form of drama in which the characters sing all or most of the words

operate VERB operates, operating, operated
❶ to make something work • *Do you know how to **operate** the camera?* ❷ If doctors operate, they cut into or take out part of someone's body to make them well.

operation NOUN operations
❶ a carefully planned activity ❷ If you have an operation, doctors cut into or take out part of your body to make you well.

operator NOUN operators
someone who operates equipment or a machine • *a radio **operator***

opinion NOUN opinions
a belief or view about something

opponent NOUN opponents
someone who is against you in a contest, war or argument

opportunity NOUN opportunities
a good time to do something

oppose VERB opposes, opposing, opposed
to be against something or someone or disagree with them
➤ **as opposed to** in contrast with • *fact, as opposed to fiction*

opposite ADJECTIVE, ADVERB
❶ on the other side; facing • *She lives on the **opposite** side of the road.* • *I'll sit **opposite**.* ❷ completely different • *They went in **opposite** directions.*

opposite NOUN opposites
something that is completely different from something else • *'Happy' is the **opposite** of 'sad'.*

🔧 **BUILD YOUR VOCABULARY**
Look at **antonym**.

opposition NOUN
❶ resistance; disagreement • *Their plans met no **opposition**.* ❷ the other side in a game or contest • *The **opposition** was getting tired.*

oppress VERB oppresses, oppressing, oppressed
❶ to treat people cruelly and unfairly ❷ to make someone feel worried or unhappy

oppressive ADJECTIVE
❶ unpleasant and making you feel tired or unhappy • *The heat was **oppressive**.* ❷ harsh and cruel • *oppressive laws*

opt VERB opts, opting, opted
To opt for something or to do something is to choose it. • *I **opted** for the cash prize.*
➤ **To opt out of something** is to decide not to have to or do it.

optical ADJECTIVE
to do with sight or the eyes

optician *(say* op-**tish**-an*) NOUN* **opticians**
someone who tests your eyesight and sells glasses
and contact lenses

optimist *NOUN* **optimists**
someone who usually expects things to turn out well
➤ **optimism** *NOUN* ➤ **optimistic** *ADJECTIVE*

⚙ **BUILD YOUR VOCABULARY**
The opposite is **pessimist**.

option *NOUN* **options**
a choice between two or more things

optional *ADJECTIVE*
If something is optional, you can choose whether
to do it or not.

or *CONJUNCTION*
used to show that there is a choice or an alternative
• *Do you want rice **or** pasta?*

oral *ADJECTIVE*
spoken, not written
➤ **orally** *ADVERB* • *You can present the information
orally.*

orange *NOUN* **oranges**
❶ a round juicy fruit with thick reddish-yellow peel
❷ a reddish-yellow colour
orange *ADJECTIVE*
reddish-yellow

orangutan *(say* o-**rang**-u-tan *or* o-rang-u-**tan***)*
NOUN **orangutans**
a large ape with long arms and reddish-brown hair

 WORD STORY
The word **orangutan** comes from Malay words
meaning 'man of the forest'.

orbit *NOUN* **orbits**
the curved path taken by something moving round a
planet or other object in space
orbit *VERB* **orbits, orbiting, orbited**
To orbit a planet or other object in space is to move
round it. • *The earth **orbits** the sun.*

orca *NOUN* **orca, orcas**
another name for **killer whale**

orchard *NOUN* **orchards**
a piece of ground with fruit trees

orchestra *NOUN* **orchestras**
a group of musicians playing different instruments
together

orchid *(say* or-kid*) NOUN* **orchids**
a type of brightly coloured flower

ordeal *NOUN* **ordeals**
a very difficult or unpleasant experience

order *NOUN* **orders**
❶ a command • *The captain gave the **order** to fire.*
❷ a request for something you want to have brought
or sent to you • *The waiter took our **order**.*
❸ the way things are arranged • *The words are
in alphabetical **order**.*
➤ **in order that** or **in order to** for the purpose of
➤ **To be out of order** is to be broken or not working.
order *VERB* **orders, ordering, ordered**
❶ To order someone to do something is to tell them
firmly to do it. ❷ to ask for something to be brought
or sent to you • *I **ordered** a lemonade.* ❸ to arrange
something in order • ***Order** these animals by size.*

orderly *ADJECTIVE*
tidy or well behaved • *an **orderly** queue*

ordinarily *ADVERB*
usually, normally • ***Ordinarily** I don't stay up this late.*

a b c d e f g h i j k l m n o p q r s t u v w x y z

ordinary ADJECTIVE
normal or usual; not special • *It began as a very
ordinary day.*
➤ **ordinariness** NOUN

ore NOUN ores
rock with metal in it • *iron ore*

organ NOUN organs
❶ a musical instrument similar to a piano with large
air pipes, played by keys and pedals ❷ a part of your
body with a particular purpose

organic ADJECTIVE
❶ grown or produced without using artificial
chemicals • *organic carrots* ❷ made by or found in
living things • *organic materials*

organisation (also **organization**) NOUN
organisations
❶ a group of people who work together to do
something • *a charity organisation* ❷ the planning
or arrangement of something • *Mum did all the
organisation for the party.*

organise (also **organize**) VERB organises,
organising, organised
❶ to plan and arrange an event • *We're organising a
concert.* ❷ to put something in order • *I'll organise
the books.*
➤ **organiser** NOUN

organism NOUN organisms
a living animal or plant

orienteering (say or-ree-en-**teer**-ing) NOUN
the sport of finding your way across countryside with
a map and compass

origin NOUN origins
The origin of something is the way in which it started.

original ADJECTIVE
❶ existing from the start; earliest • *They were the
original inhabitants.* ❷ new or imaginative • *They
came up with some original ideas.*
➤ **originally** ADVERB • *My family came from
Pakistan originally.*

originate VERB originates, originating,
originated
to start in a particular place or way • *The game of
chess originated in India.*

ornament NOUN ornaments
an object you wear or display as a decoration

ornate ADJECTIVE
highly decorated • *an ornate metal casket*

orphan NOUN orphans
a child whose parents are dead

orphanage NOUN orphanages
a home for orphans

osprey NOUN ospreys
a large fish-eating bird of prey

ostrich NOUN ostriches
a very large long-legged bird that can run fast but
cannot fly

other DETERMINER
not the same as this; different • *Try the other shoe.*
other PRONOUN others
the other person or thing • *Where are the others?*

otherwise ADVERB
❶ or else • *Write it down, otherwise you'll forget.*
❷ apart from that • *It rained a lot but otherwise the
holiday was good.*

otter NOUN otters
a wild animal with a long body, thick fur and webbed
feet that lives near water and eats fish

⚙ **BUILD** YOUR VOCABULARY
An **otter** is a **mammal**.

ought VERB
❶ If someone ought to do something, they should
do it. • *You ought to practise.* ❷ If something ought
to happen, it is likely. • *It ought to be easy.*

⚙ **BUILD** YOUR VOCABULARY
Ought is a **modal verb**.

⚠ **WATCH OUT!**
In **ought**, **bought**, **brought** and **thought**, the
letters *ough* sound like 'aw' as in the word 'saw'.

ounce NOUN ounces
a measurement of weight. There are 16 ounces in
1 pound and 1 ounce is about 28 grams.

our DETERMINER
belonging to us • *This is our house.*

ours PRONOUN
belonging to us • *Those seats are ours.*

ourselves PRONOUN
❶ used instead of 'us' when people do something and are also affected by it • *We saw ourselves in the mirror.* ❷ on our own, without help • *We wrote the play ourselves.*
➤ **by ourselves** on our own; alone • *They left us by ourselves.*

out ADVERB, ADJECTIVE
❶ away from something; not in something • *Take the seeds out.* ❷ not at home; not in a building • *I called, but she was out.* • *Let's go out.* ❸ not burning or working • *Put the fire out.* • *The lights are out.*

outbreak NOUN outbreaks
the sudden start of something bad, such as war or disease

outburst NOUN outbursts
a sudden loud expression of anger or another emotion

outcast NOUN
someone who has been rejected by their family or society

outcome NOUN outcomes
the final result of something

outcry NOUN outcries
a strong protest from many people

outdo VERB outdoes, outdoing, outdid, outdone
To outdo someone else is to do better than them.

outdoor ADJECTIVE
done or used outside • *an outdoor swimming pool*

outdoors ADVERB
in the open air • *It is cold outdoors.*

outer ADJECTIVE
outside; far from the centre • *Bark is the outer part of the tree trunk.*

BUILD YOUR VOCABULARY
The opposite is **inner**.

outer space NOUN
the universe beyond the earth's atmosphere

outfit NOUN outfits
a set of clothes you wear together

outgrow VERB outgrows, outgrowing, outgrew, outgrown
❶ To outgrow clothes is to grow too big for them. ❷ To outgrow something is to stop doing it because you are older.

outing NOUN outings
a trip to a place for pleasure

outlaw NOUN outlaws
a robber or bandit who is hiding from the law
outlaw VERB outlaws, outlawing, outlawed
to make something illegal

outlet NOUN outlets
a way for something such as water to get out • *The tank has an outlet at the bottom.*

outline NOUN outlines
the shape of something or a line around it showing its shape
outline VERB outlines, outlining, outlined
❶ to show the shape or edges of something • *The mountains were outlined against the sky.* ❷ to briefly describe a plan or idea

outlying ADJECTIVE
far from a town or city • *They passed an outlying cottage.*

outnumber VERB outnumbers, outnumbering, outnumbered
to be greater in number than something else • *Girls outnumber boys in our team.*

outpost NOUN outposts
a distant settlement

output NOUN outputs
❶ the amount produced by a factory or machine ❷ information produced by a computer

outrage NOUN outrages
❶ great anger and shock • *I stared at him in outrage.* ❷ something very shocking and unacceptable • *This is an outrage!*
➤ **outraged** ADJECTIVE

outrageous ADJECTIVE
very shocking or unacceptable

outright ADVERB
completely or at once • *I told him the truth outright.*

outside NOUN outsides
the outer side, surface or part • *There's a picture on the outside of the box.*
outside ADVERB, PREPOSITION
on or to the outside of something • *Come outside.* • *He's outside the door.*
outside ADJECTIVE
on the outside of something • *The bag has an outside pocket.*

outsider NOUN outsiders
someone who is not a member of a group

outskirts NOUN
the parts around the edge of a town or city

outstanding ADJECTIVE
extremely good

outward ADJECTIVE
❶ going outwards • *the outward journey* ❷ on the outside • *his outward appearance*

outwards ADVERB
away from something or towards the outside • *The door opens outwards.*

outwit VERB outwits, outwitting, outwitted
to deceive or defeat someone by being more clever

oval ADJECTIVE
shaped like an egg or a number 0
oval NOUN ovals
an oval shape

oven NOUN ovens
the part of a cooker where you can bake or roast food

over PREPOSITION
❶ above or covering something • *There's a shelf over the bed.* • *Clouds came over the moon.* ❷ across something • *We crossed over the road.* ❸ more than an amount • *We ran over a mile.* ❹ concerning or about something • *They argue over money.*
over ADVERB
❶ down or sideways • *He fell over.* • *She leaned over.* ❷ across to a place • *Come over here.* ❸ so that a different side shows • *I turned the page over.* ❹ left or remaining • *There was some food left over.*

over ADJECTIVE
finished • *The lesson is over.*

over NOUN overs
in cricket, a series of six balls bowled by one person

overall ADVERB, ADJECTIVE
including everything; in total • *The team with the most points overall wins.*

overalls NOUN
a piece of clothing that you wear over other clothes to protect them

overboard ADVERB
over the side of a boat into the water

overcast ADJECTIVE
An overcast sky is covered with cloud.

overcoat NOUN overcoats
a thick warm coat

overcome VERB overcomes, overcoming, overcame, overcome
❶ To overcome a problem or difficulty is to succeed in dealing with it. • *She overcame injury to win.* ❷ To be overcome by something is to become helpless because of it. • *He was overcome by grief.*

overdo VERB overdoes, overdoing, overdid, overdone
to do something too much

overflow VERB overflows, overflowing, overflowed
to flow over the edges or limits of something

overgrown ADJECTIVE
❶ thickly covered with weeds or unwanted plants ❷ much bigger than normal • *The creature looked like an overgrown frog.*

overhanging ADJECTIVE
sticking out across something • *We bent to avoid overhanging branches.*

overhead ADJECTIVE, ADVERB
above your head; in the sky

overhear VERB overhears, overhearing, overheard
to hear something accidentally or without the speaker knowing

overlap VERB overlaps, overlapping, overlapped
to lie across part of something • *The two circles **overlapped**.*

overlook VERB overlooks, overlooking, overlooked
❶ to forget or not notice something ❷ to have a view over a place • *The house **overlooks** the lake.*

overnight ADVERB, ADJECTIVE
during a night
• *It rained **overnight**.*
• *We had an **overnight** stop on the way back.*

overpower VERB overpowers, overpowering, overpowered
to be too strong for someone
➤ **overpowering** ADJECTIVE • *an **overpowering** smell*

overrun VERB overruns, overrunning, overran, overrun
to spread over a place in large numbers • *The place is **overrun** with mice.*

overseas ADVERB
to another country • *They travelled **overseas**.*
overseas ADJECTIVE
from another country • ***overseas** students*

oversleep VERB oversleeps, oversleeping, overslept
to sleep longer than you intended to • *I **overslept** and was late.*

overtake VERB overtakes, overtaking, overtook, overtaken
to catch someone or something up and go past them

overthrow VERB overthrows, overthrowing, overthrew, overthrown
to remove someone from power by force

overturn VERB overturns, overturning, overturned
If you overturn something or it overturns, it turns completely upside down.

overweight ADJECTIVE
too heavy for your size

overwhelm VERB overwhelms, overwhelming, overwhelmed
❶ to have a very strong effect on someone • *I was **overwhelmed** by their kindness.* ❷ to completely defeat someone

owe VERB owes, owing, owed
❶ If you owe something, especially money, you must pay or give it to someone. • *I **owe** you a pound.*
❷ If you owe something to someone, you have it because of them. • *He **owed** her his life.*

owl NOUN owls
a bird of prey with large eyes and a short beak, that usually flies at night

own ADJECTIVE
belonging to you or just for you • *I have my **own** bedroom.*
➤ **on your own** by yourself; alone • *I did it all **on my own**.* • *She sat **on her own**.*

own VERB owns, owning, owned
If you own something, it belongs to you.
➤ **owner** NOUN • *the car's **owner***

ox NOUN oxen
a bull kept for its meat and for pulling carts

oxygen NOUN
Oxygen is one of the gases in the air that people need to stay alive.

> 🔘 **BUILD** YOUR VOCABULARY
> **Oxygen** is an **element**.

oyster NOUN oysters
a kind of shellfish with rough shells that sometimes contain a pearl

> 🔘 **BUILD** YOUR VOCABULARY
> An **oyster** is a **mollusc**.

oz ABBREVIATION
the abbreviation for **ounce**

ozone NOUN
a strong-smelling gas that forms a layer high in the earth's atmosphere, absorbing harmful radiation from the sun

a b c d e f g h i j k l m n **o** p q r s t u v w x y z

P is for **palindrome**, which is a word or phrase that reads the same when you spell it backwards, for example *madam* or *nurses run*.

Can you think of any more palindromes?

CLUE To find a palindrome with 4 letters, look at letter **D** in this dictionary.

p *ABBREVIATION*
short for **penny** or **pence**

pace *NOUN* **paces**
❶ one step in walking, marching or running ❷ speed
• *He set a fast pace.*

pace *VERB* **paces, pacing, paced**
to walk up and down with slow or regular steps
The rat, in the dungeon below, was pacing and muttering in the darkness, waiting to take his revenge on the princess.—THE TALE OF DESPEREAUX, Kate DiCamillo

pack *NOUN* **packs**
❶ a packet or bundle of things ❷ a set of playing cards ❸ a group of wolves or dogs

pack *VERB* **packs, packing, packed**
to put things in a suitcase, bag or box to store them or take them somewhere

package *NOUN* **packages**
a parcel or packet

packet *NOUN* **packets**
a small parcel

pad *NOUN* **pads**
❶ a piece of thick soft material used to protect or shape something ❷ the soft part under an animal's paw or at the end of your finger ❸ a flat place on the ground for helicopters to take off or land or for rockets to be launched

❹ a number of sheets of paper joined along one edge

pad *VERB* **pads, padding, padded**
❶ to put thick soft material on or into something in order to protect or shape it ❷ to walk softly
• *He padded around in bare feet.*

paddle *VERB* **paddles, paddling, paddled**
❶ to walk in shallow water ❷ to move a boat with a short oar

paddle *NOUN* **paddles**
a short oar with a wide blade

paddock *NOUN* **paddocks**
a small field for keeping horses

padlock *NOUN* **padlocks**
a lock with a metal loop for locking a gate or bicycle

pagan *NOUN* **pagans**
someone who believes in a religion which is not one of the main world religions

page *NOUN* **pages**
❶ one side of a piece of paper in a book or newspaper ❷ a single piece of paper ❸ a single screen on a website

pageant *(say* paj-ent*) NOUN* **pageants**
a historical play or a procession involving people in costume

pagoda *(say* pag-oh-da*) NOUN* **pagodas**
a Buddhist tower or Hindu temple

paid *VERB (past tense and past participle of* **pay***)*
• *Mum paid the bus driver.* • *I've paid for the cake.*

pail *NOUN* **pails**
a bucket

pain *NOUN* **pains**
an unpleasant feeling because you are hurt or ill • *Are you in pain?*

painful *ADJECTIVE*
causing pain
➤ **painfully** *ADVERB* • *The shoes were painfully tight.*

pagoda

paint *NOUN* **paints**
a liquid substance put on something to colour or cover it

paint *VERB* **paints, painting, painted**
❶ to put paint on something • *The classroom is being painted.* ❷ to make a pictures using paints • *I've painted a horse.*
➤ **painter** *NOUN*

painting *NOUN* **paintings**
a painted picture

pair *NOUN* **pairs**
❶ two things or people that go together or are the same kind • *a pair of socks* ❷ something made of two parts joined together • *a pair of glasses*

pal *NOUN* **pals** *(informal)*
a friend

WORD STORY

Pal comes from a Romany (Gypsy) word meaning 'brother'.

palace *NOUN* **palaces**
a large and splendid house, especially one where a king or queen lives

pale *ADJECTIVE* **paler, palest**
❶ If you are pale, your face looks white. • *She was pale with shock.* ❷ not bright in colour • *The sky was a pale blue.*
➤ **paleness** *NOUN*

palisade *NOUN* **palisades**
a fence made of wooden posts or railings

pallid *ADJECTIVE*
pale, especially because of illness

pallor *NOUN*
paleness in a person's face, especially because they are ill

palm *NOUN* **palms**
❶ the inside surface of your hand, between your fingers and wrist ❷ a tropical tree with large leaves and no branches

pamper *VERB* **pampers, pampering, pampered**
to make someone feel very comfortable and give them a lot of treats

pamphlet *NOUN* **pamphlets**
a thin book with a paper cover

pan *NOUN* **pans**
a pot or dish with a flat base, used for cooking

pancake *NOUN* **pancakes**
a flat round cake of batter fried on both sides

panda *NOUN* **pandas**
a large black and white animal similar to a bear found in China

pandemonium *NOUN*
a lot of loud noise or disturbance

WORD STORY

The word **pandemonium** was invented by the poet John Milton in the 17th century and means 'the place of all demons'.

pane *NOUN* **panes**
a sheet of glass in a window

panel *NOUN* **panels**
❶ a flat piece of wood, metal or other material that is part of a door, wall or piece of furniture ❷ a group of people whose job is to discuss or decide something • *The winner will be chosen by a panel of judges.*

pang *NOUN* **pangs**
a sudden feeling of pain or strong emotion

panic *NOUN*
sudden fear or anxiety that makes you unable to think or act sensibly

a
b
c
d
e
f
g
h
i
j
k
l
m
n
o
p
q
r
s
t
u
v
w
x
y
z

panic VERB panics, panicking, panicked
to be so afraid or anxious that you cannot think or act sensibly

pannier NOUN panniers
a bag or basket hung on one side of a bicycle or horse

pansy NOUN pansies
a small brightly coloured garden flower

pant VERB pants, panting, panted
to take short quick breaths through your mouth

panther NOUN panthers
a black leopard

pantomime NOUN pantomimes
a Christmas entertainment based on a fairy tale

pantry NOUN pantries
a cupboard or small room for storing food

pants NOUN
❶ underpants or knickers ❷ (North American) trousers

papaya NOUN papayas
a juicy orange tropical fruit with black seeds

paper NOUN papers
❶ Paper is thin material that you write on and use for wrapping things. ❷ A paper is a newspaper. ❸ Papers are documents.

paperback NOUN paperbacks
a book with thin flexible covers

papier mâché (say pap-yay-**mash**-ay) NOUN
a mixture of wet paper and glue used to make models or ornaments

papyrus (say pap-**eye**-rus) NOUN
a kind of paper made from the stems of reeds, used in ancient Egypt

parable NOUN parables
a short story meant to teach you something

parachute NOUN parachutes
a large umbrella-shaped piece of fabric used for falling safely from an aircraft

parade NOUN parades
a long line of people or vehicles moving past while people watch

parade VERB parades, parading, paraded
to move past in a long line while people watch

paradise NOUN
a wonderful place, especially one where people are said to go when they die; heaven

✷ **WORD STORY**
The word **paradise** comes from an old Persian word meaning 'garden'.

paraffin NOUN
a kind of oil used as fuel

paragraph NOUN paragraphs
one of the groups of sentences that a piece of writing is divided into, beginning on a new line

parallel ADJECTIVE
Parallel lines are the same distance apart for their whole length, like railway lines.

⚠ **WATCH OUT!**
The word **parallel** has double l in the middle and single l at the end.

parallelogram NOUN parallelograms
a four-sided figure with its opposite sides parallel and equal in length

Paralympic Games
(also **Paralympics**) NOUN
an international sports contest for athletes with disabilities

paralyse VERB paralyses, paralysing, paralysed
to make someone unable to move or to feel their body

paralysis (say pa-**ral**-iss-iss) NOUN
inability to move or to feel anything

paramedic NOUN paramedics
a person trained to give emergency medical treatment, often as part of an ambulance crew

parapet NOUN parapets
a low wall along the edge of a bridge, roof or balcony

parasite *NOUN* **parasites**
an animal or plant that lives on or inside another animal or plant • *The plant is a **parasite** which lives on vines and smells really bad.*

parasol *NOUN* **parasols**
a light umbrella for shading yourself from the sun

parcel *NOUN* **parcels**
something wrapped up to be posted or carried

parched *ADJECTIVE*
very dry or thirsty

parchment *NOUN*
a kind of heavy paper originally made from animal skin

pardon *VERB* **pardons, pardoning, pardoned**
to forgive someone
pardon *NOUN*
➤ **I beg your pardon?** or **Pardon?** used when you do not hear or understand what someone says

parent *NOUN* **parents**
Your parents are your father and mother.

parenthesis (*say* pa-renth-iss-iss) *NOUN* **parentheses**
❶ something put into the middle of a sentence between brackets or dashes ❷ one of a pair of brackets (like these) used in the middle of a sentence

parish *NOUN* **parishes**
a district that has its own church

park *NOUN* **parks**
a large public area with grass and trees
park *VERB* **parks, parking, parked**
to stop a vehicle and leave it somewhere

parliament *NOUN* **parliaments**
the group of people that make a country's laws

> ⚠ **WATCH OUT!**
> Don't forget that **parliament** has **-ia-** in the middle.

parlour *NOUN* **parlours**
a sitting room

parrot *NOUN* **parrots**
a brightly coloured tropical bird with a curved beak

parsley *NOUN*
a plant with green leaves used to flavour food

parsnip *NOUN* **parsnips**
a pale yellow vegetable similar to a carrot

part *NOUN* **parts**
❶ some but not all of something; a bit or piece belonging to something • *I like the first **part** of the story.* • *The machine has tiny **parts**.* ❷ a role in a play or film • *I got a **part** in the school play.*
part *VERB* **parts, parting, parted**
If people or things part or something parts them, they separate.

partial *ADJECTIVE*
not complete or total • *It was a **partial** success.*
➤ **To be partial to something** is to like it.

participate *VERB* **participates, participating, participated**
to take part in something
➤ **participation** *NOUN*

participle *NOUN* **participles**
a word formed from a verb and used as part of the verb or as an adjective or noun, for example *frightened, frightening* or *meeting*

> ⚙ **BUILD YOUR VOCABULARY**
> Look at **past participle** and **present participle**.

particle *NOUN* **particles**
a very small piece or amount

a
b
c
d
e
f
g
h
i
j
k
l
m
n
o
p
q
r
s
t
u
v
w
x
y
z

particular *ADJECTIVE*

❶ only one and no other; special • *Are you looking for a particular book?* ❷ fussy • *He is very particular about what he eats.*

➤ **in particular** especially

> ⚠ **WATCH OUT!**
> Remember that **particular** starts with *part-*.

particularly *ADVERB*

especially

> ⚠ **WATCH OUT!**
> Remember to spell **particularly** as *particular + ly*, even though people do not always pronounce it that way.

partition *NOUN* **partitions**

a thin dividing wall

partly *ADVERB*

not completely; in some ways

partner *NOUN* **partners**

❶ one of a pair of people who do something together, for example working or dancing ❷ Someone's partner is the person they are married to or live with.

part of speech *NOUN* **parts of speech**

one of the groups into which words can be divided in grammar, such as *adjectives*, *nouns* and *verbs*

> ⚙ **BUILD YOUR VOCABULARY**
> Look at **word class**.

partridge *NOUN* **partridges**

a bird with brown feathers that is hunted for sport and food

part-time *ADJECTIVE, ADVERB*

working for only some of the normal working hours • *a part-time job* • *Mr Seed works part-time.*

party *NOUN* **parties**

❶ a time when people get together to enjoy themselves • *I'm having a birthday party.* ❷ a group of people doing something together • *a party of campers*

pass *VERB* **passes, passing, passed**

❶ to go past someone or something • *We pass the shop on our way to school.* ❷ to give or hand something to someone • *Can you pass me my bag?* ❸ to be successful in a test

passage *NOUN* **passages**

❶ a corridor or narrow space between two walls ❷ a section of a piece of writing or music

passageway *NOUN* **passageways**

a passage or way through, especially between buildings

passenger *NOUN* **passengers**

someone who is travelling in a vehicle and is not the driver or a member of the crew

passer-by *NOUN* **passers-by**

someone who is going past when something happens

passion *NOUN* **passions**

a very strong feeling

passionate *ADJECTIVE*

full of strong feeling, especially love or enthusiasm

➤ **passionately** *ADVERB*

passive *ADJECTIVE*

❶ letting things happen without reacting or doing anything ❷ *(in grammar)* A passive verb is one in which the subject receives the action, for example in *I was stung by a wasp*, the subject is *I* and *was stung* is a passive verb.

➤ **passively** *ADVERB*

> ⚙ **BUILD YOUR VOCABULARY**
> Look at **active**.

Passover *NOUN*

a Jewish religious festival held in spring

passport *NOUN* **passports**

an official document that allows you to travel abroad

password *NOUN* **passwords**

a secret word or phrase that you need to know to get into a place or computer system

past *NOUN*

the time before now • *Try to forget the past.*

past *ADJECTIVE*

Past events happened in the time before now.

past *PREPOSITION, ADVERB*

❶ beyond; continuing to the other side • *Go past the school and turn right.* • *A taxi drove past.* ❷ later than • *It's ten past midnight.*

> ⚠ **WATCH OUT!**
> Past as in **a drive past** is different from **passed**, which is a form of the verb *to pass*: *She passed me in the street.*

pasta NOUN
an Italian food made from flour, water and often eggs, formed into different shapes such as spaghetti and lasagne

paste NOUN pastes
a soft, moist or gluey substance

paste VERB pastes, pasting, pasted
❶ to stick something onto a surface with paste ❷ to put something into a computer document that you have cut or copied from somewhere else

pastel NOUN pastels
❶ a crayon that is like greasy chalk ❷ a light delicate colour

pastime NOUN pastimes
something you do in your spare time; a hobby

past participle NOUN past participles
a form of a verb such as *done*, *given* or *played*. A past participle is used with the verb *have* to talk about a finished or earlier action, for example *I have done it* or with the verb *be* to make a passive, for example *I was given a prize*.

pastry NOUN pastries
❶ a mixture of flour, fat and water used for making pies ❷ a small cake made from pastry

past tense NOUN
a form of a verb such as *took*, *went* or *played*, used to describe an action that happened at a time before now

pasture NOUN pastures
land covered with grass that cattle, sheep or horses can eat

pasty (*say* pass-tee) NOUN pasties
a small savoury pie

pasty (*say* pay-stee) ADJECTIVE pastier, pastiest
looking pale and unhealthy

pat VERB pats, patting, patted
to tap someone or something gently with your flat hand

patch NOUN patches
❶ a piece of material put over a hole or damaged place ❷ a small area that is different from its surroundings • *a black cat with a white patch*

patch VERB patches, patching, patched
to put a piece of material on something to repair it

patchwork NOUN
something made of pieces of different coloured cloth sewn together or something that looks like this • *a patchwork of fields*

patchy ADJECTIVE patchier, patchiest
present in some places but not others • *Patchy snow lay on the ground.*

patent (*say* pay-tent *or* pat-ent) NOUN patents
the official right to make something you have invented and to stop other people from copying it

paternal ADJECTIVE
to do with a father or like a father

> ⚙ **BUILD** YOUR VOCABULARY
> Look at **maternal**.

path NOUN paths
❶ a narrow way to walk or ride along ❷ the line along which something moves • *The line shows the path of the meteor.*

pathetic ADJECTIVE
❶ making you feel pity • *The lamb gave a pathetic cry.* ❷ very bad or unsuccessful • *That was a pathetic effort.*
➤ **pathetically** ADVERB

patience (*say* pay-shens) NOUN
the ability to stay calm, especially when you have to wait for a long time

patient (*say* pay-shent) ADJECTIVE
able to wait for a long time without getting angry or bored
➤ **patiently** ADVERB • *He waited patiently.*

patient (*say* pay-shent) NOUN patients
a person who is getting medical treatment

patio (*say* pat-ee-oh) NOUN patios
a paved area beside a house

patriot (*say* pay-tree-ot *or* pat-ree-ot) NOUN patriots
someone who loves and always supports their country
➤ **patriotic** ADJECTIVE ➤ **patriotism** NOUN

a b c d e f g h i j k l m n o p q r s t u v w x y z

patrol VERB patrols, patrolling, patrolled
If guards, police or soldiers patrol a place, they move round it regularly to check there is no trouble.

patrol NOUN patrols
a group of people patrolling a place

patron (say pay-tron) NOUN patrons
someone who supports a person or organisation with money or encouragement

patter NOUN patters
a series of light tapping sounds • the **patter** of rain against the window

patter VERB patters, pattering, pattered
to make light tapping sounds

pattern NOUN patterns
a decorative arrangement of lines or shapes

pause NOUN pauses
a short stop before continuing with something

pause VERB pauses, pausing, paused
❶ to stop for a short time before continuing with something ❷ To pause a recording is to make it stop playing for a short time.

pave VERB paves, paving, paved
to put a hard surface on a road or path

pavement NOUN pavements
a path with a hard surface, along the side of a street

pavilion NOUN pavilions
❶ a building at a sports ground for players and spectators to use ❷ a large decorated tent

paw NOUN paws
an animal's foot

pawn NOUN pawns
❶ in chess, one of the sixteen pieces that are the least valuable ❷ a person who is used by someone else

pay VERB pays, paying, paid
to give money in return for something • Have you **paid** for your lunch? • He **paid** me £5 to wash his car.

pay NOUN
money that someone earns for working

payment NOUN payments
money that is given in return for something

PC NOUN PCs
a computer designed for one person to use; short for personal computer

PE ABBREVIATION
short for **physical education**

pea NOUN peas
a small round green vegetable that is a seed growing inside a pod

peace NOUN
❶ quietness and calm ❷ a time when there is no war or violence

peaceful ADJECTIVE
❶ quiet and calm ❷ not involving violence
➤ **peacefully** ADVERB

peach NOUN peaches
a soft round juicy fruit with a slightly furry skin and a large stone

peacock NOUN peacocks
a large male bird with a long, brightly coloured tail that it can spread like a fan

peak NOUN peaks
❶ the top of a mountain ❷ the highest or best point of something ❸ the part of a cap that sticks out in front

peal VERB peals, pealing, pealed
When bells peal, they make a loud ringing sound.

peal NOUN peals
a loud ringing sound made by bells

peanut NOUN peanuts
a small round nut that grows in a pod in the ground

pear NOUN pears
a juicy fruit that is round at the bottom and narrower at the top

pearl NOUN pearls
a small shiny white jewel found in the shells of some oysters
➤ **pearly** ADJECTIVE

peasant NOUN peasants
a poor person who farms land, especially land that belongs to someone else

peat NOUN
rotted plant material that is dug up and used as fuel or fertiliser

pebble NOUN pebbles
a small round stone found on the beach

peck VERB pecks, pecking, pecked
When a bird pecks something, it bites at it with its beak.

peckish ADJECTIVE (informal)
hungry

peculiar ADJECTIVE
strange or unusual
➤ **peculiarly** ADVERB

peculiarity NOUN peculiarities
something peculiar or special

pedal NOUN pedals
a lever that you press with your foot, for example on a bicycle or piano
pedal VERB pedals, pedalling, pedalled
to push or turn pedals with your feet

pedestal NOUN pedestals
the base that supports a statue or pillar

pelican

pedestrian NOUN pedestrians
someone who is walking
➤ **pedestrian** ADJECTIVE • *a pedestrian area*

pedigree ADJECTIVE
A pedigree animal has a record of its ancestors to show that it is from a single breed.

peel NOUN peels
the skin of some fruit and vegetables
peel VERB peels, peeling, peeled
❶ to remove the peel from fruit or vegetables
❷ to come off in a thin layer • *The paint is **peeling**.*

peep VERB peeps, peeping, peeped
to look quickly or secretly or through a narrow opening
peep NOUN peeps
a quick look

peer VERB peers, peering, peered
to look at someone or something closely or with difficulty

peewit NOUN peewits
a kind of wading bird

peg NOUN pegs
a clip or pin for fixing something in place or for hanging things on

Pekinese (or **Pekingese**)
(say peek-in-**eez**) NOUN Pekinese, Pekingese
a small breed of dog with short legs and long silky hair

pelican NOUN pelicans
a large bird with a pouch in its long beak for storing fish

pelican crossing NOUN
pelican crossings
a place on a road for pedestrians to cross, controlled by lights

⚙ **BUILD** YOUR VOCABULARY
Look at **zebra crossing**.

pellet NOUN pellets
a small ball of metal, food, paper or other material

pelt VERB pelts, pelting, pelted
❶ to throw a lot of things at someone • *We **pelted** him with snowballs.* ❷ to run fast
➤ **To pelt down** is to rain very hard.

pelt NOUN pelts
an animal skin with fur or hair on it

pelvis NOUN pelvises
the large bone around your hips, to which the bones of your legs are attached

pen NOUN pens
❶ a device with a metal point for writing with ink
❷ a fenced area for cattle or other animals

penalty NOUN penalties
❶ a punishment ❷ an advantage given to one side in a game when the other side breaks a rule

pence NOUN
pennies • *I need fifty **pence** for the bus.*

pencil NOUN pencils
a device for drawing or writing, usually made of wood with a stick of soft material called **graphite** in the middle

pendant NOUN pendants
a piece of jewellery that hangs on a long chain or string

pendulum NOUN pendulums
a weight hung at the end of a rod so that it swings regularly, used in old clocks

penetrate VERB penetrates, penetrating, penetrated
to find a way through or into something • *Sunlight could not **penetrate** the thick jungle.*

penguin NOUN penguins
an Antarctic seabird that cannot fly but uses its wings as flippers for swimming

penicillin NOUN
a drug that kills bacteria, made from mould

BUILD YOUR VOCABULARY
Penicillin is an **antibiotic**.

peninsula NOUN peninsulas
a piece of land that is almost surrounded by water

penis NOUN penises
the part of the body a male person or animal uses for urinating

penknife NOUN penknives
a small folding knife

penniless ADJECTIVE
having no money; very poor

penny NOUN pennies, pence
a unit of money in Britain. There are 100 pennies or pence in 1 pound.

pension NOUN pensions
regular payments made to someone who has retired

pentagon NOUN pentagons
a flat shape with five sides
➤ **pentagonal** (*say* pent-**ag**-on-al) ADJECTIVE

WORD STORY
Pentagon comes from the Greek and Latin *pent-* meaning 'five'.

peony (*say* pee-o-nee) NOUN peonies
a plant with large round red, pink or white flowers

people NOUN
human beings; men, women and children

pepper NOUN peppers
❶ a hot-tasting powder made from the dried berries of a plant, used to flavour food ❷ a hollow green, red, yellow or orange vegetable
➤ **peppery** ADJECTIVE

peppermint NOUN peppermints
❶ a kind of mint plant with a strong taste ❷ a sweet flavoured with peppermint

per PREPOSITION
for each • *The charge is £2 **per** person.*

perceive VERB perceives, perceiving, perceived
to see, notice or understand something

per cent ADVERB
used after a number to mean 'for every hundred'. The symbol % can be used instead. • *50 **per cent** (50%) is the same as half.*

percentage NOUN percentages
an amount shown as a proportion of 100 • *The **percentage** 75% is the same as the fraction $\frac{3}{4}$.*

perception NOUN
the ability to see, notice or understand something

perch NOUN perches
❶ a place where a bird sits ❷ a fish that lives in rivers and lakes

perch VERB perches, perching, perched
to sit or stand on the edge of something or on something small
Matilda, who was perched on a tall stool at the kitchen table, ate her bread and jam slowly.—MATILDA, Roald Dahl

percussion NOUN
musical instruments that you play by hitting or shaking them, such as drums or tambourines

perfect *(say* **per**-fect*) ADJECTIVE*
so good that it cannot be any better; without faults
➤ **perfection** *NOUN* ➤ **perfectly** *ADVERB*

perfect *(say* per-**fect***) VERB* perfects,
perfecting, perfected
to make something as good as it can be • *I'm trying to* **perfect** *my diving.*

perform *VERB* performs, performing,
performed
❶ to act, dance, sing, play music or present something to entertain an audience • *We're going to* **perform** *a play.* ❷ To perform an experiment or operation is to carry it out.
➤ **performance** *NOUN* • *The actor gave a wonderful* **performance***.*
➤ **performer** *NOUN* • *Thanks go to all our* **performers** *and to everyone involved with the show.*

perfume *NOUN* perfumes
❶ a pleasant-smelling liquid that people put on their skin ❷ a pleasant smell

perhaps *ADVERB*
maybe; possibly

peril *NOUN* perils
danger • *She was in great* **peril***.*

perilous *ADJECTIVE*
dangerous • *They made a* **perilous** *voyage.*

perimeter *(say* per-**rim**-it-er*) NOUN*
perimeters
❶ the distance round the edge of something • *How do you work out the* **perimeter** *of a square?* ❷ the edge or boundary of something

period *NOUN* periods
❶ a length of time • *We waited for a short* **period***.* ❷ the time every month when a woman or girl bleeds from her womb

A synonym is **menstruation**.

periscope *NOUN* periscopes
a tube with mirrors that lets you see things above and behind you, used for example in submarines

perish *VERB* perishes, perishing, perished
❶ to die or be destroyed • *Many sailors* **perished** *in the shipwreck.* ❷ to rot or go bad • *The tyres have* **perished***.*

permanent *ADJECTIVE*
lasting forever or for a long time • *Will there be any* **permanent** *damage?*
➤ **permanently** *ADVERB*

BUILD YOUR VOCABULARY
The opposite is **temporary**.

permeable *ADJECTIVE*
letting water soak through it • *Chalk is a* **permeable** *rock.*

BUILD YOUR VOCABULARY
The opposite is **impermeable**.

permission *NOUN*
If you have permission to do something, you are allowed to do it.

permit *(say* per-**mit***) VERB* permits,
permitting, permitted
to allow something or allow someone to do something • *Dogs are not* **permitted** *on the beach.*

permit *(say* **per**-mit*) NOUN* permits
an official document that says you are allowed to do something

perpendicular *ADJECTIVE*
A perpendicular line is at 90° to another line.

perpetual *ADJECTIVE*
lasting for ever or happening all the time
➤ **perpetually** *ADVERB*

perplex *VERB* perplexes, perplexing,
perplexed
to puzzle someone very much

persecute *VERB* persecutes, persecuting,
persecuted
to continually treat someone cruelly and unfairly, especially because of their beliefs
➤ **persecution** *NOUN*

persevere *VERB* perseveres, persevering,
persevered
to go on with something even though it is difficult

persist *VERB* persists, persisting, persisted
❶ to keep trying to do or say something, even though you have no success or people want you to stop • *'But why?' she* **persisted***.* ❷ If something persists, it continues for a long time. • *The rain* **persisted***.*
➤ **persistance** *NOUN*

persistent ADJECTIVE
❶ refusing to give up ❷ lasting for a long time
• *persistent rain*
➤ **persistently** ADVERB

person NOUN persons, people
a human being; a man, woman or child

> ⚙ **BUILD** YOUR VOCABULARY
> Look at **first person**, **second person** and **third person**.

personal ADJECTIVE
❶ belonging or relating to a particular person
• *Mums and dads can leave their personal belongings in the head teacher's office.* ❷ private
• *You can't read the message. It's personal.*

personality NOUN personalities
❶ your nature and character • *She has a cheerful personality.* ❷ a well-known person • *a TV personality*

personally ADVERB
❶ If you do something personally, you do it yourself. • *You should thank them personally.* ❷ speaking for myself • *Personally, I'd rather stay.*

perspective NOUN perspectives
❶ the impression of depth and distance in a picture ❷ Your perspective is your point of view.

perspire VERB perspires, perspiring, perspired
to sweat

persuade VERB persuades, persuading, persuaded
❶ to get someone to agree to do something ❷ to make someone believe something

persuasion NOUN
a successful attempt to get someone to do something or believe something

persuasive ADJECTIVE
good at persuading people

Pesach NOUN
the Hebrew name for Passover

pesky ADJECTIVE peskier, peskiest *(informal)*
annoying • *a swarm of pesky midges*

pessimist NOUN pessimists
someone who usually expects things to turn out badly
➤ **pessimism** NOUN ➤ **pessimistic** ADJECTIVE

> ⚙ **BUILD** YOUR VOCABULARY
> The opposite is **optimist**.

pest NOUN pests
❶ a destructive insect or animal, such as a locust or a mouse ❷ a nuisance

pester VERB pesters, pestering, pestered
to keep annoying someone with questions or interruptions

pesticide NOUN pesticides
a chemical used to kill insects and grubs

pet NOUN pets
❶ a tame animal that you keep at home ❷ a person treated as a favourite

petal NOUN petals
each of the separate coloured outer parts of a flower

petition NOUN petitions
a written request for something, usually signed by a large number of people

petrify VERB petrifies, petrifying, petrified
to terrify someone

> ✳ **WORD STORY**
> The word **petrify** comes from a Greek word *petra* meaning 'rock' and originally meant 'to turn into stone'.

petrol NOUN
a liquid used as fuel for vehicle engines

petty ADJECTIVE pettier, pettiest
unimportant or caring too much about unimportant things • *a petty argument*

pew NOUN pews
a long wooden seat in a church

pewter NOUN
a grey metal that is a mixture of tin and lead

phantom NOUN phantoms
a ghost

pharaoh *(say* fair-oh*) NOUN* pharaohs
a ruler in ancient Egypt

pharmacy *NOUN* pharmacies
a shop that sells medicines

phase *NOUN* phases
a stage in the progress or development of something

pheasant *(say* fez-ant*) NOUN* pheasants
a bird with a long tail, which is hunted for sport and food

phenomenon *NOUN* phenomena
an event or fact, especially an unusual one

phew *EXCLAMATION*
a word you say when you feel relieved • *Phew! That was lucky!*

phial *(say* fy-al*) NOUN* phials
a small glass flask • *a phial of magic potion*

philosophy *(say* fil-**oss**-o-fee*) NOUN* philosophies
❶ the study of human ideas and beliefs and of what is true ❷ a way of thinking or system of beliefs
➤ **philosopher** *NOUN*

phobia *(say* foh-bee-a*) NOUN* phobias
a great or unusual fear of something

phoenix *(say* fee-niks*) NOUN* phoenixes
a mythical bird that was said to burn itself to death and be born again from the ashes

phone *NOUN* phones
a short word for telephone
phone *VERB* phones, phoning, phoned
To phone someone is to telephone them.

photo *NOUN* photos
a short word for photograph

photocopier *NOUN* photocopiers
a machine that makes photocopies

photocopy *NOUN* photocopies
a copy of a document made by a machine that photographs it

photocopy VERB photocopies, photocopying, photocopied
to make a copy of a document with a photocopier

photograph NOUN photographs
a picture made using a camera

photograph VERB photographs, photographing, photographed
to take a photograph of someone or something

photography (say fo-**tog**-re-fee) NOUN
the activity or job of taking photographs
➤ **photographer** NOUN

photosynthesis NOUN
the process by which green plants use sunlight to make their food from carbon dioxide and water

phrase NOUN phrases
a group of words used together

BUILD YOUR VOCABULARY
Look at **noun phrase**.

physical ADJECTIVE
❶ to do with the body rather than the mind or feelings • *physical* illness ❷ to do with things you can touch or see • the *physical* world
➤ **physically** ADVERB

physical education NOUN
activities at school that include sport and physical exercise

physician NOUN physicians
a doctor

physics NOUN
the study of matter and energy, including movement, heat, light and sound
➤ **physicist** NOUN

pianist NOUN pianists
someone who plays the piano

piano NOUN pianos
a large musical instrument with a row of black and white keys on a keyboard

WORD STORY
The word **piano** is short for *pianoforte*, an Italian word meaning 'quiet (and) loud'.

pick VERB picks, picking, picked
❶ to choose something or someone • *Pick any card.*
❷ To pick a flower or fruit is to cut or break it from where it is growing.
➤ **To pick something** or **someone up** is to lift them from the ground or a surface.
➤ **To pick someone** or **something up** is to collect them. • *I'll pick you up from the station.*

pickaxe NOUN pickaxes
a heavy pointed metal tool with a long handle

pickle NOUN pickles
a strong-tasting food made of vegetables preserved in vinegar

pickle VERB pickles, pickling, pickled
to preserve food in vinegar or salt water

pick-up (also **pick-up truck**) NOUN pick-ups, pick-up trucks
an open truck for small loads

picnic NOUN picnics
a meal eaten in the open air away from home

picnic VERB picnics, picnicking, picnicked
to have a picnic

pictogram NOUN pictograms
a picture or symbol that stands for a word or a phrase

pictorial ADJECTIVE
with or using pictures

picture NOUN pictures
a painting, drawing or photograph

picture VERB pictures, picturing, pictured
to imagine someone or something • *I pictured myself holding the trophy.*

picturesque (say pik-cher-**esk**) ADJECTIVE
A picturesque place is attractive or charming.

pie NOUN pies
a baked dish of meat or fruit covered with pastry

piece NOUN pieces
❶ a part of something; a bit • *Have a piece of cake.*
❷ an individual thing of a particular kind • *I like this piece of music.* ❸ a coin • *a twenty-pence piece*

⚠ **WATCH OUT!**
To remember the spelling, think of a **piece** of **pie**.

pie chart NOUN pie charts
a diagram in the form of a circle divided into slices, showing how a quantity or amount is divided up

pier NOUN piers
a long structure built out into the sea for people to walk on

pierce VERB pierces, piercing, pierced
to make a hole through something

piercing ADJECTIVE
❶ A piercing sound is loud and high. • *We heard a piercing shriek.* ❷ Something piercing seems to go right through you. • *He had piercing blue eyes.*

pig NOUN pigs
a farm animal with pink or black skin, short legs and a large snout, kept for its meat

⚙ **BUILD YOUR VOCABULARY**
Look at **boar**, **hog** and **sow**.

pigeon NOUN pigeons
a common grey bird with a small head and large chest

piglet NOUN piglets
a young pig

pigment NOUN pigments
a substance that colours something

pigsty NOUN pigsties
a place for keeping pigs

pigtail NOUN pigtails
a plait of hair

pike NOUN pikes
❶ a large fish that lives in rivers and lakes
❷ a heavy spear

pilchard NOUN pilchards
a small sea fish

pile NOUN piles
a number of things on top of one another • *a pile of rubbish*
pile VERB piles, piling, piled
To pile things is to put them into a pile.
➤ **To pile up** is to form a pile. • *Dead leaves had piled up in the playground.*

pilgrim NOUN pilgrims
someone who goes on a journey to a holy place

pilgrimage NOUN pilgrimages
a journey to a holy place

pill NOUN pills
a small piece of medicine that you swallow

pillar NOUN pillars
a tall stone or wooden post

pillow NOUN pillows
a cushion to rest your head on in bed

pilot NOUN pilots
❶ someone who flies an aircraft ❷ someone who steers a ship in and out of a port
pilot VERB pilots, piloting, piloted
To pilot an aircraft is to fly it.

pin NOUN pins
a short piece of metal with a sharp point, used to hold paper or cloth in place
pin VERB pins, pinning, pinned
to fasten something with a pin

pinafore NOUN pinafores
a dress without sleeves, worn over a blouse or jumper

pincer NOUN pincers
the claw of a shellfish such as a crab

a b c d e f g h i j k l m n o **p** q r s t u v w x y z

pincers *PLURAL NOUN*
a tool for gripping and pulling things, especially for pulling out nails

pinch *VERB* pinches, pinching, pinched
❶ to squeeze something tightly between two things, especially between the finger and thumb
❷ *(informal)* to steal something

pinch *NOUN* pinches
❶ a firm squeezing movement ❷ the amount you can pick up between the tips of your finger and thumb • *Add a **pinch** of salt.*

pine *NOUN* pines
an evergreen tree with leaves shaped like needles

pine *VERB* pines, pining, pined
to feel very sad because you miss something or someone

pineapple *NOUN* pineapples
a large tropical fruit with yellow flesh and prickly leaves and skin

ping-pong *NOUN*
another word for **table tennis**

pink *ADJECTIVE* pinker, pinkest
pale red

pink *NOUN* pinks
a pink colour

pint *NOUN* pints
a measurement of the volume of liquid. 8 pints make 1 gallon and 1 pint is about 570 millilitres.

pioneer *NOUN* pioneers
one of the first people to go to a place or do something new

pious *ADJECTIVE*
very religious
➤ **piously** *ADVERB*

pip *NOUN* pips
a small hard seed of a fruit such as an apple or orange

pipe *NOUN* pipes
❶ a tube for carrying water, gas or oil ❷ a small tube-shaped musical instrument that you blow into

pipe *VERB* pipes, piping, piped
to send liquid or gas along pipes somewhere • *Water is **piped** into our homes.*

pipeline *NOUN* pipelines
a pipe for carrying oil, water or gas over a long distance

piracy *NOUN*
the crime of attacking and robbing ships at sea

piranha *NOUN* piranhas
a fish with sharp teeth that tear the flesh of its prey

pirate *NOUN* pirates
a sailor who attacks and robs other ships

pistil *NOUN* pistils
the part of a flower that produces the seed

BUILD YOUR VOCABULARY
Look at **anther** and **stamen**.

pistol *NOUN* pistols
a small gun

piston *NOUN* pistons
a disc that moves up and down inside a cylinder in an engine

pit *NOUN* pits
❶ a deep hole or hollow ❷ a coal mine

pitch *NOUN* pitches
❶ a piece of ground marked out for football, cricket or another game ❷ The pitch of a sound is how high or low it is. ❸ a sticky black substance like tar

pitch *VERB* pitches, pitching, pitched
❶ to throw something somewhere with a lot of force ❷ To pitch a tent is to set it up.

pitfall *NOUN* pitfalls
a hidden danger or difficulty

pitiful *ADJECTIVE*
❶ making you feel pity • *a pitiful cry* ❷ very bad
• *a pitiful attempt to be funny*
➤ **pitifully** *ADVERB*

pitiless *ADJECTIVE*
having or showing no pity

pity *NOUN*
❶ The feeling of being sorry because someone is in
pain or in trouble. • *He felt no pity for his victims.*
❷ If something is a pity, it is disappointing. • *It's a
pity we can't meet.*
pity *VERB* pities, pitying, pitied
To pity someone is to feel sorry for them.

pivot *NOUN* pivots
a point on which something turns or balances
pivot *VERB* pivots, pivoting, pivoted
to turn on a pivot or central point

pixel *NOUN* pixels
one of the tiny dots on a screen from which an
image is formed

pixie *NOUN* pixies
a small fairy or elf

pizza *(say* peet-sa*) NOUN* pizzas
a dish made from a flat piece of dough, covered with
tomatoes, cheese and other ingredients

❈ **WORD STORY**
Pizza is an Italian word that originally meant 'pie'.

placard *NOUN* placards
a poster or notice, especially one carried at a
demonstration

place *NOUN* places
❶ a particular area, building, point or position • *Put
it in a safe place.* • *We stayed in a nice place.*
❷ a position in a race or competition • *I came in
fourth place.* ❸ If you get a place at a school or on
a team, you are allowed to join it.
➤ **To take place** is to happen.
place *VERB* places, placing, placed
to put something somewhere

placid *ADJECTIVE*
calm and peaceful

plague *NOUN* plagues
❶ a dangerous illness that spreads very quickly
❷ a large number of pests • *The crops were
destroyed by a plague of locusts.*
plague *VERB* plagues, plaguing, plagued
to pester or annoy someone continuously • *They
have been plagued with complaints.*

plaice *NOUN* plaice
a flat sea fish

plaid *(say* plad*) NOUN* plaids
tartan or other cloth with a pattern of squares

plain *ADJECTIVE* plainer, plainest
❶ with no decoration or anything added • *a plain
blue dress* ❷ easy to understand or see • *He made
his feelings plain.*
plain *NOUN* plains
a large area of flat country without trees

plainly *ADVERB*
❶ clearly or obviously • *I could see them plainly.*
❷ simply • *She was plainly dressed.*

plaintive *ADJECTIVE*
sounding sad • *the plaintive cry of a bird*
➤ **plaintively** *ADVERB*

plait *(say* plat*) NOUN* plaits
a length of hair with three strands twisted together
plait *(say* plat*) VERB* plaits, plaiting, plaited
To plait hair or rope is to twist three strands together
to make one thick strand.

plan *NOUN* plans
❶ something you intend to do and a way of doing it
that you have thought out in advance ❷ a drawing
or map showing how the parts of something are
arranged • *a plan of the school*
plan *VERB* plans, planning, planned
❶ to think out in advance how you are going to do
something ❷ To plan to do something is to intend to
do it. • *I don't plan to come.*

plane *NOUN* planes
❶ an aeroplane ❷ a tool for making wood smooth
plane *VERB* planes, planing, planed
to smooth wood with a plane

planet *NOUN* **planets**
a large sphere that moves in an orbit round a star. The planets which orbit the sun are Mercury, Venus, Earth, Mars, Jupiter, Saturn, Uranus and Neptune.

✳ **WORD STORY**
The word **planet** comes from a Greek word meaning 'wanderer', because the planets appear to move among the stars.

plank *NOUN* **planks**
a long flat piece of wood

plankton *NOUN*
a mass of tiny creatures that float in the sea and lakes

plant *NOUN* **plants**
a living thing that grows out of the ground. Plants include flowers, bushes, trees and vegetables.

plant *VERB* **plants, planting, planted**
❶ to put something like a flower or tree in the ground to grow ❷ to put something firmly somewhere • *She planted her feet carefully on the ground.*

plantation *NOUN* **plantations**
a large area of land where a crop such as coffee, tea or rubber is grown

plaque *(say plak or plahk) NOUN* **plaques**
❶ a metal or porcelain plate fixed on a wall as a memorial ❷ a substance that forms a thin layer on your teeth and can cause decay

plasma *(say plaz-ma) ADJECTIVE*
a plasma screen uses a special type of gas to show colours

plaster *NOUN* **plasters**
❶ a small sticky strip you put over cut skin to protect it ❷ a soft mixture that dries hard, used to make a smooth surface on walls or to cover a broken leg or arm while it heals

plaster *VERB* **plasters, plastering, plastered**
❶ to cover a surface with plaster ❷ to cover something thickly • *His clothes were plastered with mud.* ❸ to make something stick somewhere because of being wet • *His hair was plastered to his forehead.*

plastic *NOUN* **plastics**
a strong light artificial material that can be moulded into different shapes

plastic *ADJECTIVE*
made of plastic • *I don't want a plastic bag.*

plate *NOUN* **plates**
❶ a flat or almost flat dish, used for eating ❷ a thin flat sheet of metal, glass or other hard material

plateau *(say plat-oh) NOUN* **plateaux, plateaus**
a flat area of high land

plateful *NOUN* **platefuls**
an amount that fills a plate

platform *NOUN* **platforms**
❶ a flat raised area along a railway, where a train stops ❷ a small stage • *The teachers walked up on to the platform.*

platinum NOUN
a valuable silver-coloured metal

BUILD YOUR VOCABULARY
Platinum is an **element**.

platoon NOUN platoons
a small unit of soldiers

platypus NOUN platypuses
an Australian animal that is a mammal but lays eggs and has a beak and feet like a duck's

play VERB plays, playing, played
❶ to do something for fun, such as taking part in a game or using a toy • *We went out to play.*
❷ To play a sport is to take part in it. • *She plays football for the school.* ❸ To play an instrument is to make music with it. ❹ To play a part in a film or play is to perform in it.
➤ **player** NOUN

play NOUN plays
a story acted out on stage, television or radio

playful ADJECTIVE
wanting to play; full of fun • *a playful kitten*

playground NOUN playgrounds
a place out of doors where children can play

playgroup NOUN playgroups
a group of very young children who meet to play, with adults to look after them

playmate NOUN playmates
someone that you play with

playtime NOUN playtimes
a time in the school day when children go out to play

playwright NOUN playwrights
someone who writes plays

WATCH OUT!
The word **playwright** ends in **-wright**, meaning 'a person who makes something', not -*write*.

plea NOUN pleas
❶ If you make a plea, you beg or ask urgently for something. ❷ in a law court, a statement of 'guilty' or 'not guilty' by someone accused of a crime

plead VERB pleads, pleading, pleaded
to beg for something • *He pleaded with them for help.*
➤ **To plead guilty** is to state in a law court that

you are guilty of a crime. If you plead not guilty, you say you are not guilty of the crime.

pleasant ADJECTIVE pleasanter, pleasantest
nice, pleasing, enjoyable or friendly
➤ **pleasantly** ADVERB

please ADVERB
used when you want to ask for something politely
• *Can I have some more, please?*
please VERB pleases, pleasing, pleased
to make someone happy or satisfied

pleasure (say plezh-er) NOUN pleasures
a feeling of happiness or satisfaction

WATCH OUT!
Watch out for **pleasure**, **measure** and **treasure**, which are all pronounced -*ezh*-er but spelt **-easure**.

pledge NOUN pledges
a solemn promise to do something
pledge VERB pledges, pledging, pledged
to promise solemnly to do something

plentiful ADJECTIVE
large in amount • *a plentiful crop of fruit*

plenty NOUN
Plenty of something is a lot of it or more than enough. • *We have plenty of food.*

pliers NOUN
a small tool with jaws for gripping something or for breaking wire

plight NOUN plights
a very difficult situation • *We were shocked at the plight of these sea creatures.*

plinth NOUN plinths
the thick base of a column or statue

plod VERB plods, plodding, plodded
to walk slowly with heavy steps • *We plodded through the rain.*

plonk VERB plonks, plonking, plonked (*informal*)
to put something down without taking care
• *She plonked her cup down.*

plop NOUN plops
the sound of something dropping into liquid

301

plop VERB plops, plopping, plopped
to fall into liquid with a plop

plot NOUN plots
❶ a secret plan, especially to do something bad
❷ the story of a novel, film or play

plot VERB plots, plotting, plotted
❶ to make a secret plan to do something ❷ To plot a chart or graph is to make it, marking all the points on it.
➤ **plotter** NOUN • The **plotters** were captured.

plough (say plow) NOUN ploughs
a tool used on farms for turning over soil

plough (say plow) VERB ploughs, ploughing, ploughed
to turn over soil with a plough

plover (say pluv-er) NOUN plovers
a long-legged wading bird

pluck VERB plucks, plucking, plucked
❶ To pluck a flower or fruit is to pick it. ❷ To pluck a bird is to pull the feathers off it. ❸ To pluck a string on an instrument is to play it with your fingers.

plucky ADJECTIVE pluckier, pluckiest
brave; courageous

plug NOUN plugs
❶ an object used to block the hole in a sink or bath
❷ part of an electrical device that you put into a socket

plug VERB plugs, plugging, plugged
To plug a hole is to block it.
➤ **To plug something in** is to connect it to an electric socket using a plug.

plum NOUN plums
a soft juicy fruit with a stone in the middle

plumage (say ploo-mij) NOUN
A bird's plumage is its feathers.

plumber NOUN plumbers
someone who fits and mends water pipes in a building

plume NOUN plumes
❶ a large feather ❷ a column of smoke, steam, dust or liquid • We saw a **plume** of smoke in the distance.

plump ADJECTIVE plumper, plumpest
rounded or slightly fat

plunder VERB plunders, plundering, plundered
to violently steal things, especially during a war
The chief brigand counted out the jewels and gold coins they'd plundered and divided them all into twenty heaps.—THE SCARECROW AND HIS SERVANT, Philip Pullman

plunder NOUN
valuable things stolen by plundering

plunge VERB plunges, plunging, plunged
to jump, dive or fall into something

plural NOUN plurals
the form of a word meaning more than one thing or person, such as *books* and *children*

plural ADJECTIVE
in the plural • *'Mice' is a* **plural** *noun.*

⚙ **BUILD** YOUR VOCABULARY
Look at **singular**.

plus PREPOSITION
with the next number or thing added • *Two* **plus** *two equals four: 2 + 2 = 4.*

p.m. ABBREVIATION
in the afternoon or evening • *The film starts at 7* **p.m.**

✳ **WORD STORY**
p.m. is short for Latin *post meridiem*, meaning 'after midday'.

⚙ **BUILD** YOUR VOCABULARY
Look at **a.m.**

pneumatic (say new-mat-ik) ADJECTIVE
filled with air or worked by compressed air
• *a pneumatic drill*

pneumonia (say new-**moh**-nee-a) NOUN
a serious disease of the lungs

poach VERB poaches, poaching, poached
❶ To poach animals is to hunt them illegally on someone else's land. ❷ To poach an egg is to cook it out of its shell in gently boiling water.
➤ **poacher** NOUN • The **poachers** were caught.

pocket NOUN pockets
part of a piece of clothing, shaped like a small bag, for keeping things in

pocket money NOUN
money given to a child to spend

pod NOUN pods
a long seed container on a pea or bean plant

podgy *ADJECTIVE* podgier, podgiest (informal)
small and plump

poem *NOUN* poems
a piece of writing arranged in short lines, in which words are chosen for their rhythm, rhyme or effect

poet *NOUN* poets
someone who writes poetry

poetic *ADJECTIVE*
like poetry

poetry *NOUN*
poems as a form of literature • *She writes **poetry** and plays.*

point *NOUN* points
❶ the narrow or sharp end of something • *Use the **point** of the scissors.* ❷ the purpose or the most important part • *What's the **point** of this task?* ❸ an idea or opinion expressed by someone • *That's a good **point**.* ❹ a single mark in a game or quiz • *How many **points** did I get?* ❺ a particular place or time • *At one **point** he nearly fell.*

BUILD YOUR VOCABULARY
Look at **bullet point** and **decimal point**.

point *VERB* points, pointing, pointed
❶ to show where something is by holding out your finger ❷ To point something is to aim it or direct it. • *She **pointed** her telescope at the moon.*
➤ **To point something out** is to show it or explain it.

pointed *ADJECTIVE*
with a thin sharp end

pointless *ADJECTIVE*
with no purpose or meaning

point of view *NOUN* points of view
a way of looking at something; an attitude or perspective • *The story is told from the dog's **point of view**.*

poised *ADJECTIVE*
waiting in a position ready to do something • *She sat, hands **poised** above the keyboard.*

poison *NOUN* poisons
a substance that can kill or harm you if you eat or touch it

poison *VERB* poisons, poisoning, poisoned
❶ to kill or harm someone with poison ❷ to put poison in something

poisonous *ADJECTIVE*
If something is poisonous, it can kill or harm you because it contains poison.

poke *VERB* pokes, poking, poked
to push someone or something with a finger or pointed object
poke *NOUN* pokes
a push with a finger or sharp object

poker *NOUN* pokers
a metal rod for stirring a fire

polar *ADJECTIVE*
to do with or near the North or South Pole • *a **polar** expedition*

BUILD YOUR VOCABULARY
Look at **Arctic** and **Antarctic**.

polar bear *NOUN* polar bears
a large white bear living in the Arctic (around the North Pole)

pole *NOUN* poles
❶ a long thin piece of wood or metal ❷ The earth's poles are the ends of its axis, the **North Pole** and the **South Pole**. ❸ each end of a magnet

police *NOUN*
people whose job is to catch criminals and make sure that people obey the law • *Call the **police**!*

policeman *or* **policewoman** *NOUN*
policemen, policewomen
a police officer

police officer *NOUN* police officers
a member of the police

policy *NOUN* policies
a plan or set of plans for how to do something

polish (say pol-ish) *VERB* polishes, polishing, polished
to make a surface shiny and smooth
polish (say pol-ish) *NOUN* polishes
a substance used to make something shiny

a
b
c
d
e
f
g
h
i
j
k
l
m
n
o
p
q
r
s
t
u
v
w
x
y
z

polite ADJECTIVE **politer, politest**
having good manners; showing respect towards other people
➤ **politely** ADVERB ➤ **politeness** NOUN

BUILD YOUR VOCABULARY
Opposites are **impolite** and **rude**.

politician (say poli-**tish**-an) NOUN **politicians**
someone whose job is being part of a country's government

politics NOUN
activities and work to do with governing a country
➤ **political** ADJECTIVE • *political issues*

poll NOUN **polls**
a survey asking what people think about something

pollen NOUN
yellow powder found inside flowers, containing male seeds for fertilising other flowers

pollinate VERB **pollinates, pollinating, pollinated**
to put pollen into a flower or plant to fertilise it • *Bees **pollinate** many plants.*
➤ **pollination** NOUN

pollute VERB **pollutes, polluting, polluted**
to make something or somewhere dirty and dangerous to use or live in
➤ **pollution** NOUN • *the **pollution** of our oceans*

polygon NOUN **polygons**
a flat shape with many sides

BUILD YOUR VOCABULARY
Look at **heptagon, hexagon, octagon** and **pentagon**.

polythene NOUN
a thin light plastic used to make bags and wrappings

pomp NOUN
the dignified and solemn way in which an important ceremony is carried out

pompous ADJECTIVE
behaving as if you think you are very important

pond NOUN **ponds**
a small lake

ponder VERB **ponders, pondering, pondered**
to think carefully and seriously about something

ponderous ADJECTIVE
heavy and awkward

pony NOUN **ponies**
a small horse

ponytail NOUN **ponytails**
a bunch of long hair tied at the back of the head

poodle NOUN **poodles**
a dog with long curly hair

pool NOUN **pools**
❶ a puddle or pond • *The waterfall tumbled into a **pool** of clear water.* ❷ a swimming pool

poor ADJECTIVE **poorer, poorest**
❶ having very little money • *He came from a **poor** family.* ❷ not good or adequate • *This work is **poor**.* ❸ unfortunate • ***Poor** boy!*

BUILD YOUR VOCABULARY
Look at **poverty**.

poorly ADVERB
badly; not well enough • *They played **poorly**.*
poorly ADJECTIVE
ill • *He's **poorly** today.*

pop NOUN **pops**
❶ modern popular music ❷ a small explosive sound ❸ a fizzy drink
pop VERB **pops, popping, popped**
❶ to burst with a small explosive sound ❷ (informal) to go somewhere quickly • *I'm just **popping** out.*

popcorn NOUN
a snack made from maize heated until it bursts and becomes fluffy

Pope NOUN **Popes**
the leader of the Roman Catholic Church

poplar NOUN **poplars**
a tall straight tree

poppadom NOUN **poppadoms**
a thin crisp Indian bread fried in oil

poppy NOUN **poppies**
a plant with large flowers, usually red

popular ADJECTIVE
liked or enjoyed by a lot of people
➤ **popularity** NOUN • *Snowboarding quickly grew in popularity.*

populated ADJECTIVE
If a place is populated, people live there.

population NOUN populations
The population of a place is all the people who live there or the number of people who live there.
• *What is the population of London?*

porcelain *(say* por-sel-in*)* NOUN
a kind of fine china

porch NOUN porches
a small roofed area outside the door of a building

porcupine NOUN porcupines
a small animal covered with long prickles

 WORD STORY
The word **porcupine** comes from old French words meaning 'prickly pig'.

pore NOUN pores
Your pores are the tiny holes in your skin which sweat can pass through.
pore VERB pores, poring, pored
➤ **To pore over something** is to study it closely.

pork NOUN
meat from a pig

porous ADJECTIVE
allowing liquid to pass through • *Limestone is porous.*

porpoise *(say* por-pus*)* NOUN porpoises
a sea mammal similar to a dolphin with a rounded nose

porridge NOUN
a food made by boiling oats in water or milk

port NOUN ports
❶ a harbour or a town with a harbour
❷ the left-hand side of a ship or aircraft

BUILD YOUR VOCABULARY
Look at **starboard**.

portable ADJECTIVE
able to be carried easily • *a portable charger*

portcullis NOUN portcullises
a heavy gate at the entrance to a castle that can be raised and lowered

porter NOUN porters
someone whose job is to carry luggage or goods

porthole NOUN portholes
a small round window in a ship or aircraft

portion NOUN portions
❶ an amount of food for one person ❷ a part or share of something • *A portion of the wall collapsed.*

portrait NOUN portraits
a picture of a person

portray VERB portrays, portraying, portrayed
to describe or show someone or something
• *The story portrays the king as kind and noble.*

pose VERB poses, posing, posed
❶ to stay in a particular position to be photographed, drawn or painted ❷ To pose as someone is to pretend to be them. • *He posed as a waiter to get into the party.* ❸ To pose a question or problem is to present it. • *Thick fog poses a danger.*
pose NOUN poses
a way of standing or sitting for a portrait or photograph to be made of you • *Hold that pose!*

posh ADJECTIVE posher, poshest *(informal)*
expensive or upper-class • *a posh hotel*

position NOUN positions
❶ The position of something is where it is. ❷ Your position is the way you are standing, sitting or lying.
• *He was in a crouched position.* ❸ a situation or condition • *You have put me in a difficult position.*
position VERB positions, positioning, positioned
to place something somewhere

positive ADJECTIVE
❶ sure or definite • *I am positive I saw him.*
❷ agreeing or saying 'yes' • *We received a positive answer.* ❸ A positive number is greater than zero.
❹ good or beneficial • *the positive effects of tourism*
➤ **positively** ADVERB

BUILD YOUR VOCABULARY
An opposite for meanings 2, 3 and 4 is **negative**.

a b c d e f g h i j k l m n o **p** q r s t u v w x y z

positive NOUN positives
an advantage or good thing

> **BUILD YOUR VOCABULARY**
> The opposite is **negative**.

possess VERB possesses, possessing, possessed
to own or have something • *I will give you everything I* **possess***.*

> **WATCH OUT!**
> **Possess** has two sets of double **s**.

possession NOUN possessions
something that you own • *The ring was her most treasured* **possession***.*

possessive NOUN possessive *(in grammar)*
a word or form of a word that shows something belongs to someone or is part of something • *We use apostrophes to mark* **possessives***.*

possessive ADJECTIVE *(in grammar)*
showing that something belongs to someone or is part of something

possessive pronoun NOUN possessive pronouns
a pronoun that shows something belongs to someone, for example *mine* or *hers*

possibility NOUN possibilities
something that is possible • *There is a* **possibility** *of success.*

possible ADJECTIVE
able to happen or be done

> **BUILD YOUR VOCABULARY**
> The opposite is **impossible**.

possibly ADVERB
❶ perhaps • *We will finish at four or* **possibly** *earlier.*
❷ in any way • *That cannot* **possibly** *be right.*

post NOUN posts
❶ an upright piece of wood, concrete or metal fixed in the ground ❷ the system of collecting and delivering letters and parcels • *I sent it by* **post***.*
❸ letters and parcels carried by post • *Has any* **post** *come?*
➤ **postal** ADJECTIVE • *the* **postal** *service*

post VERB posts, posting, posted
❶ to send a letter or parcel ❷ to display information or a message somewhere public, for example on the Internet

postcard NOUN postcards
a card that you can write a message on and post without an envelope

postcode NOUN postcodes
a group of letters and numbers included at the end of an address

poster NOUN posters
a large notice giving information or advertising something

postman *or* **postwoman** NOUN postmen, postwomen
someone who collects and delivers letters and parcels

post office NOUN post offices
a place where you can post letters and parcels and get stamps and official documents

postpone VERB postpones, postponing, postponed
to arrange for something to take place later than was originally planned • *The match has been* **postponed***.*

posture NOUN postures
the way that a person stands, sits or walks

pot NOUN pots
a deep round container • *a* **pot** *of stew*

potato NOUN potatoes
a vegetable with a brown or red skin that grows underground and is eaten cooked • *We had roast* **potatoes***.*

> **WATCH OUT!**
> Remember to put an **e** in the plural **potatoes**, but not in the singular **potato**.

potent *ADJECTIVE*
powerful

potential *ADJECTIVE*
capable of happening or becoming something in future • *She is a **potential** national champion.*
➤ **potentially** *ADVERB*

potential *NOUN*
To have potential is to be capable of becoming successful or useful in future.

pothole *NOUN* **potholes**
❶ a hole in a road surface ❷ a deep natural hole in the ground

potion *(say poh-shun) NOUN* **potions**
a drink containing medicine or poison

potter *NOUN* **potters**
someone who makes pottery

pottery *NOUN*
pots, plates and other things made of baked clay

pouch *NOUN* **pouches**
❶ a small bag or pocket ❷ a pocket of skin in which a mother kangaroo keeps its young

poultry *NOUN*
birds such as chickens and turkeys, kept for eggs and meat

pounce *VERB* **pounces, pouncing, pounced**
to jump on or attack someone or something suddenly
The Pelican opened his gigantic beak and immediately the policemen pounced upon the burglar who was crouching inside.—THE GIRAFFE AND THE PELLY AND ME, Roald Dahl

pound *NOUN* **pounds**
❶ a unit of money. In Britain, there are 100 pence in 1 pound, which is written as £1 ❷ a measurement of weight. There are 16 ounces in 1 pound, which is about 450 grams.

> **BUILD YOUR VOCABULARY**
> The abbreviation for the measurement of weight is **lb**.

pound *VERB* **pounds, pounding, pounded**
❶ to hit something repeatedly and hard, for example to crush it ❷ If your heart pounds, it beats heavily.
• *My heart was **pounding** with fear.*

pour *VERB* **pours, pouring, poured**
❶ to make a liquid flow out of a container • *She poured me a cup of tea.* ❷ to flow in a large amount • *People **poured** out of the hall.* ❸ If it is pouring, it is raining heavily.

pout *VERB* **pouts, pouting, pouted**
to stick out your lips because you are annoyed or sulking

poverty *NOUN*
the state of being poor • *They live in **poverty**.*

powder *NOUN* **powders**
a mass of tiny pieces of something dry, like flour or dust
➤ **powdery** *ADJECTIVE* • *powdery snow*

power *NOUN* **powers**
❶ the ability to make something happen or to control other people • *The king had a lot of **power**.* ❷ a special ability • *The ring had magic **powers**.* ❸ energy or force, for example electricity • *Switch the **power** on.*

powerful *ADJECTIVE*
having a lot of power or strength • *a **powerful** magic potion*
➤ **powerfully** *ADVERB*

powerless *ADJECTIVE*
unable to do anything or control things

power station *NOUN* **power stations**
a building where electricity is produced

practical *ADJECTIVE*
❶ able to do or make useful things • *She is a very **practical** person.* ❷ likely to work or be useful • *a **practical** solution*

practically *ADVERB*
❶ almost • *I've got **practically** no money left.* ❷ in a practical way

practice *NOUN* **practices**
❶ regular training or repeating of something so that you get better at it • *Your playing will get better with **practice**.* ❷ A doctor's or dentist's practice is their business.

> ⚠ **WATCH OUT!**
> Don't confuse **practice** (a noun, spelt **-ice**) with to **practise** (a verb, spelt **-ise**).

a
b
c
d
e
f
g
h
i
j
k
l
m
n
o
p
q
r
s
t
u
v
w
x
y
z

practise VERB practises, practising, practised
❶ to do something often so that you get better at it • *We kept practising the song until the whole class knew it.* ❷ To practise a religion or activity is to regularly take part in it. ❸ To practise medicine or law is to work as a doctor or lawyer.

prairie NOUN prairies
a large area of flat grass-covered land

praise VERB praises, praising, praised
to say that someone or something is good or has done well

praise NOUN praises
words that praise someone or something

pram NOUN prams
a small bed on wheels in which a baby is pushed along

prance VERB prances, prancing, pranced
to jump about in a lively or happy way
The Scarecrow leaped all over the room, capering and skipping and prancing like a goat.—THE SCARECROW AND HIS SERVANT, Philip Pullman

prank NOUN pranks
a trick played on someone for a joke

prawn NOUN prawns
a small shellfish with a large head and a long tail that you can eat

BUILD YOUR VOCABULARY
A **prawn** is a **crustacean**.

pray VERB prays, praying, prayed
to talk to God

prayer NOUN prayers
something someone says when they talk to God

preach VERB preaches, preaching, preached
to give a talk about religion or about right and wrong
➤ **preacher** NOUN

precaution NOUN precautions
something you do to prevent trouble or danger in the future

precede VERB precedes, preceding, preceded
If one thing precedes another, it comes or goes before it. • *The film was preceded by adverts and trailers.*

⚠ WATCH OUT!
Precede meaning 'come before' starts with **pre-**, meaning 'before'. Don't confuse it with **proceed** meaning 'go on'.

precious (say presh-us) ADJECTIVE
very valuable or loved
Remembering her precious cordial, Lucy poured a few drops into her brother's mouth.—THE LION, THE WITCH AND THE WARDROBE, C. S. Lewis

precipice (say press-ip-iss) NOUN precipices
a very steep cliff or mountain face

precise ADJECTIVE
exact or very accurate • *It was a long time ago—850 years, to be precise.*
➤ **precisely** ADVERB

predator (say pred-at-er) NOUN predators
an animal that hunts other animals

predecessor (say pre-dis-ess-er) NOUN predecessors
Someone's predecessor is the person who had their job before them.

predicament NOUN predicaments
a difficult or unpleasant situation • *There seemed to be no way out of their predicament.*

predict VERB predicts, predicting, predicted
to say that something will happen in the future
➤ **prediction** NOUN • *His prediction came true.*

preen VERB preens, preening, preened
❶ When a bird preens its feathers, it tidies them with its beak. ❷ If you preen or preen yourself, you admire your own appearance.

preface (say pref-ass) NOUN prefaces
an introduction at the beginning of a book

prefect NOUN prefects
a pupil chosen to have special duties and help the teachers

prefer VERB prefers, preferring, preferred
If you prefer one thing to another, you like it better.

preference NOUN preferences
Your preference is what you prefer.

prefix NOUN prefixes
a group of letters joined to the front of a word to make a new word, like *un-* in **un**happy or *mis-* in **mis**understand

 BUILD YOUR VOCABULARY
Look at **suffix**.

pregnant ADJECTIVE
A pregnant woman has a baby developing inside her womb.
➤ **pregnancy** NOUN

prehistoric ADJECTIVE
belonging to a very long time ago, before anything was written down

prejudice (say **prej-u-diss**) NOUN prejudices
an unfair bad opinion that people have about someone or something without really knowing what they are like

✳ **WORD STORY**
The word **prejudice** comes from Latin words meaning 'judgement in advance'.

premature ADJECTIVE
happening or arriving before the proper time
• *a premature baby*

premier (say **prem-ee-er**) NOUN premiers
the leader of a government

premiere (say **prem-yair**) NOUN premieres
the first public performance of a play or showing of a film

premises NOUN
the buildings and land an organisation uses

preoccupied ADJECTIVE
thinking hard about something so you do not notice other things

preparation NOUN preparations
❶ the act of getting ready for something • *They practised in **preparation** for the concert.*
❷ Preparations are things you do in order to get ready for something.
He had made wonderful preparations for her birthday.
—A LITTLE PRINCESS, Frances Hodgson Burnett

prepare VERB prepares, preparing, prepared
to get something ready
➤ **To be prepared to do something** is to be ready or willing to do it.

preposition NOUN prepositions
a word you put in front of a noun or pronoun to show how it is linked to another word, often showing place, position or time. In these sentences, the words in bold are prepositions: *Put the plates **on** the table. I'll come **at** ten.*

 BUILD YOUR VOCABULARY
Preposition is a **word class**.

prescribe VERB prescribes, prescribing, prescribed
To prescribe a medicine is to say a patient should take it.

presence NOUN
Someone's presence is the fact that they are there.
• *She was surprised at his **presence**.*

present (say **prez-ent**) ADJECTIVE
❶ in a particular place; there • *How many people were **present**?* ❷ existing or happening now • *the **present** time*

present (say **prez-ent**) NOUN
❶ a gift • *He gave me a birthday **present**.* ❷ The present is the time now. • *She is away at **present**.*

present (say **priz-ent**) VERB
presents, presenting, presented
❶ to give something to someone, especially at a ceremony • *The headteacher will **present** the prizes.*
❷ to show or perform something in front of people
• *We **presented** our work in assembly.*
❸ To present a television or radio show is to introduce it.
➤ **presenter** NOUN
• *a TV **presenter***

presentation
NOUN presentations
❶ a formal talk or display • *You could make a **presentation** to the class.* ❷ a ceremony when a prize or medal is given

presently ADVERB
soon; soon after

present participle NOUN present participles
a form of a verb such as *smiling* or *walking*. A present participle is used with the verb *be* to talk about an action that is happening now, for example *He is smiling*, or that continues for some time, for example *We were walking for hours*.

present tense NOUN
a form of a verb used to describe something that happens or is true now, for example *likes* in *He likes football*.

preserve VERB preserves, preserving, preserved
to keep something safe or in good condition

president NOUN presidents
the head of a country that has no king or queen
➤ **presidential** ADJECTIVE

press VERB presses, pressing, pressed
❶ to push or squeeze something firmly • *Press the red button.* ❷ To press clothes is to iron them. ❸ to try to make someone do something • *She pressed him to answer.*

press NOUN
The press is newspapers and journalists.

pressure NOUN pressures
❶ a force pushing against something • *Pressure built up inside the container.* ❷ If there is pressure on you, someone is trying to make you do something.

⚠ **WATCH OUT!**
The word **pressure** is spelt **press** + *ure*.

presumably ADVERB
probably; I suppose

presume VERB presumes, presuming, presumed
to believe without knowing for certain; to suppose • *I presume that's his mum.*

pretence NOUN pretences
an attempt to pretend something

pretend VERB pretends, pretending, pretended
to behave as if something untrue or imaginary is true • *He pretended to be surprised.*

pretty ADJECTIVE prettier, prettiest
attractive; pleasant to look at
➤ **prettily** ADVERB ➤ **prettiness** NOUN

pretty ADVERB (informal)
quite; fairly • *It's pretty cold outside.*

prevail VERB prevails, prevailing, prevailed
to succeed or win • *At the end of the story, good prevails.*

prevent VERB prevents, preventing, prevented
to stop something from happening • *How could we have prevented this accident?*

previous ADJECTIVE
coming before this; preceding • *I remembered our previous conversation.*
➤ **previously** ADVERB • *The building was previously a church.*

prey (say pray) NOUN
an animal that is hunted or killed by another animal for food

prey (say pray) VERB preys, preying, preyed
➤ **To prey on something** is to hunt and kill it for food. • *Owls prey on mice.*

price NOUN prices
the amount of money that you have to pay for something

price VERB prices, pricing, priced
To price something is to decide its price.

priceless ADJECTIVE
very valuable

prick VERB pricks, pricking, pricked
to stick something small, sharp and pointed into something or someone

prickle NOUN prickles
a sharp point on a plant or animal
➤ **prickly** ADJECTIVE • *a prickly cactus*

prickle VERB prickles, prickling, prickled
to feel or make you feel as though lots of sharp little points are sticking into your skin • *His skin prickled.*

pride *NOUN* prides
① a feeling of being pleased with yourself or someone else who has done well • *I was full of pride when the team walked out.* ② a feeling that you are important and deserve respect • *I had to forget my pride and ask for help.* ③ A pride of lions is a group of them that live together.

priest *NOUN* priests
someone who leads religious ceremonies, especially in the Christian church

prim *ADJECTIVE* primmer, primmest
always neat and correct and disapproving of anything rude
➤ **primly** *ADVERB*

primary *ADJECTIVE*
first or most important • *The children are his primary concern.*

primary school *NOUN* primary schools
a school for the first stage of a child's education, between the ages of 5 and 11

primate *NOUN* primates
an animal of the group that includes human beings, apes and monkeys

prime *ADJECTIVE*
① main or most important • *He was the prime suspect.* ② of the best quality • *prime beefburgers* ③ *(in mathematics)* able to be divided only by itself and the number 1 with no remainders • *How do you know if a number is prime?* • *The prime factors of 15 are 5 and 3.*

prime *NOUN* primes
the best part or stage of someone's life • *He was in his prime.*

prime minister *NOUN* prime ministers
the leader of a government

prime number *NOUN* prime numbers
a number that can only be divided by itself and the number 1 with no remainders, for example 2, 3, 5, 7 or 11

primitive *ADJECTIVE*
not very developed or advanced • *Primitive humans were hunters.*

primrose *NOUN* primroses
a pale yellow flower that comes out in spring

prince *NOUN* princes
a male member of a royal family, especially the son of a king or queen

princess *NOUN* princesses
a female member of a royal family, especially the daughter of a king or queen or the wife of a prince

principal *ADJECTIVE*
main or most important • *Our principal goal is to raise money.*

principal *NOUN* principals
the head of a college or school

⚠ **WATCH OUT!**
Don't confuse **principal** meaning 'most important' or 'head' with **principle** meaning 'basic rule'.

principle *NOUN* principles
① a general rule or truth • *the principles of mathematics* ② a basic belief about behaviour and what is right and wrong

print *VERB* prints, printing, printed
① To print words or pictures is to put them on paper using a machine. ② To print letters is to write them separately, not joined together. • *Print your name at the top.*

print *NOUN* prints
① Print is printed letters and numbers. ② A print is a mark made by something pressing on a surface. • *Her thumb left a print on the glass.*

printer *NOUN* printers
a machine that prints information on paper from a computer

printout *NOUN* printouts
a piece of paper with information printed on it from a computer

priority *(say* pry-or-rit-ee*) NOUN* priorities
something that is more important than other things • *His children are his priority.*

prise *VERB* prises, prising, prised
to force or lever something • *She prised open the lid with a spoon.*

a b c d e f g h i j k l m n o **p** q r s t u v w x y z

prism *NOUN* prisms
❶ a piece of glass that breaks up light into the colours of the rainbow ❷ *(in mathematics)* a solid object with parallel ends that are equal triangles or polygons

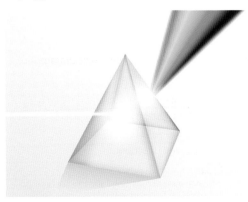

prison *NOUN* prisons
a place where people are held as a punishment for crime

prisoner *NOUN* prisoners
someone who is kept somewhere, especially in a prison and not allowed to leave

privacy *NOUN*
the state of being private or away from other people

private *ADJECTIVE*
❶ only for a particular person or group to have or use • *They have a private pool.* ❷ only for you or particular people to know • *That message was private.* ❸ away from other people • *Let's go somewhere private to talk.*
➤ **privately** *ADVERB* • *Let's talk privately.*

> ⚙ **BUILD** YOUR VOCABULARY
> An opposite is **public**.

private *NOUN* privates
a soldier of the lowest rank
➤ **in private** where only particular people can see or hear

privilege *NOUN* privileges
a special right or advantage given to one person or group of people
➤ **privileged** *ADJECTIVE*

> ⚠ **WATCH OUT!**
> The word **privilege** has a tricky spelling. It is made up of *privi* (two 'i's) + *lege* (two 'e's).

prize *NOUN* prizes
something you get for winning something or for doing well
prize *VERB* prizes, prizing, prized
to value something highly

probability *NOUN* probabilities
The probability of something is how likely it is to happen.

probable *ADJECTIVE*
likely to be true or to happen

> ⚙ **BUILD** YOUR VOCABULARY
> An opposite is **improbable**.

probably *ADVERB*
If something will probably happen or is probably true, it is likely to happen or be true.

probe *VERB* probes, probing, probed
❶ to gently push or feel something to find out about it ❷ to investigate or ask questions about something
probe *NOUN* probes
a device used to look inside something

problem *NOUN* problems
❶ something that causes difficulties • *The problem is, we haven't got enough people.* ❷ a puzzle or question that you have to solve

procedure *NOUN* procedures
a fixed or special way of doing something

proceed *(say pro-seed)* *VERB* proceeds, proceeding, proceeded
to go on or continue

> ⚠ **WATCH OUT!**
> Proceed means 'go on' and is related to **process**. Don't confuse it with **precede**, which means 'come before' and starts with *pre-* meaning 'before'.

proceedings *NOUN*
things that happen or are done; activities

process *NOUN* processes
a series of actions for making or doing something • *Growth is a natural process.*
process *VERB* processes, processing, processed
to put something through a series of actions or treatments to make something with it • *The leaves are processed into a paste.*

procession *NOUN* processions
a number of people or vehicles moving steadily forwards

proclaim *VERB* proclaims, proclaiming, proclaimed
to announce something officially or in public

prod *VERB* prods, prodding, prodded
to poke or push someone or something with your finger

produce *(say* prod-uce*) VERB* produces, producing, produced
❶ to make or create something • *Hens produce eggs.* ❷ to bring something out of a bag or other container • *She produced a camera and took a photo.* ❸ To produce a film, play or programme is to be responsible for organising it.

produce *(say* prod-uce*) NOUN*
food that is grown on farms or in gardens

producer *NOUN* producers
someone who produces a film, play or programme

product *NOUN* products
❶ something that is made for sale • *They sell beauty products.* ❷ The number that is the result of multiplying two numbers. • *12 is the product of 4 and 3.*

production *NOUN* productions
❶ the process of making or creating something • *oil production* ❷ a version of a play or film • *We saw a production of 'Romeo and Juliet'.*

profession *NOUN* professions
a type of work for which you need special knowledge and training, for example medicine, law or teaching

professional *ADJECTIVE*
❶ doing something as a paid job or profession • *She dreamed of being a professional footballer.* ❷ done to a high standard • *The show was very professional.*

professional *NOUN* professionals
someone who does something as their paid job

professor *NOUN* professors
a senior teacher in a university

profile *NOUN* profiles
❶ the outline of a person's face seen from the side
❷ a short description of someone

profit *NOUN* profits
money made from selling something for more than it cost to buy or make

⚠ **WATCH OUT!**
Don't confuse a **profit** which relates to money with a **prophet**, which sounds the same but has a different meaning.

profit *VERB* profits, profiting, profited
To profit from something is to get an advantage from it.

profitable *ADJECTIVE*
If something is profitable, it makes money.

profound *ADJECTIVE*
very deep or intense • *'This book,' said Mr Brown, 'had a profound effect on me.'*
➤ **profoundly** *ADVERB*

program *NOUN* programs
a series of coded instructions for a computer

program *VERB* programs, programming, programmed
to write instructions for a computer

programme *NOUN* programmes
❶ a show on radio or television ❷ a planned series of events ❸ a leaflet that gives information about a play, concert or event

progress *(say* pro-gress*) NOUN*
❶ forward movement • *The march made slow progress.* ❷ development or improvement • *You have made a lot of progress this term.*

progress *(say* pro-gress*) VERB* progresses, progressing, progressed
❶ to continue or move forward • *As the meal progressed, more and more dishes appeared.*
❷ to develop or improve

prohibit *VERB* prohibits, prohibiting, prohibited
to forbid something, especially by law • *Smoking is prohibited.*

project *(say* proj-ect*) NOUN* projects
❶ a task in which you find out about a subject and write about it ❷ a plan or scheme

project *(say* pro-ject*) VERB* projects, projecting, projected
❶ to stick out • *A flat rock projected from the cliff.*
❷ to display something on a screen with a projector
➤ **projection** *NOUN*

a
b
c
d
e
f
g
h
i
j
k
l
m
n
o
p
q
r
s
t
u
v
w
x
y
z

projector NOUN projectors
a machine for showing films or photographs on a large screen

prologue (say proh-log) NOUN prologues
an introduction to a poem or play or long story

prolong VERB prolongs, prolonging, prolonged
to make something last longer

promenade (say prom-en-ahd) NOUN promenades
a path or area for walking, especially by the sea

prominent ADJECTIVE
❶ important • a prominent person ❷ large or noticeable • a prominent nose

promise NOUN promises
❶ a statement that you will definitely do something ❷ If someone or something shows promise, they are likely to be successful.
➤ **promising** ADJECTIVE • a promising young player

promise VERB promises, promising, promised
to say that you will definitely do something
• I promise not to tell anyone.

promote VERB promotes, promoting, promoted
❶ to give someone a more important job or higher rank • She was promoted to captain. ❷ To promote a product or cause is to try to make it more popular or well known.
➤ **promotion** NOUN

prompt ADJECTIVE prompter, promptest
happening soon or without delay • We need a prompt reply.
➤ **promptly** ADVERB

prompt VERB prompts, prompting, prompted
to encourage someone to speak or remind them of what to say, for example in a play
'Perhaps you could tell us a bit about your last school, Polly?' she prompted.—FROZEN IN TIME, Ali Sparkes

prone ADJECTIVE
lying face downwards
➤ **To be prone to something** is to be likely to do or suffer from it. • The area is prone to flooding.

prong NOUN prongs
one of the pointed parts at the end of a fork

pronoun NOUN pronouns
a word used instead of a noun, such as he, her, it, them or those

🔧 **BUILD** YOUR VOCABULARY
Pronoun is a **word class**.
Look at **possessive pronoun** and **relative pronoun**.

pronounce VERB pronounces, pronouncing, pronounced
❶ to say a word in a particular way • 'Too' and 'two' are pronounced the same. ❷ to declare something formally • I now pronounce you husband and wife.

pronunciation (say pro-nun-see-ay-shun) NOUN pronunciations
the way a word is pronounced

proof NOUN proofs
a fact which shows that something is true or exists
• Do you have any proof it was him?

prop VERB props, propping, propped
If you prop something somewhere, you lean it there so it does not fall over. • I propped my bike against the wall.

prop NOUN props
❶ an object used to support something ❷ an object or piece of furniture used on stage in a play

propel VERB propels, propelling, propelled
to move something forward

propeller NOUN propellers
a device with spinning blades that drives an aircraft or ship

proper ADJECTIVE
suitable or correct • This is the proper way to hold a bat.

proper fraction NOUN proper fractions
a fraction that is less than 1, such as $\frac{1}{2}$ or $\frac{3}{5}$

🔧 **BUILD** YOUR VOCABULARY
Look at **improper fraction** and **mixed fraction**.

properly ADVERB
in a way that is correct or suitable

proper noun *NOUN* proper nouns
the name given to a particular person or place, such as *Mary* or *Tokyo*, written with a capital first letter

property *NOUN* properties
❶ Your property is something that belongs to you.
❷ a building and the land belonging to it ❸ a quality or characteristic • *Rubber has elastic* **properties**.

prophecy *(say* prof-iss-see*)* *NOUN* prophecies
something that someone has said will happen in the future

prophesy *(say* prof-iss-eye*)* *VERB* prophesies, prophesying, prophesied
to say that something will happen in the future
• *She* **prophesied** *disaster if the team failed to score more goals.*

prophet *NOUN* prophets
❶ someone who says what will happen in the future ❷ a religious teacher who is believed to speak the word of God

⚠ **WATCH OUT!**
Don't confuse with **profit**, which sounds the same but means 'money'.

proportion *NOUN* proportions
❶ a fraction or share of something • *Water covers a large* **proportion** *of the earth's surface.* ❷ The proportion of one thing to another is its amount or size compared to the other. • *What is the* **proportion** *of boys to girls in the class?*

propose *VERB* proposes, proposing, proposed
❶ To propose something is to suggest it.
❷ To propose to someone is to ask them to marry you.
➤ **proposal** *NOUN*

proprietor *(say* pro-**pry**-et-er*)* *NOUN* proprietors
the owner of a shop or business

prose *NOUN*
writing that is not poetry or a play

prosecute *VERB* prosecutes, prosecuting, prosecuted
to make someone go to court to be tried for a crime

prospect *NOUN* prospects
a possibility or chance • *I was excited at the* **prospect** *of a holiday.*

prosper *VERB* prospers, prospering, prospered
to be successful or do well

prosperity *NOUN*
success or wealth

prosperous *ADJECTIVE*
successful or rich

protect *VERB* protects, protecting, protected
to keep someone or something safe
➤ **protection** *NOUN* • *The tent offered little* **protection** *against the rain.*

protective *ADJECTIVE*
❶ wanting to protect someone or something • *He's just being* **protective** *of his little brother.* ❷ intended to protect someone or something • *They wore* **protective** *gloves.*

protein *(say* proh-teen*)* *NOUN* proteins
a substance found in some types of food, for example meat, eggs and cheese. Your body needs protein to help you grow.

⚠ **WATCH OUT!**
The word **protein** is an exception to the spelling rule 'i before e except after **c**'.

protest *(say* pro-**test***)* *VERB* protests, protesting, protested
to say or show that you disapprove of or disagree with something
'No, no! Don't do that!' protested the scarecrow.
—THE SCARECROW AND HIS SERVANT, Phillip Pullman

protest *(say* **pro**-test*)* *NOUN* protests
something you say or do because you disapprove of someone or something

Protestant *(say* **prot**-est-ant*)* *NOUN* Protestants
a member of a western Christian Church that is not the Roman Catholic Church

prototype *NOUN* prototypes
the first example of something, used as a model for making others

a b c d e f g h i j k l m n o **p** q r s t u v w x y z

protractor *NOUN* protractors
a semicircular device for measuring and drawing angles

protrude *VERB* protrudes, protruding, protruded
to stick out • *He had **protruding** ears.*

proud *ADJECTIVE* prouder, proudest
❶ very pleased with yourself or with someone who has done well • *I am **proud** of my team.* ❷ feeling that you are important or deserve a lot of respect • *They were too **proud** to ask for help.*
➤ **proudly** *ADVERB*

prove *VERB* proves, proving, proved
❶ to show that something is true • *Can you **prove** who did it?* ❷ to prove to be something is to turn out to be that way • *The forecast **proved** to be correct.*

proverb *NOUN* proverbs
a short well-known saying that states a truth or gives advice, for example *Don't judge a book by its cover.*

provide *VERB* provides, providing, provided
to give or supply something to someone • *The school **provides** drinking water.*

province *NOUN* provinces
a division of a large country

provisions *NOUN*
supplies of food and drink

provoke *VERB* provokes, provoking, provoked
❶ To provoke someone is to deliberately make them angry. ❷ To provoke a reaction is to cause it. • *His words **provoked** laughter.*

prow *NOUN* prows
the front end of a ship

prowl *VERB* prowls, prowling, prowled
to move quietly and secretly, as some animals do when they are hunting

proximity *NOUN*
To be in the proximity of something is to be near it.

prudent *(say* **pru**-dent*) ADJECTIVE*
careful and sensible
➤ **prudence** *NOUN*

prune *NOUN* prunes
a dried plum

prune *VERB* prunes, pruning, pruned
To prune a tree or bush is to cut off unwanted parts from it.

pry *VERB* pries, prying, pried
to try to find out someone's private business

PS *ABBREVIATION*
used when adding something after the end of a letter or note; short for *postscript*

psalm *(say* sahm*) NOUN* psalms
a religious song, especially one from the Book of Psalms in the Bible

psychiatry *(say* sy-**ky**-at-ree*) NOUN*
the treatment of mental illness
➤ **psychiatrist** *ADJECTIVE*

⚠ **WATCH OUT!**
Words that start ps–, like **psychiatry**, **psychology** and **psalm** all have a silent **p**.

psychic
(say **sy**-kik*)*
ADJECTIVE
able to tell the future or read other people's minds

psychology
(say sy-**kol**-oj-ee*) NOUN*
the study of the mind and the way people behave
➤ **psychologist** *NOUN*

pterodactyl
(say teh-ro-**dak**-til*) NOUN*
pterodactyls
an extinct flying reptile with a long head and neck

pterodactyl

pub *NOUN* pubs
a place where people can buy drinks and food and meet friends

puberty *(say* **pew**-ber-tee*) NOUN*
the time when a young person starts to become an adult and their body starts to change

public ADJECTIVE
❶ for anyone to have or use • *The city has good public transport.* ❷ for anyone to know • *The information was made public.* ❸ with many people able to hear or see something • *I was embarrassed to sing in a public place.*

BUILD YOUR VOCABULARY
The opposite is **private**.

public NOUN
people in general
➤ **in public** where anyone can see or hear

publication NOUN publications
❶ a book, magazine or newspaper ❷ the act of making something available to read • *Following publication, the story was read by millions.*

publicity NOUN
information or advertising to attract attention to something

publish
VERB publishes, publishing, published
❶ to print and sell books, magazines or newspapers ❷ To publish information is to make it known.
➤ **publisher** NOUN

pucker VERB puckers, puckering, puckered
to form into wrinkles • *Her mouth puckered in disgust.*

pudding NOUN puddings
❶ the sweet course of a meal • *What's for pudding?*

BUILD YOUR VOCABULARY
A synonym is **dessert**.

❷ a sweet food, usually a kind of sponge cake eaten hot

puddle NOUN puddles
a small pool, especially of rainwater

pudgy ADJECTIVE pudgier, pudgiest (informal)
small and plump

puff VERB puffs, puffing, puffed
to blow out smoke, steam or air
➤ **To puff something out** is to make something swell or fill with air. • *He puffed out his cheeks.*

puff NOUN puffs
a small amount of breath, wind, smoke or steam • *He vanished in a puff of smoke.*

puffin NOUN puffins
a seabird with a large striped beak

puffy ADJECTIVE puffier, puffiest
swollen • *Her eyes looked red and puffy.*

pull VERB pulls, pulling, pulled
❶ to move something firmly towards you • *Pull the string.* • *She pulled her hand away.* ❷ to move something along behind you while holding it or attached to it • *The car was pulling a caravan.* ❸ to move somewhere with effort • *He pulled himself up on to the branch.*

pulley NOUN pulleys
a wheel with a rope or chain over it, used for lifting heavy things

pullover NOUN pullovers
a knitted piece of clothing for the top half of your body, which you put on over your head

pulp NOUN pulps
a soft wet mass

pulpit NOUN pulpits
a raised platform in a church, from which the preacher speaks

pulse NOUN pulses
Your pulse is the regular beat you can feel in your wrist as your heart pumps.

puma NOUN pumas
a large wild cat

a
b
c
d
e
f
g
h
i
j
k
l
m
n
o
p
q
r
s
t
u
v
w
x
y
z

pumice
(say **pum**-iss) NOUN
light sponge-like rock made
from lava

pummel VERB
pummels, pummelling, pummelled
to hit someone hard many times

pump NOUN **pumps**
a device that forces air or liquid into or out of
something
pump VERB **pumps, pumping, pumped**
to force air or liquid into or out of something
• *Pump more air into the tyres.*

pumpkin NOUN **pumpkins**
a very large round orange vegetable with a hard skin

pun NOUN **puns**
a joke made by using a word with two different
meanings or two words that sound the same, as in
Choosing where to bury him was a grave decision.

punch VERB **punches, punching, punched**
❶ to hit someone or something with your fist
❷ To punch a hole is to make a hole in something.
punch NOUN **punches**
a hit with the fist

punctual ADJECTIVE
arriving exactly on time

punctuate VERB **punctuates, punctuating,
punctuated**
to put commas, full stops and other punctuation
in a piece of writing

punctuation NOUN
the marks such as commas, full stops and brackets put
into a piece of writing to make it easier to understand

puncture NOUN **punctures**
a small hole made in a tyre by accident

pungent ADJECTIVE
smelling or tasting very strong or sharp

punish VERB **punishes, punishing, punished**
to make someone suffer for doing something wrong
➤ **punishment** NOUN • *There were harsh
punishments for stealing.*

puny (say pew-nee) ADJECTIVE **punier, puniest**
small and weak • *He looked too **puny** to be a superhero.*

pupa (say pew-pa) NOUN **pupae**
an insect such as a butterfly or mosquito at the stage
when it is transforming from a larva into an adult

⚙ **BUILD** YOUR VOCABULARY
Look at **chrysalis** and **larva**.

pupil NOUN **pupils**
❶ someone who is being taught by a teacher ❷ the
dark circular opening in the centre of your eye

⚙ **BUILD** YOUR VOCABULARY
Look at **iris**.

puppet NOUN **puppets**
a doll that can be made to move by putting your
hand inside it or by pulling its strings

puppy NOUN **puppies**
a young dog

purchase VERB **purchases, purchasing,
purchased**
to buy something
purchase NOUN **purchases**
something you have bought

pure ADJECTIVE **purer, purest**
❶ not mixed with anything else • *Use **pure** olive oil.*
❷ clean or clear • *The mountain air was **pure**.*

purely ADVERB
only; simply • *They did it **purely** for the money.*

purify VERB **purifies, purifying, purified**
to make something pure

purity NOUN
the state of being pure

purple NOUN, ADJECTIVE
a deep reddish-blue

purpose NOUN **purposes**
the reason for something; what something is for
➤ **on purpose** deliberately

purposeful ADJECTIVE
determined to do or say something

A B C D E F G H I J K L M N O P Q R S T U V W X Y Z

purr *VERB* **purrs, purring, purred**
When a cat purrs, it makes a low rumbling sound because it is happy.

purse *NOUN* **purses**
a small bag for holding money

pursue *VERB* **pursues, pursuing, pursued**
❶ to chase someone or something ❷ To pursue an activity is to continue to work at it. • *She **pursued** a career in medicine.*

pursuit *NOUN* **pursuits**
❶ Pursuit is the action of chasing someone.
❷ A pursuit is a hobby or activity.

push *VERB* **pushes, pushing, pushed**
to move something or someone away from you by pressing against them

push *NOUN* **pushes**
a pushing movement

put *VERB* **puts, putting, put**
❶ To put something somewhere is to move or place it there. • *Where shall I **put** my shoes?* • ***Put** butter on the bread.* ❷ To put someone into a certain state means to cause them to be in it. • *It **put** me in a bad mood.*
➤ **To put something off** is to decide to do it later instead of now.
➤ **To put up with something** is to be willing to accept it.

puzzle *NOUN* **puzzles**
❶ a tricky question or game that you have to solve
❷ something difficult to explain or understand

puzzle *VERB* **puzzles, puzzling, puzzled**
If something puzzles you, you cannot explain or understand it.

pyjamas *NOUN*
a set of loose light trousers and a top that you wear in bed

✴ **WORD STORY**
The word **pyjamas** comes from Urdu and Persian words meaning 'leg clothing'.

pylon *NOUN* **pylons**
a metal tower for supporting electric cables

pyramid *NOUN* **pyramids**
❶ a solid shape with a square base and four triangular sides coming to a point ❷ a very large ancient Egyptian monument shaped like this, built from stone over the tomb of a dead ruler

python *NOUN* **pythons**
a large snake that crushes its prey

a
b
c
d
e
f
g
h
i
j
k
l
m
n
o
p
q
r
s
t
u
v
w
x
y
z

⚙ Q is one of the rarest letters in the English language. Q is for **queueing**, which is the only word in English to have five vowels in a row.

quack NOUN quacks
the loud sound made by a duck

quack VERB quacks, quacking, quacked
When a duck quacks, it makes a loud sound.

quad NOUN quads
a rectangular courtyard with buildings round it

quadrant NOUN quadrants
a quarter of a circle

quadrilateral NOUN quadrilaterals
a flat shape with four straight sides

quail NOUN quails
a small bird that is hunted for sport and food

quail VERB quails, quailing, quailed
to feel or show fear

quaint ADJECTIVE quainter, quaintest
attractive in an unusual or old-fashioned way

quake VERB quakes, quaking, quaked
to tremble or shake

qualification NOUN qualifications
Your qualifications are the exams you have passed or certificates you have that show your skills and abilities.

qualify VERB qualifies, qualifying, qualified
❶ If someone **qualifies**, they pass a test or exam to show that they have the skills and abilities to do a job. • She **qualified** as a doctor. ❷ To **qualify** for a competition is to be good enough to be allowed to take part or compete.

quality NOUN qualities
❶ how good something is • The work was of a high quality. ❷ Someone's or something's qualities are what they are like.

quantity NOUN quantities
an amount that you can count or measure

quarantine NOUN
a period when a person or an animal is kept apart from others to prevent a disease from spreading

✳ **WORD STORY**
From the Italian word *quarantina* meaning 'forty days', because of a rule during the Black Death epidemic that people had to wait for 40 days before going ashore from a ship.

quarrel NOUN quarrels
an angry argument

quarrel VERB quarrels, quarrelling, quarrelled
to argue angrily with someone

quarrelsome ADJECTIVE
liking to quarrel or start arguments

quarry NOUN quarries
a place where stone or slate is dug out of the ground

quart (say kwort) NOUN quarts
a measurement of the volume of liquid, equal to 2 pints or about 1.136 litres

quarter NOUN quarters
❶ one of four equal parts into which something is divided. It can be written as $\frac{1}{4}$. ❷ Someone's quarters are where they live for a time.
➤ **quarter past** or **to** 15 minutes after or before the hour • It's a **quarter past** three.

quartet (say kwor-tet) NOUN quartets
❶ a group of four musicians ❷ a piece of music for four instruments or voices

quartz (say kworts) NOUN
a hard mineral, used in making accurate watches and clocks

quaver VERB quavers, quavering, quavered
to tremble

quaver NOUN quavers
a musical note equal to half a crotchet, written (♪)

BUILD YOUR VOCABULARY
Look at **crotchet**, **minim** and **semibreve**.

quay (say kee) NOUN quays
a place where ships can be loaded and unloaded

queasy ADJECTIVE queasier, queasiest
feeling slightly sick

queen NOUN queens
❶ a woman who has been crowned as the ruler of a country or the wife of a king ❷ a female bee or ant that produces eggs

queer ADJECTIVE queerer, queerest
strange or odd

quench VERB quenches, quenching, quenched
To quench your thirst is to drink until you are not thirsty any more.

query (say kweer-ee) NOUN queries
a question

quest NOUN quests
a long search, especially for something valuable
'Is this a proper quest we are on?' asked Tootles.
'A person could get killed!'—PETER PAN, J. M. Barrie

question NOUN questions
something you ask; a sentence asking for information • *If you don't understand, ask a question.*
➤ **out of the question** impossible

question VERB questions, questioning, questioned
❶ To question someone is to ask them questions.
❷ To question something is to doubt it.

question mark NOUN question marks
the punctuation mark (?) put at the end of a question

questionnaire (say kwess-chun-air) NOUN questionnaires
a set of questions for collecting information from a group of people

queue (say kew) NOUN queues
a line of people or vehicles waiting for something

queue (say kew) VERB queues, queueing, queued
to wait in a queue

WATCH OUT!
Queue has a tricky spelling—the letters **ue** appear twice!

quick ADJECTIVE quicker, quickest
taking only a short time • *We had a quick snack.*
➤ **quickly** ADVERB

quicken VERB quickens, quickening, quickened
If something quickens or you quicken it, it becomes quicker. • *She quickened her pace.*

quicksand NOUN quicksands
an area of loose wet sand that sucks in anything that falls into it

quid NOUN quid (informal)
a pound (£1)

quiet ADJECTIVE quieter, quietest
❶ without any noise • *It's very quiet here at night.*
❷ A quiet sound is not loud. • *He spoke in a quiet voice.*
➤ **quietly** ADVERB
quiet NOUN
silence • *Let's have a bit of quiet now.*

quieten VERB quietens, quietening, quietened
If something or someone quietens or you quieten them, they become quiet. • *The class quietened.*

quill NOUN quills
❶ A bird's quills are its large feathers. ❷ a pen made from a large feather
❸ A porcupine's quills are its long spines.

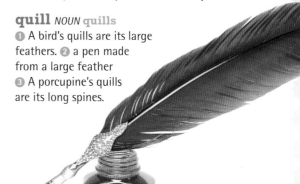

quilt NOUN quilts
a thick soft cover for a bed

quit VERB quits, quitting, quitted, quit
to leave or abandon something

quite ADVERB
① rather fairly • He's **quite** a good swimmer.
② completely • Are you **quite** sure?

quiver VERB quivers, quivering, quivered
to tremble

quiver NOUN quivers
a container for arrows

quiver

quiz NOUN quizzes
a series of questions, especially as a game

quota (say kwoh-ta) NOUN quotas
a set minimum or maximum amount • They have a **quota** of fish they can catch each week.

quotation NOUN quotations
words taken from a book or speech • It's a **quotation** from Shakespeare.

quotation marks NOUN
inverted commas (" " or ' ') that you put around quotations

BUILD YOUR VOCABULARY
Look at **inverted commas** and **speech marks**.

quote VERB quotes, quoting, quoted
to repeat words someone has said or written

Qur'an NOUN
another spelling of **Koran**

Rr

⚙ R is for **rhythm** —a word without vowels? In fact, **y** often works as a vowel letter, making a vowel sound.

⚙ Can you think of any other words where **y** makes the only vowel sound?

rabbi *(say rab-eye)* NOUN rabbis
a Jewish religious leader

rabbit NOUN rabbits
a furry animal with long ears that digs burrows

rabies *(say ray-beez)* NOUN
a fatal disease causing madness, that affects dogs and can be passed to humans

raccoon NOUN raccoons
a small North American animal with a bushy striped tail

race NOUN races
❶ a competition to be the fastest to reach somewhere or do something ❷ a large group of people who share certain physical features such as the colour of their skin
race VERB races, racing, raced
❶ to take part in a race • *I'll race you to the corner.* ❷ to move very fast • *The train raced towards him.*

racial ADJECTIVE
to do with a person's race • *racial discrimination*

racism *(say ray-sizm)* NOUN
disliking people or treating them unfairly because of the race they belong to

racist NOUN racists
someone who treats other people unfairly or dislikes them because of the race they belong to
➤ **racist** ADJECTIVE • *a racist remark*

rack NOUN racks
a frame for holding something • *a bike rack*
rack VERB racks, racking, racked
➤ **To rack your brains** is to try hard to remember or think of something.

racket NOUN rackets
❶ a bat with strings stretched across an oval frame, used in tennis ❷ a loud unpleasant noise

radar *(say ray-dar)* NOUN
a system that uses radio waves to show the position of ships or aircraft

✳ **WORD STORY**
The word **radar** comes from the first letters of *radio detection and ranging.*

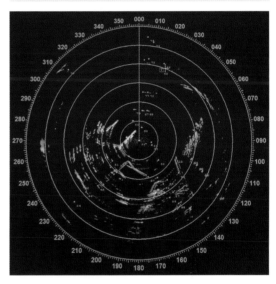

radiant ADJECTIVE
❶ producing light or heat ❷ looking very happy and beautiful

radiate VERB radiates, radiating, radiated
to produce heat, light or other energy that spreads out

radiation NOUN
❶ waves or particles sent out by something radioactive ❷ heat and light energy produced by something

radiator NOUN radiators
a metal object in a room that gives out heat from hot water inside it

radii NOUN (plural of **radius**)

radio NOUN radios
❶ a system of sending or receiving sound using electrical waves ❷ a piece of electrical equipment for listening to radio programmes or sending or receiving radio messages

radioactive ADJECTIVE
Radioactive substances have atoms that break up and send out harmful waves or particles.
➤ **radioactivity** NOUN

radish NOUN radishes
a small hard red vegetable with a hot taste eaten raw in salads

radius NOUN radii
a straight line or the distance from the centre of a circle to the edge

BUILD YOUR VOCABULARY
Look at **circumference** and **diameter**.

raffle NOUN raffles
a way of raising money by selling numbered tickets, some of which win prizes
raffle VERB raffles, raffling, raffled
To raffle something is to offer it as a prize in a raffle.

raft NOUN rafts
a floating platform of logs or barrels tied together

rafter NOUN rafters
one of the long sloping pieces of wood that hold up a roof

rag NOUN rags
❶ a piece of old cloth ❷ Rags are very old, torn clothes.

rage NOUN rages
great or violent anger

rage VERB rages, raging, raged
If something rages, it is very intense and violent.
The storm was raging outside. Rain lashed against the windows, the wind howled through the telegraph wires.
—GRANNY NOTHING, Catherine MacPhail

ragged (say rag-id) ADJECTIVE
torn or frayed • *a girl dressed in ragged clothes*

raid NOUN raids
a sudden attack
raid VERB raids, raiding, raided
To raid a place is to make a sudden attack on it.
➤ **raider** NOUN

rail NOUN rails
❶ a metal or wooden bar that is part of a fence
❷ a long metal strip that is part of a railway track
➤ **by rail** on a train

railings NOUN
a fence made of metal bars

railway NOUN railways
❶ a route that trains travel on ❷ a system of transport using trains

rain NOUN
drops of water that fall from the sky
rain VERB rains, raining, rained
❶ When it rains, rain falls from the sky. ❷ to fall like rain • *Arrows rained down on them.*

rainbow NOUN rainbows
a curved band of colours that you sometimes see in the sky when the sun shines through rain

raincoat NOUN raincoats
a waterproof coat

raindrop NOUN raindrops
a single drop of rain

rainfall NOUN
the amount of rain that falls in a particular place or time

rainforest NOUN rainforests
a thick tropical forest in an area that has a lot of rain

raise VERB raises, raising, raised
❶ to move something to a higher or more upright position • *Raise your hand if you know the answer.*
❷ To raise your voice is to speak loudly. ❸ To raise money is to collect it for a purpose. • *They raised £1000 for Sport Relief.*

raisin NOUN raisins
a dried grape

rake NOUN rakes
a gardening tool with a row of short spikes fixed to a long handle

rake VERB rakes, raking, raked
to tidy something with a rake

rally VERB rallies, rallying, rallied
to revive or recover after an illness or setback • *The team **rallied** when they realised they could win.*

RAM (say ram) ABBREVIATION
a type of computer memory; short for *random-access memory*

ram NOUN rams
a male sheep

BUILD YOUR VOCABULARY
A female sheep is a **ewe**.

ram VERB rams, ramming, rammed
to push one thing hard against another

Ramadan (say ram-a-dan) NOUN
the ninth month of the Muslim year, when Muslims do not eat or drink during daylight

BUILD YOUR VOCABULARY
Look at **Eid**.

ramble NOUN rambles
a walk in the country
ramble VERB rambles, rambling, rambled
❶ to go for a walk in the country ❷ to talk a lot in a confused way, without sticking to a subject

ramp NOUN ramps
a slope joining two different levels

rampage VERB rampages, rampaging, rampaged
to rush about wildly or violently
rampage NOUN
➤ **To go on the rampage** is to rampage.

ran VERB (past tense of **run**)
• *The dog **ran** along the beach.*

ranch NOUN ranches
a large cattle farm, especially in North America or Australia

random NOUN
➤ **at random** by chance; without any plan
random ADJECTIVE
done or taken at random • *They took a **random** sample.*

rang VERB (past tense of **ring**)
• *The doorbell **rang**.*

range NOUN ranges
❶ a collection of different things of the same type • *We do a wide **range** of activities.* ❷ a set of numbers from lowest to highest • *The book is aimed at the 8-11 age **range**.* ❸ a line of hills or mountains ❹ the distance that something can travel
range VERB ranges, ranging, ranged
To range between two limits is to extend from one to the other. • *Prices **range** from £1 to £20.*

ranger NOUN rangers
someone who looks after a park or forest

rank NOUN ranks
a title or position which shows how important someone or something is • *He had the **rank** of captain.*

ransack VERB ransacks, ransacking, ransacked
to go through a place searching for something to steal and leave it in a mess

ransom NOUN ransoms
money demanded for setting free someone who has been kidnapped

rap VERB raps, rapping, rapped
to knock quickly and loudly
rap NOUN raps
❶ a quick loud knock ❷ a type of poetry that is spoken aloud with a strong rhythm, often to music

rapid ADJECTIVE
moving or working quickly
➤ **rapidly** ADVERB

rapids NOUN
part of a river where the water flows very fast

rare ADJECTIVE rarer, rarest
not happening or seen often • *They saw a **rare** bird.*
➤ **rarely** ADVERB • *She's very **rarely** late.*

rarity NOUN rarities
something that does not often happen or is not often seen

rascal NOUN rascals
a naughty or dishonest person

rash ADJECTIVE **rasher, rashest**
too quick to do something, without thinking about it first
By the time Hallowe'en arrived, Harry was regretting his rash promise to go to the Deathday Party.—HARRY POTTER AND THE CHAMBER OF SECRETS, J. K. Rowling

rash NOUN **rashes**
red spots or patches that appear on your skin when you are ill or allergic to something

rasher NOUN **rashers**
a slice of bacon

raspberry NOUN **raspberries**
a small soft red fruit

rat NOUN **rats**
an animal like a large mouse

BUILD YOUR VOCABULARY
A **rat** is a **rodent**.

rate NOUN **rates**
how fast or how often something happens • *The seedlings grow at a fast rate.*

rather ADVERB
❶ quite; fairly • *It was getting rather dark.*
❷ If you would rather do something, you would prefer to do it. • *I'd rather do this later.* ❸ more accurately • *'No!' she said or rather shouted.*

ratio (say **ray-shee-oh**) NOUN **ratios**
The relationship between two numbers; how many times one number is bigger than another. • *The ratio of teachers to pupils in this school is 1 to 25.*

ration (say **rash-un**) NOUN **rations**
the amount of something one person is allowed to have

ration (say **rash-un**) VERB **rations, rationing, rationed**
to give something out in fixed amounts because there is not very much of it

rational (say **rash-un-al**) ADJECTIVE
reasonable or sensible • *That was not a rational decision.*
➤ **rationally** ADVERB

rattle VERB **rattles, rattling, rattled**
If something rattles or if you rattle it, it makes a series of short hard sounds when it is shaken.

rattle NOUN **rattles**
a baby's toy that rattles

rattlesnake NOUN **rattlesnakes**
a poisonous American snake that makes rattling sounds with its tail

rave VERB **raves, raving, raved**
❶ to talk in an uncontrolled way that does not make sense ❷ To rave about something is to talk very enthusiastically about it.

raven NOUN **ravens**
a large black bird

ravenous (say **rav-en-us**) ADJECTIVE
very hungry

ravine (say **rav-een**) NOUN **ravines**
a very deep narrow gorge

raw ADJECTIVE **rawer, rawest**
❶ Raw food is not cooked. ❷ A raw material is in its natural state before being made into something.

ray NOUN **rays**
❶ a thin line of light, heat or other energy ❷ a large sea fish with a flat body and a long tail

ray

razor NOUN **razors**
a device with a very sharp blade, used for shaving

reach VERB **reaches, reaching, reached**
❶ When you reach a place, you arrive there. ❷ to stretch out your hand to get or touch something

reach NOUN
the distance someone or something can reach • *The kite hung just beyond his reach.*

react *VERB* **reacts, reacting, reacted**
to do something in response to another person
or thing

reaction *NOUN* **reactions**
Your reaction to something is what you do or feel in
response to it.

reactor *NOUN* **reactors**
an apparatus for producing nuclear power

read *VERB* **reads, reading, read** *(say* red*)*
❶ to look at something written or printed and
understand it or say it aloud • *Have you* **read** *this
book?* ❷ If a sign or instrument reads something,
that is what it says. • *The sign* **read**: *'Beware of
the dog.'*
➤ **reader** *NOUN* • *Millions of* **readers** *love her
books.*

readily *ADVERB*
❶ willingly; eagerly • *She* **readily** *agreed to help.*
❷ quickly and easily • *All the ingredients are* **readily**
available.

readiness *NOUN*
the state of being ready

reading *NOUN* **readings**
❶ the action of reading something written or
printed ❷ an amount shown on a gauge or
instrument

ready *ADJECTIVE* **readier, readiest**
able or willing to do something or to be used at
once; prepared • *Are you* **ready** *to go?* • *Dinner's*
ready!

real *ADJECTIVE*
❶ true or existing; not imaginary • *Ghosts are not*
real. ❷ genuine; not a copy or fake • *Is that* **real**
gold?

realise *(also* **realize***) VERB* **realises,
realising, realised**
to understand something or accept that it is true
• *We began to* **realise** *that something was wrong.*
➤ **realisation** *NOUN*

realistic *ADJECTIVE*
❶ true to life • *It is a very* **realistic** *painting.*
❷ seeing things as they really are • *She is* **realistic**
about her chances of winning.

reality *NOUN* **realities**
❶ what is really true • *We need to face* **reality**.
❷ a reality is something that is real • *My dream had
become a* **reality**.

really *ADVERB*
❶ very • *I'm* **really** *tired.* ❷ truly; in real life • *Did he*
really *say that?*

realm *(say* relm*) NOUN* **realms**
a kingdom or land • *I felt like I had entered a
magical* **realm**.

reap *VERB* **reaps, reaping, reaped**
❶ to cut and gather corn ❷ to get a reward or
punishment

reappear *VERB* **reappears, reappearing,
reappeared**
to appear again

rear *NOUN* **rears**
the back part of something

rear *ADJECTIVE*
placed or found at the back • *They left by the* **rear** *exit.*

rear *VERB* **rears, rearing, reared**
❶ To rear children is to bring them up. ❷ When a
horse rears, it stands up on its back legs.

rearrange *VERB* **rearranges, rearranging,
rearranged**
to arrange something differently

reason *NOUN* **reasons**
❶ The reason for something is why it happens.
❷ Reason is clear logical thinking. • *He won't listen
to* **reason**.

reason *VERB* **reasons, reasoning, reasoned**
❶ to think in a logical way ❷ To reason with
someone is to try to persuade them to be logical or
sensible.

reasonable *ADJECTIVE*
sensible or fair

reasonably *ADVERB*
❶ in a sensible or fair way • *She agreed quite*
reasonably. ❷ fairly; quite • *The room is* **reasonably**
tidy.

reassure *VERB* **reassures, reassuring,
reassured**
To reassure someone is to make them feel less worried.
➤ **reassurance** *NOUN*

a
b
c
d
e
f
g
h
i
j
k
l
m
n
o
p
q
r
s
t
u
v
w
x
y
z

rebel *(say re-bel)* VERB **rebels, rebelling, rebelled**
to refuse to obey rules or authority

rebel *(say reb-el)* NOUN **rebels**
❶ someone who refuses to obey rules or authority ❷ someone who fights against the authorities or the government

rebellion NOUN **rebellions**
❶ Rebellion is refusing to obey rules or authority.
❷ A rebellion is a fight against the authorities or the government.

rebellious ADJECTIVE
refusing to obey rules or authority

rebound VERB **rebounds, rebounding, rebounded**
to bounce back after hitting something

rebuild VERB **rebuilds, rebuilding, rebuilt**
to build something again after it has been destroyed

recall VERB **recalls, recalling, recalled**
to remember

recapture VERB **recaptures, recapturing, recaptured**
❶ to catch someone again after they have escaped ❷ to get something back again

recede VERB **recedes, receding, receded**
to move back • *The floods **receded**.*

receipt *(say re-seet)* NOUN **receipts**
a note proving that something has been paid for or delivered

receive VERB **receives, receiving, received**
to get something when it is given or sent to you
• *I never **received** your text.*

⚠️ **WATCH OUT!**
The word **receive** follows the rule 'i before e except after c'.

receiver NOUN **receivers**
❶ a part of a radio or satellite that receives signals
❷ the part of an old-fashioned telephone that you hold to your ear

recent ADJECTIVE
made or happening a short time ago
➤ **recently** ADVERB • *Have you seen her **recently**?*

reception NOUN **receptions**
❶ a desk in a hotel or office where visitors go when they arrive ❷ a formal party • *a wedding **reception***

receptionist NOUN **receptionists**
someone who works at a hotel or office reception, welcoming visitors and answering the phone

recess NOUN **recesses**
a small hollow or space

recipe *(say ress-ip-ee)* NOUN **recipes**
a list of ingredients and instructions for preparing a dish

recite VERB **recites, reciting, recited**
To recite something such as a poem is to say it aloud.

reckless ADJECTIVE
doing things without thinking or caring about what might happen
➤ **recklessly** ADVERB ➤ **recklessness** NOUN

reckon VERB **reckons, reckoning, reckoned**
❶ to calculate or count something • *How many do you **reckon** we need?* ❷ to think or believe something • *I **reckon** it's about to rain.*

reclaim VERB **reclaims, reclaiming, reclaimed**
❶ to get something back after losing it ❷ To reclaim land is to make it suitable for use by clearing or draining it.

recline VERB **reclines, reclining, reclined**
to lean or lie back

recognise *(also* **recognize***) VERB*
recognises, recognising, recognised
❶ to know who someone is because you have seen them before • I **recognised** his face. ❷ to recognise a fact is to admit it is true
➤ **recognisable** *(also* **recognizable***) ADJECTIVE*

recognition *NOUN*
the feeling or act of recognising someone or something • She gave a smile of **recognition**.

recoil *VERB* recoils, recoiling, recoiled
to move backwards suddenly • He **recoiled** in horror.

recollect *VERB* recollects, recollecting, recollected
to remember
➤ **recollection** *NOUN*

recommend *VERB* recommends, recommending, recommended
❶ to suggest something because you think it is good • I **recommend** the strawberry ice cream. ❷ to advise someone to do something • I **recommend** that you see a doctor.
➤ **recommendation** *NOUN*

reconcile *VERB* reconciles, reconciling, reconciled
To be reconciled is to become friends again after quarrelling or to learn to accept something after not liking it.

record *(say* rec-ord*) NOUN* records
❶ the best or most that has ever been achieved in an activity • She broke the world **record** for the women's 100 metres. ❷ If you keep a record of something, you write down when it happens. ❸ A record in a database is an individual piece of information stored in it. ❹ a plastic disc with music recorded on it
record *(say* re-cord*) VERB* records, recording, recorded
❶ to store music, sound or pictures on a disk, tape or computer ❷ to write down things that have happened
➤ **recording** *NOUN*

recorder *NOUN* recorders
❶ a small musical instrument that you play by blowing into one end and covering holes with your fingers

🔵 **BUILD YOUR VOCABULARY**
A **recorder** is a **woodwind instrument**.

❷ a machine for recording sounds and pictures

recount *VERB* recount, recounting, recounted
to tell someone about something that has happened • We **recounted** our adventures.

recover *VERB* recovers, recovering, recovered
❶ to get better after being ill ❷ To recover something is to get it back after losing it.
➤ **recovery** *NOUN*

recreation *NOUN* recreations
something you do for enjoyment in your spare time

recruit *NOUN* recruits
someone who has just joined the armed forces, a company or a club
recruit *VERB* recruits, recruiting, recruited
to get someone to join an organisation or help with something

rectangle *NOUN* rectangles
a shape with four straight sides and four right angles, usually one that is not a square
➤ **rectangular** *ADJECTIVE*

recuperate *VERB* recuperates, recuperating, recuperated
to get better after you have been ill

recycle *VERB* recycles, recycling, recycled
To recycle waste material is to use it again.

red *ADJECTIVE* redder, reddest
❶ of the colour of blood ❷ Red hair is orange-brown in colour.
red *NOUN* reds
a red colour

redden *VERB* reddens, reddening, reddened
to turn red • He **reddened** with embarrassment.

reddish *ADJECTIVE*
almost red or with some red in it

reduce *VERB* reduces, reducing, reduced
❶ to make something smaller or less ❷ To be reduced to something is to be forced into a very bad state. • He was **reduced** to begging for money.

a b c d e f g h i j k l m n o p q r s t u v w x y z

reduction *NOUN* reductions
If there is a reduction in something, it becomes smaller or less.

reed *NOUN* reeds
a plant that grows in or near water

reef *NOUN* reefs
a line of rocks or sand near the surface of the sea

reek *VERB* reeks, reeking, reeked
to have a strong unpleasant smell

reel *NOUN* reels
❶ a round object on which thread is wound
❷ a lively Scottish dance
reel *VERB* reels, reeling, reeled
to stagger • *He reeled back in shock.*

refer *VERB* refers, referring, referred
❶ If you refer to someone or something, you mention them or speak about them. ❷ If you refer to a book, you look something up in it.

referee *NOUN* referees
someone who makes sure that people obey the rules of a game

reference *NOUN* references
❶ a mention of something or someone
❷ a description of someone and of their work, which helps them when they apply for a job • *Dad asked his old boss for a reference.*

referendum (say ref-er-en-dum) *NOUN* referendums, referenda
a vote on one question by all the people in a country

refill *VERB* refills, refilling, refilled
to fill something again

refined *ADJECTIVE*
❶ A refined substance has been made pure. • *refined oil* ❷ Refined foods have lost some of their goodness when being processed. ❸ very polite and cultured

refinery *NOUN* refineries
a factory for purifying a product, such as oil

reflect *VERB* reflects, reflecting, reflected
❶ to send light or heat back from a surface ❷ If a mirror or lake reflects something, it shows an image of it. ❸ To reflect on something is to think seriously about it.

reflection *NOUN* reflections
the image you can see in a mirror or other shiny surface

reflective *ADJECTIVE*
❶ sending back light • *The coat has a reflective stripe.* ❷ suggesting or showing serious thought • *There was a reflective silence.*

reflex *NOUN* reflexes
a movement or action that you do without conscious thought
reflex *ADJECTIVE*
A reflex angle is between 180° and 360°.

⚙ **BUILD** YOUR VOCABULARY
Look at **acute**, **obtuse** and **right angle**.

reform *VERB* reforms, reforming, reformed
❶ to make changes to a system or organisation in order to improve it ❷ If someone reforms or is reformed, they improve their behaviour.

refrain *VERB* refrains, refraining, refrained
If you refrain from doing something, you do not do it.

refresh *VERB* refreshes, refreshing, refreshed
to make someone feel fresh and strong again

refreshments *PLURAL NOUN*
food and drink

refrigerator *NOUN* refrigerators
an appliance for keeping food fresh and drinks cold

refuel *VERB* refuels, refuelling, refuelled
to put more fuel into a plane or other vehicle

refuge *NOUN* refuges
a place where someone can go to be safe from danger

refugee (say ref-yoo-**jee**) *NOUN* refugees
someone who has had to leave their home or country because of war, cruel treatment or disaster

refund (say rif-**und**) *VERB* refunds, refunding, refunded
to refund money that someone has spent is to give it back

refund (say **ree**-fund) *NOUN* refunds
money you have spent that is given back to you

refusal NOUN refusals
the act of refusing to do something or of saying 'no' to something

refuse (say re-fewz) VERB refuses, refusing, refused
to say that you will not do something or to say 'no' to something • They **refuse** to listen. • He **refused** my offer.

refuse (say ref-yooss) NOUN
rubbish or waste material

regain VERB regains, regaining, regained
to get something back

regard VERB regards, regarding, regarded
❶ If you regard someone or something as something, you think they are that thing. • I **regard** her as a friend. ❷ to look at someone or something • She **regarded** him suspiciously.

regard NOUN regards
❶ consideration or respect ❷ Your **regards** are kind wishes you send in a message.

regarding PREPOSITION
on the subject of; about • They wrote to us **regarding** the trip.

regardless ADJECTIVE
paying no attention to something • Buy it, **regardless** of the cost.

regiment NOUN regiments
a large unit of soldiers, often divided into several smaller groups

region NOUN regions
❶ a large part of a country ❷ an area • These plants only grow in tropical **regions**.

register NOUN registers
an official list, especially of the names of pupils in a class

register VERB registers, registering, registered
❶ to record something on an official list • They **registered** the baby's birth. ❷ to notice or realise something • It took him a moment to **register** what was happening.

registration NOUN
❶ the act of officially recording something ❷ the time when a teacher reads the names of all the pupils in a class to see who is present

regret NOUN regrets
If you feel regret, you feel sorry or sad about something.
regret VERB regrets, regretting, regretted
To regret something is to feel sorry or sad about it.

regretful ADJECTIVE
feeling sorry or sad about something

regular ADJECTIVE
❶ happening with the same amount of time between each one • They have **regular** meetings. ❷ even or symmetrical • a **regular** row of teeth ❸ usual; following normal rules • For a **regular** plural you just add 's'.
➤ **regularly** ADVERB

BUILD YOUR VOCABULARY
An opposite is **irregular**.

WORD STORY
The word **regular** comes from a Latin word regula meaning 'a rule'.

regulate VERB regulates, regulating, regulated
to adjust or control something • This knob **regulates** the temperature.

regulation NOUN regulations
an official rule

rehearsal NOUN rehearsals
a time when you practise something before performing it

rehearse VERB rehearses, rehearsing, rehearsed
to practise something like a play before you perform it

reign VERB reigns, reigning, reigned
to be king or queen
reign NOUN reigns
Someone's reign is the time when they are king or queen.

WATCH OUT!
Reign has a silent g. Do not confuse it with a **rein** which means 'a strap for a horse'.

a b c d e f g h i j k l m n o p q r s t u v w x y z

rein *NOUN* reins
a strap used by a rider to guide a horse

reindeer *NOUN* reindeer
a kind of deer that lives in Arctic regions

reinforce *(say* ree-in-**force***) VERB* reinforces,
reinforcing, reinforced
to make something stronger

reinforcements *NOUN*
extra people sent to help in a battle or fight

reject *VERB* rejects, rejecting, rejected
to refuse to accept something • *They rejected my
offer of help.*
➤ **rejection** *NOUN*

rejoice *VERB* rejoices, rejoicing,
rejoiced
to celebrate and be very happy

relate *VERB* relates, relating, related
❶ If things relate to each other, there is a
connection between them. ❷ To relate a story
is to tell it.

related *ADJECTIVE*
❶ If people are related, they belong to the same
family. ❷ If things are related, there is a connection
between them.

relation *NOUN* relations
❶ someone who belongs to the same family as you
❷ the way that one thing is connected with another

relationship *NOUN* relationships
❶ the way people or things are connected with each
other ❷ the way people get on • *He has a good
relationship with his sister.* ❸ a close friendship,
especially a romantic one

relative *NOUN* relatives
Your relatives are the people who are related to you.
relative *ADJECTIVE*
compared with something else • *After that there was
relative peace.*

relative clause *NOUN (in grammar)*
a clause that is linked to a noun or main clause and
gives more information about it, often starting with
who, *which* or *that*. In this sentence the relative
clause is in bold: *We had pizza, **which I love.***

relatively *ADVERB*
compared with other things; fairly • *Books are
relatively cheap.*

relative pronoun *NOUN* relative pronouns
(in grammar)
a word such as *who*, *which* or *that*, used to begin
a relative clause

relax *VERB* relaxes, relaxing, relaxed
❶ to become less worried or tense ❷ to stop working
and rest or enjoy yourself

relay *VERB* relays, relaying, relayed
To relay a message is to pass it on.
relay *NOUN* relays
a race between teams in which each team member
runs part of the distance

release *VERB* releases, releasing,
released
to let someone or something go or to unfasten them

relent *VERB* relents, relenting, relented
to be less angry or severe than you were going
to be

relentless *ADJECTIVE*
never stopping or getting less • *She was sick of the relentless wind.*

relevant *ADJECTIVE*
related to what you are discussing or dealing with
➤ **relevance** *NOUN*

BUILD YOUR VOCABULARY
The opposite is **irrelevant**.

WATCH OUT!
Relevant ends in **-ant**, like **important**.

reliable *ADJECTIVE*
able to be trusted or depended on

relic *NOUN* relics
something that has survived from an ancient time

relief *NOUN* reliefs
a good feeling you get because something unpleasant has stopped or is not going to happen • *It was such a relief when we reached dry land.*

relieve *VERB* relieves, relieving, relieved
To relieve pain or suffering is to end or lessen it.

relieved *ADJECTIVE*
feeling good because something unpleasant has stopped or is not going to happen

religion *NOUN* religions
a system of beliefs about God or gods and how to worship them

religious *ADJECTIVE*
❶ to do with religion • *a religious ceremony*
❷ Someone who is religious follows a religion.

relish *VERB* relishes, relishing, relished
to enjoy something very much
'A little nonsense now and then, is relished by the wisest men,' Mr Wonka said.—CHARLIE AND THE GREAT GLASS ELEVATOR, Roald Dahl

relish *NOUN* relishes
❶ enjoyment • *The dogs ate the leftovers with relish.* ❷ a spicy sauce or pickle

reluctant *ADJECTIVE*
If you are reluctant to do something, you do not want to do it.
➤ **reluctance** *NOUN* ➤ **reluctantly** *ADVERB*

rely *VERB* relies, relying, relied
➤ **To rely on someone** or **something** is to trust them or need them to help or support you.

remain *VERB* remains, remaining, remained
to continue in the same place or condition • *It will remain cloudy all day.*

remainder *NOUN* remainders
❶ something left over ❷ *(in mathematics)* the amount that is left over when you divide one number into another

remains *NOUN*
what is left of something • *On the table were the remains of a meal.*

remark *VERB* remarks, remarking, remarked
to say something that you have thought or noticed • *'It's very cold,' she remarked.*
remark *NOUN* remarks
something you say • *He made a rude remark.*

remarkable *ADJECTIVE*
so unusual or impressive that you notice or remember it
➤ **remarkably** *ADVERB* • *It was remarkably simple.*

remember *VERB* remembers, remembering, remembered
to keep something in your mind or bring it into your mind when you need to • *Do you remember our holiday?* • *I can't remember his name.*

remembrance *NOUN*
the act of remembering something or someone

remind *VERB* reminds, reminding, reminded
❶ To remind someone is to help them remember something. • *Mum reminded me to take my bag.*
❷ If something reminds you of a person or thing, it makes you think of them because it is similar. • *The girl in that painting reminds me of you.*

reminder *NOUN* reminders
something that makes you think about or remember something or someone

remnant NOUN remnants
a small piece of something left over

remorse NOUN
deep regret for something wrong you have done

remote ADJECTIVE remoter, remotest
❶ far away • *He lived on a remote island.*
❷ unlikely or slight • *Their chances of winning were remote.*

remote control NOUN remote controls
an electrical or radio device for controlling something such as a television or toy from a distance

removal NOUN removals
the act of removing or moving something

remove VERB removes, removing, removed
to take something away or take it off

render VERB renders, rendering, rendered
to cause someone to be in a particular condition • *The shock rendered her speechless.*

rendezvous *(say* ron-day-voo) NOUN rendezvous
a meeting or a meeting place

✻ **WORD STORY**

The word **rendezvous** comes from French words meaning 'present yourself'.

renew VERB renews, renewing, renewed
❶ to replace something with a new version • *I need to renew my passport.* ❷ to begin something again • *They renewed their attack.*

renewable ADJECTIVE
Renewable resources are never completely used up. • *The wind and the sun are renewable sources of energy.*

renowned ADJECTIVE
famous • *The city was renowned for its beauty.*

rent NOUN rents
a regular payment for using something, especially a house or room

rent VERB rents, renting, rented
To rent something is to pay money to use it.

repair VERB repairs, repairing, repaired
to mend something

repair NOUN repairs
something you do to mend something • *The car needs some repairs.*

repay VERB repays, repaying, repaid
❶ to pay back money ❷ to do something for someone in return for something they did for you

repeat VERB repeats, repeating, repeated
to say or do something again

repeatedly ADVERB
several times; again and again

repel VERB repels, repelling, repelled
❶ to drive or force something or someone away • *They repelled the intruders.* ❷ If magnets repel each other, they push each other away.

⚙ **BUILD YOUR VOCABULARY**

The opposite of this meaning is **attract**.

❸ to disgust someone

repent VERB repents, repenting, repented
to be sorry for what you have done
➤ **repentance** NOUN ➤ **repentant** ADJECTIVE

repetition NOUN repetitions
the act of saying or doing something again

repetitive ADJECTIVE
boring because of being repeated many times

replace VERB replaces, replacing, replaced
❶ to put something back in its place • *Don't forget to replace the lid.* ❷ To replace someone or something is to take their place.
➤ **replacement** NOUN

replica *(say* rep-lic-a) NOUN replicas
an exact copy

reply NOUN replies
an answer

reply VERB replies, replying, replied
If you reply to someone, you answer them.

report VERB reports, reporting, reported
to describe or tell someone about something that has happened

report NOUN reports
❶ a description or account of something
❷ a statement written by a teacher about what a pupil has learned and done at school

reporter *NOUN* reporters
someone whose job is to collect news for a newspaper or for radio or television

represent *VERB* represents, representing, represented
❶ to be a picture, model or symbol of something • *This graph **represents** different ways pupils travel to school.* ❷ To represent someone is to speak or act on their behalf.

representative *NOUN*
a person or thing that represents others

repress *VERB* represses, repressing, repressed
to control something with effort or force • *She struggled to **repress** a smile.*

reproach *VERB* reproaches, reproaching, reproached
to blame or criticise someone • *I **reproached** myself for losing my temper.*
reproach *NOUN*
blame or criticism

reproduce *VERB* reproduces, reproducing, reproduced
❶ to copy something or make something that is the same • *She tried to **reproduce** her mother's recipe.* ❷ When living things reproduce, they produce new living things.

reproduction *NOUN* reproductions
❶ the process of producing new living things • *reproduction in plants* ❷ A reproduction is a copy.

reptile *NOUN* reptiles
a cold-blooded animal with dry scaly skin, such as a snake or lizard

 WORD STORY
The word **reptile** comes from a Latin word meaning 'to crawl'.

republic *NOUN* republics
a country ruled by a president chosen by the people, not by a king or queen

repulsive *ADJECTIVE*
disgusting

reputation *NOUN* reputations
the opinion most people have of a person or thing • *The school has a good **reputation**.*

request *VERB* requests, requesting, requested
to ask politely or formally for something
request *NOUN* requests
If you make a request, you ask politely or formally for something.

require *VERB* requires, requiring, required
❶ If you require something, you need or want it. • *We will give you any help that you **require**.* ❷ If you are required to do something, you have to do it.

requirement *NOUN* requirements
something that is needed or must be done

rescue *VERB* rescues, rescuing, rescued
to save someone from danger or capture
➤ **rescuer** *NOUN*
rescue *NOUN* rescues
an act of rescuing someone

research *NOUN* researches
study or investigation to find out about a subject
research *VERB* researches, researching, researched
to find out about a subject by studying or investigating
➤ **researcher** *NOUN*

resemblance NOUN resemblances
If there is a resemblance between things or people, they are or look similar.

resemble VERB resembles, resembling, resembled
To resemble someone or something is to be or look similar to them.

resent VERB resents, resenting, resented
to feel angry and hurt about something
➤ **resentment** NOUN • *He feels a lot of resentment about how he was treated.*

resentful ADJECTIVE
angry and hurt about something

reservation NOUN reservations
❶ an arrangement to have a seat saved for you on a train, plane or coach or at a restaurant • *He checked our ticket reservations.* ❷ an area of land kept for a special purpose ❸ If you have reservations about something, you are not sure that it is good or right.

reserve VERB reserves, reserving, reserved
to keep something for a particular person or for a special use
reserve NOUN reserves
❶ something or someone kept ready to be used if necessary ❷ an area of land kept for a special purpose • *This island is a nature reserve.*

reserved ADJECTIVE
❶ saved for someone • *These seats are reserved.* ❷ shy or unwilling to show your feelings

reservoir (say rez-er-vwar) NOUN reservoirs
a lake built for storing water

residence NOUN residences
a place where someone lives

resident NOUN residents
someone who lives in a particular place

resign VERB resigns, resigning, resigned
to give up your job or position
➤ **To resign yourself to something** is to accept that it will happen, although you do not like it.
➤ **resignation** NOUN

resilient ADJECTIVE
able to put up with or recover quickly from difficult conditions • *Children are more resilient than many parents realise.*
➤ **resilience** NOUN

resin (say rez-in) NOUN resins
a sticky substance that comes from plants or is made artificially

resist VERB resists, resisting, resisted
❶ to oppose or fight against something or someone ❷ If you can resist something, you are not affected or tempted by it.
➤ **resistant** ADJECTIVE • *The plant is resistant to frost.*

resistance NOUN
fighting or taking action against someone or something • *The Roman soldiers met with resistance.*

resolute (say rez-o-loot) ADJECTIVE
determined or firm
➤ **resolutely** ADVERB

resolution NOUN resolutions
❶ determination • *She set off full of resolution.* ❷ a decision that you are determined to do something • *I made a resolution to exercise more.*

resolve VERB resolves, resolving, resolved
❶ To resolve a problem or disagreement is to find a way of dealing with it. ❷ to decide firmly to do something

resort NOUN resorts
a place where people go on holiday • *Blackpool is a seaside resort.*
➤ **a last resort** something you try because everything else has failed
resort VERB resorts, resorting, resorted
to use or try something when other things have failed • *In the end they resorted to threats.*

resound VERB resounds, resounding, resounded
to fill a place with sound; to echo

resource NOUN resources
things that you have and can use • *The land is rich in natural resources.*

respect *NOUN* respects
❶ admiration for someone's good qualities or achievements ❷ consideration or concern • *Have* **respect** *for people's feelings.* ❸ a detail or aspect *That child is hard to understand in some respects.* —ANNE OF GREEN GABLES, L. M. Montgomery

respect *VERB* respects, respecting, respected
to have respect for someone or something

respectable *ADJECTIVE*
having good manners and character

respectful *ADJECTIVE*
showing respect
➤ **respectfully** *ADVERB* • *She listened* **respectfully**.

respective *ADJECTIVE*
belonging to each of the different people • *We went to our* **respective** *rooms.*

respiration *NOUN*
breathing

respond *VERB* responds, responding, responded
to reply or react to someone or something

response *NOUN* responses
a reply or reaction to something

responsibility *NOUN* responsibilities
❶ the fact of being responsible for something • *I take* **responsibility** *for my decision.* ❷ something for which you are responsible • *She has a lot of* **responsibilities**.

responsible *ADJECTIVE*
❶ in charge of something and likely to take the blame if anything goes wrong ❷ sensible and able to be trusted

🔵 BUILD YOUR VOCABULARY
An opposite of the second meaning is **irresponsible**.

❸ To be responsible for something is to be the cause of it. • *Who is* **responsible** *for all this mess?*

rest *NOUN* rests
❶ a time when you can relax or sleep • *Have a good* **rest** *over the weekend.* ❷ a support for something • *a chair with arm* **rests**
➤ **the rest** the part that is left; the others

rest *VERB* rests, resting, rested
❶ to relax or sleep ❷ If you rest something on something or it rests there, it is leaning or supported there.

restaurant *NOUN* restaurants
a place where you can buy a meal and eat it

restless *ADJECTIVE*
unable to relax or keep still
➤ **restlessly** *ADVERB*

restore *VERB* restores, restoring, restored
to put something back to its original state or give it back to its original owner

restrain *VERB* restrains, restraining, restrained
to control someone or something or hold them back

restraint *NOUN*
control or self-control • *They are free to act without* **restraint**.

restrict *VERB* restricts, restricting, restricted
to put limits on what someone or something can do • *The tight clothes* **restricted** *his movement.*
➤ **restriction** *NOUN*

result *NOUN* results
❶ The result of something is what happens because of it. ❷ the final score or mark at the end of something
result *VERB* results, resulting, resulted
to happen as the result of something

resume *VERB* resumes, resuming, resumed
If something resumes or you resume it, it starts again after stopping. • *They* **resumed** *their game.*

retain *VERB* retains, retaining, retained
to keep something

retina *(say* ret-in-a*) NOUN* retinas
a layer at the back of your eyeball that is sensitive to light

retire *VERB* retires, retiring, retired
❶ If someone retires, they stop working because of their age. ❷ to retreat, withdraw or go to bed
➤ **retirement** *NOUN*

a
b
c
d
e
f
g
h
i
j
k
l
m
n
o
p
q
r
s
t
u
v
w
x
y
z

retort VERB retorts, retorting, retorted
to reply quickly or angrily
*'Swallows can't read, silly,' said Peter. 'Silly yourself,'
retorted Phyllis; 'how do you know?'*–THE RAILWAY
CHILDREN, Edith Nesbit

retort NOUN retorts
a quick or angry reply

retrace VERB retraces, retracing, retraced
To retrace your steps is to go back the way you came.

retreat VERB retreats, retreating, retreated
to move back from an attack or from something
dangerous

retrieve VERB retrieves, retrieving, retrieved
to get something back or find it again

retriever NOUN retrievers
a type of dog that can be used to fetch birds and
animals that have been hunted

return VERB returns, returning, returned
❶ to come or go back to a place • He *returned* home.
❷ To return something is to give or send it back.

return NOUN returns
❶ a time when someone or something comes back
• the *return* of winter ❷ (also **return ticket**)
a ticket for a journey to a place and back again

> **BUILD** YOUR VOCABULARY

An opposite for the second meaning is **single**.

reunion NOUN reunions
a meeting of people who have not seen each other
for some time

rev VERB revs, revving, revved (informal)
To rev an engine is to make it run quickly.

reveal VERB reveals, revealing, revealed
to show something or make it known

revelation NOUN revelations
a surprising fact that is revealed or discovered

revenge NOUN
To take revenge on someone is to harm them because
they have harmed you.

> **BUILD** YOUR VOCABULARY

Look at **vengeance**.

revenue (say rev-en-yoo) NOUN revenues
money that a business or person receives

revere (say riv-eer) VERB reveres, revering,
revered
to deeply respect or worship someone

reverence NOUN
great respect or worship

Reverend NOUN
a title for a Christian priest or minister

reverse NOUN
the opposite way or side
> **in reverse** going in the opposite direction

reverse VERB reverses, reversing, reversed
❶ To reverse something is to turn it the opposite
way. ❷ If you reverse a vehicle or it reverses, you
drive it backwards.

reversible ADJECTIVE
a reversible change can be changed back

review NOUN reviews
something someone writes giving their opinion
of a book, film or play

review VERB reviews, reviewing,
reviewed
to write something giving your opinion of a book,
film or play

revise VERB revises, revising, revised
❶ If you revise for a test, you go over work you
have already done to prepare for it. ❷ to correct or
change something
> **revision** NOUN

revive VERB revives, reviving, revived
If you revive or something revives you, you feel
stronger or better after fainting or feeling weak.

revolt VERB revolts, revolting, revolted
❶ If something revolts you, it disgusts you.
❷ to rebel
> **revolting** ADJECTIVE • *That smells revolting!*

revolution NOUN revolutions
❶ a rebellion that violently gets rid of a government
❷ a complete change

revolutionise (also **revolutionize**)
VERB revolutionises, revolutionising,
revolutionised
to change something completely • *Einstein's ideas
revolutionised science.*

revolve *VERB* revolves, revolving, revolved
to go round in a circle
In the middle of the floor was a giant telescope, which revolved slowly, keeping watch on the sky.—COMET IN MOOMINLAND, Tove Jansson

revolver *NOUN* revolvers
a pistol that can fire several times without being loaded again

reward *NOUN* rewards
something given to a person in return for something good they have done
reward *VERB* rewards, rewarding, rewarded
to give someone a reward for something • *Her kindness was **rewarded**.*

rewarding *ADJECTIVE*
satisfying

rewind *VERB* rewinds, rewinding, rewound
To rewind a tape or film is to make it go backwards quickly.

rewrite *VERB* rewrites, rewriting, rewrote, rewritten
to write something again or differently

rheumatism
(say **roo**-mat-izm*) NOUN*
a disease that causes pain and stiffness in joints and muscles

rhinoceros *NOUN*
rhinoceroses, rhinoceros
a large heavy mammal with a horn or two horns on its nose and thick folded skin

WORD STORY
The word **rhinoceros** comes from Greek words meaning 'nose horn'.

rhododendron *NOUN*
rhododendrons
an evergreen shrub with large flowers

rhombus *NOUN* rhombuses
a shape which has four equal sides but is not a square

BUILD YOUR VOCABULARY
Look at **diamond**.

rhubarb *NOUN*
a plant with pink or green stalks that are cooked and eaten

rhyme *NOUN* rhymes
❶ a word that ends with the same sound as another word • *Can you find a **rhyme** for 'sister'?* ❷ a short rhyming poem
rhyme *VERB* rhymes, rhyming, rhymed
If words or lines rhyme, they have the same sound at the end. • *'Fish' **rhymes** with 'dish'.* • *Your poem does not have to **rhyme**.*

⚠ **WATCH OUT!**
The words **rhyme** and **rhythm** both start the same way, with **rhy-**.

rhythm *NOUN* rhythms
a regular pattern of beats, sounds or movements
➤ **rhythmic** *ADJECTIVE* • *rhythmic footsteps*

rib *NOUN* ribs
Your ribs are the curved bones in your chest that protect your heart and lungs.

ribbon *NOUN* ribbons
a long narrow strip of cloth, used as a decoration

rice

rice *NOUN*
white seeds from a cereal plant, used as food

rich *ADJECTIVE* richer, richest
❶ If someone is rich, they have a lot of money or property.
❷ containing a large amount or a lot of different things • *Oranges are **rich** in vitamin C.* • *a **rich** vocabulary*
➤ **richly** *ADVERB* • *The floors were **richly** decorated with mosaics.*

riches *PLURAL NOUN*
wealth

a b c d e f g h i j
n o p q r s t u v w x y z

rickety *ADJECTIVE*
unsteady and likely to break or fall down • *a rickety little bridge*

ricochet *(say* rik-o-shay*)* *VERB* **ricochets, ricocheting, ricocheted**
to bounce off something • *The bullets ricocheted off the wall.*

rid *VERB* **rids, ridding, rid**
To rid a person or place of something unwanted is to free them from it. • *He rid the town of rats.*
➤ **To get rid of something** or **someone** is to make them go or throw them away.

riddance *NOUN*
➤ **good riddance** used to say that you are glad that something or someone has gone

riddle *NOUN* **riddles**
a puzzling question, especially as a joke

ride *VERB* **rides, riding, rode, ridden**
❶ To ride a horse or bicycle is to sit on it and control it as it moves. • *He rode away on his horse.* ❷ To ride in a car, bus or train is to travel in it. • *Have you ever ridden on the top deck of the bus?*
➤ **rider** *NOUN* • *As we overtook the horses, one of the riders signalled 'thank you'.*
ride *NOUN* **rides**
a journey on a horse or bicycle or in a vehicle

ridge *NOUN* **ridges**
a long narrow piece of high land • *a mountain ridge*

ridicule *VERB* **ridicules, ridiculing, ridiculed**
to make fun of someone or something in an unkind way

ridiculous *ADJECTIVE*
extremely silly or absurd
➤ **ridiculously** *ADVERB*

rifle *NOUN* **rifles**
a long gun that you hold against your shoulder to fire

rift *NOUN* **rifts**
❶ a crack or split ❷ a disagreement or a break in a friendship

rig *VERB* **rigs, rigging, rigged**
to fit a ship with sails and ropes
➤ **To rig something up** is to make it quickly.
• *They rigged up a shelter.*
rig *NOUN* **rigs**
a large structure, especially one used in drilling for oil

rigging *NOUN*
the ropes that support a ship's masts and sails

right *ADJECTIVE*
❶ on or towards the east if you are facing north
• *I write with my right hand.*

BUILD YOUR VOCABULARY
The opposite for this meaning is **left**.

❷ correct • *Is this the right spelling?*

BUILD YOUR VOCABULARY
The opposite for this meaning is **wrong**.

❸ fair or morally good • *It's not right to cheat.*
➤ **rightly** *ADVERB* • *The children are rightly proud of their success.*

BUILD YOUR VOCABULARY
The opposite for meaning 4 is **wrong**.

right *ADVERB*
❶ on or towards the right • *Turn right.* ❷ completely or exactly • *We sat right in the middle.*
➤ **right away** immediately
right *NOUN* **rights**
❶ the right side • *The bus stop is on the right.*
❷ If you have a right to do something, you are or should be allowed to do it. • *They wanted the right to vote.*

right angle *NOUN* **right angles**
an angle of 90°, like an angle in a rectangle

BUILD YOUR VOCABULARY
Look at **acute**, **obtuse** and **reflex**.

righteous *ADJECTIVE*
morally right or good

rightful *ADJECTIVE*
deserved or proper • *The bike was returned to its rightful owner.*

right-hand *ADJECTIVE*
on the right side of something

BUILD YOUR VOCABULARY
The opposite is **left-hand**.

rigid *(say* rij-id*)* *ADJECTIVE*
firm or stiff; impossible to bend
➤ **rigidly** *ADVERB*

BUILD YOUR VOCABULARY
An opposite is **flexible**.

rim *NOUN* **rims**
the outer edge of a cup, wheel or other round object

rind *NOUN* **rinds**
the tough skin on bacon, cheese or fruit

ring *NOUN* **rings**
❶ a circular piece of jewellery that you wear on your finger ❷ something in the shape of a circle • *We sat in a ring.*

ring *VERB* **rings, ringing, rang, rung**
❶ If a bell rings or you ring it, it makes a sound. • *The bell rang for playtime.* ❷ To ring someone is to telephone them. • *I've rung him twice but he never answers.*

ringleader *NOUN* **ringleaders**
someone who leads other people in mischief or crime

ringlet *NOUN* **ringlets**
a long curled piece of hair

rink *NOUN* **rinks**
a place made for skating

rinse *VERB* **rinses, rinsing, rinsed**
to wash something in clean water without soap

rinse *NOUN* **rinses**
a wash in clean water without soap

riot *NOUN* **riots**
wild or violent behaviour by a crowd in a public place

riot *VERB* **riots, rioting, rioted**
If people riot, they behave violently in a public place.

rip *VERB* **rips, ripping, ripped**
to tear something roughly

rip *NOUN* **rips**
a place where something is torn

ripe *ADJECTIVE* **riper, ripest**
ready to be harvested or eaten
➤ **ripeness** *NOUN*

ripen *VERB* **ripens, ripening, ripened**
to become ripe or to make something ripe

ripple *NOUN* **ripples**
a small wave on the surface of water

ripple *VERB* **ripples, rippling, rippled**
When water ripples, it forms small waves on its surface.

rise *VERB* **rises, rising, rose, risen**
❶ to move upwards • *Smoke rose from the fire.*
❷ When the sun or moon rises, it becomes visible

a b c d e f g h i j k l m n o p q r s t u v w x y z

rink

above the horizon. • *The sun **rises** in the east.*
❸ to stand up or get up • *She **rose** early that morning.* ❹ to increase • *Prices have **risen** this year.*

rise NOUN rises
an increase • *There was a **rise** in temperature.*

risk VERB risks, risking, risked
To risk something is to take a chance of damaging or losing it. • *They **risked** their lives to help others.*

risk NOUN risks
a chance that something bad will happen • *There's a **risk** the river might flood.*
➤ **risky** ADJECTIVE • *That was a **risky** thing to do.*

rite NOUN rites
a ceremony or ritual

ritual NOUN rituals
❶ a traditional or religious ceremony ❷ a series of actions always done in the same way

rival NOUN rivals
Your rival is someone who competes with you and wants to do better than you.
➤ **rivalry** NOUN • *There has always been **rivalry** between the two teams.*

river NOUN rivers
a large natural stream of water flowing along a channel

riveted ADJECTIVE
unable to stop looking at something or paying attention to something • *The children were **riveted** by his story.*

road NOUN roads
a wide path with a hard surface, built for vehicles

roam VERB roams, roaming, roamed
to wander around in a place

roar VERB roars, roaring, roared
to make a loud deep sound, like the sound a lion makes • *The engine **roared**.*

roar NOUN roars
a loud deep sound, like the sound a lion makes
• *I heard the **roar** of the crowd.*

roast VERB roasts, roasting, roasted
to cook food in an oven or over a fire

rob VERB robs, robbing, robbed
to steal from a person or place
➤ **robber** NOUN ➤ **robbery** NOUN

robe NOUN robes
a long loose piece of clothing

robin NOUN robins
a small brown bird with a red breast

robot NOUN robots
a machine that imitates the movements of a person or does the work of a person

✳ **WORD STORY**
The word **robot** comes from a Czech word meaning 'forced labour'.

rock NOUN rocks
❶ A rock is a large stone. ❷ Rock is the hard mineral substance that mountains and the ground are made of.
➤ **rocky** ADJECTIVE • *rocky ground*

rock VERB rocks, rocking, rocked
If something rocks or if you rock it, it moves gently backwards and forwards or from side to side.

rocket NOUN rockets
❶ a pointed tube-shaped object that travels fast through the air, as a space vehicle or weapon
❷ a firework that shoots high into the air

rod NOUN rods
❶ a long thin stick or bar ❷ a long pole with a line attached for fishing

rode VERB (past tense of **ride**)
• *I **rode** my bike around the park.*

rodent NOUN rodents
an animal that has large front teeth for chewing through things. Rats, mice and squirrels are **rodents**.

✳ **WORD STORY**
The word **rodent** comes from a Latin word that means 'gnawing'.

rogue NOUN rogues
a dishonest or mischievous person

role NOUN roles
❶ the job someone or something does or the part they play • *Plants have an important **role** in keeping the air clean.* ❷ a part in a play, film or story

roll VERB rolls, rolling, rolled
❶ If something rolls or if you roll it, it moves along on wheels or by turning over and over, like a ball. ❷ If you roll something or roll it up, you form it into a tube or ball. • *She rolled up the map.* ❸ If you roll dough or roll it out, you flatten it using a cylinder-shaped object.

roll NOUN rolls
❶ a tube made by rolling up cloth or paper ❷ a small loaf of bread for one person

roller NOUN rollers
❶ a cylinder-shaped object, especially one for flattening things ❷ a long rolling wave in the sea

roller skate NOUN roller skates
boots with small wheels underneath, so you can skate on the ground
➤ **roller skating** NOUN

ROM (say rom) ABBREVIATION
a type of computer memory with information that can be seen but not changed by the user; short for *read-only memory*

Roman ADJECTIVE
from or to do with ancient Rome • *the Roman empire*
➤ **Roman** NOUN • *the time of the Romans*

Roman Catholic NOUN Roman Catholics
a member of the Church with the Pope in Rome at its head

romance NOUN romances
❶ experiences and feelings connected with love ❷ a love affair or a love story

Roman numeral NOUN Roman numerals
a symbol used to represent a number in ancient Rome, for example X for 10 or C for 100

BUILD YOUR VOCABULARY
Look at **Arabic numeral**.

romantic ADJECTIVE
❶ to do with love • *a romantic relationship* ❷ to do with emotions or imagination • *I had a romantic idea of what France would be like.*

romp VERB romps, romping, romped
to play in an energetic way

roof NOUN roofs
❶ the part that covers the top of a building or vehicle ❷ the ceiling of a cave

rook NOUN rooks
a black bird similar to a crow

room NOUN rooms
❶ a part of a building with its own walls and ceiling ❷ space for someone or something • *Is there room for me?*

roomy ADJECTIVE roomier, roomiest
with plenty of space inside

roost NOUN roosts
the place where a bird settles or rests
roost VERB roosts, roosing, roosted
When birds roost, they rest or settle for the night.

root NOUN roots
the part of a plant that grows under the ground

root word NOUN root words
a word that can be used to make other words by adding a group of letters before or after it. For example, the root word *help* can make *helper*, *helpful* and *helpless*.

BUILD YOUR VOCABULARY
Look at **prefix** and **suffix**.

rope NOUN ropes
a strong thick cord made of strands twisted together

rose VERB (past tense of **rise**)
• *Clouds of smoke rose from the building.*

rose NOUN roses
a sweet-smelling flower with a long thorny stem

rosette NOUN rosettes
a large circular badge made of ribbons

Rosh Hashana NOUN
the Jewish New Year festival

rosy ADJECTIVE rosier, rosiest
pink

a b c d e f g h i j k l m n o p q r s t u v w x y z

rot VERB rots, rotting, rotted
to go bad and become soft or fall apart • *The wood has rotted.*

rotate VERB rotates, rotating, rotated
to go round like a wheel
➤ **rotation** NOUN

rotor NOUN rotors
the part of a machine that goes round, especially the large propeller of a helicopter

rotten ADJECTIVE
❶ decayed; gone bad • *a rotten apple* ❷ (informal) bad or unpleasant • *We had rotten weather.*

Rottweiler NOUN Rottweilers
a large dog with short black and tan hair, often kept as a guard dog

rough ADJECTIVE rougher, roughest
❶ not smooth or flat • *We walked across rough ground.* ❷ violent • *Ice hockey is a rough game.*

> ⚙ **BUILD YOUR VOCABULARY**
> An opposite of the second meaning is **gentle**.

❸ not exact or accurate • *Just make a rough guess.*

> ⚠ **WATCH OUT!**
> In **rough**, **enough** and **tough**, the letters *ough* sound like 'uff'.

roughly ADVERB
❶ approximately • *There were roughly a hundred people there.* ❷ not gently • *She pushed him roughly out of the way.*

round ADJECTIVE rounder, roundest
shaped like a circle or ball • *a round table*
round ADVERB
❶ turning in a circle or curve • *The wheels spin round.* • *Turn your chair round.* ❷ from place to place or from person to person • *Let's have a look round.* • *Hand the cakes round.* ❸ to someone's house • *Come round on Saturday.*
round PREPOSITION
❶ on all sides of • *I painted a border round the edge.* ❷ in a curve or circle around • *The earth moves round the sun.* ❸ to every part of • *Show them round the house.*

round NOUN rounds
❶ each stage in a competition • *The winners go on to the next round.* ❷ a series of calls or deliveries • *The postman is on his round.*
round VERB rounds, rounding, rounded
❶ To round a bend is to travel along and past it. • *They rounded the corner.* ❷ To round a number is to increase or decrease it to the nearest 1, 10, 100 or 1000. • *The number of tickets sold, rounded to the nearest 10, was 180.* • *One third as a percentage can be rounded down to 33%.*

roundabout NOUN roundabouts
❶ a road junction where traffic passes round a circular island ❷ a circular platform in a playground that spins around

rounded ADJECTIVE
round in shape

rounders NOUN
a game in which players try to hit a ball and run round a circuit

rouse VERB rouses, rousing, roused
❶ to wake someone up • *A voice roused me from a deep sleep.* ❷ to make someone have a particular emotion • *Her curiosity was roused.*

route (say root) NOUN routes
the way you have to go to get to a place

routine (say roo-teen) NOUN routines
a regular or fixed way of doing things

rove VERB roves, roving, roved
to roam or wander
The Trunchbull's dangerous glittering eyes roved around the classroom.—MATILDA, Roald Dahl

row (rhymes with **go**) NOUN rows
a line of people or things • *Our seats were in the front row.*

row (rhymes with **go**) VERB rows, rowing, rowed
To row a boat is to use oars to make it move.
➤ **rower** NOUN

row (rhymes with **cow**) NOUN rows
❶ a quarrel or argument ❷ a great noise or disturbance

rowdy *ADJECTIVE* **rowdier, rowdiest**
noisy and rough

royal *ADJECTIVE*
to do with a king or queen

royalty *NOUN*
❶ the state of being royal ❷ a royal person or royal people • *We were in the presence of **royalty**.*

rub *VERB* **rubs, rubbing, rubbed**
to press and move your hand or a cloth backwards and forwards over something • *She **rubbed** her eyes.* • *Try **rubbing** the mark with a cloth.*
➤ **To rub something out** is to remove it with a rubber.

rubber *NOUN* **rubbers**
❶ a strong elastic substance used for making tyres, balls and hoses ❷ a piece of rubber or soft plastic for removing mistakes done in pencil
➤ **rubbery** *ADJECTIVE*

rubbish *NOUN*
❶ things that are not wanted or needed ❷ nonsense

rubble *NOUN*
broken pieces of brick or stone

ruby *NOUN* **rubies**
a precious red stone

ruby

rucksack *NOUN*
rucksacks
a bag that you carry on your back

BUILD YOUR VOCABULARY
A synonym is **backpack**.

rudder *NOUN* **rudders**
a flat hinged device at the back of a ship or aircraft, for steering it

ruddy *ADJECTIVE* **ruddier, ruddiest**
red and healthy-looking • *He had a **ruddy** complexion.*

rude *ADJECTIVE* **ruder, rudest**
❶ not polite; not showing respect for other people • *It is **rude** to stare at someone.* ❷ offensive or indecent • *a **rude** word*
➤ **rudely** *ADVERB* ➤ **rudeness** *NOUN*

ruffian *NOUN* **ruffians**
a violent person

ruffle *VERB* **ruffles, ruffling, ruffled**
to disturb the smooth surface of something
• *The bird **ruffled** its feathers.*

rug *NOUN* **rugs**
❶ a thick piece of material that partly covers a floor ❷ a thick blanket

rugby (*also* **rugby football**) *NOUN*
a team game using an oval ball that players can kick or carry

✳ **WORD STORY**
The game of **rugby** is named after Rugby School in Warwickshire, where it was first played.

rugged (*say* **rug**-id) *ADJECTIVE*
rough or uneven
We round the headland and pass along the rugged coastline of rocky inlets and deep shelving coves.
—WHITE DOLPHIN, Gill Lewis

ruin *VERB* **ruins, ruining, ruined**
to spoil or destroy something completely
ruin *NOUN* **ruins**
a building that has been so badly damaged that it has almost all fallen down
➤ **To be in ruins** is to be destroyed. • *My plans were in ruins.*

rule *NOUN* **rules**
something that tells you what you must or must not do
rule *VERB* **rules, ruling, ruled**
to govern or be in charge of a country

ruler *NOUN* **rulers**
❶ someone who governs a country ❷ a straight wooden, plastic or metal strip for drawing straight lines and measuring

a
b
c
d
e
f
g
h
i
j
k
l
m
n
o
p
q
r
s
t
u
v
w
x
y
z

rum NOUN rums
a strong alcoholic drink made from sugar cane that used to be given to sailors

rumble VERB rumbles, rumbling, rumbled
to make a long deep sound like thunder • *His stomach was rumbling.*

rumble NOUN rumbles
a long deep sound • *There was a rumble of thunder.*

rummage VERB rummages, rummaging, rummaged
to feel around, in or under something, because you are trying to find something
Mrs Whiffy hurriedly rummaged in her bag and gave me 10p.—DOGSBOTTOM SCHOOL GOES TOTALLY MENTAL, John Blake

rumour NOUN rumours
a story or piece of information that many people repeat, but that may not be true

rump NOUN rumps
the back part of an animal, above its hind legs

run VERB runs, running, ran, run
❶ to move quickly, taking both feet off the ground during each stride ❷ to flow • *The river runs into the sea.* ❸ If you run something, you are in charge of it. • *She runs the drama club.*
➤ **To run away** is to leave a place suddenly or secretly.
➤ **To run out of something** is to have used it all up.
➤ **runner** NOUN • *She is a fast runner.*

run NOUN runs
❶ If you go for a run, you run for sport or exercise. ❷ a point scored in cricket or baseball

runaway NOUN runaways
someone who has run away from home

rung VERB (past participle of **ring**)
• *Have you rung your friend yet?*

rung NOUN rungs
The rungs of a ladder are the short bars that you stand on.

runner bean NOUN runner beans
a kind of bean from a climbing plant

runny ADJECTIVE runnier, runniest
flowing like a liquid

runway NOUN runways
a strip of land for an aeroplane to take off and land

rural ADJECTIVE
in or to do with the countryside • *a rural community*

BUILD YOUR VOCABULARY
Look at **urban**.

rush VERB rushes, rushing, rushed
to hurry • *Everyone was rushing around.* • *Don't rush your work.*

rush NOUN
❶ a hurry • *I can't stop—I'm in a rush.* ❷ a plant with a thin stem that grows in or near rivers and lakes

rust NOUN
a reddish-brown substance that forms on iron when it comes into contact with water and oxygen
➤ **rusty** ADJECTIVE • *The gate was broken and rusty.*

rust VERB rusts, rusting, rusted
If metal rusts, it develops rust.

rustic ADJECTIVE
typical of the countryside • *a rustic scene*

rustle VERB rustles, rustling, rustled
to make a gentle sound like dry leaves

rut NOUN ruts
a deep groove made by wheels in soft ground

ruthless ADJECTIVE
not feeling any pity or caring if you hurt other people

rye NOUN
a cereal used to make bread and biscuits

There are more English words that begin with **s** than any other letter. This is why it takes up the most pages in this dictionary.

However, **s** is not the most frequently used letter—can you guess what it is?

CLUE It is a vowel.

sabbath (also **the Sabbath**) NOUN sabbaths
the weekly day for rest and prayer in some religions: Saturday for Jewish people, Sunday for Christians

sabotage (say sab-o-tahzh) NOUN
deliberate damage to machines or equipment

sabotage (say sab-o-tahzh) VERB sabotages, sabotaging, sabotaged
to damage machines or equipment deliberately

sabre NOUN sabres
a type of sword with a curved blade

sac NOUN sacs
any bag-like part of an animal or plant
• a spider's egg **sac**

sachet (say sash-ay) NOUN sachets
a small sealed packet of something such as shampoo or sugar

sack NOUN sacks
a large bag made of strong material
➤ **To get the sack** (informal) is to be dismissed from a job.

sack VERB sacks, sacking, sacked
to dismiss someone from their job

sacred ADJECTIVE
to do with God or a god; holy

sacrifice VERB sacrifices, sacrificing, sacrificed
If you sacrifice something important to you, you give it up, usually for something more important. • They **sacrificed** a lot for their children.

sacrifice NOUN sacrifices
something good or important that you give up

sad ADJECTIVE sadder, saddest
feeling or making you feel unhappy
• She looks **sad**. • a **sad** story
➤ **sadly** ADVERB ➤ **sadness** NOUN

sadden VERB saddens, saddening, saddened
If something saddens you, it makes you sad.

saddle NOUN saddles
❶ a seat that you put on an animal's back so you can ride it ❷ the seat of a bicycle

saddle VERB saddles, saddling, saddled
If you saddle a horse, you put a saddle on it.

safari (say sa-far-ee) NOUN safaris
an expedition to see or hunt wild animals

safe ADJECTIVE safer, safest
❶ not in any danger • You're **safe** here.
❷ not dangerous • The water is **safe** to drink.
➤ **safely** ADVERB • We got home **safely**.

safe NOUN safes
a strong metal box with a lock where you can keep money or valuable things

safeguard NOUN safeguards
a rule that protects against danger

safeguard VERB safeguards, safeguarding, safeguarded
to protect something or someone from danger

safety NOUN
the state of being safe or protected • We listened to a talk on road **safety**.

sag VERB sags, sagging, sagged
to dip or droop downwards • This mattress **sags** in the middle.

saga NOUN sagas
a long story with many adventures

a
b
c
d
e
f
g
h
i
j
k
l
m
n
o
p
q
r
s
t
u
v
w
x
y
z

said VERB (past tense and past participle of **say**)
• Did you hear what he **said**? • You haven't **said** much today.

sail NOUN sails
a large piece of strong cloth attached to a mast on a boat. When the wind blows against the sail, the boat moves.

sail VERB sails, sailing, sailed
❶ To sail somewhere is to travel there in a ship or boat.
❷ When a ship sails, it sets off across water.

sailor NOUN sailors
❶ a member of a ship's crew ❷ someone who goes sailing

saint NOUN saints
a holy or very good person
➤ **saintly** ADJECTIVE

sake NOUN
➤ **for the sake of something** in order to do something or get something • They did it **for the sake of** peace.
➤ **for someone's sake** in order to help or please someone • **For his sake**, I agreed to go.

salad NOUN salads
a mixture of vegetables eaten cold and often raw

salary NOUN salaries
an amount of money someone earns each month

sale NOUN sales
❶ the selling of something ❷ a time when a shop sells things at reduced prices
➤ **for sale** or **on sale** able to be bought

saliva (say sa-**ly**-va) NOUN
the liquid in your mouth

salmon NOUN salmon
a large fish with pink flesh, eaten as food

salt NOUN
a white substance found in sea water that is used to flavour and preserve food
➤ **salty** ADJECTIVE

salute VERB salutes, saluting, saluted
to raise your hand to your forehead as a sign of respect or greeting

salute NOUN salutes
the act of saluting

salvage VERB salvages, salvaging, salvaged
to manage to save something from a disaster or wreck
They'd salvaged what they could from the boat.—THE FLIP FLOP CLUB: WHALE SONG, Ellen Richardson

salvation NOUN
the act of saving someone or something

same ADJECTIVE
not different; exactly equal or alike
• We are the **same** age. • Look, these two leaves are exactly the **same**.

BUILD YOUR VOCABULARY
The opposite is **different**.

sample NOUN samples
a small amount that shows what something is like

sample VERB samples, sampling, sampled
to try something • She **sampled** the cake.

samurai NOUN samurai
a warrior in ancient Japan

sanctuary NOUN sanctuaries
❶ a safe place, especially for someone being chased or attacked
❷ a place where wildlife is protected
• a bird **sanctuary**

sand NOUN
❶ tiny grains of rock found on beaches and in deserts ❷ **Sands** means a beach or sandy area.
• They ran across the **sands**.
➤ **sandy** ADJECTIVE

sandal NOUN sandals
a light shoe with straps, for warm weather

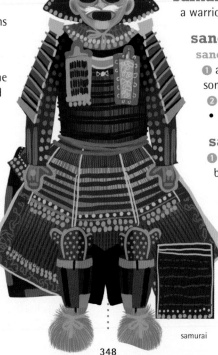
samurai

348

sandstone *NOUN*
rock made of sand pressed together

BUILD YOUR VOCABULARY
Sandstone is **permeable**.

sandwich *NOUN* sandwiches
slices of bread with a filling such as cheese or meat between them

✳ WORD STORY
The word **sandwich** is named after the Earl of *Sandwich*, who is said to have invented it so that he could eat at the same time as playing cards.

sane *ADJECTIVE* saner, sanest
having a healthy mind; not mad

sang *VERB (past tense of sing)*
• We **sang** a song.

sanity *NOUN*
the state of being sane

sank *VERB (past tense of sink)*
• The boat hit a rock and **sank**.

sap *NOUN*
the juice inside a tree or plant

sap *VERB* saps, sapping, sapped
To sap someone's strength or energy is to weaken it.

sapling *NOUN* saplings
a young tree

sapphire *NOUN* sapphires
a bright blue precious stone

sarcastic *ADJECTIVE*
If you are being sarcastic, you are saying the opposite of what you mean in order to make fun of someone.
➤ **sarcastically** *ADVERB*

sardine *NOUN* sardines
a small sea fish, eaten as food

sari *(say* sah-ree*) NOUN* saris
a long length of cloth worn as a dress, especially by Indian women and girls

sash *NOUN* sashes
a strip of cloth worn round the waist or over one shoulder

sat *VERB (past tense and past participle of sit)*
• She **sat** next to her friend. • I've **sat** here all morning waiting.

satchel *NOUN* satchels
a bag with a long strap, especially for school books

satellite

satellite *NOUN* satellites
❶ a spacecraft sent into space to orbit the earth and collect information or send out signals
❷ a moon that orbits a planet

satellite dish *NOUN* satellite dishes
an object shaped like a large dish that can receive signals from a satellite

satin *NOUN*
a silky shiny material

satisfaction *NOUN*
the feeling of being satisfied

satisfactory *ADJECTIVE*
good enough; acceptable • He tried to think of a **satisfactory** excuse.

satisfy *VERB* satisfies, satisfying, satisfied
to give someone what they want or need
➤ **satisfied** *ADJECTIVE* • The teacher was not **satisfied** with our work.

satsuma *NOUN* satsumas
a kind of tangerine with a loose skin

sauce *NOUN* sauces
a thick liquid served with food to add flavour

saucepan *NOUN* saucepans
a metal cooking pan with a long handle

saucer *NOUN* saucers
a small curved plate for a cup to stand on

saucy *ADJECTIVE* saucier, sauciest
rude or cheeky

saunter *VERB* saunters, sauntering, sauntered
to walk in a very casual confident way

sausage *NOUN* sausages
a cylinder-shaped food made of minced meat and flavourings

savage *ADJECTIVE*
wild, fierce and cruel
➤ **savagely** *ADVERB*

savannah *(say* sa-**van**-a*) NOUN* savannahs
a grassy plain in a hot country, with few trees

a
b
e
f
g
h
i
j
k
l
m
n
o
p
q
r
s
t
u
v
w
x
y
z

save VERB saves, saving, saved
① to rescue someone or something from danger or harm ② to keep something so that it can be used later • *Save some cake for me!* ③ To save something on a computer is to store a copy of it on the hard disk. • *Don't forget to save your work.*

savings NOUN
Your savings are money that you have saved.

saviour NOUN saviours
a person who saves someone

savoury ADJECTIVE
salty rather than sweet

saw VERB (past tense of **see**)
• *I saw them both yesterday.*

saw NOUN saws
a tool with sharp teeth for cutting wood
saw VERB saws, sawing, sawed, sawn
to cut something with a saw • *He sawed off a branch.*

sawdust NOUN
powder that comes from wood when it is cut with a saw

saxophone NOUN saxophones
a metal musical instrument with a tube that curves upward

BUILD YOUR VOCABULARY
The **saxophone** is a **wind instrument**.

say VERB says, saying, said
to make words with your voice • *'Hello,' he said.*
• *Nobody has said anything about lunch.*

saying NOUN sayings
a well-known phrase telling you something that people think is true

scab NOUN scabs
a hard crust that forms over a cut while it is healing

scabbard NOUN scabbards
a cover for a sword or dagger

scaffold NOUN scaffolds (old use)
a platform on which criminals used to be executed

scaffolding NOUN
a structure of poles and planks for workers to stand on when working on a building

scald VERB scalds, scalding, scalded
to burn something with very hot liquid or steam

scale NOUN scales
① a series of units or marks for measuring something • *We use the Celsius temperature scale.* ② The scale of a map or model is the relationship between its size and the size of something in real life. • *The scale of this map is one centimetre to one kilometre.* ③ one of the thin overlapping parts on the skin of a fish or snake ④ a series of musical notes going up or down ⑤ **Scales** are a device for weighing things.

scale VERB scales, scaling, scaled
to climb up something • *They had to scale a sheer cliff.*

scalene triangle NOUN scalene triangles
a triangle with sides that are different lengths

BUILD YOUR VOCABULARY
Look at **equilateral triangle** and **isosceles triangle**.

scalp NOUN scalps
the skin on the top of your head

scamper VERB scampers, scampering, scampered
to run quickly with short steps

scan VERB scans, scanning, scanned
① to move your eyes across a place looking for something • *He scanned the horizon.* ② When a machine scans something, it moves a light beam or X-ray over it, for example in order to copy it or examine it. • *We scanned the photograph and saved it on the computer.*
scan NOUN scans
a search or examination with a light beam or X-ray

scandal NOUN scandals
① a shocking or shameful situation ② gossip that can hurt someone's reputation

scanner NOUN scanners
① a machine used to examine something using an X-ray or electronic beam ② a machine that scans documents so they can be saved on a computer

scanty ADJECTIVE scantier, scantiest
hardly big enough

scapegoat NOUN scapegoats
someone who gets all the blame for something that is not their fault or not only their fault

scar NOUN scars
a mark left on your skin by an injury after it has healed

scar VERB scars, scarring, scarred
if an injury scars you, it leaves a permanent mark on your skin.

scarab NOUN scarab
an ancient Egyptian symbol in the shape of a beetle

scarce ADJECTIVE scarcer, scarcest
rare; not enough • *Water is scarce in the desert.*

scarcely ADVERB
hardly; only just • *I could scarcely believe it.*

scare VERB scares, scaring, scared
to frighten someone

scare NOUN scares
a fright • *You gave me quite a scare.*

scarecrow NOUN scarecrows
a model of a person dressed in old clothes, put in a field to frighten birds away from crops

scarf NOUN scarves
a strip of material that you wear round your neck or head

scarlet ADJECTIVE
bright red

scary ADJECTIVE scarier, scariest (informal)
frightening • *We told scary ghost stories.*

scatter VERB scatters, scattering, scattered
❶ to throw or drop things in all directions • *Cushions were scattered on the floor.* ❷ to move quickly in all directions • *The herd scattered.*

scavenge VERB scavenges, scavenging, scavenged
❶ To scavenge for something is to search through waste or rubbish for it. ❷ If an animal scavenges, it eats dead animals that it has not killed itself.
➤ **scavenger** NOUN

scene NOUN scenes
❶ the place where something happens • *It was a peaceful scene.* • *the scene of the crime* ❷ one part of a play or film

scenery NOUN
❶ the natural features of an area • *We were admiring the scenery.* ❷ things put on a stage to make it look like a particular place

scent (say sent) NOUN scents
❶ a pleasant smell or perfume ❷ an animal's smell, that other animals can follow
➤ **scented** ADJECTIVE

sceptical (say skep-tik-al) ADJECTIVE
If you are sceptical about something, you are not sure if you believe it.

scarab

sceptre (say sep-ter) NOUN sceptres
a ceremonial stick carried by a king or queen

schedule (say shed-yool) NOUN schedules
a timetable of things that have to be done

scheme NOUN schemes
a plan of what to do

scheme VERB schemes, scheming, schemed
to make secret plans

scholar NOUN scholars
someone who studies a subject thoroughly

scholarship NOUN scholarships
❶ an amount of money given to someone to pay for their education ❷ knowledge and learning

school NOUN schools
❶ a place where children go to be taught ❷ a group of fish or whales

schooner (say skoo-ner) NOUN schooners
a sailing ship with two or more masts

science NOUN
the study of living things, objects and events in the world that can be observed and tested

⭐ **WORD STORY**
The word **science** comes from a Latin word meaning 'knowledge'.

science fiction NOUN
stories about imaginary worlds, especially in space and in the future

scientific ADJECTIVE
❶ to do with science • *scientific knowledge*
❷ studying things carefully and logically
• *That's not very scientific.*

scientist *NOUN* **scientists**
someone who studies science or is an expert
in science

scissors *NOUN*
a tool with two sharp blades for cutting paper
or cloth

⚠ **WATCH OUT**
There is a silent c in **scissors**.

scoff *VERB* **scoffs, scoffing, scoffed**
to make fun of someone or something
'No one would ever believe a story like that!' Sam scoffed.
—THE DAY OF THE CAMERA CARNAGE, Steve Cole

scold *VERB* **scolds, scolding, scolded**
to tell someone off

scone *(say* skon *or* skohn*) NOUN* **scones**
a small heavy cake, usually eaten with butter
or cream and jam

scoop *VERB* **scoops, scooping, scooped**
to pick something up with a spoon or with your
curved hand • *She scooped up a handful of sand.*
scoop *NOUN* **scoops**
a deep spoon for serving soft food such as ice cream

scooter *NOUN* **scooters**
❶ a simple bicycle that you ride by standing on a
platform and pushing it along with your foot
❷ a kind of motorcycle with small wheels

scope *NOUN*
❶ opportunity or possibility for something
• *There is lots of scope for imagination in
the game.* ❷ the range or extent of something
• *Some subjects are outside the scope of this book.*

scorch *VERB* **scorches, scorching, scorched**
to slightly burn something so it goes brown

scorching *ADJECTIVE*
very hot

score *NOUN* **scores**
❶ the number of points or goals in a game
• *The score is 2-2.* ❷ A score is twenty. **Scores of**
means 'a large number of'. • *Scores of children
ran around.*
score *VERB* **scores, scoring, scored**
❶ To score a goal or point is to get one. ❷ to make a
deep scratch in a surface

scorn *NOUN*
a feeling of no respect at all for someone or
something • *She looked at him with scorn.*

scornful *ADJECTIVE*
feeling or showing no respect at all
➤ **scornfully** *ADVERB*
'Don't be so feeble,' Ingrid said scornfully.—THE DEMON
HEADMASTER AND THE PRIME MINISTER'S BRAIN, Gillian Cross

scorpion *NOUN*
scorpions
a small animal
with pincers
and a poisonous
sting in its
curved tail

Scots *NOUN*
a language spoken in lowland Scotland

scour *VERB* **scours, scouring, scoured**
❶ to rub something hard with a rough cloth
to clean it ❷ to search an area thoroughly

scout *NOUN* **scouts**
someone sent out ahead of a group in order to
collect information

scowl *VERB* **scowls, scowling, scowled**
to frown angrily
scowl *NOUN* **scowls**
an angry look

scramble *VERB* **scrambles, scrambling,
scrambled**
❶ to move quickly using hands and feet
• *We scrambled over the rocks to safety.*
❷ To scramble eggs is to cook them by mixing
and heating them.

scrap *NOUN* **scraps**
❶ a small piece of something ❷ rubbish, especially
unwanted metal or paper
scrap *VERB* **scraps, scrapping, scrapped**
to get rid of something • *Let's scrap that idea.*

scrape *VERB* **scrapes, scraping, scraped**
❶ to rub against something with something hard
or sharp • *He scraped at the rock with his
fingernails.* • *Scrape off the old paint.* ❷ to cut
yourself slightly by rubbing against something hard
or sharp • *I've scraped my elbow.*

scrape NOUN scrapes
a sound or mark made by something scraping against something

scratch VERB scratches, scratching, scratched
❶ to damage a surface by rubbing something sharp over it ❷ to rub your skin with your fingernails because it itches
scratch NOUN scratches
a mark or small cut made by scratching

scrawl VERB scrawls, scrawling, scrawled
to write something in a quick untidy way
scrawl NOUN scrawls
untidy writing

scream NOUN screams
a loud high cry of pain, fear or anger
scream VERB screams, screaming, screamed
to make a loud high cry
Things happened to me that will probably make you scream when you read about them. That can't be helped.
—THE WITCHES, Roald Dahl

screech NOUN screeches
an unpleasant high sound • *There was a screech of tyres.*
screech VERB screeches, screeching, screeched
to make an unpleasant high sound • *Seagulls rose screeching into the air.*

screen NOUN screens
❶ a surface on which a film, a television programme, computer information or phone information is shown ❷ a panel used to hide or protect something • *The bed was behind a screen.*
screen VERB screens, screening, screened
to form a screen that hides or protects something • *Their den was screened by thick bushes.*

screw NOUN screws
a pointed piece of metal that can be twisted into things to fix them together
screw VERB screws, screwing, screwed
❶ to fix something somewhere using a screw • *She screwed a shelf to the wall.* ❷ to put something in place by twisting it • *Screw the lid on.*
➤ **To screw something up** is to twist or squeeze it into a tight ball.

screwdriver NOUN screwdrivers
a tool for putting in or taking out screws

scribble VERB scribbles, scribbling, scribbled
to write or draw something in a quick careless untidy way

script NOUN scripts
the words of a play, film or programme, written down for people to say

scripture NOUN scriptures
a holy book, especially the Bible

scroll NOUN scrolls
a roll of paper or parchment with writing on it
scroll VERB scrolls, scrolling, scrolled
If you scroll up or down on a computer screen, you move the text up or down.

scrub VERB scrubs, scrubbing, scrubbed
to rub something with a hard brush
scrub NOUN
❶ the action of scrubbing • *Give the pan a good scrub.* ❷ ground covered with bushes and low trees

scruffy ADJECTIVE scruffier, scruffiest
untidy; not smart • *a scruffy pair of jeans*

scrum NOUN scrums
in rugby, a group of players who push against each other and try to win the ball

scrutinise (also **scrutinize**) VERB scrutinises, scrutinising, scrutinised
to examine or look at something closely

scrutiny NOUN
close examination of something

scuba diving NOUN
the sport of swimming underwater using breathing equipment

scuffle NOUN scuffles
a confused struggle or fight
scuffle VERB scuffles, scuffling, scuffled
to fight in a confused way

sculptor NOUN sculptors
someone who makes sculptures

a
b
c
d
e
f
g
h
i
j
k
l
m
n
o
p
q
r
s
t
u
v
w
x
y
z

seahorse

sculpture *NOUN* **sculptures**
a piece of art carved or shaped out of a material such as stone or sand

scum *NOUN*
froth or dirt on the top of a liquid

scurry *VERB* **scurries, scurrying, scurried**
to run or hurry with short steps • *A large black beetle scurried across the floor.*

scurvy *NOUN*
a disease caused by lack of fresh fruit and vegetables

scuttle *VERB* **scuttles, scuttling, scuttled**
❶ To scuttle a ship is to sink it deliberately by making holes in it. ❷ to run with short quick steps *'Oh! Oh! Oh!' said Mrs Crabbity and she turned and scuttled into her cottage like a small frightened spider.* —UNDER THE MOON, Vivian French

scuttle *NOUN* **scuttles**
a container for coal, kept by a fireplace

scythe *(say* sythe*) NOUN* **scythes**
a tool with a long curved blade for cutting grass or corn

sea *NOUN* **seas**
❶ the salty water that covers most of the earth's surface ❷ a large area of something • *I looked out at a sea of faces.*

seafaring *ADJECTIVE, NOUN*
travelling or working on the sea
➤ **seafarer** *NOUN*

seafood *NOUN*
fish or shellfish from the sea eaten as food

seagull *NOUN* **seagulls**
a sea bird with long wings

seahorse *NOUN* **seahorses**
a small fish that swims upright, with a head that looks like a horse's head

seal *NOUN* **seals**
❶ a sea mammal with thick fur and flippers ❷ something that closes an opening and stops anything getting in or out

seal *VERB* **seals, sealing, sealed**
to close something by sticking two parts together • *He sealed the envelope.*

sea level *NOUN*
the level of the sea halfway between high and low tide • *The village is at 1000 metres above sea level.*

sea lion *NOUN* **sea lions**
a large type of seal. The male has a kind of mane.

seam *NOUN* **seams**
❶ the line where two edges of cloth join together ❷ a layer of coal in the ground

seaman *NOUN* **seamen**
a sailor

search *VERB* **searches, searching, searched**
❶ to try hard to find something or someone • *I've searched for my shoes everywhere.* ❷ To search a person or place is to examine them closely trying to find something.

search *NOUN* **searches**
❶ an attempt to find someone or something ❷ the operation of looking for information in a computer or on the Internet • *Let's do a search for her name.*

search engine *NOUN* **search engines**
a computer program that helps you find information on the Internet

searchlight *NOUN* **searchlights**
a light with a strong beam that can be turned in any direction

seashore *NOUN*
the land close to the sea

seasick ADJECTIVE
feeling or being sick because of the movement of a ship
➤ **seasickness** NOUN

seaside NOUN
The seaside is a place by the sea where people go on holiday.

season NOUN seasons
❶ one of the four main parts of the year: spring, summer, autumn or winter ❷ the time of year when a sport or other activity happens • When does the football **season** start?
➤ **seasonal** ADJECTIVE • seasonal rain

seat NOUN seats
a piece of furniture for sitting on
seat VERB seats, seating, seated
If a place seats a number of people, it has seats for that many people. • The hall **seats** 500.

seat belt NOUN seat belts
a strap to hold a person safely in a car, bus or plane

seaward (also **seawards**) ADVERB
towards the sea

seaweed NOUN seaweeds
plants that grow in the sea

secluded ADJECTIVE
away from large numbers of people; quiet and hidden • They found a **secluded** beach for their picnic.

second ADJECTIVE
The second thing is next after the first. • February is the **second** month. • I won **second** prize.
second ADVERB
after the first • Who came **second**?
second NOUN seconds
❶ a very short period of time. There are 60 seconds in one minute. ❷ a person or thing that is second

secondary school NOUN secondary schools
a school for children who are 11 years old and older

second-hand ADJECTIVE, ADVERB
owned after someone else has owned it • a **second-hand** bike • Did you buy it **second-hand**?

secondly ADVERB
as the second thing • **Secondly**, I'd like to thank my parents.

second person NOUN
the use of the word you and the verbs that go with it

⚙ BUILD YOUR VOCABULARY
Look at **first person** and **third person**.

secrecy NOUN
the act of keeping something secret

secret ADJECTIVE
known or seen only by a small number of people and hidden from others • a **secret** message
➤ **secretly** ADVERB • I was **secretly** pleased.
secret NOUN secrets
something that is secret
➤ **To do something in secret** is to do it secretly.

secretary (say sek-rit-tree) NOUN secretaries
someone whose job is to deal with letters, emails and phone calls and to organise meetings

secretive (say seek-rit-iv) ADJECTIVE
liking or trying to keep things secret

section NOUN sections
a part of something • Our school library has a large history **section**. • The tail **section** of the plane broke off.

secure ADJECTIVE
❶ firmly and safely fixed • Is that ladder **secure**?
❷ safe and protected • She felt **secure** at home.
➤ **securely** ADVERB
secure VERB secures, securing, secured
❶ to make something safe and firmly fixed
❷ to manage to get something • She **secured** tickets for the show.

security NOUN
❶ a feeling of being secure or safe ❷ things that are done to prevent theft or attack

sediment NOUN
solid matter that settles at the bottom of a liquid

see VERB sees, seeing, saw, seen
❶ to notice or observe something with your eyes • I **saw** him yesterday. • We've **seen** that film already. ❷ to understand something • I **see** what you mean. ❸ To see that something happens is to make sure of it. • **See** that the door is locked.

a b c d e f g h i j k l m n o p q r **s** t u v w x y z

A
B
C
D
E

seed NOUN seeds
a tiny part of a plant that can grow in the ground to make a new plant

seedling NOUN seedlings
a very young plant

F
G
H
I
J
K
L
M
N
O
P
Q
R

seek VERB seeks, seeking, sought
to try to find or get something or someone
• We **sought** shelter in a cave. • They have **sought** him everywhere.

seem VERB seems, seeming, seemed
to look, sound or appear to be a certain thing
• It **seems** strange. • She **seemed** to be annoyed.

seemingly ADVERB
as something appears • He was staring ahead, **seemingly** at nothing.

seen VERB (past participle of **see**)
• Have you **seen** my book anywhere?

seep VERB seeps, seeping, seeped
to flow very slowly

see-saw NOUN see-saws
a toy made of a plank balanced in the middle, which goes up and down when people sit on each end

★ **WORD STORY**
The word **see-saw** comes from an old rhyme that people used when sawing wood.

seethe VERB seethes, seething, seethed
❶ to boil or bubble ❷ If you are seething, you are very angry.

segment NOUN segments
a part that can be separated from the rest of something • I ate a few **segments** of an orange.

seize (say seez) VERB seizes, seizing, seized
to take hold of something or someone suddenly or firmly

seldom ADVERB
rarely; not often • I **seldom** go there.

select VERB selects, selecting, selected
to choose someone or something carefully

select ADJECTIVE
small and carefully chosen • a **select** team of top players

selection NOUN selections
❶ the act of choosing people or things carefully
❷ a number of things that have been chosen
• The book contains a **selection** of poems.

self NOUN selves
the type of person you are; your individual nature

self-conscious ADJECTIVE
embarrassed or shy because you know people are watching you

self-control NOUN
the ability to control your own behaviour or feelings

self-defence NOUN
ways of fighting or other things that are done to protect yourself when you are being attacked

selfie NOUN selfies
a photograph that you take by pointing a phone or camera towards yourself

selfish ADJECTIVE
taking or doing what you want without thinking of other people
➤ **selfishly** ADVERB
➤ **selfishness** NOUN

sell VERB sells, selling, sold
to offer goods or services for people to buy • I **sold** my old bike.

semaphore NOUN
a signalling system that uses flags held in different positions to send messages

segment

S
T
U
V
W
X
Y
Z

semibreve *NOUN* semibreves
the longest musical note normally used, written (o)

> ⚙ **BUILD YOUR VOCABULARY**
Look at **crotchet**, **minim** and **quaver**.

semicircle *NOUN* semicircles
half a circle • *We sat in a semicircle.*
➤ **semicircular** *ADJECTIVE*

semicolon *NOUN* semicolons
a punctuation mark (;) used between two clauses
that could stand on their own

semi-final *NOUN* semi-finals
a match played to decide who will take part in
the final

send *VERB* sends, sending, sent
❶ to arrange for something to go or be taken
somewhere • *I've sent you a message.* ❷ To send
someone somewhere is to tell them to go there.
• *She was sent home.*

senior *ADJECTIVE*
❶ more important or experienced
*One of the spells he was working with was a very
dangerous one indeed. It was reserved for the most
senior wizards and Sheepshank had no business even
knowing it, let alone playing with it.*—MEASLE: THE MONSTER
OF MUCUS!, Ian Ogilvy
❷ older or for older children • *the senior team*

> ⚙ **BUILD YOUR VOCABULARY**
Look at **junior**.

sensation *NOUN* sensations
❶ a feeling • *I had a sensation of warmth.*
❷ great interest or excitement • *The news caused
a sensation.*

sensational *ADJECTIVE*
❶ very exciting or shocking ❷ very good

sense *NOUN* senses
❶ the ability to see, hear, smell, touch or taste
things ❷ the ability to make sensible judgements
• *She had the sense to call an ambulance.*
➤ **To make sense** is to have a meaning you can
understand.
sense *VERB* senses, sensing, sensed
to feel or be aware of something • *I sensed someone
was there.*

senseless *ADJECTIVE*
❶ stupid; pointless • *a senseless waste*
❷ unconscious • *He was knocked senseless.*

sensible *ADJECTIVE*
reasonable and wise • *She's a sensible girl.*
➤ **sensibly** *ADVERB* • *Sensibly, he decided to stay
where he was.*

> ⚠ **WATCH OUT**
Remember that **sensible** ends in –ible, like
incredible, **possible** and **terrible**.

sensitive *ADJECTIVE*
❶ easily offended or upset ❷ understanding and
careful of other people's feelings ❸ easily affected
by something such as the sun or a substance • *I have
sensitive skin.*

sensor *NOUN* sensors
a device or instrument for detecting something such
as heat or light

sent *VERB* (past tense and past participle of **send**)
• *She sent me an email.* • *He has been sent home
because he's ill.*

sentence *NOUN* sentences
❶ a group of words which are all connected
grammatically. A sentence starts with a capital
letter and ends with a full stop, question mark
or exclamation mark. ❷ a punishment given to
someone who has been found guilty in court
sentence *VERB* sentences, sentencing,
sentenced
to give someone a punishment in a law court

sentiment *NOUN* sentiments
a feeling or emotion

sentimental *ADJECTIVE*
showing or making you feel emotion, especially
too much sad emotion

sentinel *NOUN* sentinels
a guard who keeps watch

sentry *NOUN* sentries
a soldier who guards a place

separate (say sep-er-at) *ADJECTIVE*
❶ not joined to anything • *The sports hall is in a
separate building.* ❷ not together • *We went in
separate directions.*
➤ **separately** *ADVERB* • *They arrived separately.*

A
B
C
D
E
F
G
H
I
J
K
L
M
N
O
P
Q
R
S
T
U
V
W
X
Y
Z

separate *(say* sep-er-ayt*)* VERB separates, separating, separated
❶ To separate things or people is to take them away from others. • *He was* **separated** *from his friends.*
❷ If things separate, they move away from each other. • *The branches* **separate**.
➤ **separation** NOUN • *He had endured a long* **separation** *from his mother.*

⚠ **WATCH OUT**
Remember the **a** in the middle of **separate**.

sequel *(say* see-kwel*)* NOUN sequels
a book or film that continues the story of an earlier one

sequence *(say* see-kwenss*)* NOUN sequences
❶ a series of things • *What comes next in the* **sequence**: *1, 1.5, 2, 2.5, 3 . . . ?* ❷ the order in which things should follow each other • *Put the events in* **sequence**.

sequin *(say* see-kwin*)* NOUN sequins
a small shiny disc sewn on clothes to decorate them

serene ADJECTIVE
calm and peaceful
➤ **serenely** ADVERB

sergeant *(say* sar-jent*)* NOUN sergeants
a soldier or police officer who is in charge of others

serial NOUN serials
a story that is told or broadcast in separate parts over a period of time

⚠ **WATCH OUT**
Do not confuse **serial**, which is connected with the word *series* and **cereal**, which is a grain you can eat.

series NOUN series
❶ a number of things following each other or connected with each other • *We had a* **series** *of problems.* ❷ a television or radio programme that is on regularly with the same title

serious ADJECTIVE
❶ important • *This is a* **serious** *matter.* ❷ very bad • *There's been a* **serious** *accident.* ❸ not funny or laughing • *His face was* **serious**.
➤ **seriously** ADVERB ➤ **seriousness** NOUN

sermon NOUN sermons
a talk given by a preacher

serpent NOUN serpents
a snake

servant NOUN servants
a person whose job is to work in someone else's house

serve VERB serves, serving, served
❶ To serve food or drink is to bring it to people.
❷ To serve customers in a shop is to help them to buy things. ❸ in tennis or similar games, to start the game by hitting the ball to your opponent's side of the net

service NOUN services
❶ something provided for people • *There is a good bus* **service** *into town.* ❷ help or work done for someone • *They were grateful for his* **services**.

sesame NOUN
a plant whose seeds are used in cooking or to make oil

session NOUN sessions
a time spent doing one thing • *We had a training* **session**.

set VERB sets, setting, set
❶ To set something somewhere is to put or place it there. • *She* **set** *the bags down.* ❷ To set a device is to adjust the controls so it will work as you want. • *Have you* **set** *the alarm?* ❸ To set is to become solid or hard. • *The jelly has* **set** *now.* ❹ When the sun sets, it disappears below the horizon at the end of the day.
➤ **To set off** or **set out** is to begin a journey.
➤ **To set something up** is to start it or get it ready to use. • *We* **set up** *a chess club.* • *Have you* **set up** *the new computer?*

set NOUN sets
❶ a group of people or things that belong together • *a* **set** *of art materials* ❷ *(in mathematics)* a group of things that have something in common, for example a group of odd numbers

sett NOUN setts
a badger's burrow

settee NOUN settees
a sofa

setting NOUN settings
the place and time in which a story happens

settle VERB settles, settling, settled
❶ to sort something out or decide about it • *To* **settle** *the argument, we looked the word up in the dictionary.* ❷ to sit or lie still in a comfortable

way somewhere • *He **settled** down on the sofa.*
❸ to make somewhere your home • *The family
settled in Canada.*

settlement *NOUN* settlements
a group of houses; a town or village

settler never *NOUN* settlers
one of the first people to start living in a new area

sever *VERB* severs, severing, severed
to cut something off

several *DETERMINER, PRONOUN*
more than two; quite a few • *We've been there
several times.* • *I ate two biscuits and Sam ate
several.*

severe *ADJECTIVE* severer, severest
❶ strict or harsh; not gentle or kind
*'It's my opinion that you never think at all,' the Rose
said, in a rather severe tone.*—ALICE THROUGH THE
LOOKING-GLASS, Lewis Carroll
❷ very bad or serious • *a **severe** injury*
➤ **severely** *ADVERB*

sew *(say so) VERB* sews, sewing, sewed,
sewn *or* sewed
to use a needle and thread to mend cloth or make it
into something

sewage *(say soo-ij) NOUN*
dirty water and waste carried away in drains

sewer *(say soo-er) NOUN* sewers
an underground drain that carries away sewage

sex *NOUN* sexes
❶ one of the two groups, male or female, that people
and animals belong to ❷ the physical activity by
which people and animals produce young

shabby *ADJECTIVE* shabbier, shabbiest
very old and worn
*The stranger was wearing an extremely shabby set
of wizard's robes which had been darned in several
places.*—HARRY POTTER AND THE PRISONER OF AZKABAN,
J. K. Rowling

shack *NOUN* shacks
a roughly built hut

shade *NOUN* shades
❶ an area that is darker because sunlight cannot
reach it • *We sat in the **shade**.* ❷ a colour or how

light or dark it is • *a nice **shade** of blue* ❸ an object
that decreases or blocks bright light
➤ **shady** *ADJECTIVE* • *We sat in a **shady** spot.*

shade *VERB* shades, shading, shaded
❶ to stop bright light from reaching something
• *She **shaded** her eyes with her hand.* ❷ To shade a
drawing is to make parts of it darker than the rest.

shadow *NOUN* shadows
❶ a dark shape that falls on a surface when
something blocks the light • *She used her hands to
create different **shadows** on the wall.* ❷ an area that
is dark because the light is blocked • *The stranger's
face was in **shadow**.*

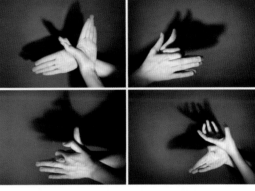

shadow *VERB* shadows, shadowing,
shadowed
To shadow someone is to follow them secretly.

shadowy *ADJECTIVE*
❶ dark and full of shadows • *a **shadowy** corner of
the room* ❷ not seen clearly • *a **shadowy** figure*

shaft *NOUN* shafts
❶ a long thin rod or straight part of something
❷ a deep narrow hole in a mine or building
• *a lift **shaft*** ❸ a beam of light

shaggy *ADJECTIVE* shaggier, shaggiest
having long untidy hair

shake *VERB* shakes, shaking, shook, shaken
❶ to move something quickly up and down or
from side to side • *Have you **shaken** the bottle?*
❷ If something shakes, it moves around.
• *The ground **shook**.* ❸ To shake is to tremble
from fear or cold. • *His voice was **shaking**.*

shake *NOUN* shakes
a quick movement up and down or from side to side
• *Give the box a **shake**.*

shaky ADJECTIVE **shakier, shakiest**
trembling or weak • *I took a **shaky** step.*
➤ **shakily** ADVERB • *He got up **shakily**.*

shall VERB *(past tense **should**)*
used to say what is going to happen • *We **shall** arrive tomorrow.* • *You **shall** go to the ball.*

BUILD YOUR VOCABULARY
Shall is a **modal verb**.

shallow ADJECTIVE **shallower, shallowest**
not deep • *The stream is quite **shallow** here.*

sham NOUN **shams**
something or someone that is not what they claim to be; a fake

shamble VERB **shambles, shambling, shambled**
to walk in an awkward way, dragging your feet

shame NOUN
❶ a feeling of sorrow or guilt because you have done something bad ❷ If something is a shame, you are sad about it. • *What a **shame** you won't be able to come.*
shame VERB **shames, shaming, shamed**
to make someone feel ashamed

shameful ADJECTIVE
causing shame • *a **shameful** deed*

shameless ADJECTIVE
feeling or showing no shame

shampoo NOUN **shampoos**
liquid soap for washing your hair

shamrock NOUN
a small plant similar to clover, with leaves divided in three, which is the national symbol of Ireland

shan't
short for *shall not* • *I **shan't** be long.*

shanty NOUN **shanties**
❶ a traditional song sung by sailors ❷ a rough hut

shape NOUN **shapes**
❶ the outline of something or the way it looks • *He saw a dark **shape** moving outside.* • *a card in the **shape** of a butterfly* ❷ something that has a definite form, such as a square, circle or triangle

shape VERB **shapes, shaping, shaped**
to give something a shape • *a ballon **shaped** like a sausage*

shapeless ADJECTIVE
having no definite shape • *a **shapeless** bundle*

share VERB **shares, sharing, shared**
❶ to divide something between people or things • *We **shared** the money equally.* ❷ To share something is to use it with someone else. • *My sister and I **share** a bedroom.*
share NOUN **shares**
A share of something is one of the parts given to different people or things.

shark NOUN **sharks**
a large sea fish with sharp teeth and a large fin on its back

sharp ADJECTIVE **sharper, sharpest**
❶ with an edge or point that can cut or make holes • *This is a **sharp** knife.* ❷ quick to learn or notice things • *She has **sharp** eyes.* ❸ sudden or severe • *We came to a **sharp** bend in the road.*
❹ tasting slightly sour
➤ **sharpness** NOUN
sharp ADVERB
❶ with a sudden change of direction • *Turn **sharp** right.* ❷ exactly; punctually • *Be there at six o'clock **sharp**.*

sharpen VERB **sharpens, sharpening, sharpened**
to make something sharp or pointed
➤ **sharpener** NOUN • *a pencil **sharpener***

sharply ADVERB
in a critical or severe way

shatter VERB **shatters, shattering, shattered**
If something shatters or if you shatter it, it breaks suddenly into lots of tiny pieces.

shave VERB **shaves, shaving, shaved**
to remove hair from skin with a razor
shave NOUN **shaves**
the act of shaving • *Dad was having a **shave**.*

shawl NOUN **shawls**
a large piece of material for covering the shoulders or wrapping a baby

she PRONOUN
a female person or animal who does something

BUILD YOUR VOCABULARY
She is used as the **subject** of a verb.

sheaf NOUN **sheaves**
❶ a bundle of papers ❷ a bundle of corn stalks tied together

shear VERB **shears, shearing, sheared, shorn** or **sheared**
To shear a sheep is to cut the wool from it.
• The sheep have been **shorn**.

shears PLURAL NOUN
a tool like a large pair of scissors for trimming plants or shearing sheep

sheath (rhymes with **heath**) NOUN **sheaths**
a cover for the blade of a sword or dagger

sheathe (rhymes with **breathe**) VERB **sheathes, sheathing, sheathed**
To sheathe a weapon is to put it into its sheath.

shed NOUN **sheds**
a small simple building for storing things
shed VERB **sheds, shedding, shed**
To shed something is to let it fall or flow. • The trees had **shed** their leaves.

she'd
short for she had or she would • **She'd** (= she had) already gone. • **She'd** (= she would) like that.

sheen NOUN
a soft shine on a surface

sheep NOUN **sheep**
a grass-eating animal kept by farmers for wool and meat

WATCH OUT
The word **sheep** does not change in the plural: a herd of sheep.

sheepdog NOUN **sheepdogs**
a dog trained to guard and control sheep

sheepish ADJECTIVE
embarrassed
➤ **sheepishly** ADVERB

sheer ADJECTIVE **sheerer, sheerest**
❶ complete or total • That is **sheer** nonsense!
❷ extremely steep; vertical • a **sheer** cliff

WATCH OUT
Do not confuse the adjective **sheer** with to **shear** a sheep.

sheet NOUN **sheets**
❶ a large piece of thin material put on a bed
❷ a thin flat piece of paper, glass or metal

shelf NOUN **shelves**
a flat piece of wood, metal or plastic fixed to a wall or inside a cabinet or cupboard, for storing things on

shell NOUN **shells**
❶ the hard outer covering of a nut or egg ❷ the hard part protecting the body of an animal such as a snail, crab or tortoise

shellfish NOUN **shellfish**
a sea animal that has a shell

shelter NOUN **shelters**
❶ a place where people are protected from danger or from the weather • They built a **shelter**.
❷ protection from danger or from the weather
• We found **shelter** under a rock.
shelter VERB **shelters, sheltering, sheltered**
❶ to stay somewhere where you are protected from danger or from the weather • We **sheltered** under the trees. ❷ To shelter something or someone is to protect or cover them. • The hill **shelters** the house from the wind.

shepherd NOUN **shepherds**
someone whose job is to look after sheep

WATCH OUT
The word **shepherd** ends in **herd**, with a silent **h**.

sheriff NOUN **sheriffs**
the chief law officer of a county in some countries

she's
short for she is or she has • **She's** (= she is) my sister.
• **She's** (= she has) been away.

shield NOUN **shields**
a large piece of metal, wood or plastic that soldiers or police carry to protect themselves

shield VERB shields, shielding, shielded
to protect someone or something • *She **shielded** her eyes from the sun.*

shift VERB shifts, shifting, shifted
to move or change position or to make something do this • *He **shifted** uncomfortably in his chair.* • *I **shifted** my feet.*

shift NOUN shifts
a period in the day when one group of people work • *Dad was working a night **shift**.*

shilling NOUN shillings
a coin that was used in Britain in the past. There were 20 shillings in a pound.

shimmer VERB shimmers, shimmering, shimmered
to shine with a quivering light • *The sea **shimmered** in the midday sun.*

shin NOUN shins
the bony front part of your leg between your knee and ankle

shine VERB shines, shining, shone
❶ to give out or reflect bright light • *The sun has **shone** all day.* ❷ To shine a light somewhere is to point it in that direction. • *He **shone** his torch into the cave.*

shingle NOUN
pebbles on a beach

shiny ADJECTIVE shinier, shiniest
bright or glossy

ship NOUN ships
a large boat, especially one that goes to sea

ship VERB ships, shipping, shipped
to send something somewhere, usually by ship

shipping NOUN
ships • *Attention all **shipping**! There are warnings of a gale.*

shipwreck NOUN shipwrecks
❶ the destruction of a ship at sea by a storm or accident ❷ the remains of a wrecked ship
➤ **shipwrecked** ADJECTIVE • ***shipwrecked** sailors*

shirt NOUN shirts
a piece of clothing you wear on the top half of your body, with a collar and sleeves

shiver VERB shivers, shivering, shivered
to tremble with cold or fear

shiver NOUN shivers
an act of shivering • *I felt a **shiver** down my spine.*

shoal NOUN shoals
a large number of fish swimming together

shock NOUN shocks
a sudden unpleasant surprise

shock VERB shocks, shocking, shocked
to upset and unpleasantly surprise someone
➤ **shocking** ADJECTIVE • *a **shocking** lie*

shoe NOUN shoes
an item of clothing that you wear as a covering and protection for your foot

shoelace NOUN shoelaces
a cord for tying a shoe

shone VERB (past tense and past participle of **shine**)
• *The doctor **shone** a light into my eyes.* • *The sun has **shone** all day.*

shook VERB (past tense of **shake**)
• *The ground **shook**.*

shoot VERB shoots, shooting, shot
❶ To shoot a gun or other weapon is to fire it.
• *She **shot** an arrow.* ❷ to injure a person or animal by firing a weapon at them • *The lion had been **shot**.*
❸ To shoot a film is to make it. • *The film was **shot** in New Zealand.*

shoot NOUN shoots
a new growth of a plant

shooting star NOUN shooting stars
a meteor

shop NOUN shops
❶ a building where people buy things
• a toy **shop** ❷ a workshop • a bike repair **shop**
shop VERB shops, shopping,
shopped
to go and buy things at shops
➤ **shopper** NOUN

shopkeeper NOUN shopkeepers
someone who owns or looks after a shop

shopping NOUN
❶ the activity of buying things • I like **shopping**.
❷ things that you have bought in shops • Let me
help you carry your **shopping**.

shore NOUN shores
the land along the edge of a sea or lake

shorn VERB (a past participle of **shear**)
• The sheep have been **shorn**.

short ADJECTIVE shorter, shortest
❶ not tall • My grandma is quite **short**. ❷ not long
• She has **short** hair. ❸ not lasting long • It's only a
short book.
➤ **for short** as a shorter form of something
• His name is Mohamed—Mo **for short**.
➤ **short for something** a shorter form of
something • 'Advert' is **short** for 'advertisement'.
➤ **To be short of something** is to not have
enough of it. • We are **short** of chairs.
➤ **shortness** NOUN

shortage NOUN shortages
If there is a shortage of something, there is not
enough.

short cut NOUN short cuts
a route or method that is quicker than the usual one

shorten VERB shortens, shortening,
shortened
to make something shorter

shortly ADVERB
soon • I'll be there **shortly**.

shorts NOUN
trousers with legs that stop at or above the knee

shot VERB (past tense and past participle of **shoot**)
• He **shot** a gun. • She had **shot** a lot of film.

shot NOUN shots
❶ the firing of a gun • They heard a **shot**.
❷ a photograph • I got some great **shots** of
sports day. ❸ an act of hitting or kicking a ball,
especially when trying to score • Good **shot**!

should VERB
❶ If someone should do something, they ought to
do it. • You **should** tell your parents. ❷ If something
should happen, you expect it will happen.
• They **should** be here soon.

⚙ **BUILD YOUR VOCABULARY**
Should is a **modal verb**.

shoulder NOUN shoulders
the part of your body between your neck and your arm
shoulder VERB shoulders, shouldering,
shouldered
to carry or rest something on your shoulder
• The woodcutter **shouldered** his axe.

shoulder blade NOUN shoulder blades
each of the two large flat bones at the top of your back

shout VERB shouts, shouting, shouted
to speak or call very loudly
shout NOUN shouts
a loud cry or call

shove (say shuv) VERB shoves, shoving,
shoved
to push something or someone hard

shovel (say shuv-el) NOUN shovels
a tool like a spade with the sides turned up, for
moving snow, earth or coal
shovel (say shuv-el) VERB shovels, shovelling,
shovelled
to move or clear something with a shovel

show VERB shows, showing, showed, shown
❶ to let someone see something • She **showed** me
her picture. ❷ to explain or demonstrate something
to someone • Can you **show** me how to print this
out? ❸ to guide or lead someone somewhere
• I'll **show** you to your seats. ❹ to be visible
• She was nervous, but it didn't **show**.
➤ **To show off** is to try to impress people.
show NOUN shows
❶ an entertainment on television or at the theatre
• We watched a quiz **show**. ❷ a display or exhibition
• Have you been to the flower **show**?

a
b
c
d
e
f
g
h
i
j
k
l
m
n
o
p
q
r
s
t
u
v
w
x
y
z

shower NOUN showers
❶ a brief fall of rain or snow • *It's only a shower.*
❷ a device or cabinet with a water spray for washing
❸ If you have a shower, you wash yourself using a water spray.
shower VERB showers, showering, showered
❶ To shower someone with things is to drop a lot of things on them. • *The apple tree showered us with blossom.* ❷ to fall like rain • *Rubble showered down.* ❸ to have a wash in the shower

showy ADJECTIVE showier, showiest
likely to attract attention

shrank VERB (past tense of **shrink**)
• *My jumper shrank in the wash.*

shred NOUN shreds
a small torn strip or piece • *His cloak had been ripped to shreds.*
shred VERB shreds, shredding, shredded
to tear or cut something into small strips or pieces

shrew NOUN shrews
a small animal similar to a mouse

shrewd ADJECTIVE shrewder, shrewdest
with a good understanding of something
➤ **shrewdly** ADVERB

shriek NOUN shrieks
a loud high scream
shriek VERB shrieks, shrieking, shrieked
to give a loud high cry or scream • *They shrieked with laughter.*

shrill ADJECTIVE
A shrill sound is very high and loud. • *the shrill blast of a whistle*
➤ **shrilly** ADVERB

shrimp NOUN shrimps
a small prawn

BUILD YOUR VOCABULARY
A **shrimp** is a **crustacean**.

shrine NOUN shrines
a place of worship connected to a particular holy person or object

shrink VERB shrinks, shrinking, shrank, shrunk
❶ to become smaller • *The pile of cookies was shrinking.* ❷ to make something smaller, usually by washing it • *You've shrunk my jeans!* ❸ to move away from something because you are afraid or disgusted • *The girls shrank back in horror.*

shrivel VERB shrivels, shrivelling, shrivelled
to become wrinkled and dry

shroud NOUN shrouds
a sheet in which a dead body is wrapped
shroud VERB shrouds, shrouding, shrouded
to cover or conceal something • *The mountain was shrouded in mist.*

shrub NOUN shrubs
a bush or small tree

shrug VERB shrugs, shrugging, shrugged
If you shrug, you raise your shoulders slightly to show that you do not care or do not know.
shrug NOUN shrugs
the act of shrugging

shrunk VERB (past participle of **shrink**)
• *My jeans have shrunk in the wash.*

shrunken ADJECTIVE
having got smaller, especially because of being dried out • *a shrunken apple*

shudder VERB shudders, shuddering, shuddered
to shake, especially because of fear or disgust
shudder NOUN shudders
the act of shuddering

shuffle VERB shuffles, shuffling, shuffled
to drag your feet along the ground as you walk

shut VERB shuts, shutting, shut
❶ to move something so that it is not open
• *Have you shut the window?* • *We shut our books.*
❷ If a shop or place shuts, you cannot go into it.
• *The park shuts at 8.*
shut ADJECTIVE
closed • *Keep your eyes shut.*

shutter NOUN shutters
a screen that can be closed over a window

shuttle NOUN **shuttles**
a bus, train or aircraft that makes frequent journeys between two places

shuttlecock NOUN **shuttlecocks**
a light object with plastic or real feathers round it, used in the game of **badminton**

shy ADJECTIVE **shyer, shyest**
timid about meeting or talking to other people
➤ **shyly** ADVERB
➤ **shyness** NOUN
• *I soon got over my shyness.*

sibling NOUN **siblings**
Your siblings are your brothers and sisters.

sick ADJECTIVE **sicker, sickest**
❶ ill or unwell • *He looks after sick animals.*
❷ If you are sick, you vomit; if you feel sick, you feel that you are going to vomit.
➤ **sick of something** or **someone** tired of or fed up with them

sicken VERB **sickens, sickening, sickened**
If something sickens you, it makes you feel sick.

sickly ADJECTIVE **sicklier, sickliest**
❶ unhealthy; often ill • *a sickly child*
❷ unpleasantly sweet • *There was a sickly smell.*

sickness NOUN **sicknesses**
an illness or disease

side NOUN **sides**
❶ an outside surface of something that is not the top, bottom, front or back • *The ingredients are on the side of the packet.* ❷ a position or space to the left or right of something • *We stopped at the side of the road.* ❸ a line that forms the edge of a shape • *A triangle has three sides.* ❹ one surface of something such as a piece of paper or a coin • *Write on both sides.* ❺ Your sides are the parts of your body from your armpits to your hips. • *I had a pain in my side from laughing.* ❻ a group of people playing, arguing or fighting against another group • *We're on the same side.*

side VERB **sides, siding, sided**
To side with someone is to support them in a quarrel or argument.

sideboard NOUN **sideboards**
a piece of furniture with drawers and cupboards and a flat top that you can put things on

sidecar NOUN **sidecars**
a small compartment fixed to the side of a motorcycle, for a passenger

sideways ADVERB, ADJECTIVE
❶ to or from the side • *Crabs walk sideways.*
• *She gave me a sideways glance.* ❷ with one side facing forward • *We sat sideways in the bus.*

sidle VERB **sidles, sidling, sidled**
to move sideways • *She sidled up to me and whispered in my ear.*

siege (say seej) NOUN **sieges**
an attack by an army that surrounds a place until the people inside surrender

sieve (say siv) NOUN **sieves**
a container made of net or with small holes in it, used to separate solid parts or lumps

sift VERB **sifts, sifting, sifted**
to pour a substance through a sieve to get rid of lumps • *sift the flour.*

sigh NOUN **sighs**
a sound you make by breathing out heavily when you are sad, tired or relieved
sigh VERB **sighs, sighing, sighed**
to give a sigh or say something with a sigh

sight NOUN **sights**
❶ Sight is the ability to see. • *Owls have very good sight.* ❷ A sight is something that you see.
• *The northern lights are a wonderful sight.*
❸ **Sights** are interesting places or buildings that are worth seeing. • *We went to London to see the sights.*
➤ **in sight** able to be seen
➤ **out of sight** no longer able to be seen

⚠ **WATCH OUT**
Do not confuse **sight** with **site**, which means a place used for something, as in *campsite*.

sightseeing NOUN
the activity of going round looking at interesting places

sign NOUN **signs**
❶ a mark or symbol that stands for something
• *a minus sign* ❷ a board or notice that tells or shows people something • *The sign says 'No Entry'.*

❸ an action or signal telling someone something • *She made a sign to be quiet.* **❹** something that shows that a thing exists or is there • *There was no sign of anyone in the house.*

sign *VERB* **signs, signing, signed**
If you sign something, you write your signature on it.

signal *NOUN* **signals**
a movement, sound or light that tells you something • *A red light is a signal meaning 'Stop'.*

signal *VERB* **signals, signalling, signalled**
To signal to someone is to give them a signal.

signature *NOUN* **signatures**
your name written by you, for example at the end of a letter

significance *NOUN*
The significance of something is its meaning or importance.

significant *ADJECTIVE*
If something is significant, it means something or is important.
➤ **significantly** *ADVERB*

signify *VERB* **signifies, signifying, signified**
to mean or indicate something • *What does this mark signify?*

sign language *NOUN*
a language that uses hand movements instead of sounds

signpost *NOUN* **signposts**
a sign by a road showing the names of places and how far they are

Sikh *(say* seek*) NOUN* **Sikhs**
someone who believes in **Sikhism,** a religion with one God founded in India by Guru Nanak
➤ **Sikh** *ADJECTIVE*

silence *NOUN* **silences**
complete quiet, with no sound at all

silence *VERB* **silences, silencing, silenced**
To silence someone or something is to make them silent.

silent *ADJECTIVE*
without any sound; not speaking
➤ **silently** *ADVERB*

silhouette *(say* sil-oo-et*) NOUN* **silhouettes**
a dark outline of something seen against a light background

silicon *NOUN*
a substance found in rocks, used in making microchips

silk *NOUN*
❶ a fine soft thread produced by caterpillars called **silkworms ❷** smooth shiny cloth made from this thread

➤ **silky** *ADJECTIVE* • *My dog's ears felt silky.*

sill *NOUN* **sills**
a strip of stone, wood or metal underneath a window or door

silly *ADJECTIVE* **sillier, silliest**
foolish; not sensible
➤ **silliness** *NOUN*

silver *NOUN*
❶ a precious shiny white metal

BUILD YOUR VOCABULARY
Silver is an **element.**

❷ a grey-white colour
➤ **silvery** *ADJECTIVE*

similar *ADJECTIVE*
If one thing is similar to another, it is like it in some ways but not exactly the same.
➤ **similarly** *ADVERB* • *They were similarly dressed.*

similarity *NOUN* **similarities**
a way in which one thing is like another • *There are some similarities between the two books.*

simile *(say* sim-il-ee*) NOUN* **similes**
a way of describing something by comparing it with something else, for example 'Her hand was as cold as ice.'

BUILD YOUR VOCABULARY
Look at **metaphor** and **imagery.**

simmer *VERB* **simmers, simmering, simmered**
❶ to boil gently over a low heat **❷** If you are simmering, you are very angry but trying not to show it.

simple ADJECTIVE **simpler, simplest**
❶ easy • *The answer is* **simple**. ❷ not complicated; plain in style • *They lived in a* **simple** *cottage*.
➤ **simplicity** NOUN • *I like the* **simplicity** *of the design*.

simplify VERB **simplifies, simplifying, simplified**
to make something simple or easy to understand

simply ADVERB
❶ in a simple way • *Explain it* **simply**. ❷ just
• *I was* **simply** *trying to help*.

simultaneously *(say* sim-ul-**tay**-nee-us-lee*)* ADVERB
at exactly the same time
Lorna leapt into the air as a dozen robots fired simultaneously.—VILLAIN.NET 3: POWER SURGE, Andy Briggs

sin NOUN **sins**
a bad act that breaks a religious or moral law
➤ **sinful** ADJECTIVE • *It's* **sinful** *to lie*.
sin VERB **sins, sinning, sinned**
to commit a sin
➤ **sinner** NOUN

since CONJUNCTION
❶ from the time when • *A lot has happened* **since** *I last saw you*. ❷ because • **Since** *you won't do it, I will*.
since PREPOSITION
from a certain time • *I've known him* **since** *Year 1*.
since ADVERB
between then and now • *He has not been seen* **since***.*

sincere ADJECTIVE **sincerer, sincerest**
meaning what you say; expressing your true feelings
• *He thanked us in a* **sincere** *way*.
➤ **sincerely** ADVERB

sinew NOUN **sinews**
strong tissue that joins a muscle to a bone

sing VERB **sings, singing, sang, sung**
❶ to make musical sounds with your voice
• *We* **sang** *a song*. • *Have you ever* **sung** *in a choir?*
❷ When birds or insects sing, they make musical sounds.
➤ **singer** NOUN

singe *(say* sinj*)* VERB **singes, singeing, singed**
to burn something slightly

single ADJECTIVE
❶ only one • *This all happened on a* **single** *day*.
• *a* **single** *page* ❷ suitable for one person
• *a* **single** *bed* ❸ If someone is single, they do not have a wife, husband, girlfriend or boyfriend.
single NOUN *(also* **single ticket***)* **singles**
a ticket for a journey to a place but not back again

🔵 **BUILD YOUR VOCABULARY**
The opposite is **return**.

single VERB **singles, singling, singled**
➤ **To single someone out** is to pick them from other people.

single file NOUN
➤ **in single file** in a line, one behind the other

single-handed ADVERB
alone, without any help • *She sailed around the world* **single-handed***.*

singular NOUN **singulars**
the form of a word meaning only one thing or person, such as *book* and *child*
singular ADJECTIVE
in the singular • *'Mouse' is a* **singular** *noun*.

🔵 **BUILD YOUR VOCABULARY**
Look at **plural**.

sinister ADJECTIVE
seeming evil or harmful • *The jailer gave a* **sinister** *laugh*.

✳ **WORD STORY**
The word **sinister** comes from the Latin word for 'left', because the Romans thought the left side was unlucky.

sink VERB **sinks, sinking, sank, sunk**
❶ to go under water • *The boat* **sank**. ❷ to go or fall down • *The sun had* **sunk** *behind the hills*.
sink NOUN **sinks**
a basin with taps, for washing things

sip VERB **sips, sipping, sipped**
to drink something slowly in small mouthfuls
sip NOUN **sips**
a small mouthful of a drink • *She took a* **sip** *of the magic potion*.

sir NOUN
❶ a word used for speaking or writing politely to a man • *Can I help you,* **sir**?

🔵 **BUILD YOUR VOCABULARY**
Look at **madam**.

❷ **Sir** is the title given to a knight. • **Sir** *Francis Drake*

sire NOUN sires (old use)
a word used in the past when speaking to a king
The tailor smiled and bowed his head. 'O honoured sire,'
he softly said, 'This marvellous magic cloth has got
Amazing ways to keep you hot.' –RHYME STEW, Roald Dahl

siren NOUN sirens
a device that makes a loud sound as a warning

sister NOUN sisters
Your sister is a girl or
woman who has the
same parents as you.

sister-in-law NOUN
sisters-in-law
A person's sister-in-law is the sister
of their husband or wife or the wife
of their brother or sister.

sit VERB sits, sitting, sat
❶ to rest on your bottom • *We **sat** on the floor.*
• *Who is **sitting** next to you?* ❷ to be placed or
positioned somewhere • *The box had **sat** there*
all day unopened.

site NOUN sites
a piece of ground where something happens or
happened • *a caravan **site*** • *This was the **site** of a*
Roman town.

sitting room NOUN sitting rooms
a room with comfortable chairs for sitting in

situated ADJECTIVE
placed or positioned somewhere • *The town is*
situated close to the sea.

situation NOUN situations
the things that are happening at a particular time
• *We are in a difficult **situation**.*

sixpence NOUN sixpences
a coin that was used in Britain in the past. It was
worth half a **shilling**.

size NOUN sizes
❶ how big a person or thing is ❷ a measurement for
something such as clothes or shoes • *What **size** are*
your shoes?

sizzle VERB sizzles, sizzling, sizzled
If food sizzles, it makes a crackling sound as you
fry it.

skate NOUN skates
❶ an ice skate or roller skate ❷ a large flat sea fish
skate VERB skates, skating, skated
to move around on skates
➤ **skater** NOUN

skateboard NOUN skateboards
a small board with wheels, for standing and riding on
➤ **skateboarder** NOUN
➤ **skateboarding** NOUN

skeletal ADJECTIVE
to do with or like a skeleton

skeleton NOUN skeletons
the framework of bones in a person's or
animal's body

skeleton

sketch NOUN
sketches
a quick or rough
drawing
sketch VERB sketches,
sketching, sketched
to make a quick drawing of
someone or something

skewer NOUN skewers
a long sharp object that can be stuck through pieces
of food to hold them for cooking
skewer VERB skewers, skewering, skewered
to stick something sharp through something

ski (say skee) NOUN skis
a long flat strip you can fasten to boots, for moving
over snow
ski (say skee) VERB skis, skiing, skied
to move on snow wearing skis
➤ **skier** NOUN

skid VERB skids, skidding, skidded
to slide accidentally, especially in a vehicle
skid NOUN skids
a skidding movement • *The car went into a **skid***
on the icy road.

skilful ADJECTIVE
showing a lot of skill • *a **skilful** footballer*
➤ **skilfully** ADVERB

⚠ **WATCH OUT**
There is only one l in the middle of **skilful**.

skill *NOUN* **skills**
❶ the ability to do something well ❷ a type of ability that needs special knowledge or practice
• *We practised our map-reading skills.*
➤ **skilled** *ADJECTIVE* • *a skilled chef*

skim *VERB* **skims, skimming, skimmed**
❶ to move quickly over a surface ❷ to remove something from the surface of a liquid ❸ to read a piece of writing quickly, in order to get the general idea

skin *NOUN* **skins**
❶ Your skin is the part of you that covers your whole body. ❷ The skin of a fruit or vegetable is its outer covering that you can peel off.

skinny *ADJECTIVE* **skinnier, skinniest**
very thin

skip *VERB* **skips, skipping, skipped**
❶ to jump or move along by hopping from one foot to the other ❷ to jump with a skipping rope ❸ To skip something is to miss it out or ignore it.
• *You can skip the last chapter.*

skipper *NOUN* **skippers**
the captain of a ship or team

skirt *NOUN* **skirts**
a piece of clothing for that hangs from the waist
skirt *VERB* **skirts, skirting, skirted**
to go round the edge of something • *We skirted the field.*

skittle *NOUN* **skittles**
an object shaped like a bottle, that you try to knock down with a ball in a game called **skittles**

skull *NOUN* **skulls**
the framework of bones around your brain

skunk *NOUN* **skunks**
a black and white furry animal from North America that can make an unpleasant smell

sky *NOUN* **skies**
the space above the earth, where you can see the sun, moon and stars

skylark *NOUN* **skylarks**
a small brown bird that sings as it hovers high in the air

skylight *NOUN* **skylights**
a window in a roof

skyscraper *NOUN* **skyscrapers**
a very tall building

slab *NOUN* **slabs**
a thick flat piece of something

slack *ADJECTIVE* **slacker, slackest**
not pulled tight; loose • *The rope was slack.*

slacken *VERB* **slackens, slackening, slackened**
❶ to make something looser or to become looser
• *She slackened the belt.* ❷ to make something slower or to become slower • *He slackened his pace.*

slain *VERB* (past participle of **slay**)
• *The knight said he had slain the dragon.*

slam *VERB* **slams, slamming, slammed**
to shut something hard or loudly • *She slammed the lid down.*

slang *NOUN*
informal language, especially words used by a particular group • *Parents sometimes don't understand teenage slang.*

slant *VERB* **slants, slanting, slanted**
to slope or be at an angle
slant *NOUN* **slants**
a slope or a leaning position • *The writing had a slant.*

slap *VERB* **slaps, slapping, slapped**
to hit someone with the palm of your hand
slap *NOUN* **slaps**
To give someone a slap is to slap them.

slash *VERB* **slashes, slashing, slashed**
to make a long deep cut in something
slash *NOUN* **slashes**
❶ a long deep cut ❷ a sloping line (/) used to separate words or letters

slat *NOUN* **slats**
a thin strip of wood or plastic, for example in a blind or fence

slate *NOUN* **slates**
a kind of grey rock that splits easily into flat pieces, used to cover roofs or in the past for writing on at school

BUILD YOUR VOCABULARY
Slate is **impermeable**.

slaughter (say slor-ter) VERB **slaughters, slaughtering, slaughtered**
❶ To slaughter an animal is to kill it for food.
❷ To slaughter people or animals is to kill a lot of them.
slaughter (say slor-ter) NOUN
the act of killing animals or a lot of people

slave NOUN **slaves**
a person who is owned by someone else and has to work for them without being paid

slavery NOUN
the state of being a slave or the system of having slaves

slay VERB **slays, slaying, slew, slain** (old use)
to kill someone or something • He **slew** his enemy.
• The dragon had been **slain**.

sledge NOUN **sledges**
a vehicle for travelling over snow on strips of metal or wood

sledgehammer NOUN **sledgehammers**
a very large heavy hammer

sleek ADJECTIVE **sleeker, sleekest**
smooth and shiny • The cat was **sleek** and black.

sleep VERB **sleeps, sleeping, slept**
❶ to close your eyes and rest your body and mind
• Did you **sleep** well? • I **slept** until ten. ❷ to spend the night somewhere • My parents **sleep** in this room. • Have you ever **slept** in a tent?
sleep NOUN
a time when you are sleeping • You need some **sleep**.

sleepless ADJECTIVE
unable to sleep; without sleep • We had a **sleepless** night.

sleepy ADJECTIVE **sleepier, sleepiest**
wanting to fall asleep or having recently been asleep
➤ **sleepily** ADVERB • She rubbed her eyes **sleepily**.

sleet NOUN
a mixture of rain and snow

sleeve NOUN **sleeves**
the part of a piece of clothing that covers your arm

sleigh (say slay) NOUN **sleighs**
a large sledge pulled by horses

slender ADJECTIVE **slenderer, slenderest**
slim; thin

slept VERB (past tense and past participle of **sleep**)
• I **slept** at my friend's house. • You've **slept** late this morning!

slew VERB (past tense of **slay**)
• The knight **slew** the dragon.

slice NOUN **slices**
a thin flat piece cut off something
slice VERB **slices, slicing, sliced**
to cut something into slices

slick ADJECTIVE **slicker, slickest**
slippery • Her face was **slick** with sweat.

slide VERB **slides, sliding, slid**
❶ to move smoothly across a surface
• He **slid** down the grassy bank. ❷ to move something smoothly • She **slid** the phone into her pocket.
slide NOUN **slides**
a structure for children to play on, with a smooth slope for sliding down

slight ADJECTIVE **slighter, slightest**
❶ small and not serious or important • There are some **slight** differences. ❷ Someone who is slight is slim and light.

slightly ADVERB
a little • I feel **slightly** better.

slim ADJECTIVE **slimmer, slimmest**
❶ thin in an attractive way ❷ A slim chance is small.

slime NOUN
an unpleasant wet slippery substance
➤ **slimy** ADJECTIVE • What's that **slimy** stuff?

sling VERB **slings, slinging, slung**
❶ to throw something somewhere carelessly
• She **slung** her shoes into a corner. ❷ to hang something loosely somewhere • He **slung** the sack over his shoulder.
sling NOUN **slings**
a piece of cloth tied round your neck to support an injured arm

slink VERB **slinks, slinking, slunk**
to move somewhere in a secret or guilty way
• He **slunk** off to bed.

slip VERB slips, slipping, slipped
❶ to slide or fall over accidentally ❷ to move somewhere quickly and quietly • *He **slipped** out before anyone was awake.* ❸ to put something somewhere quickly without being seen • *She **slipped** the letter into her pocket.*

slip NOUN slips
❶ an accidental slide or fall • *One **slip** and you could fall into the river.* ❷ a small mistake ❸ a small piece of paper

slipper NOUN slippers
a soft comfortable shoe for wearing indoors

slippery ADJECTIVE
wet or very smooth, so that it is difficult to stand on or hold

slit NOUN slits
a long narrow cut or opening

slit VERB slits, slitting, slit
to make a slit in something

slither VERB slithers, slithering, slithered
to slide across something • *The snake **slithered** away.*

sliver (say sliv-er) NOUN slivers
a small thin piece of something

slogan NOUN slogans
a short memorable phrase, used in advertising or politics

slop VERB slops, slopping, slopped
If you slop liquid or it slops, it spills over the edge of something.

slope VERB slopes, sloping, sloped
to go gradually downwards or upwards; to have one end higher than the other

slope NOUN slopes
❶ a sloping surface or piece of ground ❷ the amount by which a surface slopes • *The hill has a **slope** of 30°.*

sloppy ADJECTIVE sloppier, sloppiest
❶ very wet and soft • *sloppy mud* ❷ careless • *Their work is **sloppy**.*

slosh VERB sloshes, sloshing, sloshed (informal)
If you slosh liquid or if it sloshes, it splashes in a messy way.

slot NOUN slots
a narrow opening to put something in • *Put the coin in the **slot**.*

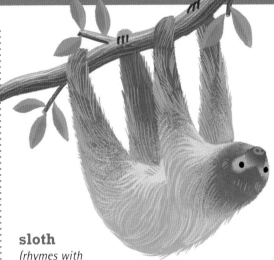

sloth
(rhymes with both) NOUN sloths
❶ a long-haired South American animal that lives in trees and moves very slowly ❷ laziness

slouch VERB slouches, slouching, slouched
to move, stand or sit lazily with your head and shoulders bent forwards

slow ADJECTIVE slower, slowest
❶ not fast • *I'm a **slow** reader.* ❷ If a clock or watch is slow, it shows a time earlier than the correct time.
➤ **slowly** ADVERB • *We walked home **slowly**.*

slow ADVERB
slowly • *Go **slower**.*
➤ **slowness** NOUN

slow VERB slows, slowing, slowed
If something slows or slows down or if you slow it or slow it down, it becomes slower. • *The car was slowing down.* • *I **slowed** my steps.*

sludge NOUN
thick sticky mud

slug NOUN slugs
a small slimy animal like a snail without a shell

BUILD YOUR VOCABULARY
A **slug** is a **mollusc**.

slum NOUN slums
a poor and crowded area of a city

slumber NOUN (old use)
peaceful sleep

a
b
c
d
e
f
g
h
i
j
k
l
m
n
o
p
q
r
s
t
u
v
w
x
y
z

slumber *VERB* slumbers, slumbering, slumbered
to sleep peacefully

slump *VERB* slumps, slumping, slumped
To slump is to fall heavily or suddenly.
slump *NOUN* slumps
A slump is a sudden fall in prices or trade.

slung *VERB (past tense and past participle of* sling*)*
• He **slung** the bag over his shoulder. • Her things had been **slung** in the corner.

slunk *(past tense and past participle of* slink*)*
• He **slunk** out, embarrassed. • The thieves had **slunk** away.

slush *NOUN*
snow that is melting on the ground
➤ **slushy** *ADJECTIVE*

sly *ADJECTIVE* slyer, slyest
cunning or mischievous
➤ **slyly** *ADVERB*

smack *VERB* smacks, smacking, smacked
to hit someone with your flat hand, especially as a punishment
smack *NOUN* smacks
a hit with your flat hand

small *ADJECTIVE* smaller, smallest
❶ not large in size • She carried a **small** bag.
❷ not important • There's a **small** problem.

smallpox *NOUN*
a serious disease that causes a fever and spots that can leave scars on the skin

smart *ADJECTIVE* smarter, smartest
❶ neat and well dressed ❷ clever; quick
➤ **smartly** *ADVERB* • They were **smartly** dressed.
smart *VERB* smarts, smarting, smarted
If something smarts, it stings painfully.

smartphone *NOUN* smartphones
a mobile phone that can connect to the Internet and run apps

smash *VERB* smashes, smashing, smashed
❶ If you smash something or if it smashes, it breaks into pieces noisily and violently. • I dropped a glass and it **smashed**. ❷ To smash into something is to hit it with great force. • A wave **smashed** against the side of the boat.

smear *VERB* smears, smearing, smeared
to rub something dirty or greasy across a surface
smear *NOUN* smears
a dirty or greasy mark

smell *VERB* smells, smelling, smelt or smelled
❶ If you smell something, you sense it using your nose. • I can **smell** something burning. ❷ To smell is to have a smell. • The cheese **smells** funny.
smell *NOUN* smells
❶ something you can smell • What's that horrible **smell**? ❷ Your sense of smell is your ability to smell things.

smelly *ADJECTIVE* smellier, smelliest
having an unpleasant smell

smile *VERB* smiles, smiling, smiled
When you smile, your lips stretch and curve upwards, showing that you are happy or friendly.
smile *NOUN* smiles
a happy or friendly expression made with your lips

smite *VERB* smites, smiting, smote, smitten
❶ *(old use)* to hit someone hard • He **smote** his enemy with a spear. ❷ to affect someone with a strong emotion • He was **smitten** with remorse.

smith *NOUN* smiths
someone who makes things out of metal

smock *NOUN* smocks
a loose piece of clothing like a long shirt

smog *NOUN*
a mixture of smoke and fog

smoke *NOUN*
grey or blue gas and particles that rise from a fire
➤ **smoky** *ADVERB* • a **smoky** room
smoke *VERB* smokes, smoking, smoked
❶ to give out smoke • The fire is **smoking**.
❷ to breathe in smoke from a cigarette or pipe

smooth *ADJECTIVE* smoother, smoothest
❶ A smooth surface is even, with no roughness or bumps. ❷ A smooth mixture has no lumps.
❸ A smooth movement has no bumps or jolts.
• We had a **smooth** ride.
➤ **smoothly** *ADVERB* • The boat floated **smoothly** downstream.
➤ **smoothness** *NOUN*

smooth VERB smooths, smoothing, smoothed
to make something flat and smooth • *He smoothed his hair.*

smoothie NOUN smoothies
a thick smooth drink made from crushed fruit

smote VERB *(past tense of* **smite***)*
• *He smote his enemy.*

smother VERB smothers, smothering, smothered
❶ to cover something with a lot of something • *She smothered the toast with butter.* ❷ to cover someone's face so that they cannot breathe • *Her hug almost smothered me.*

smoulder VERB smoulders, smouldering, smouldered
to burn slowly without a flame

smudge NOUN smudges
a dirty or messy mark made by rubbing something

smudge VERB smudges, smudging, smudged
To smudge paint or ink is to touch it while it is still wet and make a smudge.

smug ADJECTIVE smugger, smuggest
too pleased with yourself
➤ **smugly** ADVERB

smuggle VERB smuggles, smuggling, smuggled
to bring something into or out of a place secretly, breaking the law or rules
➤ **smuggler** NOUN

snack NOUN snacks
a quick light meal

snag NOUN snags
an unexpected difficulty or problem

snag VERB snags, snagging, snagged
to catch on something sharp • *Her trousers snagged on the brambles.*

snail NOUN snails
a small animal with a soft body and a hard spiral shell

BUILD YOUR VOCABULARY
A **snail** is a **mollusc**.

snake NOUN snakes
an animal with a long narrow body and no legs

BUILD YOUR VOCABULARY
A **snake** is a **reptile**.

snap VERB snaps, snapping, snapped
❶ to break suddenly with a sharp noise • *A twig snapped under his feet.* ❷ If an animal snaps, it makes a biting movement with its jaws. • *The dog was snapping and snarling.* ❸ to say something quickly and angrily • *'No, you can't!' snapped Mum.*

snap NOUN snaps
a snapping sound

snare NOUN snares
a trap for catching animals

snare VERB snares, snaring, snared
to catch something or someone in a trap

snarl VERB snarls, snarling, snarled
If an animal snarls, it growls and shows its teeth.

snarl NOUN snarls
a snarling sound

snatch VERB snatches, snatching, snatched
to grab something quickly • *She snatched the letter.*

sneak VERB sneaks, sneaking, sneaked
to move somewhere quietly and secretly

sneaky ADJECTIVE sneakier, sneakiest
cleverly deceitful or secretive

sneer VERB sneers, sneering, sneered
If you sneer at someone or something, you say or do something that shows you think they are stupid.

sneeze VERB sneezes, sneezing, sneezed
to push air through your nose suddenly and uncontrollably • *She was sneezing a lot because of her cold.*

sneeze NOUN sneezes
the action or sound of sneezing

sniff VERB sniffs, sniffing, sniffed
to draw air in through your nose so that it makes a sound, often when smelling something

sniffle VERB sniffles, sniffling, sniffled
to keep sniffing because you have a cold or are crying

snigger VERB sniggers, sniggering, sniggered
to laugh quietly in an unkind way

snip VERB snips, snipping, snipped
to make a small quick cut with scissors

snivel VERB snivels, snivelling, snivelled
to cry or complain in an annoying way

373

snoop *VERB* snoops, snooping, snooped
to try to find out about someone else's business

snooze *NOUN* snoozes
a short sleep or nap • *Grandad had a snooze on the sofa.*

snooze *VERB* snoozes, snoozing, snoozed
to have a short sleep or nap

snore *VERB* snores, snoring, snored
to breathe noisily while you are sleeping

snorkel *NOUN* snorkels
a tube for breathing when you are swimming just under the surface of water

snort *VERB* snorts, snorting, snorted
to make a loud noise by forcing air out through your nose

snort *NOUN* snorts
a snorting noise

snout *NOUN* snouts
An animal's snout is a part that sticks out and includes its nose and mouth.

snow *NOUN*
frozen drops of water falling from the sky as small white flakes

snow *VERB* snows, snowing, snowed
When it snows, snow falls from the sky.

snowball *NOUN* snowballs
snow formed into a ball for throwing

snowboard *NOUN* snowboards
a board like a short wide ski, used for riding downhill on snow
➤ **snowboarder** *NOUN*
➤ **snowboarding** *NOUN*

snowdrop *NOUN* snowdrops
a small white flower that blooms in early spring

snowflake *NOUN* snowflakes
a flake of snow

snowman *NOUN* snowmen
a figure of a person made of snow

snowstorm *NOUN* snowstorms
a storm with snow falling

snowy *ADJECTIVE* snowier, snowiest
❶ with a lot of snow or covered in snow
• *We went out in the snowy garden.* ❷ like snow • *The rabbit's fur was snowy white.*

snug *ADJECTIVE* snugger, snuggest
warm and cosy • *It was very snug under the blanket.*
➤ **snugly** *ADVERB*

snuggle *VERB* snuggles, snuggling, snuggled
to curl up in a warm comfortable place
• *She snuggled down in bed.*

so *ADVERB*
❶ to such an extent; in this way • *Why are you so cross?* ❷ very • *This is so boring.* ❸ also • *I was wrong but so were you.*

so *CONJUNCTION*
for that reason • *I was tired, so I went home.*

soak *VERB* soaks, soaking, soaked
❶ to make someone or something very wet
❷ to leave something in a liquid
➤ **To soak something up** is to take in a liquid in the way that a sponge does.

soap *NOUN* soaps
a substance you use with water for washing yourself
➤ **soapy** *ADJECTIVE*

soar *VERB* soars, soaring, soared
to rise or fly high in the air • *An eagle soared above them.*

sob *VERB* sobs, sobbing, sobbed
to cry loudly with gasping noises

sob *NOUN* sobs
a sobbing sound

sober *ADJECTIVE*
❶ not drunk ❷ calm and serious
• *She had a sober expression.*
➤ **soberly** *ADVERB*

so-called *ADJECTIVE*
named in what may be the wrong way
• *None of his so-called friends defended him.*

soccer *NOUN*
another name for the game of **football**

sociable *(say soh-sha-bul) ADJECTIVE*
enjoying meeting and being with other people

social (*say* soh-shal) ADJECTIVE
❶ to do with meeting other people • *social activities*
❷ living in groups, not alone • *Bees are social insects.*

social media NOUN
websites where people post personal messages and photographs to share with friends

society NOUN societies
❶ all the people living together as a community or country at one time • *In our society it's usual for children to go to school.* ❷ a club • *He's joined a drama society.*

sock NOUN socks
a soft piece of clothing that covers your foot and the lower part of your leg

socket NOUN sockets
❶ a place where an electric plug or light bulb fits into, to connect it ❷ a hole or part that something fits into

soda (*also* **soda water**) NOUN
fizzy water, often mixed with other drinks

sodium (*say* soh-dee-um) NOUN
a soft silver-white metal

⚙ **BUILD YOUR VOCABULARY**
Sodium is an **element**.

sofa NOUN sofas
a long soft seat with sides and a back

✳ **WORD STORY**
The word **sofa** comes from an Arabic word *suffa*, which has the same meaning.

soft ADJECTIVE softer, softest
❶ not hard, stiff or firm • *The bed was very soft.*
❷ gentle or quiet • *He spoke in a soft voice.*
➤ **softly** ADVERB • *She spoke softly.*
➤ **softness** NOUN

soften VERB softens, softening, softened
If something softens or if you soften it, it becomes softer.

software NOUN
computer progams and applications

⚙ **BUILD YOUR VOCABULARY**
Look at **hardware**.

soggy ADJECTIVE soggier, soggiest
very wet and heavy • *The ground was soggy underfoot.*
➤ **sogginess** NOUN

soil NOUN
the loose earth that plants grow in
The soil began to fly out furiously behind Mr Fox as he started to dig for dear life with his front feet.—FANTASTIC MR FOX, Roald Dahl

soil VERB soils, soiling, soiled
to make something dirty • *They wore soiled clothes.*

solar ADJECTIVE
to do with or coming from the sun • *The house is heated by solar power.*

solar system NOUN
the sun and the planets that move in orbit around it

sold VERB (*past tense and past participle of* **sell**)
• *He sold his bike.* • *Shops have sold thousands of copies of the book.*

soldier NOUN soldiers
a member of an army

⚠ **WATCH OUT!**
Remember the **-di-** in the middle of **soldier**.

sole NOUN soles
❶ the bottom part of a shoe or foot ❷ a flat sea fish

sole ADJECTIVE
single or only • *He was my sole supporter.*
➤ **solely** ADVERB • *They lived solely on fruit.*

solemn ADJECTIVE
very serious and dignified
➤ **solemnly** ADVERB

⚠ **WATCH OUT!**
Remember the silent **n** at the end of **solemn**.

solicitor NOUN solicitors
a lawyer who gives legal advice and prepares legal documents

solid ADJECTIVE
❶ keeping its shape; not a liquid or gas ❷ not hollow
• *The egg is solid chocolate.* ❸ firm or strong
• *It's good to be back on solid ground.*

solid *NOUN* solids
❶ an object or substance that is solid, not liquid or gas
❷ a three-dimensional shape, such as a cube, sphere or cone

solidify *VERB* solidifies, solidifying, solidified
to change into a solid

solitary *ADJECTIVE*
alone; single • *A solitary building stood on the hill.*

solitude *NOUN*
the state of being alone

solo *NOUN* solos
something sung or performed by one person alone

soluble *ADJECTIVE*
❶ able to dissolve • *Salt is soluble in water.* ❷ able to be solved • *The problem should be soluble.*

> **BUILD YOUR VOCABULARY**
> The opposite is **insoluble**.

solution *NOUN* solutions
❶ the answer to a problem or puzzle ❷ a liquid with something dissolved in it • *a sugar solution*

solve *VERB* solves, solving, solved
To solve a problem or puzzle is to find an answer to it.

> **BUILD YOUR VOCABULARY**
> Look at **soluble**, **insoluble** and **solution**.

solvent *NOUN* solvents
a liquid in which other substances can be dissolved

sombre *ADJECTIVE*
❶ Sombre colours are dark or dull. ❷ very serious or sad

some *DETERMINER, PRONOUN*
❶ a number or amount of something • *I've invited some friends.* • *Would you like some cake?* • *Would you like some?* ❷ part of a number or amount, but not all • *Some people didn't like the film, but I did.* • *I ate some of my meal.*

somebody *PRONOUN*
someone; a person

somehow *ADVERB*
in some way • *We must finish the work somehow.*

somersault

someone *PRONOUN*
a person • *Ask someone to help you.*

somersault *(say* sum-er-solt*)* *NOUN* somersaults
a roll or turn forwards or backwards, in which your body goes over your head

something *PRONOUN*
a thing • *Can I say something?* • *I've found something.*

sometimes *ADVERB*
at times but not always • *We sometimes walk to school.*

somewhat *ADVERB*
rather; a little • *He was somewhat confused.*

somewhere *ADVERB*
in or to some place • *Let's sit down somewhere.* • *We're going somewhere after school.*

son *NOUN* sons
Someone's son is a boy or man who is their child.

> **! WATCH OUT**
> Do not confuse **son** meaning 'male child' with **sun** meaning 'star'.

song *NOUN* songs
❶ a tune with words for singing ❷ A bird's song is the musical sounds it makes.

songbird *NOUN* songbirds
a bird that sings pleasantly

sonic *ADJECTIVE*
to do with sound or sound waves • *sonic vibrations*

sonnet *NOUN* sonnets
a kind of poem with 14 lines

soon *ADVERB* sooner, soonest
in a short time; quickly • *We have to go soon.* • *She soon got better.*

soot *NOUN*
black powder left by smoke from a fire
➤ **sooty** *ADJECTIVE*

soothe *VERB* soothes, soothing, soothed
❶ to make someone calm ❷ to ease a pain

sophisticated (say sof-**iss**-tee-kay-tid)
ADJECTIVE
❶ A sophisticated person has had a lot of different experiences and knows about fashion or culture. ❷ complicated and advanced • very **sophisticated** equipment

soppy ADJECTIVE soppier, soppiest (informal)
sentimental or silly

sorcerer NOUN sorcerers
someone who can do magic

sorcery NOUN
magic or witchcraft

sore ADJECTIVE sorer, sorest
painful • I've got a **sore** throat.
➤ **soreness** NOUN
sore NOUN sores
a red and painful place on your skin

sorely ADVERB
seriously; very much • He **sorely** missed her.

sorrow NOUN sorrows
sadness or regret
➤ **sorrowful** ADJECTIVE • He looked **sorrowful**.

sorry ADJECTIVE sorrier, sorriest
❶ If you are sorry that you did something, you regret it or want to apologise. • I'm **sorry** I forgot your birthday. ❷ If you feel sorry for someone, you feel pity for them or are sad that something bad has happened to them. • I'm **sorry** you've been ill.

sort NOUN sorts
a kind; a type • What **sort** of fruit do you like?
sort VERB sorts, sorting, sorted
to arrange things in different groups or in order • We **sorted** the books into piles. • The computer will **sort** the names alphabetically.
➤ **To sort something out** is to organise it or deal with it.

sought VERB (past tense and past participle of **seek**)
• We **sought** answers to our questions. • They have **sought** him everywhere.

soul NOUN souls
a person's spirit that some people believe continues to exist after death

sound VERB sounds, sounding, sounded
❶ If something sounds or if you sound it, it makes a sound. • He **sounded** the alarm. ❷ If something or someone sounds a certain way, they seem that way from what you hear. • Her new film **sounds** amazing.
sound NOUN sounds
❶ Sound is vibrations in the air that you can detect with your ear. ❷ A sound is something that you hear. • What was that clicking **sound**?

BUILD YOUR VOCABULARY
Look at **sonic**.

soundly ADVERB
If you sleep soundly, you sleep deeply and well.

soup NOUN soups
a liquid food made with vegetables, meat or fish

sour ADJECTIVE sourer, sourest
❶ having a sharp taste like vinegar or lemons
❷ bad-tempered
➤ **sourly** ADVERB • 'Lucky you,' she said **sourly**.

source NOUN sources
❶ a place where something comes from • This is a good **source** of information. ❷ A river's source is where it starts.

south NOUN
the direction to the right of a person facing east or a place that is in this direction • They live in the **south** of the country.
south ADVERB
towards the south • We marched **south**.
south ADJECTIVE
coming from the south • a **south** wind

south-east NOUN, ADJECTIVE, ADVERB
midway between south and east

southern (say **suth**-ern) ADJECTIVE
from or to do with the south

south-west NOUN, ADJECTIVE, ADVERB
midway between south and west

souvenir (say soo-ven-**eer**) NOUN souvenirs
something that you buy or keep to remind you of a person, place or event

WORD STORY
The word **souvenir** comes from a French word meaning 'to remember'.

a
b
c
d
e
f
g
h
i
j
k
l
m
n
o
p
q
r
s
t
u
v
w
x
y
z

A
B
C
D
E
F
G
H
I
J
K
L
M
N
O
P
Q
R
S
T
U
V
W
X
Y
Z

sovereign *(say* sov-rin*) NOUN* **sovereigns**
❶ a king or a queen ❷ a gold coin that was used in Britain in the past, worth £1

sow *(rhymes with* **go***) VERB* **sows, sowing, sowed, sown, sowed**
To sow seeds is to put them into the ground so that they will grow into plants.

sow *(rhymes with* **cow***) NOUN* **sows**
a female pig

> ⬤ **BUILD** YOUR VOCABULARY
> A male pig is a **boar**.

soya bean *NOUN* **soya beans**
a kind of bean that is used to make oil, flour and milk

space *NOUN* **spaces**
❶ the area outside and beyond the earth, where the stars and planets are • *Would you like to travel in* **space***?* ❷ an empty area; room • *Leave a* **space** *for your name.* • *There isn't enough* **space** *to get past.*
space *VERB* **spaces, spacing, spaced**
To space things or space them out is to arrange them with gaps between them.

spacecraft *NOUN* **spacecraft**
a vehicle for travelling in outer space

spaceship *NOUN*
spaceships
a spaceship

spacious *ADJECTIVE*
with plenty of space • *a* **spacious** *kitchen*

spade *NOUN* **spades**
a tool with a long handle and a wide blade for digging

spaghetti *(say* spa-get-ee*) NOUN*
pasta that looks like pieces of string

> ⚠ WATCH OUT
> There is a silent **h** and a double **t** in **spaghetti**.

span *NOUN* **spans**
❶ the length of something from one end to the other • *The huge bird's wings had a* **span** *of two metres.* ❷ the distance between the tips of your thumb and little finger when your hand is spread out
span *VERB* **spans, spanning, spanned**
to reach from one side of something to the other • *A rope bridge* **spanned** *the river.*

spaniel *NOUN* **spaniels**
a breed of dog with long ears and silky fur

spanner *NOUN* **spanners**
a tool for tightening or loosening a **nut**

spar *NOUN* **spars**
a strong pole used as a mast on a ship

spar *VERB* **spars, sparring, sparred**
to box, fight or argue without trying to hurt each other

spare *ADJECTIVE*
available to be used if it is needed; extra • *They have a* **spare** *bedroom.*
spare *VERB* **spares, sparing, spared**
❶ If you can spare something, you are able to give it to someone. • *Can you* **spare** *ten minutes?* ❷ To be spared something unpleasant is to avoid suffering it.

spark *NOUN* **sparks**
❶ a tiny flash of electricity ❷ a tiny glowing piece of something hot
spark *VERB* **sparks, sparking, sparked**
to give off sparks

sparkle *VERB* **sparkles, sparkling, sparkled**
to shine with a lot of tiny bright flashes • *The sea* **sparkled** *in the sunlight.*
➤ **sparkly** *ADJECTIVE* • *a* **sparkly** *dress*

sparrow *NOUN* **sparrows**
a small brown bird

sparse ADJECTIVE sparser, sparsest
small in number or amount and thinly spread out
• *sparse trees*
➤ **sparsely** ADVERB • *The land is **sparsely** populated.*

spat VERB (past tense and past participle of **spit**)
• *He **spat** out the disgusting liquid.*

spatter VERB spatters, spattering, spattered
to splash or scatter something in small drops
• *The lorry **spattered** mud all over the pavement.*

spawn NOUN
the eggs of frogs, fish or other water animals

🔧 **BUILD YOUR VOCABULARY**
The eggs of frogs, which develop into **tadpoles**, are called **frogspawn**.

speak VERB speaks, speaking, spoke, spoken
❶ to say something • *I've never **spoken** to her.*
• *Nobody **spoke**.* ❷ To speak a language is to be able to talk in it. • *Do you **speak** German?*

speaker NOUN speakers
❶ a person who is speaking ❷ the part of a radio, music player or computer that sound comes out of

spear NOUN spears
a long pole with a sharp point, used as a weapon
spear VERB spears, spearing, speared
to stick a spear or pointed object into something

special ADJECTIVE
❶ different from others and usually better or more important • *This ring is very **special**.* ❷ for a particular person or purpose • *You need **special** training for this job.*

specialise (also **specialize**) VERB
specialises, specialising, specialised
to study a subject in detail • *She's a biologist who **specialises** in insects.*

specialist NOUN specialists
an expert

speciality NOUN specialities
Your speciality is something you know a lot about or are very good at.

specially ADVERB
especially

species (say spee-shiz) NOUN species
a group of animals or plants that have similar features and can breed with each other. Humans are a **species**.

specific ADJECTIVE
definite or exact • *It's a dog, but I don't know what specific breed.*
➤ **specifically** ADVERB • *I **specifically** asked for a vegetarian meal.*

specimen NOUN specimens
a sample or example of something

speck NOUN specks
❶ a tiny piece of something • *a **speck** of dust*
❷ a tiny mark or spot

speckled ADJECTIVE
covered with small spots

spectacle NOUN spectacles
❶ an exciting sight or display ❷ Someone's **spectacles** are their glasses.

spectacular ADJECTIVE
exciting and impressive to see

spectator NOUN spectators
a person watching a game or show

spectre (say spek-ter) NOUN spectres
a ghost

spectrum NOUN spectra
a band of colours like those seen in a rainbow

speech NOUN speeches
❶ the ability to speak or a person's way of speaking
❷ A speech is a talk given to an audience.

speechless ADJECTIVE
unable to speak, especially because you are surprised or angry

speech marks PLURAL NOUN
inverted commas (" ") or (' ') that you put around speech

🔧 **BUILD YOUR VOCABULARY**
Look at **inverted commas** and **quotation marks**.

speed *NOUN* speeds
❶ the rate at which something moves or happens
• *They were going at a* **speed** *of 20 miles per hour.*
❷ the fact that something is quick or fast • *He ate with* **speed**.

speed *VERB* speeds, speeding, sped
to go very fast • *She* **sped** *along the path.*
➤ **speed up** *(past tenses* **sped up**, **speeded up**)
to become quicker

spell *VERB* spells, spelling, spelt or spelled
to say or write the letters of a word in order
'Esio trot is simply tortoise spelled backwards,' Mr Hoppy said.—ESIO TROT, Roald Dahl

spell *NOUN* spells
a piece of magic for making a particular thing happen
• *A witch cast a* **spell** *on the princess.*

spellcheck *VERB* spellchecks, spellchecking, spellchecked
to check the spellings in a document using a computer program

spelling *NOUN* spellings
❶ the order of the letters in a word • *That is not the correct* **spelling** *of 'friend'.* ❷ how well someone can spell • *His* **spelling** *is good.*

spend *VERB* spends, spending, spent
❶ To spend money is to use it to pay for things.
❷ To spend time is to pass it. • *We* **spent** *the day in the park.*

sphere *NOUN* spheres
a round solid shape; a globe or ball

spice *NOUN* spices
a seed or powder from a plant added to food to flavour it

bay leaves

pink peppercorn

sumac

star anise

cinnamon sticks

cumin seeds

spicy *ADJECTIVE* spicier, spiciest
tasting strongly of spices

spider *NOUN* spiders
a small animal with eight legs that spins webs to catch insects for food

spied *VERB (past tense and past participle of* **spy***)*
• *He* **spied** *on them from behind a bush.* • *Have you* **spied** *anything interesting?*

spike *NOUN* spikes
a sharp point, often made of metal

spiky *ADJECTIVE* spikier, spikiest
with a lot of sharp points • *He had* **spiky** *hair.*

spill *VERB* spills, spilling, spilt or spilled
If you spill something or if it spills, it falls out of a container by accident. • *Careful or you'll* **spill** *your juice.*

spin *VERB* spins, spinning, spun
❶ If something or someone spins, they turn round quickly. • *The wheels were* **spinning**. • *He* **spun** *round.* ❷ to make fibres into thread by pulling and turning them • *She had* **spun** *all the cotton into thread.* ❸ When a spider spins a web, it makes it with threads that it produces.

spinach *NOUN*
a vegetable with dark green leaves

spindle *NOUN* spindles
a thin rod on which thread is wound

spindly *ADJECTIVE* spindlier, spindliest
long or tall and thin • *The baby giraffe stood on its* **spindly** *legs.*

spine *NOUN* spines
❶ the line of bones down the middle of your back

⚙ **BUILD YOUR VOCABULARY**
A synonym is **backbone**.

❷ a sharp point on an animal or plant • *This cactus has sharp* **spines**. ❸ The back part of a book where the pages are joined together.

spiral *ADJECTIVE*
❶ going round and round a central point, getting further from it with each turn • *a* **spiral** *pattern*
❷ going round and round a central line • *a* **spiral** *staircase*

spiral *NOUN* spirals
something with a spiral pattern or shape

spire *NOUN* spires
a tall pointed part on top of a church tower

spirit *NOUN* spirits
❶ A person's spirit is their soul. ❷ a ghost or supernatural being ❸ liveliness, energy and courage

spiritual *ADJECTIVE*
to do with feelings and beliefs, especially religious ones, rather than physical things

spit *VERB* spits, spitting, spat
❶ to push liquid or saliva out of your mouth • *He **spat** into the basin.* ❷ to say something very angrily • *'Get out!' she **spat**.*

spit *NOUN* spits
❶ saliva ❷ a long thin rod for roasting meat over a fire

spite *NOUN*
a desire to hurt or annoy someone
➤ **in spite of something** although something has happened or is happening • *In spite of the problems, it was a good day.*

spiteful *ADJECTIVE*
mean; wanting to hurt or annoy someone
➤ **spitefully** *ADVERB*

spittle *NOUN*
saliva, especially when it is spat out

splash *VERB* splashes, splashing, splashed
❶ if liquid splashes or if you splash it, it flies around in drops • *The paint **splashed** everywhere.* ❷ To splash someone or something is to wet them with drops of liquid. • *The bus **splashed** us.*

splash *NOUN* splashes
the action or sound of splashing

splendid *ADJECTIVE*
very good or impressive
➤ **splendidly** *ADVERB*

splendour *NOUN*
a magnificent or impressive quality or appearance

splint *NOUN* splints
a straight piece of wood or metal used to keep a broken leg or arm straight

splinter *NOUN* splinters
a small sharp piece of wood or glass broken off a larger piece

splinter *VERB* splinters, splintering, splintered
to break into splinters

split *VERB* splits, splitting, split
❶ to burst or break in two • *The bag has **split**.* ❷ to share or divide something • *We **split** the money between us.*

split *NOUN* splits
a crack or tear where something has split

splodge *NOUN* splodges *(informal)*
a patch or smear of something soft

splutter *VERB* splutters, spluttering, spluttered
❶ to speak quickly and unclearly because you are angry or embarrassed ❷ to make quick spitting or coughing sounds • *The engine **spluttered**.*

spoil *VERB* spoils, spoiling, spoilt or spoiled
❶ to stop something from being good or useful • *The rain **spoilt** our holiday.* ❷ to always let someone have what they want • *He has always been **spoilt** by his grandma.*

spoke *VERB* (past tense of **speak**)
• *Suddenly a voice **spoke**.*

spoke *NOUN* spokes
The spokes of a wheel are the rods that go from the centre to the rim.

spoken *VERB* (past participle of **speak**)
• *Nobody had **spoken**.*

sponge *(say* spunj*)* *NOUN* sponges
❶ a soft material with tiny holes that soaks up liquid easily ❷ a soft light cake or pudding
➤ **spongy** *ADJECTIVE* • *The ground was soft and spongy.*

sponsor *VERB* sponsors, sponsoring, sponsored
❶ to provide money to support a person or event ❷ to promise to give money to a charity if someone does something difficult

sponsor *NOUN* sponsors
someone who sponsors a person or an event

a b c d e f g h i j k l m n o p q r s t u v w x y z

spontaneous *(say* spon-tay-nee-us*)* ADJECTIVE
happening or done without being planned • *There was a **spontaneous** cheer from the class.*

spooky ADJECTIVE **spookier, spookiest**
strange in a frightening way • *a **spooky** old house*

spool NOUN **spools**
a round object for winding something such as thread or tape

spoon NOUN **spoons**
an implement for eating soft or liquid food or for stirring or measuring, with a rounded part and a handle

BUILD YOUR VOCABULARY
A spoon that you eat with is a piece of **cutlery**.

spoon VERB **spoons, spooning, spooned**
to lift or take something with a spoon

spoonful NOUN **spoonfuls**
the amount a spoon holds • *a **spoonful** of sugar*

sport NOUN **sports**
❶ a game that exercises your body, especially one you play outside • *My favourite **sport** is cricket.*
❷ sport is games like this • *Are you interested in **sport**?*

spot NOUN **spots**
❶ a small round mark • *A leopard has **spots**.*
❷ a pimple on your skin ❸ a place • *This is the **spot** where it happened.*

spot VERB **spots, spotting, spotted**
to notice someone or something • *She **spotted** something moving in the distance.*

spotless ADJECTIVE
perfectly clean

spotlight NOUN **spotlights**
a light with a beam that shines on a small area

spotted ADJECTIVE
marked with spots • *a **spotted** tablecloth*

spotty ADJECTIVE **spottier, spottiest**
having spots or pimples

spout NOUN **spouts**
❶ a pipe or opening from which liquid can pour
❷ a jet of liquid

spout VERB **spouts, spouting, spouted**
❶ to come out in a jet of liquid ❷ *(informal)* to talk a lot in a boring way

sprain VERB **sprains, spraining, sprained**
If you sprain your ankle or wrist, you injure it by twisting it.

sprain NOUN **sprains**
an injury caused by spraining

sprang VERB *(past tense of* **spring***)*
• *He **sprang** to his feet.*

sprawl VERB **sprawls, sprawling, sprawled**
to sit or lie with your arms and legs spread out

spray VERB
sprays, spraying, sprayed
to scatter liquid in tiny drops over something
• *Spray the plants with water.*

spray NOUN
sprays
❶ tiny drops of liquid sprayed on something
❷ a device for spraying liquid

spread VERB **spreads, spreading, spread**
❶ to lay or stretch something out as widely as possible • *The bird **spread** its wings and flew away.* ❷ to cover a surface with something • *He **spread** jam on his toast.* ❸ If something spreads, it becomes widely known. • *The news had **spread** quickly.*

sprightly ADJECTIVE **sprightlier, sprightliest**
lively and energetic

spring NOUN **springs**
❶ the season of the year when most plants start to grow, between winter and summer ❷ a coil of wire that bounces back to its original shape after being squeezed ❸ a place where water rises out of the ground and becomes a stream

spring VERB **springs, springing, sprang, sprung**
to jump or bounce up suddenly • *He **sprang** to his feet.* • *The lock had **sprung** open.*

springy ADJECTIVE springier, springiest
bouncy • *The wooden floor was springy.*

sprinkle VERB sprinkles, sprinkling, sprinkled
to make tiny drops or pieces of powder fall on something • *I sprinkled the cakes with sugar.*

sprint VERB sprints, sprinting, sprinted
to run very fast for a short distance
➤ **sprinter** NOUN
sprint NOUN sprints
a short fast race

sprite NOUN sprites
a fairy or elf

sprout VERB sprouts, sprouting, sprouted
When something sprouts, it starts to grow.
sprout NOUN sprouts
a **Brussels sprout**

spruce NOUN spruces
a kind of fir tree

sprung VERB (past participle of **spring**)
• *The box had sprung open.*

spun VERB (past tense and past participle of **spin**)
• *He spun around. • I have spun the wheel.*

spur NOUN spurs
a sharp device on the heel of a boot, used to make a horse go faster
spur VERB spurs, spurring, spurred
to encourage someone • *Their shouts spurred him to try harder.*

spurt VERB spurts, spurting, spurted
When a liquid spurts, it gushes out or up.
• *Juice spurted from the orange.*
spurt NOUN spurts
❶ a jet of liquid ❷ a sudden increase in speed

spy NOUN spies
someone who works secretly to find out things about another country or person
spy VERB spies, spying, spied
❶ to watch someone secretly • *Have you been spying on me?* ❷ to work as a spy • *He spied for his country.* ❸ to notice something • *We spied a ship on the horizon.*

squabble VERB squabbles, squabbling, squabbled
to quarrel about something unimportant
squabble NOUN squabbles
a quarrel

squad NOUN squads
a team of people

squadron NOUN squadrons
part of an army, navy or air force

squall NOUN squalls
a sudden short storm or strong wind

squander VERB squanders, squandering, squandered
To squander money or time is to waste it.

square NOUN squares
❶ a shape with four equal sides and four right angles ❷ *(in mathematics)* the result of multiplying a number by itself • *9 is the square of 3.* ❸ an open area in a town surrounded by buildings

⚙ **BUILD** YOUR VOCABULARY
Look at **cube**.

square ADJECTIVE
❶ shaped like a square • *a square table*
❷ *(in mathematics)* A square number is the result of multiplying a number by itself. • *16 (or 4 x 4) is a square number.* ❸ used in measurements for area. For example, a square metre is an area one metre wide by one metre long.

squared ADJECTIVE
multiplied by itself. It can be written as ^{2}.
• *4 squared or 4^2 = 4 x 4 = 16*

⚙ **BUILD** YOUR VOCABULARY
Look at **cubed**.

squarely ADVERB
directly or exactly • *The ball hit him squarely in the mouth.*

squash VERB squashes, squashing, squashed
❶ to squeeze something so that it loses its shape
❷ to force something or someone into a place that is too small • *I squashed everything into one bag.*
squash NOUN squashes
a sweet fruit-flavoured drink

squat VERB squats, squatting, squatted
to sit back on your heels

a
b
c
d
e
f
g
h
i
j
k
l
m
n
o
p
q
r
s
t
u
v
w
x
y
z

squat ADJECTIVE squatter, squattest
short and fat

squawk VERB squawks, squawking, squawked
to make a loud harsh cry

squawk NOUN squawks
a loud harsh cry

squeak VERB squeaks, squeaking, squeaked
to make a short high sound or cry

squeak NOUN squeaks
a short high sound or cry
➤ **squeaky** ADJECTIVE • *a squeaky floorboard*

squeal VERB squeals, squealing, squealed
to make a long high sound

squeal NOUN squeals
a long high sound

squeeze VERB squeezes, squeezing, squeezed
❶ to press something from opposite sides
• *Squeeze the juice from the lemon.* ❷ to force a way through or into a small space • *We all squeezed into the lift.*

squelch VERB squelches, squelching, squelched
to make a sound like someone treading in thick mud

squelch NOUN squelches
a squelching sound

squid NOUN squid, squids
a sea animal with eight short arms and two long tentacles

squiggle NOUN squiggles
a short curly or wavy line

squint VERB squints, squinting, squinted
to look at something with half-shut eyes, usually because it is difficult to see

squire NOUN squires
❶ someone who owns a large house and a lot of land in the countryside ❷ in the Middle Ages, a young nobleman who served a knight

squirm VERB squirms, squirming, squirmed
to wriggle about, especially when you feel embarrassed

squirrel NOUN squirrels
a small grey or red animal with a bushy tail that lives in trees and eats nuts

BUILD YOUR VOCABULARY
A **squirrel** is a **rodent**.

squirt VERB squirts, squirting, squirted
If you squirt something or if it squirts, it comes out in a strong jet. • *The orange juice squirted in his eye.*

squish VERB squishes, squishing, squished (informal)
to squash something • *Don't squish that bug!*

stab VERB stabs, stabbing, stabbed
to stick something sharp into someone or something • *She stabbed the tomato with a knife.*

stability NOUN
the quality of being steady or staying the same

stable ADJECTIVE stabler, stablest
steady and firm; unlikely to fall, move or change • *The pile of bricks was not very stable.*

stable NOUN stables
a building where horses are kept

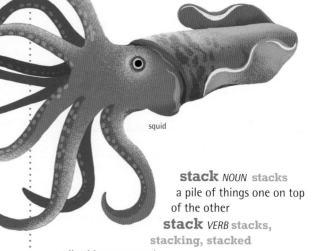
squid

stack NOUN stacks
a pile of things one on top of the other

stack VERB stacks, stacking, stacked
to pile things up neatly

stadium *NOUN* stadiums
a sports ground surrounded by seats for spectators

WORD STORY

From a Greek word *stadion*, meaning a measure of
length of about 185 metres, which was the usual
length of a race in an ancient stadium.

staff *NOUN* staffs
❶ the people who work in an organisation
• *the staff of the school* ❷ a set of five lines on
which music is written

stag *NOUN* stags
a male deer

stage *NOUN* stages
❶ a platform for performances in a theatre or hall
❷ a point in a process or journey • *We've reached
the final stage of the competition.*
stage *VERB* stages, staging, staged
to organise a performance or event

stagger *VERB* staggers, staggering,
staggered
❶ to walk unsteadily ❷ to amaze or shock someone
• *I was staggered by the price.*
➤ **staggering** *ADJECTIVE* • *The amount of choice
is staggering.*

stagnant *ADJECTIVE*
Stagnant water is not flowing or fresh.

stain *NOUN* stains
a dirty mark that is difficult to remove
stain *VERB* stains, staining, stained
to make a stain on something • *The ink has stained
the carpet.*

stair *NOUN* stairs
Stairs are steps that take you from one floor to
another in a building.

staircase *NOUN* staircases
a set of stairs

stake *NOUN* stakes
a thick pointed stick or post
➤ **To be at stake** is to be at risk of being lost.
stake *VERB* stakes, staking, staked
to risk losing something, depending on a result
• *He staked everything on winning.*

stalactite *NOUN* stalactites
a stony spike hanging like an icicle from the roof of
a cave

stalagmite *NOUN* stalagmites
a stony spike standing like a pillar on the floor of
a cave

stale *ADJECTIVE* staler, stalest
no longer fresh • *The bread has gone stale.*

stalk *NOUN* stalks
the main part of a plant, from which the leaves and
flowers grow

BUILD YOUR VOCABULARY
A synonym is **stem**.

stalk *VERB* stalks, stalking, stalked
❶ To stalk a person or animal is to follow them
without being seen. ❷ to walk proudly or stiffly

stall *NOUN* stalls
❶ a table or stand where you can buy something
or get information • *We're running a stall at the
summer fair.* ❷ a place for one animal in a stable
❸ The **stalls** in a theatre are the seats on the
ground floor.

stall VERB **stalls, stalling, stalled**
❶ If an engine stalls, it suddenly stops.
❷ to delay something or someone • *Try to stall him until I get there.*

stallion NOUN **stallions**
an adult male horse

stamen *(say* stay-men*)* NOUN **stamens**
the part of a flower that produces pollen

⚙ **BUILD** YOUR VOCABULARY
Look at **anther** and **pistil**.

stamina *(say* stam-in-a*)* NOUN
strength and energy to keep doing something for a long time

stammer VERB **stammers, stammering, stammered**
to keep repeating the sounds at the beginning of words

stammer NOUN **stammers**
If someone has a stammer, they often stammer when they speak.

stamp NOUN **stamps**
a small piece of sticky paper with a picture on it that you put on a letter or parcel before sending it

stamp VERB **stamps, stamping, stamped**
❶ to bang your foot heavily on the ground
❷ to make a mark on a piece of paper using a special block with a design on it, dipped in ink • *The cashier stamped the document and handed it to Mum.*

stampede NOUN **stampedes**
a sudden rush of animals or people

stampede VERB **stampedes, stampeding, stampeded**
If animals or people stampede, they all rush in the same direction.

stand VERB **stands, standing, stood**
❶ to be on your feet without moving • *She stood at the back of the hall.* ❷ If something stands somewhere, it is there. • *The house has stood here for 400 years.* ❸ If you cannot stand something, you dislike it strongly or cannot bear it. • *I can't stand this heat.*
➤ **To stand for something** is to be short for something. • *'Dr' stands for 'Doctor'.*

stand NOUN **stands**
❶ a table or object for displaying or selling something • *a newspaper stand* ❷ a building at a sports ground for spectators

standard NOUN **standards**
❶ the level of quality of something • *Their work was of a high standard.* ❷ an agreed level or measurement for judging something • *We have certain standards for behaviour.*

standard ADJECTIVE
of the usual or agreed kind or size • *Standard units are used for measuring.*

standstill NOUN
a complete stop • *Snow brought traffic to a standstill.*

stank VERB *(past tense of* **stink***)*
• *The room stank of sweat.*

stanza NOUN **stanzas**
a group of lines in a poem

staple NOUN **staples**
a small piece of metal used to fasten things together

staple VERB **staples, stapling, stapled**
to fasten things together with a staple

staple ADJECTIVE
main or usual • *Rice is their staple food.*

star NOUN stars
❶ a large mass of burning gas that looks like a bright speck of light in the night sky ❷ a shape with five or six points ❸ a famous actor, musician or sports player

star VERB stars, starring, starred
If a film or show stars someone or if they star in it, they are one of its main performers.

starboard NOUN
the right-hand side of a ship or aircraft

BUILD YOUR VOCABULARY

Look at **port**.

starch NOUN starches
❶ a substance found in bread, potatoes, pasta and rice, which gives you energy ❷ a substance used to stiffen clothes

stare VERB stares, staring, stared
to look at someone or something for a long time, usually in an unfriendly or surprised way

stare NOUN stares
a long look, usually an unfriendly or surprised one • I gave him a hard **stare**.

starfish NOUN starfish, starfishes
a sea animal shaped like a star with five points

starfish

starling NOUN starlings
a noisy black or brown speckled bird

starry ADJECTIVE
A starry sky or night is full of stars.

start VERB starts, starting, started
❶ If you start something, you begin doing it. • He **started** to laugh. • She has **started** learning the violin. • Shall we **start**? ❷ When something starts, it begins. • School **starts** at nine.

start NOUN starts
The start of something is the point or place where it begins.

startle VERB startles, startling, startled
to surprise and slightly frighten a person or animal

starve VERB starves, starving, starved
to suffer or die from lack of food

starving ADJECTIVE (informal)
very hungry • I'm absolutely **starving**.

state NOUN states
❶ The state of something or someone is the condition they are in. • The room was in a terrible **state**. ❷ part of a country that can make its own laws • the **state** of Texas ❸ a country and its government

state VERB states, stating, stated
to say something clearly or formally

statement NOUN statements
❶ a sentence that is not a question, exclamation or command • He made the **statement** 'I am hungry'. ❷ a formal account or report • The witness gave a **statement** to the police.

static (also **static electricity**) NOUN
an electrical charge caused by friction

station NOUN stations
❶ a building where people get on or off trains or buses ❷ a building for police or firefighters ❸ a radio or television company • It's my favourite radio **station**.

stationary ADJECTIVE
not moving • The bus hit a **stationary** vehicle.

WATCH OUT

Do not confuse **stationary** meaning 'still' with **stationery** meaning 'things for writing'. Think of the er in paper to help you remember!

stationery NOUN
paper, envelopes and other things used for writing

statistics NOUN
the study of information that is expressed as numbers

statue NOUN statues
a model made of stone, clay or metal to look like a person or animal

status NOUN statuses
❶ high rank or importance ❷ the condition or level of something or someone at a particular time • The website said his **status** was 'inactive'.

staunch ADJECTIVE
loyal and strong • They are her **staunch** supporters.

stave NOUN staves
a **staff** in music

stay VERB stays, staying, stayed
❶ to continue to be in a place or condition; to remain • *Stay where you are.* • *I tried to stay calm.*
❷ to sleep somewhere as a visitor or guest • *On Friday night I stayed at my friend's house.*

steady ADJECTIVE steadier, steadiest
❶ not shaking or moving; firm • *Hold the camera steady.* ❷ not changing; regular • *They kept up a steady pace.*
➤ **steadily** ADVERB

steady VERB steadies, steadying, steadied
to make something steady • *He steadied his breathing.*

steak NOUN steaks
a thick slice of meat or fish

steal VERB steals, stealing, stole, stolen
❶ to take something that does not belong to you and keep it • *Someone has stolen my purse.*
❷ to move somewhere quietly and secretly • *He stole away in the night.*

stealthy ADJECTIVE stealthier, stealthiest
in a quiet or secret way, in order not to be seen
➤ **stealthily** ADVERB • *The tiger moves stealthily.*

steam NOUN
the hot gas that comes from boiling water
➤ **steamy** ADJECTIVE • *steamy windows*

steam VERB steams, steaming, steamed
to give off steam

steamer (also **steamship**) NOUN
steamers, steamships
a ship driven by steam

steed NOUN steeds (old use)
a horse

steel NOUN
a strong metal made from iron and carbon

steely ADJECTIVE steelier, steeliest
tough or hard • *She had a steely look in her eyes.*

steep ADJECTIVE steeper, steepest
rising or sloping sharply
➤ **steeply** ADVERB • *a steeply sloping roof*

steeple NOUN steeples
a church tower with a tall pointed part called a **spire**

steer VERB steers, steering, steered
to make a vehicle go in the direction you want

stegosaur NOUN
stegosaurs
a dinosaur with a double row of bony plates along its back

stem NOUN stems
the central part of a plant that grows out of the ground, from which flowers and leaves grow

> ⚙ **BUILD** YOUR VOCABULARY
> A synonym is **stalk**.

stench NOUN stenches
a very unpleasant smell

stencil NOUN stencils
a piece of card or metal or plastic with pieces cut out, used to make a picture or design

step NOUN steps
❶ If you take a step, you move your foot when walking, running or dancing. ❷ a stair, especially one that is outside • *There are steps down to the beach.* ❸ one of a series of actions in a process • *The first step is to switch the oven on.*

step VERB steps, stepping, stepped
to tread or walk

stepchild NOUN stepchildren
Someone's stepchild is a child that their husband or wife had with another person. A boy is a **stepson** and a girl is a **stepdaughter**.

stepfather NOUN stepfathers
Your stepfather is a man who is married to your mother but is not your own father.

stepmother NOUN stepmothers
Your stepmother is a woman who is married to your father but is not your own mother.

stereo NOUN
a piece of equipment that plays recorded music through two speakers

stern *ADJECTIVE* sterner, sternest
strict and serious • *The teacher looked stern.*
➤ **sternly** *ADVERB*

stern *NOUN* sterns
The stern of a ship is the back part.

stew *NOUN* stews
a dish of meat or vegetables cooked slowly in liquid

stew *VERB* stews, stewing, stewed
to cook food slowly in liquid • *stewed apples*

steward *NOUN* stewards
❶ a person whose job is to look after passengers
on a ship or aircraft ❷ an official who helps at a
public event

stick *NOUN* sticks
❶ a long thin piece of wood ❷ a walking stick
❸ a long object used to hit the ball in hockey and
some other games

stick *VERB* sticks, sticking, stuck
❶ If you stick something sharp into something, you
push it in. • *He stuck a pin in the map.* ❷ to fasten
or join things using glue or tape • *Stick some glitter
on the card.* ❸ If something sticks, it becomes fixed
or jammed. • *The drawer keeps sticking.*
➤ **To stick out** is to poke out from a surface.

sticker *NOUN* stickers
a label or picture that can stick to things

stick insect *NOUN* stick insects
an insect with a long thin body that looks like a twig

sticky *ADJECTIVE* stickier, stickiest
able or likely to stick to things • *There was a sticky
mess on the floor.*

stiff *ADJECTIVE* stiffer, stiffest
❶ firm and not bending easily • *Use stiff cardboard
for the back.* ❷ If your body is stiff, you cannot
move it easily. • *My arm was stiff and sore.*
➤ **stiffly** *ADVERB* • *She was walking stiffly.*

stiffen *VERB* stiffens, stiffening, stiffened
to become stiff or still • *The dog stiffened as if it
had heard something.*

stifle *VERB* stifles, stifling, stifled
If you stifle a noise or expression, you try to stop it
from being heard or seen.
With the greatest difficulty he stifled a smile.—TOM
SCATTERHORN: THE HIDDEN WORLD, Henry Chancellor
➤ **stifled** *ADJECTIVE* • *I heard a stifled cry.*

stifling *ADJECTIVE*
so hot that it is difficult to breathe

stile *NOUN* stiles
steps or bars for climbing over a wall

still *ADJECTIVE* stiller, stillest
❶ not moving at all • *Stay still.* • *We looked out at
the still water.* ❷ not fizzy
➤ **stillness** *NOUN*

still *ADVERB*
❶ even now • *Are you still hungry?* • *I still don't
understand.* ❷ however • *We lost. Still, we played
well.*

stilts *PLURAL NOUN*
❶ a pair of long poles on which someone can walk
❷ long poles supporting a house built over water

stimulate *VERB* stimulates, stimulating,
stimulated
to cause or encourage a feeling or response
• *Books stimulate your imagination.*

sting *VERB* stings, stinging, stung
If an insect or a plant stings you, it jabs your skin
painfully. • *She was stung by a wasp.*

sting *NOUN* stings
❶ a painful jab from an insect or a plant • *I had bad
nettle stings.* ❷ part of an insect or plant that can
jab you • *A scorpion has a sting in its tail.*

a
b
c
d
e
f
g
h
i
j
k
l
m
n
o
p
q
r
s
t
u
v
w
x
y
z

stingray NOUN **stingrays**
a large sea fish with a flat body and a long tail with a poisonous sting

stink NOUN **stinks**
an unpleasant smell
➤ **stinky** ADJECTIVE • *stinky cheese*
stink VERB **stinks, stinking, stank, stunk**
to have an unpleasant smell • *The room stank of smoke.* • *That dog has always stunk!*

stir VERB **stirs, stirring, stirred**
❶ To stir something liquid or soft is to move it round and round, especially with a spoon. ❷ to move slightly or start to move after being still • *She didn't stir all afternoon.*
➤ **To stir something up** is to cause or excite it.
• *They are always stirring up trouble.*

stirrup NOUN **stirrups**
a metal loop that hangs down on each side of a horse's saddle to support the rider's foot

stitch NOUN **stitches**
a loop of thread in sewing or knitting

stoat NOUN **stoats**
a small wild animal similar to a weasel, with a black-tipped tail

stock NOUN **stocks**
❶ a supply of things ready to be sold or used
• *His stocks of food were running low.* ❷ farm animals

BUILD YOUR VOCABULARY
A synonym is **livestock**.

stock VERB **stocks, stocking, stocked**
❶ If a shop stocks goods, it has them to sell.
• *They stock all kinds of books.* ❷ to put a supply of things somewhere • *We stocked the fridge with food.*

stockade NOUN **stockades**
a fence made of large stakes

stocking NOUN **stockings**
a piece of clothing that covers the whole of someone's leg and foot

stocky ADJECTIVE **stockier, stockiest**
short and solidly built

stoke VERB **stokes, stoking, stoked**
To stoke a fire is to add fuel to it.

stole VERB (past tense of **steal**)
• *They stole a famous painting.*

stolen VERB (past participle of **steal**)
• *Someone had stolen the jewels.*

stomach NOUN **stomachs**
❶ the part of your body where food starts to be digested ❷ the front part of your body that contains your stomach

BUILD YOUR VOCABULARY
A synonym for the second meaning is **abdomen**.

stomp VERB **stomps, stomping, stomped**
to step heavily and noisily • *Debra stomped angrily up the stairs.*

stone NOUN **stones**
❶ rock • *The walls are made of stone.* ❷ a small piece of rock • *Someone threw a stone.* ❸ the large hard seed in the middle of some fruits, such as plums or peaches ❹ (plural **stone**) a measurement of weight. There are 14 pounds in 1 stone, which is about 6.35 kilograms. • *She weighs 6 stone.*
➤ **stony** ADJECTIVE • *stony ground*

stood VERB (past tense and past participle of **stand**)
• *Everyone stood up.* • *The tree has stood there for centuries.*

stool NOUN **stools**
a small seat without a back

stoop VERB **stoops, stooping, stooped**
to bend forwards and down • *He stooped to pick something up.*

stop VERB **stops, stopping, stopped**
❶ If something stops or if you stop it, it no longer happens or continues. • *The rain has stopped.*
• *We had to stop the game.* • *Please stop making that noise.* ❷ If something or someone stops or if you stop them, they are no longer moving or travelling.
• *I stopped to listen.* • *Stop the car!* ❸ To stop a hole or stop it up is to fill it.

stop NOUN **stops**
❶ the action of stopping • *He skidded to a stop.*
❷ a place where a bus or train stops regularly

stopper NOUN **stoppers**
something that fits into the top of a bottle or jar to close it

storage NOUN
a place for storing things

store VERB stores, storing, stored
to keep things somewhere until they are needed
store NOUN stores
❶ a shop, especially a big one ❷ a supply of things for future use • *a store of food* ❸ a place where things are stored • *a log store*
➤ **in store** waiting to happen • *There was a surprise in store.*

storey NOUN storeys
one whole floor or level of a building

stork NOUN storks
a large bird with long legs and a long beak

storm NOUN storms
a period of bad weather with strong winds, rain or snow and often thunder and lightning
➤ **stormy** ADJECTIVE • *stormy weather*
storm VERB storms, storming, stormed
❶ to go somewhere angrily • *He stormed out of the room.* ❷ If soldiers storm a place, they attack it suddenly.

story NOUN stories
a spoken or written account of events, imaginary or real • *She read us a story about a horse.*

stout ADJECTIVE stouter, stoutest
❶ rather fat ❷ thick and strong • *She wore stout boots.* ❸ brave • *a stout heart*
➤ **stoutly** ADVERB • *'I'm not afraid,' she said stoutly.*

stove NOUN stoves
a device that produces heat for cooking or for warming a room

stow VERB stows, stowing, stowed
to pack or store away something • *She stowed the map in her rucksack.*
➤ **To stow away** is to travel secretly, hidden on a ship or aircraft.

stowaway NOUN stowaways
someone who travels secretly, hidden on a ship or aircraft

straddle VERB straddles, straddling, straddled
to stand, sit or be situated across something, with one leg or part on either side • *He straddled the path, blocking our way.*

straggle VERB straggles, straggling, straggled
❶ to walk slowly and not keep up with a group
❷ to grow in an untidy way • *Brambles straggled across the path.*
➤ **straggler** NOUN • *At last a few stragglers arrived.*
➤ **straggly** ADJECTIVE • *straggly hair*

straight ADJECTIVE straighter, straightest
❶ not curving, bending or curly • *a straight road* • *My hair is straight.* ❷ level • *Is this picture straight?*
straight ADVERB
❶ in a straight line • *Go straight on.*
❷ directly; immediately • *I went straight to bed.*
➤ **straight away** at once

straighten VERB straightens, straightening, straightened
to make something straight

straightforward ADJECTIVE
❶ not complicated; simple • *It's a straightforward question.* ❷ honest or frank

strain VERB strains, straining, strained
❶ to use or stretch something like a muscle so much that it hurts • *I strained my eyes trying to see the screen.* ❷ to make a great effort to do something • *She strained to reach the key.* ❸ To strain liquid is to put it through a sieve to remove lumps or solids.
strain NOUN strains
If there is strain on something, it is stretched or pulled too hard. • *The rope broke under the strain.*

strait NOUN straits
a narrow stretch of water connecting two seas

strand NOUN strands
a piece of hair or thread

stranded ADJECTIVE
stuck somewhere and unable to leave • *A whale was stranded on the beach.*

strange ADJECTIVE stranger, strangest
❶ unusual or surprising ❷ not known or experienced before • *a strange land*
➤ **strangely** ADVERB • *The house was strangely quiet.*
➤ **strangeness** NOUN

stranger NOUN strangers
a person you do not know

a
b
c
d
e
f
g
h
i
j
k
l
m
n
o
p
q
r
s
t
u
v
w
x
y
z

strangle VERB strangles, strangling, strangled
to kill someone by squeezing their throat

strap NOUN straps
a flat strip of leather, cloth or plastic for fastening or holding something • *a bag with a shoulder strap*

strategy NOUN strategies
a plan to achieve or win something

straw NOUN straws
❶ dry cut stalks of corn ❷ a narrow tube that you can drink through

strawberry NOUN strawberries
a small red juicy fruit with its seeds on the outside

stray VERB strays, straying, strayed
to wander or become lost
stray ADJECTIVE
A stray dog or cat does not have a home.
stray NOUN strays
a stray dog or cat

streak NOUN streaks
a long thin line or mark
streak VERB streaks, streaking, streaked
❶ to mark something with streaks • *Tears streaked his face.* ❷ to move very quickly

stream NOUN streams
❶ a small narrow river ❷ a steady flow of something • *a stream of traffic*
stream VERB streams, streaming, streamed
❶ to move in a fast steady flow • *People streamed out of the stadium.* ❷ To stream music or a video is to listen to it or watch it while it is being sent over the Internet.

streamer NOUN streamers
a long strip of paper or ribbon

street NOUN streets
a road with houses along it

strength NOUN strengths
❶ how strong a person or thing is • *The Hulk has superhuman strength.* ❷ Your strengths are the things you are good at.

⚠ **WATCH OUT**
The word **strength** has a **g** in it, like the related adjective **strong**.

strengthen VERB strengthens, strengthening, strengthened
to make something or someone stronger

strenuous ADJECTIVE
needing or using great effort and determination

stress NOUN stresses
❶ emphasis put on part of a word or phrase when you say it • *In the word 'visit', the stress is on the first syllable.* ❷ a lot of worry or pressure ❸ a force that pulls, pushes or twists something
stress VERB stresses, stressing, stressed
❶ To stress part of a word or phrase is to put emphasis on it when you say it. ❷ To stress a point or idea is to emphasise it. • *She stressed the importance of being on time.* ❸ To stress someone is to make them feel very worried and under pressure.

stretch VERB stretches, stretching, stretched
❶ If you stretch something or if it stretches, it becomes longer or wider because of being pulled. ❷ If you stretch or stretch out, you hold out your arms or legs as far as you can. ❸ to extend somewhere • *An amazing view stretched before us.*
stretch NOUN stretches
an area of land or water • *They walked along a wide stretch of the river.*

stretcher NOUN stretchers
a framework like a light bed with handles, for carrying a sick or injured person

strew VERB strews, strewing, strewed, strewn or strewed
to scatter things over a surface • *Petals were strewn over the grass.*

stricken ADJECTIVE
strongly affected by a feeling or illness • *She was stricken with guilt.*

strict ADJECTIVE stricter, strictest
❶ insisting that people obey rules; firm
❷ complete or exact • *He had strict instructions not to touch anything.*
➤ **strictly** ADVERB • *Smoking is strictly forbidden.*

stride VERB strides, striding, strode, stridden
to walk with long steps • *He strode confidently into the room.*

stride NOUN strides
a long step you take when walking or running

strike VERB strikes, striking, struck
❶ to hit someone or something • *They were **struck** by falling rocks.* ❷ When a clock strikes, it makes a number of sounds to show the time. • *The clock was **striking** twelve.* ❸ To strike a match is to light it. ❹ If something strikes you, you think of it. • *A thought has just **struck** me.*

string NOUN strings
❶ thin rope or cord for tying things ❷ a line or series of similar things • *a **string** of numbers* ❸ a piece of stretched wire or nylon that is part of a musical instrument • *a guitar **string***
string VERB strings, stringing, strung
❶ to hang or thread something on a string • *They had **strung** lights in the trees.* ❷ to put a string or strings on something • *Robin Hood **strung** his bow.*

stringed instrument NOUN
stringed instruments
a musical instrument that has strings, such as a violin

🔧 **BUILD** YOUR VOCABULARY

Look at **brass instrument**, **percussion**, **wind instrument** and **woodwind instrument**.

strip NOUN strips
a long narrow piece of something • *Cut a **strip** of cardboard.*
strip VERB strips, stripping, stripped
❶ to take a covering off something • *The bed had been **stripped** of its sheets.* ❷ to undress

stripe NOUN stripes
a long narrow band of colour
➤ **striped** or **stripy** ADJECTIVE • *A lemur has a **stripy** tail.*

strive VERB strives, striving, strove, striven
to try hard to do something • *She **strove** to free herself.* • *He had **striven** to hide his true feelings.*

strode VERB (past tense of **stride**)
• *He **strode** into the room.*

stroke VERB strokes, stroking, stroked
to move your hand gently over something
• *She **stroked** my hair.*
stroke NOUN strokes
❶ a swinging movement when hitting something, swimming or rowing • *He split the log with one **stroke** of the axe.* • *She swam with strong **strokes**.* ❷ one sudden action or event • *We had a **stroke** of luck.*
➤ **the stroke of ten, midnight, etc.** exactly ten o'clock, midnight, etc.

stroll VERB strolls, strolling, strolled
to walk slowly
stroll NOUN strolls
a short leisurely walk

strong ADJECTIVE stronger, strongest
❶ A strong person has a lot of physical power.
• *His arms are very **strong**.* ❷ A strong person has a lot of courage and determination. • *She's **strong** enough to cope with this.* ❸ A strong object is not easily broken or damaged. • *a **strong** box* ❹ intense; having a great effect • *strong feelings* ❺ having a lot of flavour or smell • *This tea is too **strong**.*
➤ **strongly** ADVERB • *The room smelt **strongly** of perfume.*

stronghold NOUN strongholds
a place that is well defended

strove VERB (past tense of **strive**)
• *I **strove** to do my best.*

struck VERB (past tense and past participle of **strike**)
• *The clock **struck** two.* • *He had been **struck** by a car.*

structure NOUN structures
❶ the way something is made, built or organised
• *the **structure** of a leaf* ❷ something that has been built or put together • *A crane is a tall **structure**.*

struggle VERB struggles, struggling, struggled
❶ to move around violently while you are fighting or trying to get free ❷ to make strong efforts to do something or move somewhere • *We **struggled** on through the snow.* ❸ to find it difficult to do something • *I **struggled** to understand.*

a
b
c
d
e
f
g
h
i
j
k
l
m
n
o
p
q
r
s
t
u
v
w
x
y
z

struggle NOUN struggles
something that is very difficult or takes a lot of effort • *Her life has been a struggle.*

strung VERB (past tense and past participle of **string**)
• *I strung beads on a cord.* • *Lights had been strung in the trees.*

strut VERB struts, strutting, strutted
to walk proudly and stiffly
strut NOUN struts
❶ a wooden or metal bar that strengthens a framework ❷ a proud stiff walk

stub NOUN stubs
a short piece of something left after the rest has been used

stubble NOUN
❶ short stalks of corn left in the ground after a harvest ❷ short stiff hairs growing on a man's chin when he has not shaved

stubborn ADJECTIVE
not willing to change your ideas or ways, even if they may be wrong
➤ **stubbornly** ADVERB

○ **BUILD** YOUR VOCABULARY
A synonym is **obstinate.**

stuck VERB (past tense and past participle of **stick**)
• *Dylan stuck his hands in his pockets.* • *Have you stuck a stamp on the envelope?*
stuck ADJECTIVE
unable to move or make progress • *The car got stuck in the mud.*

stud NOUN studs
a small metal button fixed into something

student NOUN students
❶ someone who studies, especially at a college or university ❷ a school pupil

studio NOUN studios
❶ a place where radio or television broadcasts, films or music recordings are made ❷ the room where an artist works

study VERB studies, studying, studied
❶ to spend time learning about something
❷ To study something is to look at it carefully.

study NOUN studies
❶ the process of studying ❷ a room used for studying or writing

stuff NOUN
❶ a substance or material • *What's this stuff on my shoe?* ❷ Someone's stuff is their possessions.
• *Please move your stuff.*
stuff VERB stuffs, stuffing, stuffed
❶ to push something roughly into something else
• *He stuffed the blanket into a bag.* ❷ to fill something with something else • *We stuffed the rolls with cheese.*

stuffy ADJECTIVE stuffier, stuffiest
with not enough fresh air

stumble VERB stumbles, stumbling, stumbled
❶ to trip or fall over ❷ to make mistakes or hesitate when speaking

stump NOUN stumps
❶ the bottom of a tree trunk left in the ground when the rest of the tree has gone ❷ each of the three upright sticks of a wicket in cricket

○ **BUILD** YOUR VOCABULARY
Look at **bail** and **wicket.**

stun VERB stuns, stunning, stunned
❶ to knock a person or animal unconscious
❷ to shock or confuse someone • *I was stunned by the news.*

stung VERB (past tense and past participle of **sting**)
• *My cut finger stung.* • *She has been stung by a wasp.*

stunk VERB (past participle of **stink**)
• *The cheese had stunk for days before I threw it out.*

stunt NOUN stunts
something daring or dangerous done in a film or as part of a performance

stupefied ADJECTIVE
unable to think or feel properly

stupid ADJECTIVE stupider, stupidest
silly; not intelligent or reasonable • *That was a stupid idea.*
➤ **stupidity** NOUN ➤ **stupidly** ADVERB

sturdy ADJECTIVE sturdier, sturdiest
strong and solid
➤ **sturdiness** NOUN

stutter VERB stutters, stuttering, stuttered
to keep repeating the sounds at the beginning of words
stutter NOUN stutters
If someone has a stutter, they often stutter when they speak.

sty NOUN sties
a pigsty

style NOUN styles
❶ the way that something is done, made, said or written • *The letter is written in a formal style.*
• *I like this style of cooking.* ❷ Style is being fashionable and elegant.
➤ **stylish** ADJECTIVE • *a stylish hat*

subdivide VERB subdivides, subdividing, subdivided
to divide something that has already been divided into smaller parts • *The group 'animals' can be subdivided into mammals, reptiles and so on.*

subdue VERB subdues, subduing, subdued
❶ to defeat someone or bring them under control
❷ to make someone calmer and quieter

subject (*say* sub-ject) NOUN subjects
❶ something or someone that is talked or written about • *Did anyone mention the subject of money?*
❷ something that is studied • *English is my favourite subject.* ❸ (*in grammar*) the person or thing that does the action stated by the verb in a sentence, for example *the boy* in the sentence *The boy kicked the ball.*

⚙ **BUILD YOUR VOCABULARY**
Look at **object**.

subject (*say* sub-ject) VERB subjects, subjecting, subjected
To subject someone to something bad is to make them experience it.

submarine NOUN submarines
a type of ship that can travel under water

submerge VERB submerges, submerging, submerged
If something submerges or is submerged, it goes under water.

submit VERB submits, submitting, submitted
❶ to give in to someone or agree to obey them
• *They had to submit to Roman rule.* ❷ To submit a report or essay is to hand it in.

subordinate clause NOUN subordinate clauses (*in grammar*)
a clause that cannot stand on its own as a sentence, but gives more information about a word or another part of the sentence it is in. In this sentence the subordinate clause is in bold: *Although I was tired, I agreed to go.*

subsequent ADJECTIVE
coming later or after something else • *Subsequent events proved that she was right.*
➤ **subsequently** ADVERB

subside VERB subsides, subsiding, subsided
❶ to sink into the ground • *The building had subsided.* ❷ to go away or become quieter
• *We waited for the noise to subside.*

substance NOUN substances
any liquid, solid or gas; a material

substantial ADJECTIVE
❶ large or important ❷ strong and solid

substitute VERB substitutes, substituting, substituted
to use one thing or person instead of another
• *In this recipe you can substitute oil for butter.*
➤ **substitution** NOUN
substitute NOUN substitutes
a person or thing that is used instead of another

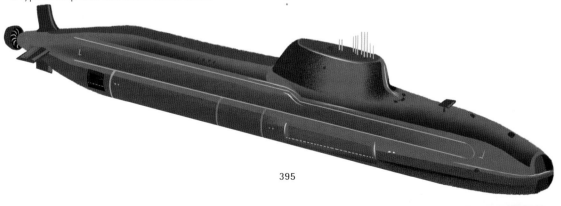

a b c d e f g h i j k l m n o p q r s t u v w x y z

subtle (say sut-el) ADJECTIVE **subtler, subtlest**
delicate or not obvious • a **subtle** flavour

subtract VERB **subtracts, subtracting, subtracted**
To subtract one number from another is to take it away. • If you **subtract** 2 from 7, you get 5.
➤ **subtraction** NOUN

suburb NOUN **suburbs**
an area of houses on the edge of a city or large town

subway NOUN **subways**
an underground passage for pedestrians

succeed VERB **succeeds, succeeding, succeeded**
❶ to do or get what you wanted or intended
❷ To succeed someone is to come after them and take their place, especially as king or queen.

success NOUN **successes**
❶ Success is doing or getting what you wanted or intended. ❷ A success is a person or thing that succeeds. • The plan was a complete **success**.

successful ADJECTIVE
having success
➤ **successfully** ADVERB • We **successfully** finished the quiz.

succession NOUN **successions**
❶ A succession of things is a series of them one after the other. • I heard a **succession** of thuds.
❷ the right to be the next person to do something, especially to become king or queen

successor NOUN **successors**
Someone's successor is the person who comes after them and takes their place.

such DETERMINER
❶ so much; used to emphasise something
• That was **such** hard work! • It's **such** a good book. ❷ of this or that kind • He takes no interest in **such** things as fashion. • A suit would be best for **such** an occasion.

suck VERB **sucks, sucking, sucked**
to pull something with the inside of your mouth
• I was **sucking** an ice lolly.

sudden ADJECTIVE
quick and unexpected • a **sudden** shower of rain
➤ **suddenly** ADVERB • He **suddenly** jumped up.
➤ **suddenness** NOUN

sue VERB **sues, suing, sued**
to start a claim against someone in a law court

suede (say swayd) NOUN
leather with one soft velvety side

suffer VERB **suffers, suffering, suffered**
to feel pain or unhappiness

suffering NOUN **sufferings**
pain or great unhappiness

sufficient ADJECTIVE
enough • Two loaves of bread should be **sufficient**.
➤ **sufficiently** ADVERB • We'll go when you're **sufficiently** well.

BUILD YOUR VOCABULARY
The opposite is **insufficient.**

suffix NOUN **suffixes**
a group of letters joined to the end of a word to make a new word, like -ish in childish or -ness in sadness

BUILD YOUR VOCABULARY
Look at **prefix.**

suffocate VERB **suffocates, suffocating, suffocated**
If someone suffocates or is suffocated, they suffer or die because they cannot breathe.

suffragette NOUN **suffragettes**
in the past, a woman who campaigned for women to have the right to vote

sugar NOUN
a sweet substance obtained from some plants, added to food and drinks
➤ **sugary** ADJECTIVE • Try to avoid **sugary** drinks.

suggest VERB **suggests, suggesting, suggested**
to offer something as an idea or possibility

suggestion NOUN **suggestions**
something that you mention as an idea or possibility

suicide NOUN **suicides**
If someone commits suicide, they deliberately kill themselves.

suit NOUN **suits**
① a matching set of jacket and trousers or jacket and skirt ② clothing for a particular activity
• *a diving suit*

suit VERB **suits, suiting, suited**
① to be suitable or convenient for someone • *Does it suit you if we meet here?* ② If something suits you, it looks good on you. • *Those glasses suit you.*

suitable ADJECTIVE
satisfactory or right for a person, purpose or occasion
• *The film is suitable for young children.*
➤ **suitably** ADVERB • *They were not suitably dressed for walking.*

suitcase NOUN **suitcases**
a large stiff bag for carrying clothes and other things on journeys

suitor NOUN **suitors**
A woman's suitor is a man who wants to marry her or to start a relationship with her.

sulk VERB **sulks, sulking, sulked**
to be silent and bad-tempered because you are annoyed
➤ **sulky** ADJECTIVE • *What is he so sulky about?*

sullen ADJECTIVE
sulking and gloomy
➤ **sullenly** ADVERB

sulphur NOUN
a yellow chemical which burns with a bad smell, like rotten eggs

🔧 **BUILD YOUR VOCABULARY**
Sulphur is an **element**.

sultana NOUN **sultanas**
a dried grape without seeds

sum NOUN **sums**
① the amount you get when you add two or more numbers together ② A sum is a question with numbers. • *We were doing some hard sums.*
③ an amount of money • *He sold it for a large sum.*

sum VERB **sums, summing, summed**
➤ **To sum something up** is to describe it in just a few words.

summarise *(also* **summarize***)* VERB **summarises, summarising, summarised**
to give the main points of something • *Can you summarise the main ideas in the article?*

summary NOUN **summaries**
a short statement of the main points of something

summer NOUN **summers**
the season between spring and autumn, when it is warm

summit NOUN **summits**
the top of a mountain or hill

summon VERB **summons, summoning, summoned**
to order someone to come or appear
➤ **To summon something up** is to manage to find it in yourself. • *She summoned up the courage to speak.*

sun NOUN
① the star that the earth orbits around and that gives us heat and light ② any star in the universe
③ the light and heat of the sun • *Don't stay in the sun for too long.*

🔧 **BUILD YOUR VOCABULARY**
Look at **solar**.

A
B
C
D
E
F
G
H
I
J
K
L
M
N
O
P
Q
R
S
T
U
V
W
X
Y
Z

sundial *NOUN*
sundials
a device that shows the time by a shadow made by the sun

sunflower *NOUN* **sunflowers**
a tall flower with a large round yellow head

sung *VERB (past participle of* **sing***)*
• *We have* **sung** *that song in assembly before.*

sunglasses *PLURAL NOUN*
dark glasses you wear in strong sunlight

sunk *VERB (past participle of* **sink***)*
• *The sun had* **sunk** *below the horizon.*

sunlight *NOUN*
light from the sun

sunny *ADJECTIVE* **sunnier, sunniest**
having a lot of sunshine • *It's a* **sunny** *day.*

sunrise *NOUN* **sunrises**
the time when the sun first appears • *They left at* **sunrise***.*

sunset *NOUN* **sunsets**
the time when the sun sets

sunshine *NOUN*
warmth and light from the sun

super *ADJECTIVE*
excellent or very good

superb *ADJECTIVE*
magnificent or excellent

superhero *NOUN* **superheroes**
in stories, a character with special powers such as very great strength

superior *ADJECTIVE*
better or more important than something else
• *This robot's brain is* **superior** *to ours.*

BUILD YOUR VOCABULARY
The opposite is **inferior**.

superiority *NOUN*
the fact of being better or more important

superlative *NOUN* **superlatives**
the form of an adjective or adverb that expresses 'most' • *The* **superlative** *of 'big' is 'biggest' and the* **superlative** *of 'bad' is 'worst'.*

supermarket *NOUN* **supermarkets**
a large self-service shop that sells food and other goods

supernatural *ADJECTIVE*
not belonging to the natural world or having a natural explanation

superpower *NOUN* **superpowers**
an ability that humans do not normally have

superstition *NOUN* **superstitions**
a belief about luck and magic that is not based on evidence • *According to* **superstition***, the number 13 is unlucky.*

superstitious *ADJECTIVE*
believing in traditional ideas about luck and magic that are not based on evidence

supervise *VERB* **supervises, supervising, supervised**
to be in charge of people or an activity and make sure the activity is done correctly

supper *NOUN* **suppers**
a meal or snack eaten in the evening

supple *ADJECTIVE* **suppler, supplest**
able to bend easily

supply *VERB* **supplies, supplying, supplied**
to give or sell something to people who need it

supply *NOUN* **supplies**
❶ an amount of something kept to be used when needed • *We keep a* **supply** *of paper in the cupboard.* ❷ **Supplies** are food, medicines or equipment needed for doing something.
• *The truck was carrying medical* **supplies***.*

support *VERB* **supports, supporting, supported**
❶ to hold something up so that it does not fall down
• *The beams* **support** *the roof.* ❷ to give someone or something encouragement or help • *We went there to* **support** *our team.*
➤ **supporter** *VERB* • *Her friends are her greatest* **supporters***.*

support *NOUN* **supports**
❶ help or encouragement • *My parents give me a lot of* **support***.* ❷ something that holds an object up

suppose *VERB* supposes, supposing, supposed

to think that something is likely or true • *I suppose he's tired.*

➤ **To be supposed to do something** is to have to do it according to a rule or duty. • *You're not supposed to walk on the grass.*

supposedly *ADVERB*

so people believe or think • *They are supposedly rich.*

suppress *VERB* suppresses, suppressing, suppressed

to manage to prevent something from being noticed • *He tried to suppress a smile.*

supreme *ADJECTIVE*

greatest or most important

sure *ADJECTIVE* surer, surest

❶ having no doubts • *Are you sure you locked the door?* ❷ If something is sure, it is definitely true or going to happen. • *She's sure to wonder where you've been.*

> **BUILD YOUR VOCABULARY**
> A synonym is **certain**.

surely *ADVERB*

used when you feel something must be true • *Surely he would help his best friend.*

surf *NOUN*

white foam made by waves breaking

surf *VERB* surfs, surfing, surfed

❶ to balance on a board and ride towards the shore on big waves ❷ To surf the Internet is to look at different things on it.

➤ **surfer** *NOUN* ➤ **surfing** *NOUN*

surface *NOUN* surfaces

the top or outside part of something • *The surface of the water was smooth.*

surface *VERB* surfaces, surfacing, surfaced

to come up to the surface from under water • *The submarine surfaced.*

surge *VERB* surges, surging, surged

❶ to make a sudden powerful movement • *The crowd surged forward.* ❷ to suddenly appear or increase • *Fear surged inside him.*

surge *NOUN* surges

a sudden powerful movement or feeling

surgeon *NOUN* surgeons

a doctor who performs operations

surgery *NOUN* surgeries

❶ a place where a doctor or dentist works ❷ If someone has surgery, they have an operation in which a surgeon cuts into their body.

surname *NOUN* surnames

your last name, which you share with other members of your family

surpass *VERB* surpasses, surpassing, surpassed

to do better or be better than someone or something else

surprise *NOUN* surprises

❶ A surprise is something that you did not expect. ❷ Surprise is the feeling you have when something unexpected happens.

surprise *VERB* surprises, surprising, surprised

to give someone a surprise

➤ **surprised** *ADJECTIVE* • *He looked very surprised.*
➤ **surprising** *ADJECTIVE* • *a very surprising result*

> ⚠ **WATCH OUT**
> It might surprise you to know that **surprise** starts with **sur-** and ends with **-ise**, never 'ize'!

surrender *VERB* surrenders, surrendering, surrendered

to stop fighting and admit that you have been beaten

surrender *NOUN*

the act of surrendering

a b c d e f g h i j k l m n o p q r s t u v w x y z

surround VERB surrounds, surrounding, surrounded
to stand or be situated all the way around something • *A fence* **surrounded** *the field.*

surroundings NOUN
the things or conditions around a person or place

survey (*say* ser-vay) NOUN surveys
❶ a set of questions that you ask people in order to find out about something ❷ a detailed inspection of something

survey (*say* ser-vay) VERB surveys, surveying, surveyed
❶ to look at something all over • *He stood back and* **surveyed** *the scene.* ❷ to inspect an area or building in detail

survive VERB survives, surviving, survived
❶ to remain alive despite danger or difficulty • *Cacti can* **survive** *in very dry climates.*
❷ to continue to exist • *The original painting has not* **survived***.*
➤ **survival** NOUN • *The* **survival** *of the planet depends on us.*
➤ **survivor** NOUN • *She was the only* **survivor** *of the crash.*

suspect (*say* sus-pect) VERB suspects, suspecting, suspected
❶ to think that something is likely or possible • *I* **suspect** *he's right.* ❷ to think that someone has done something wrong or cannot be trusted

suspect (*say* sus-pect) NOUN suspects
someone who is thought to have done something wrong

suspend VERB suspends, suspending, suspended
❶ to hang something up ❷ to stop or delay something temporarily ❸ to stop someone coming to work for a time

suspense NOUN
the anxious or excited feeling when you do not know what will happen

suspicion NOUN suspicions
a feeling that someone has done something wrong or cannot be trusted

suspicious ADJECTIVE
❶ If you are suspicious, you do not trust someone or something. ❷ If something is suspicious, it makes you think something is wrong. • *That email looks* **suspicious***.*
➤ **suspiciously** ADVERB

sustain VERB sustains, sustaining, sustained
❶ to keep something or someone going • *We have enough food to* **sustain** *us.* ❷ To sustain damage or an injury is to suffer it.

swagger VERB swaggers, swaggering, swaggered
to move or act confidently as if you have a very high opinion of yourself
He was so obnoxious too. Well, he had been on the day of the competition, swaggering about.—HOW TO GET FAMOUS, Pete Johnson

swallow VERB swallows, swallowing, swallowed
to make something go down your throat and into your stomach

swallow NOUN swallows
a small bird with a forked tail and pointed wings

swam VERB (past tense of **swim**)
• *I* **swam** *ten lengths of the pool today.*

swamp NOUN swamps
an area of very soft wet land

swamp VERB swamps, swamping, swamped
To swamp a place is to fill or cover it.

swan NOUN swans
a large white water bird with a long neck

swap VERB swaps, swapping, swapped
to exchange something for something else • *Do you want to swap places?*

swap NOUN swaps
If you make a swap, you exchange something for something else.

swarm NOUN
swarms
a large number of insects flying together

swarm
VERB swarms, swarming, swarmed
❶ When bees or other insects swarm, they fly in a swarm. ❷ To be swarming with people is to be very crowded.

swat (*say* swot) VERB swats, swatting, swatted
To swat a fly is to hit and kill it.

sway VERB sways, swaying, swayed
to move gently from side to side

swear VERB swears, swearing, swore, sworn
❶ to make a solemn promise • *She swore to tell the truth.* • *He has sworn an oath.* ❷ to use very rude or offensive words

sweat (*say* swet) VERB sweats, sweating, sweated
to give off salty liquid through your skin, especially when you are hot

sweat (*say* swet) NOUN
salty liquid that comes through your skin when you are hot

➤ **sweaty** ADJECTIVE • *I was sweaty after football.*

sweater (*say* swet-er) NOUN
sweaters
a jumper

sweatshirt NOUN
sweatshirts
a warm top made of thick stretchy cotton

swede NOUN swedes
a large round root vegetable with purple skin and yellow flesh

sweep VERB sweeps, sweeping, swept
❶ to clean or clear a place with a broom or brush • *I swept the floor.* ❷ to take or push something away quickly • *The flood has swept away the bridge.* ❸ to pass quickly through or across something • *Laughter swept around the room.*

sweet ADJECTIVE sweeter, sweetest
❶ tasting of sugar or honey ❷ very pleasant • *the sweet smell of roses* ❸ charming or delightful • *a sweet little kitten*
➤ **sweetly** ADVERB • *She smiled sweetly.*
➤ **sweetness** NOUN

sweet NOUN sweets
❶ a small piece of sweet food made of sugar or chocolate ❷ something sweet eaten at the end of a meal

⚙ **BUILD YOUR VOCABULARY**
A synonym for the second meaning is **dessert**.

sweetcorn *NOUN*
the juicy yellow seeds of the maize plant, which grow on a long stalk called a **cob**

sweeten *VERB* sweetens, sweetening, sweetened
to make something sweet

sweetheart *NOUN* sweethearts
a person you love very much

sweet pea *NOUN* sweet peas
a climbing plant with sweet-smelling flowers

sweet potato *NOUN* sweet potatoes
a root vegetable with a reddish skin and white or orange flesh

swell *VERB* swells, swelling, swelled, swollen or swelled
to get bigger or louder • *My ankle has swollen up.*

swell *NOUN* swells
the rise and fall of the sea's surface

swelling *NOUN* swellings
a swollen place on your body

swept *VERB (past tense and past participle of sweep)*
• *Cinderella swept the floor.* • *The flood has swept away the bridge.*

swerve *VERB* swerves, swerving, swerved
to move suddenly to one side • *The car swerved to avoid a bike.*

swift *ADJECTIVE* swifter, swiftest
quick
➤ **swiftly** *ADVERB*

swift *NOUN* swifts
a small bird similar to a swallow

swim *VERB* swims, swimming, swam, swum
to move through water using your arms and legs
• *She swam to the end of the pool.* • *Have you ever swum in the lake?*
➤ **swimmer** *NOUN* • *I'm a good swimmer.*

swim *NOUN* swims
a time spent swimming • *Let's go for a swim.*

swimming costume *NOUN* swimming costumes
a piece of clothing worn for swimming

swimming pool *NOUN* swimming pools
a specially built pool for people to swim in

swimming trunks *NOUN*
a piece of clothing worn by a boy or man for swimming

swine *NOUN* swine, swines
❶ *(old use)* a pig ❷ *(informal)* an unpleasant person

swing *VERB* swings, swinging, swung
to move smoothly backwards and forwards or from side to side • *He swung his legs.* • *The gate had swung open.*

swing *NOUN* swings
❶ a seat hung on chains or ropes so that it can move backwards and forwards ❷ a swinging movement • *He took a swing at the ball.*

swipe *VERB* swipes, swiping, swiped
❶ to hit, push or take something with a quick sideways movement of your hand ❷ to touch a screen and move your finger sideways to see a different image

swirl *VERB* swirls, swirling, swirled
to move around quickly in circles

swirl *NOUN* swirls
a swirling movement or pattern

swish *VERB* swishes, swishing, swished
to make a hissing or rustling sound

switch *NOUN* switches
something that you press or turn to start or stop an electrical device or machine • *Where's the light switch?*

switch *VERB* switches, switching, switched
❶ To switch a device on or off is to use a switch to make it work or stop working. ❷ to change something suddenly • *She switched to a different topic of conversation.*

swivel *VERB* swivels, swivelling, swivelled
to turn round or from side to side

swollen *VERB (past participle of swell)*
• *The rains had swollen the river.*

swollen *ADJECTIVE*
having swelled or puffed up • *His finger was very swollen.*

swoon *VERB* swoons, swooning, swooned *(old use)*
to faint

swoop *VERB* swoops, swooping, swooped
to dive or come down suddenly

swop *VERB* swops, swopping, swopped
another spelling of **swap**

sword *(say* sord*) NOUN* swords
a weapon with a long pointed blade fixed in a handle

swore *VERB (past tense of* swear*)*
• *She swore to tell the truth.*

sworn *VERB (past participle of* swear*)*
• *She has sworn to tell the truth.*

swum *VERB (past participle of* swim*)*
• *Have you ever swum in the sea?*

swung *VERB (past tense and past participle of* swing*)*
• *She swung her bag.* • *The door had swung open.*

sycamore *NOUN* sycamores
a tall tree with winged seeds

syllable *NOUN* syllables
one separate sound or beat when you say a word
• *'Ant' has one syllable and 'elephant' has three syllables.*

syllabus *(say* sil-a-bus*) NOUN* syllabuses
a list of things to be studied by a class or for an examination

symbol *NOUN* symbols
a mark, shape or thing that means or represents something • *This (%) is the per cent symbol.* • *The dove is a symbol of peace.*

symmetrical
(say sim-et-rik-al*) ADJECTIVE*
able to be divided into two halves that are exactly the same, but the opposite way round • *An equilateral triangle is symmetrical.*

symmetry *NOUN*
If something has symmetry, it can be divided into two halves that are exactly the same, but the opposite way round.
➤ **A line of symmetry** is a line that you can draw to divide something into two halves that are exactly the same, but the opposite way round. • *A square has four lines of symmetry.*

sympathetic *ADJECTIVE*
understanding and caring about someone's feelings
➤ **sympathetically** *ADVERB*

sympathise *(also* **sympathize***)*
VERB sympathises, sympathising, sympathised
to understand and care about someone's feelings

sympathy *NOUN* sympathies
If you have sympathy for someone, you understand and care about their feelings.

symphony *NOUN* symphonies
a long piece of music for an orchestra

symptom *NOUN* symptoms
A symptom of an illness is a sign that you have it.

synagogue *(say* sin-a-gog*) NOUN* synagogues
a building where Jewish people meet to worship

synonym *(say* sin-o-nim*) NOUN* synonyms
a word that means the same or nearly the same as another word. For example, *big* and *large* are synonyms, and *unhappy* is a synonym of *sad*.

syringe *NOUN* syringes
a tube-shaped device for sucking in a liquid and squirting it out

syrup *NOUN* syrups
a thick sweet liquid
➤ **syrupy** *ADJECTIVE*

system *NOUN* systems
❶ a set of parts, things or ideas that work together • *the digestive system* • *the solar system* ❷ a well-organised way of doing something • *We have a system for organising the reading books.*

symmetrical

Tt

⚙ T is for **time**, which is the most commonly used noun in English. The most commonly used word overall also begins with **t**.

Can you guess what it is?

CLUE It is used twice in the two sentences to the left of this clue, and twice in this sentence.

tab *NOUN* **tabs**
a small strip or flap that sticks out

table *NOUN* **tables**
❶ a piece of furniture with a flat top supported on legs ❷ a list of facts or numbers arranged in rows and columns

tablecloth *NOUN* **tablecloths**
a cloth for covering a table

tablespoon *NOUN* **tablespoons**
a large spoon used for serving food
➤ **tablespoonful** *NOUN* • *a tablespoonful of flour*

tablet *NOUN* **tablets**
❶ a pill ❷ a flat piece of stone or wood with writing on it ❸ a small flat computer with a touch screen

tablet

table tennis *NOUN*
a game played with bats and a small ball, on a table with a net in the middle

tack *NOUN* **tacks**
❶ a short nail with a flat top ❷ equipment for horses, such as harnesses and saddles
tack *VERB* **tacks, tacking, tacked**
❶ to nail something with tacks ❷ to sail a zigzag course to catch the wind

tackle *VERB* **tackles, tackling, tackled**
❶ To tackle a task is to start doing it. ❷ to try to get the ball from an opposing player in a game such as football or hockey

tackle *NOUN* **tackles**
❶ equipment, especially for fishing ❷ an attempt to get the ball from an opposing player

tact *NOUN*
skill in not offending or upsetting people

tactful *ADJECTIVE*
careful not to offend or upset people by what you say
➤ **tactfully** *ADVERB*

tactics *NOUN*
methods used to achieve or win something

tadpole *NOUN* **tadpoles**
a young frog or toad at a stage when it has a round head and a long tail and lives in water

⚙ **BUILD** YOUR VOCABULARY
Look at **spawn**.

taekwondo *(say ty-kwon-doh) NOUN*
a Korean martial art similar to karate

tag *NOUN* **tags**
a label tied or stuck to something
tag *VERB* **tags, tagging, tagged**
➤ **To tag along** is to follow or go with other people.

tail *NOUN* **tails**
❶ the long part at the end of an animal's or bird's body ❷ the part at the back of something, such as an aeroplane or comet ❸ **Tails** is the side of a coin that does not have a head shown on it.

⚙ **BUILD** YOUR VOCABULARY
The other side of a coin is **heads**.

tail *VERB* **tails, tailing, tailed**
To tail someone is to follow them without them seeing you.

tailor *NOUN* **tailors**
someone who makes and repairs clothes, especially men's clothes

take *VERB* **takes, taking, took, taken**
❶ to get hold of something • *He took a cake from the plate.* • *Who has taken my pen?* ❷ to transport or

404

carry someone or something to a place • *Mum took me to school.* • *You should take a coat with you.*
❸ Take is used with some nouns to say someone does an activity. • *I'm taking my piano exam today.*
• *He took a nap.* ❹ To take one number from another is to subtract it. • *Take two from ten and you get eight.*
❺ To take a photograph is to make it with a camera.
➤ **To take off** is to leave the ground at the beginning of a flight.
➤ **To take part in something** is to be involved in doing it.
➤ **To take place** is to happen.

takeaway *NOUN* takeaways
❶ a place that sells cooked food for customers to take away ❷ a meal from a takeaway

talcum powder *NOUN*
a sweet-smelling powder put on the skin to dry it

tale *NOUN* tales
a story, especially a traditional one

talent *NOUN* talents
a natural ability or skill • *She has a talent for drawing.*
➤ **talented** *ADJECTIVE* • *a talented musician*

talk *VERB* talks, talking, talked
to speak or have a conversation

talk *NOUN* talks
❶ a conversation or discussion ❷ a lecture • *She gave a talk about her latest book.*

talkative *ADJECTIVE*
talking a lot

tall *ADJECTIVE* taller, tallest
❶ A tall person, tree or building is higher than average. • *You're very tall for your age.* ❷ used to talk about how much someone or something measures from top to bottom • *a tiny man only twelve inches tall*

tally chart *NOUN* tally charts
a record that is a quick way of counting things, using groups of lines to represent numbers

Talmud *NOUN*
a book of Jewish religious writings

talon *NOUN* talons
a strong claw, especially on a bird of prey

tambourine *NOUN* tambourines
a small musical instrument with metal discs around the edge that jingle when you shake it or hit it

● **BUILD** YOUR **VOCABULARY**
A **tambourine** is a **percussion** instrument.

tame *ADJECTIVE* tamer, tamest
A tame animal is gentle and not afraid of people.

tame *VERB* tames, taming, tamed
To tame a wild animal is to make it gentle and not afraid of people.

tamper *VERB* tampers, tampering, tampered
➤ **To tamper with something** is to interfere with it or change it.

tan *NOUN* tans
❶ If someone has a tan, their skin has turned browner in the sun. ❷ a yellow-brown colour

tang *NOUN*
a strong flavour or smell

tangerine (*say* tan-jer-**een**) *NOUN* tangerines
a kind of small orange

✱ **WORD STORY**
The word **tangerine** is named after *Tangier* in Morocco, where the fruit originally came from.

tangle *VERB* tangles, tangling, tangled
If you tangle something or if it tangles, it becomes twisted and difficult to separate. • *The wires have tangled.*

tangle *NOUN* tangles
a twisted mass of things, such as hair or wires, that is difficult to separate

tank *NOUN* tanks
❶ a large container for a liquid or gas ❷ a heavy armoured vehicle used in war

tankard *NOUN* tankards
a large heavy mug

tanker NOUN **tankers**
❶ a large ship for carrying oil ❷ a large lorry for carrying liquid

tantrum NOUN **tantrums**
an outburst of bad temper

tap NOUN **taps**
❶ a device that you turn to let liquid or gas flow out or to stop it flowing out • *Which one is the hot water* **tap**? ❷ a quick light hit • *I gave him a* **tap** *on the shoulder.*
tap VERB **taps, tapping, tapped**
to hit something or someone gently • *Try* **tapping** *on the window.*

tape NOUN **tapes**
❶ paper, cloth or plastic in a thin strip ❷ a strip of plastic with a magnetic coating, used to record sound
tape VERB **tapes, taping, taped**
❶ to fasten something by sticking or tying it with tape ❷ to record sound or music on tape

tape measure NOUN **tape measures**
a long strip marked in centimetres or inches for measuring things

taper VERB **tapers, tapering, tapered**
to get narrower towards one end
taper NOUN **tapers**
a piece of string thinly coated with wax, for lighting things

tapestry (*say* tap-iss-tree) NOUN **tapestries**
a piece of heavy cloth with designs embroidered on it

tapir NOUN **tapirs**
a large tropical animal that looks similar to a pig with a long snout

tar NOUN
a thick black sticky substance used in making roads

tarantula (*say* ta-**ran**-tew-la) NOUN **tarantulas**
a large hairy poisonous tropical spider

target NOUN **targets**
something that you aim at and try to hit or reach

tarmac NOUN (trademark)
a mixture of tar and broken stone, used for making a hard surface on roads and airfields

tarnish VERB **tarnishes, tarnishing, tarnished**
If metal tarnishes, it becomes stained and less shiny.

tarpaulin NOUN **tarpaulins**
a large sheet of waterproof canvas

tart NOUN **tarts**
a sweet pie, usually without pastry on top

tart ADJECTIVE **tarter, tartest**
tasting sour • The apples are **tart**.

tartan NOUN **tartans**
a woollen cloth from Scotland, with a pattern of squares and stripes

task NOUN **tasks**
a piece of work that needs to be done

tassel NOUN **tassels**
a decoration made of a bundle of threads tied together at the top

taste VERB **tastes, tasting, tasted**
❶ To taste food is to eat a small amount to see what it is like. ❷ The way something tastes is the flavour that it has. • The soup **tasted** horrible.

taste NOUN **tastes**
❶ The taste of something is its flavour. • The milk has a strange **taste**. ❷ Your sense of taste is your ability to taste things. ❸ Your taste is what kind of things you like. • We have the same **taste** in books—we both like adventure stories.

tea

tasty ADJECTIVE **tastier, tastiest**
Tasty food has a strong pleasant taste.

tattered ADJECTIVE
very torn and ragged

tatters NOUN
➤ **in tatters** badly torn

tattoo NOUN **tattoos**
a design made on someone's skin with a needle and dye

tattoo VERB **tattoos, tattooing, tattooed**
If someone is tattooed, they have a tattoo or tattoos.

tatty ADJECTIVE **tattier, tattiest**
old and in bad condition

BUILD YOUR VOCABULARY
A synonym is **shabby**.

taught VERB (past tense and past participle of **teach**)
• Mr Kelly **taught** us last year. • I've **taught** my dog to roll over.

taunt VERB **taunts, taunting, taunted**
to make fun of someone in an insulting way

taunt NOUN **taunts**
an insulting or mocking remark

taut ADJECTIVE **tauter, tautest**
stretched tightly

tavern NOUN **taverns** (old use)
an inn or pub

tawny ADJECTIVE
yellow-brown

tax NOUN **taxes**
money that people and businesses have to pay to the government for public services

tax VERB **taxes, taxing, taxed**
to charge someone a tax or put a tax on something

taxi NOUN **taxis**
a car with a driver that people hire for journeys

tea NOUN **teas**
❶ a drink made by pouring hot water on the dried leaves of the tea plant ❷ a meal eaten in the late afternoon or early evening

teach VERB **teaches, teaching, taught**
❶ to show someone how to do something or give them knowledge about something
• He **taught** me to swim. • Has anyone **taught** you how to use the microscope? ❷ To teach a subject is to give lessons in it. • She **teaches** French.
➤ **teacher** NOUN

team NOUN **teams**
a group of people who play on the same side in a game or sport or who work together

teapot NOUN **teapots**
a pot with a handle and spout, for making and pouring out tea

a
b
c
d
e
f
g
h
i
j
k
l
m
n
o
p
q
r
s
t
u
v
w
x
y
z

tear *(rhymes with* **fair***)* VERB tears, tearing, tore, torn
to make a split in something or to pull it apart
• *I've **torn** my T-shirt.* • *She **tore** open the packet.*

tear *(rhymes with* **fair***)* NOUN tears
a hole or split made by tearing something

tear *(rhymes with* **fear***)* NOUN tears
a drop of water that comes from your eye when you cry

tearful ADJECTIVE
feeling, looking or sounding like you want to cry or are crying

tease VERB teases, teasing, teased
to make fun of someone or try to embarrass them

teaspoon NOUN teaspoons
a small spoon for stirring tea
➤ **teaspoonful** NOUN • *a **teaspoonful** of sugar*

technical ADJECTIVE
to do with machines or technology or the way things work

technically ADVERB
If something is technically true or possible, it is true or possible in theory, but may not actually happen.

technician NOUN technicians
someone whose job is to look after scientific equipment and do practical work in a laboratory

technique *(say* tek-**neek***)* NOUN techniques
a method for doing something skilfully

technology NOUN technologies
the use of science, machines and computers to help people do things

teddy bear NOUN teddy bears
a stuffed toy bear

tedious *(say* tee-dee-us*)* ADJECTIVE
boring; slow or long • *It was a long **tedious** wait.*

teenage ADJECTIVE
A teenage boy or girl is aged between 13 and 19.
• *She has two **teenage** sons.*

teenager NOUN teenagers
a person aged between 13 and 19

teens NOUN
the time when you are aged 13 to 19 • *My sisters are in their **teens**.*

teeth NOUN *(plural of* **tooth***)*

telecommunications NOUN
methods of sending news and information over long distances, such as the telephone or Internet

telegram NOUN telegrams
in the past, a message sent by telegraph

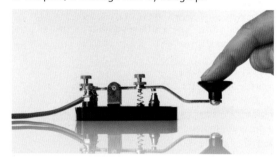

telegraph NOUN telegraphs
a way of sending messages using electrical or radio signals

telepathy *(say* tel-**ep**-ath-ee*)* NOUN
communication of thoughts from one person's mind to another without speaking
➤ **telepathic** ADJECTIVE

telephone NOUN telephones
a device for speaking to someone who is far away using wires or radio signals

telephone VERB
telephones, telephoning, telephoned
to speak to someone by telephone

✷ **WORD STORY**
The word **telephone** comes from Greek words meaning 'far-off sound'.

telescope NOUN
telescopes
a tube with lenses at each end, for making distant objects look larger and clearer

television NOUN
televisions
a device with a screen for watching programmes sent by radio waves, satellite or cable

telescope

tell *VERB* **tells, telling, told**
① To tell something to someone is to give them information by speaking. • *She **told** us the answer.*
② To tell someone to do something is to order them to do it. • *I have **told** you to be quiet.* ③ If you can tell something, you can recognise it or say what it is. • *I can't **tell** the difference.* • *He is learning to **tell** the time.*
➤ **To tell someone off** is to scold them.

temper *NOUN* **tempers**
① a person's mood • *He is in a good **temper**.*
② an angry mood • *She was in a **temper**.*
➤ **To lose your temper** is to become very angry.

temperament *NOUN* **temperament**
Someone's temperament is the way they usually behave and react to things.

temperate *ADJECTIVE*
A temperate climate is not very hot and not very cold.

temperature *NOUN* **temperatures**
① The temperature of something is how hot or cold it is. ② an unusually high body temperature • *She's ill and has a **temperature**.*

tempest *NOUN* **tempests**
a violent windy storm

temple *NOUN* **temples**
① a building where a god or goddess is worshipped • *an ancient Egyptian **temple*** ② Your temples are the sides of your head between your forehead and your ear.

tempo *NOUN* **tempos**
The tempo of a piece of music is its speed.

temporary *ADJECTIVE*
only lasting or used for a short time • *They were using a **temporary** classroom.*
➤ **temporarily** *ADVERB*

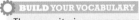 **BUILD YOUR VOCABULARY**
The opposite is **permanent**.

tempt *VERB* **tempts, tempting, tempted**
to make someone want to do something wrong or foolish
➤ **tempting** *ADJECTIVE* • *It was so **tempting** just to take the sweets.*

temptation *NOUN* **temptations**
a feeling of wanting to do something wrong or foolish • *She felt a strong **temptation** to lie.*

tend *VERB* **tends, tending, tended**
① If something tends to happen, it usually happens. • *This room **tends** to get cold.* ② to look after something or someone • *She **tended** the young plants.*

tendency *NOUN* **tendencies**
the way a person or thing is likely to behave • *She has a **tendency** to be lazy.*

tender *ADJECTIVE* **tenderer, tenderest**
① gentle and loving • *She looked after them with **tender** care.* ② not tough or hard • *The chicken was **tender**.* ③ sore or sensitive • *My stomach feels **tender**.*
➤ **tenderly** *ADVERB* ➤ **tenderness** *NOUN*

tendon *NOUN* **tendons**
a strong cord in the body that joins a muscle to a bone

tendril *NOUN* **tendrils**
a thin twisting part of something such as a plant

tennis *NOUN*
a game played with rackets and a ball on a court with a net across the middle

tense *ADJECTIVE* **tenser, tensest**
① tightly stretched • *All his muscles were **tense**.*
② nervous and not able to relax
➤ **tensely** *ADVERB*

tense *NOUN* **tenses**
a form of a verb that shows when something happens

BUILD YOUR VOCABULARY
Look at **past tense** and **present tense**.

tension *NOUN* **tensions**
a feeling of worry or nervousness

tent *NOUN* **tents**
a shelter made of canvas or cloth supported by poles

tentacle *NOUN* **tentacles**
a long bending part of the body of an octopus and some other animals

tepee (say tee-pee) *NOUN* **tepees**
a traditional Native American tent, made from skins or canvas on a frame of poles

term *NOUN* **terms**
① the time when a school is open for teaching
② a word or expression used in a particular subject
• *'Modal verb' is a grammatical **term**.*

terminal *NOUN* **terminals**
① a building where passengers arrive or depart
• *an airport **terminal*** ② a keyboard and screen connected to a main computer

termite *NOUN* **termites**
an insect that eats wood and lives in large groups

terrace *NOUN* **terraces**
① a row of houses joined together ② a flat paved area outside a house

terrapin *NOUN* **terrapins**
a kind of small turtle that lives in water

terrible *ADJECTIVE*
awful; very bad
➤ **terribly** *ADVERB*

terrier *NOUN* **terriers**
a kind of small dog

terrific *ADJECTIVE*
① very good; excellent • *That's a **terrific** idea!*
② very great • *They went at a **terrific** speed.*

terrify *VERB* **terrifies, terrifying, terrified**
to make someone extremely frightened

territory *NOUN* **territories**
an area of land that belongs to a country or group

terror *NOUN* **terrors**
very great fear

terrorise (also **terrorize**) *VERB* **terrorises, terrorising, terrorised**
to frighten someone with threats and violence

terrorism *NOUN*
the use of violence for a political purpose
➤ **terrorist** *NOUN*

test *NOUN* **tests**
① a set of questions to show what you have learned
② an experiment or process to find out information
• *We did a **test** to find out which substance melted first.*

test *VERB* **tests, testing, tested**
① To test someone is to give them a test. ② To test something is to use it so that you can find out whether it works or find out more about it.

tether *VERB* **tethers, tethering, tethered**
to tie an animal to something

tetrahedron *NOUN* **tetrahedrons**
a solid shape that has four triangular sides

text *NOUN* **texts**
① the words of something printed or written
② a written message sent using a mobile phone
text *VERB* **texts, texting, texted**
to send someone a text on a mobile phone

textbook *NOUN* **textbooks**
a book that gives information about a subject

textile *NOUN* **textiles**
a kind of cloth
🔘 **BUILD YOUR VOCABULARY**
A synonym is **fabric**.

texture *NOUN* **textures**
the way something feels • *Silk has a smooth texture.*

than *CONJUNCTION, PREPOSITION*
compared with another person or thing • *You are taller **than** I am.* • *You are taller **than** me.*

thank *VERB* **thanks, thanking, thanked**
to tell someone you are grateful for something they have given you or done for you
➤ **thank you** words that you say when you thank someone

that *DETERMINER, PRONOUN*
the one there • *What is **that** book?* • *What book is **that**?*
that *PRONOUN*
which or who • *This is the book **that** I like.* • *Are you the person **that** has the key?*
that *CONJUNCTION*
used as a linking word after some verbs, adjectives and nouns or to introduce a result • *I hope **that** you are well.* • *It's possible **that** he's wrong.* • *I was so tired **that** I fell asleep.*

thaw *VERB* **thaws, thawing, thawed**
When something thaws, it melts and is no longer frozen. • *The icicles were thawing.*

the *DETERMINER*
a particular one • *That is the bike I want.*

> **BUILD YOUR VOCABULARY**
>
> The word **the** is called the **definite article**.

theatre *NOUN* **theatres**
❶ a building where plays or shows are performed
❷ a room in a hospital where operations are done

theft *NOUN* **thefts**
the crime of stealing

their *DETERMINER*
belonging to them • *This is their house.*

> **! WATCH OUT!**
>
> Do not confuse **their** meaning 'belonging to them' with **they're** meaning 'they are'.

theirs *PRONOUN*
the one that belongs to them • *This house is theirs.*

them *PRONOUN*
a word used instead of *they* when it comes after a verb or a preposition • *I saw them yesterday.* • *I'll speak to them.*

> **BUILD YOUR VOCABULARY**
>
> **Them** is used as the **object** of a verb.

theme *NOUN* **themes**
the main idea or subject of something such as a book, film or poem

themselves *PRONOUN*
❶ used instead of 'them' when the same people do something and are affected by it • *They hurt themselves.* ❷ on their own; without help
• *The children made the cake themselves.*
➤ **by themselves** on their own; alone
• *They shouldn't go off by themselves.*

then *ADVERB*
❶ after that; next • *Then I went to bed.* ❷ at that time • *I was only five then.* ❸ in that case; therefore • *If you are going, then I'll go too.*

theory *NOUN* **theories**
an idea or a set of ideas that is meant to explain something
➤ **in theory** according to what should happen

therapy *NOUN* **therapies**
a way of treating a mental or physical illness
➤ **therapist** *NOUN* • *a speech therapist*

there *ADVERB*
in or to that place • *We're going there tomorrow.*
➤ **there is** used to say that something exists
• *There's a spider in the bath.* • *I knew there was something wrong.*

> **! WATCH OUT!**
>
> **There** is used to say where something is and is spelt like *where*. Do not confuse it with **their**, which means 'belonging to them'.

therefore *ADVERB*
for that reason; so

thermal *ADJECTIVE*
to do with heat

thermometer *NOUN* **thermometers**
a device for measuring temperature

thesaurus *NOUN* **thesauri, thesauruses**
a kind of dictionary in which words with similar meanings are listed in groups together

> **✳ WORD STORY**
>
> The word **thesaurus** comes from a Greek word meaning 'treasure-house'.

these *DETERMINER, PRONOUN*
the ones here • *Whose are these shoes?* • *Whose shoes are these?*

a
b
c
d
e
f
g
h
i
j
k
l
m
n
o
p
q
r
s
t
u
v
w
x
y
z

they PRONOUN
① a number of people or things that do something
② people in general • *They say it's a good film.*

BUILD YOUR VOCABULARY
They is used as the **subject** of a verb.

they'd
Short for *they had* or *they would* • *They'd (= they had) already gone.* • *They'd (= they would) like to come.*

thick ADJECTIVE thicker, thickest
① wide; not thin • *He cut a thick slice of bread.*
② used to talk about how much something measures from one side to the other • *The wall is ten centimetres thick.* ③ dense or closely packed • *thick fog* ④ a thick liquid does not flow easily • *a dollop of thick cream*
➤ **thickness** NOUN • *Measure the thickness of the stem.*

thicken VERB thickens, thickening, thickened
If you thicken something or it thickens, it becomes thicker.

thief NOUN thieves
someone who steals things

thigh NOUN thighs
the part of your leg above your knee

thin ADJECTIVE thinner, thinnest
① measuring a small amount from one side to the other • *a thin slice of bread* ② not fat ③ not dense or closely packed together • *He had thin hair.*
④ runny or watery • *The pancake mix should be quite thin.*

thing NOUN things
① an object or anything that you can see, touch or think about ② Your things are your belongings.
• *You can leave your things here.*

think VERB thinks, thinking, thought
① to use your mind; to have thoughts or ideas
• *Have you thought about what you want for your birthday?* ② to believe something • *I think that's a good idea.* • *I thought you liked pizza.* ③ To be thinking of doing something is to be planning to do it.

third ADJECTIVE
The third thing is next after the second. • *March is the third month.* • *I won third prize.*

third ADVERB
after the second • *Who came third?*

third NOUN thirds
① one of three equal parts into which something is divided. It can be written as $\frac{1}{3}$ ② the person or thing that is third

third person NOUN
the use of the words *he, him, she, her, it, they, them* and the verbs that go with them, for example to tell a story • *The story is told in the third person, beginning 'She woke up.'*

BUILD YOUR VOCABULARY
Look at **first person** and **second person**.

thirst NOUN
the feeling that you need to drink

thirsty ADJECTIVE thirstier, thirstiest
When you are thirsty, you feel that you need to drink.
➤ **thirstily** ADVERB

this DETERMINER, PRONOUN
the one here • *Whose is this pen?* • *Whose pen is this?*

thistle NOUN thistles
a wild plant with prickly leaves and purple flowers

thorax NOUN thoraces, thoraxes
the middle part of an insect's body, to which the legs or wings are joined

BUILD YOUR VOCABULARY
Look at **abdomen**.

thorn NOUN thorns
a small pointed growth on the stem of roses and other plants

thorough (say thuh-ruh) ADJECTIVE
done properly and carefully
➤ **thoroughly** ADVERB • *She checked her work thoroughly.*

WATCH OUT!
Thorough has a tricky spelling. It is spelt like and sounds like **borough**.

those DETERMINER, PRONOUN
the ones there • *Whose are **those** shoes?* • *Whose shoes are **those**?*

though *(rhymes with* **go***)* CONJUNCTION
although; in spite of the fact that • *Though it was very cold, it did not snow.*

though *(rhymes with* **go***)* ADVERB
however; even so • *It's a strange book. I like it, **though**.*

thought VERB *(past tense and past participle of* **think***)*
• *I **thought** Anna would come, but I wasn't sure.*
• *Have you **thought** carefully about this?*

thought NOUN thoughts
❶ something that you think; an idea ❷ thinking
• *I can see you've put a lot of **thought** into this.*

⚠ **WATCH OUT!**
In **bought**, **brought**, **ought** and **thought**, the letters *ough* sound like 'aw' in the word 'thaw'.

thoughtful ADJECTIVE
❶ thinking hard about something • *He looked thoughtful.* ❷ a thoughtful person thinks of what other people would like
➤ **thoughtfully** ADVERB

thoughtless ADJECTIVE
not thinking of other people and what they want or need

thousand NOUN thousands
the number 1000

thrash VERB thrashes, thrashing, thrashed
❶ to beat someone with a stick or whip ❷ to defeat someone easily in a game or sport ❸ to move part of your body violently • *The dinosaur **thrashed** its tail.*

thread NOUN threads
a long piece of cotton, nylon or other material used for sewing or weaving

thread VERB threads, threading, threaded
to put thread through a needle or bead

threadbare ADJECTIVE
Threadbare clothes are worn thin.

threat NOUN threats
❶ a statement that you will harm someone if they do not do what you want ❷ a danger

threaten VERB threatens, threatening, threatened
❶ to tell someone that you will harm them if they do not do what you want ❷ to be a danger to something • *Pollution **threatens** the oceans.*

three-dimensional *(also* **3-D***)* ADJECTIVE
solid rather than flat; having length, width, and height or depth

cylinder

threw VERB
(past tense of **throw***)*
• *Someone **threw** a snowball.*

thrill NOUN thrills
a sudden feeling of excitement

thrill VERB thrills, thrilling, thrilled
If something thrills you, it gives you a sudden feeling of excitement.

thrive VERB thrives, thriving, thrived
or thrives, thrived or thriven
to grow well and be strong or successful

throat NOUN throats
❶ the part at the back of your mouth where you swallow food and drink ❷ the front of your neck

throb VERB throbs, throbbing, throbbed
to beat or vibrate strongly and regularly • *My twisted ankle **throbbed** terribly.*

throne NOUN thrones
a special chair for a king or queen

a b c d e f g h i j k l m n o p q r s t u v w x y z

throng NOUN throngs
a large crowd of people

throttle VERB throttles, throttling, throttled
to squeeze someone's throat and strangle them

through PREPOSITION
from one end or side of something to the other
• We crawled **through** the tunnel.

through ADVERB
from one end or side to the other • Push the needle **through**.

> **WATCH OUT!**
> Do not confuse **through** with **threw**, which is the past tense of throw.

throughout PREPOSITION, ADVERB
all the way through • The knight searched **throughout** the land. • Jake's behaviour was excellent **throughout**.

throve VERB (a past tense of **thrive**)
• She **throve** at her new school.

throw VERB throws, throwing, threw, thrown
to send something or someone through the air
• Who **threw** that snowball?
➤ **To throw something away** is to get rid of it.
• I have **thrown away** my old trainers.

throw NOUN throws
a throwing action or movement • That was a good **throw**.

thrush NOUN thrushes
a bird that has a white front with brown spots

thrust VERB thrusts, thrusting, thrust
to push something somewhere with force • He **thrust** his hands into his pockets.

thud NOUN thuds
the dull sound of something heavy falling
thud VERB thuds, thudding, thudded
to fall with a thud

thumb NOUN thumbs
Your thumbs are the short thick fingers at the side of your hands.

thump VERB thumps, thumping, thumped
❶ to hit someone or something heavily ❷ to make a dull heavy sound
thump NOUN thumps
❶ a hard hit ❷ a dull heavy sound

thunder NOUN
the loud rumbling noise that you hear during a storm
thunder VERB thunders, thundering, thundered
❶ to make a loud rumbling noise like thunder
❷ to say something in a very loud or angry voice

thunderous ADJECTIVE
extremely loud • There was **thunderous** applause.

thunderstorm NOUN thunderstorms
a storm with thunder and lightning

thus ADVERB
in this way
'Thus was Wonka-Vite invented!' said Mr Wonka. 'And thus was it made safe for all to use!'–CHARLIE AND THE GREAT GLASS ELEVATOR, Roald Dahl

tick NOUN ticks
❶ a small mark (✓), made next to something to show that it is correct or has been done ❷ a regular clicking sound made by a clock or watch
tick VERB ticks, ticking, ticked
❶ to mark something with a tick • She **ticked** the correct answers. ❷ to make regular clicking sounds

ticket NOUN tickets
a piece of paper or card that shows you have paid for a journey or to get into a place

tickle VERB tickles, tickling, tickled
to touch someone's skin lightly in a way that makes them laugh or wriggle

tidal ADJECTIVE
to do with tides or affected by tides

tidal wave NOUN tidal waves
a huge sea wave moving with the tide
> **BUILD YOUR VOCABULARY**
> Look at **tsunami**.

tide NOUN tides
the regular rising or falling of the sea, which usually happens twice a day

BUILD YOUR VOCABULARY
Look at **ebb**.

tidy ADJECTIVE tidier, tidiest
❶ neat and orderly, with things in the right place • *Her bedroom was quite tidy.* ❷ If you are tidy, you keep things neat and in the right place.

tidy VERB tidies, tidying, tidied
to make a place neat by putting things away in the right place

tie VERB ties, tying, tied
❶ to fasten something using knotted string, rope, ribbon or cloth • *They tied the boat to a tree.* • *She tied a scarf around her neck.* ❷ To tie a knot or bow is to make one.

tie NOUN ties
❶ a thin strip of material tied round a collar, with a knot at the front ❷ If there is a tie in a game, two teams or people have the same number of points.

tiger NOUN tigers
a large wild animal of the cat family, with yellow and black stripes

tight ADJECTIVE tighter, tightest
❶ fitting closely; slightly too small • *These shoes are tight.* ❷ fully stretched • *Is the string tight?*
➤ **tightly** ADVERB

tight ADVERB
firmly • *Hold on tight.*

tighten VERB tightens, tightening, tightened
If you tighten something, you make it tighter or firmer. • *These screws need to be tightened.*

tightrope NOUN tightropes
a tightly stretched rope above the ground, for acrobats to perform on

tightrope

tights PLURAL NOUN
a piece of clothing worn under other clothes that cover a person's legs, feet and bottom

tile NOUN tiles
a thin piece of hard material used to cover roofs, walls or floors

till PREPOSITION, CONJUNCTION
until • *We waited till the end of the day.* • *I'll wait till Mum gets home.*

till NOUN tills
a machine that stores and records money received in a shop

BUILD YOUR VOCABULARY
A synonym is **cash register**.

till VERB tills, tilling, tilled
To till soil is to plough it.

tiller NOUN tillers
a handle used to steer a boat

BUILD YOUR VOCABULARY
The **tiller** moves the **rudder**.

tilt VERB tilts, tilting, tilted
If something tilts or if you tilt it, it slopes or leans.

timber NOUN timbers
❶ wood for building or making things ❷ A timber is a beam of wood.

time NOUN times
❶ Time is what we measure in seconds, minutes, hours, days, weeks, months and years. • *We haven't got much time.* ❷ A time is a particular point in the day. • *What time is it?* • *It's time for you to go to bed.* ❸ A time is an occasion when something happens. • *I've told you three times!* • *Come back another time.*
➤ **in time** or **on time** soon or early enough; not late • *Make sure you get there on time.*
➤ **times** PLURAL NOUN multiplied by • *5 times 3 is 15. (5 x 3 = 15)*

time VERB times, timing, timed
❶ to measure how long something takes
❷ to choose the time when something happens • *He timed his shot perfectly.*

timetable NOUN timetables
a list of the times when things happen, such as buses or trains leaving and arriving

timid ADJECTIVE
nervous or shy
➤ **timidly** ADVERB

a b c d e f g h i j k l m n o p q r s t u v w x y z

tin NOUN tins
1 a soft white metal

> **BUILD YOUR VOCABULARY**
> Tin is an **element**.

2 a metal container for preserving food

tin VERB tins, tinning, tinned
To tin food is to preserve it in tins.

tingle VERB tingles, tingling, tingled
If part of your body tingles, you have a slight stinging or tickling feeling there. • *The cold water made my skin* **tingle**.

tinkle VERB tinkles, tinkling, tinkled
to make a gentle ringing sound

tinsel NOUN
strips of sparkly material used for decoration

tint NOUN tints
a shade or small amount of a colour

tiny ADJECTIVE tinier, tiniest
very small

tip NOUN tips
1 the end part of something long and thin • *I tasted it with the* **tip** *of my tongue.* 2 a small amount of money given to thank someone who has helped you 3 a piece of useful advice • *The website gives* **tips** *on how to write great stories.* 4 a rubbish dump

tip VERB tips, tipping, tipped
to move something upside down or to tilt it
• *She* **tipped** *the water out of the bucket.*
• *Don't* **tip** *your chair back.*

tiptoe VERB tiptoes, tiptoeing, tiptoed
to walk quietly on your toes

tiptoe NOUN
➤ **on tiptoe** walking or standing on your toes

tire VERB tires, tiring, tired
1 To tire someone is to make them tired. 2 To tire is to become tired. • *She soon* **tired** *of his complaints.*

tired ADJECTIVE
feeling that you need to sleep or rest
➤ **To be tired of something** is to have had enough of it.
➤ **tiredness** NOUN
➤ **tiresome** ADJECTIVE annoying

tissue NOUN tissues
1 *(also* **tissue paper***)* thin soft paper
2 A tissue is a paper handkerchief.

tit NOUN tits
a small bird. There are several kinds, for example a **blue tit** and a **great tit**.

title NOUN titles
1 the name of something such as a book, film, painting or piece of music • *Give your story a* **title**.
2 a word that shows a person's position or profession, such as *Dr, Mrs* or *Sir*

titter VERB titters, tittering, tittered
to laugh in a silly way

to PREPOSITION
1 towards a place or person • *We went* **to** *town.*
• *Give it* **to** *me.* 2 as far as; up to • *The water came* **to** *my knees.* 3 compared with; rather than • *I prefer cats* **to** *dogs.*

toad NOUN toads
an animal similar to a large frog

> **BUILD YOUR VOCABULARY**
> A **toad** is an **amphibian**.

toadstool NOUN toadstools
a plant that looks like a mushroom, but is often poisonous

> **BUILD YOUR VOCABULARY**
> A **toadstool** is a **fungus**.

toast NOUN toasts
bread that has been grilled until it is crisp and brown

toast VERB toasts, toasting, toasted
to grill food in a toaster, under a grill or in front of a fire

toaster NOUN toasters
an electrical device for toasting bread

tobacco NOUN
the dried leaves of a tobacco plant that some people smoke in pipes, cigarettes and cigars

toboggan NOUN toboggans
a small sledge for sliding downhill
➤ **tobogganing** NOUN

today NOUN
this day • *Today is Monday.*

today ADVERB
❶ on this day • *It's my birthday today.* ❷ nowadays
• *Dodos are extinct today.*

toddler NOUN **toddlers**
a young child who is just learning to walk

toe NOUN **toes**
❶ Your toes are the five separate parts at the end of
each of your feet. ❷ the part of a shoe or sock that
covers your toes

toffee NOUN **toffees**
a sticky sweet made from butter and sugar

toga NOUN **togas**
a long loose piece of clothing worn by men in
ancient Rome

together ADVERB
❶ with another person; with each other • *Let's read
the story together.* ❷ If you put things together,
you join, mix or attach them. • *Glue the two parts
together.*

toil VERB **toils, toiling, toiled**
to work hard

toil NOUN
hard work

toilet NOUN **toilets**
❶ a large bowl with a seat, where you get rid of
waste from your body ❷ a room with a toilet in it

token NOUN **tokens**
❶ something such as a voucher or plastic coin that
you can use to pay for something ❷ a sign or symbol
• *This ring is a token of my love.*

told VERB *(past tense and past participle of* **tell***)*
• *She told everyone her story.* • *I've told you not to
do that.*

tolerant ADJECTIVE
accepting other people's behaviour and opinions
even when you do not agree with them

tolerate VERB **tolerates, tolerating, tolerated**
to allow or put up with something • *We will not
tolerate fighting in school.*

tomato NOUN **tomatoes**
a soft round red fruit with seeds inside it, eaten as a
vegetable

> ⚠️ **WATCH OUT!**
> Remember to put an **e** in the plural: *a tin of tomatoes.*

tomb (*say* toom) NOUN **tombs**
a place, especially a building, where a dead body is
buried

tombstone NOUN **tombstones**
a stone put over a grave

tomorrow NOUN, ADVERB
the day after today • *Tomorrow is Friday.*
• *He's coming tomorrow.*

> ⚠️ **WATCH OUT!**
> The word **tomorrow** has two **r**s but only one **m**!

ton NOUN **tons**
a measurement of weight. There are 2240 pounds in
1 ton, which is about 1016 kilograms.

tone NOUN **tones**
❶ The tone of someone's voice is the way it sounds.
❷ a shade of a colour

tongs PLURAL NOUN
a tool with two parts joined at one end, for picking
up and holding things

tongue NOUN **tongues**
❶ the long soft part that moves about inside your
mouth ❷ a language • *He spoke in his native
tongue.*

> ⚠️ **WATCH OUT!**
> The 'g' sound is spelt **-gue** in **tongue** and **league**.
> Both these words come from French.

tonic NOUN **tonics**
something that makes a person healthier or stronger

tonight ADVERB, NOUN
this evening or night • *It will be cold tonight.*
• *Tonight is New Year's Eve.*

tonne NOUN **tonnes**
a measurement of weight. There are 1000 kilograms
in a tonne.

a
b
c
d
e
f
g
h
i
j
k
l
m
n
o
p
q
r
s
t
u
v
w
x
y
z

too ADVERB
❶ also • *My sister has freckles too.* ❷ more than is wanted, correct or good • *You've used too much water.*

> ⚠ **WATCH OUT!**
> Do not confuse **too** with **to**, which is used to talk about a place or direction.

took VERB (past tense of **take**)
• *Grandma took us shopping.*

tool NOUN tools
something, such as a hammer or a saw, that you use to do a particular job

tooth NOUN teeth
❶ Your teeth are the hard white parts in your mouth that you use for biting and chewing.

> ⚙ **BUILD YOUR VOCABULARY**
> Look at **dental**.
> Look at **canine**, **incisor** and **molar**.

❷ one of the points of a comb, zip or saw

toothache NOUN
a pain in one of your teeth

toothbrush NOUN toothbrushes
a small brush on a long handle, for cleaning your teeth

toothpaste NOUN toothpastes
a substance for cleaning your teeth

top NOUN tops
❶ The top of something is the highest part. • *They climbed to the top of the hill.* ❷ the lid of a jar, bottle or tube ❸ a piece of clothing you wear on the upper part of your body ❹ a toy that spins on its point
top ADJECTIVE
❶ highest • *the top floor* ❷ The top things or people are the best or most important.
top VERB tops, topping, topped
to be at or on the top of something • *The cake was topped with thick pink icing.*

top hat NOUN top hats
a man's tall hat worn with formal clothes

topic NOUN topics
a subject that you are writing, talking or learning about

topmost ADJECTIVE
highest • *the topmost branches*

topple VERB topples, toppling, toppled
to fall over

topsy-turvy ADJECTIVE
upside down; muddled

torch NOUN torches
❶ a small electric lamp that you hold in your hand ❷ a burning stick used as a light

tore VERB (past tense of **tear**)
• *I tore my jeans when I fell over.*

torment (say tor-ment) VERB torments, tormenting, tormented
❶ to make someone suffer or feel pain ❷ to keep annoying someone deliberately
➤ **tormentor** NOUN

torment (say tor-ment) NOUN torments
great suffering

torn VERB (past participle of **tear**)
• *Someone has torn this book.*

tornado (say tor-**nay**-doh) NOUN tornadoes
a violent storm or whirlwind

> ✳ **WORD STORY**
> The word **tornado** comes from a Spanish word meaning 'thunder'.

torpedo NOUN torpedoes
a long tube-shaped bomb sent under water
torpedo VERB torpedoes, torpedoing, torpedoed
To torpedo a ship is to attack it with a torpedo.

torrent NOUN torrents
a very strong stream or fall of water
The wind howled, the rain came down in torrents and the waves got so high, they splashed right over the boat.
—THE STORY OF DOCTOR DOLITTLE, Hugh Lofting

torrential ADJECTIVE
falling very heavily • *torrential rain*

torso NOUN torsos
the main part of the human body, not including the head, arms or legs

tortoise (say tor-tus) NOUN tortoises
a slow-moving animal with a shell over its body

> ⚙ **BUILD YOUR VOCABULARY**
> A **tortoise** is a **reptile**.

torture VERB tortures, torturing, tortured
to make someone feel great pain, especially so that they will give information

torture NOUN tortures
something that causes someone great pain

toss VERB tosses, tossing, tossed
❶ to throw something into the air ❷ To toss a coin is to throw it in the air and see which way it lands, as a way of deciding something.

total NOUN totals
the amount you get by adding everything together

total ADJECTIVE
❶ including everything • What is the **total** amount? ❷ complete • There was **total** silence.
➤ **totally** ADVERB • It's **totally** safe.

total VERB totals, totalling, totalled
to add amounts together

totter VERB totters, tottering, tottered
to walk unsteadily or to wobble

toucan NOUN toucans
a tropical bird with a large, brightly coloured beak

touch VERB touches, touching, touched
❶ to feel something with your hand or fingers • Don't **touch** the pan.
❷ to come into contact with something • Their noses were almost **touching**. ❸ to make you feel emotional • I was **touched** by his story.

touch NOUN touches
❶ an act of touching • You can find the information with one **touch** of the screen.
❷ Your sense of touch is your ability to feel things by touching them. ❸ a small thing that greatly improves something • You should now be adding the finishing **touches** to your work.

tough ADJECTIVE tougher, toughest
❶ strong; hard to break or damage • The rope is very **tough**.
❷ Tough food is hard to chew.
❸ Someone who is tough is brave and strong.

⚠ **WATCH OUT!**
In **tough**, **enough** and **rough**, the letters ough sound like 'uff'.

tour NOUN tours
a journey or visit in which you see several places
• a **tour** of the city

tourist NOUN tourists
someone who is visiting a place on holiday
➤ **tourism** NOUN • **Tourism** is very important to this town.

tournament NOUN tournaments
a competition in which there is a series of games or contests

tow (rhymes with **go**) VERB tows, towing, towed
to pull something along behind you • The car was **towing** a caravan.

towards (also **toward**) PREPOSITION
❶ in the direction of • We walked **towards** the village. ❷ in relation to • He was friendly **towards** us.

towel NOUN towels
a piece of soft cloth that you use for drying yourself

tower NOUN towers
a building or part of a building that is tall or narrow

tower VERB towers, towering, towered
To tower over things or people is to be much taller than them.

town NOUN towns
a place where a lot of people live, with many houses, shops and other buildings

toxic ADJECTIVE
poisonous • The planet has a **toxic** atmosphere.

toy NOUN toys
an object to play with

trace VERB traces, tracing, traced
❶ To trace a picture is to copy it by drawing over it on thin paper that you can see through. ❷ To trace someone or something is to find them after a search.

trace NOUN traces
a tiny amount of something or a mark that shows someone or something was there • He vanished without a **trace**.

toucan

a
b
c
d
e
f
g
h
i
j
k
l
m
n
o
p
q
r
s
t
u
v
w
x
y
z

track NOUN **tracks**
❶ Tracks are marks left by a person or thing.
❷ a path ❸ a set of rails for trains or trams
❹ an area of ground for racing

track VERB **tracks, tracking, tracked**
to follow someone or something by following the marks they leave

tracksuit NOUN **tracksuits**
a loose suit of trousers and a top, worn for sports and exercise

tractor NOUN **tractors**
a farm vehicle used for pulling machinery or other heavy loads

trade NOUN **trades**
❶ the activity of buying, selling or exchanging things ❷ a job, especially a skilled craft

trade VERB **trades, trading, traded**
to buy, sell or exchange things
➤ **trader** NOUN

trademark NOUN **trademarks**
a symbol or name that only one manufacturer is allowed to use

tradition NOUN **traditions**
a custom or belief that is passed on from one generation to the next

traditional ADJECTIVE
❶ passed down from one generation to the next • *a traditional* folk tale ❷ following older ideas rather than modern ones • *a very traditional* school
➤ **traditionally** ADVERB

traffic NOUN
vehicles, ships or aircraft moving along a route

traffic lights NOUN
a set of coloured lights used to control traffic

tragedy NOUN **tragedies**
❶ a very sad event, especially one in which people are hurt or killed ❷ a serious story or play with a sad ending

tragic ADJECTIVE
very sad and usually involving death or disaster
➤ **tragically** ADVERB

trail NOUN **trails**
❶ a rough path through the countryside or through a forest ❷ the marks or scents left behind by something as it moves • *He left a **trail** of dirty handprints.*

trail VERB **trails, trailing, trailed**
❶ to follow behind someone • *The children **trailed** after them.* ❷ If you trail something or if it trails, it follows, hangs or drags along behind you.

trailer NOUN **trailers**
❶ a small vehicle that is pulled along by a car or lorry ❷ a short film advertising a film or television programme

train NOUN **trains**
a group of coaches or trucks pulled by an engine, that carry passengers or goods along a railway

train VERB **trains, training, trained**
❶ to teach a person or animal how to do something • *The dog is **trained** to herd sheep.* ❷ to learn how to do a job • *She **trained** as a doctor.* ❸ to practise for a sporting event • *I'm **training** hard for the race.*

trainer NOUN **trainers**
❶ a soft shoe with a rubber sole, worn for running and sport ❷ someone who trains people or animals

traitor NOUN **traitors**
someone who betrays their country or friends

tram NOUN **trams**
a passenger vehicle that runs along rails in the road

tramp NOUN **tramps**
❶ a person without a home or job ❷ the sound of heavy footsteps

tramp VERB **tramps, tramping, tramped**
to walk with heavy footsteps

trample VERB tramples, trampling, trampled
to crush something by treading heavily on it

trampoline NOUN trampolines
a large piece of canvas joined to a frame by springs, used for jumping on

trance NOUN trances
a dreamy or partly conscious condition, in which someone can see or hear some things but not others

tranquil ADJECTIVE
quiet and peaceful

transfer VERB transfers, transferring, transferred
To transfer something from one place to another is to move it.

transform VERB transforms, transforming, transformed
If someone or something transforms or is transformed, their form or appearance changes completely.
• The caterpillar is **transformed** into a butterfly.
➤ **transformation** NOUN

transistor NOUN transistors
a tiny electronic device that controls a flow of electricity

transitive ADJECTIVE
A transitive verb is used with an object, for example *tell* in *I told you.*

🔧 **BUILD YOUR VOCABULARY**
Look at **intransitive**.

translate VERB translates, translating, translated
To translate something is to say or write it in another language.
➤ **translation** NOUN ➤ **translator** NOUN

translucent ADJECTIVE
allowing light to shine through, without being fully transparent

transmission NOUN transmissions
a signal, message or broadcast that is sent out

transmit VERB transmits, transmitting, transmitted
❶ to send out a signal or broadcast ❷ to send or pass something from one person or place to another
➤ **transmitter** NOUN • *a radio* **transmitter**

transparent ADJECTIVE
possible to see through

transplant VERB transplants, transplanting, transplanted
❶ To transplant an organ is to remove it from one person's body and put it in another. ❷ to move a plant from one place to another
transplant NOUN transplants
an operation to transplant an organ • *a heart* **transplant**

transport *(say* trans-port*)* VERB transports, transporting, transported
to take people or things from one place to another
transport *(say* trans-port*)* NOUN
something used to transport people or things, such as cars, bicycles or lorries • *What form of* **transport** *do you use to get to school?*

trap NOUN traps
❶ a device used to catch an animal ❷ a plan or trick to catch or deceive someone • *They laid a* **trap** *to catch the thief.*
trap VERB traps, trapping, trapped
❶ to catch an animal in a trap ❷ to catch or trick someone ❸ To be trapped is to be stuck somewhere dangerous and unable to escape. • *They were* **trapped** *in a burning building.*

trapdoor NOUN trapdoors
a door in a floor, ceiling or roof

trapeze NOUN trapezes
a bar hanging from two ropes, used as a swing by acrobats

trapezium NOUN trapeziums
a four-sided figure that has two parallel sides of different lengths

trash NOUN
rubbish or nonsense

travel VERB travels, travelling, travelled
to go from one place to another
travel NOUN
journeys • *Do you enjoy* **travel**?

traveller NOUN travellers
❶ someone who is travelling ❷ a person who lives in a vehicle and does not settle in one place

a
b
c
d
e
f
g
h
i
j
k
l
m
n
o
p
q
r
s
t
u
v
w
x
y
z

trawler *NOUN* trawlers
a fishing boat that pulls a large net

tray *NOUN* trays
a flat piece of wood, metal or plastic with raised edges used for carrying food, drinks and other things

treacherous *ADJECTIVE*
❶ betraying someone; not loyal ❷ dangerous
The snow was deep and treacherous, with a thick, shiny crust of ice on top.—ODD AND THE FROST GIANTS, Neil Gaiman

treachery *NOUN*
behaviour or an act that betrays someone • *He was shocked by his friend's treachery.*

treacle *NOUN*
thick sweet sticky liquid made from sugar

tread *VERB* treads, treading, trod, trodden
to walk on something or put your foot on it
• *He trod on my toe.* • *I've trodden in something sticky.*

tread *NOUN* treads
the sound of someone walking • *I heard a heavy tread on the stairs.*

treason *NOUN*
the crime of betraying your country

treasure *NOUN* treasures
❶ gold, silver, jewels or other valuable things
❷ A treasure is a precious thing.

treasure *VERB* treasures, treasuring, treasured
To treasure something is to think that it is very precious.

> ! **WATCH OUT!**
> Watch out for **treasure**, **measure** and **pleasure**, which are all pronounced -e*zh*-er but spelt **–easure**.

treasury *NOUN* treasuries
a place where treasure is stored

treat *VERB* treats, treating, treated
❶ to behave towards someone or something in a particular way • *Treat your pets well.* • *He treated us with respect.* ❷ to give someone medical care
• *She was treated in hospital.*

treat *NOUN* treats
something special that you enjoy • *Mum promised me a treat.*

treatment *NOUN* treatments
❶ the way you behave towards someone or something • *I can't bear cruel treatment of animals.* ❷ medical care

treaty *NOUN* treaties
a formal agreement between two or more countries

treble *ADJECTIVE*
❶ three times as much or three times as many
• *a treble score*

> ⚙ **BUILD YOUR VOCABULARY**
> A synonym for this meaning is **triple**.

❷ A treble voice or instrument has a high sound.
❸ In music, a treble clef is a symbol put on a staff to show the notes in it are high.

> ⚙ **BUILD YOUR VOCABULARY**
> Look at **bass**.

treble *VERB* trebles, trebling, trebled
If you treble something or if it trebles, it becomes three times as big. • *He trebled the price.*

> ⚙ **BUILD YOUR VOCABULARY**
> A synonym is **triple**.

tree *NOUN* trees
a tall plant with leaves, branches and a thick wooden stem called a *trunk*

trek *VERB* treks, trekking, trekked
to go on a long walk or journey

trek *NOUN* treks
a long walk or journey

tremble *VERB* trembles, trembling, trembled
to shake slightly, especially because you are afraid

tremendous *ADJECTIVE*
❶ very large or very great
Then, without warning, there was a tremendous SPLASH! right at Measle's side and Measle received a great wave of water directly in his face.—MEASLE: THE MONSTER OF MUCUS!, Ian Ogilvy
❷ excellent
➤ **tremendously** *ADVERB* very or very much
• *It is tremendously exciting.*

tremor *NOUN* tremors
❶ a shaking or trembling ❷ a small earthquake

trench *NOUN* trenches
a long hole or ditch dug in the ground

trend *NOUN* trends
the general direction in which something is going or developing

trespass *VERB*
trespasses, trespassing, trespassed
to go on someone's land or property without their permission

trestle table *NOUN*
trestle tables
a table consisting of a board resting on triangular supports

T-rex *NOUN* T-rexes
short for **tyrannosaurus rex**

trial *NOUN* trials
❶ the process of hearing evidence about a crime in a law court in order to find out whether someone is guilty ❷ If you give something a trial, you try or test it to see how well it works.

triangle *NOUN* triangles
❶ a flat shape with three straight sides and three angles

⚙ **BUILD YOUR VOCABULARY**
Look at **equilateral triangle**, **isosceles triangle** and **scalene triangle**.

❷ a musical instrument made from a metal triangle

⚙ **BUILD YOUR VOCABULARY**
A **triangle** is a **percussion** instrument.

triangular *ADJECTIVE*
in the shape of a triangle

tribe *NOUN* tribes
a group of families living together as a community
➤ **tribal** *ADJECTIVE* • *a tribal leader*

tributary *NOUN* tributaries
a river or stream that flows into a larger river

tribute *NOUN* tributes
❶ something said or done to show respect or admiration ❷ money that people in one country used to have to pay a powerful ruler in another country

triceratops
NOUN triceratops
a dinosaur with three horns and a bony frill above its neck

trick *NOUN*
tricks
❶ something done to deceive or fool someone ❷ a skilful act that creates an illusion
• *My brother likes doing magic tricks.*

trick *VERB* tricks, tricking, tricked
to deceive or fool someone

trickle *VERB* trickles, trickling, trickled
to flow slowly in small quantities
trickle *NOUN* trickles
a slow gradual flow

tricky *ADJECTIVE* trickier, trickiest
❶ difficult or awkward • *There were some tricky questions.* ❷ cunning or deceitful

tricycle *NOUN* tricycles
a bicycle with three wheels

trident *NOUN* tridents
a spear with three prongs

tried *VERB (past tense and past participle of try)*
• *I tried not to cry.* • *Have you ever tried roller skating?*

trifle *NOUN* trifles
❶ a pudding made with layers of sponge cake, custard, fruit and cream ❷ something with little importance or value

trifling *ADJECTIVE*
very small or unimportant

trigger *NOUN* triggers
a lever that is pulled to fire a gun
trigger *VERB* triggers, triggering, triggered
to start something happening

a b c d e f g h i j k l m n o p q r s t u v w x y z

trilobite (say tril-o-bite or tri-lo-bite) NOUN
trilobites
a type of fossil with a body divided into three parts

trim VERB **trims, trimming, trimmed**
❶ to cut the edges or unwanted parts from something ❷ to decorate the edges of clothing
• *The cloak was **trimmed** with fur.*
trim ADJECTIVE **trimmer, trimmest**
neat and tidy
trim NOUN
❶ If you give something a trim, you cut a little off it.
• *My hair needs a **trim**.* ❷ a decoration along the edges of something

trio NOUN **trios**
❶ a group of three people or things ❷ a piece of music for three players or singers

trip VERB **trips, tripping, tripped**
❶ to catch your foot on something and fall or stumble ❷ To trip someone, or trip them up, is to make them fall or stumble.
trip NOUN **trips**
a short journey or outing

triple ADJECTIVE
❶ three times as much or three times as many
• *a **triple** helping* ❷ having three parts or suitable for three people • *a **triple**-decker sandwich* • *a **triple** room*
triple VERB **triples, tripling, tripled**
If you triple something or if it triples, it becomes three times as big. • *The price has **tripled**.*

triplet NOUN **triplets**
one of three children born at the same time to the same mother

tripod (say tri-pod) NOUN **tripods**
a stand with three legs, for supporting a camera or other instrument

triumph NOUN **triumphs**
❶ a great success or victory ❷ a feeling of victory or success • *She raised her arms in **triumph**.*
triumph VERB **triumphs, triumphing, triumphed**
to win or succeed

triumphant ADJECTIVE
enjoying or celebrating a victory
➤ **triumphantly** ADVERB

trivial ADJECTIVE
not important

trod VERB (past tense of **tread** VERB)
• *Someone **trod** on my toe.*

trodden VERB (past participle of **tread** VERB)
• *You've **trodden** all over the flowers.*

troll NOUN **trolls**
a creature in Scandinavian mythology, either a dwarf or a giant

trolley NOUN **trolleys**
a container on wheels, for carrying things around in

trombone NOUN **trombones**
a large metal musical instrument with a sliding tube

BUILD YOUR VOCABULARY
The **trombone** is a **brass instrument**.

troop NOUN **troops**
❶ **Troops** are soldiers. ❷ A troop of animals or people is a group of them.
troop VERB **troops, trooping, trooped**
If people troop somewhere, they move there in large numbers.

trophy NOUN **trophies**
a cup or other prize for winning a competition

trophy

tropic NOUN **tropics**
one of two imaginary lines around the earth showing the limits of the earth's hottest regions. The **Tropic of Cancer** is north of the equator and the **Tropic of Capricorn** is south of the equator.

BUILD YOUR VOCABULARY
These lines are lines of **latitude**.

➤ **the tropics** the hot regions between these two lines

tropical ADJECTIVE
found in or relating to the tropics • *a **tropical** bird*

trot VERB **trots, trotting, trotted**
❶ When a horse trots, it runs with short steps, not very fast.

BUILD YOUR VOCABULARY
Look at **canter** and **gallop**.

❷ If a person trots, they run slowly with small steps.

trouble *NOUN* **troubles**
something that causes problems or worry
➤ **To be in trouble** is to have a problem or to have someone cross with you.

trouble *VERB* **troubles, troubling, troubled**
to worry or disturb someone

troublesome *ADJECTIVE*
causing trouble or worry

trough *(say* trof*)* *NOUN* **troughs**
a long narrow box for animals to eat or drink from

⚠ **WATCH OUT!**
In **trough** and **cough**, the letters *ough* sound like 'off'.

trousers *NOUN*
a piece of clothing worn over the lower half of your body, with two parts to cover your legs

trout *NOUN* **trout**
a fish that lives in rivers and lakes

trowel *NOUN* **trowels**
a tool like a small spade, for gardening or building

truant *NOUN*
➤ **To play truant** is to stay away from school without permission.

truce *NOUN* **truces**
an agreement to stop fighting for a while

truck *NOUN* **trucks**
❶ a lorry ❷ a railway wagon for carrying goods

trudge *VERB* **trudges, trudging, trudged**
to walk slowly and heavily

true *ADJECTIVE* **truer, truest**
❶ real or correct; that actually exists or actually happened • *This is a* **true** *story.* ❷ loyal and faithful • *You are a* **true** *friend.*

truly *ADVERB*
really • *I am* **truly** *sorry.*

trump *NOUN* **trumps**
a type of card that beats all the others in one game or round

trumpet *NOUN* **trumpets**
a metal musical instrument with a narrow tube that widens at the end

🔧 **BUILD YOUR VOCABULARY**
A **trumpet** is a **brass instrument**.

trumpet *VERB* **trumpets, trumpeting, trumpeted**
When an elephant trumpets, it makes a loud sound.

truncheon *NOUN* **truncheons**
a short thick stick carried by a police officer

trundle *VERB* **trundles, trundling, trundled**
to move along heavily, especially on wheels • *A lorry* **trundled** *across the bridge.*

trunk *NOUN* **trunks**
❶ the main thick stem of a tree ❷ an elephant's long nose ❸ a large box with a hinged lid, for carrying or storing things

trunks *PLURAL NOUN*
a piece of clothing worn by a boy or a man for swimming

trust *VERB* **trusts, trusting, trusted**
to believe that someone is good, truthful or reliable • *I don't* **trust** *him.* • *She can be* **trusted** *to keep a secret.*

trust *NOUN*
the feeling that you can trust someone • *There must be* **trust** *between teammates.*

trustworthy *ADJECTIVE*
able to be trusted

trusty *ADJECTIVE* **trustier, trustiest**
reliable • *He came on his* **trusty** *old bike.*

truth *NOUN* **truths**
the true facts about something

truthful *ADJECTIVE*
telling the truth; honest
➤ **truthfully** *ADVERB*

try *VERB* **tries, trying, tried**
❶ to make an effort to do something • *I* **tried** *to keep still.* ❷ to use something to see if it works or taste something to see if you like it • *Have you* **tried** *lemon ice cream?* ❸ To try someone in a law court is to listen to evidence in order to decide whether they are guilty of a crime.
➤ **To try something on** is to put on clothes to see if they fit or look good.

try *NOUN* **tries**
❶ a go at something; an attempt • *Have another* **try**. ❷ in rugby, an act of putting the ball on the ground behind your opponents' goal to score points

a
b
c
d
e
f
g
h
i
j
k
l
m
n
o
p
q
r
s
t
u
v
w
x
y
z

T-shirt NOUN **T-shirts**
a shirt or vest with short sleeves

tsunami (say soo-nah-mee) NOUN **tsunamis**
a huge sea wave caused by an earthquake

tub NOUN **tubs**
a container with a wide top • a **tub** of ice cream

tuba (say tew-ba) NOUN **tubas**
a large metal musical instrument that makes a deep sound

BUILD YOUR VOCABULARY
A **tuba** is a **brass instrument**.

tube NOUN **tubes**
❶ a long round hollow object made of metal, plastic, rubber or glass ❷ a long container that you can squeeze, for a thick liquid such as toothpaste

tuck VERB **tucks, tucking, tucked**
to push something into a thing that hides it or holds it in place
• She **tucked** her hair under her cap. • Now **tuck** in the flap of the envelope.

tuft NOUN **tufts**
a bunch of something soft such as grass or hair growing together

tug VERB **tugs, tugging, tugged**
to pull something hard

tug NOUN **tugs**
❶ a hard or sudden pull ❷ a small powerful boat for towing ships

tulip NOUN **tulips**
a bright cup-shaped flower that grows on a tall stem from a bulb

tumble VERB **tumbles, tumbling, tumbled**
to fall over or fall down clumsily

tumble NOUN **tumbles**
a clumsy fall

tumbler NOUN **tumblers**
❶ a drinking glass with no stem or handle ❷ an acrobat

tumult (say tew-mult) NOUN
an uproar or state of great confusion

tuna (say tew-na) NOUN **tuna, tunas**
a large sea fish, often used for food

tundra NOUN
a large area of flat land in cold regions, which has no trees and is frozen for most of the year

tune NOUN **tunes**
a series of notes that make a pleasant short piece of music
➤ **To be in tune** is to be at the correct musical pitch.

tune VERB **tunes, tuning, tuned**
to adjust a musical instrument so it is in tune

tunic (say tew-nik) NOUN **tunics**
a piece of clothing that is like a long loose shirt

tunnel NOUN **tunnels**
a passage made underground or through a hill

tunnel VERB **tunnels, tunnelling, tunnelled**
to make a tunnel • They **tunnelled** under the wall.

turban NOUN **turbans**
a head covering made by wrapping round a long piece of cloth, worn especially by Sikhs and by some Muslims

turbine NOUN **turbines**
a machine or motor that is driven by a flow of water, gas or wind

turbulent ADJECTIVE
❶ moving violently • a **turbulent** sea ❷ full of confusion and disorder • his **turbulent** thoughts
➤ **turbulence** NOUN

turf NOUN
Turf is short grass with the soil it is growing in.

turkey NOUN **turkeys**
a large bird kept on farms for its meat

turmoil NOUN
great disturbance or confusion

turn VERB **turns, turning, turned**
❶ To turn is to move round or move to a new direction. • She **turned** and saw him. • **Turn** left at the corner. ❷ If you turn something, you make it move round or face a different direction. • I **turned**

the door handle. ❸ to become a certain thing
• *His face **turned** red.* • *The days are **turning** cold.*
❹ To turn a device on, off, up or down is to use a switch to make it do something. • *Don't forget to **turn** off the lights.*
➤ **To turn into something** is to become it.
• *The caterpillar **turned into** a butterfly.*
➤ **To turn out** is to happen a certain way. • *It all **turned out** fine in the end.*
➤ **To turn up** is to appear or arrive. • *The other team finally **turned up**.*

turn NOUN turns
If it is your turn to do something, you are the next person who can or must do it.

turnip NOUN turnips
a round white root vegetable

turquoise *(say* ter-kwoiz*)*
NOUN
❶ a sky-blue or green-blue colour ❷ a blue stone used to make jewellery

turret NOUN turrets
a small tower in a castle

turtle NOUN turtles
a sea animal similar to a tortoise

⚙ **BUILD** YOUR VOCABULARY
A **turtle** is a **reptile**.

tusk NOUN tusks
one of a pair of long pointed teeth belonging to an elephant, walrus or boar

tutor NOUN tutors
a teacher who teaches one person or a small group at a time

TV NOUN TVs
television • *What's on **TV** tonight?*

twang NOUN twangs
the vibrating sound made by a spring, a string or a piece of elastic being pulled and let go
twang VERB twangs, twanging, twanged
to make a twanging sound

tweak VERB tweaks, tweaking, tweaked
to twist or pull something sharply

tweed NOUN
a thick rough woollen cloth

twice ADVERB
❶ on two occasions • *I've told you **twice**.* ❷ double
• *This one costs **twice** the amount.*

twiddle VERB twiddles, twiddling, twiddled
to turn something quickly round and round
• *He started **twiddling** the controls.*

twig NOUN twigs
a short thin branch

twilight NOUN
the time just after sunset, when it starts to get dark

⚙ **BUILD YOUR VOCABULARY**
A synonym is **dusk**.

twin NOUN twins
one of two children born at the same time to the same mother

twine VERB twines, twining, twined
to twist and curl something around something
• *The snake **twined** itself around a branch.*
twine NOUN
strong thin string

twinge NOUN twinges
a sudden pain or unpleasant feeling

twinkle VERB twinkles, twinkling, twinkled
to sparkle or shine with flashes of bright light

twirl VERB twirls, twirling, twirled
If something twirls or if you twirl it, it turns round and round quickly. • *He **twirled** his cane.*
twirl NOUN twirls
a twirling movement

twist VERB twists, twisting, twisted
❶ to turn the ends of something in opposite directions or bend it out of shape • *The trees were **twisted** by the wind.* ❷ to bend or turn around
• *He **twisted** round to try and see.* ❸ to injure part of your body by twisting it • *I've **twisted** my ankle.*
twist NOUN twists
a twisting movement or action

twitch VERB twitches, twitching, twitched
to make a sudden small jerky movement

twitter *VERB* **twitters, twittering, twittered**
When birds twitter, they make quick high sounds.

two-dimensional *(also* **2-D***) ADJECTIVE*
flat; having length and width

tying *VERB (present participle of* **tie***)*
• *I'm just* **tying** *my shoelaces.*

type *NOUN* **types**
A type is a group or class of similar people or things. • *What* **type** *of food do you like?*

type *VERB* **types, typing, typed**
to write something using the keys on a keyboard or touchscreen

typhoon *NOUN* **typhoons**
a violent windy storm

typical *ADJECTIVE*
usual, normal or expected • *What time do you get up on a* **typical** *Sunday?* • *It's* **typical** *of her to forget something!*
➤ **typically** *ADVERB*

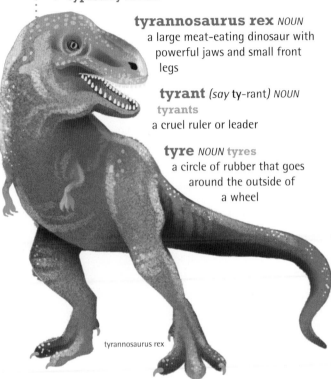

tyrannosaurus rex *NOUN*
a large meat-eating dinosaur with powerful jaws and small front legs

tyrant *(say* ty-rant*) NOUN*
tyrants
a cruel ruler or leader

tyre *NOUN* **tyres**
a circle of rubber that goes around the outside of a wheel

tyrannosaurus rex

Can you think of any English words that contain uu? They are hard to find, but there is one in this dictionary!

CLUE a word meaning *'a completely empty space with nothing, including air, in it'*

UFO NOUN UFOs
an object or spacecraft in the sky, believed to have come from another planet; short for *unidentified flying object*

ugly ADJECTIVE uglier, ugliest
not beautiful; unpleasant-looking
➤ **ugliness** NOUN

✳ WORD STORY
The word **ugly** comes from an Old Norse (Viking) word meaning 'to dread'.

ultimate ADJECTIVE
❶ final • *What is your ultimate goal?* ❷ the best possible example of something • *Winning Player of the Year is the ultimate honour.*

ultimately ADVERB
in the end; finally • *Ultimately, the decision is yours.*

ultraviolet light NOUN
light that is not visible and causes tanning and damage to your skin

umbrella NOUN umbrellas
a round cloth cover over a frame with a handle, which you use to protect yourself from rain

✳ WORD STORY
The word **umbrella** comes from an Italian word meaning 'a little shade'.

umpire NOUN
umpires
a person who makes sure that people obey the rules in cricket, tennis and some other games

unable ADJECTIVE
not able • *She was unable to hear.*

unaware ADJECTIVE
not knowing about something • *They were unaware of the danger.*

unawares ADVERB
without knowing or being prepared • *His question caught me unawares.*

unbearable ADJECTIVE
so painful or unpleasant that you cannot bear it

unbelievable ADJECTIVE
❶ difficult to believe • *His story sounded unbelievable.* ❷ amazing; wonderful • *The flavour is unbelievable.*
➤ **unbelievably** ADVERB

uncanny ADJECTIVE
strange and slightly frightening • *The resemblance between them was uncanny.*

uncertain ADJECTIVE
not sure; doubtful
➤ **uncertainty** NOUN

uncle NOUN uncles
your mother's or father's brother or your aunt's husband

uncomfortable ADJECTIVE
❶ not comfortable to sit in or wear • *uncomfortable shoes* ❷ not relaxed • *There was an uncomfortable silence.*
➤ **uncomfortably** ADVERB • *The room was uncomfortably cold.*

uncommon ADJECTIVE
unusual
➤ **uncommonly** ADVERB

a b c d e f g h i j k l m n o p q r s t u v w x y z

unconscious ADJECTIVE
❶ not aware of things around you because you have fainted or been knocked out ❷ not aware of something • *He was quite **unconscious** of her anger.*
➤ **unconsciously** ADVERB
➤ **unconsciousness** NOUN

uncontrollable ADJECTIVE
not possible to control
➤ **uncontrollably** ADVERB • *He was shivering **uncontrollably**.*

uncouth (say un-kooth) ADJECTIVE
behaving in a rude, rough way

uncover VERB uncovers, uncovering, uncovered
❶ to take the cover or top off something
❷ To uncover a secret is to find it out.

under PREPOSITION
❶ below; beneath • *We sat **under** a tree.*
❷ less than • *a competition for children **under** 10*
❸ experiencing something • *They were **under** attack.*

undercarriage NOUN undercarriages
the wheels and other parts underneath an aircraft

underfoot ADVERB
under someone's feet • *The ground was boggy **underfoot**.*

undergo VERB undergoes, undergoing, underwent, undergone
to experience or go through something • *She **underwent** surgery.* • *The city has **undergone** huge changes.*

underground ADJECTIVE, ADVERB
under the ground • *an **underground** cave* • *The train goes **underground** here.*

undergrowth NOUN
bushes and other plants that grow thickly together under trees

underline VERB underlines, underlining, underlined
to draw a line under something you have written

undermine VERB undermines, undermining, undermined
to weaken something • *All that criticism **undermines** his confidence.*

underneath PREPOSITION, ADVERB
below or beneath • *We sat **underneath** the trees.* • *Sam was wearing his football shirt **underneath** his school shirt.*

underpants NOUN
a piece of men's or boys' underwear worn under trousers

underpass NOUN underpasses
a place where one road or path goes under another

understand VERB understands, understanding, understood
❶ to know what something means or how it works • *I didn't **understand** all the words.*
❷ to see why someone behaves as they do • *It's fine—I **understand**.*

understandable ADJECTIVE
❶ reasonable or normal • *It is **understandable** to be upset.* ❷ able to be understood • *Make sure your speech is **understandable**.*
➤ **understandably** ADVERB

understanding NOUN
❶ the ability to understand or think ❷ sympathy or tolerance • *Thank you for your **understanding**.*

understanding ADJECTIVE
sympathetic • *He was very **understanding** when I was ill.*

undertake VERB undertakes, undertaking, undertook, undertaken
to agree or promise to do something

undertaking NOUN undertakings
something that someone agrees to do

underwater ADJECTIVE, ADVERB
placed, used or done below the surface of water

underwear NOUN
clothes you wear next to your skin, under other clothes

underworld NOUN
In mythology, the underworld is a place for the spirits of the dead.

undo VERB undoes, undoing, undid, undone
❶ to open something so that it is no longer tied or fastened. • *I **undid** my shoe laces* ❷ to cancel the

effect of something that has been done. • *He has **undone** all our work.* ❸ On a computer, when you undo a change, you change it back.

undress VERB **undresses, undressing, undressed**
to take your clothes off

unearth VERB **unearths, unearthing, unearthed**
to dig something up or discover it

unearthly ADJECTIVE
strange and slightly frightening • *We heard an **unearthly** sound.*

uneasy ADJECTIVE **uneasier, uneasiest**
anxious or worried
➤ **uneasily** ADVERB
➤ **uneasiness** NOUN • *Her **uneasiness** grew as she waited.*

unemployed ADJECTIVE
without a job
➤ **unemployment** NOUN

uneven ADJECTIVE
not level; flat or regular • *The path was **uneven**.*

unexpected ADJECTIVE
not expected; surprising
➤ **unexpectedly** ADVERB

unfair ADJECTIVE
not right or reasonable; unjust

unfamiliar ADJECTIVE
that you have not seen or experienced before
• *An **unfamiliar** face appeared.*

unfasten
VERB **unfastens, unfastening, unfastened**
to open something so it is no longer fastened

unfit ADJECTIVE
❶ not suitable • *The food was **unfit** to eat.*
❷ If someone is unfit, they are not fit or fully healthy.

unfold VERB **unfolds, unfolding, unfolded**
❶ to open or spread something out • *I **unfolded** the map.* ❷ When a story unfolds, it becomes known gradually.

unforgettable ADJECTIVE
impossible to forget

unfortunate ADJECTIVE
unlucky; regrettable
➤ **unfortunately** ADVERB • *Unfortunately, I have to leave early.*

unfriendly ADJECTIVE
not friendly

ungrateful ADJECTIVE
not grateful

unhappy ADJECTIVE **unhappier, unhappiest**
not happy or pleased
➤ **unhappily** ADVERB ➤ **unhappiness** NOUN

unharmed ADJECTIVE
not hurt • *The animals escaped the fire **unharmed**.*

unhealthy ADJECTIVE **unhealthier, unhealthiest**
❶ not in good health ❷ not good for you
• *an **unhealthy** diet of fast food*

unicorn NOUN **unicorns**
an imaginary animal that looks like a horse with a long straight horn growing from its forehead

unicorn

uniform NOUN **uniforms**
special clothes worn by members of a school, army or organisation

unimportant ADJECTIVE
not important
➤ **unimportance** NOUN

uninhabited ADJECTIVE
If a place is uninhabited, no one lives there.

union NOUN **unions**
an organisation of workers, countries, people or groups that agree to do something together or help each other

unique (say yoo-**neek**) ADJECTIVE
If something is unique, it is the only one of its kind.
• *Everyone's fingerprints are* **unique***.*

unison (say yoo-niss-on) NOUN
➤ **in unison** said or done by several people at exactly the same time

unit NOUN **units**
❶ an amount used in measuring or counting, such as a centimetre or a pound • *An hour is a* **unit** *of time.*
❷ (in mathematics) any whole number less than 10
❸ a section in a textbook or course of study • *We're on unit 4.* ❹ a piece of furniture or equipment that fits with others like it • *kitchen* **units** ❺ a section within an organisation

unite VERB **unites, uniting, united**
If people unite or if something unites them, they join together and act as one group.

universal ADJECTIVE
including everyone and everything

universe NOUN
The universe is everything that exists, including the earth and all the stars and planets.

university NOUN **universities**
a place where you study for a degree

unjust ADJECTIVE
not fair or just
➤ **unjustly** ADVERB

unkempt ADJECTIVE
untidy and not looked after • *He looked dirty and* **unkempt***.*

unkind ADJECTIVE **unkinder, unkindest**
not kind; mean or cruel
➤ **unkindly** ADVERB ➤ **unkindness** NOUN

unknown ADJECTIVE
If someone or something is unknown, you do not know who or what they are or anything about them.
• *It was painted by an* **unknown** *artist.*

unleaded ADJECTIVE
unleaded petrol does not contain lead

unless CONJUNCTION
except if • *We cannot go* **unless** *we are invited.*

unlike PREPOSITION
not like; different to • ***Unlike*** *me, she enjoys sport.*

unlikely ADJECTIVE **unlikelier, unlikeliest**
not likely to happen or be true

unload VERB **unloads, unloading, unloaded**
to take things out of a container or off a vehicle

unlock VERB **unlocks, unlocking, unlocked**
to open a door or container with a key

unlucky ADJECTIVE **unluckier, unluckiest**
not lucky; unfortunate
➤ **unluckily** ADVERB

unmistakable ADJECTIVE
impossible to mistake for something else
➤ **unmistakably** ADVERB • *That is* **unmistakably** *her writing.*

unnatural ADJECTIVE
not natural or normal
➤ **unnaturally** ADVERB

unnecessary ADJECTIVE
not needed
➤ **unnecessarily** ADVERB

unpack VERB **unpacks, unpacking, unpacked**
to take things out of a suitcase or bag

unpleasant ADJECTIVE
not enjoyable or not nice • *There was an* **unpleasant** *smell.*
➤ **unpleasantly** ADVERB • *He smiled* **unpleasantly***.*

unplug VERB **unplugs, unplugging, unplugged**
to disconnect an electrical device by taking its plug out of the socket

unpopular ADJECTIVE
not liked by many people

unravel VERB **unravels, unravelling, unravelled**
❶ If something knitted or tangled unravels, it loosens and all the knots or tangles come apart.
❷ To unravel a mystery is to solve it.

unreal ADJECTIVE
not really existing or happening

unreasonable ADJECTIVE
not reasonable or fair

unrest NOUN
discontent and trouble among a group of people

unroll VERB unrolls, unrolling, unrolled
to open something that has been rolled up

unruly (say un-roo-lee) ADJECTIVE
badly behaved or difficult to control

unsafe ADJECTIVE
not safe; dangerous

unscrew VERB unscrews, unscrewing, unscrewed
to undo something by turning it or by removing screws

unseen ADJECTIVE
not seen or noticed • He slipped into the building unseen.

unselfish ADJECTIVE
not selfish; thinking of others rather than yourself

unsteady ADJECTIVE unsteadier, unsteadiest
shaking, wobbling or likely to fall
➤ **unsteadily** ADVERB

unsuccessful ADJECTIVE
not successful
➤ **unsuccessfully** ADVERB

unsuitable ADJECTIVE
not suitable
➤ **unsuitably** ADVERB

unsure ADJECTIVE
not sure; uncertain • I was unsure of what to do.

unthinkable ADJECTIVE
so bad or unlikely that you do not want to think about it

untidy ADJECTIVE untidier, untidiest
messy; not tidy

untie VERB unties, untying, untied
to undo something that has been tied

until PREPOSITION, CONJUNCTION
up to a particular time or event • The shop is open until 8 o'clock. • I'll wait until she gets here.

untold ADJECTIVE
impossible to measure or describe • The storm caused untold damage.

untrue ADJECTIVE
not true; false

unused ADJECTIVE (say un-yoozd)
not yet used
➤ **unused to something** (say un-yoost)
not familiar with something • The creature was unused to daylight.

unusual ADJECTIVE
not usual; not normal
➤ **unusually** ADVERB • She looked unusually pale.

unwanted ADJECTIVE
not wanted

unwell ADJECTIVE
ill

unwilling ADJECTIVE
If you are unwilling to do something, you do not want to do it.
➤ **unwillingly** ADVERB ➤ **unwillingness** NOUN

unwind VERB (rhymes with find) unwinds, unwinding, unwound
to remove something that has been wound around something • She unwound her scarf.

unwise ADJECTIVE
foolish • It would be unwise to go alone.

unworthy ADJECTIVE unworthier, unworthiest
not good enough for something; not deserving something

unwrap VERB unwraps, unwrapping, unwrapped
to take the wrapping off something

up ADVERB
❶ towards a higher place • Lift the lid up slowly.
❷ upright • Sit up. ❸ towards a higher level
• The temperature has gone up.

a
b
c
d
e
f
g
h
i
j
k
l
m
n
o
p
q
r
s
t
u
v
w
x
y
z

up *PREPOSITION*
in or to a higher position on something • *We ran* **up** *the stairs.*

update *VERB* **updates, updating, updated**
to make something more modern or new; to replace something with the latest version • *You need to* **update** *the software.*

upheaval *NOUN* **upheavals**
a sudden major change or disturbance

uphill *ADVERB*
up a slope • *The path led* **uphill**.

uphold *VERB* **upholds, upholding, upheld**
to support something

uplands *NOUN*
the highest part of a country or region

> **BUILD** YOUR VOCABULARY
> Look at **lowlands** and **highlands**.

upload *VERB* **uploads, uploading, uploaded**
To upload data is to copy it from a computer or phone onto the Internet.

upon *PREPOSITION*
on

upper *ADJECTIVE*
higher • *the* **upper** *floors of the building*

upper case *NOUN*
capital letters

> **BUILD** YOUR VOCABULARY
> Look at **lower case**.

upright *ADJECTIVE, ADVERB*
straight up; vertical • *an* **upright** *position* • *He was sitting* **upright** *in bed.*

uproar *NOUN*
a loud or angry noise or disturbance • *The room was in* **uproar**.

upset *ADJECTIVE*
unhappy or worried about something
upset *VERB* **upsets, upsetting, upset**
❶ to make someone unhappy or worried ❷ to knock something over and spill its contents

upside-down (*or* **upside down**)
ADJECTIVE, ADVERB
with the upper part underneath; the wrong way round
'We're UPSIDE DOWN!' *gasped Mr Twit. 'We must be upside down. We are standing on the ceiling looking down at the floor!'*—THE TWITS, Roald Dahl

upstairs *ADVERB, ADJECTIVE*
to or on a higher floor in a building

upstream *ADVERB*
in the direction opposite to the flow of a river or stream

> **BUILD** YOUR VOCABULARY
> The opposite is **downstream**.

upward (*also* **upwards**) *ADJECTIVE, ADVERB*
going towards what is higher

> **BUILD** YOUR VOCABULARY
> The opposite is **downward** or **downwards**.

urban *ADJECTIVE*
in or to do with towns or cities • *the* **urban** *environment*

> **BUILD** YOUR VOCABULARY
> Look at **rural**.

urchin *NOUN* **urchins**
a dirty or raggedly dressed child

Urdu *NOUN*
a language spoken in northern India and Pakistan

> ✳ WORD STORY
> The words **khaki** and **pyjamas** come from Urdu.

urge *VERB* **urges, urging, urged**
to try to persuade someone to do something

urge *NOUN* **urges**
a sudden strong desire to do something • *I had an* **urge** *to giggle.*

urgent *ADJECTIVE*
needing to be done or dealt with immediately
➤ **urgently** *ADVERB*

urine (*say* **yoor**-in) *NOUN*
waste liquid that you pass out of your body in the toilet

urn NOUN urns
a large vase

us PRONOUN
a word used instead of *we*
when it comes after a verb or
a preposition • *I think they
saw us.* • *They are waving
to us.*

BUILD YOUR VOCABULARY
Us is used as the **object** of a verb.

use *(say yooz)* VERB uses, using, used
to do an action or job with something • *You can use
my pen.* • *What is this used for?*
➤ **used to** If you used to do something, you did it
in the past but do not do it now. • *We used to live in
London when I was a baby.*

use *(say yooss)* NOUN uses
something that a thing can be used for; a purpose
• *Can you find a use for this box?*

used ADJECTIVE
(say yoozd) owned before; second-hand • *They sell
used bicycles.*
➤ **used to something** familiar with something
(say yoost) because you have seen it or done it a lot
• *She soon got used to her new school.*

BUILD YOUR VOCABULARY
An opposite is **unused**.

useful ADJECTIVE
helpful; good for doing something • *This dictionary
is very useful.*

useless ADJECTIVE
❶ not having any use ❷ *(informal)* very bad at doing
something • *I'm useless at drawing.*

user NOUN users
someone who uses something • *a wheelchair user*

usher VERB ushers, ushering, ushered
to lead someone into or out of a place • *We were
ushered into the dining room.*

usual ADJECTIVE
as happens often or all the time; normal • *He sat in
his usual place.* • *She was late as usual.*

usually ADVERB
on most occasions; normally • *We usually have pizza
on Fridays.*

utensil *(say yoo-ten-sil)*
NOUN utensils
a tool or device, especially one
you use in the house

utmost ADJECTIVE
greatest • *Guard this letter
with the utmost care.*

utensil

utter VERB utters, uttering,
uttered
to say something or make a
sound • *The creature uttered a
high-pitched shriek.*

utter ADJECTIVE
complete; absolute • *He stared at me in utter
amazement.*
➤ **utterly** ADVERB • *The day was utterly ruined.*

a
b
c
d
e
f
g
h
i
k
l
m
n
o
p
q
r
s
t
u
v
w
x
y
z

Vv

⚙ **V** is the only letter in the English language that is never silent. The letter *g* is silent in *gnome*, and *b* is silent in *lamb* but when **v** is used in a word it is always pronounced.

⚙ Try finding some other examples of silent letters!

V *ABBREVIATION*
5 in Roman numerals

vacancy *NOUN* **vacancies**
a job or a room that is available and not taken

vacant *ADJECTIVE*
❶ free; not taken • *There were no **vacant** seats.*
❷ not showing any expression • *He had a **vacant** look.*

vacation *(say* vay-kay-shun*) NOUN* **vacations**
a holiday

vaccinate *(say* vak-sin-ayt*) VERB* **vaccinates, vaccinating, vaccinated**
to inject someone with a vaccine to protect them against a disease
➤ **vaccination** *NOUN*

vaccine *(say* vak-seen*) NOUN* **vaccines**
a medicine injected into people to protect them from a disease

vacuum *NOUN* **vacuums**
a completely empty space with nothing, including air, in it

vacuum *VERB* **vacuums, vacuuming, vacuumed**
to clean something using a vacuum cleaner

vacuum cleaner *NOUN* **vacuum cleaners**
an electrical device that sucks up dust and dirt from the floor

vagina *(say* vaj-**eye**-na*) NOUN* **vaginas**
A woman's vagina is the passage that leads from the outside of her body to her womb.

vague *ADJECTIVE* **vaguer, vaguest**
not definite or clear • *I only have a **vague** memory of his face.*
➤ **vaguely** *ADVERB*

vain *ADJECTIVE* **vainer, vainest**
❶ too proud of yourself, especially of how you look
❷ A vain attempt is unsuccessful or useless.
➤ **in vain** unsuccessfully • *I tried **in vain** to find it.*
➤ **vainly** *ADVERB*

valentine *NOUN* **valentines**
❶ a card you send to someone you love on St Valentine's Day, 14th February ❷ Someone's valentine is the person they love and send a valentine to.

valiant *ADJECTIVE*
brave; courageous
➤ **valiantly** *ADVERB*

valid *ADJECTIVE*
legally able to be used or accepted • *Your ticket is not **valid**.*

valley *NOUN* **valleys**
an area of low land between hills

valour *NOUN*
bravery; courage

valuable *ADJECTIVE*
❶ worth a lot of money ❷ very useful or important
• *She gave me valuable advice.*

valuables *NOUN*
things that are worth a lot of money

value *NOUN* values
❶ the amount of money that something is worth ❷ the usefulness or importance of something
value *VERB* values, valuing, valued
to think something is important or worth having
• *I value her friendship.*

valve *NOUN* valves
a device used to control the flow of gas or liquid

vampire *NOUN* vampires
in stories, a creature that sucks people's blood

van *NOUN* vans
a vehicle with a large covered back part for carrying goods

vandal *NOUN* vandals
someone who deliberately breaks or damages things

vanilla *NOUN*
a sweet flavouring made from the pods of a tropical plant

vanish *VERB*
vanishes, vanishing, vanished
to disappear • *The magician vanished in a puff of smoke.*

vanity *NOUN*
too much pride in yourself, especially in how you look

vanquish *VERB* vanquishes, vanquishing, vanquished
to defeat someone

vaporise *(also* **vaporize***) VERB* vaporises, vaporising, vaporised
to turn into vapour

vapour *NOUN* vapours
a mass of tiny drops of liquid in the air, for example mist or steam

variation *NOUN* variations
a change or difference • *There have been slight variations in temperature.*

varied *ADJECTIVE*
of various kinds • *She has varied interests.*

variety *NOUN* varieties
❶ a number of different kinds of something
• *He's had a variety of jobs.* ❷ a particular kind of something • *There are many varieties of butterfly.*

various *ADJECTIVE*
several of different kinds • *We talked about various things.*

varnish *NOUN* varnishes
a liquid that dries to form a hard shiny surface
varnish *VERB* varnishes, varnishing, varnished
to put varnish on something

vary *VERB* varies, varying, varied
to change or be different • *The weather varies a lot here.*

vase *(say* vahz*) NOUN* vases
a jar used for holding flowers or as an ornament

a b c d e f g h i j k l m n o p q r s t u **v** w x y z

vast ADJECTIVE
very large or wide • *the vast expanse of outer space*
➤ **vastly** ADVERB

vat NOUN **vats**
a very large container for holding liquid

vault VERB **vaults, vaulting, vaulted**
If you vault something or vault over it, you jump over it using your hands or a pole to help you.

vault NOUN **vaults**
❶ a secure room for storing money and valuables
❷ an arched roof

veal NOUN
meat from a calf

Veda NOUN
the ancient writings of the Hindu religion

veer VERB **veers, veering, veered**
to swerve or change direction suddenly
• *He suddenly veered to the left.*

vegan (say **vee**-gan) NOUN **vegans**
someone who does not use or eat any products made from animals

vegan (say **vee**-gan) ADJECTIVE
containing no animal products

vegetable NOUN **vegetables**
a plant that can be used as food

vegetarian (say vej-it-**tair**-ee-an) NOUN **vegetarians**
someone who does not eat meat

vegetarian (say vej-it-**tair**-ee-an) ADJECTIVE
containing no meat

vegetation NOUN
plants that are growing somewhere

vehicle NOUN **vehicles**
something that is used for transporting people or things, especially on land. Cars, buses, trains and lorries are vehicles.

veil NOUN **veils**
a piece of thin material to cover a woman's face or head

veil VERB **veils, veiling, veiled**
to cover something with a veil or thin layer • *Mist veiled the mountains.*

vein NOUN **veins**
Your veins are the tubes that carry blood towards your heart from other parts of your body.

⚙ BUILD YOUR VOCABULARY
Look at **artery**.

velociraptor NOUN **velociraptors**
a small fast-moving dinosaur with large claws on its back legs

velocity (say vil-**oss**-it-ee) NOUN **velocities**
speed in a particular direction

velvet NOUN
a soft material with short furry fibres on one side
➤ **velvety** ADJECTIVE • *The rabbit has velvety ears.*

venerable ADJECTIVE
worthy of respect because of being so old

vengeance NOUN
the act of harming or punishing someone because they have done harm to you

vengeful ADJECTIVE
wanting revenge

venison NOUN
meat from a deer

Venn diagram NOUN **Venn diagrams**
a diagram using circles to show how sets of things relate to one another

venom NOUN
❶ poison from a snake ❷ bitter hatred
➤ **venomous** ADJECTIVE • *a venomous snake*

vent NOUN **vents**
an opening in something, especially to let out smoke or gas

ventilation NOUN
pipes, openings and other things that allow fresh air to enter and move around a place

venture VERB **ventures, venturing, ventured**
to go somewhere or try something even though it might be risky

venture NOUN **ventures**
something new or risky that you decide to do

veranda (say ver-**an**-da) NOUN **verandas**
an open terrace with a roof along the outside of a house

verb NOUN verbs
a word that shows what someone or something is doing or what is happening, such as *go, make, think* or *be*. Every clause must have a verb.

BUILD YOUR VOCABULARY
Verb is a **word class**.

verbal ADJECTIVE
spoken rather than written • *We had a verbal agreement.*
➤ **verbally** ADVERB

verdict NOUN verdicts
the decision reached by a judge or jury about whether someone is guilty of a crime

verge NOUN verges
a strip of grass beside a road or path
➤ **on the verge of something** very close to doing something • *She was on the verge of tears.*

vermin NOUN
animals or insects that damage crops or food or carry disease, such as rats or fleas

verse NOUN verses
❶ one part of a song or poem that is not the chorus • *Let's sing the last verse.* ❷ poetry

version NOUN versions
one form of something, which is different from other forms • *I downloaded the latest version of the app.*

versus PREPOSITION
against or competing with • *The final was Brazil versus Russia.*

vertebrate NOUN vertebrates
an animal with a backbone

BUILD YOUR VOCABULARY
Look at **invertebrate**.

vertex NOUN vertices
❶ a point where the sides of a shape meet • *A square has four vertices and a cube has eight.* ❷ the highest point of something pointed

BUILD YOUR VOCABULARY
A synonym for the second meaning is **apex**.

vertical ADJECTIVE
going straight up at a right angle to a surface
➤ **vertically** ADVERB

very ADVERB
extremely • *It is very cold today.*
very ADJECTIVE
exact; actual • *You're the very person I wanted to see.*

Vesak (say ves-ak) NOUN
the most important Buddhist festival, usually held in May

vessel NOUN vessels
❶ a boat or ship ❷ a container for liquids
❸ *(also* **blood vessel***)* a tube inside your body that carries blood

vest NOUN vests
a piece of underwear worn on the top half of your body

vet NOUN vets
a person trained to treat sick animals

veteran NOUN veterans
❶ a person with long experience of something
❷ a soldier who has fought in a war

veterinary (say vet-trin-ree or vet-in-ree) ADJECTIVE
to do with the medical treatment of animals

vex VERB vexes, vexing, vexed
to annoy someone or cause them worry
➤ **vexation** NOUN

via (say vy-a) PREPOSITION
going through • *The train goes from Edinburgh to London via York.*

viaduct (say vy-a-dukt) NOUN viaducts
a high bridge carrying a road or railway across a valley

vibrate VERB vibrates, vibrating, vibrated
to move quickly from side to side with small movements • *Sound waves make your eardrum vibrate.*
➤ **vibration** NOUN

vicar NOUN vicars
a Christian religious leader in charge of a parish (a district with its own church)

blood vessels

a
b
c
d
e
f
g
h
i
j
k
l
m
n
o
p
q
r
s
t
u
v
w
x
y
z

vice *NOUN* **vices**
a bad or evil habit

vicinity *NOUN* **vicinities**
the area near or surrounding a place • *Is there a supermarket in the vicinity?*

vicious *(say vish-us) ADJECTIVE*
violent and cruel
➤ **viciously** *ADVERB* • *She kicked and fought viciously.*

victim *NOUN* **victims**
someone who is harmed by an accident, disaster or crime • *He was the victim of a robbery.*

victor *NOUN* **victors**
the winner of a battle, contest or game

Victorian *ADJECTIVE*
from the time when Queen Victoria reigned (1837-1901)

victorious *ADJECTIVE*
If someone is victorious, they win a battle, contest or game.

victory *NOUN* **victories**
the act of winning a battle, contest or game

video *(say vid-ee-oh) NOUN* **videos**
❶ the recording of moving pictures and sound
❷ a film or recorded programme you can watch on a phone or computer

video *(say vid-ee-oh) VERB* **videoes, videoing, videoed**
to record moving pictures and sound

view *NOUN* **views**
❶ everything you can see from one place • *We had a lovely view from the top of the hill.* ❷ an opinion • *We'd like to hear your views.*

view *VERB* **views, viewing, viewed**
to look at something • *She viewed the mess with alarm.*

viewer *NOUN* **viewers**
someone who watches something, especially a television programme

viewpoint *NOUN* **viewpoints**
a point of view; a way of looking at something • *Whose viewpoint is the story told from?*

vigorous *ADJECTIVE*
full of strength and energy • *He gave the rug a vigorous shake.*
➤ **vigorously** *ADVERB*

vigour *NOUN*
strength and energy

Viking *NOUN* **Vikings**
a Scandinavian pirate or trader in the 8th-11th centuries
➤ **Viking** *ADJECTIVE* • *a Viking longship*

vile *ADJECTIVE* **viler, vilest**
disgusting; very bad • *What a vile smell.*

villa *NOUN* **villas**
a house, especially a large one in its own grounds

village *NOUN* **villages**
a group of houses and other buildings in the country, smaller than a town

villager *NOUN* **villagers**
someone who lives in a village

villain *NOUN* **villains**
a wicked person or criminal

vine *NOUN* **vines**
a plant on which grapes grow

vinegar *NOUN*
a sour liquid used to flavour food

vineyard *(say vin-yard) NOUN* **vineyards**
an area of land where grapes are grown for making wine

viola *(say vee-oh-la) NOUN* **violas**
a musical instrument like a slightly larger violin with a lower pitch

BUILD YOUR VOCABULARY
A **viola** is a **stringed instrument**.

violence *NOUN*
❶ behaviour that involves using force to hurt or kill people ❷ great power that can cause damage • *We weren't prepared for the violence of the storm.*

violent *ADJECTIVE*
❶ using force to hurt or kill people ❷ A violent storm or emotion is very powerful.
➤ **violently** *ADVERB*

violet NOUN **violets**

❶ a blue-purple colour ❷ a small plant that usually has purple flowers

violin NOUN **violins**

a musical instrument with four strings. You hold it under your chin and play it with a bow.

BUILD YOUR VOCABULARY

A **violin** is a **stringed instrument**.

viper NOUN **vipers**

a small poisonous snake

virtual ADJECTIVE

using computers to create an image or environment that is like the real world • *Click here to go on a virtual tour of the gallery.*

virtually ADVERB

in effect; almost • *They are virtually identical.*

virtual reality NOUN

an image or environment created by a computer that allows you to experience something that is like the real world

virtue NOUN **virtues**

❶ moral goodness ❷ a good quality in a person's character • *He has many virtues.*

virus *(say* vy-rus*)* NOUN **viruses**

❶ a tiny organism that can cause disease ❷ a disease caused by a virus • *He was off school with a virus.* ❸ a computer program that is designed to cause damage or problems

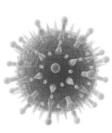

virus

visibility NOUN

the distance that you can see clearly • *Visibility was only 10 metres in the fog.*

visible ADJECTIVE

able to be seen • *A ship was visible on the horizon.*
➤ **visibly** ADVERB • *She was visibly shocked.*

vision NOUN **visions**

❶ the ability to see • *She has good vision.*
❷ something that you see or imagine

visit VERB **visits, visiting, visited**

To visit a place or person is to go to see them or stay there.
➤ **visitor** NOUN • *We had a visitor.*

visit NOUN **visits**

a short stay at a place or with a person

visor *(say* vy-zer*)* NOUN **visors**

the part of a helmet that closes over your face

vital ADJECTIVE

extremely important; essential
➤ **vitally** ADVERB • *Sleep is vitally important.*

vitamin NOUN **vitamins**

a substance found in foods, which your body needs to stay healthy. There are several different types of vitamin. • *Fresh fruit contains a lot of vitamin C.*

vivid ADJECTIVE

❶ Vivid colours are bright and strong. ❷ clear and powerful • *She wrote a vivid description of the storm.*
➤ **vividly** ADVERB • *I remember it vividly.*

vixen NOUN **vixens**

a female fox

vlog NOUN **vlogs**

a website on which someone regularly posts short videos about something

vlog VERB **vlogs, vlogged, vlogging**

to make and post videos for a vlog
➤ **vlogger** NOUN ➤ **vlogging** NOUN

vocabulary NOUN **vocabularies**

❶ the words used in a language ❷ Someone's vocabulary is the words that they know and use.

a b c d e f g h i j k l m n o p q r s t u v w x y z

vocal *ADJECTIVE*
to do with or using the voice

voice *NOUN* voices
the sound you make when you speak or sing
voice *VERB* voices, voicing, voiced
to express something • *He voiced his concerns.*

void *NOUN* voids
an empty space or hole

volcano *NOUN* volcanoes
a mountain with a hole at the top through which hot liquid rock sometimes bursts from inside the earth
➤ **volcanic** *ADJECTIVE*

BUILD YOUR VOCABULARY
Look at **crater, dormant, erupt, extinct** and **lava.**

✳ **WORD STORY**
The word **volcano** comes from *Vulcan*, the Roman god of fire.

vole *NOUN* voles
a small animal similar to a rat with a rounded nose

BUILD YOUR VOCABULARY
A **vole** is a **rodent.**

volley *NOUN* volleys
a number of bullets or missiles fired at the same time

volleyball *NOUN*
a game in which two teams hit a large ball over a net with their hands

volt *NOUN* volts
a unit for measuring the force of an electric current

voltage *NOUN* voltages
electric force measured in volts

volume *NOUN* volumes
❶ the amount of space something takes up • *What is the volume of liquid in this jug?* ❷ the loudness of a sound • *Turn down the volume!* ❸ a book, especially one of a set

voluntary *ADJECTIVE*
done because someone wants to, not because they are paid or made to do it

volunteer *VERB* volunteers, volunteering, volunteered
to offer to do something that you do not have to do

volunteer *NOUN* volunteers
someone who offers to do something that they are not paid or made to do

vomit *VERB* vomits, vomiting, vomited
to bring food back from your stomach through your mouth

vortex *NOUN*
vortices
a whirling spiral; a whirlpool or whirlwind

vote *VERB* votes, voting, voted
to show your choice or opinion by putting up your hand or making a mark on a piece of paper
➤ **voter** *NOUN*
vote *NOUN* votes
a choice you make by putting up your hand or making a mark on a piece of paper

voucher *NOUN* vouchers
a piece of paper that can be used instead of money to pay, or pay less, for something

vow *VERB* vows, vowing, vowed
to make a solemn promise to do something
vow *NOUN* vows
a solemn promise

vowel *NOUN* vowels
Vowels are the letters **a, e, i, o, u** and sometimes **y.**

BUILD YOUR VOCABULARY
Look at **consonant.**

voyage *NOUN* voyages
a long journey by ship or in a spacecraft

vulgar *ADJECTIVE*
rude; without good manners

vulnerable *ADJECTIVE*
able to be harmed or attacked easily

vulture *NOUN* vultures
a large bird that eats dead animals
BUILD YOUR VOCABULARY
A **vulture** is a **scavenger.**

The sound /w/ used to be written as *vv* or *uu—double v* or *double u*. Eventually *double u* began to be written and thought of as a single, separate letter.

In many other languages, for example French, Danish, Norwegian and Swedish, the name of this letter is *double v*.

wad NOUN **wads**
a thick bundle of paper or cloth

waddle VERB **waddles, waddling, waddled**
to walk with short steps, rocking from side to side, like a duck
Aunt Sponge, fat and pulpy as a jellyfish, came waddling up behind her sister to see what was going on.—JAMES AND THE GIANT PEACH, Roald Dahl

wade VERB **wades, wading, waded**
to walk through water or mud

wafer NOUN **wafers**
a thin kind of biscuit, often eaten with ice cream

waffle NOUN **waffles**
a crisp square pancake with a pattern of squares on it

waffle VERB **waffles, waffling, waffled**
to talk or write a lot without saying anything important or interesting

wag VERB **wags, wagging, wagged**
❶ When a dog wags its tail, it moves it quickly from side to side. ❷ If you wag your finger, you move it up and down or from side to side.

wage NOUN (also **wages**)
money paid regularly to someone for the job they do

wage VERB **wages, waging, waged**
To wage a war is to fight it.

wager VERB **wagers, wagering, wagered** (old use)
to bet • *I wager he'll be back.*
wager NOUN **wagers**
a bet

waggle VERB **waggles, waggling, waggled**
to move something quickly from side to side

wagon NOUN **wagons**
a cart with four wheels, pulled by a horse or ox

wagtail NOUN **wagtails**
a small bird with a long tail

wail VERB **wails, wailing, wailed**
to make a long sad cry
wail NOUN **wails**
a sound of wailing

waist NOUN **waists**
the narrow part in the middle of your body

waistcoat NOUN **waistcoats**
a piece of clothing without sleeves, worn over a shirt and under a jacket

wait VERB **waits, waiting, waited**
to stay somewhere until something happens • *Wait here until I come back.* • *I waited an hour for the bus.*
wait NOUN **waits**
a time spent waiting • *We had a long wait.*

⚠ **WATCH OUT!**
Do not confuse **wait** with **weight**, the amount that something or someone **weighs**.

waiter NOUN **waiters**
a man who takes food to tables in a restaurant

a b c d e f g h i j k l m n o p q r s t u v w x y z

waitress NOUN waitresses
a woman who takes food to tables in a restaurant

wake VERB wakes, waking, woke, woken
❶ When you wake or wake up, you stop sleeping.
• *He woke early.* ❷ To wake someone or wake them up is to make them stop sleeping. • *You've woken the baby.*

wake NOUN wakes
the trail left on the water by a ship or boat

waken VERB wakens, wakening, wakened
to wake up or to wake someone

walk VERB walks, walking, walked
to move along on your feet at normal speed
➤ **walker** NOUN
walk NOUN walks
A walk is a journey on foot.

wall NOUN walls
❶ The walls of a building are the parts that hold up the roof and that separate the rooms. ❷ a structure built from stone, bricks or concrete around an area

wallaby (*say* wol-a-bee) NOUN wallabies
an animal similar to a small kangaroo

BUILD YOUR VOCABULARY
A wallaby is a **marsupial**.

wallet NOUN wallets
a small flat folding case for holding money and bank cards

wallop VERB wallops, walloping, walloped
(*informal*)
to hit someone or something hard

wallow VERB wallows, wallowing, wallowed
to roll about in water or mud

wallpaper NOUN wallpapers
paper used to cover the walls of rooms

walnut NOUN walnuts
a kind of nut with a wrinkled surface

walrus NOUN walruses
a large Arctic sea animal that looks like a large seal with two long tusks

waltz NOUN waltzes
a dance with three beats to a bar
waltz VERB waltzes, waltzing, waltzed
to dance a waltz

wand NOUN wands
a short thin rod used by a magician, wizard or fairy

wander VERB wanders, wandering, wandered
❶ to walk around in no particular direction
❷ to stray or get lost • *Don't let the dog wander off.*
➤ **wanderer** NOUN

wane VERB wanes, waning, waned
❶ When the moon wanes, the bright part seen in the sky gets smaller.

BUILD YOUR VOCABULARY
The opposite is **wax**.

❷ to become less, smaller or weaker
• *His enthusiasm was waning.*

want VERB wants, wanting, wanted
If you want something, you would like to have it or do it.

war NOUN wars
fighting between nations or armies

warble VERB warbles, warbling, warbled
If a bird or piece of equipment warbles, it makes a high musical sound.

ward NOUN wards
❶ a long room with beds for patients in a hospital
❷ a child looked after by a guardian
ward VERB wards, warding, warded
➤ **To ward something off** is to keep it away.

warden NOUN wardens
an official who looks after a place, for example a college, prison or park, and makes sure rules are obeyed there

wardrobe NOUN wardrobes
a tall cupboard for hanging clothes

warehouse NOUN **warehouses**
a large building where goods are stored

wares PLURAL NOUN
goods offered for sale

warfare NOUN
fighting a war

warlike ADJECTIVE
enjoying war or likely to start a war

warm ADJECTIVE **warmer, warmest**
❶ fairly hot; not cold • *a warm day* • *It's nice and warm in here.* ❷ Warm clothes keep you warm. ❸ friendly and enthusiastic • *a warm smile*
➤ **warmly** ADVERB

warm VERB **warms, warming, warmed**
to make something warm • *I felt the sun warming my face.*

warmth NOUN
❶ the quality of being fairly hot or not cold • *We huddled together for warmth.* ❷ friendliness and enthusiasm • *We were greeted with such warmth and kindness that we never felt homesick.*

warn VERB **warns, warning, warned**
to tell someone about a danger or difficulty that might affect them

warning NOUN **warnings**
something said or written to warn someone

warp (*say* worp) VERB **warps, warping, warped**
If something warps or is warped, it becomes bent or twisted out of shape.

warrant NOUN **warrants**
a document that gives the police the right to arrest someone or search a place

warren NOUN **warrens**
❶ an area where there are many rabbit burrows ❷ a complicated set of streets or passageways through which it is difficult to find your way

warrior NOUN **warriors**
a fighter in battles; a soldier

wart NOUN **warts**
a small hard lump on your skin

warthog NOUN **warthogs**
an African wild pig with curved tusks

wary (*rhymes with* **fairy**) ADJECTIVE **warier, wariest**
cautious and suspicious
➤ **warily** ADVERB • *We looked at one another warily.*

⚠ **WATCH OUT!**
Do not confuse **wary**, meaning 'cautious', with **weary**, meaning 'tired'.

was VERB (the past tense of **be** used with I, he, she and it)
• *Miss Cale was my teacher last year.*

wash VERB **washes, washing, washed**
❶ to clean something with water and soap • *I'll wash the cups.* ❷ to clean yourself with water and soap • *Go and wash.*
➤ **To wash up** is to wash the dishes and cutlery after a meal.

washing NOUN
clothes that need to be washed or have been washed

washing machine NOUN **washing machines**
a machine for washing clothes

washing-up NOUN
dishes and cutlery that need to be washed after a meal

wasp NOUN **wasps**
a stinging insect with black and yellow stripes

waste VERB **wastes, wasting, wasted**
❶ to use more of something than you need to ❷ to fail to use something • *You wasted an opportunity.*

waste NOUN **wastes**
❶ A waste of something is the action of wasting it. • *It's a waste of time.* ❷ things that are thrown away or not wanted

waste ADJECTIVE
left over or thrown away because it is not wanted • *Recycle your waste paper.*

wasteful ADJECTIVE
wasting things or not using them well • *It's wasteful to use so much packaging.*

a b c d e f g h i j k l m n o p q r s t u v w x y z

watch *VERB* watches, watching, watched
❶ to look at someone or something for some time
• *Watch! I'm going to dive in.* • *We watched a film.*
❷ to pay attention to something or to guard it
• *Watch for the traffic lights to change.*
➤ **To watch out** is to be careful about something.
watch *NOUN* watches
a device like a small clock, usually worn on your wrist

watchful *ADJECTIVE*
alert and watching carefully

watchman *NOUN* watchmen
someone whose job is to guard a building at night

water *NOUN* waters
the clear colourless liquid that falls from the sky as rain and that all living things need
water *VERB* waters, watering, watered
❶ To water a plant is to pour water on it. ❷ If your eyes water, they produce tears. If your mouth waters, it produces saliva.

water cycle *NOUN*
the process by which water falls as rain and snow, runs into rivers and lakes, flows into the sea, evaporates into the air to form clouds and then falls again

waterfall *NOUN* waterfalls
a place where a river or stream flows over a cliff or large rock

watermelon *NOUN* watermelons
a large melon with juicy red flesh and a hard green skin

waterproof *ADJECTIVE*
able to keep water out • *a waterproof jacket*

watertight *ADJECTIVE*
made so that water cannot get in or out

waterway *NOUN* waterways
a river or canal that ships can travel on

watery *ADJECTIVE*
❶ like water ❷ full of water or tears • *His eyes were red and watery.* ❸ made weak or thin by adding too much water • *watery soup*

watt *NOUN* watts
a measurement of electric power. 1000 watts is 1 kilowatt.

✳ **WORD STORY**
The **watt** is named after the Scottish engineer James Watt (1736-1819), who invented a type of steam engine.

wave *VERB* waves, waving, waved
❶ to lift your hand and move it from side to side, usually to say hello or goodbye ❷ If something waves or if you wave it, it moves from side to side or up and down. • *Flags were waving in the wind.*
wave *NOUN* waves
❶ a moving ridge on the surface of water, especially on the sea

⚙ **BUILD YOUR VOCABULARY**
Look at **breaker** and **roller**.

❷ *(in science)* a movement in which sound, light or electricity travels

wavelength *NOUN* wavelengths
the size of a sound wave or electric wave

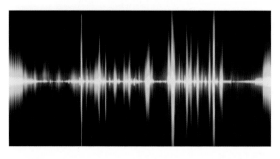

waver *VERB* wavers, wavering, wavered
to be unsteady or uncertain

wavy *ADJECTIVE* wavier, waviest
Wavy hair or a wavy line has smooth curves.

wax *NOUN* waxes
a soft substance that melts easily, used for making candles
➤ **waxy** *ADJECTIVE*

wax VERB waxes, waxing, waxed
When the moon waxes, the bright part seen in the sky gets larger.

BUILD YOUR VOCABULARY
The opposite is **wane**.

way NOUN ways
❶ The way you do something is how you do it. ❷ The way to a place is how you get there. ❸ a distance • *Is it a long way?* ❹ an aspect of something • *It's a good idea in some **ways**.*
➤ **in the way** blocking something

we PRONOUN
I and someone else; I and others

BUILD YOUR VOCABULARY
We is used as the **subject** of a verb.

weak ADJECTIVE weaker, weakest
❶ without much strength or energy ❷ easy to break or bend
➤ **weakly** ADVERB

weaken VERB weakens, weakening, weakened
If something weakens or is weakened, it becomes weaker.

weakness NOUN weaknesses
❶ the state of being weak ❷ Your weaknesses are your faults or the things you do not do well.

wealth NOUN
a large amount of money or property that someone owns

wealthy ADJECTIVE wealthier, wealthiest
having a lot of money or property

weapon NOUN weapons
something used to harm or kill people in a battle or fight

wear VERB wears, wearing, wore, worn
❶ When you wear an item of clothing, you have it on. • *She **wore** a blue dress.* ❷ If something wears or is worn, it becomes damaged by being rubbed or used. • *The carpet has **worn** thin.*
➤ **To wear off** is to become less strong or intense.
➤ **To wear out** is to become old, thin or useless from being used.

weary (rhymes with **cheery**) ADJECTIVE wearier, weariest
very tired
➤ **wearily** ADVERB • *They trudged **wearily** up the hill.*

WATCH OUT!
Do not confuse **weary** meaning 'tired' with **wary** meaning 'cautious'.

weasel NOUN weasels
a small wild animal with a long slim body, similar to a stoat

weather NOUN
the rain, snow, wind, sunshine and temperature at a particular time or place

weather VERB weathers, weathering, weathered
If something weathers or is weathered, it gradually changes shape or colour because of being exposed to weather.

weave VERB weaves, weaving, wove, woven
❶ to make something by crossing threads or strips over and under each other • *The baskets were **woven** from grass.* ❷ (past tense also **weaved**) to move from side to side to get round things in the way • *He **weaved** through the crowd.*

web NOUN webs
❶ a net of thin sticky threads that a spider spins to catch insects ❷ The Web is the Internet. • *I downloaded it from the **Web***

webbed ADJECTIVE
Webbed feet are feet like a duck's, with toes joined by skin.

webcam NOUN webcams
a camera that broadcasts film live over the Internet

website NOUN websites
a place on the Internet where you can get information

wed VERB weds, wedding, wedded, wed
to marry

we'd
Short for *we had* or *we would*. • *We'd (= we had) already left.* • *We'd (= we would) like some more.*

wedding NOUN weddings
the ceremony that takes place when two people get married

wedge NOUN wedges
❶ a piece of wood, metal or plastic that is thick at one end and thin at the other, used to push something apart or hold it still ❷ something shaped like a wedge • *a wedge of cheese*

wedge VERB wedges, wedging, wedged
to push something firmly into place so it stays there • *He wedged a chair under the door handle.*

weed NOUN weeds
a wild plant that grows where it is not wanted

weed VERB weeds, weeding, weeded
to remove weeds from the ground

week NOUN weeks
❶ a period of seven days ❷ the part of the week that does not include the weekend • *We go to bed earlier during the week.*

weekday NOUN weekdays
any day except Saturday and Sunday

weekend NOUN weekends
Saturday and Sunday

weekly ADJECTIVE, ADVERB
every week • *She writes a weekly blog.* • *She updates her blog weekly.*

weep VERB weeps, weeping, wept
to cry • *He wept bitterly.*

weeping willow NOUN weeping willows
a kind of willow tree that has drooping branches

weigh VERB weighs, weighing, weighed
❶ to find out how heavy something or someone is using scales • *We weighed the ingredients.* ❷ If something or someone weighs a particular amount, that is their weight. • *How much do you weigh?*

weight NOUN weights
❶ The weight of something or someone is how heavy they are. ❷ a heavy object or an object that has a certain weight • *He was lifting weights in the gym.*

weir (say weer) NOUN weirs
a small dam across a river or canal to control the flow of water

weird (say weerd) ADJECTIVE weirder, weirdest
very strange or unnatural
➤ **weirdly** ADVERB • *The house was weirdly silent.*

welcome VERB welcomes, welcoming, welcomed
To welcome someone or something is to show that you are pleased when they arrive.

welcome NOUN welcomes
a friendly greeting when someone arrives

welcome ADJECTIVE
❶ If someone is welcome, you are happy they have come. ❷ If something is welcome, you are glad to get it or see it. • *a welcome change*

welfare NOUN
people's health, happiness and comfort

well NOUN wells
a deep hole dug or drilled to get water or oil out of the ground

well ADVERB better, best
❶ in a good or successful way • *You played very well.* ❷ thoroughly • *Stir the mixture well.*
➤ **as well** also

well ADJECTIVE
❶ in good health • *I hope you're well.* ❷ good or satisfactory • *All is well.*

wellingtons or **wellington boots** or (informal) **wellies** PLURAL NOUN
rubber or plastic waterproof boots that cover the lower part of your leg

well-known ADJECTIVE
known to many • *He is a well-known footballer.*

went VERB (past tense of **go**)
• *We went on a class trip to the museum.*

wept VERB (past tense and past participle of **weep**)
• *She wept as she said goodbye.* • *I could have wept when I saw the mess.*

were VERB (the past tense of **be** used with **you**, **we** and **they**) • *The questions were quite difficult.*

werewolf NOUN werewolves
in stories, a person who changes into a wolf when there is a full moon

west NOUN
the direction where the sun sets or a place that is in this direction • *The city is in the **west**.*
west ADVERB
towards the west • *They travelled **west**.*
west ADJECTIVE
coming from the west • *a **west** wind*

western ADJECTIVE
from or to do with the west

wet ADJECTIVE wetter, wettest
❶ covered or soaked in water ❷ not yet set or dry • *The paint is still **wet**.* ❸ rainy • *It's been **wet** all day.*
➤ **wetness** NOUN
wet VERB wets, wetting, wet, wetted
to make something wet

whack VERB whacks, whacking, whacked
to hit someone or something hard
whack NOUN whacks
a hard hit

whale NOUN whales
a very large sea mammal that breathes through a hole on its head

wharf (say worf) NOUN wharves, wharfs
a flat area where ships are loaded or unloaded

what DETERMINER
❶ used to ask which thing • *What kind of bike have you got?* • *What time is it?* ❷ used to emphasise something • *What a lovely day!*

what PRONOUN
❶ which thing or things • *What did you say?* ❷ the thing that • *This is **what** you must do.*

whatever PRONOUN
❶ anything or everything • *Do **whatever** you like.* ❷ no matter what • *I'll be there **whatever** happens.*

wheat NOUN
a cereal plant from which flour is made

wheel NOUN wheels
a round device that turns around its centre, used to move vehicles or to work machinery
wheel VERB wheels, wheeling, wheeled
❶ To wheel a bicycle is to push it along rather than ride it. ❷ to turn in a curve or circle • *She **wheeled** round to face him.*

wheelbarrow NOUN wheelbarrows
a small cart with one wheel at the front and two handles at the back

wheelchair NOUN wheelchairs
a chair with large wheels, for a person who cannot walk well

wheeze VERB wheezes, wheezing, wheezed
to make a whistling or gasping noise as you breathe

whelk NOUN whelks
a shellfish that looks like a snail

BUILD YOUR VOCABULARY
A **whelk** is a **mollusc**.

when ADVERB
at what time • *When can you come to play?*
when CONJUNCTION
at the time that • *The bird flew away **when** I moved.*

whenever CONJUNCTION
at any time; every time • *You can come **whenever** you like.* • *Whenever I see him, he's smiling.*

where ADVERB
in or to what place • *Where have you put the glue?*
where CONJUNCTION
in the place that • *Leave it **where** it is.*

whereabouts NOUN
Something's or someone's whereabouts are the place where they are. • *His **whereabouts** are a mystery.*

whereas CONJUNCTION
while; but • *Owls see better in the dark, **whereas** we see better by day.*

whereupon CONJUNCTION
after which; and then

wherever ADVERB
in or to any place; no matter where • *Sit **wherever** you like.*

a
b
c
d
e
f
g
h
i
j
k
l
m
n
o
p
q
r
s
t
u
v
w
x
y
z

whether CONJUNCTION
if • *I don't know **whether** he's coming.*

which DETERMINER
what particular • *Which way did he go?*

which PRONOUN
what person or thing • *Which is your desk?*

which PRONOUN
the thing just mentioned • *We played football,*
***which** is my favourite sport.*

whichever PRONOUN, DETERMINER
any; no matter which • *Take **whichever** you like.*
• *Take **whichever** bus comes first.*

whiff NOUN whiffs
something you smell for a short time • *There was a*
***whiff** of cheese from the fridge.*

while CONJUNCTION
❶ during the time that • *She sang **while** she*
worked. ❷ but; although • *She is fair, **while** her*
sister is dark.

while NOUN
a period of time • *We rested for a short **while**.*

whilst CONJUNCTION
while

whim NOUN whims
a sudden desire to do or have something

whimper VERB whimpers, whimpering,
whimpered
to cry quietly with a trembling sound

whine VERB whines, whining, whined
❶ to make a long high sad sound ❷ to complain
in an annoying way

whine NOUN whines
a whining sound

whinny VERB whinnies, whinnying,
whinnied
When a horse whinnies, it neighs gently.

whip NOUN whips
a leather cord or strip with a handle, used for hitting
people or animals

whip VERB whips, whipping, whipped
❶ to beat a person or animal with a whip ❷ To whip
cream is to beat it until it becomes thick.

whirl VERB whirls, whirling, whirled
If you whirl something round or if it whirls, it turns
or spins very quickly.

whirlpool NOUN whirlpools
a strong current of water going round in a circle and
pulling things towards it

whirlwind NOUN whirlwinds
a column of strong wind that spins around as it
moves along

whirr VERB whirrs, whirring, whirred
to make a continuous buzzing sound

whirr NOUN whirrs
a continuous buzzing sound

whisk VERB whisks, whisking, whisked
❶ To whisk cream or eggs is to stir them round and
round quickly. ❷ to move something somewhere very
quickly • *A waiter **whisked** my plate away.*

whisk NOUN whisks
a device for whisking eggs or cream

whisker NOUN whiskers
❶ A cat's whiskers are the long stiff hairs on its
face. ❷ A man's whiskers are the hairs growing on
his face.

whisky NOUN whiskies
a very strong alcoholic drink

whisper VERB whispers, whispering,
whispered
to speak very softly or secretly

whisper NOUN whispers
a very soft voice or sound

whistle VERB whistles, whistling, whistled
❶ to make a shrill or musical sound by blowing through your lips ❷ to make a high sound like someone whistling • *The wind* **whistled** *through the forest.*

whistle NOUN
whistles
a small object that makes a shrill sound when you blow into it

white
ADJECTIVE whiter, whitest
❶ of the colour of snow or milk ❷ White people are people with pale skin, especially those whose families originally come from Europe. ❸ White bread or rice has had some parts of the grain removed.

BUILD YOUR VOCABULARY
An opposite of the third meaning is **brown**.

white NOUN whites
❶ a white colour ❷ The white of an egg is the substance round the yolk, which turns white when cooked.

whiteboard NOUN whiteboards
a board with a white surface for writing on with special pens or for projecting information on to from a computer

whiten VERB whitens, whitening, whitened
to make something white

whizz VERB whizzes, whizzing, whizzed
to move very quickly
Blue and yellow smoke shot out from every part of the machine. Wheels whizzed. Levers clicked.—PROFESSOR BRANESTAWM STORIES, Norman Hunter

whizz NOUN
the sound of something passing very quickly
• *the* **whizz** *of an arrow*

who PRONOUN
which person or people • *Who are you?*

who PRONOUN
the person or people just mentioned • *That is the man* **who** *brought the parcel.*

whoever PRONOUN
any person who • *Whoever comes is welcome.*

whole ADJECTIVE
❶ all of something • *We stayed there the* **whole** *day.* ❷ not broken; in one piece • *The snake can swallow an egg* **whole**.

whole NOUN wholes
The whole of something is all of it. • *I read the* **whole** *of the book in one weekend.*

wholemeal ADJECTIVE
Wholemeal flour or bread is made from the whole grain of wheat.

whole number NOUN whole numbers
a number without a fraction

wholesome ADJECTIVE
healthy and good for you

wholly ADVERB
completely; entirely

whom PRONOUN
a word used instead of *who* when it comes after a verb or preposition • *This is not the man* **whom** *I saw.* • *To* **whom** *should I give this letter?*

BUILD YOUR VOCABULARY
Whom is used as the **object** of a verb.

whoop NOUN whoops
a loud excited cry
The little man gave a great whoop of joy and threw his bowl of mashed caterpillars right out of the tree-house window.—CHARLIE AND THE CHOCOLATE FACTORY, Roald Dahl

whoop VERB whoops, whooping, whooped
to give a loud excited cry

whoosh NOUN whooshes
a sudden rushing sound when something moves
Out of the darkness came a whoosh of wings.—THE SHIP BETWEEN THE WORLDS, Julia Golding

whoosh VERB whooshes, whooshing, whooshed
to move quickly with a rushing sound

who's
Short for *who is* or *who has*. • *Who's (= who is) that?* • *Who's (= who has) been invited?*

WATCH OUT!
Do not confuse **who's** with **whose**, meaning 'belonging to which person'.

a
b
c
d
e
f
g
h
i
j
k
l
m
n
o
p
q
r
s
t
u
v
w
x
y
z

whose *DETERMINER, PRONOUN*
belonging to which person • *Whose bike is that?*
• *Whose is this?*

whose *PRONOUN*
of which; of whom • *the girl whose party we went to*

⚠ WATCH OUT!
Do not confuse **whose** with **who's**, which is short for 'who is' or 'who has'.

why *ADVERB*
for what reason or purpose

wick *NOUN* **wicks**
the string in the middle of a candle or lamp that you light

wicked *ADJECTIVE* **wickeder, wickedest**
❶ very bad; evil ❷ mischievous • *He gave a wicked grin.*
➤ **wickedly** *ADVERB* ➤ **wickedness** *NOUN*

wicker *NOUN*
material or things made from reeds or canes woven together • *a wicker basket*

wicket *NOUN* **wickets**
in cricket, each set of three stumps with two bails on top of them

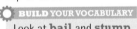

🔧 BUILD YOUR VOCABULARY
Look at **bail** and **stump**.

wide *ADJECTIVE* **wider, widest**
❶ measuring a lot from one side to the other
• *We had to cross a wide river.* ❷ used to talk about how much something measures from one side to the other • *The gap is only a few inches wide.*
❸ including a large range • *They sell a wide variety of toys.*

wide *ADVERB* **wider, widest**
To open or spread something wide is to open or spread it as far as possible.
➤ **wide awake** completely awake

widespread *ADJECTIVE*
very common; found in many places

widow *NOUN* **widows**
a woman whose husband or wife has died

widower *NOUN* **widowers**
a man whose wife or husband has died

width *NOUN* **widths**
how much something measures from one side to the other

wield *(say* weeld*)* *VERB* **wields, wielding, wielded**
To wield a weapon is to hold and use it.

wife *NOUN* **wives**
the woman that someone is married to

Wi-Fi *NOUN (trademark)*
a wireless connection to the Internet

wig *NOUN* **wigs**
a covering of false hair worn on the head

wiggle *VERB* **wiggles, wiggling, wiggled**
to move something from side to side repeatedly

wild *ADJECTIVE* **wilder, wildest**
❶ Wild animals and plants live or grow in a natural state and are not looked after by people. ❷ Wild land is in its natural state and not farmed or used by people. ❸ Wild behaviour is not controlled or calm.
• *The crowd went wild.*
➤ **wildly** *ADVERB* • *She waved her arms wildly.*

wild *NOUN* **wilds**
If animals live in the wild, they live free in their natural environment.

wilderness *NOUN* **wildernesses**
an area of wild country

wildlife *NOUN*
wild animals in their natural setting

wilful *ADJECTIVE*
❶ determined to do what you want ❷ deliberate
• *a wilful act of destruction*

will *VERB (past tense* **would***)*
If something will happen, it is going to happen.
• *I will be there at 12 o'clock.*

🔧 BUILD YOUR VOCABULARY
Will is a **modal verb**.

will *NOUN* **wills**
❶ Your will is what you choose or want. • *He was taken there against his will.* ❷ determination to do something • *She has a strong will to win.* ❸ a legal document saying what someone wants to be done with their possessions after they die

willing ADJECTIVE
ready and happy to do something • *We're willing to help.*
➤ **willingly** ADVERB ➤ **willingness** NOUN

willow NOUN willows
a tree with thin flexible branches, often growing near water

wilt VERB wilts, wilting, wilted
If a plant wilts, it droops because it is dry or not healthy.

wily ADJECTIVE wilier, wiliest
crafty or cunning

win VERB wins, winning, won
❶ To win a contest, game or battle is to beat your opponents. • *Our team has **won** every game.*
❷ To win something is to get it using effort or in a competition. • *She **won** second prize.*

win NOUN wins
a success or victory

wince VERB winces, wincing, winced
to make a slight movement because you are in pain or embarrassed

winch NOUN winches
a device for lifting or pulling things, using a rope or cable that winds round a cylinder

winch VERB winches, winching, winched
to lift or pull something with a winch

wind (rhymes with **tinned**) NOUN winds
air that moves over the earth • *Trees swayed in the **wind**.*

wind (rhymes with **find**) VERB winds, winding, wound
❶ If a road, path or river winds, it twists and turns.
• *The path **winds** up the hill.* ❷ to wrap or twist something round something else • *She **wound** her scarf round her neck.* ❸ To wind a clock or a machine is to turn a key or knob so it works.

wind instrument NOUN wind instruments
a musical instrument played by blowing, such as a flute or clarinet

BUILD YOUR VOCABULARY
Look at **brass instrument**, **percussion**, **stringed instrument** and **woodwind instrument**.

windmill NOUN windmills
a building with long arms called **sails** that are turned by the wind to make a machine work

window NOUN windows
❶ an opening in a wall or roof to let light in, usually filled with glass ❷ an area on a computer screen used by a particular program

✳ WORD STORY
The word **window** comes from Old Norse (Viking) words meaning 'wind eye'.

windpipe NOUN windpipes
the tube through which air reaches your lungs

windscreen NOUN windscreens
the big window in front of the driver in a vehicle

wind turbine NOUN wind turbines
a tall upright machine with large parts that move in the wind to produce electricity

windy ADJECTIVE windier, windiest
with a lot of wind • *It's **windy** today.*

wine NOUN wines
❶ an alcoholic drink made from grapes ❷ a dark red colour

wing NOUN wings
❶ A bird's or insect's wings are the parts it uses for flying. ❷ An aircraft's wings are the long flat parts that stick out from its sides and support it in the air.
➤ **winged** ADJECTIVE • *a **winged** insect*

wink VERB winks, winking, winked
❶ to close and open one of your eyes quickly ❷ If a light winks, it flickers or twinkles.

wink NOUN winks
the action of closing and opening one of your eyes quickly

wind turbine

A
B
C
D
E
F
G
H
I
J
K
L
M
N
O
P
Q
R
S
T
U
V
W
X
Y
Z

winner *NOUN* **winners**
a person who wins something

winter *NOUN* **winters**
the coldest season of the year, between autumn and spring

wintry *ADVERB* **wintrier, wintriest**
cold; like winter

wipe *VERB* **wipes, wiping, wiped**
to rub something in order to dry it or clean it

wire *NOUN* **wires**
a long thin strip of metal used to carry electricity or for making things
wire *VERB* **wires, wiring, wired**
To wire something or wire it up is to connect it using electrical wires.

wireless *ADJECTIVE*
able to send and receive signals without using wires
• *wireless headphones*

wireless *NOUN* **wirelesses** *(old use)*
a radio

wiry *ADJECTIVE* **wirier, wiriest**
❶ A wiry person is lean and strong. ❷ Wiry hair is tough and stiff.

wisdom *NOUN*
the quality of being wise

wise *ADJECTIVE* **wiser, wisest**
knowing or understanding a lot, so you are able to make sensible decisions
➤ **wisely** *ADVERB* • *He **wisely** decided to tell the truth.*

wish *VERB* **wishes, wishing, wished**
❶ If you wish that something would happen, you would really like it to happen. • *I **wish** it would stop raining.* ❷ To wish for something is to say that you would like to have it. ❸ To wish someone something is to say that you hope they will get it. • *They **wished** us luck.*

wish *NOUN* **wishes**
the act of wishing for something; something you wish for • *Make a **wish**.* • *She got her **wish**.*

wisp *NOUN* **wisps**
a thin piece or streak of something such as hair or smoke

wistful *ADJECTIVE*
thinking sadly about something you would like to have
➤ **wistfully** *ADVERB*

wit *NOUN* **wits**
❶ clever jokes or humour ❷ intelligence; good sense

witch *NOUN* **witches**
in stories, a woman or girl who has magic powers

witchcraft *NOUN*
the use of magic, especially to make bad things happen

with *PREPOSITION*
❶ If someone or something is with someone or something else, they are together. • *I'll come **with** you.* ❷ using • *Stir the mixture **with** a wooden spoon.* ❸ having • *a crocodile **with** powerful jaws*

withdraw *VERB* **withdraws, withdrawing, withdrew, withdrawn**
❶ to take something away or take it back
• *She **withdrew** her offer.* ❷ If you withdraw from something, you do not continue with it. • *He has **withdrawn** from the race because of injury.*

wither *VERB* **withers, withering, withered**
If a plant withers, it becomes dry and dies.

withhold *VERB* **withholds, withholding, withheld**
to refuse to give something • *He **withheld** his permission.*

within *PREPOSITION*
❶ inside • *There was a mystery **within** those walls.*
❷ not more than • *She was **within** ten metres of the finish line.*
within *ADVERB*
inside a place • *There were noises **within**.*

without *PREPOSITION*
❶ not together with • *Don't go **without** me!* ❷ not having or using • *An invertebrate is an animal **without** a backbone.*

withstand *VERB* **withstands, withstanding, withstood**
to experience or suffer something without being seriously harmed • *The building had **withstood** an earthquake.*

witness *NOUN* **witnesses**
a person who sees an event happen and can describe it • *There were no* **witnesses** *to the accident.*

witness *VERB* **witnesses, witnessing, witnessed**
to see an event happening

witty *ADJECTIVE* **wittier, wittiest**
clever and amusing

wizard *NOUN* **wizards**
in stories, a man or boy who has magic powers

 WORD STORY
The word **wizard** comes from an old meaning of *wise* and originally meant 'a wise person'.

wizened *ADJECTIVE*
shrivelled or wrinkled with age • *a* **wizened** *old man*

wobble *VERB* **wobbles, wobbling, wobbled**
to move unsteadily from side to side

wobble *NOUN* **wobbles**
a wobbling movement
➤ **wobbly** *ADJECTIVE*

woe *NOUN* **woes**
great sorrow

woke *VERB (past tense of* **wake***)*
• *I* **woke** *early.*

woken *VERB (past participle of* **wake***)*
• *You've* **woken** *the baby.*

wolf *NOUN* **wolves**
a wild animal like a large fierce dog

wolf *VERB* **wolfs, wolfing, wolfed**
To wolf down food is to eat it greedily.

woman *NOUN* **women**
a grown-up female human being

womb *(say* woom*) NOUN* **wombs**
the part of a female's body where babies develop before they are born

wombat *NOUN* **wombats**
an Australian animal like a small bear with short legs

BUILD YOUR VOCABULARY
A **wombat** is a **marsupial**.

won *VERB (past tense and past participle of* **win***)*
• *Who* **won** *first prize?*

wonder *VERB* **wonders, wondering, wondered**
to ask yourself something; to want to know something • *I* **wonder** *how it happened.*

wonder *NOUN* **wonders**
a feeling of surprise and admiration

wonderful *ADJECTIVE*
marvellous; excellent
➤ **wonderfully** *ADVERB* • *The sky was* **wonderfully** *blue.*

won't
short for *will not* • *We* **won't** *forget.*

a
b
c
d
e
f
g
h
i
j
k
l
m
n
o
p
q
r
s
t
u
v
w
x
y
z

wood NOUN woods
❶ Wood is the substance that trees are made of.
❷ A wood is a lot of trees growing together.
➤ **woody** ADJECTIVE

wooded ADJECTIVE
covered with trees • the **wooded** shore

wooden ADJECTIVE
made of wood

woodland NOUN woodlands
land covered with trees

woodlouse NOUN woodlice
a small animal with seven pairs of legs that lives in rotten wood or damp soil

woodpecker NOUN woodpeckers
a bird that taps tree trunks with its beak to find insects

woodwind instrument NOUN woodwind instruments
a musical instrument that is played by blowing and that is made of wood or plastic

🔩 **BUILD** YOUR VOCABULARY
Look at **brass instrument, percussion, stringed instrument** and **wind instrument.**

woodwork NOUN
❶ the activity of making things with wood
❷ The parts of a building that are made of wood.

woof NOUN woofs
the barking sound made by a dog

wool NOUN
❶ the thick soft hair of sheep or goats ❷ thread or cloth made from sheep's or goats' hair
➤ **woolly** ADJECTIVE • a warm **woolly** jumper

woollen ADJECTIVE
made of wool

word NOUN words
❶ a group of sounds or letters that has a meaning and is written with a space before and after it ❷ a short talk with someone • Can I have a **word** with you? ❸ Your word is your promise. • I gave my **word** and I will keep it.

word VERB words, wording, worded
to express something in words • Can you **word** it differently?

word class NOUN word classes
one of the groups into which words can be divided in grammar, such as adjectives, nouns and verbs

🔩 **BUILD** YOUR VOCABULARY
Look at **part of speech.**

wore VERB (past tense of **wear**)
• I **wore** my new shoes to the party.

work VERB works, working, worked
❶ to spend time doing something that needs effort or energy • I have to **work** on my project. ❷ to have a job • She **works** in a bank. ❸ If something works, it operates correctly or successfully. • Is the lift **working**? • My plan didn't **work**.
➤ **To work something out** is to find the answer to it.
➤ **To work your way somewhere** is to gradually get there.
➤ **worker** NOUN

A B C D E F G H I J K L M N O P Q R S T U V W X Y Z

work NOUN **works**
❶ something you have to do that needs effort or energy • *Please get on with your* **work** *quietly.* • *Digging is hard* **work**. ❷ a job • *What* **work** *does she do?* ❸ A work is a piece of writing or music or painting. • *The book has all the* **works** *of Shakespeare.*
➤ **To be at work** is to be working.

worker NOUN **workers**
❶ someone who works ❷ a bee or ant that does the work in a hive or colony but does not produce eggs

workmanship NOUN
skill in making something

workshop NOUN **workshops**
a place where things are made or mended

world NOUN **worlds**
❶ the earth with all its countries and people ❷ a particular subject or activity • *He knows a lot about the* **world** *of sport.*

worldly ADJECTIVE **worldlier, worldliest**
to do with ordinary life and material things, rather than anything spiritual or religious

worldwide ADJECTIVE, ADVERB
over the whole world

World Wide Web NOUN
a system of linked computers all over the world so that people can find information using the Internet

worm NOUN **worms**
a small thin wriggling animal without legs, especially an earthworm

worm VERB **worms, worming, wormed**
To worm your way somewhere is to get there by wriggling or crawling.

worn VERB
(past participle of **wear**) • *Have you ever* **worn** *fancy dress?*

worn ADJECTIVE
damaged because of being rubbed or used a lot • *His shoes were old and* **worn**.
➤ **worn out** very tired

worried ADJECTIVE
anxious or troubled • *Don't look so* **worried**!
➤ **worriedly** ADVERB

worry VERB **worries, worrying, worried**
❶ to feel anxious or troubled about something • *Don't* **worry**—*everything will be fine.* ❷ If something worries you, it makes you feel anxious or troubled. • *The spelling test was* **worrying** *her.*

worry NOUN **worries**
❶ a problem that makes you worry ❷ the feeling of worrying • *They were frantic with* **worry**.

worse ADJECTIVE, ADVERB
more bad or badly; less good or well • *The pain is getting* **worse**. • *The team did* **worse** *than expected.*

worship VERB **worships, worshipping, worshipped**
to give praise and respect to God or to a god
➤ **worshipper** NOUN

worship NOUN
ceremonies or other things done to worship

worst ADJECTIVE, ADVERB
most bad or badly; least good or well • *We had our* **worst** *result so far.* • *That was the* **worst** *I've ever felt.*

worth ADJECTIVE
❶ If something is worth an amount, that is its value. • *This stamp is* **worth** *£100.* ❷ If something is worth doing, it is good or useful enough to do. • *That book is* **worth** *reading.*

worth NOUN
A thing's worth is its value or usefulness.

worthless ADJECTIVE
having no value

worthwhile ADJECTIVE
important or good enough to be worth doing

worthy ADJECTIVE **worthier, worthiest**
deserving respect or support • *The event is for a* **worthy** *cause.*

a
b
c
d
e
f
g
h
i
j
k
l
m
n
o
p
q
r
s
t
u
v
w
x
y
z

would VERB
❶ used in polite questions or requests • *Would you like some tea?* ❷ used to talk about imaginary situations • *If I won the lottery, I **would** buy a big house for my family.*

BUILD YOUR VOCABULARY
Would is a **modal verb**.

wound VERB (rhymes with **round**) (past tense and past participle of **wind**)
• *The path **wound** through the woods.* • *She had **wound** a bandage round her wrist.*

wound (rhymes with **spooned**) NOUN **wounds**
a cut or injury to someone's body

wound (rhymes with **spooned**) VERB **wounds, wounding, wounded**
❶ to cut or injure someone ❷ to hurt someone's feelings

wove VERB (past tense of **weave**)
• *She **wove** beautiful golden cloth.*

woven VERB (past participle of **weave**)
• *The baskets were **woven** from grass.*

wrap VERB **wraps, wrapping, wrapped**
to put paper, cloth or some other covering around something

wrap NOUN **wraps**
❶ a shawl or cloak ❷ a sandwich made of flat bread wrapped around a filling

wrapper NOUN **wrappers**
a piece of paper or plastic that something is wrapped in

wrapping NOUN **wrappings**
material used to wrap something, especially a present

wrath (rhymes with **cloth**) NOUN (old use)
anger

wreath (say reeth) NOUN **wreaths**
a decorative circle made of flowers and leaves

wreathe (say reeth) VERB **wreathes, wreathing, wreathed**
To be wreathed in something is to be covered or decorated with it. • *The mountains were **wreathed** in mist.*

wreck VERB **wrecks, wrecking, wrecked**
to damage something so badly that it is ruined or completely broken

wreck NOUN **wrecks**
a car, ship or plane that has been very badly damaged in an accident

wreckage NOUN
pieces of something that has been wrecked

wren NOUN **wrens**
a very small brown bird

wrench VERB **wrenches, wrenching, wrenched**
to pull or twist something suddenly and violently • *He **wrenched** the door open.*

wrench NOUN **wrenches**
❶ a violent pulling or twisting movement ❷ a tool for gripping and turning bolts or nuts

wrestle VERB **wrestles, wrestling, wrestled**
❶ to fight by holding someone and trying to throw them to the ground ❷ To wrestle with a problem or difficulty is to struggle with it and try to solve it.
➤ **wrestler** NOUN
➤ **wrestling** NOUN

wrench

wretch
NOUN **wretches**
a person who you pity or dislike

wretched (say rech-id) ADJECTIVE
unfortunate and unhappy; to be pitied • *a **wretched** beggar*

wriggle VERB **wriggles, wriggling, wriggled**
to twist and turn your body

wring VERB **wrings, wringing, wrung**
to squeeze or twist something hard, especially to get water out of it • *Have you **wrung** out the cloth?* • *She **wrung** her hands in despair.*

wrinkle NOUN **wrinkles**
a small crease or fold, especially in someone's skin

wrinkle VERB **wrinkles, wrinkling, wrinkled**
If something wrinkles, small creases or folds appear in it or on it.
➤ **wrinkled** ADJECTIVE

wrist NOUN **wrists**
the joint that connects your hand to your arm

write VERB **writes, writing, wrote, written**
① to put words or signs on paper or some other surface so that people can read them • *Write your name here.* • *I wrote him a letter.* ② to be the author or composer of something • *I've **written** a poem.*
➤ **writer** NOUN

writhe VERB **writhes, writhing, writhed**
to twist your body about because you are in pain

writing NOUN **writings**
① Writing is something written. • *The card had some writing on the back.* ② Your writing is the way you write. • *He has neat **writing**.*

written VERB (past participle of **write**)
• *Have you **written** your name at the top?*

wrong ADJECTIVE
① not fair or not morally right • *It is **wrong** to cheat.* ② incorrect • *Your answer is **wrong**.*
③ not working properly • *There's something **wrong** with the engine.*
➤ **wrongly** ADVERB
wrong ADVERB
wrongly • *You guessed **wrong**.*

wrote VERB (past tense of **write**)
• *I **wrote** a story about a goblin.*

wrung VERB (past tense and past participle of **wring**)
• *She **wrung** her hands.* • *Have you **wrung** out the wet towel?*

wry ADJECTIVE **wryer, wryest**
slightly mocking or amused • *He gave a **wry** smile.*
➤ **wryly** ADVERB

a
b
c
d
e
f
g
h
i
j
k
l
m
n
o
p
q
r
s
t
u
v
w
x
y
z

When **x** starts a word it often sounds like /z/, as in *xylophone*.

x is the least common starting letter for English words.

Can you guess the most common?

CLUE Which letter takes up the most pages in this dictionary?

X *ABBREVIATION*
10 in Roman numerals

Xmas *NOUN (informal)*
Christmas

X-ray *NOUN* X-rays
a photograph of the inside of something, especially your body, made using a kind of radiation called **X-rays**

X-ray *VERB* X-rays, X-raying, X-rayed
to make an X-ray of something • *The doctor X-rayed my hand.*

xylophone *(say* zy-lo-fohn*) NOUN* xylophones
a musical instrument with a row of wooden bars that you hit with small hammers

WORD STORY

The word **xylophone** comes from Greek words meaning 'wood sound'.

Is **Y** a consonant or a vowel? The answer is both. In *yes* and *yellow* it makes a consonant sound, but in *rhythm* and *gypsy* it makes vowel sounds.

yacht *NOUN* **yachts**
a sailing boat used for racing or pleasure trips

yam *NOUN* **yams**
a tropical vegetable that grows underground

yank *VERB* **yanks, yanking, yanked**
to pull something strongly and suddenly

yap *VERB* **yaps, yapping, yapped**
If a small dog yaps, it makes a high barking sound.

yard *NOUN* **yards**
❶ a measurement of length. There are 3 feet or 36 inches in 1 yard, which is about 91 centimetres.
❷ a piece of hard ground outside a building or used for a type of work • *a builder's* **yard**

yarn *NOUN* **yarns**
❶ thread spun by twisting fibres together
❷ *(informal)* a tale or story

yawn *VERB* **yawns, yawning, yawned**
❶ to open your mouth wide and breathe in deeply because you are tired or bored ❷ If a hole yawns, it is wide and open in front of someone.
yawn *NOUN* **yawns**
an act of yawning

year *NOUN* **years**
❶ the time that the earth takes to go round the sun, about 365 days or twelve months ❷ the time from 1 January to 31 December ❸ any period of twelve months • *the school* **year** ❹ a group of students of roughly the same age • *Is she in your* **year**?

yearly *ADJECTIVE*
every year • *Your pets should have a* **yearly** *check-up.*

BUILD YOUR VOCABULARY
A synonym is **annual**.

yearn *VERB* **yearns, yearning, yearned**
to long for something

yeast *NOUN*
a substance used in baking bread and in making beer

BUILD YOUR VOCABULARY
Yeast is a **fungus**.

yell *NOUN* **yells**
a loud cry or shout
yell *VERB* **yells, yelling, yelled**
to shout loudly

yellow *ADJECTIVE* **yellower, yellowest**
of the colour of lemons or butter
yellow *NOUN* **yellows**
a yellow colour

yelp *NOUN* **yelps**
a sudden high bark or cry, usually of pain
yelp *VERB* **yelps, yelping, yelped**
to give a yelp

yes *EXCLAMATION*
a word used to agree with something or to answer your name • *Yes, I'd love to come.* • *'Mum!'–'Yes?'*

yesterday *NOUN, ADVERB*
the day before today • *Yesterday was fun.* • *It was her birthday* **yesterday**.

yet *ADVERB*
❶ up to now; by now • *He hasn't arrived* **yet**. • *Have you finished* **yet**? ❷ until later • *Don't print it* **yet**.
yet *CONJUNCTION*
but • *It is strange,* **yet** *it is true.*

yeti *(say* yet-ee*) NOUN* **yetis**
a creature like a huge hairy ape or bear that according to legends lives in the Himalayas

yew *NOUN* **yews**
an evergreen tree with red berries and dark leaves like needles

yield *VERB* **yields, yielding, yielded**
to surrender or give in • *He refused to* **yield**.

a b c d e f g h i j k l m n o p q r s t u v w x y z

yoga NOUN
a Hindu system of exercise and meditation

yoghurt *(also* **yogurt***) (say* **yog**-ert*) NOUN*
yoghurts, yogurts
a thick liquid made from milk, sometimes flavoured
with fruit

yoke NOUN **yokes**
a curved object put across the necks of animals
pulling a cart

yoke VERB **yokes, yoking, yoked**
to harness or link animals with a yoke

yolk *(rhymes with* **coke***) NOUN* **yolks**
the yellow part of an egg

Yom Kippur NOUN
an important Jewish religious festival

yonder ADVERB, ADJECTIVE *(old use)*
over there

you PRONOUN
❶ the person or people someone is speaking to
• *You can sit here.* • *Who told you?* ❷ people;
anyone • *You can never be sure.*

⚙ **BUILD YOUR VOCABULARY**
You can be used as the **subject** or **object** of a verb.

you'd
short for *you had* or *you would* • *You'd (= you had)
already done it.* • *You'd (= you would) be welcome.*

young ADJECTIVE **younger, youngest**
having lived or existed only a short time; not old

young NOUN
An animal's or bird's young are its babies.

youngster NOUN **youngsters**
a young person or child

your DETERMINER
belonging to you • *Is this **your** pencil?*

⚠ **WATCH OUT!**
Do not confuse **your** meaning 'belonging to you' with
you're, which is short for 'you are'.

yours PRONOUN
belonging to you • *Is this book **yours**?*
➤ **Yours faithfully, Yours sincerely, Yours
truly** ways of ending a letter before you sign it

yourself PRONOUN **yourselves**
❶ used instead of 'you' when a person does
something and is also affected by it • *Have you hurt
yourself?* ❷ on your own; without help • *Did you
make the food **yourselves**?*
➤ **by yourself** or **yourselves** on your own;
alone • *Have you been **by yourself** all day?*

youth NOUN **youths**
❶ the time when you are young • *She was a dancer
in her **youth**.* ❷ a boy or young man ❸ young people
• *Today's **youth** have grown up with computers.*

youthful ADJECTIVE
young or seeming young

yo-yo NOUN **yo-yos**
a round wooden or plastic toy that moves up and
down on a string

yuck EXCLAMATION
a word you say when you feel disgust

yummy ADJECTIVE **yummier, yummiest**
(informal)
delicious

Zz

⚙ Z occurs three times in **zzz**, used for the sound of someone sleeping.

⚙ Not many English words have the same letter three times in a row. Can you think of any others?

CLUE They are mostly other words for sounds, like the sound you make when you are very cold, or a sound for telling someone to be quiet.

zap *VERB* **zaps, zapping, zapped** *(informal)*
to attack or destroy something or someone with a ray or special power
He was feeling more than a little pleased with himself now. And why not? Hadn't he just zapped a villain single-handed?–FOLLOW ME DOWN, Julie Hearn

zeal *NOUN*
eagerness, especially to do what you believe to be right

zebra *NOUN* **zebras**
an African animal similar to a horse with black and white stripes

zebra crossing *NOUN* **zebra crossings**
a place on a road for pedestrians to cross, marked with white stripes

⚙ **BUILD YOUR VOCABULARY**
Look at **pelican crossing**.

zero *NOUN* **zeros**
nought; the figure 0

zigzag *NOUN* **zigzags**
a line or route with many sharp turns left and right
zigzag *VERB* **zigzags, zigzagging, zigzagged**
to move in a series of sharp turns from left to right
• *They walked up the zigzagging cliff path.*

zinc *NOUN*
a silver-white metal used to coat iron and steel to stop them rusting

⚙ **BUILD YOUR VOCABULARY**
Zinc is an **element**.

zip *NOUN* **zips**
a device for joining two pieces of cloth, with rows of small teeth that fit together
zip *VERB* **zips, zipping, zipped**
to fasten something with a zip

zodiac *(say* zoh-dee-ak*) NOUN*
a group of twelve constellations, each called a **sign of the zodiac** and each with its own special name and symbol, for example *Leo* (the lion) or *Pisces* (the fish)

zombie *NOUN* **zombies**
in stories, a dead person who turns into a creature that eats people

zone *NOUN* **zones**
an area of a particular kind • *They flew across three time zones.*

zoo *NOUN* **zoos**
a place where wild animals are kept so that people can look at them or study them

zoology *(say* zoo-ol-oj-ee*) NOUN*
the scientific study of animals

zoom *VERB* **zooms, zooming, zoomed**
to move or travel very quickly
➤ **To zoom in** is to look at an object or image very close up with a camera or computer.

a b c d e f g h i j k l m n o p q r s t u v w x y z

Contents

Find the answers for the questions at each alphabetical letter opener on page 481

Word classes used in this dictionary

adjective

a word which gives more information about a noun. It normally goes before the noun. In this sentence the words in bold are adjectives: •*The **little green** bird flew away.*

adverb

a word that tells you how, when, where or why something happens. In these sentences, the words in bold are adverbs: *He listened **carefully**. • I heard voices **upstairs**.*

conjunction

a word that joins other words and parts of a sentence, for example **and**, **but** and **whether**

determiner

a word that goes before a noun and any adjectives, for example **a**, **the**, **some** and **many**. It helps to tell you which person or thing the sentence is about, or how much or how many there are.

noun

a word that stands for a person, place or thing, for example **girl**, **sun**, **school** or **truth**. Most nouns can be used after 'the'.

preposition

a word you put in front of a noun or pronoun to show how it is linked to another word, often showing place, position or time. In these sentences, the words in bold are prepositions: *Put the plates **on** the table. • I'll come **at** ten.*

pronoun

a word used instead of a noun, such as **he**, **her**, **it**, **them** or **those**

verb

a word that shows what someone or something is doing or what is happening, such as **go**, **make**, **think** or **be**. All sentences have a verb.

Some grammar terms

active An active verb is one where the subject of the sentence does the action. For example, in *the girl caught the ball* the subject is 'the girl' and the verb 'caught' is active.
» Look at **passive** (page 468).

adverbial a word or phrase that gives more information about a verb or clause. It can be an adverb, a phrase or a subordinate clause. Adverbials tell you about **when, where, why, how** or **how much** something happened, for example the bold parts of these sentences: *The dog slept **under the table**.* or ***Next**, I had my breakfast.*

antonym Antonyms are words that mean the opposite of each other, such as **wet** and **dry** or **full** and **empty**.

auxiliary verb a 'helping' verb such as be, have or do that is used with another verb (a main verb) to make questions, negatives and tenses. In *we have finished* the auxiliary verb is 'have' and the main verb is 'finished.'
» Look at **modal verb** (page 468).

capital letter the large form of a letter (A, B, C, D etc) used at the start of a sentence or the start of the name of a person or place

clause a phrase which has a verb as its key word. A clause can be a whole sentence or part of a sentence. For example, the sentence *I called the cat and it jumped on to my lap.* contains two clauses joined by 'and': *I called the cat* and *it jumped on to my lap.*

cohesion the way that ideas in a text are linked using words or phrases called cohesive devices. These might be conjunctions (linking words) like **and**, pronouns like **it** to refer back to something you have already mentioned, or adverbials like **later** or **not far away** that show links in time or place.

command a sentence which gives an order or instruction. It usually has the verb first and often ends with an exclamation mark (!), for example *Give me that!*

compound a word which is made from two or more other words, such as **bathroom** or **bookshelf**

consonant A consonant or consonant letter is a letter that is not a vowel.
» Look at **vowel letter** (page 469).

direct speech the exact words that someone says, written between inverted commas or speech marks (" " and ' ')

hyphen to join words, or join a prefix to a root word: *hard-working, co-operate*

main clause a clause that works on its own as a sentence
» Look at **relative clause** (page 468) and **subordinate clause** (page 469).

Some grammar terms

modal verb a kind of auxiliary verb that is used with another verb (a main verb) to say what is possible, what is necessary or what is going to happen in the future. Modal verbs are: **will, would, can, could, may, might, shall, should, must** and **ought to**.

noun phrase a group of words that has a noun as its key word. In this sentence the noun phrase is in bold: *The book with the torn pages on the table over there is not mine.* The key word is the noun **book**.

object The object of a verb is the person or thing that is acted upon by the verb. In *the girl carried a bag* the verb is 'carried' and the object is 'a bag'.
» Look at **subject** (page 469).

passive A passive verb is one whose subject is the person or thing that had something done to it. For example, in *the ball* was caught the subject is 'the ball' and the verb 'was caught' is passive. In a passive sentence, the person or thing that does the action is not mentioned or comes after 'by'.
» Look at **active** (page 467).

past tense the form of a verb that tells us that something happened earlier. It usually ends with **-ed**, as in *We played football yesterday.*

plural The plural form of a noun tells us that there is more than one. It usually ends with **-s**, as in *There was a bowl of apples and bananas.*
» Look at **singular** (page 469).

possessive pronoun a pronoun that shows something belongs to someone, for example **mine** or **hers**.

present tense the form of a verb that tells us that something happens now. It usually has no ending, or ends with **-s**, as in *This milk smells bad.*

punctuation the marks such as commas, full stops and brackets put into a piece of writing to make it easier to understand.
» Look at the section on **Punctuation**.

question a sentence which asks something. It usually ends with a question mark (**?**), as in *Who is that?*

relative clause a type of subordinate clause that gives more information about the noun in the main clause. It starts with a relative pronoun. For example, the bold part of this sentence is the relative clause: *He finished the homework **that his teacher had given him earlier**.*

relative pronoun a word such as **who, which, that** or **whose** that is used to connect a relative clause to a main clause

Some grammar terms

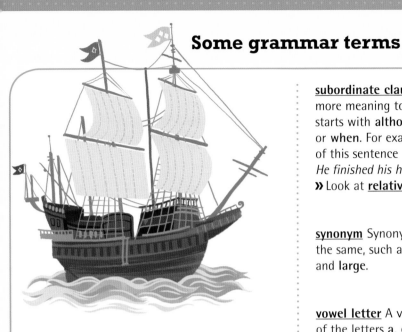

sentence a group of words that tells you something (a statement), asks something (a question), tells you to do something (a command), or exclaims about something (an exclamation). It must have at least one verb and can have one more more clauses. In writing, it starts with a capital letter and ends with a full stop, a question mark, or an exclamation mark.

singular The singular form of a noun tells us that there is just one, for example *I ate a banana*.
» Look at **plural** (page 468).

statement a sentence that tells you something, for example *I am hungry*.

subject The subject of a verb is the person or thing that does something. In *the girl carried a bag* the verb is 'carried' and the subject is 'the girl'.
» Look at **object** (page 468).

subordinate clause a clause that helps to give more meaning to the main clause. It often starts with **although**, **because**, **before**, **if**, **since** or **when**. For example, the bold part of this sentence is the subordinate clause: *He finished his homework **before going to bed**.*
» Look at **relative clause**.

synonym Synonyms are words that mean the same, such as **shut** and **closed** or **big** and **large**.

vowel letter A vowel or vowel letter is one of the letters **a**, **e**, **i**, **o** and **u** that are in most words. The letter **y** sometimes also acts as a vowel, as in 'gypsy'.

word family a group of words that are related to each other by spelling, grammar and meaning. For example, **write**, **writer** and **writing** are in the same word family and **medicine**, **medical** and **medicinal** are in the same word family. If you know how to spell one, you can use it to help spell the others.

See also
Apostrophes,
Punctuation and
Word classes
used in this
dictionary.

Spelling help

Here are some useful rules:

To make a noun plural

Normally just add **–s**:
skirts   ties   pianos   stars

But watch out for some words ending in **–o** that need **–es**:
echoes, heroes, potatoes, tomatoes, volcanoes, etc.

To words ending in **–ch**, **–s**, **–sh**, **–x** or **–z**, add **–es**:
dress – dresses   box – boxes   stitch – stitches

To words ending in **–f** and **–fe**, change to **–ves**:
scarf – scarves   life – lives   half – halves

⚠ But watch out for these exceptions:
beliefs, proofs, roofs, etc.

To words ending in a consonant followed by **–y**, change the **y** to **i** and add **–es**:
copy – copies   cry – cries   party – parties

Adding –ing and –ed to verbs

Normally just add **–ing** or **–ed**:
load – loading – loaded   open – opening – opened
stay – staying – stayed

For short words ending in **–e** usually leave off the **e**:
race – racing – raced   blame – blaming – blamed

For many short words that end with one consonant, double the last consonant:
slam – slamming – slammed   tip – tipping – tipped

For longer words ending with one consonant and having the stress on the last syllable, double the last consonant:
compel – compelling – compelled   prefer – preferring – preferred

For words ending in **–y** after a consonant, change the **y** to an **i** before adding **–ed**:
try – trying – tried

For words ending in **–ie**, change the **ie** to **y** before adding **–ing**:
lie – lying – lied   tie – tying – tied

⚠ Watch out for these exceptions:
lay – laid   pay – paid   say – said

Spelling help

Adding –er and –est to adjectives

Normally just add **–er** and **–est**, unless the word already ends in **–e**:
cold – colder – coldest   **wide – wider – widest**

For many short words that end with one consonant, change to a double consonant:
wet – wetter – wettest   **dim – dimmer – dimmest**

If the word has two syllables and ends in **y**, change the **y** to an **i**:
dirty – dirtier – dirtiest   **happy – happier – happiest**

Adding –ly

Adding **–ly** to an adjective makes it into an adverb:
slowly, badly, awkwardly

If the word ends in **–ll** just add **–y**:
full – fully

For words ending in **–y** and with more than one syllable, leave off the **–y** and add **–ily**:
happy – happily   **hungry – hungrily**

For words ending in **–le**, leave off the **e**:
idle – idly   **simple – simply**

For adjectives ending in **–ic**, usually add **–ally**:
basic – basically   **drastic – drastically**

! Watch out for other special ones:
public – publicly

Homophones

Activity Some words sound the same but have different spellings and meanings. Choose the right word for each sentence. You can check them in the dictionary.

I need another 25p for my bus . . .	fair	fare	
Don't drop it! You'll . . . it.	brake	break	
I just want some . . . and quiet.	peace	piece	
Everyone . . . me got a present.	accept	except	
Don't . . . with things that don't concern you.	medal	meddle	
She took hold of the horse's . . .	rains	reigns	reins
Some children ran . . . us.	passed	past	
We don't wear high . . . at school.	heals	heels	
Eating in lessons is not . . .	allowed	aloud	
I need to . . . my speech.	practice	practise	

UK / US differences

UK	US	UK	US
autumn	fall	on holiday	on vacation
bonnet (of a car)	hood (of a car)	petrol	gas
boot (of a car)	trunk (of a car)	trousers	pants
bumper	fender	trainers	sneakers or tennis shoes
chips	fries		
crisps	chips	spelling **–our** *behaviour, colour neighbourhood*	**–or** *behavior, color, neighborhood*
flat	apartment		
football	soccer	word ends **–re** *centre, metre, theatre*	word ends **–er** *enter, meter, theater*
lift	elevator		

472

Punctuation

 full stop

at the end of a statement or command
It's raining today. Don't forget your umbrella.

 question mark

at the end of a question
What's your favourite colour?

 exclamation mark

at the end of an exclamation
I don't believe it!

 comma

after items in a list or with direct speech
I need pens, pencils, paper and glue.
Dan asked, 'Can I come?'
'No,' said Mum.

 colon

before a list or explanation
You will need: flour, eggs, sugar and butter.
Today's aim: to learn more about fractions.

 apostrophe

to show that some letters are missing
to show ownership
» Look at **Apostrophes** (page 474)

 inverted commas/speech marks

to show the words someone says
'What's the time?' asked Raj.
Tara said, "It's almost time to go home."

 semicolon

between two connected sentences
I like peas; Aisha prefers beans.

 dash

to put before something extra added at the end of a sentence, or before and after something extra inserted into the middle
Then they poured out on to the observation roof—which is the place where tourists stand—just at the bottom of the big spike.
—JAMES AND THE GIANT PEACH, Roald Dahl

 brackets

to put around something extra inserted into the middle of a sentence:
'Anna Maria,' said the old man rat (whose name was Samuel Whiskers), 'Anna Maria, make me a kitten dumpling roly-poly pudding for my dinner.'
—THE ROLY-POLY PUDDING, Beatrix Potter

⚠ *Inserting something into the middle of a sentence between dashes or brackets is called* **parenthesis** */ pa-REN-the-sis /. Sometimes brackets themselves are called* **parentheses** */ pa-re-the-seez /.*

 ellipsis

to show a pause or that a sentence is not finished:
'It's Christmas! Speaking of which . . . '
I dipped into my bag and reached for his presents.—SAMMIE'S BACK, Helena Pielichaty

 hyphen

to join words or join a prefix to a root word
hard-working, co-operate.

Apostrophes

Apostrophes are used:

1 to show that a letter or group of letters has been missed out e.g.

do not ⟶ **don't**   **it is** ⟶ **it's** (see the next section on contractions)

2 with an s to show ownership e.g. **Sara's book, mum's car, the children's work**

! with a plural ending in s, the apostrophe comes after the s e.g. **the boys' toilets, the horses' hooves** (there are two or more horses)

! possessives like *its*, *hers* and *yours* never have an apostrophe. To remember this, think of other possessives such as *my*, *mine* and *your* that don't happen to end in s - and, obviously, don't have an apostrophe.

Activity — Choose the right word

1	_____ time to go.	Its	It's	Its'
2	_____ shoes are these?	Whose	Who's	Whos
3	_____ my best friend.	You're	Your	Yore
4	I'm in the _____ football team.	girl's	girls	girls'
5	They sell _____ clothes.	men's	mens'	mens's
6	The cat licked _____ paw.	its	it's	its'
7	_____ that?	Whose	Who's	Whos
8	This jacket is _____	her	her's	hers

Answers: 1. It's 2. Whose 3. You're 4. girls' 5. men's 6. its 7. Who's 8. hers

Contractions

- didn't → did not
- doesn't → does not
- don't → do not
- can't → cannot
- won't → will not
- musn't → must not
- couldn't → could not
- wouldn't → would not
- shouldn't → should not
- hadn't → had not
- hasn't → has not
- haven't → have not
- isn't → is not
- aren't → are not
- wasn't → was not

- weren't → were not
- it's → it is/has
- he's → he is/has
- she's → she is/has
- we're → we are
- I'm → I am
- I've → I have
- I'll → I will
- you're → you are
- you've → you have
- you'll → you will
- he'll → he will
- she'll → she will
- we'll → we will
- we've → we have

Word building

Prefix	Meaning	Examples
anti–	against (the opposite is **pro-**)	*anti-bacterial, antiwar*
co–	together	*co-exist, cooperate*
de–	take away; opposite of	*deforestation, deactivate*
dis–	not; opposite of	*disagree, dishonest*
ex–	former, past	*ex-boyfriend, ex-president*
extra–	more than usual	*extra-special*
extra–	beyond	*extraterrestrial*
im–	not; opposite of (before root word beginning **m** or **p**)	*immature, impossible*
in–	not; opposite of	*incorrect, inactive*
inter–	between two or more people/things	*interchangeable, inter-school*
mid–	in the middle of	*mid-July, midsummer*
mini–	much smaller or shorter than usual	*mini-dictionary*
mis–	wrong, wrongly	*misunderstanding, misspell*
mono–	having one	*monosyllable*
multi–	having many	*multicolour, multi-purpose*
non–	not	*non-existent, non-toxic*
over–	too, too much	*over-excited, oversleep*
poly–	many	*polygon*
post–	after (the opposite is **pre-**)	*post-war*
pre–	before (the opposite is **post-**)	*pre-war*
pro–	in favour of (the opposite is **anti-**)	*pro-independence*
re–	again	*reappear, rebuild*
semi–	half	*semi-final*
sub–	under	*submarine, subway*
super–	over; beyond	*superhuman, superhero*
trans–	across	*transatlantic*
ultra–	beyond	*ultraviolet*
ultra–	extremely	*ultra-difficult*
un–	not; opposite of	*unbelievable, unlock*
under–	below	*underground, underwater*

Suffix	Meaning or use	Examples
–able	possible to do	*enjoyable, drinkable*
–ation	forms a noun	*information, preparation*
–er	person who does . . .	*teacher, viewer*
–er/–est	more/most	*smaller, smallest, happier, happiest*
–ful	the amount that fills something	*roomful, pocketful*
–ful	with a lot of . . .	*hopeful, wasteful*
–hood	state of being a . . .	*childhood, fatherhood*

–ify	forms a verb	*classify, solidify*
–ion	forms a noun	*subtraction, confusion*
–ise / –ize	forms a verb	*magnetise, terrorise*
–ish	slightly, rather	*coldish, greenish*
–ish	like a . . .	*boyish, childish*
–less	without; free from	*harmless, hopeless*
–ly	in a . . . way	*cleverly, comfortably*
–ment	forms a noun	*agreement, movement*
–ness	the state of being . . .	*coldness, unhappiness*
–or	person who does . . .	*actor, sailor*
–ous	forms an adjective	*poisonous, mountainous*
–proof	resistant, not affected	*heatproof, waterproof*
–sized	of a certain size	*medium-sized, football-sized*
–y	forms an adjective meaning 'like . . .'	*watery, muddy*

Activity

Try inventing some new words!

Use the words in blue plus a prefix or suffix from the box to make a word that means . . .

1. not **ridiculous**
2. not affected by **chocolate**
3. like **bread**
4. the size of a **pumpkin**
5. the amount that fills a **sock**
6. without a **nose**
7. too **pink**
8. the state of not being **stinky**
9. slightly **wrong**
10. a person who pats **heads**

non–	over–	un–
–er	–ful	–ish
–less	–nes	–proof
–sized	–y	

Suggested answers: **1.** unridiculous **2.** chocolate-proof **3.** bready **4.** pumpkin-sized **5.** a sockful **6.** noseless **7.** over-pink **8.** non-stinkiness **9.** wrongish **10.** a head-patter

Spelling

For spelling rules when adding word endings, see the section on **Spelling help** (pages 470 – 471).

It can be hard to predict which words end in –er (like *teacher*) and which in –or (like *actor*), although –er is more common.

Check the spelling in the dictionary.

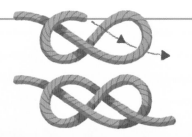

Numbers and ordinal numbers

1	one	first	21	twenty-one	twenty-first	
2	two	second	22	twenty-two	twenty-second	
3	three	third	30	thirty	thirtieth	
4	four	fourth	40	forty	fortieth	
5	five	fifth	50	fifty	fiftieth	
6	six	sixth	60	sixty	sixtieth	
7	seven	seventh	70	seventy	seventieth	
8	eight	eighth	80	eighty	eightieth	
9	nine	ninth	90	ninety	ninetieth	
10	ten	tenth	100	hundred	hundredth	
11	eleven	eleventh	1,000	thousand	thousandth	
12	twelve	twelfth	1,000,000	million	millionth	
13	thirteen	thirteenth	1,000,000,000,00	billion	billionth	
14	fourteen	fourteenth				
15	fifteen	fifteenth				
16	sixteen	sixteenth				
17	seventeen	seventeenth				
18	eighteen	eighteenth				
19	nineteen	nineteenth				
20	twenty	twentieth				

Activity

There are many words that you use when you are working with numbers. Find these words in the dictionary to see how they are used.

degree   odd   negative

digit   even

factor   positive

Roman numerals

I	1	XXI	21
II	2	XXX	30
III	3	L	50
IV	4	LX	60
V	5	LXX	70
VI	6	LXXX	80
VII	7	XC	90
VIII	8	C	100
IX	9	CL	150
X	10	CC	200
XI	11	D	500
XII	12	M	1,000
XIII	13	MM	2,000
XIV	14		
XV	15		
XX	20		

Planet names

Mercury	named after the Roman messenger of the gods
Venus	named after the Roman goddess of love and beauty
Earth	from an Old English word
Mars	named after the Roman god of war
Jupiter	named after the most important Roman god
Saturn	named after the Roman god of agriculture
Uranus	named after the Greek god of the sky

Days

Monday	from an old English word meaning 'day of the moon'
Tuesday	from *Tiw*, the Anglo-Saxon god of war
Wednesday	from *Woden* or *Odin*, the most important Norse god
Thursday	from *Thor*, the Norse god of thunder
Friday	from *Frigga*, the Norse goddess of love, who was Odin's wife
Saturday	from the Roman god *Saturn*
Sunday	from an old English word meaning 'day of the sun'

Months

January	from *Janus*, the Roman god of doors and beginnings
February	from *Februa*, an ancient Roman festival ⚠ Don't forget the **r** in the middle.
March	from *Mars*, the Roman god of war
April	from *Aprillis*, the fourth month of the ancient Roman calendar
May	from *Maia*, a Roman goddess connected with springtime
June	from *Juno*, the most important Roman goddess
July	after Roman emperor Julius Caesar, who was born in this month
August	after Augustus, the first Roman emperor
September	from Latin *septem* 'seven'. It was the 7th month in the old Roman calendar.
October	from Latin *octo* 'eight'. It was the 8th month in the old Roman calendar.
November	from Latin *novem* 'nine'. It was the 9th month in the old Roman calendar.
December	from Latin *decem* 'ten'. It was the 10th and last month in the old Roman calendar.

Dictionary Treasure Hunt!

Look up the word in blue to find the answer to the question.

What do you call the bush a **blackberry** grows on?

Can you name some types of **fossil**?

What do you call it when someone **betrays** you?

What kind of animal is an **otter**?

What colour is a **cornflower**?

What do you call the noise a **donkey** makes?

What kind of instrument is an **oboe**?

The Romans used **Roman numerals** – but what do you call the numbers we use?

What do you call it when someone **deceives** you?

What do you call an **angle** that's more than 180°?

What's the difference between an **arc** and an **ark**?

What do you call the three parts of an **insect's** body?

An animal that eats meat is a **carnivore**, but what do you call an animal that eats plants and meat?

What do you call a male **duck**?

Where does the word **hippopotamus** come from?

What adjective means 'like a **cow**'?

Can you find words for two different types of **wave**?

What type of verb is **may**?

How do you pronounce **chasm**?

What is the opposite of **concave**?

What word do you use to describe something that is impossible to **dissolve**?

What words can you use to describe a volcano that is not **active**?

Can you name a chemical **element**?

Can you name some types of **micro-organism**?

What type of animal is a **koala**?

What do you call a type of drug, **penicillin** for example, that kills bacteria?

What is the opposite of a **pessimist**?

Answers for letter openers

A *synonym*

B **Some answers**: *sea* or *see, gee, eye, jay, oh* or *owe, pea, queue, are, tea, you* or *yew, why*

C **Some answers**: *centenary, centigrade, centipede, per cent*

E The letter *s*

G For some UK / US differences, look at page 472.

I *a* (the indefinite article) and *o* (an old, poetic way of spelling *oh!*)

J *onomatopoeia*

K The Roman numeral for 1000 was M. For more on Roman numerals, look at page 479.

L **Some answers**: *scratched, stretched, strengths*

M *purple, orange, silver*

N **Some ideas**: *Brexit, fidget spinner, hangry, selfie, story* (on social media), *swipe* (on a touchscreen)

O **Some answers**: *beep, boom, clatter, click, fizz, hiss, hum, rustle, sizzle, slurp, splash, whizz, whoosh, zap, zip*

P *deed*

R **Some answers**: *my, try, myth, gym*

S The letter *e*

T The word *the*

U The word *vacuum*

V A few answers: *autumn, debt, island, knight, psychology, reign, shepherd, spaghetti, write*

X The letter *s*

Z *brr, shhh*

pelican

worm

shuttlecock

conker

vanilla

gecko

mistletoe

flamingo

trophy

newt

chrysalis

starfish

acorn

scarab

sundial

wheat

oyster

galleon